endorsed for
BTEC

Pearson
BTEC National
Sport

Student Book 2

Dale Forsdyke
Dr Adam Gledhill
Amy Gledhill
Chris Lydon
Chris Manley
Alex Sergison
Richard Taylor

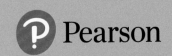
Pearson

Published by Pearson Education Limited, 80 Strand, London, WC2R 0RL.

www.pearsonschoolsandfecolleges.co.uk

Copies of official specifications for all Pearson qualifications may be found on the website: qualifications.pearson.com

Text © Pearson Education Limited 2017
Edited by Cambridge Publishing Management Ltd
Typeset by Tech-Set Ltd, Gateshead
Original illustrations © Pearson Education Ltd 2017
Illustrated by Tech-Set Ltd, Gateshead
Cover photo © Shutterstock.com / Rocksweeper

The rights of Dale Forsdyke, Adam Gledhill, Amy Gledhill, Katherine Howard, Chris Lydon, Chris Manley, Alex Sergison and Richard Taylor to be identified as authors of this work have been asserted by them in accordance with the Copyright, Designs and Patents Act 1988.

First published 2017

19 18 17
10 9 8 7 6 5 4 3 2

British Library Cataloguing in Publication Data

A catalogue record for this book is available from the British Library

ISBN 978 1 292 13406 2

Copyright notice

Printed in Slovakia by Neografia

Acknowledgements

We would like to thank Nicky Bourne, Gretel Redwood and David Spencer-Smith for their invaluable help in reviewing this book. We would also like to thank Matthew Fleet for his work supporting the early development of this book.

The authors and publisher would like to thank the following individuals and organisations for permission to reproduce photographs:

(Key: b-bottom; c-centre; l-left; r-right; t-top)

123RF.com: andresr 97bl, Marcin Ciesielski 8cl, Rostislav Sedláček 295tr, Wavebreak Media Ltd 392tl; **Alamy Stock Photo:** ableimages 122br, Action Plus Sports Images 353bl, Adolphe Pierre-Louis / Albuquerque Journal / ZUMA Press Inc 176br, Bill Cheyrou 69tr, Chronicle 370br, Corey Jenkins / Cultura RM 251bl, Dave & Les Jacobs / Blend Images 6br, Dominic Steinmann 54bl, Gato Desaparecido 173, Henry Westheim Photography 378cl, Hero Images Inc. 73cr, 309br, Holger Weitzel / imageBROKER 1, Ian Francis stock 286br, Image Source 360br, JIM YOUNG / REUTERS 332c, John Green / Cal Sport Media 376cl, Juice Images 12cr, Laszlo Szirtesi 367, Luiz Souza 284tr, Miso Lisanin / Xinhua 347br, NIGEL RODDIS / REUTERS 303bc, REUTERS 89, 199, 219tl, ROBERT GALBRAITH / REUTERS 350br, Split Seconds 31, Tony Tallec 263, Wavebreak Media Ltd 236, Wavebreakmedia Ltd PH85 165br; **Alex Sergison:** 41bl; **DJO UK Ltd:** 216tr, 299; **Down's Syndrome Association:** 310cl; **Fotolia.com:** Andrey Popov 316t, antgor 103cl, AntonioDiaz 76br, 100tc, 126br, DragonImages 68br, icsnaps 61tr, Lee Torrens 148br, Lorelyn Medina 88tl, luckybusiness 154, 164bl, 171tr, lunamarina 119, michaeljung 151tr, Paul Hakimata 335tr, pressmaster 132tr, Rido 184tl, 198tl, Syda Productions 159tr, 329tr, WavebreakMediaMicro 36tl, 68cr, 87tr, 117tr, 118tl, 197tr, zeremskimilan 110c; **Getty Images:** Bloomberg 113, Eric Thayer / Sports Illustrated 333c, FABRICE COFFRINI / AFP 42cl, Fuse / Corbis 106, Jeff J Mitchell 43c, Julian Finney - FIFA 272tl, Jupiter Images / Stockbyte 391tr, Media for Medical / UIG 223tl, Scot Barbour 288tl, Stephen McCarthy / SPORTSFILE 221bl, Stockbyte 152tl, sturti / E+ 247bl, Visionhaus / Gary Prior (Photo by Ben Radford / Corbis) 382tl; **Pearson Education Ltd:** Studio 8 252cl, Jon Barlow 320c, 365tr; **PhotoDisc:** 1999 63, Doug Menuez 262tl; **Rex Shutterstock:** Jed Leicester 278cr; **Shutterstock.com:** Elina Manninen 157br, Maxisport 341, Monkey Business Images 35tr, 366tl, paul prescott 195tl, Robert Kneschke 96tl, Shahjehan 347tr, snowblurred 172tl, Thor Jorgan Udvang 261tr, vgstudio 233tl, wavebreakmedia 62tr, 187tl, 191cl, ZouZou 234tl; **Sport England:** 267cl

Cover images: *Front:* **Shutterstock.com:** Rocksweeper

All other images © Pearson Education

The authors and publisher would like to thank the following individuals and organisations for permission to reproduce materials:

pp.16–17 Republished with the permission of Sport England, Retrieve from https://www.sportengland.org/funding/our-investments-explained/

Websites

Notes from the publisher

1.

Contents

How to use this book

Welcome to your BTEC National Sport course!

A BTEC National in Sport is one of the most popular BTEC courses. It is a vocational qualification that will help prepare you for a huge range of careers. You may be thinking of pursuing a career as an elite sports performer or as a coach. At present, there are around 1.2 million coaches in Britain. You may be considering joining the health and fitness industry as an exercise professional. This job requires you to supervise and instruct people who are taking part in exercise classes or training sessions.

Research shows a clear link between an active lifestyle and good health. As a result, the health and fitness industry has grown significantly over the last ten years, and will probably continue to grow. There is a demand for exercise professionals and there are good employment opportunities, some of which you will find out more about in this book.

How your BTEC is structured

Your BTEC National is divided into **mandatory units** (the ones you must do) and **optional units** (the ones you can choose to do).

The number of mandatory and optional units will vary depending on the type of BTEC National you are doing. The book supports mandatory units and popular optional units to allow you to complete the:

▶ Diploma

▶ Diploma in Fitness Services.

▶ Extended Diploma

This book should be used in combination with Pearson's BTEC National Sport Student Book 1 that covers the remaining mandatory and optional units for these qualifications.

Your learning experience

You may not realise it but you are always learning. Your educational and life experiences are constantly shaping your ideas and thinking, and how you view and engage with the world around you.

You are the person most responsible for your own learning experience so you must understand what you are learning, why you are learning it and why it is important both to your course and to your personal development. Your learning can be seen as a journey with four phases.

Phase 1	Phase 2	Phase 3	Phase 4
You are introduced to a topic or concept and you start to develop an awareness of what learning is required.	You explore the topic or concept through different methods (e.g. research, questioning, analysis, deep thinking, critical evaluation) and form your own understanding.	You apply your knowledge and skills to a task designed to test your understanding.	You reflect on your learning, evaluate your efforts, identify gaps in your knowledge and look for ways to improve.

During each phase, you will use different learning strategies to secure the core knowledge and skills you need. This student book has been written using similar learning principles, strategies and tools. It has been designed to support your learning journey, to give you control over your own learning, and to equip you with the knowledge, understanding and tools you need to be successful in your future studies or career.

Features of this book

This student book contains many different features. They are there to help you learn about key topics in different ways and understand them from multiple perspectives. Together, these features:

▶ explain what your learning is about

▶ help you to build your knowledge

▶ help you to understand how to succeed in your assessment

▶ help you to reflect on and evaluate your learning

▶ help you to link your learning to the workplace.

Each individual feature has a specific purpose, designed to support important learning strategies. For example, some features will:

▶ encourage you to question assumptions about what you are learning

▶ help you to think beyond what you are reading about

▶ help you to make connections between different areas of your learning and across units

▶ draw comparisons between your own learning and real-world workplace environments

▶ help you to develop some of the important skills you will need for the workplace, including teamwork, effective communication and problem solving.

Features that explain what your learning is about

Getting to know your unit

This section introduces the unit and explains how you will be assessed. It gives an overview of what will be covered and will help you to understand why you are doing the things you are asked to do in this unit.

Getting started

This is designed to get you thinking about the unit and what it involves. This feature will also help you to identify what you may already know about some of the topics in the unit and act as a starting point for understanding the skills and knowledge you will need to develop to complete the unit.

Features that help you to build your knowledge

Research

This asks you to research a topic in greater depth. These features will help to expand your understanding of a topic and develop your research and investigation skills. All of this will be invaluable for your future progression, both professionally and academically.

Worked example

Our worked examples show the process you need to follow to solve a problem, such as a maths or science equation or the process for writing a letter or memo. This will also help you to develop your understanding and your numeracy and literacy skills.

Theory into practice

In this feature you are asked to consider the workplace or industry implications of a topic or concept from the unit. This will help you to understand the close links between what you are learning in the classroom and the affects it will have on a future career in your chosen sector.

Discussion

Discussion features encourage you to talk to other students about a topic, working together to increase your understanding of the topic and to understand other people's perspectives on an issue. These features will also help to build your teamworking skills, which will be invaluable in your future professional and academic career.

Safety tip

This provides advice around health and safety when working on the unit. It will help build your knowledge about best practice in the workplace, as well as make sure that you stay safe.

Key terms

Concise and simple definitions are provided for key words, phrases and concepts, giving you, at a glance, a clear understanding of the key ideas in each unit. Key terms are highlighted in **bold** in the index.

Link

Link features show any links between units or within the same unit, helping you to identify knowledge you have learned elsewhere that will help you to achieve the requirements of the unit. Remember, although your BTEC National is made up of several units, there are common themes that are explored from different perspectives across the whole of your course.

Further reading and resources

This contains a list of other resources – such as books, journals, articles or websites – you can use to expand your knowledge of the unit content. This is a good opportunity for you to take responsibility for your own learning, as well as preparing you for research tasks you may need to do academically or professionally.

Features connected to your assessment

Your course is made up of mandatory and optional units. There are two different types of mandatory unit:

▶ externally assessed

▶ internally assessed.

The features that support you in preparing for assessment are below. But first, what is the difference between these two different types of unit?

Externally assessed units

These units will give you the opportunity to demonstrate your knowledge and understanding, or your skills, in a direct way. For these units you will complete a task, set directly by Pearson, in controlled conditions. This could take the form of an exam or it could be another type of task. You may have the opportunity to prepare in advance, to research and make notes about a topic which can be used when completing the assessment.

Internally assessed units

Most of your units will be internally assessed and will involve you completing a series of assignments, set and marked by your tutor. The assignments you complete will allow you to demonstrate your learning in a number of different ways, from a written report to a presentation to a video recording and observation statements of you completing a practical task. Whatever the method, you will need to make sure you have clear evidence of what you have achieved and how you did it.

Assessment practice

These features give you the opportunity to practise some of the skills you will need during the unit assessment. They do not fully reflect the actual assessment tasks but will help you to prepare for them.

Plan – Do – Review

You will also find handy advice on how to plan, complete and evaluate your work. This is designed to get you thinking about the best way to complete your work and to build your skills and experience before doing the actual assessment. These questions will prompt you to think about the way you work and why particular tasks are relevant.

Getting ready for assessment

For internally assessed units, this is a case study of a BTEC National student, talking about how they planned and carried out their assignment work and what they would do differently if they were to do it again. It will give you advice on preparing for your internal assessments, including Think about it points for you to consider for your own development.

Getting ready for assessment

This section will help you to prepare for external assessment. It gives practical advice on preparing for and sitting exams or a set task. It provides a series of sample answers for the types of question you will need to answer in your external assessment, including guidance on the good points of these answers and ways in which they could be improved.

Features to help you reflect on and evaluate your learning

PAUSE POINT

Pause Points appear regularly throughout the book and provide opportunities to review and reflect on your learning. The ability to reflect on your own performance is a key skill you will need to develop and use throughout your life, and will be essential whatever your future plans are.

Hint

Extend

These also give you suggestions to help cement your knowledge and indicate other areas you can look at to expand it.

Features which link your learning with the workplace

Case study

Case studies are used throughout the book to allow you to apply the learning and knowledge from the unit to a scenario from the workplace or the industry. Case studies include questions to help you consider the wider context of a topic. This is an opportunity to see how the unit's content is reflected in the real world, and for you to build familiarity with issues you may find in a real-world workplace.

THINK ▶FUTURE

This is a case study in which someone working in the industry talks about their job role and the skills they need. The *Focusing your skills* section suggests ways for you to develop the employability skills and experiences you will need to be successful in a career in your chosen sector. This will help you to identify what you could do, inside and outside your BTEC National studies, to build up your employability skills.

About the authors

Dale Forsdyke

Dale Forsdyke has over 12 years of teaching experience and is a senior lecturer in Sports Injury Management at York St John University. He has previously written text books on sports therapy and his research has been published in practitioner- and peer-reviewed journals. Alongside teaching, Dale is a practising spotters therapist (MSST) and has the role of Head of Science and Medicine in a Tier One Regional Talent Club. He has also worked in Women's Super League (WSL) football and for the Football Association.

Dr Adam Gledhill

Adam has 15 years' experience working within further and higher education. He works within qualification development for Pearson and is a co-author of previous editions of this book. He achieved his PhD from Loughborough University, where he completed a programme of study examining psychosocial factors associated with talent development in UK female youth football players.

Adam has experience of providing interdisciplinary sport science support to different athlete populations; from youth and senior international football players, to youth athletes in a range of sports. Among his consultancy roles, he has worked as Head of Sport Science for an FA Women's Super League team and as Head of Psychosocial Development for a Football Association Licensed Girls' Football Centre of Excellence.

Amy Gledhill

Amy Gledhill is the course leader for Sport and Exercise Sciences at a further education college and has taught BTEC Sport qualifications for six years, following the completion of an MSc in Sport and Exercise Physiology. She has experience working with a range of athletes across football and track and field athletics, including as Head of Sport Science for a regional Cerebral Palsy Football Centre of Excellence.

Chris Lydon

Chris has worked in further and higher education for twenty years as a senior sports science lecturer specialising in anatomy and physiology and fitness training. He has also worked as an external standards verifier for Pearson and an external examiner for a number of universities. He is currently employed as an Assistant Principal at a large FE college where he is responsible for the recruitment and support of staff and students. Chris has previously written a number of books relating to BTEC sports qualifications.

Chris Manley

Chris splits his time between roles as a Postgraduate Education Tutor at Canterbury Christ Church University and as a Senior Practitioner at an FE college. Chris has been a National League basketball coach, tutor and referee and was a successful slalom canoeist. He has a Master's degree in Education and postgraduate qualifications in the sociology of sport, and works in a variety of roles related to BTEC for Pearson. Chris has published for BTEC and for teaching professionals studying teaching qualifications.

Alex Sergison

Alex has worked in the sports industry for over 15 years and specialises in outdoor education. He has acted as a consultant for a number of small businesses as well as running his own. He manages Weymouth College's outdoor education department, based in Portland. Alex has been involved with Pearson as a course writer and study guide writer for the last 7 years.

Richard Taylor

Richard is a former rower and personal trainer with several years of experience in teaching further and higher education sports programmes and PE in schools. Currently a tutor for Gillingham FC's academy, Richard has worked with a number of professional football clubs, written several higher education sports programmes and contributed to previous editions of this book.

Research Methods in Sport 9

Getting to know your unit

Assessment
You will be assessed by a
series of assignments set
by your tutor.

Evidence-based practice has become much more prominent in sport in recent years. When working with clients, it is important to base your work on sound evidence that will help you to justify your work: the service you provide to clients is only as good as the evidence you base your work on. Therefore, having a good skill set and understanding of research methods is central to becoming an effective practitioner and, in doing so, being able to offer your clients the highest quality of support.

This unit will help you to develop knowledge and skills that you can use to collect and analyse data with a range of clients. In turn, this will aid their sport performance or overall health and well-being. You will learn about what it means to work ethically and why this is central to everything that you do as a practitioner in sport.

Whether you want to progress into related work or higher education, studying this unit will set you on a journey to becoming a capable, evidence-based practitioner.

How you will be assessed

This unit will be assessed by a series of internally assessed tasks set by your tutor. There will also be opportunities for formative assessment where you will be able to receive feedback on your progress, strengths and areas for improvement.

The assignments set by your tutor may take the form of:
▶ a written report on the importance of research and factors affecting the quality of research
▶ a presentation about the different approaches to research and the application of research methods.

The activities within this unit are designed to help you gain knowledge, understanding and skills that will help you complete your assignments. Your understanding of research methods is best gained through using the different concepts and research methods in a practical manner.

The skills that you learn throughout this unit will also be directly beneficial in *Unit 11: Research Project in Sport* where you will have the opportunity to plan and carry out your own research project.

To pass this unit you must ensure that you have provided sufficient evidence to cover all the Pass assessment criteria which are listed in the table opposite.

If you are seeking a Merit or Distinction grade, then you must be able to show both an understanding and application of the concepts and techniques in sport-based contexts.

Assessment criteria

This table shows what you must do to achieve a **Pass**, **Merit** or **Distinction** grade, and where you can find activities to help you.

Pass	**Merit**	**Distinction**
Learning aim A Understand the importance of research in sporting environments		
A.P1 Discuss the different types of research in a sport-based environment. **Assessment activity 9.1**	**A.M1** Analyse how the different types of research can be used to inform your work with clients in a sport-based environment. **Assessment activity 9.1**	**A.D1** Evaluate the importance of research in sporting environments and key issues that impact on the effectiveness and quality of research. **Assessment activity 9.1**
A.P2 Discuss the importance of using research to inform your work with clients in a sport-based environment. **Assessment activity 9.1**		
Learning aim B Examine key issues that impact on the effectiveness and quality of research in sport		
B.P3 Explain the importance of validity, reliability, accuracy and precision in sport-based research. **Assessment activity 9.1**	**B.M2** Analyse the relationship between validity, reliability, accuracy and precision, and the ability to conduct ethical research in sport. **Assessment activity 9.1**	**B.D2** Justify the relationship between validity, reliability, accuracy and precision, and the ability to conduct ethical research in sport. **Assessment activity 9.1**
B.P4 Explain research ethics and their importance in sport-based research. **Assessment activity 9.1**		
Learning aim C Apply appropriate research methods to a selected research problem in sport		
C.P5 State the appropriate research methods for a sport-based research problem. **Assessment activity 9.2**	**C.M3** Assess the research methods for a sport-based research problem. **Assessment activity 9.2**	**C.D3** Justify the choice of research methods for a selected sport-based research problem. **Assessment activity 9.2**
C.P6 Demonstrate skills in appropriate research methods to address a selected research problem. **Assessment activity 9.2**		

Getting started

Every year, sports teams spend significant amounts of money on developing athletes and buying the best talent available. Outside sport, the government and various government agencies spend large amounts of public funds on health initiatives to try to improve the health of the nation. Produce a mind map of all the ways that research could help to inform how this money is best spent.

A Understand the importance of research in sporting environments

Link

This unit links to *Unit 11: Research Project in Sport* as it introduces you to the different types of research that could be used as part of a project.

'Research' means different things to different people. Some believe research is reading around a topic; others believe research is the collection and analysis of new data. While both ideas are correct, it is important that you are familiar with the different types of research that you can use.

There are different definitions of 'research'. However, one definition that encompasses many of the different aspects of research is: a systematic process of discovery and advancement of knowledge, understanding and skills that is guided by seeking answers to specific questions, problems or **hypotheses**.

Different types of research

There are five main types of research: primary, secondary, quantitative, qualitative and mixed-methods.

Primary research

Primary research collects original data specific to a particular project. For example, if you want to investigate the effects of sports massage on hamstring flexibility, you could measure flexibility before and after sports massage and record the results to see if there is any difference.

Discussion

Based on the definition of 'hypothesis' given in the key term box, what do you think are the key aspects of research?

Secondary research

Secondary research uses previously published data found in books, journals, government publications, websites and other forms of media. Secondary research is used to form **rationales** for your research and to support or counter-argue your research findings.

Quantitative research

Quantitative research is a formal, objective and systematic process in which numerical data is used to obtain information. It involves testing a hypothesis or trying to discover relationships. It is generally deductive research (meaning a scientist would start from a hypothesis and then make observations to prove the hypothesis). It is designed to establish differences, relationships or **causality**.

Key terms

Hypothesis – the predicted, testable relationship between two or more variables, for example imagery training will improve basketball free throw performance.

Rationale – the reason for a decision.

Causality – the relationship between a cause and its effect.

Because quantitative research relies on measurement and statistical analysis, its success often depends on the accuracy and precision of data collection. It is conducted using large sample sizes, where possible, in order to help 'smooth out' readings that might be false having been generated by a smaller sample size.

As an example of quantitative research, Soligard et al. (2008) investigated the effectiveness of a warm-up programme to prevent injuries in female youth football players. Their investigation used 1,892 female football players and had treatment and control groups. They found that the treatment group had fewer injuries than the control group, and this comprehensive warm-up programme is now widely used in women's football.

Qualitative research

Qualitative research is generally **subjective** and involves words rather than numbers. It looks at feelings, opinions and emotions and is concerned with trying to explain **why** rather than **what** or **how many**. It tends to be inductive, which means you collect data and then analyse it to create explanations, models or theories. It tries to explain differences, relationships or causality. Qualitative data can also produce quantitative data. For example, you may record how many people said that they like playing sport because they can spend time with their friends; you might explore why this is the case.

Key term

Subjective – based on or influenced by personal feelings, beliefs or opinions.

Mixed-methods research

Mixed-methods research is an approach that adopts and combines qualitative and quantitative principles and methods in the same study.

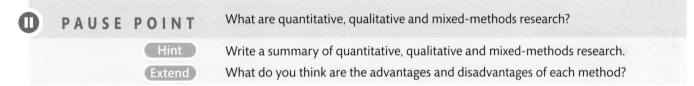

⏸ PAUSE POINT   What are quantitative, qualitative and mixed-methods research?

    Hint   Write a summary of quantitative, qualitative and mixed-methods research.

    Extend   What do you think are the advantages and disadvantages of each method?

The importance of research

Research is important for those working in sport because it helps people to keep up to date with the latest trends and develop new ideas. Before researching, search for sources of information to check your proposed research has not already been done by someone else and, if it has, find out what their results were.

Literature searching

The first stage of developing a good sport-based project is to search for and read appropriate sources of information. At this point you need to look for any differences of opinion or any popular topics within a subject area.

To find sources of information, explore basic versus advanced searches in search engines or journal databases, the use of key words and filtering journals. For example, going to www.google.com/advanced_search allows you to be much more precise about the results returned. You can add an author name and specify where you want the search engine to look for specific words.

You should always judge the literature for validity and reliability, especially when you have found it on the Internet. This is explored in more detail later in this unit, starting on page 7.

Using research to develop knowledge and understanding

There are many examples of research to develop knowledge and understanding. The following two studies demonstrate how you can refine and develop subject knowledge through research, to benefit clients.

▶ First, Holt and Dunn (2004) produced a theory associated with talent development in elite youth football that made predictions about different qualities that would give players the best chance of reaching elite level. However, as this theory was based mainly on players who had been successful in their youth football career, it was not known whether less successful football players possessed these same qualities.

▶ As a result, Holt and Mitchell (2006) examined the experiences of less successful and

Key term

Evidence-based practice (EBP) – making sure that evidence uncovered in research is included in your everyday work practices for the benefit of your clients.

lower-level youth players and produced a revised theory. However, both of these studies had the limitation that it was not known if any of the players studied had successfully achieved and maintained a professional career.

The use of research

When you work in a sport-related occupation, you should always use research to plan and review your work. This is **evidence-based practice (EBP)**. This does not mean you have to read article after article every time you plan a session with clients, but rather, as a professional, that you have a good working knowledge of the research in your area and know how to apply it to your clients.

It also means you should update your knowledge on a regular basis by keeping up to date with the latest research. For example, if you are a strength and conditioning coach or a sports therapist responsible for the post-event recovery of athletes, you should ensure you are familiar with the different recovery strategies available for those athletes, as well as the physiological and psychological benefits of those strategies.

The ultimate aim of research is to benefit clients, for example, by improving their sport performance through helping sports coaches and performance analysts gain better understanding, or by developing understanding to allow the development of new technology or equipment to help clients' performance.

The importance of EBP in sporting environments

As a sport-based practitioner, the welfare and safety of your participants is always your main concern. In research and practice environments, this means that you should not place any undue physiological or psychological stress on your clients (for example, you should not conduct any work that might significantly increase the risk of injury). EBP is important in this context, as the available evidence will help you to stay within the normal working limits for clients, or levels of work that will not significantly pose an increased risk to a client's well-being.

▶ If you were the yoga instructor shown here, why would EBP be important for you?

PAUSE POINT   What is 'evidence-based practice'?

> Hint   Close this book and define evidence-based practice.
>
> Extend   Discuss why evidence-based practice is important for people working in sport-related occupations.

B Examine key issues that impact on the effectiveness and quality of research in sport

Validity, reliability, accuracy and precision in research

When conducting research, you will need to consider its **validity**, **reliability**, accuracy and precision.

Validity

The first important consideration is validity. Definitions of validity can vary depending on the context.

▶ If your research involves **collecting** data, 'validity' can be defined as whether you are measuring what you intended to measure.

▶ If your research involves **analysing** data, 'validity' is the soundness of the interpretation of test results.

Validity is also connected to the conclusions drawn through research, i.e. that you correctly draw conclusions from the data that you have collected and analysed.

Types of validity

There are different types of validity but the two key types are 'internal validity' and 'external validity'.

▶ **Internal validity** relates to whether the results of the study can be attributed to the different treatments in the study. This means that, for your research to claim internal validity, you need to ensure that you have controlled everything that could affect the results of the study.

▶ **External validity** relates to whether or not the results of the study can be generalised and applied to other people or situations.

Other types of validity include **ecological validity** (which relates to the extent to which results of a study can be applied to real-world settings) and **face validity** (which relates to whether an investigation clearly measures the performance variable – for example, why do you think that some people have questioned the face validity of the sit and reach test for measuring hamstring flexibility?).

> **Link**
>
> This content links to *Unit 11: Research Project in Sport* – whenever you collect data in a project, you need to make sure that it is both valid and reliable so that you can reach meaningful conclusions.

> **Key terms**
>
> **Validity** (in data collection) – whether you are measuring what you intended to measure.
>
> **Validity** (in data analysis) – the soundness of the interpretation of results.
>
> **Reliability** – the consistency or repeatability of a measure.

Case study

Valid research

As part of a project investigating the effects of sports massage on hamstring flexibility in athletes, a sports massage therapist decides to use the sit and reach test to measure the hamstring flexibility of rugby players. When the massage therapist talks through their idea with their research supervisor, they raise the point that sit and reach scores can also be influenced by lower back condition. The supervisor also asks why, if the aim is to measure

hamstring flexibility in athletes, has the sports massage therapist only selected rugby players for the research?

Check your knowledge

1 Which types of validity would be affected by the way the sports massage therapist had originally planned the project?

2 How would they have been affected?

3 If you offered advice to the therapist about potential changes to the project, what would it be and why?

Reliability

Reliability refers to the consistency or repeatability of a measure/test or of their results. It is important to remember that reliability can be achieved without validity: you could ask the wrong questions and get the same wrong answers consistently. In this case, your work is **reliable** (the answers you received were consistent and repeatable), but not **valid** (as you did not find out information about the subject you intended to investigate).

In quantitative research (i.e. research looking at numbers, statistics or other 'countable' data), reliability can be achieved by one researcher conducting the same test on the same individual on a number of occasions, and getting the same or similar results. Alternatively, it can be achieved by different researchers conducting the same test on the same individual and getting the same or similar results.

In qualitative research (i.e. research looking at non-numerical data such as words, images or behaviours), reliability relates to the same researcher placing results into the same categories on different occasions, or different researchers placing results into the same or similar categories.

There are certain factors you should take into account that can affect reliability. Errors may occur if:

▶ researchers do not know how to use the equipment correctly
▶ equipment is poorly maintained
▶ the wrong type of equipment is chosen.

Types of reliability

There are three types of reliability.

▶ **Inter-observer or inter-researcher reliability** examines whether different researchers in the same situation would get the same (or similar) results. An example of when inter-observer reliability can be a problem is when measuring body composition. When people are learning to use the skinfold calliper technique of assessing body composition, it is difficult to take accurate measurements from the correct sites, meaning researchers come up with different values. When this happens, you cannot claim to have achieved inter-observer reliability.
▶ **Test-retest reliability** relates to doing the same test on different occasions and getting the same (or similar) results. An example of a test–retest reliability issue in sport or exercise research is the measurement of heart rate. Heart rate can be affected by different factors such as temperature, time of day, diet, sleep patterns, physical activity levels and alcohol. If you measured the heart rate on the same person at the same time of day but on different days, you could get different measurements.
▶ **Internal consistency reliability** relates to whether the items in a survey or questionnaire all measure the same thing. For example, if you were measuring sport anxiety and had a seven-item questionnaire where all the questions measured sport anxiety appropriately, it would have good internal consistency reliability.

▶ Measuring body composition using skinfold callipers

PAUSE POINT

What are the different types of validity and reliability?

Hint Close this book then list and define each of the types of validity and reliability.

Extend Explain why you think it is important to consider validity and reliability in research settings.

Accuracy and precision

Key term

Accuracy – how close your measurement is to the 'gold standard'.

Accuracy relates to how close your measurement is to the 'gold standard' or what you are intending to measure. Imagine looking at the weight of a boxer before a fight. If the boxer has an actual weight of 100 kg and your weighing device shows he weighs 100.1 kg, you could say this is accurate. However, if the measuring device shows he weighs 103 kg, you would say this is not accurate as it is not close to his body weight.

Any measurement you take will have some unpredictability. The degree of unpredictability relates to the amount of **precision** of the tool selected for measurement. Precision is related to the refinement of the measuring process. It is concerned with how small a difference the measuring device can detect. Precision is closely related to repeatability/reliability.

▶ **Figure 9.1:** Accuracy and precision can affect the validity and reliability of research

An easy way to get to grips with accuracy and precision is to think about target sports such as archery. If you hit the bullseye on the archery board with all of your arrows, you would say that you had been both accurate and precise. However, if you missed the board completely in different directions with your arrows, you would say that you had been neither accurate nor precise. This is shown in Figure 9.1.

Impact of accuracy and precision on validity and reliability

Accuracy and precision can affect validity and reliability: if you do not follow the relevant protocol (i.e. the way of conducting the data), it is likely the data collected will be less accurate and precise. If this is the case, you are less likely to measure what you intended to measure, reducing the validity of data collection.

Equally, if you are less accurate and precise with your data collection, there is likely to be a degree of variance in the errors you make. In this instance, you will produce different results, reducing the reliability of your data.

Research ethics

There are many different definitions of research ethics. However, a common definition is: standards of conduct that differentiate between acceptable and unacceptable behaviour while conducting research activities. You should always make sure that you adhere to a relevant code of conduct, such as the codes of the British Association of Sport and Exercise Sciences (BASES) or Sports Coach UK.

The BASES Code of Conduct

The ethical issues relevant to you are outlined in the BASES Code of Conduct. This governs how you work as practitioners and researchers, and outlines ethical standards essential for safe research within sport and exercise sciences.

Ethical clearance

When conducting research, to ensure that you are working ethically and legally, you need to gain ethical clearance from an appropriate body before you start. If you conduct any research as part of your course, ethical clearance will come from your tutor, college or school **ethics committee**.

Informed consent

Once you have gained ethical approval for your research project, it is an ethical and legal requirement for you to gain informed consent from your participants. This can be given verbally, but it is safer for both you and your participants if you obtain it in writing. An informed consent form consists of:
▶ a description of the investigation
▶ details of the procedure to be followed
▶ details of any risks to the participant

> **Key term**
>
> **Precision** – how fine or small a difference a measuring device can detect.
>
> **Ethics committee** – a panel that looks at research proposals and decides whether they are safe and ethical.

> **Theory into practice**
>
> **Research measurement of body composition using skinfold callipers.**
>
> Think about the key errors that could be made when measuring body composition this way. How would this affect accuracy, precision, validity and reliability?

- details of the potential benefits of taking part in the research
- a section that offers to answer any questions and confirms these have been answered fully
- an indication that the participant can withdraw at any time without being penalised
- a section which explains that any information collected about the participant will remain confidential
- a section for you, the participant and any other relevant individual (such as a parent or carer) to sign and date.

Confidentiality, data protection and responsibility

Any data you collect is governed by the terms of the Data Protection Act (1998). You may only disclose information important to the study you are conducting, and no data that makes the participants personally identifiable should be included in your research project. Data collected should be stored in a secure location (such as a locked filing cabinet or a password-protected computer), accessible only by you and your research supervisor.

Competence

Competence refers to you only working within your specific skill sets. If you are not suitably qualified, experienced or skilled in a certain technique, you should not perform it during research without adequate supervision. Neither should you interpret results from areas where you do not have sufficient subject knowledge, as this may mislead clients and bias the results of your study, not to mention potentially having a negative impact on the clients' safety and well-being if they change their lifestyle based on your interpretations.

If you are ever asked to work within an area in which you are not competent, **refer** this to another appropriate professional (for example, somebody within a different discipline of sport and exercise sciences, a sports therapist or a sports medicine professional).

Personal and professional conduct

Working in a professional manner is the cornerstone of being an effective practitioner. In addition to the factors discussed above, some of the key considerations within this context are outlined below.

- **Safety of the participants** – when conducting research, this is a key concern. The researcher must maintain the highest professional standards so as not to endanger participants or themselves. This is especially important if the research involves participants exerting themselves and getting towards their maximum effort. The researcher should treat all participants equally and only work within their own area of competence.
- **Acting with due regard for equality and impartiality** – to preserve the reputation of sport and exercise science, you must remain totally unbiased in your actions and practices. This means you cannot let factors such as race, age or gender affect your work with clients or interpretation of results. You must not exploit personal relationships for personal gain. Any decisions must be completely objective (based on facts rather than opinions).
- **Responding to member or client queries** – there may be a time when a senior member of BASES or your client asks why you have worked in a particular way. As a practitioner, you have the professional responsibility to answer these queries in an open, honest and timely manner.

Impact of ethical issues in research settings

The primary role of research ethics is to ensure the safety and well-being of the research participants and the researcher. If you do not consider ethical issues, it is not possible to offer these safeguards.

Centring more on the research process, ethical issues also play a role in helping to ensure a high quality of data collection and analysis, allowing you to investigate research aims in the best manner, resulting in the most useful research for the widest audience. Working

---

Key terms

Competence – having knowledge, skills and experience within a given area and recognising your associated limitations.

Referral – when you recognise that you are not competent to work with a particular client or conduct research in a particular area based on your skill set, contacting another professional who is competent so that they can conduct that work.

Research

Research the Society of Sports Therapists' standard of conduct, performance and ethics. What are the similarities and differences between this and the BASES Code of Conduct?

in this way is also likely to reduce the potential for bias in the research, enhancing the credibility of sport and exercise sciences as a professional discipline.

Ⅱ PAUSE POINT   What are the key ethical considerations when conducting research?

> **Hint**   Think about a specific topic you would like to research. What are the key ethical considerations relating to this project?

> **Extend**   Why are these ethical considerations in place and what might be the consequences of breaching them?

Assessment practice 9.1   `A.P1` `A.P2` `A.M1` `A.D1` `B.P3` `B.P4` `B.M2` `B.D2`

You are applying for a strength and conditioning internship at a Football Association Regional Talent Club. The head of science and medicine is very keen on evidence-based practice, so part of the application process requires you to write a report that examines the importance of research when working with clients within a football setting and justifies the factors that can influence the effectiveness of research.

Within your report, consider how you can use football-specific examples to illustrate the work (for example, why evidence-based practice is used in football; football-specific examples of validity and reliability).

Plan
- If I were applying for this internship, what football-based examples could I provide of the different types of research?
- What am I being asked to show about research and the factors affecting the quality of research, and why is this important?

Do
- Have I spent some time planning my approach to the task and sought others' opinions?
- Have I recorded any problems I experienced and looked for ways to resolve them?

Review
- Can I explain how I approached the task and how I could approach it differently next time?
- Can I say whether I met the task's criteria?.

C Apply appropriate research methods to a selected research problem in sport

Quantitative research designs

You will use a number of different research designs within sport and exercise sciences. A research design is the overall structure of your research. The main quantitative designs are experimental, cross-sectional or survey-based, and longitudinal.

Experimental research design

The aim of experimental research is to explore the effects something has on something else that depends on it. To use this research design effectively, you need to understand the terms **independent variable** and **dependent variable**. The independent variable affects the dependent variable. For example, an athletics coach might want to find out whether her lower-back flexibility training is benefiting the athlete's high-jump performance. As the coach wants to find out if flexibility affects performance, in this example:

▸ the independent variable = flexibility
▸ the dependent variable = high-jump performance – i.e. it depends on the flexibility.

In this type of design, having **treatment** and **control groups** is important so that you can isolate any treatment effects – you need to know for sure that it is the independent variable affecting any changes, not something else. Other variables that might 'skew'

> **Key terms**
>
> **Independent variable** – a variable whose variation does not depend on that of another.
> **Dependent variable** – a variable whose variation depends on that of another.
> **Treatment group** – a group of participants who undergo the treatment condition in an investigation.
> **Control group** – a group of participants who undergo the control condition in an experiment or study, for example receiving no treatment or 'sham treatment' when they think they are being treated.

results need to be controlled and reduced as much as possible.

Cross-sectional or survey-based design

Cross-sectional research involves using a range of participants with different backgrounds, ages and gender from the overall population. For example, if you want to look at preferences for team sports or individual sports in people in the UK, cross-sectional research would be useful. This would allow you to obtain opinions from a range of people from different backgrounds.

Cross-sectional research is often questionnaire- or survey-based. You would send your participants a survey-type questionnaire that allowed them to say which type of sport they prefer. Then you could produce some descriptive statistics for the results of the study (for example, 73 per cent of men prefer team sports, 20 per cent of men prefer individual sports and 7 per cent of men have no preference).

This type of research can identify trends or relationships within or between different groups of people.

> **Theory into practice**
>
> In small groups, discuss how you think the application of longitudinal research designs would differ between qualitative and quantitative research?

Longitudinal design

Longitudinal research involves measuring the same variables over a long period of time. It requires greater resources than other research types, so be careful when approaching it. Measurements are taken at multiple time points over a period of weeks, months or even years, and you then see how and when these change.

Longitudinal research is useful if you want to examine developmental characteristics of a group. For example, it would be a good option if you were investigating factors associated with talent development in a particular sport, allowing you to focus on developmental issues over an extended period of time.

Longitudinal designs can be used in either quantitative or qualitative research, but the application is slightly different.

Quantitative data collection methods

Laboratory-based data collection

Laboratory-based data collection involves collecting data in an environment where all the conditions and potential **extraneous variables** are controlled, so that you are only measuring the variables that your research is focusing on.

One advantage of laboratory-based data collection is that it has high levels of internal validity: you are controlling all your variables so you know that you are only measuring the aspect you mean to measure, making it easier to isolate treatment effects.

One disadvantage of laboratory-based data collection is that it has low levels of 'ecological validity' because the data is not collected in an environment that reflects the situation in which the activity is performed. Another disadvantage is that it normally requires the use of expensive or technical equipment to collect data, making it difficult to use if you have few resources.

> **Key term**
>
> **Extraneous variable** – a variable outside the scope of a study that could adversely affect the results, reducing the validity and reliability of findings.
>
> **Closed questions** – questions that are worded to provoke a single-word response, such as 'yes' or 'no'.

▶ VO$_2$ max tests are a form of laboratory-based data collection

Field-based data collection

Field-based data is collected in an environment that simulates the one in which the sport is played. One of the key strengths of field-based data collection is that it mimics the performance environment so you can claim ecological validity when you are collecting data in this setting.

Field-based data collection can be cheaper than laboratory-based collection, making it more accessible to people with fewer resources. However, one limitation is that you do not control all of the extraneous variables in this setting, so it can be difficult to claim internal validity.

Survey-based data collection

Surveys are used when you are trying to collect a large amount of data from large groups and when the data you want to collect is not in-depth. As such, surveys predominantly use **closed questions**. If you need to obtain more in-depth information, surveys would not be suitable alone. However, they could be effective if used alongside other qualitative methods of data collection (such as interviews). As with other data collection methods, surveys have advantages and disadvantages, shown in Table 9.1.

▶ **Table 9.1:** Advantages and disadvantages of surveys

Advantages	Disadvantages
They are people-friendly if the form is designed correctly.	Questions can be too complex if the form is designed incorrectly.
They provide an opportunity to reduce participant bias.	There are control issues (e.g. potential issues with controlling the return rate; clarity and understanding of questions).
The participant can be anonymous.	There is no opportunity for probing questions.
The data is structured so you can analyse the results more easily.	There is a potential for a low response rate.
They are usually accessible to most people.	

When you start to design your survey, you need to think carefully about a number of factors.

▶ Consider what you want to find out.
▶ Consider your sample (as this will affect how you write your survey).
▶ Consider the length and appearance of your survey (as when you design it, you must not make it too long or difficult to answer).
▶ Decide how and when you are going to distribute your survey. If this will be by hand, wait for it to be completed rather than going away and returning later. If you decide to distribute it by post or email, this reduces the chances of it being returned. Include a return address, a covering letter to explain why your questionnaire is being sent and prepaid postage if possible.
▶ Consider the best way to analyse the results.

If your survey looks poorly organised and unprofessional, people may throw it away, particularly if they have received it by post or online. If it looks well organised and purposeful, you have a better chance of it being completed. Ensure your survey design is geared towards its audience, for example by making it simple to use if it is to be used by young children.

When designing your survey, remember that if it is more than one page long, it is much less likely to be filled in. Keep it as short as possible while still containing sufficient information to answer your research question(s).

Always consider why you are asking a question – this will stop you including unnecessary ones. The quality of your survey will increase as its validity increases. Decide which format would be most appropriate for the question you want to ask, i.e. a 'closed question' that invites a one-word answer or an 'open question' (who? what? where? when? why? how?) that invites a longer response.

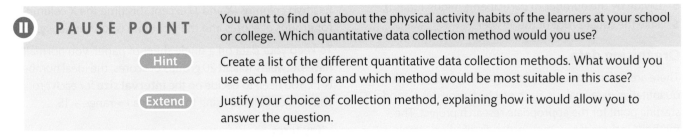

PAUSE POINT You want to find out about the physical activity habits of the learners at your school or college. Which quantitative data collection method would you use?

Hint Create a list of the different quantitative data collection methods. What would you use each method for and which method would be most suitable in this case?

Extend Justify your choice of collection method, explaining how it would allow you to answer the question.

Quantitative data analysis methods

Quantitative data analysis involves using different statistical methods for different purposes to answer your research questions.

Descriptive statistics

Common descriptive statistics are the mean, median, mode and standard deviation.

▶ **Mean** – the average or 'measure of central tendency' that is calculated by adding up all the values and dividing the answer by the number of values. For example, if all the values added up to 125 and there were eight of them, the measure of central tendency would be 15.625.

▶ **Median** – the middle value in a series of numbers. For example, if the series featured the numbers 4, 6, 7, 10 and 11, 7 would be the median because it is the middle number in the series.

▶ **Mode** – the value that occurs most frequently. For example, if the values were 3, 4, 6, 6, 7 and 8, 6 would be the mode because it occurs twice.

▶ **Standard deviation** – a number that indicates how much each of the values in the distribution deviates from the mean (or centre) of the distribution. If the data points are all close to the mean, then the standard deviation is close to zero. If many data points are far from the mean, then the standard deviation is far from zero. If all the data values are equal, then the standard deviation is zero. The formula for calculating standard deviation (sd) is as follows:

$$sd = \sqrt{\frac{\Sigma(X - M)^2}{n - 1}}$$

Where:
- Σ = sum of
- X = individual score
- M = mean
- n = number of participants

Here is how to calculate standard deviation.
1 Calculate the mean.
2 Subtract the mean from each subject's score $(X - M)$.
3 Square the answer $(X - M)^2$.
4 Sum the squared scores $\Sigma (X - M)^2$ for each one.
5 Divide by the number of participants minus 1 $(n - 1)$.
6 Take the square root of the answer.

Organising data

There are different methods for organising your data during quantitative data analysis, each of which provides a good starting point for the appropriate research project. The methods include range, rank–order distribution, simple frequency distribution and grouped frequency distribution.

▶ **Range** is the distance in numerical value from the highest to the lowest value collected. You calculate the range by subtracting the lowest value from the highest value. For example, if the highest value was 15 and the lowest value was 7, the range would be 8.

▶ **Rank–order distribution** means placing your data into an ordered list from the lowest to the highest in a single column, ensuring you include all the scores. Rank–order distribution is used when the number of participants is less than or equal to 20 ($n \leq 20$).

▶ **Simple frequency distribution** is used when the number of participants is greater than 20 ($n > 20$) and when the range is less than or equal to 20 ($r \leq 20$). You use simple frequency distribution with a table that has two columns, one for raw data scores (X) and one for frequency scores (f). The frequency column is the number of times that particular score was achieved.

Worked example

A basketball coach is looking at the number of free throws missed in each game over a season. He has 25 games to assess ($n > 20$) and the number of missed shots per game ranges from 1 to 7 ($r \leq 20$), so simple frequency distribution is suitable. The data is set out as shown in Table 9.2.

▶ **Table 9.2:** Simple frequency distribution example

Number of missed shots (X)	Frequency (f)
7	3
6	5
5	14
3	2
1	1
	n = 25

Grouped frequency distribution

In quantitative research, you often work with ranges greater than 21 ($r > 21$) and with more than 20 participants ($n > 20$) – this is when grouped frequency distribution can be used. As with simple frequency distribution, the table has two columns (X and f) except this time the X column is for groups of scores and the f column is for frequency.

To keep your data on a single sheet of paper, you normally have between 10 and 20 groups of scores; the ideal number is 15. You need to decide on the **interval size** for each group, which is calculated using the formula i = range ÷ 15.

Key term

Interval size – the range of values that each group will cover.

Worked example

An athletics coach is looking at the times recorded (in seconds) of athletes who want to represent the college at 5000 metres. She has 30 times to look at ranging from 900 seconds to 1094 seconds. Grouped frequency distribution is a suitable method because both $r > 21$ and $n > 20$. The interval size for each group is 13 seconds ($r = 194$ seconds; $194 \div 15 = 12.93$ seconds, which is rounded up to 13). The data is shown in Table 9.3.

▶ **Table 9.3:** Example of grouped frequency distribution

Time (X)	Frequency (f)
1082–1094	1
1068–1081	1
1054–1067	1
1040–1053	1
1026–1039	5
1012–1025	8
998–1011	3
984–997	2
970–983	2
956–969	1
942–955	1
928–941	1
914–927	1
900–913	2
	n = 30

Although using grouped frequency distribution is a useful way of organising large amounts of data, some information is lost through this process. Once scores have been placed into groups, it is impossible to know the individual values. For example, if you look at the 1012–1025 seconds row in Table 9.3, it is only possible to identify that eight athletes fell within that range, but you will not know what the individual times were.

Distribution curves

Distribution curves help you to understand the relationship of your data to the mean value.

Normal distribution curves

A normal distribution of data means that most of the examples in a set of data are close to the 'average', while a few examples are at one extreme or the other. In a normal distribution graph (see Figure 9.2):

▶ the curve has a single peak
▶ the curve is bell-shaped
▶ the mean (average) lies at the centre of the distribution and the distribution is symmetrical around the mean
▶ the two 'tails' of the distribution extend indefinitely and never touch the x axis
▶ the shape of the distribution is determined by the mean and standard deviation.

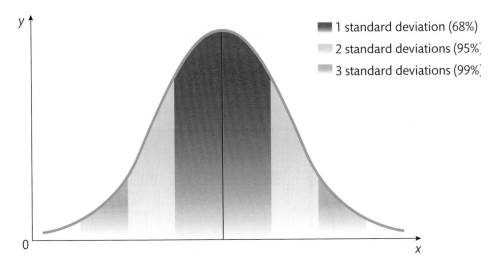

1 standard deviation (68%)
2 standard deviations (95%)
3 standard deviations (99%)

▶ **Figure 9.2:** An example of a normal distribution curve

Not all sets of data have graphs as perfect as Figure 9.2. Some have relatively flat curves; others will be steeper. Sometimes the mean will lean to one side or the other. However, all normally distributed data will have something similar to this bell-shaped curve. Generally, if you go right or left one standard deviation from the mean (the red area on the graph) you will include about 68 per cent of the scores in the distribution. Two standard deviations away from the mean (the red and yellow areas) account for about 95 per cent of scores, whereas three standard deviations (the red, yellow and green areas) account for about 99 per cent of scores.

Standard deviation tells you how tightly all the various examples are clustered around the mean in a set of data. When the examples are tightly bunched together and the bell-shaped curve is steep, the standard deviation is small. When the examples are spread apart and the bell curve is flat, this tells you that you have a relatively large standard deviation.

Positively skewed curves and negatively skewed curves

If the shape of the curve is asymmetrical, your data is not distributed normally and is said to be positively or negatively skewed.

▸ Positively skewed means the longer tail of the curve points to the positive (higher) end of the scale and the scores are bunched to the left of the centre.
▸ Negatively skewed means the longer tail of the curve points to the negative (lower) end of the scale and the scores are bunched to the right of the centre.

Figure 9.3(a) shows an example of a positively skewed curve and Figure 9.3(b) demonstrates a negatively skewed curve.

Inferential statistics

Inferential statistics assess relationships or differences between data sets. For example, if you wanted to find out whether PNF stretching increases hamstring flexibility, you could use an appropriate inferential test to get your answer. Inferential tests are further subdivided into two groups: parametric tests and non-parametric tests (see Figure 9.4). The over-arching purpose of inferential statistics is to test your 'null hypothesis' so that you are able to either accept or reject it.

(a)

(b)

▸ **Figure 9.3:** Examples of (a) positively and (b) negatively skewed curves

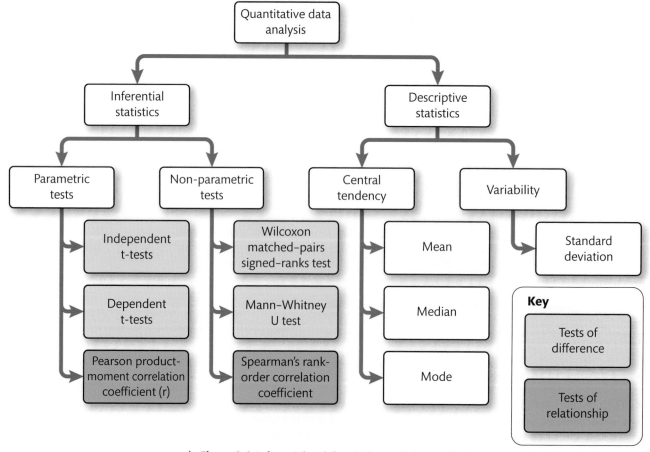

▸ **Figure 9.4:** Inferential and descriptive statistics used in sport research

Selecting appropriate inferential tests

A good way to select your test is to use a decision tree like that in Figure 9.5. If you follow the decision tree using the information available, you will find the test that you need to use. The process of using the decision tree is similar to planning a bus or a train journey – follow the line and find your stops to get to the destination.

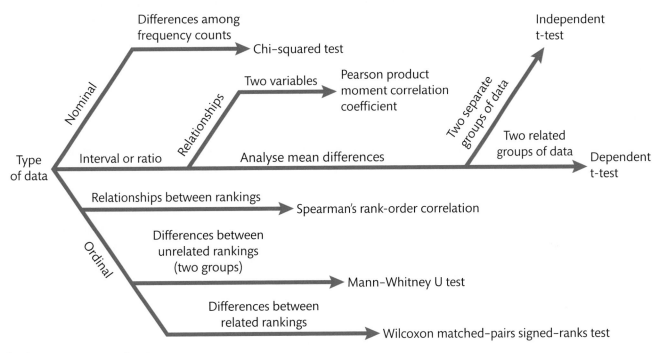

▶ **Figure 9.5:** Statistics decision tree

To be able to use this decision tree and appropriately select parametric or non-parametric tests, you need to understand the types of data: nominal, ordinal, interval and ratio data.

▶ **Parametric tests** use **interval or ratio data** and assume that the data is drawn from a normal distribution and has the same variance.

▶ **Non-parametric tests** use **ordinal or nominal data**.

Nominal data

A nominal scale is where you put participants into categories and count them, for example you group basketball players under their team. You would group the players in this way to count them, not necessarily to say that one group is better than another.

Ordinal data

Ordinal data is ranked data that gives no indication of the difference between levels. It allows you to say who is best and second best, but does not tell you the difference between the two.

This type of data provides the researcher with a rank order, but does not give an exact value. For example, on a badminton ladder, the person at the top is assigned a rank of 1, the person second down is awarded a rank of 2, the third person is awarded a rank of 3, and so on. There is nothing to say, however, that the person at the top of the ladder is three times as good as the person in third place on the ladder.

Interval

Interval data is based on a scale that has equal intervals of measurement with equal intervals between each score. For example, in a figure skating scoring scale there is the same difference between scoring 5 and 5.5 as there is between scoring 5.5 and 6.

Ratio

Ratio data has proportional equal units of measurement. Ratio scales range from zero upwards and cannot have negative scores. For example, if a rugby team scores 40 points, it is worth twice as much as their opponents who have scored 20 points.

How to conduct appropriate inferential statistical tests

This section contains step-by-step instructions, formulae and **tables of critical values** for each of the statistical tests listed in your unit specification. While these will help you learn how to conduct the tests by hand, they will not show you how to complete the tests using different ICT packages (such as Microsoft Excel® or IBM SPSS® statistics). For these programs, you should refer to the appropriate user manual.

> **Key term**
>
> **Table of critical values** – a table that compares statistical testing results to find out if they are significant at a given level.

Parametric tests

The most common t-tests are the dependent t-test (also known as the paired–samples t-test) and the independent t-test. When you complete your t-test and want to see if your result is significant or not, you need to know whether you are completing a **one-tailed test** or a **two-tailed test**.

Dependent t-test

The dependent (paired–samples) t-test examines significant differences between two sets of related scores, for example whether the mean high–jump scores of one group are different when measured pre- and post-training (see the following worked example). The test is calculated using the formula:

$$t = \frac{\Sigma D}{\sqrt{[n\Sigma D^2 - (\Sigma D)^2 \div (n-1)]}}$$

where:

▶ D = difference between before and after

▶ n = number of paired scores

▶ Σ = sum of.

One-tailed test – a test that assumes one group will be better than the other, or at least no worse than the other. For example, girls will be better than boys.

Two-tailed test – a test that assumes there will be a difference between both groups, but does not say which will be better. For example, there will be a difference between girls and boys.

Degree of freedom – used as a correction factor for bias and to limit the effects of outliers, and based on the number of participants you have.

Follow the steps below to carry out the dependent t-test.

1 Calculate your t value using the formula above.

2 Calculate your **degree of freedom** (df) using the formula $df = n - 1$.

3 Compare your t value to the critical values shown in Table 9.4. Find your df value (in this case 9), then go across and see if your result is greater than or equal to the number in the column below the 0.05 level. If the value achieved for your t-test is equal to or greater than the number shown, your results are significant to that level. Note that if $df > 120$, use the infinity row at the end of Table 9.4 (∞).

▶ **Table 9.4:** Critical values of *t*

Level of significance for one-tailed test						
	.10	.05	.025	.01	.005	.0005
Level of significance for two-tailed test						
df	.20	.10	.05	.02	.01	.001
1	3.078	6.314	12.706	31.821	63.657	636.619
2	1.886	2.920	4.303	6.965	9.925	31.598
3	1.638	2.353	3.182	4.541	5.841	12.941
4	1.533	2.132	2.776	3.747	4.604	8.610
5	1.476	2.015	2.571	3.365	4.032	6.589
6	1.440	1.943	2.447	3.143	3.707	5.959
7	1.415	1.895	2.365	2.998	3.499	5.405
8	1.397	1.860	2.306	2.896	3.355	5.041
9	1.383	1.833	2.262	2.821	3.250	4.781
10	1.372	1.812	2.228	2.764	3.169	4.587
11	1.363	1.796	2.201	2.718	3.106	4.437
12	1.356	1.782	2.179	2.681	3.055	4.318
13	1.350	1.771	2.160	2.650	3.012	4.221
14	1.345	1.761	2.145	2.624	2.977	4.140
15	1.341	1.753	2.131	2.602	2.947	4.073
16	1.337	1.746	2.120	2.583	2.921	4.015
17	1.333	1.740	2.110	2.567	2.898	3.965
18	1.330	1.734	2.101	2.552	2.878	3.922
19	1.328	1.729	2.093	2.539	2.861	3.883
20	1.325	1.725	2.086	2.528	2.845	3.850
21	1.323	1.721	2.080	2.518	2.831	3.819
22	1.321	1.717	2.074	2.508	2.819	3.792
23	1.319	1.714	2.069	2.500	2.807	3.767
24	1.318	1.711	2.064	2.492	2.797	3.745
25	1.316	1.708	2.060	2.485	2.787	3.725
26	1.315	1.706	2.056	2.479	2.779	3.707
27	1.314	1.703	2.052	2.473	2.771	3.690
28	1.313	1.701	2.048	2.467	2.763	3.674
29	1.311	1.699	2.045	2.462	2.756	3.659
30	1.310	1.697	2.042	2.457	2.750	3.646
40	1.303	1.684	2.021	2.423	2.704	3.551
60	1.296	1.671	2.000	2.390	2.660	3.460
120	1.289	1.658	1.980	2.358	2.617	3.373
∞	1.282	1.645	1.960	2.326	2.576	3.291

Worked example

Dependent t-test

An investigation explored the effects of a 12-week plyometric training programme on high–jump performance using a dependent t-test. The investigation generated the data shown in Table 9.5.

$$t = \frac{43}{\sqrt{(2490 - 1849) \div 9}}$$

$$t = \frac{43}{\sqrt{641 \div 9}}$$

$$t = \frac{43}{\sqrt{71.22}}$$

$$t = \frac{43}{8.44}$$

$$t = 5.09$$

As you can see, the t value calculated (5.09) is greater than the critical value of t (2.262) meaning the result is significant to the 0.05 level. This means we can say that there is a significant difference between high–jump scores pre- and post-training.

Table 9.5: Effects of a 12-week plyometric training programme on high–jump performance

Subject	Pre-training height (cm)	Post-training height (cm)	D (post-training minus pre-training)	D²
1	176	179	3	9
2	169	172	3	9
3	171	175	4	16
4	173	177	4	16
5	164	166	2	4
6	170	171	1	1
7	161	168	7	49
8	159	169	10	100
9	163	166	3	9
10	170	176	6	36
$n = 10$			$D = 43$	$D^2 = 249$

Independent t-test

The independent t-test is used when you have two groups and are trying to discover whether the mean scores of the two groups can be considered to be significantly different.

It is suitable when the data you have collected is interval or ratio data, when your groups are randomly assigned, and when the variance (or spread) in the two groups is equal. It is calculated using the formula:

$$t = \frac{M_1 - M_2}{\sqrt{s_1^2/n_1 + s_2^2/n_2}}$$

Where:

- M_1 = mean value of group 1
- M_2 = mean value of group 2
- s_1 = standard deviation of group 1
- s_2 = standard deviation of group 2
- n_1 = number of participants in group 1
- n_2 = number of participants in group 2

Worked example

Independent t-test

A research team produced Cooper 12-minute run data (see Table 9.6) and then used the independent t-test formula to see if there was a significant difference between the two groups.

Calculate the degrees of freedom (*df*) using the formula: $df = n_1 + n_2 - 2$ and then compare the *t* value calculated to critical values in Table 9.4.

Where:

$s_1 = 238.3$ $M_1 = 3183.3$ $s_1{}^2 = 56786.89$ $n_1 = 10$

$s_2 = 94.6$ $M_2 = 2468.7$ $s_2{}^2 = 8949.16$ $n_2 = 10$

$$t = \frac{3183.3 - 2468.7}{\sqrt{(238.3)^2 \div 10 + (94.6)^2 \div 10}}$$

$$t = \frac{714.6}{\sqrt{(56786.89) \div 10 + (8949.16) \div 10}}$$

$$t = \frac{714.6}{\sqrt{5678.69 + 894.92}}$$

$$t = \frac{714.6}{\sqrt{6573.61}}$$

$$t = \frac{714.6}{81.08}$$

$$t = 8.81$$

As you can see, the *t* value calculated (8.81) is greater than the critical value of *t* (1.734) meaning the result is significant to the 0.05 level. This means we can say that there is a significant difference between Cooper 12–minute run data in the two groups.

Table 9.6: Cooper 12-minute run data

Subject	Group 1 (12-minute run after 70% VO$_2$ max training)	Group 2 (12-minute run after 40% VO$_2$ max training)
1	3200 m	2513 m
2	3600 m	2601 m
3	2894 m	2444 m
4	3001 m	2361 m
5	3187 m	2541 m
6	3651 m	2486 m
7	3109 m	2611 m
8	2997 m	2419 m
9	3056 m	2400 m
10	3138 m	2311 m
Mean	3183.3 m	2468.7 m
Standard deviation	238.3	94.6

Pearson product-moment correlation coefficient (r)

A correlation is the value of the relationship between two or more variables, which can be positive or negative. Whether it is positive or negative depends on the direction of

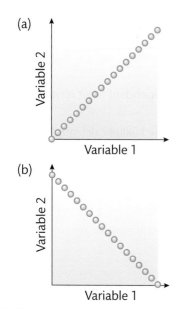

(a)

Variable 2 / Variable 1

(b)

Variable 2 / Variable 1

▶ **Figure 9.6:** Examples of perfect positive and negative correlations

the line when the results are plotted on a graph. Figure 9.6 shows examples of perfect positive and perfect negative correlations, but it is rare to record such correlations during data analysis.

The Pearson product-moment correlation coefficient is a parametric test that is suitable when you have interval or ratio data and you are trying to identify a relationship between two variables. It is a test of association, which means it looks at whether two or more variables are related.

The test can be used in two ways:

▸ *either* you can try to find out a relationship between two variables

▸ *or* you can try to predict one score from another.

In a simple correlation that is trying to find out a relationship between two variables, it does not matter which variable is assigned *X* and which *Y*. However, if you are trying to predict one score from another, then *X* is the independent variable and *Y* is the dependent variable.

There are three stages to using the Pearson product-moment correlation:

1 summing each set of scores

2 squaring and summing each set of scores

3 multiplying each pair of scores and obtaining the cumulative sum of these products.

The formula for this is:

$$r = \frac{n\Sigma XY - (\Sigma X)(\Sigma Y)}{[\sqrt{n\Sigma X^2 - (\Sigma X)^2}][\sqrt{n\Sigma Y^2 - (\Sigma Y)^2}]}$$

where:

▸ *n* = number of paired scores

▸ Σ = sum of

▸ *X* = scores for one variable

▸ *Y* = scores for the other variable

▸ $\Sigma (X)^2$ = sum of raw scores for *X*, squared

▸ $\Sigma (Y)^2$ = sum of raw scores for *Y*, squared

▸ ΣX^2 = sum of all the X^2 scores

▸ ΣY^2 = sum of all the Y^2 scores.

To interpret the significance of your *r* value, select your level of significance (remember that in sport research this is normally 0.05) and find your degree of freedom (*df*) for your test. For this test, use the formula *df* = *n* – 2 and compare your *r* value to Table 9.7 to find whether your results are significant. If your result is equal to or greater than the critical value in the table, your result is significant.

▶ **Table 9.7:** Critical values of Pearson product-moment correlation coefficient

Level of significance for one-tailed test					
df	.05	.025	.01	.005	.001
Level of significance for two-tailed test					
df	**.10**	**.05**	**.02**	**.01**	**.001**
1	.9877	.9969	.9995	.9999	1.000
2	.9000	.9500	.9800	.9900	.9990
3	.8054	.8783	.9343	.9587	.9912
4	.7293	.8114	.8822	.9172	.9741
5	.6694	.7545	.8329	.8745	.9507
6	.6215	.7067	.7887	.8343	.9249
7	.5822	.6664	.7498	.7977	.8982

▶ **Table 9.7:** *Continued...*

Level of significance for two-tailed test					
8	.5494	.6319	.7155	.7646	.8721
9	.5214	.6021	.6851	.7348	.8471
10	.4973	.5760	.6581	.7079	.8233
11	.4762	.5529	.6339	.6835	.8010
12	.4575	.5324	.6120	.6614	.7800
13	.4409	.5139	.5923	.6411	.7603
14	.4259	.4973	.5742	.6226	.7420
15	.4124	.4821	.5577	.6055	.7246
16	.4000	.4683	.5425	.5897	.7084
17	.3887	.4555	.5285	.5751	.6932
18	.3783	.4438	.5155	.5614	.6787
19	.3687	.4329	.5034	.5487	.6652
20	.3598	.4227	.4921	.5368	.6524
25	.3233	.3809	.4451	.4869	.5974
30	.2960	.3494	.4093	.4487	.5541
35	.2746	.3246	.3810	.4182	.5189
40	.2573	.3044	.3578	.3932	.4896
45	.2428	.2875	.3384	.3721	.4648
50	.2306	.2732	.3218	.3541	.4433
60	.2108	.2500	.2948	.3248	.4078
70	.1954	.2319	.2737	.3017	.3799
80	.1829	.2172	.2565	.2830	.3568
90	.1726	.2050	.2422	.2673	.3375
100	.1638	.1946	.2301	.2540	.3211

Non-parametric tests

If the data is non-parametric, t-tests cannot be used. In this case, the Wilcoxon matched–pairs signed–ranks test is used in place of the dependent t-test, and the Mann–Whitney U test is used in place of the independent t-test. The Spearman rank-order correlation test purpose is similar to the Pearson product-moment correlation coefficient.

Wilcoxon matched–pairs signed–rank test

The Wilcoxon matched-pairs signed–rank test is used when you are trying to find out if there is a significant difference between two scores (or 'conditions') that are taken from the same participant (or from matched participants). It is used when the data is ordinal (ranked). To do the test, work through the following steps.

1 Disregard any results for participants who scored the same in both conditions, then count the number of paired scores left. This is your *n* score.
2 Calculate the difference between the two scores of each participant, assigning plus or minus signs (*d*).
3 Rank the differences, giving the smallest a rank of 1 (ignoring plus or minus signs, i.e. +2 is of the same value as –2). When two scores are tied, each is given the mean of the two ranks and the next rank is missed out (for example, if two participants are in joint sixth place, they are both given the rank of 6.5 and the next place is given a rank of 8).
4 Add up the ranks of all the minus scores.
5 Add up the ranks of all the plus scores.

Reflect

Can you think of examples when, as a sport-based practitioner, you might find correlation tests useful?

6 Take the smaller of the two figures calculated in points 4 and 5 to gain your *w* value.

7 Look up your value for *w* in a significance table. If it is equal to or less than the figure in the 0.05 column, the result is significant at that level. A table of significance can be found at: **www.real-statistics.com/statistics-tables/wilcoxon-signed-ranks-table//**

▶ **Table 9.8:** Using the Wilcoxon matched–pairs signed–rank test to assess effect of imagery training

Subject pair	Condition A (run times pre-imagery training)	Condition B (run times post-imagery training)	*d* (A minus B)	Rank of *d*	Rank of plus differences	Rank of minus differences
1	11.09	11.00				
2	11.23	11.25				
3	11.55	11.32				
4	11.46	11.36				
5	11.22	11.73				
6	11.13	11.43				
7	11.01	10.86				
8	10.93	10.55				
9	10.99	10.90				
10	11.39	11.10				
					Total	Total
						w =

Mann–Whitney U test

The Mann–Whitney U test is the non-parametric equivalent of the independent t-test. You would use this if you have ranked data, or not normally distributed data. You use the 'U' value to find out if one group ranks significantly higher than the other when measured against the same variable (for example assessing the number of 180s scored by darts players in the British Darts Organisation against the Professional Darts Corporation).

Spearman's rank–order correlation test

Spearman's rank–order correlation test has a similar purpose to the Pearson product-moment correlation coefficient. However, it is a non-parametric equivalent and is used when your data is ordinal (ranked).

This test should be used when you want to find a relationship between two sets of ordinal data (for example, goals scored and final league position in football, or serving accuracy and final ladder position in badminton, or golf driving distance and final leader board position).

The first step is to rank your data (goals scored/serving accuracy/golf driving distance) from highest to lowest, with 1 being the highest. After this, determine the difference between your data and the place in the tournament. This must be squared and then summed. The formula used for the test is:

$$r_s = \frac{6(\Sigma D^2)}{n(n^2 - 1)}$$

where:

▶ *n* = number of ranked pairs

▶ *D* = difference between each pair

▶ ΣD^2 = the sum of the squared differences between rank.

To interpret the significance of your r_s value, select the level of significance (0.05) and calculate the degree of freedom (*df*) for your test. For Spearman's rank–order correlation test, this is calculated using the formula *n* – 2. Compare your value to the table of significance in Table 9.9.

▶ **Table 9.9:** Table of critical values for Spearman's rank–order correlation

df	.10	.05	.01
5	0.90		
6	0.83	0.89	
7	0.71	0.79	0.93
8	0.64	0.74	0.88
9	0.60	0.68	0.83
10	0.56	0.656	0.79
11	0.52	0.61	0.77
12	0.50	0.59	0.75
13	0.47	0.56	0.71
14	0.46	0.54	0.69
15	0.44	0.52	0.66
16	0.42	0.51	0.64
17	0.41	0.49	0.62
18	0.40	0.48	0.61
19	0.39	0.46	0.60
20	0.38	0.45	0.58
21	0.37	0.44	0.56
22	0.36	0.43	0.55
23	0.35	0.42	0.54
24	0.34	0.41	0.53
25	0.34	0.40	0.52
26	0.33	0.39	0.51
27	0.32	0.38	0.50
28	0.32	0.38	0.49
29	0.31	0.37	0.48
∞	0.31	0.36	0.47

Practical meaningfulness statistics

Inferential statistics are used in quantitative research to accept or reject your null hypothesis, and therefore your hypothesis. However, inferential statistics do not give you information about the practical significance of your results, such as how effective a treatment has been. To do this, you need to use practical meaningfulness statistics. Two of the most common methods look at percentage change and effect size.

Percentage change

Calculating percentage change gives you a simple statistic that provides basic information about the effectiveness of a treatment or an intervention (such as how beneficial a particular training method has been) in a way that most people can understand quite easily. The formula for calculating percentage change is:

$$\text{percentage change} = ((X_2 - X_1) \div X_1) \times 100$$

where:

▶ X_1 = pre-test mean values

▶ X_2 = post-test mean values.

Effect size

As its name suggests, you use the effect size calculation to determine how effective

Discussion

If you were a strength and conditioning coach working with clients on a daily basis, why would you find practical meaningfulness statistics useful?

a particular treatment has been, with the test providing a result equating to a small, moderate or large effect size. A value of 0.2 to <0.5 equates to a small effect size, a value of 0.5 to <0.8 equates to a moderate effect size, while a value of >0.8 equates to a large effect size. The larger the effect size, the more effective a treatment has been. The formula for effect size is:

$$\text{effect size} = (X_1 - X_2)/SD_{control}$$

where:

▶ X_1 = treatment group
▶ X_2 = control group
▶ $SD_{control}$ = standard deviation of the control group.

Ⅱ PAUSE POINT What are the main practical meaningfulness statistics that you can use in sport-based research?

Hint List the main practical meaningfulness statistics and state how you would use each one.

Extend What are the key benefits of using this type of statistic, for coaches?

Qualitative research designs

There are four main types of qualitative research design: case studies, historical/retrospective design, grounded theories and ethnographic design.

Case study

Case study research is where you investigate a particular phenomenon (for example an individual or team) over a long period of time. It takes into account the development of the area of investigation over time and the environment in which the research takes place. Multiple case studies can also be used, where two or more cases are examined at the same time.

For example, a case study would be suitable to investigate the psychological effects of injury at different stages of injury and recovery. It allows you to investigate one person over a period of time and at different times throughout the stages of injury. This means you can draw conclusions relating to that individual and suggest these conclusions as directions for future research on a larger scale.

Historical/retrospective design

Historical or retrospective research is aimed at collecting and analysing data relating to past events to try to explain how or why those events happened. For example, Gledhill and Forsdyke (2015) conducted retrospective interviews with former female football players who had retired from the sport to investigate the role of injury in their decision to retire.

Grounded theory

Use a grounded theory when you aim to produce a theory from the data that you can collect and analyse. You would usually show the theory you have produced as a diagram. For example, you could interview former professional players in a particular sport, and the people involved in their development, and use the information you gathered to develop a theory about the factors that contribute to a successful career in that sport.

Ethnographic design

Ethnographic design aims to study a group or culture by becoming immersed within that group to carry out observations. For example, Atkinson (2007) used an ethnographic design to study the use of supplements by gym-goers who were trying to enhance their masculinity.

Reflect

Think about your favourite topic within sport. Can you think of a way that the different qualitative designs could be used to investigate the topic?

Qualitative data collection techniques

Interviews

Interviews can be separated into individual and group-based interviews. There are three main types of individual interview.

▸ **Structured interviews** – a set interview plan that you follow without change, regardless of participant responses.

▸ **Unstructured interviews** – this type of interview has a start question and then the conversation goes from there. You must be skilled at focusing your conversation to get a lot out of this type of interview.

▸ **Semi-structured interviews** – an interview that follows the original plan but allows scope for follow-up **probe questions** if a topic of interest is brought up. This is a good technique as it allows you to get deeper information from your participant through additional questioning, as well as giving the participant the opportunity to discuss things further.

Key term

Probe questions – questions used to explore a topic further when it appears as part of an interview. Examples of probe questions include elaboration, clarification and prompts to continue.

Focus groups

Focus groups are similar to individual interviews but involve more than one participant. There are usually between six and twelve participants and the researcher acts as a discussion facilitator rather than an interviewer. In this context, your role as the researcher is to ensure that the focus group keeps to the topic and does not digress.

Focus groups are more effective if everyone joins in with the discussion. They can provide a better quality of data because the discussion gets deeper as the ideas develop. They are a good at finding opinions and ideas.

Advantages and disadvantages of interviews

No one type of interview is perfect – it should be matched to the situation or participant. Interviews are used in qualitative research because they are a useful way for researchers to understand the beliefs, opinions and emotions of participants: the researcher gets a view of what the participant thinks in their own words. This gives the researcher a greater understanding of the meaning that the participant attaches to their experiences.

▸ **Table 9.10:** Advantages and disadvantages of interviews

Advantages	Disadvantages
Participants can express their views in their own words.	They require more resources and are more time-consuming than using questionnaires.
Participants can provide information from their own perspective.	They tend to use small sample sizes because they are time-consuming.
Unexpected data may come out in the interview.	The participant(s) can take the interview off in a number of directions.
You can assess body language, tone and pitch of voice, and speed of speech.	Data analysis is more difficult and takes longer than using questionnaires.
You can establish a rapport with the participant(s) and investigate target groups.	The quality of the data is dependent on the quality of the questioning and quality of responses.

Conducting effective interviews

Interviews are used in qualitative research as they help you get lots of information about a topic quickly, but this only works if you have developed good interview skills. In interviews, you will only get answers to the questions you ask. If you ask the wrong questions, you will never find out what you want.

To get the most out of an interview, establish some form of relationship with your participant by setting the tone of the interview; have a friendly chat before starting or break the ice with more general questions at the start that do not need much thought to answer. You can then progress to more specific questions likely to lead to more detailed responses. Guide the conversation around your research problem. Gently probe the participant further to provide you with examples of things they have experienced, rather than hypothetical examples.

When interviewing in research, a three-stage technique is often used.

1 The researcher asks the main question (for example, 'What motivates you to...?'). This gets the conversation started.
2 The researcher asks probe questions (for example, 'Can you give me a specific example of...?'). This clarifies or deepens understanding or knowledge.
3 Finally, the researcher asks a follow-up question (for example, 'So, am I correct in saying that...?'). This gives the researcher the opportunity to check they have understood what the participant has said and that it is taken in the correct context.

Remember that the listening part of an interview is as important as the speaking part. A good interviewer knows when to keep quiet and listen, and when to speak. Do not interrupt the participant when they are speaking as this can prevent them from wanting to answer further questions.

Ⅱ PAUSE POINT   You want to understand an injured player's experiences of injury and gain an in-depth understanding of their expectations around returning to competition. Which interview type would you use?

 Think about each interview type in turn and consider whether it would be appropriate in this case.

 Explain why you would use your chosen interview type, and justify why you would not use other available options.

Observations

Observations are qualitative data collection methods that take place in a natural setting. They allow you to observe behaviours a participant may not know they display, or would not like to disclose during an interview. As such, observations can add a different dimension to your research.

Data is often recorded in field notes, which can be handwritten or typed/recorded on a smartphone. Field notes should describe the activity or setting you are observing (for example, behaviours you have seen and when) and be as detailed as possible without spending more time writing than observing. You should reflect on your thoughts and feelings as the researcher during your observations.

▶ **Table 9.11:** Advantages and disadvantages of observations

Advantages	Disadvantages
They can be 'here and now' rather than being dependent on memory.	There is potential for the researcher to misunderstand what they are seeing.
They can take place in natural settings rather than research settings.	It can be difficult to identify and record the correct type of data.
They allow for the identification of behaviours that may not be apparent to the person and may not have been discovered through interviews.	The Hawthorne effect: if the person knows they are the subject of research, they may act differently and could invalidate the whole project – the researcher must be very careful as to how they approach the people in observational research.
They allow for the identification of behaviours that the person may not wish to disclose.	

Participant observation

Participant observation involves you being actively involved in the topic you are researching. For example, if you were studying team cohesion in rugby, you could join a rugby team to observe 'from the inside' and gain your own experiences of cohesion as a player. Data would then be recorded in the form of field notes with you recording your own thoughts, feelings, opinions, emotions and experiences. This method is useful when trying to discover the more **nuanced** aspects of group behaviour that are not easy to see from the outside.

Non-participant observation

Non-participant observation involves you observing 'from the outside'. There is no interaction with the individuals or the activity being observed. For example, if you wanted to look at injuries during a basketball match, you could watch how many injuries happened and what types of injuries they were, and record the numbers on a data recording sheet.

PAUSE POINT You want to investigate team cohesion in netball using observations. Therefore, you need to prepare a proposal for the approval panel. What type of observation would you use?

> Hint Produce a table that contrasts the two types of observation.

> Extend Discuss the advantages and disadvantages of each type of observation, and then state which method you have selected.

Qualitative data analysis methods

Appropriate methods of data analysis

Selecting an appropriate method of analysis for your qualitative data is an important aspect of the research process. Three common qualitative data analysis methods are: content analysis, coding and thematic analysis.

Content analysis

Qualitative content analysis is an umbrella term used to describe methods of analysing qualitative communications – such as interviews or focus groups – with a specific focus on the context in which the communication took place and the content of the communication. It involves you looking at the content of the interview and grouping different data together under themes, which are then refined and developed into your final data analysis.

The key differences between this and other methods (such as coding and thematic analysis) are that content analysis does not aim to develop a specific theory in the same way as coding does within grounded theory, and that it is more flexible in its use than thematic analysis.

Coding

Coding involves organising raw data (sentences, phrases or words from your questionnaires or interviews) into categories. Each category must have a valid heading and a **rule for inclusion**, which helps to decide in which category to place each piece of data.

For example, if you were researching 'factors affecting talent development in football', you could have a category called 'importance of parental tangible support'. A rule for inclusion could be 'statement made refers to concrete support given to player from parent (for example, the purchase of playing kit or transport to matches), being either a positive or negative influence on the player's development'.

Before starting your coding, you should read and re-read your transcribed data to gain an in-depth understanding of that data. The process starts with open coding, progresses to axial coding and ends with selective coding.

▸ **Open coding** – data is broken down and examined. Your aim is to identify all the key statements in the interviews relating to the aims of your research and your research problem. After identifying the key statements, you can start to put the key points into categories, but each category must be given a suitable heading. When you start to organise your data into categories, you have started the coding process.

Key terms

Nuance – a very slight, hardly noticeable difference in manner or meaning.

Rule for inclusion – a statement used to define which data is included in a category.

Research

Research the analysis method of hierarchical content analysis. What are the stages involved and why do you think this type of content analysis is popular with qualitative researchers?

▸ **Axial coding** – the next stage is to put the data back together. Part of this process means re-reading the data you have collected so that you can give precise explanations about your area of interest. To do this, you need to refine the categories that you started to create during open coding. During this stage, you may develop new categories (and therefore new codes). To be able to refine your codes at this stage, ask more questions about the categories (and the codes) you have created. Here are some questions to consider.
- Can I put certain codes together under a more general code?
- Can I place codes in a particular order?
- Can I identify any relationships between different codes?

▸ **Selective coding** is the final stage. It involves finalising your categories (and codes) so that you can group them together. When you group them together, you will produce different diagrams to show how your categories link together. The key part of this is to select a main category that will form the focal point of your diagram. You also need to look for data that contradicts previous research, rather than data that supports it. This helps you to make better arguments and draw more conclusions based on your data.

Thematic analysis

Thematic analysis is a common qualitative data analysis technique originally put forward by Braun and Clarke (2006). It is different to other methods of qualitative data analysis as it has six stages, or steps, that you progress through to reach your final analysis. This process is useful for some novice qualitative researchers as it provides a framework for analysis that you can follow while still offering you the flexibility of qualitative analysis.

Step by step: Thematic analysis

`6 steps`

1 Immersion – become familiar with your data by, for example, reading interview transcripts repeatedly so that you gain a deep understanding.

2 Generate initial codes – create codes across the full data set and produce a list of all of them. You can then ensure that you have included all the relevant data under each code.

3 Search for and identify themes – think more broadly beyond codes and progress to more general themes. Identify codes that are relevant to each other, group them together into a theme, and then give the theme a working title. At this stage, you would usually produce a thematic map – a form of mind map – that shows how the different codes link together to form a particular theme.

4 Refine themes – think critically about the themes that you produced in step 3, looking at, for example, any potential overlap or repetition so that you can produce themes that more succinctly represent the data. While doing this, consider any data that did not fall into any of the codes at step 1 and see if you can fit it into your themes.

5 Define and name themes – write a short definition (two or three sentences maximum) about the content of the theme and give the theme a name that accurately represents the content. This is another opportunity to ensure that your themes are not too broad as, by writing your description of the theme, you will be further reflecting on the content of each theme.

6 Write the report – write your report of the thematic analysis. You should use quotes or extracts from data that clearly demonstrate the themes in your study. Even at this stage, you should reflect on your analysis so far, to ensure that it fairly represents the data you collected.

Stages of qualitative data analysis

Qualitative research will generally go through three stages, originally put forward by Miles and Huberman (1994): firstly, data reduction; secondly, displaying data; and thirdly, drawing conclusions and verifying data.

> **Discussion**
>
> What do you think are the advantages and disadvantages of using thematic analysis in qualitative research?

Data reduction

Data reduction is the process of taking all the data that you have (for example, field notes from observations and interview transcripts) and organising this data into more manageable chunks. This is done in different ways, and can involve any of the methods of qualitative data analysis explored in the previous section (content analysis, coding or thematic analysis).

When going through this stage, you might be tempted to permanently discard some of your data. However, you should avoid doing this until your project is finished and you are certain that you no longer need it.

Displaying data

There are different ways to display your data. The way that you display it will affect the argument or point you are trying to make. For instance, a Venn diagram is used to show interactions between different aspects of the data, whereas a cycle diagram shows a cyclical relationship.

Diagramming is a technique that you can use throughout your data analysis to help you to understand the relationships between different aspects of your data, as well as at the end of your data analysis to represent these relationships.

Network diagrams show hierarchical relationships between different ideas. Figure 9.7 shows that there are several benefits to the use of imagery (the top of the hierarchy or the most important part of information to take away) and that these benefits include increased self-efficacy, skill acquisition and injury rehabilitation.

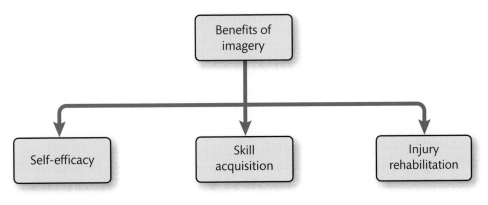

▶ **Figure 9.7:** A network diagram

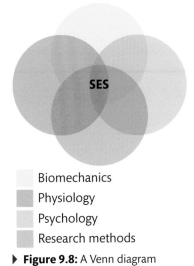

Biomechanics
Physiology
Psychology
Research methods

▶ **Figure 9.8:** A Venn diagram

Venn diagrams consist of two or more overlapping circles. They show how different topics relate to each other. In the example in Figure 9.8, you can see how the different disciplines within sport and exercise sciences (SES) interact to make up the overall discipline.

A **radial diagram** (also known as a **spider diagram**) illustrates a relationship where each item is linked to a central item. This diagram can be thought of as a simple organisation chart that starts from the centre rather than the top (see Figure 9.9 below).

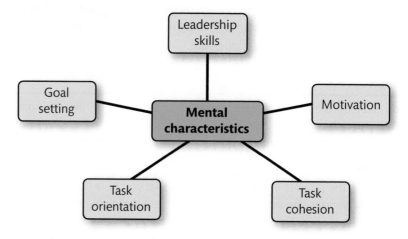

▶ **Figure 9.9:** A radial diagram

A **cycle diagram** shows the stages in a process as a continuous cycle. The process is shown as a cycle, with a break at each stage, and an arrowhead to show the direction of the process. In the example in Figure 9.10, the diagram shows that team cohesion affects team performance, which in turn affects team cohesion further, and so on.

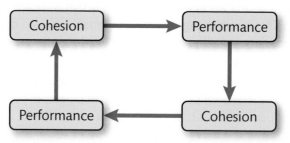

▶ **Figure 9.10:** A cycle diagram

Theory into practice

Write down when you would use each of the diagrams that are covered on this page and why.

Drawing conclusions and verifying data

Your data analysis should allow you to draw meaningful conclusions about your data and then verify these conclusions. Doing this can help you to ensure the validity and reliability of your research. Two common techniques used to do this are triangulation and member checking.

▶ **Triangulation** can refer to using different data collection methods in the same study to check that similar data is produced. For example, you could use interviews and questionnaires or you could use the same interviews with different types of participants (such as athletes and coaches). Alternatively, it can refer to asking different researchers to collect data and independently draw conclusions before checking their findings with each other.

▶ During **member checking**, you complete your data analysis and draw conclusions relating to the aims of the study. You then show the analysis to the participants who took part in the research so that they can check that you have understood and communicated everything correctly. If they agree with your analysis, you can say that the data is valid.

(II) PAUSE POINT   Produce a 'novice guide' to qualitative research that explains what happens at the different stages.

> Hint   What are the different stages of qualitative data analysis?

> Extend   Think of an example research project and explain how you would apply the different stages of qualitative data analysis to this project

---

Assessment practice 9.2   C.P5 C.P6 C.M3 C.D3

Great news! Following on from assessment activity 9.1, your application letter has got you an interview for the internship. In the interview, you are required to deliver a presentation that:

- introduces the three main approaches to research in sport so that the football club can see how well you will be able to apply these if you conduct any research with the players
- presents the methods and results from a mini-investigation that you have conducted, so that the club can see your ability to correctly select a method for a topic and your ability to appropriately present results about a topic.

You should create a PowerPoint presentation and any handouts that you can use to help you deliver your presentation.

Plan
- What are the key parts to the presentation that form the whole task?
- Do I need clarification on anything? Do I know how to interpret the results of my statistical test?
- What aspects of the task do I think will take the most/least time?

Do
- Can I make connections between what I am reading/researching and the task, and identify the important information?
- Can I set milestones and evaluate my progress and success at these intervals?

Review
- Can I explain what the task was and how I approached it?
- Can I explain how I would use this type of activity in working life or in another unit on my course, such as *Unit 11: Research Project in Sport*?
- Do I know which research methods I am confident with (and which not) and how I can improve this?

> **Further reading and resources**

Books

Gratton, C. and Jones, I. (2009) *Research Methods for Sport Studies*, 2nd edition, Oxford: Routledge.

Smith, M.F. (2010) *Research Methods in Sport*, Exeter: Learning Matters.

Sparkes, A.C. and Smith, B. (2014) *Qualitative Research Methods in Sport, Exercise and Health: From Process to Product*, Oxford: Routledge.

Thomas, J.R., Nelson, J.K., and Silverman, S.J. (2011) *Research Methods in Physical Activity*, 6th edition, Illinois: Human Kinetics.

Journals

Gledhill, A. and Harwood, C. (2015) A holistic perspective on career development in UK female soccer players: A negative case analysis, *Psychology of Sport and Exercise*, 21: 65–77.

THINK ▶FUTURE

Mohammed Khan

Strength and conditioning coach

I've been working as a strength and conditioning coach in professional basketball for two years. During this time, I have encountered so many different athletes for whom I've had to produce individualised training programmes, either for sport performance or injury rehabilitation purposes.

When I completed my BTEC Level 3 Sport, I went to university and completed a course in Performance Conditioning, then completed my UK Strength and Conditioning Association accreditation. This complemented my existing basketball coaching qualifications and playing experience so I'm happy that I have the subject-specific knowledge as well as an understanding of the sport. This gives me solid background knowledge when I carry out research.

Having an understanding of the sport you work in is essential for effective work as a strength and conditioning coach. So is the ability to develop and maintain effective working relationships with different individuals. In doing so, you are more likely to be able to get to know your players which is really useful when it comes to trying to get them to agree to try things like new training methods you have researched.

It is also important to keep up with developments when it comes to researching new strength and conditioning methods as they are regularly advancing, and if you don't know what the best methods are, you can't offer the best quality of service and support to your clients. This is important as the safety and well-being of your players is always your main concern when you are working in sport, even more important than their levels of performance. So having them train and perform in the way they should be doing is more likely to mean they will stay safe and well.

Focusing on your skills

Conducting research with athletes

Research is important for the continued development of sports teams and athletes as it helps to develop knowledge, understanding and skills. You should think about the following points.
- Before completing any research with a client, make sure that you have their consent.
- Make sure that you provide them with a clear information sheet so that they know exactly what will be required of them.
- Make sure that you have a good depth of knowledge, understanding and skills across each of the main approaches to research.
- Remember, there is no one best approach to research, only approaches that are best suited to answering research questions.

Getting ready for assessment

Jessica is working towards a BTEC National in Sport. She was given an assignment with the following title: 'The role of research in sport: Why is it important and what factors can affect it?' for learning aims A and B. The report had to:

▸ discuss the importance of research in sporting environments

▸ examine the key issues that have an impact on the effectiveness and quality of research in sport and exercise sciences.

How I got started

First, I decided on which sport I wanted to base my report on. I chose a sport that I am interested in because I knew this would make me more motivated and committed to doing a good piece of work.

I collated all my notes for these learning aims and separated them into different sections on the importance of research and the different factors that can impact on the quality and effectiveness of research.

Finally, I wrote a plan for my assignment that included key headings that I was going to include and a mind map for each section that showed what I wanted to include. The mind map started with each of the topic areas in the centre and developed outwards into what I needed to say about each of the topic areas giving steadily more detail.

How I brought it all together

To start, I wrote a short introduction that outlined the purpose of the work that I was doing. After this, I separated my assignment down into six different sub-sections:

▸ a definition of research, that I referenced from an appropriate source

▸ a discussion of the different types of research

▸ a discussion of the importance of research for those working in sport and for informing your work with clients. Within this, I talked about things like the importance of evidence-based practice.

▸ the role of validity, reliability, accuracy and precision in research

▸ ethical issues associated with sport and exercise science research

▸ a conclusion.

What I learned from the experience

There are lots of different things to think about when you are looking at how research applies in sport settings. It is important to know how they apply in sport, not just what they are. This made the assignment a little bit difficult at times but using examples in my assignment made it easier to get to grips with it, as I was talking about it in a context that I understood.

I think I spent a bit too much time focusing on defining key words like validity and reliability, rather than looking in depth at the different types. I would look at understanding the different types in more depth as they each have different roles to play and just looking at validity and reliability in general is a little too basic.

Think about it

▸ Have you planned your assignment so that you know you will be able to complete it by the submission deadline?

▸ Do you have the recommended resources as well as your class notes to help you to provide evidence and references to support and develop the arguments that you plan to make?

▸ Is your assignment written in your own words?

Sports Event Organisation 10

Getting to know your unit

Sports event organisation is a global industry worth billions of pounds every year. High-quality events are essential to sports and generate interest, raising their profile and ultimately increasing the number of participants taking part in the sport. At the very highest level, events can enhance a country's profile and act as a catalyst for future success. In this unit, you will research a variety of events, propose your own even, and then plan and deliver your event. Afterwards, you will review your successes and areas for improvement.

How you will be assessed

A series of internally set assignments will be used to assess you throughout this unit. The activities in this unit are designed to replicate real life and give you an experience which will develop your own skills and techniques, many of which will be transferable. Although completing these tasks will not guarantee you a certain grade, they will allow you to practise scenarios and gather a valuable insight into events and their organisation.

Gaining a Pass grade relies on you completing all the tasks in the unit. Ensuring that you are methodical and complete all tasks is essential to your success.

For a Merit or Distinction grade, you will need to enhance your performance in completing the tasks and ensure that you deliver in a style that fulfils the more demanding criteria. For example, when looking at other sporting events, a basic discussion will enable you to achieve a Pass but an evaluation will meet the needs of a Distinction.

The tasks in the assignment set by your tutor will be varied and allow you to use a variety of styles to demonstrate your understanding. They could include:

▶ designing a presentation to pitch an idea for a new event to a board of industry professionals
▶ organising an event for local schools to try out new sports and activities
▶ completing worksheets to review your performance while planning and delivering a sports event.

Assessment criteria

This table shows what you must do in order to achieve a **Pass**, **Merit** or **Distinction** grade, and where you can find activities to help you.

Pass	Merit	Distinction
Learning aim **A** Investigate how different types of sports events are planned and delivered		
A.P1 Discuss the planning, promotion and delivery of two different types of sports events. Assessment practice 10.1	**A.M1** Compare the planning, promotion and delivery of two different sports events. Assessment practice 10.1	**A.D1** Evaluate own feasible planned proposal for a sports event to meet targeted aims to recommend improvements. Assessment practice 10.1
Learning aim **B** Develop a proposal for a sports event for implementation approval		
B.P2 Explain own feasible planned proposal for a sports event to meet targeted aims. Assessment practice 10.2	**B.M2** Analyse own feasible planned proposal for a sports event to meet targeted aims. Assessment practice 10.2	**B.D2** Evaluate own feasible planned proposal for a sports event to meet targeted aims to recommend improvements. Assessment practice 10.3
Learning aim **C** Undertake the planning, promotion and delivery of a sports event		
C.P3 Plan for the promotion and delivery of a sports event, contributing effectively to team activities. Assessment practice 10.3	**C.M3** Manage key decisions for planning and delivering individual and team activities to meet planned outcomes for promotion and delivery of a sports event. Assessment practice 10.3	**CD.D3** Evaluate own performance in planning, promoting and delivering a sports event, justifying choices, strengths and recommendations for future practice. Assessment practice 10.4
C.P4 Perform tasks/activities fully, correctly and safely to achieve planned outcomes for the promotion and delivery of a sports event. Assessment practice 10.3		
Learning aim **D** Review the planning, promotion and delivery of a sports event and reflect on your own performance		
D.P5 Discuss the effectiveness of the planning, promotion and delivery of the sports event, explaining strengths and weaknesses and areas for development. Assessment practice 10.4	**D.M4** Analyse the effectiveness of the planning, promotion and delivery of the sports event, recommending areas for improvement for self and future events. Assessment practice 10.4	
D.P6 Explain own contribution to the planning, promotion and delivery of the sports event using personal logs and feedback from others. Assessment practice 10.4		

Getting started

Sports events are numerous and diverse. Give yourself five minutes to name as many as you can. Are there any which you feel are more successful than others? Justify your thoughts. Setting up sports events can take a large amount of time and energy. What do you think are the main challenges faced by anyone trying to organise a sports event?

A Investigate how different types of sports events are planned and delivered

Link

This unit can link with *Unit 4: Sports Leadership* if there is an opportunity to combine assignment work by running an event that requires you to demonstrate leadership skills.

There are numerous factors that must be considered and managed when planning and delivering a sports event. No matter what the scale of an event, there will be restrictions on delivery. These may come from local or national government, from working to a budget, from following governing body guidelines or meeting the expectations of the audience. A sports event that does not fulfil every demand that it is expected to cannot ultimately be deemed successful.

Different types of sports events

Understanding the purpose of a sports event is fundamental to ensuring its success. There are many types of sports events and selecting the correct type and format for your audience or to achieve your aims is the first task of any event organiser. Table 10.1 shows different types of sports events with a brief description of each one.

▶ **Table 10.1:** Different types of sports events

Type of event	Description of event
Tournaments and competitions	Where teams or individuals meet to compete to find a winner. If numerous teams or individuals are competing, there will often be a series of stages that make up a tournament. In some tournaments losers are immediately knocked out, but in others participants have an opportunity to compete against a variety of opponents in groups, with the best from each group moving on to the next stage.
Training camps	Where individuals or teams are invited to come together to develop skills and techniques. These often happen over several days and are most likely to take place off season. For individuals and teams with large budgets, these may often take place abroad in locations that increase the likelihood of good conditions that will maximise opportunities to train.
Coaching courses	Allow sports participants to come together to look at specific skills under an experienced coach. Often governing body awards in proficiency are associated with coaching courses.
Conferences	Where experts make presentations to an audience on a chosen topic, allowing time for interaction with the audience and feedback on the subject matter.
Campaign events	Designed to promote interest in a team, individual or larger event. Often the priority is ensuring maximum exposure and building a buzz around the subject. They help ensure sponsors get value for money, and that teams and individuals get the support needed to build their confidence to succeed.
Charity and fundraising events	Designed to raise funds for a charity – are numerous and varied. They can take the form of a simple competition or tournament, parades or challenges. Sponsored events such as 10k runs are popular examples of this.
Expeditions	May take place in any terrain and use any mode of transport to make progress. However, all expeditions force participants out of their normal environment and have an ultimate purpose such as climbing a challenging mountain, kayaking down a river or looking for rare animals in the wilderness.
Outdoor education	Could take the form of a competition, coaching course or expedition. Taking part in outdoor education has proven benefits for people's social and personal development. Team-building events for corporate clients are big business and use outdoor experiences to develop transferable skills such as cooperation and communication.
Social, personal or physical development	Taking part in any sport will have benefits for social, personal and physical development. It is possible to tailor an event to highlight these benefits and make them clear to participants using reflective sessions and focused briefing about tasks.

Scale

Events take place at all levels from grass-roots events that are highly localised up to global events attracting visitors from right round the world and watched on television by millions. All events have a place in the success of sports and value in making people more active. Table 10.2 shows examples of different scales of events.

▸ **Table 10.2:** Different scales of sporting events

Type	Example
Local	• School sports day • 5-a-side football league
Regional	• Dorset Schools beach event • Southwest Netball League
National	• FA Premier League • British Stand Up Paddleboarding N1SCO One Design Championships
Global	• Rugby World Cup • Olympics

Events that at first glance might seem similar can be on a very different scale. For example, both Premier League and local boys' football clubs might organise training camps but they are likely to be very different events. The Premier League club might travel to Spain for a week, stay in a luxury hotel and training complex, and end the week playing a friendly against a top-level club from anywhere else around the world. In contrast, the local boys' football club might travel for a weekend somewhere in the UK, stay in a hostel with each player paying for their own accommodation, and end the weekend by taking part in a tournament.

Research

Consider events that might have been held locally to you: there will certainly have been local events but you may have been lucky enough to live near a national or even international event. Give three examples of localised events. Describe the closest national event to your home and the closest international event to where you live. Are there any similarities between these events?

Case study

UK N1SCO National Stand Up Paddleboard Championships

Stand up paddleboarding (SUP) is a relatively young sport and it is an exciting time for its development. As more and more people start to take it up, the opportunity to run events around it is growing. One very successful event is the N1SCO National Championships. N1SCOs are inflatable boards and a very user-friendly introduction into the world of SUP racing. Having everyone racing on exactly the same board results in a fair competition. During the event, there are races for men, women and children in sprint, middle-distance and long-distance formats.

N1SCOs are built by a company called Naish. Running events is one way that Naish increases exposure for its product. People who do not own a N1SCO SUP on race day, can rent one for a nominal fee. The event is so successful and participants have so much fun that on completion all the rental boards are sold to participants and more stand up paddlers own their first board.

The organisers of the event are lucky that the focus is about exposure and there is no pressure to generate a profit from the actual event. This way, all finance can be directed at ensuring the event is of a high quality.

The event is always run from a public beach. This helps build a positive atmosphere around the event and ensures that there are plenty of spectators.

Check your knowledge

1 What things do you think the organisers might do to strengthen the image and atmosphere at the event?

2 What immediate safety considerations would there be for this event?

3 Do you think there any external parties that the event organisers may have to work with when organising an event such as this?

Planning sports events

No matter what its scale, there are a number of considerations when organising an event. Depending on the type of event, these factors may have more or less relevance, but most are still common between all events.

Aims and objectives

Understanding the overall aim of the event is fundamental to getting all other planning considerations right. The priority of the event could be financially driven, to set up a spectator event or to decide a winner from numerous competitors. Whatever it is, that aim must remain the driving factor behind planning and the focus must be kept on this above anything else (other than safety) to ensure success.

> **Research**
>
> In a small group from your class, of about four people, consider an event that has been held locally to you. What considerations do you think there are when planning this event? Discuss this as a group, conducting appropriate research as necessary. What was the timescale for planning this event?

▶ Bids to host global events involve multi-million pound budgets and take many years to put together

Bidding process

Many larger events take place regularly but are held at different locations each time. The location is often decided by a bidding process. Interested venues create a document and sometimes present their ideas to a panel governing the event. The panel will then decide the most suitable venue based on a variety of factors which might include cost of delivery, facilities, ability to run a smooth event, safety implications or potential to maximise spectator engagement.

Even smaller events are likely to need to seek permission to run an event. This is especially true if the event is run on public grounds such as in a park or could potentially cause disruption to people's normal day due to increased crowds or additional noise.

Organisation

To ensure an event is planned for and delivered successfully, organisation is key. It is vital that those people involved in the event are assigned specific roles and understand what their duties are. Updates on progress will need to be coordinated and any concerns over meeting targets managed. Smaller events may have one person making decisions. Other events have a committee steering them and ensuring they stay on track.

Time restraints

Meeting deadlines is essential to keep an event on track. There will obviously be the main deadline of when the event is due to take place. However, planning is often helped by setting other deadlines in the build-up to the event. Deadlines can be set for a number of key tasks that must be carried out to deliver the event and to ensure everything happens in good time and not at the last minute.

Physical resources

Locating appropriate venues, facilities and equipment is an early priority in the planning process. If you are expecting large numbers of participants or spectators, then you may need to consider additional infrastructure. This may include providing temporary areas to eat and drink, and toilet facilities, or closing roads and redirecting traffic. For major events, such as an Olympic Games, serious infrastructure is often required to the extent that roads and railways are built to assist with managing numbers.

Sport-specific equipment may also need to be arranged if the event is taking place at a venue where that sport is not usually played.

Financial resources

No matter what size the event, a budget will be set and must be kept to. Projections should be calculated on both expenditure and income. If needed, additional funding may have to be secured through loans or grants. For instance, local authorities may have funds available to help initiatives that promote an active lifestyle among the local population. At the other end of the scale, global events can often only take place because global companies give large sums of money through sponsorship.

Human resources

Personnel are key to any event. Larger events have the luxury of well-paid specialists to manage various elements. However, almost all events have a contingent of volunteers ready to assist with preparation and delivery. Locating paid staff and volunteers is sometimes time–consuming and must be prioritised early in the planning process.

▶ Even big events like the London 2012 Olympics rely on volunteers

Health and safety

Procedures to keep staff, spectators and participants safe will be specific to each event. An operational plan will include risk assessments, emergency procedures and an event management plan. First aid should be both available and easily accessible.

Legislative requirements must be met such as the Health and Safety at Work Act 1974 and Reporting of Injuries, Diseases and Dangerous Occurrences Regulations (RIDDOR). All events will need specific risk assessments and operating procedures drawn up in relation to them. Even events that may appear initially to be very similar will have differences such as projected numbers of visitors, time of year and predicted weather, all things which could affect the overall running and logistics.

If you are organising events where children and/or vulnerable adults are taking part, you must also make sure that they are protected from harm.

It is quite common for a stadium to host events funded and organised by separate organisations. The stadium will have its own operating procedures and action plans with which the organisations will have to familiarise themselves and work around.

Security

Unfortunately, the larger and more successful an event, the more security is likely to be needed. Events that are well published and globally popular may now become targets for terrorism and demonstrations. Having large numbers of people in one area, especially if alcohol is readily available, increases the risk of antisocial behaviour and hooliganism.

Even a small local event may attract unwanted attention, for example if thieves think there will be a large number of cars parked unattended that may have valuables kept in them.

An event may have its own security personnel to manage potential issues. Organisers will also be likely to work with local authorities and police forces to pre-empt problems and manage any risks.

Stakeholders

Stakeholders include the targeted participants and spectators who must be attracted to the event and engage with the event's delivery. However, stakeholders may also include sponsors who provide financial support, but expect brand exposure in return, and media companies broadcasting the event to their listeners or viewers. Sponsors and media companies will have their own agendas. When organising an event, you must consider these objectives, as well as the event's ultimate objective.

Contingency plans

There are many things that can go wrong when planning for and delivering an event. As part of the organisational process, you must ask 'what if' various scenarios happen: how will people cope and still ensure the event is a success?

A common scenario in planning a sports event is bad weather. If the event is outside, a well-planned event will have a strong contingency plan which may include adapting delivery or even bringing the event inside. On the day, there will be participants and spectators with high expectations. Considering in advance what to do if something does not go to plan will ensure disruption is minimised and success is more likely.

> **Discussion**
>
> Imagine that you are running a charity 10 km cross-country run. With three days to go, the forecast looks terrible with high wind and lots of rain. What are your options? What contingency might you have in place?

Ethical issues

An event that is organised in an unethical manner is sure to attract negative publicity and affect the participation of those involved – including spectators and other stakeholders – potentially damaging its reputation as a result. Ethical issues include the following.

▶ **Equality and diversity** – No matter what someone's race, religion, sex, ability or disability, all attempts must be made to ensure that they can engage with an event. This may mean that additional toilet facilities are required, specific catering is considered and access for people with limited manoeuvrability provided. There are many events that are focused around persons with disabilities, such as wheelchair basketball. For such events, the numbers of disabled people present can be higher and so facilities and resources will need to be adapted and provided. Other events may seek to encourage participation by underrepresented groups, such as women-only football events.

▶ **Environmental** – Reducing carbon footprints, using recycled materials, preventing excess waste and avoiding damage to surrounding environments are all hot topics. Considering all these topics is ethically positive. in addition, events which are actually seen to be pursuing environmental consideration may attract further participation from key partners.

▶ **Fair trade** – Large events have particular potential to pressurise small partners into providing services for less than they are worth. It is important to ensure that trade is fair and that participation is sustainable and ethically sound.

Promoting a sports event

Even the best event in the world will be a disaster if no one attends it. Prioritise the promotion of the event at an early stage in order to build excitement and potential participation from targeted groups and individuals. This section looks at planning and implementing a marketing plan.

Aims and objectives

When promoting an event, we need to understand the aims and objectives of what we are trying to achieve. Understanding who we are trying to attract and at what time is fundamental to designing a promotional plan. Promotion may be targeted at:

▶ participants

PAUSE POINT There are many considerations when planning an event. How many can you write down?

Hint What do you need to think about when you organise an event, such as a party? List as many considerations as you can in two minutes.

Extend Of these considerations, which do you believe are the most important and why?

▶ spectators
▶ sponsors
▶ media companies.

We may well wish to attract all these groups. However, it is unlikely we will want to do this all at the same time – use different promotional techniques to target each group separately.

Prioritising who to target and when will be specific to the event, but all events should do thorough market research to understand their competition and how others tackle promotion.

Target market

Many events are fairly **niche**, especially those which cater for activities which are not mainstream, for example windsurfing or rock climbing. In these cases, marketing needs to be targeted to attract those who have an interest in these activities. Events which are more mainstream, such as athletics, swimming or football, will appeal to a far more diverse audience and therefore promotion can afford to be less focused.

When organising an event, it is very easy to get carried away and lose sight of who the primary market is likely to be. This is especially true when organising a local event: take care to keep promotion focused on the local area (where the interest is likely to be). In contrast, global events often have to target audiences abroad, with different cultural and language considerations.

Budget

A promotional budget must show value for money. When setting a budget, an organiser must judge whether they are likely to see that money return by attracting additional participants or spectators. There are many things that are possible with limited or even no budget. With the popularity of social media, such as Facebook, Twitter and Instagram, there are platforms for building very successful promotional campaigns without any financial resources other than personnel to manage them.

At the other end of the scale, international events such as the Olympics and World Cup will have a promotional budget worth millions of pounds. Additionally, the build-up to such prestigious events attracts worldwide news coverage, online, on television, radio and in magazines. Sometimes this coverage might come even when not wanted, such as when an event is linked to bad news such as a delay in its preparation schedule. It may then be required to take action to counter negative publicity with a positive response.

Role of sponsors and partners

Sponsors and other partners may have separate agendas, but they also have an interest in ensuring the ultimate success of the event. Using sponsors to attract an existing client base is useful. If a client has already established the means of promotion, you can adapt and tie in the promotion to generate exposure.

Media partners promoting the event will want optimum numbers of listeners, viewers or readers and may be inclined to assist with advertising in the build-up to the event.

Variety of promotional activities

Key tools to generate interest in an event include:
▶ a strong logo and brand such as the Olympic rings
▶ selling tickets in advance to start building anticipation
▶ providing corporate hospitality to attract celebrity and corporate clients whose attendance may, in turn, help attract others
▶ negotiating media rights and securing sponsors who, in turn, will want to promote their involvement and coverage of the event
▶ advertising via social media, radio, television and written media
▶ providing merchandising and memorabilia that can be taken away and may help start to promote follow-up events.

Discussion

Split into small groups. Consider the rest of the class, their interests and what type of event might appeal to them. In your groups, prepare a brief presentation to give to the rest of your class. Remember, you are trying to sell the event, so focus on why people would want to come. As a whole class at the end of the session, vote on whose presentation was best.

Key term

Niche – an event or product that has a small, specialised audience or consumer base.

Research

Consider these three types of event:
• a skateboard competition
• a lawn bowling competition
• a Premier League football match.

How diverse do you think the audience of these events is likely to be? Do you think that any of these events are more likely to attract spectators of a specific age, sex, etc.?

Depending on the size and appeal of the event and associated budgets, some or all of these activities might be achievable. However, the key question that must always be asked before engaging in promotional activity is: will I see a return from this activity that helps fulfil my aims and objectives?

When putting together a plan for marketing, it might be useful to use the blank template shown in Figure 10.1.

EVENT DETAILS	
Event name	Event date
Event description	
Key organisational personnel	Target audience
PROMOTIONAL DETAILS	
Promotional budget	Additional resources available for promotion
Use of social media	Use of other online tools
Use of journals, magazines or papers	Use of television and radio
Use of physical events	Additional promotional strategies

▶ **Figure 10.1:** An example of a template for a marketing plan

❚❚ PAUSE POINT An event is only as good as the promotional effort that went into it. Can you remember the considerations when promoting an event?

Hint Close the book and draw a spider diagram with as many considerations as you can.

Extend Put the considerations in order of importance, with those that you think are most important first.

Delivery considerations

Just as important as planning an event is reviewing its delivery afterwards. This will help you when it comes to planning other events in the future.

There are several factors which can be used to help define whether an event has been a success or not. The following questions can be asked.

▸ Were the event's core aims and objectives achieved?
▸ Were there the expected number of participants and spectators?
▸ Was the media reaction/publicity surrounding the event positive? Did promotional activity effectively support the aims and objectives of the event?
▸ Were timescales met and kept to?
▸ Was the venue fit for task and facilities up to standard?
▸ Was the event delivered within budget? Did the event achieve the target profit?
▸ Was the event viewed in a positive light and is there demand for further events?
▸ Were there any health, safety or security issues?
▸ Is there a **legacy** from the event?

> **Key term**
>
> **Legacy** – the lasting impact of a sports event at local, regional and national levels.

London 2012

The Olympics in 2012 were built around the promise of providing a legacy for the UK and the world. Although most of the events were held in London, the sailing and windsurfing races took place in a small borough known as Weymouth and Portland located on the south coast of Dorset.

Portland in particular was an area of significant social and economic deprivation. In 1996, a previously busy Royal Navy base in the area closed. For many years, the area lay empty and the knock-on effect of the departure of the Naval personnel was significant to many local businesses, causing some to close.

Eventually, the site began to be redeveloped as a sailing and water sports centre capable of delivering both grassroots training and world-class events. When the 2012 Olympics were awarded to the UK, the Weymouth and Portland

National Sailing Academy was part of the successful bid.

The centre now hosts a variety of prestigious events every year. There are four watersports centres with various specialities. The area has attracted numerous marine businesses such as sail makers, marine engineers and boat sellers to support the Academy and new neighbouring marina. A significant grant was won as part of providing a legacy to help local people access water sports every weekend during the spring and summer.

• Were there any other sites outside London that hosted sport during the Olympics?
• Do the venues still exist and provide activity that can be classed as a legacy?
• Do you feel that the Olympics provided everything that it promised it would in promoting sport and generating a sustainable legacy?

Assessment practice 10.1

A.P1   A.M1   A.D1

Events happen every day and at various scales. Some are local and some global. However, there are key features found in all events.

Imagine that you work for the council in your local town. The senior management has asked you to evaluate how two separate sporting events have contributed to the local area, how well they were planned and promoted, and whether there is anything that the council can do to support their growth.

Choose two events. Prepare and deliver a presentation that discusses the planning process, promotion and delivery of these events, making comparisons between the two. Evaluate the two events identifying both successes and areas for improvement that the council might help support.

Make sure you choose two events that contrast with each other, for example, a charity abseil from a local building and a five-a-side football tournament.

Plan
• What is the objective of this task? What do I need to do to complete it?
• Do I have two examples of events that I can use in my assessment activity? Remember events are diverse and there are many types.

Do
• I have done plenty of research to identify two good examples.
• I have the appropriate resources in place to complete this activity.

Review
• I can explain why I tackled this task as I did.
• I can explain how I might adapt my approach next time to make improvements on my outcome.

B Develop a proposal for a sports event for implementation approval

Although we would all like to work without restrictions or expectations, in reality even when organising global events, targets must be met and boundaries adhered to. An event must be **feasible** in order to succeed. At some point during the planning process of an event, you are very likely to have to demonstrate the feasibility of the event to partners or third parties with an interest in its success. In some cases, the process of getting approval for a proposal may take many years.

When designing a feasibility proposal, it is useful to use the following headings as a format to ensure that any potential queries or questions can be answered and have been thought through. The proposal may be presented as a written document or a physical presentation, with the proposer standing up in front of a panel. Often both forms are required and for larger events you may find that multiple presentations are required during a bidding process.

Key terms

Feasible – when a plan, idea, or method is possible and likely to work.

Disclosure and Barring Service (DBS) checks – checks carried out by a government agency to make sure that someone has no history that might pose a risk to youngsters or vulnerable adults.

Aims and objectives

▶ Include in your proposal the event's aims and objectives. Keep them realistic and achievable.
▶ Include short- and long-term SMART targets (specific, measurable, achievable, realistic, timebound).
▶ Include key milestones.

Type of event

▶ Be realistic about what is achievable – do not bite off more than you can chew. It is better to run a small and successful event than a large failure. There may be an opportunity to re-run the event on a larger scale in the future.
▶ Have an idea about timescales.

Organisational structure

▶ Make sure that you use your human resources most efficiently. Understand your team and coorganisers. If they have specific skills such as marketing or budgeting, use their skills and explain why.
▶ Do not take too much on yourself. Ensure you delegate responsibility as much as possible.
▶ Note the key roles in your proposal and who is carrying them out.

Realistic budget

▶ Understand where the budget is coming from. Will it be secured upfront from sponsors or financiers?
▶ If a loan is required, will income from ticket sales, food and beverage sales or merchandising be sufficient to pay the loan back?
▶ Outline the sources of funding and income streams in your proposal.

Available resources

▶ Ensure you have all the resources required for a strong event. Consider the venue, equipment, additional facilities and possible transport requirements.
▶ Do the best you can within budget, and prioritise essentials first.

Health and safety considerations

▶ Specific risk assessments must be completed in advance alongside emergency action plans to demonstrate a thorough understanding of health and safety considerations.

Promotional plan

▶ A strategy for promoting the event alongside detailed costings and predicted returns is key to ensuring that your proposal is successful.
▶ Your proposal should state what promotional activity you intend to do and when. This could include using local media or social media, handing out flyers or putting up posters.

Organisational and legislative policies and guidelines

▶ Each event will have separate legislative requirements. These will depend upon venue and activity.
▶ All events must have insurance. When running an event linked to an established, well-governed activity, there will be clear advice from the governing body on running and insuring the event.
▶ If the event is to attract under 18-year-olds then ensuring that **Disclosure and Barring Service (DBS) checks** are complete and in place for everyone staffing and working on the event (where appropriate) is an important consideration.

Contingency plans

▶ Always have a back-up plan in case things go wrong, both during the planning and the delivery stages of the event.
▶ Consider what happens if the weather is poor, if a member of the team is sick and cannot attend, or if more or fewer participants arrive. Ensure that you have a clearly considered response for every scenario that could arise at your event.

Ethical considerations

▶ Make sure that your event is accessible and welcoming to all groups. You may need to consider access for disabled persons.

⏸ PAUSE POINT   Well-prepared proposals are clear and the aims and benefits obvious. What benefits are there from running an event that you might use to justify a proposal?

    (Hint)   What considerations do you think might be hardest to explain?

    (Extend)   Is there anything you can do to gain experience in the skills required to propose an event?

Format of the proposal

Large events may have very large proposal documents created by a team of highly skilled professionals. The proposal document shown in Figure 10.2 may help to put shape to a small-scale event in a very basic format.

EVENT PROPOSAL	
Event name	Event date
Brief description of the aims and objectives of the event	
Organisational structure	Venue for the event
1 2 3 4	
Equipment required	Additional staff required (paid and volunteers)
Promotional plan	
Health and safety considerations (Provide specific risk assessments separately)	Contingency plans
Ethical considerations	Legal considerations

▶ **Figure 10.2:** An example of a template proposal document for an event

---

Theory into practice

Think back to the most recent local event that you attended. Consider its participants and spectators. Where was the event hosted? What were the prevailing conditions? Did you see any accidents or injuries during the event? How were they dealt with?

Safety tip

Check out your school or college's policies and guidelines regarding putting on events.

Research

Choose two separate well-known sports. Identify their governing bodies. Do their governing bodies offer any support with running an event?

The proposal must include or be linked to a document that breaks down the financial considerations of the event. An example of this is shown in Figure 10.3.

EVENT FINANCES				
	During planning	**During delivery**	**During wrap-up**	**Total**
Expenditure				
Staff				
Venue				
Equipment				
Promotion and marketing				
Transport				
Catering				
Unforeseen				
TOTAL				
Income				
Ticket sales				
Sponsorship				
Merchandise				
External finance				
TOTAL				
FINAL TOTAL (Income – Expenditure)				

▶ **Figure 10.3:** An example of financial considerations for a proposal

Events coordinator for a regional cricket league

Tom Landy is the events coordinator for a regional cricket league. Every year, the league hosts a charity tournament over a weekend in July. The event attracts over 200 participants and 300 spectators. The charity that they support is well known and popular.

Tom's managers have set him the task of increasing the number of spectators by 20 per cent this year. Last year, they contributed £3,348 to the charity. This was raised through a fee for participants, tickets for spectators, an inflatable castle for children and an ice cream stall. This year they would like to raise over £4,000.

The event is always great fun and entire families come to

the venue for the weekend. The weather has so far always been kind and very hot. Tom has 6 months to plan and promote the tournament.

Check your knowledge

1. What health and safety considerations do you think Tom should prioritise?

2. Are there any planning considerations that might be more important than others?

3. What ways of generating further financial return might you suggest to Tom?

4. How do you think Tom should promote the event, remembering that he needs to make an increased financial contribution this year?

You are the sports coordinator for a partnership between local primary schools. You have been tasked with planning, promoting and delivering a sports event designed to get children to try new sports and spend more time outdoors.

The partnership has set you a budget of £4500 to source a venue, resources and any staff you might need. This is the first time this event has been tried and everyone is very keen for it to be successful.

It has already been decided to target Year 6 learners and the partnership chairman would like to see at least 100 participants.

Design a proposal for an inspiring and fun event. Ensure it is feasible and realistic. Present your proposal to other members of your class, explaining why it is feasible and meets the targeted aims.

After the presentation, evaluate the event proposal and make recommendations for improvements for the future.

Plan
- What boundaries do I have to work within?
- Do I understand what is being asked of me?

Do
- I have a clear understanding of what I need to achieve and how I am going to do this.
- I have researched many events and can use this research to help me develop a successful proposal.

Review
- I can identify what I did well in completing this activity.
- Next time there are a number of things that I might improve and I understand how I might implement these.

C Undertake the planning, promotion and delivery of a sports event

Planning and delivering an event relies upon the use of core skills within the event team. Although there is likely to be one person at the top of the team responsible for keeping focus, it is important every person in the team understands their role and responsibilities and how they are contributing to the event's ultimate success.

Roles and responsibilities within the event team

Actual roles and responsibilities of persons found within an event team will change depending on the scale, type and budget of the event. In many events, you will find that individuals are allocated more than one role. However, the following are some key roles and responsibilities that are likely to be found in all event teams.

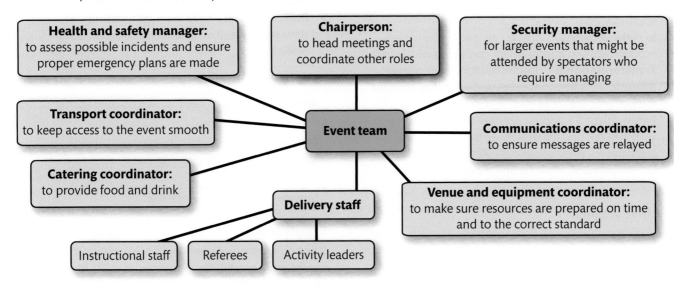

▶ **Figure 10.4:** Key roles within an event team

Skills associated with event planning and delivery

Teamwork

All members in a team must value others' roles and responsibilities. Some roles will be busier than others at various times. Team members should be prepared to assist where needed. Rather than only focusing on their own contribution, team members should be aware of how they fit into the whole set-up and offer support to others wherever possible.

Leadership

Some members of the team may have leadership responsibilities. These people must ensure they adopt an appropriate leadership style (listed below) to motivate other members as well as keep them on task. A good leader should be approachable, flexible, passionate, energetic and lead from the front.

Discussion

In small groups, discuss the five styles of leadership listed above. Without telling the rest of the group, write on a piece of paper which style of leader you feel you are. Place the paper face down. Ask the group to discuss your style without you and vote on which sort of leader they think you are. Compare results and then follow the process for someone else in the group.

Leadership styles

- **Autocratic** – Likes to be the sole decision maker, dictates tasks and does not like to consider opposing opinions. Is very goal orientated.
- **Democratic** – Wants to share responsibility and collaborate when making decisions and is a concerned coach.
- **Laissez-faire** – Steps back and has a 'hands–off' approach, placing the emphasis on the rest of the team to make decisions. This style can lead to the lowest productivity and improvement compared with others.
- **Transformational** – Uses inspiration to encourage others to push themselves beyond what they thought themselves capable of.
- **Paternalistic** – Adopts a position of complete authority but understands those they are in charge of and cares for them completely. Acts with high levels of self-discipline, kindness and moral integrity when controlling the group members.

Decision making

In all planning processes, decisions must be made. Some decisions may be quick and uncomplicated and can be made by just one member. Others may require more of the team to contribute and benefit from extra time spent ensuring the right path is taken.

Communication

Communication when organising events can be notoriously difficult to maintain. **Regular meetings** are key to successful communication and will help to ensure that progress is being made appropriately and issues are highlighted early so they may be dealt with effectively.

All meetings should have an **agenda**. Examples of agenda items could be:

▶ securing an appropriate event venue
▶ setting a date for the event
▶ deciding fee levels for ticket sales.

Ideally, agendas should be made available to the team attending the meeting before the actual day. This will allow them to prepare appropriately and consider any agenda points. Agendas are usually decided by a **chairperson**. Often other members of the team will be given the opportunity to suggest agenda points which the chairperson will plan to discuss.

During the meeting, **minutes** should be kept to ensure that records are accurate and that progress between meetings can be tracked. A well-run meeting will often follow the following format and the minutes reflect the following features.

▶ **Attendance** – who came to the meeting.
▶ **Apologies** – who was unable to attend the meeting.
▶ **Recap of minutes from the previous meeting** – so progress can be checked and any tasks assigned in the agenda can be ticked off by the team (if complete). If a task is incomplete it may need to be re-assigned or a solution discussed.
▶ **Agenda discussions** – these will include an overview of agenda items, whether items were closed, whether they were assigned to a team member and a timeframe for completion.
▶ **Any other business (AOB)** – items that have come up after the agenda was set but need urgent attention.
▶ **Date, time and venue for next meeting** – these should be agreed to ensure best attendance from the event team.

Key terms

Agenda – items that need to be discussed during a meeting.

Chairperson – the person tasked with keeping a meeting focused and ensuring that all agenda items are met.

Minutes – records of a meeting.

Organisation

Some events are more complicated than others and require more organisation. However, an ability to work to timeframes, prioritise workloads and retain focus are all important factors when trying to keep organised.

Generating **'to do' lists** is a great way to keep things on track. An example of simple headings for a 'to do' list is shown in Figure 10.5.

	TO DO LIST		
Task	Person assigned	Date to be completed	Date completed

▶ **Figure 10.5:** Example headings for a 'to do' list

Keep to the event's focus

When planning an event, it is very easy to get sidetracked. All events should focus to some degree on:

▶ keeping participants, spectators and staff safe
▶ meeting financial targets
▶ delivering quality.

All events should make safety a priority. However, the other two elements must be carefully and appropriately balanced.

Safety awareness

Generating risk assessments and emergency action plans is the first step to preventing incidents and accidents. However, to generate these documents and more importantly react to risks during the event, team members must understand the associated dangers.

Table 10.3 shows some examples of how dangers may change in different conditions for a local cricket match.

▶ **Table 10.3:** Possible dangers at a local cricket match

Air temperature	If too hot, there could be a risk of participants and spectators being sunburned, dehydrated or getting sunstroke, so water and shade need to be provided. If cold, they could suffer from a reduction in temperature instead and shelter would be required.
Rain	The grass will become slippery if there has been rain before or during the match. It might be that there is fine weather on the actual day, but due to rain a few days previously, the pitch is slippery. A pitch inspection might be required because of previous rain.
Large numbers of spectators	When some tickets are unsold and no gates prevent extra people arriving, there is always concern at local events about unexpected crowds. In the event of extra numbers, there may need to be security on standby or fences ready to be put in place.

Customer focus

All events provide a service to customers. Customers may be the participants themselves or spectators. However, members of the team must always promote the values of good customer service to all customers to ensure they have a positive experience and might want to take part in future events.

Team members should be:

▶ professional
▶ punctual
▶ approachable and positive
▶ ready to react to incidents.

PAUSE POINT

Do you feel you have strengths in any particular areas required to work within an events team?

Hint   Which roles within an events team do you feel you might be best at?

Extend   How might you go about developing the other skills which you might not possess so strongly?

Keeping to plan

Some events take years to organise and prepare for. To meet the demands of the event, it is vital that a plan is made and then kept to.

Remember that as your planning progresses, you may need to adapt your plan, adjusting it to take account of any situations that you did not foresee when you started your planning. You may need to draw up contingency plans, not just for what you might do if something happens on the day of the event, but also if something happens during the planning itself. For example, although you might have a preferred venue for the event, you might also think about a back-up venue as a contingency plan that you can put in place if necessary.

Although the final target will be delivery of the event itself, key targets should be set to keep progress on track. Remember when setting any target to keep it SMARTER.

▶ **Table 10.4:** SMARTER planning

Specific	Precise targets will encourage focused performance.
Measurable	A target will not work unless there is a clear way of measuring success.
Achievable	Is everything in place to encourage success? Targets will normally require resources such as support, resources or time.
Realistic	Targets should be challenging. Improvements are not made without pushing yourself. However, at the opposite end of the scale, a target that is set too high can damage motivation.
Timed	Having a starting point and finishing point will focus efforts.
Enthusiastic	When a goal has clear benefits for an individual's or team's performance, participants' motivation is likely to be far higher. Having enthusiasm about a goal is crucial for target setting.
Recordable	If they can review previous achievements or failures, team members can assess progress and, in return, more accurately develop further SMARTER targets.

There are many ways to generate a plan. One clear and visual method is by using a flow chart or diagram. Flow charts are particularly useful for giving an overview. 'To do' lists can then be used to meet each specific target.

Case study

Planning a national mountain biking event

Figure 10.7 below is an example of a basic flow chart for planning a national mountain biking event. The event could attract high-level competitors and plenty of spectators. From this flow chart, very specific plans will be made and the event chairperson is careful to keep them SMARTER.

1   Would you change the order of any items in this flow chart to help you work to schedule?

2   Are there any key items that are not included but which should be mentioned?

3   What would you consider the main aim of the event to be? What would you prioritise when planning for this event?

Promotion

Promoting an event is an important part of the planning process because those who attend the event are crucial to its success. Deciding where to focus the promotion will depend on the event and where you expect your customers to come from. For example, there is no point in running a national campaign to advertise a local football competition.

Figure 10.6 shows some considerations before starting a promotional campaign. Table 10.5 shows examples of some methods to promote an event.

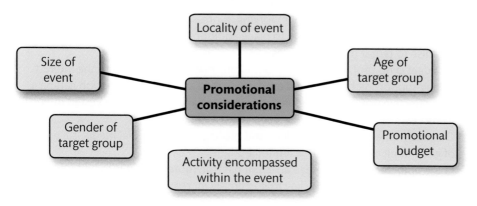

▶ **Figure 10.6:** Things to consider when promoting an event

▶ **Table 10.5:** Different ways of promoting an event

Promotional method	Positive	Negative
Social media	• Potential to be seen by large numbers. • Can be organised for little or no cost. • A variety of presentational formats can be used including written, photographic and video.	• Must be targeted to ensure it reaches the right audience. • Can take a large amount of time to keep momentum up and generate interest.
Magazines and newspapers	• When appropriate publications are selected for the client base, can be very engaging. • Take little time to manage other than designing adverts.	• Are reasonably expensive. • Can have a limited client base and once you are committed, there is little room to adapt the campaign.
Pre-events	• Small warm-up events can be very good to give a taste of the main event and generate excitement.	• Take time to organise. • May have expenses associated with them.
Word of mouth	• Excellent for established events or when there is already excitement for an event.	• Difficult to generate without other promotional techniques leading the way.
Face-to-face sales	• A good way to express passion and energy. • Help you understand the target market and can be adapted very quickly to make it more effective.	• Can be very time–consuming. • Must be run from a venue that will attract the event's target market.
Using an ambassador or sponsor	• Association with an ambassador or sponsor allows an event to utilise their own existing interest and image. • Strong ambassadors or sponsors can generate real interest in events just by their association.	• Sponsors often have their own agendas. • If a sponsor or ambassador has negative personal publicity, that can affect the event's publicity.

January
• Secure venue and negotiate fees
• Set draft budget
• Contact potential sponsors
• Contact potential delivery partners

February
• Generate risk assessments
• Write draft delivery plan
• Design logo and branding
• Finalise sponsors

March
• Start social media campaign
• Finalise delivery partners
• Advertise for volunteers
• Order delivery resources

April
• Finalise delivery plan
• Book first aid team
• Sign off legislative requirements
• Finalise contingency plans

May
• Train volunteers
• Increase social media presence
• Focus promotion through magazines, online publications and broadcast media
• Check resources and equipment

June
• Set up and deliver event

▶ **Figure 10.7:** A flow chart for organising a mountain biking event

Promotional contingencies

Even specialist and experienced promotions and marketing experts must be willing to adapt a campaign as it develops. You may focus the promotional campaign around one or two techniques, but if these fail or do not generate the interest that you require, you must be prepared to try alternative methods. It is advisable to always allow for additional budget in case promotion does not go as well as expected.

Ultimately, it will be the participants attracted to an event who will be the mark of whether promotion was successful. For events which pre-sell tickets, there is an early indication of whether promotion is working. If pre-sales indicate lower numbers than required, either you will have to place additional resources on promotion or re-organise to target the right groups.

▶ If budget is no problem, then additional pre-events might increase the interest.
▶ Asking supporting business and ambassadors to assist with promotion can be a cost-effective way of pushing promotion, especially if they have a vested interest in its success.
▶ Creating home-made, short videos and placing them on social media is a good way of generating exposure with a limited budget.
▶ In the end, the more coverage an event has, the more likely it is to hit target numbers. It may be that the key to it is simply increasing the presence of the event across all media streams.

 **PAUSE POINT**   Think about the ways in which it is possible to promote an event.

> Hint   Close the book and write a list of ways to promote – you only have three minutes.

> Extend   Give each technique a score out of three (one being the best) for affordability and effectiveness.

Assessment practice 10.3   C.P3 C.P4 C.M3

Imagine that you are working at a school or college in a sports department. Your department has been tasked with running a special sports event to try to encourage learners to become more active.

The event can take any form but must be designed to take place within an enrichment afternoon. There is no budget assigned to this event. However, you will have access to the school or college's well-stocked sports centre. You also have a team of sports learners who are keen to volunteer in running the event to get useful experience.

The event must be exciting, fun and, most importantly, inspire participants to play more sport.

As part of a team plan, promote and deliver a sports event. Make sure that you exhibit all the core skills required when working on the event. Manage key decisions effectively so that the event runs smoothly, safely and is a success.

Plan
- What is the purpose of this assessment activity?
- What strengths do I think I will bring to this activity and what might I find more demanding?

Do
- I know what I must do to contribute to this task.
- I am confident in my team and we have clear communication between us.

Review
- I can identify what we did well as a team and how we might improve in the future.
- I can explain how I contributed to the event individually and what I feel I might need to practise.

 D   # Review the planning, promotion and delivery of a sports event and reflect on your own performance

Reviewing the planning, promotion and delivery of an event is an important part of the process. Many successful events are repeated – understanding their strengths and weaknesses enables you to adapt planning for future events and implement improvements.

When conducting reviews, the overall team's performance should be considered, as well as your own personal contribution to the event.

Gathering feedback

In order to accurately review the performance of an event, you must collate feedback. Feedback can be of two main types.

▶ **Qualitative** – feedback based on words and opinions. For example, a spectator may tell you they thought that the competition was really well run, but that the catering facilities were poor.

▶ **Quantitative** – feedback that uses actual data to assess performance. For example, if an event had set a target of 220 participants but actually attracted 239, you know it over achieved by 8%.

▶ Both types of feedback are valuable, and to conduct a thorough review, both types should be collected.

▶ Feedback can be collected at various stages of an event. Naturally, much feedback will be gathered at the end, that is, the final data and thoughts that will allow improvements to be made for future events. This is known as **summative feedback**.

▶ When feedback is collected during the organisation or during an event, it is known as **formative feedback**. This type of feedback is useful for giving organisers the opportunity to react to comments, making changes and improvements where possible.

▶ Table 10.6 shows different ways of collecting feedback.

▶ **Table 10.6:** Different ways of collecting feedback

Feedback method	Description
Witness statements	A written statement from someone who observed the event discussing positives and areas for improvement.
Interviews	Interviews may be conducted by phone or face to face. To give them focus, it is useful to have bullet points listing the information you are interested to hear about.
Questionnaires and surveys	A series of focused questions presented in written format or online. Some questionnaires may ask for short written statements. However, in order to encourage people to actually complete them, most use tick boxes allowing people to work through them quickly. They are sometimes completed during or straight after the event if time allows. Many are sent out by post or email after the event is completed.
Observation forms	Anyone can complete an observation form. However, they are most useful when completed by an industry expert. Observation forms are completed during observation to ensure they are most accurate. As they are often completed by experts, they tend to pick up subtle areas for improvements or positive features that might otherwise be missed.
Comment cards	Comment cards are a good way of collecting anonymous feedback. They are usually completed at the event and then posted into a comment box. Often comment cards do not ask for personnal details which means feedback may be more honest.
Satisfaction buttons	Although still relatively rare due to the expense of setting them up, computerised satisfaction buttons allowing you to quickly and anonymously rate your satisfaction of an event as excellent, good, average or poor are great ways of getting quick feedback from large numbers of people.

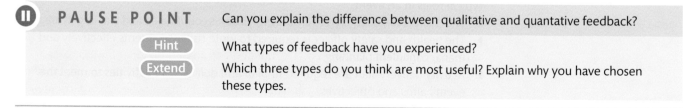

Ⅱ PAUSE POINT   Can you explain the difference between qualitative and quantative feedback?

Hint   What types of feedback have you experienced?

Extend   Which three types do you think are most useful? Explain why you have chosen these types.

Figure 10.8 shows an example of a brief questionnaire used to gather feedback after a hockey training camp.

FEEDBACK FORM				
Please rate the experience you had on this weekend's hockey training camp by ticking the most relevant circle and adding comments.				
	Excellent	**Good**	**Average**	**Poor**
Accommodation	○	○	○	○
Food	○	○	○	○
Structure of lessons	○	○	○	○
Professionalism of staff	○	○	○	○
Quality of resources	○	○	○	○
Overall satisfaction	○	○	○	○
Any other comments				

▶ **Figure 10.8:** An example of a feedback questionnaire

When analysing feedback, you must ensure you link any reflection to the event's original aims and objectives.

▶ Were target numbers of participants and spectators achieved?
▶ Were timescales and deadlines met and kept to?
▶ Was the venue fit for the task and facilities up to standard?
▶ Was the event delivered within budget?
▶ Was the target profit made from the event?
▶ Was the event viewed in a positive light and is there demand for further events?
▶ Were there any health and safety issues?
▶ Were any contingency plans used or adaptions made to the plan?
▶ Is there a legacy from the event?

Reflecting on your personal performance

Reflecting on your own personal performance after running an event is an important part of the process. This is how you identify your strengths (things you would repeat next time) and weaknesses (things you would eliminate, adapt or improve upon).

Responsibilities

It is probable that you had a specific role during the organising and delivery of the event, and you should assess your performance in this role. Every role in an event will have its own specific responsibilities. It is important that you understand your role and its responsibilities, and exactly what was expected of you. Here are some examples of typical roles in an event.

▶ The chairperson is required to ensure everybody is coordinated and that targets are met.
▶ The health and safety officer is required to write risk assessments effectively and manage incident planning.
▶ Activity delivery staff are required to plan and deliver core activities to meet the event's aims and objectives.

All these roles are different. However, they all involve transferable skills such as teamwork, flexibility and communication.

There are also the core aims of the event which are everyone's duty to promote and manage. You should assess how well you did this. The core aims of an event are likely to include:

▶ maintaining a safe environment
▶ maintaining an ethical environment
▶ promoting environmental consideration
▶ keeping to budget
▶ maintaining high levels of customer service
▶ using every opportunity to promote the event in a positive light.

Skills

Many of the skills for an individual associated with successfully delivering an event are highly transferable. Core transferable skills include:

▶ teamwork
▶ communication
▶ adaptability
▶ energy
▶ decisiveness
▶ motivation
▶ decision making
▶ leadership where appropriate.

All these skills and more can and should be used in day-to-day life; however, within an event setting they are essential. It is important that you know the skills that you may have been expected to demonstrate in your role during the event.

Assessing your personal performance

▶ It is vital that you understand the link between the various roles in event management and their associated skills. When reflecting on your own performance, it might be useful to use the following questions to structure your thoughts.

▶ **What was your role in the event?** Consider both your primary function and any additional core duties that were necessary for the event's success.

▶ **How did you perform against the 'job description' for that role?** What skills were associated with your functions in the event team and did you display them? Analyse both personal thoughts as well as feedback from participants and peers to help you identify both strengths and weaknesses.

▶ **How can I improve my performance for future events?** Once you have identified areas for improvement or weaknesses, consider ways that you might improve your own performance next time. This could be by getting further experience by volunteering or working at other events, shadowing experienced event staff or by seeking further training.

When assessing our own performance, a useful tool is a **SWOT** analysis. A SWOT analysis is a written document that should start with a brief summary of what you wanted to achieve and then use the following headings.

▶ **Strengths** – The positive elements of our performance within our role should be recognised so that they might be used again in the future.

▶ **Weaknesses** – No matter how minor, areas for improvement should be highlighted so that they might be eliminated from subsequent performance.

▶ **Opportunities** – Change is an important part of the development process. Opportunities to learn new techniques, develop resources or practise skills should be identified and pursued.

> **Theory into practice**
>
> Gaining experience is the best way of developing the skills needed for the work in the events industry. Try and find an event to volunteer at. Shadow someone working there. What are their role and responsibilities? Did they have to do anything that you might not have expected as part of the event process? What core skills do you think they needed to fulfil this role?

> **Key term**
>
> **SWOT** – Strengths, Weaknessess, Opportunities, Threats.

▶ **Threats** – Elements that might prevent success are varied. They might be time constraints or access to appropriate resources. However, they should be identified so that solutions can be found wherever possible.

⏸ PAUSE POINT   Reviewing an event is an important exercise for identifying both strengths and areas for improvement for the future.

Hint   List five ways of gathering information on how participants and/or spectators might have found an event.

Extend   What core aims of an event should you use to judge personal performance?

Assessment practice 10.4   D.P5   D.P6   D.M4   CD.D3

During the last assessment activity, you were tasked with planning, promoting and delivering a sports event for a school or college.

Analyse how successful this event was and what strengths it had, as well as what areas for improvement there were. Make sure that you look at both the performance of the team and your personal performance in the analysis.

Evaluate your thoughts, justifying both highlighted strengths and areas for improvement.

Plan
- Did I ensure I completed the previous task?
- Do I understand how to gather feedback to help my evaluation?

Do
- I have identified the most effective way of gathering feedback.
- I have a range of feedback to work from as well as my own thoughts and observations.

Review
- I can explain why this task is an important part of my development.
- I can explain how I might approach this task differently next time.

Further reading and resources

Capell, Laura (2013) *Event Management for Dummies*, Chichester: John Wiley & Sons.

Masterman, Guy (2009) *Strategic Sports Event Management*, London: Routledge.

Supovitz, Frank and Goldwater, Robert (2013) *The Sports Event Management and Marketing Playbook 2nd Edition*, John Wiley & Sons.

THINK ▶FUTURE

Gary Peterson

Charity volleyball tournament chairman

The charity that I work for has been running an annual fundraising event for 12 years. Every year it gets bigger and more popular. We invite local businesses to enter teams for the tournament and charge a fee for participation. Last year, we had 36 teams enter and this year we would like to have over 40.

We have a number of local sponsors who help finance logistics and assist with advertising the event. During the event, we have bands playing, a BBQ and plenty of refreshments for spectators and participants to buy. We have worked very hard to ensure there is a great atmosphere at our tournament. Many teams come back every year and it is a real highlight in our local calendar.

My day-to-day role for the charity is head of marketing and so managing the volleyball event is something that I must fit in around my other commitments. I didn't really have any sports event management experience before we started this project so I have had to learn fast. Luckily, I have played plenty of sports in my life and managed fêtes and charity auctions in my last role. I've acquired lots of transferable skills in managing our tournament, such as teamwork, communication and motivation.

Focusing your skills

Prioritising safety

When running a sports event, there are many things that can go wrong and lots of ways people might get injured.

- What documents must be created to help manage safety?
- What are common ways in which participants in sports might become injured?
- When working on a busy event, what could you do to help control people and how they move around the event site?
- In the event of a serious incident, what would the priorities be for event staff?

Ensuring success

If no one attends an event or no one has a good time, then the event can only be classed as a failure.

- What tools are there that you can use to promote events effectively and cheaply?
- How would you make sure that you generate a positive and exciting atmosphere at an event?
- What core skills would you expect team members working with you on an event to possess to help organise a success?

Getting ready for assessment

Andre is working towards his BTEC National Extended Diploma in Sport. He has been looking forward to the sports event unit as he knows there is plenty of opportunity to practise real skills and work in a team.

Andre has the assignment brief for learning aim C. His tutor has asked them to attract children from local primary schools to attend his college for a one-off event in one month's time. He and four other members of his class must plan and deliver an event for up to 65 children aged 8 to 10 years old. The aim of the event is to encourage teamwork among the youngsters. The event is to last three hours and the college is able to supply a wide range of sports equipment.

Andre discusses his experiences below.

How I got started

Working on a project as part of a team immediately gave us some challenges. We all had different ideas and it was hard to make any decisions. Eventually we decided to elect a chairperson to oversee things and make sure that everyone had opportunity to speak. In the end, we had three good ideas and so we took a vote to decide which was the best.

We looked at our event and decided what jobs needed to be done. We tried to allocate jobs evenly so that we all had a fair amount of work to do. Each of us wrote a 'to do' list and gave ourselves specific timescales on when each task should be completed. We decided to meet up three times a week to check how we were all progressing and make sure we didn't need to adapt our plan.

How I brought it all together

We booked meetings to go and see teachers in the local primary schools. Molly is the best one of us at doing presentations and so we voted for her to talk to the teachers. To give them a taste of our event, we ran very brief team challenges for their classes. We kept the challenges really short and made sure we gave them lots of energy. In the end, we managed to get three schools to send learners to our event.

Because of the time of year, we decided to run the event indoors, so we booked the college sports hall. We wanted to keep the event as energetic and high paced as possible and so we decided to run a rotation of four activities. This also allowed us to split the ability groups.

We prepared a presentation to welcome all the learners and really reinforce the aim of the event, which was 'teamwork'. We had some good video clips from the Internet lined up to show them of inspirational team players.

What I learned from the experience

We left a lot of the preparation until the day before the event. Some of the equipment that we thought we would have access to was not there and we had to come up with an on-the-spot contingency. If we had taken stock of our resources much earlier in the process, we would not have had such a last-minute panic.

Within our small team, two of us were much more vocal than the others. It was our ideas that really shaped the event. Although we were really pleased with the outcome and feedback, I think that we could have spent more time listening to the rest of the group. They had some good ideas but we didn't get to hear them until we were too far into the process to make massive changes.

Think about it

▶ Do you have a clear plan and are you sure that you have assessed all options and your plan meets the aims of the event?

▶ Does everyone in your team know what their roles are? Has workload been evenly distributed?

▶ Are you able to evidence your thinking with clear notes and explanations on your decision making?

Self-employment in the Sports Industry 12

Getting to know your unit

Within the sports industry there are many opportunities for professionals to be self-employed. They may either run their own business or provide services for other businesses on a short-term contractual basis. There are many benefits to being self-employed, including managing your own goals and having a flexible schedule. However, there are also many considerations and hurdles that must be thought about and understood.

How you will be assessed

This unit is split into three clear learning aims. Your tutor will set a range of assignments to give you the opportunity to fulfil these learning aims at Pass, Merit and Distinction grades. It is important that you complete all the assignments to pass the unit. Completion of every task will not guarantee you the highest grade.

To receive a Pass you must ensure that you complete all assignments to the required level and incorporate all the information as instructed by your tutor.

If you would like to gain a Merit or Distinction, all the information in your assignment must be presented in the style required by the relevant assessment criterion. Merit criteria, for example, may require you to assess, while Distinction criteria require you to evaluate.

The assignments set by your tutor will be varied and designed to enable you to vary your approach and make you think. Assignments might include:

▶ preparing a PowerPoint® presentation to explain and evaluate the legal requirements, financial demands and other start-up considerations of becoming self-employed within the sports industry

▶ presenting a vlog on research into various ideas for starting a small business and becoming self-employed

▶ producing a written business plan and evaluating both its content and your original research.

Assessment criteria

This table shows what you must do in order to achieve a **Pass**, **Merit** or **Distinction** grade, and where you can find activities to help you.

Pass	**Merit**	**Distinction**
Learning aim **A** Investigate self-employment in the sports industry and the legalities of becoming self-employed to safeguard the business and individual		
A.P1 Explain the types of self-employment appropriate to an individual in the sports industry. Assessment activity 12.1	**A.M1** Assess the different self-employed roles available to individuals in the sports industry. Assessment activity 12.1	**A.D1** Evaluate the impact of legal requirements, financing of the business and start-up considerations on different self-employed roles available to individuals in the sports industry. Assessment activity 12.1
A.P2 Explain the legal influences on a self-employed individual in the sports industry. Assessment activity 12.1	**A.M2** Assess the importance of legal requirements, financing of the business and start-up considerations on self-employed individuals in the sports industry. Assessment activity 12.1	
A.P3 Explain how financing of the business and start-up considerations affect self-employed individuals in the sports industry. Assessment activity 12.1		
Learning aim **B** Research your market to generate business ideas		
B.P4 Research to generate ideas for starting a business. Assessment activity 12.2	**B.M3** Assess the results of the market research related to starting a realistic business in the sports industry. Assessment activity 12.2	**B.D2** Evaluate the quality of the research and the results of market research, drawing valid conclusions about business opportunities in the sports industry. Assessment activity 12.2
Learning aim **C** Develop a business plan to gain investment and/or contracts		
C.P5 Produce a basic business plan, using an appropriate template for a service in the sports industry. Assessment activity 12.3	**C.M4** Produce a detailed business plan for a service in the sports industry. Assessment activity 12.3	**C.D3** Evaluate the content of a professional and strategic business plan for a service in the sports industry, recommending improvements to the plan. Assessment activity 12.3
C.P6 Review the content of own business plan for a service in the sports industry. Assessment activity 12.3	**C.M5** Assess the content of own business plan for a service in the sports industry. Assessment activity 12.3	

Getting started

Setting up your own business and becoming self-employed is an exciting prospect. Draw a quick spider diagram with as many examples of self-employed people in the sports industry as you can. It can take courage and certainly takes determination; however, the rewards can be fantastic. What do you think attracts people to becoming self-employed? What concerns might you have about setting up your own business?

 A Investigate self-employment in the sports industry and the legalities of becoming self-employed to safeguard the business and individual

The sports industry is vast and worth billions of pounds across the globe every year. As the industry continues to grow, opportunities for entrepreneurs and fitness professionals increase dramatically – and many of these people will work on a self-employed basis.

With the sports industry being so diverse, the potential for specialists to find opportunities is almost limitless. When considering the sports industry, do not just limit your thinking to the conventional roles of coaches and instructors: think about all the services that support sports businesses, such as those shown in Table 12.1.

For many individuals, the possibility of running their own business and managing themselves is an appealing prospect. When you are reliant upon yourself, investing in your own training and development is an important consideration. This is especially true for small business where the primary function is to deliver a physical service such as sports instruction, strength and conditioning coaching or sports massage. You should keep up to date with trends and new techniques, ensure your personal qualifications are valid and current, and use any opportunity to gain further experience to broaden your skills base. This can involve setting aside money each year to fund training and development, which can be tricky to do when your business is just starting out.

Discussion

Consider the roles listed below with the rest of your class. As a group can you come up with any further potential roles? Individually, choose a role that most appeals to you.

▶ **Table 12.1:** Self-employed roles in the sports industry

Role	Description
Coach	A practitioner who works with participants to develop skills which normally already exist in order to improve performance
Fitness instructor	A practitioner who introduces new skills and techniques, normally in a practical environment
Sports therapist	Someone who uses a variety of practices to prevent or rehabilitate people from injury
Manager	Someone who oversees a group's or individual's performance as a whole and is responsible for both motivation and discipline. This person often has unseen duties such as logistical organisation (e.g. organising travel) and budget control
Business and sales executive	Someone who generates sales of a product or service and manages the business supporting that product or service
Marketing and public relations executive	Someone who promotes and advertises a product or service. They will be responsible for ensuring that the product or service is viewed positively and gains the exposure required to be successful
Health and safety advisor	A person who designs and manages procedures to ensure incidents and accidents are prevented where possible and ensures processes are in place, should an accident happen, to manage the situation effectively
Consultant	Anyone who provides an external service to a company or business offering support and advice on how to improve systems and performance

Types of self-employment

There are several types of employment available in all industries, including the sports industry; some of the most common are described below. Each of them has different benefits and advantages.

▶ **Full time** – a role that is able to generate work to justify employment across a full year and fill a working week, generating a sufficient wage.

▶ **Part time** – a role that does not fill a conventional working week. This may be due to choice, i.e. it is combined with another job, or it generates sufficient income to allow the person to work just part time. It may also be through necessity, such as the business not generating sufficient work for full-time employment or only needing certain staff at certain times or for certain tasks.

▶ **Seasonal** – businesses that deliver services outdoors can be very seasonal. This means that they will only run when prevailing conditions are right. This might result in people working longer and harder for certain periods of the year to generate income so that they are able to survive during quieter spells. For example, a surfing instructor is likely to be busy during the summer but have very little work during the cooler months of the year.

▶ **Flexible hours** – this is when a self-employed person is able or may have to pick and choose when they work to fit round either personal commitments or other working commitments. For many self-employed people who own small businesses, the need to work flexibly is vital to ensure it runs efficiently. A self-employed person who provides one-off classes for an organisation such as a leisure centre may also need to be flexible about when they work.

▶ **Franchise** – established brands often offer opportunities for other people to become a 'franchise' of their business. This is when a person buys a licence to run a business under the brand name and structure already established by another person. Franchises can be good ways for a brand to grow without the original owner having to invest additional amounts of finance or excessive time. An example is the sport retailer, Intersport.

▶ **Consultant** – a consultant is someone who has in-depth knowledge of subject matter relevant to an industry and usually experience and qualifications to back up this knowledge. For a fee, they offer advice to both established and new businesses or other organisations to help them achieve efficiency and best practice.

▶ **Volunteer** – this is when time and skills are provided for free. This might be for purely selfless reasons or in order to gain valuable experience. Volunteers are most often associated with clubs and charities.

Business–ownership structures

There are three main business structures that self-employed people usually use to own their own business:

▶ **Sole trader** – when you as an individual are solely responsible for the business. Even if there are other employees within the business, the liability for the business's success or failure sits upon the owner. Debt or profit to the business is directly linked to the owner's personal finances, so if the business fails, the person running it could also be dragged into personal financial difficulties.

▶ **Limited company** – when a legal organisation is set up to run your company. Personal and business finances are separate and one is not liable for the other. Profits belong to the company but can be shared between shareholders through annual dividends.

▶ **Partnerships** – when responsibility and liability is shared personally between partners, each with a vested interest in the business. There are two types of partnership:

- a **business partnership** – where the partners are both individually responsible for the business, and the liability for the business's success or failure sits on the owners together
- a **limited liability partnership** – which is more like a limited company where the partnership is a separate legal entity from its owners.

The best type of structure to choose will depend on your own individual circumstances, but often someone just setting out in self-employment will do so as a sole trader or in a business partnership because these structures have fewer legal requirements. They might choose to enter into a limited liability partnership or form a limited company as the business grows over time.

PAUSE POINT   Describe the different ways in which a business can be structured.

> Hint   List and briefly describe the three business structures.
>
> Extend   Explain which might be the most popular structure and justify your choice.

The following case studies are examples of small businesses that have many similarities but were initially set up under different business structures. Each structure has been chosen for reasons linked to the owners' aspirations about how the buisness might grow and how they want to manage their business.

Case study

Sole trader

Rob is a circuit trainer and registered as a sole trader. He provides classes for nine sports centres within the local area. He loves what he does, the variety of clients he gets to meet and the fact that he moves between centres and experiences a wide range of workplaces.

His classes are well received and there is demand for his sessions. Sometimes it is difficult to negotiate a schedule between centres that satisfies everyone. His peak times are mornings and evenings and it is at these times that there is demand for his services; centres sometimes compete with each other for him to work there.

It took almost 12 months for his business to be financially viable without him having to work part time elsewhere. However, as all the resources are provided by the centres he works at, the initial outlay was minimal other than for insurance and marketing. The biggest demand was time and effort in establishing connections and proving the quality of his work.

Limited company

Jess owns a small limited company that runs climbing and kayaking sessions for tourists during the spring and summer.

She has between 5 and 7 months to generate enough income for the entire year. Within these months she has to work long hours and can go weeks with no day off. However, she gets to work outside delivering activities she enjoys and then, during the winter, she has extended time off in which she likes to travel.

She was able to secure a start-up loan for her business which will take a further 5 years to pay back. However, her business is financially stable and she has the security of knowing that she is not financially liable for its success or failure.

Jess is paid a minimal wage from her business each year. The rest of her income is received through dividends from the company's profits. This means her personal income varies from year to year depending on the company's success.

Partnership

Brad, Saanvi and Steff have a business partnership that provides sports nutrition services for gyms in the North East of England. The business was initially financed equally by each of them from their own pockets. This was a risk for their personal finances and caused them quite a lot of stress.

They provide meals and supplements tailored to individual needs. The gyms through which they supply take a cut of the profits and so have an interest in supporting sales.

The use of meal plans and supplements varies and is heavily influenced by trends and so they need to adapt their products regularly to meet consumer demand.

Having three people working together in the team, each with a stake in its success, means that a wide range of skills is brought to the table. It also means that responsibility is shared and each of them is able to work more flexibly as they have one another's support.

Check your knowledge

Many businesses could have been set up as either sole traders, limited companies or business partnerships. Consider the case studies above.

1 What do you consider to be the three biggest benefits of each structure? Think about how each structure is financed and where liability falls.

2 What reasons do you think influence whether individuals set up business as sole traders, partnerships or limited companies?

Personal skills associated with self-employment

Being self-employed is not for everyone. Being successful in business takes hard work and determination. There are constant challenges to overcome, but the rewards associated with success can include both an improved lifestyle and financial compensation. Below are some of the skills associated with being successfully self-employed.

> **Reflect**
>
> Consider the skills that you possess. What skills do you have that might help you if you were to become self-employed? Are there any skills that you might need to improve or practise?

Motivation

When you are self-employed there is no escaping the fact that you are responsible for your own income and success. Especially in the early stages of setting up a business, the effort required to drive the business forward can be phenomenal. Having high levels of motivation is vital to ensure you keep momentum up and put in the work required to generate and maintain business. People wanting to become self-employed must ensure they are motivated by the right reasons and understand that setting up a business is not an easy task.

Positivity

Projecting positivity even when things are difficult is a vital skill. Being positive will give those around you – whether they are partners, financers, suppliers or clients – the confidence that you have the energy to succeed.

Communication

Communication is a priority for any business so self-employed people must have good communication skills. Communication can take place face to face, by phone, letter or email. It can take the form of presentations or adverts. No matter what happens, there must be continuity within the communication and a clear message projected and maintained.

Good communication also involves listening to the views of others with respect and understanding. This can apply to talking to your clients or talking to third parties whom you approach for advice.

Discipline

When you are only accountable to yourself, for some people it is too easy to take short cuts, put jobs off or avoid tasks altogether. Being responsible for your own business means that at times you may have to do tasks that you do not want to do, so having the discipline to keep up standards and meet targets is crucial.

Leadership

Even for the smallest business (a sole trader who employs no one else), it is very likely that at some point they will work with third parties. This might be to assist with the management of the business, using accountants, solicitors or marketing specialists, or it might involve working with other people sent to you by your own clients. Being able to lead others to achieve an objective will involve energy, focus and determination, all of which are key elements of leadership.

Openness to advice

An ability to listen and accept advice is really important, epecially for those new to running their own business. There are many very experienced business people who may offer support, either casually or through organised schemes. Ultimately, you as the self-employed person must make your own decisions, but you may find consideration of other people's ideas and views beneficial.

At some point, you are likely to engage an external specialist such as an accountant or insurance broker. Remember, these people are professionals and often will be able to advise you of the best way to proceed.

Integrity

Within business there are many opportunities to take short cuts and possibly act unscrupulously. Although sometimes hard decisions must be made when you are self-employed, it is important to maintain your integrity.

Your business is likely to be in competition with at least one other organisation. To attract a client's business, you could be tempted to damage the competition's reputation, undercut them with unsustainable prices or use aggressive marketing that is designed to be visible specifically to the competition's clients. This may give you a temporary boost, but will not help to build a reputation for your company for honest dealing.

Having pride in your business usually comes from focusing on building your own reputation and creating a service or product that clients and customers want to purchase for its own strengths.

Self-awareness

Knowing your own limits is an important skill. You may be approached by a potential client who wants something that is not quite within your field of expertise, or you may already be working to capacity. If you are unable to offer a service for a client or customer, rather than just apologising and turning them away, consider where else they may be able to receive that service. This could potentially be another business close to your own. By pointing the client to somewhere they can obtain what they want, not only are you providing them with a solution and keeping them happy, but you are also building a relationship with another business which may return the gesture.

Organisation and planning

Being self-employed and owning your own business means that you have total responsibility for your own success or failure as well as that of the business. At times you may need to juggle many different tasks, meet deadlines and still keep looking ahead. Being highly organised is very important to any self-employed person.

To help maintain organisation, having a clear plan that you are able to stick to is vital. Although sometimes plans need to be adapted as you progress, having a schedule helps 'tick off' tasks and meet deadlines. Both momentum and focus can be well maintained by following a clear plan.

Time management

Having a plan is one thing; keeping to it is quite another. You must manage your time effectively and prioritise tasks in order to keep to your plan and schedule.

Literacy and numeracy

There is no denying that both literacy and numeracy skills are essential for success in business. Projecting revenue streams, recording expenses and income as well as setting service charges all rely on good numeracy skills. Simple tasks such as writing an email, designing a brochure or reading a letter need literacy skills. Numeracy and literacy skills are sometimes undervalued by those intent on becoming self-employed and this can hold them back from being more successful.

> **Discussion**
>
> In groups of 3–4, discuss what other skills, qualities or characteristics might be beneficial to people running their own business. Individually, take your final list and place the points in order of importance.

Skills relevant to example roles

Yoga instructor

Natalie has been a self-employed yoga instructor for 5 years. She is lucky enough to be able to spend her summers in the UK teaching yoga in her home town to residents and holiday makers, and her winters in India teaching at a specialist instructor's camp. She feels that being self-employed has allowed her to develop exactly the lifestyle she wants. The following are the key skills that she feels have been most important to her.

- **Motivation** to drive her dreams forward and not be too affected by setbacks or disappointments.
- **Openness to advice** from other small business owners. She had little business experience to start with and so the advice from others was invaluable.
- **Organisation** as her schedule is often busy moving between classes and private bookings. She needs to ensure she accounts for travel time when planning sessions and keeps a schedule that is manageable.
- **Integrity** as there have been opportunities to sacrifice quality in the name of profit. She wants to maintain a product she is proud of and so shunned any opportunities that did not fit her moral values.

Studio manager

Justin has had a studio space from which he has run fitness classes for just under 3 years. In that time his small business has grown quickly and he now has an administrator working for him two and a half days a week and other fitness professionals renting space from him. It has been a hard process setting up his business and he never envisaged renting space to other trainers. However, he has adapted his plans and now has a business that is doing well and looks set to expand in the future. These are the skills he feels have been most useful to him.

- **Positivity** has been really important. There have been some big challenges along the way and some disappointments. Being able to keep going and stay positive has carried him through.
- **Numeracy and literacy** have been invaluable. They weren't his priorities at college. However, as soon as he realised how relevant they were to his own success, he enrolled on evening classes to upskill himself.
- **Leadership** to keep the studio focused has been tough. Even though the other trainers only rent space from him, it has been important for the reputation of the studio as a whole.
- **Planning** schedules and strategies to attract further business has become a large part of his role. Being both organised and thorough has been important in the planning process.

Surfing instructor

Naomi started Water Born Surf School in 2007. She had previously worked managing a successful retail store for someone else. The position within the store was fantastic experience and helped her learn about the logistics of running a business. Eventually, she decided that she wanted a career that allowed her to spend more time outdoors doing what she loved. An opportunity came up to take on a long-term licence to run a surf school from a beach in the south-west and she jumped at the chance. There are a number of skills that she developed while working in retail that have really helped her within her own business.

- **Time management** is really important. All the surf school's bookings are dependent upon tide and so start times must be adhered to. Sometimes there is more than one group a day and so groups must finish on time so the next one is not delayed.
- **Self-awareness** is important when the beach is really busy and her surfing groups have to be well controlled in order not to get in the way of swimmers.
- **Positivity** is essential every day. Many last–minute bookings are made when beach-goers see her lessons and want to join in. To encourage this process, Naomi makes sure that she looks positive all day every day, even when she is tired. She knows that when she looks like she is having fun, clients will want to join in.
- **Motivation** is especially important during high season. Her business is very seasonal and, as such, she has to work hard during the summer months to ensure her cash flow is strong enough to survive the winter.

> **Research**
>
> Does a particular role appeal to you as a self-employed person within the sports industry? What skills do you think are most relevant to success in this role? How might you gain experience to help you improve your own skills?

Sector requirements and specialist training

Within the sports industry there are several sectors that specialise in different activities and support the industry as a whole. In many of these roles, the people working in them will need to have specific skills to meet the requirements of their job. In most cases, if you are interested in working in these jobs, you will need to have undertaken some specialist training to help you develop these skills. Many professionals are required to hold qualifications to show evidence of their specialist training. This training is required to ensure that standards are maintained and also services are delivered safely.

Table 12.2 shows examples of self-employed roles and the qualifications required to perform them. The qualifications are examples and may only be one option of many to show evidence of competency.

▶ **Table 12.2:** Qualifications for different self-employed roles

Role	Examples of associated qualifications
Windsurfing instructor	Royal Yachting Association windsurfing instructors' certificate
Yoga teacher	Yoga Alliance UK 200-hour teacher training certificate
Sports physio	Approved degree in physiotherapy or sport rehabilitation
Personal trainer	Level 3 Diploma in Personal Training
Sports nutritionist	Approved degree in sports nutrition

 **PAUSE POINT**   What skills are involved in being self-employed?

 Hint   Try to remember as many relevant skills as you can and draw a spider diagram.

Extend   Are there any additional skills not discussed here that might be useful for someone who is self-employed?

Legal requirements

The sports industry is well regulated. This is both to keep clients safe and to ensure that standards are high within the industry. Requirements between sectors within the industry vary, but there are also many laws and pieces of legislation that apply across the board.

Insurance

All businesses need insurance, but the type and extent of that insurance will vary depending on the specialism of the business (such as a fitness instructor's liability insurance) and its size. Table 12.3 shows the elements within a business that should be insured.

▶ **Table 12.3:** Insurance for the self-employed

Assets such as buildings and equipment	If a business is lucky enough to own its own premises and expensive equipment, it is sensible to insure these assets. In the event of a fire or theft, insurance could be what determines whether a business can carry on.
Personal insurance for self-employment	For many self-employed people within the sports industry, their ability to work dictates their income. In the event of a personal accident resulting in injury, the ability to work might be taken away from them. Having insurance in place to ensure that there is financial cover is sensible practice.
Clients and third parties – personal indemnity	All businesses must insure against injury to clients and third parties exposed to the business. This insurance is known as business insurance and it will vary heavily between different businesses depending upon their size and specialism. For example, professional indemnity insurance covers you if you make a mistake when giving your client advice. Public liability insurance covers you if a client injures themselves on your premises.
Employees	As soon as a business takes on an employee, that business must have employers' insurance. This is to protect them and their employees against injury within the workplace that might prevent them working.

Professional bodies, governing bodies and associations

The various sectors within the sports industry have different professional bodies, governing bodies and associations which it is possible – and sometimes compulsory – to join.

Professional bodies (also sometimes referred to as 'associations') focus on developing the interests of individual professionals within that sport. This could include offering continued professional development and training or providing advice on working within the industry, all important things for self-employed people.

Examples include:

▶ the Chartered Institute for the Management of Sport and Physical Activity
▶ the British Association of Sport and Exercise Science (BASES)
▶ the Association for Physical Education.

Governing bodies focus on a specific sport as a whole and tend to prioritise increasing participation and generating sporting success. They may require that a coach operating within their field is qualified to a certain standard in order to help ensure that standards are maintained and improved. Examples include:

▶ the Rugby Football Union (rugby)
▶ the Royal Yachting Association (sailing, windsurfing, power boating)
▶ the England and Wales Cricket Board (cricket).

There is often a great deal of overlap between professional bodies and governing bodies, and sometimes governing bodies in particular will encompass the role of an association into their own organisation.

> **Research**
>
> Some sports require coaches and instructors to hold qualifications designed by the governing body. Can you identify the governing body responsible for the following sports: football, kayaking and gymnastics? What qualifications are required by these bodies before you are recognised as a coach or instructor?

Working with children

For any business or person who might work with children and young people there are strict requirements regarding checks to ensure their suitability for these roles. These checks are known as DBS (Disclosure and Barring Service) checks. When you are contracted by a company that requires these checks, they should ensure they are done before your employment begins. However, when you are self-employed, you may have to conduct them yourself to ensure that legal requirements are met. It is now possible to get a 'transportable' DBS check so that if you work between employers on a freelance self-employed basis you do not have to go through the process more than once.

▶ Working with children brings extra responsibilities for self-employed coaches

> **Theory into practice**
>
> As a group, list as many sports as you can that you have tried. There are likely to be a great number. Consider less well-known sports such as croquet and paragliding.
>
> **1** Take the list and rate each sport according to whether it is *likely*, *average* or *unlikely* that contact will normally happen between young people.
> **2** Consider which sports young people are most likely to engage in.
> **3** Consider the requirements of these sports. Does it involve physical contact between participants? Is there a need to change into specialist clothing or equipment? Is it considered to be higher risk as an activity?
> **4** For each sport that was rated *likely* in step 1, as a group suggest a sensible way to minimise the risk adults may pose to young people.

Key laws and legislation

The laws and legislation relevant to self-employment and running a business in the sports industry are many and varied. Table 12.4 lists the most important items of legislation for anyone working for themselves or running a business. You should be aware of all your obligations under these Acts before you start your own business. Guidance and assistance can be found through the Health and Safety Executive, your local Chamber of Commerce or your local council.

Act	Date introduced	Description
Children and Families Act	2014	Introduced to help local authorities and other organisations access and implement procedures where needed to protect the well-being of children. The Act makes it possible for anyone with concerns over the well-being of a child to report their observations, triggering appropriate intervention. All businesses working with children should have a procedure in place where concerns can be reported to a nominated person and suitable actions taken in response.
Health and Safety at Work Act	1974	The Health and Safety Executive (HSE), working alongside local authorities, is responsible for enforcing health and safety in the workplace. Health and safety is relevant to employees and to clients. The Act clearly states the standards expected within the workplace as well as the procedures that should be followed to ensure health and safety is maintained. It also advises what to do when reporting an accident or incident.
Health and Safety (First Aid) Regulations	1981	In the event of an accident that causes injury to an employee or client, a business has a clear responsibility to be able to administer appropriate first aid. The size of the organisation and environment in which it operates will dictate the extent of first aid resourcing that should be available. These regulations state an employer should conduct an in-depth assessment to establish what level of first aid is required.
Disability Discrimination Acts	1995 and 2005	Designed to ensure that everybody – irrespective of their ability or disability – is protected against discrimination. A person should be recruited for employment for their ability to do the job. A person with disabilities should be given an equal opportunity to access resources and services. By law, any reasonable support required to enable disabled people to access employment or services must be provided.
Sex Discrimination Act	1975	This Act clearly states that people should be recruited for employment for their ability and not discriminated against because of their sex.
Equality Act	2010	This is the most recent of the Acts and goes some way towards combining all previous Acts relating to discrimination into one simplified piece of legislation.

 **PAUSE POINT**

What is the key legislation that relates to being self-employed within the sports industry?

Hint　　From memory, name three Acts or regulations that are relevant to being self-employed.

Extend　　Describe each Act and explain why it is relevant.

Contracts

A contract is an agreement between two or more parties in which an item of value, either a product or a service, is exchanged, normally for remuneration (payment) but sometimes in return for another product or service. A contract will also set out the conditions of employment and the responsibilities and duties of the employee (for example working hours and any particular responsibilities, such as managing a team).

Examples of contracts might be between:
▶ employer and employee – a contract of employment (for example, between a small business owner and someone they hire)
▶ personal trainer and client – a contract for services (for the client to receive training)
▶ small business owner and property owner – a contract for premises (for the business owner to have a place to base their business)
▶ yoga teacher and sports centre – a contract for facility usage (for the yoga teacher to hire space in the sports centre).

A contract should contain basic elements to ensure that it is fair to all parties and easy to interpret. The following questions are useful guidelines when looking at creating a contract:
▶ Who is it between?
▶ What dates does it run between? Is there a start and end date?

▶ What service or product is to be delivered? What will the payment be and when should it be made?

▶ What are the responsibilities of either party to ensure the contract is met?

▶ What circumstances might result in the contract being terminated?

▶ Has the contract been witnessed by a third party?

It is important to note that a contract can be either verbal or written. Unless you are very familiar with the second party, it is usually sensible to ensure that a written document is produced and signed by both of you (and potentially a witness) as this is easier to refer to as evidence if there is a later dispute.

A contract is **legally binding** and designed to protect both the supplier and client.

Theory into practice

You are in negotiations with a sports centre about offering private gym instruction to their clients. You are well qualified in sports strength and conditioning and have a strong reputation. You have many clients of your own who you see on a regular basis. You normally charge £32 per hour for one to one training but realise that the sports centre will want to make a margin (their own profit) from the service and will also help market your work.

Consider the key questions in the main text that you should ask when creating a mutually beneficial contract. Draft notes for a contract between yourself and the centre.

Finance

Securing adequate finance to start a new business and then ensuring adequate **cash flow** to keep it afloat are often the most challenging aspects of owning your own business. Depending on the size of the business and what it is providing, the levels of finance required can vary hugely. It is well documented that a large number of new businesses fail within their first year. Often this is due to insufficient start-up finance and overly optimistic projections of initial income. It is therefore vitally important to be realistic, making sure you secure finance and manage to keep your business running.

Research

Grants can sometimes be available from local organisations looking to support innovation and business enterprise. Are there any initiatives in your area through which you might be able to access funding to help set up a business?

Funding opportunities

There are numerous opportunities for financial support to start a new business or inject cash flow into an existing one. Table 12.5 gives some examples.

▶ **Table 12.5:** Sources of funding for small businesses

Small business loans	Many banks will lend to businesses. However, just as if they were lending to private individuals, they need to know that their money will be paid back at some point. Securing money from a bank relies on a strong plan and realistic projections of income and expenditure. The safer the loan looks, often the better the terms of the loan.
Private investors	Sometimes you might be lucky enough to find a private investor who has faith in you and wants to support your business ideas. That could take the form of a family member or friend. Alternatively, it could be someone completely separate. Depending on the person, they might wish to see their investment paid back with interest or alternatively take a share of the business so they also share some of the profits.
Crowd funding	There are a number of crowd-funding platforms now online on which individuals can pitch an idea and interested investors can inject cash into the business for various degrees of return. These platforms include GoFundMe and Kickstarter.
Start-up grants	In order to stimulate new business and encourage entrepreneurs, government and other organisations sometimes offer start-up grants to support your first few steps. For example, the Princes' Trust offers financial support to young people looking to start small businesses.

Considerations

When looking at the finances that a business relies upon, it is important to grasp which considerations are relevant to your picture of expenditure. These might include:

- personal salary – what will you pay yourself from the business?
- employees' salaries (if any)
- premises and facilities costs
- **capital resources**
- **consumables**
- transport costs.

Registering a business with HMRC

Regardless of whether you choose to work as a sole trader or as a limited company, you will need to contact HM Revenue and Customs (the government agency that is responsible for collecting tax, also known as HMRC) and let it know.

If you have chosen to set up a limited company, you must register the company with HMRC. In order to do this, you need to contact HMRC and have the following in place:

- a name and address for the company
- at least one director
- at least one shareholder
- be set up to pay corporation tax (the tax that businesses pay on the profit they make).

Correctly registering the company will allow HMRC to request and receive tax. Failing to register a company can result in heavy fines and prosecutions.

If you decide to operate as a sole trader, you also need to let HMRC know that you are becoming self-employed. This means that you will then be sent an annual tax return that you need to fill in, rather than having tax deducted automatically by your employer.

Tax returns

Most businesses and all self-employed people have to file a tax return once a year. This is where they calculate their total expenditure and income for the year and provide an accurate figure for their profit. This could be a positive or negative figure (a loss). Depending on what this figure is, the amount of tax owed will be calculated by HMRC. Individuals who are either sole traders or gain an income from a limited company will also need to pay **National Insurance** contributions.

Most businesses will calculate their own financial figures showing a profit or loss. There is a great deal of trust involved with submitting that figure to HMRC and some businesses may be tempted to falsify accounts to avoid tax. If HMRC suspects this is the case, it will conduct an audit of the business's accounts. Potential penalties if you are caught are high.

For this reason, it is very important that all accounts for a business are kept up to date. All expenditure and income should be recorded in a spreadsheet or other accountancy software program, and receipts, invoices and bank returns kept to provide evidence of company accounts. Many self-employed people and small businesses hire a third-party accountant to help them keep on top of their financial records and submit their tax return.

> ### Key terms
>
> **Capital resources** – resources that may lose value over time but will hold some value, such as a rowing machine or squat rack.
>
> **Consumables** – resources that have a limited life expectancy, such as pens and paper or cleaning products.
>
> **National Insurance** – a contribution from a person's income towards nationally distributed benefits which might include a state pension, maternity allowance and bereavement benefits.

Premises

When choosing premises, it is important to consider your business needs. A well-financed business may be in a position to buy premises, but others may need to lease or rent space. Making use of space at an established centre for sport may make it easier to find clients. This could be an office or studio space, or simply having access to popular sports facilities such as a gym or pool.

Some sports businesses, such as those delivering fitness training in a local park, might not seem to have any premises requirements – but they may have to pay the local council for access to the park.

▶ Securing the right premises is an important step for any new small business

The following three questions should help you make a decision on choosing premises.

1. What is my budget?
2. How much space do I need and what is that space for?
3. How long do I envisage needing the space?

Supply chains

All businesses need to buy resources of one sort or another. These could be anything from gym equipment to stationery or uniforms. When we start buying products from other suppliers we become part of a supply chain.

When choosing where to source goods, you can look at suppliers locally, nationally or even internationally, including online. There could be strengths and weaknesses in any supplier and it is up to you as a business owner to decide which fits your needs best.

Buying local is often good when it is important to be able to check products personally and you are keen to meet suppliers face to face. However, local products may come with a higher price tag, and limiting yourself to local suppliers may mean you are limiting your options.

Buying from further afield means communication will need to be via phone and email, but you may be able to find cheaper prices and will certainly have more variety and choice. If you buy internationally, there are likely to be import taxes added.

Here are a few more things you should consider before making a purchase:

▶ Set a budget and do not exceed it.
▶ All supplies come with 'lead times' (how long it will take to be delivered) – when will it be available and will it arrive before you need it? What would be the impact if the product was delayed before delivery?
▶ For specialist equipment, how easy are repairs and will you be able to source replacement parts easily?
▶ Are you able to generate **leverage** by buying in bulk?

> **Key term**
>
> **Leverage** – when you are able to offer something to enable you to encourage a supplier to give a better price. This could be by buying in bulk or by offering useful brand exposure.

Assessment practice 12.1

`A.P1` `A.P2` `A.P3` `A.M1` `A.M2` `A.D1`

You have been recruited by a local charity as a consultant to give assistance to people thinking about starting a new business and becoming self-employed, offering them advice and support in getting started.

One of your first tasks is to design some literature that they can take away and which will help them understand some options as well as the challenges associated with being self-employed.

Design a leaflet that explains and evaluates:
- the various types of self-employment available and roles that might be appropriate within the sports industry
- the legal considerations relevant to a self-employed person in the sports industry
- the financial considerations relevant to a self-employed person in the sports industry.

Plan
- Do I understand the task thoroughly?
- Have I gathered enough background knowledge from my classes and own research into local sports businesses to allow me to complete this task?

Do
- Do I know how I am going to structure the information required for this task?
- Am I able to write a clear list of points that must be covered within this task?

Review
- Can I justify why I approached this task as I did and how it has helped me gain further knowledge about self-employment?
- If I were to do this task again, I could make suggestions on how I might improve my work.

B Research your market to generate business ideas

Market research

Understanding who your clients are and what your potential market might be is a vital aspect of running a successful business. First and foremost, you need to understand who you want to aim your business at and this means understanding your clients. The types of clients aimed at by sports businesses vary immensely. The following are some questions that you should ask yourself when deciding who to target and where your market actually is.

▶ Are you aiming at private individuals, groups or other businesses?

- Is age a consideration?
- Is ability a consideration, i.e. are you aiming at beginners or people already engaged in activity?
- Does your product's **price point** restrict the number of people who might be able to afford it?

Consumer research

Ensuring your product is right and actually sellable involves engaging with your market and gathering feedback. It is usual for this consumer research to be done before launching a product. However, the needs of consumers do change and, as such, it is good practice to ensure that you keep up to date with both their likes and dislikes. Table 12.6 describes a few ways of conducting consumer research.

▶ **Table 12.6:** Methods of consumer research

Questionnaires and surveys	Questionnaires can be sent out by post, emailed or shared over social media. When done well, they can reach a large audience and gather useful data. Often, to encourage engagement with questionnaires, companies offer incentives such as being entered into a prize draw.	**Primary research** This type of research is specifically conducted by or for a business. It can be precisely tailored to ensure the required information is captured and can be reactive to gather additional information should the opportunity arise.
Interviews and focus groups	Meeting potential clients face to face allows someone doing consumer research to take every opportunity to gather information. It is possible to have frank conversations and adapt questions during the process to allow for a better understanding of the consumer's thoughts.	
Observation	Often, it can be fairly straightforward to see what consumers like and dislike. This is especially relevant when looking at practical delivery services such as personal training or classes. A great method is to take part in sessions similar to yours but delivered by others, and observe both strengths and weaknesses.	
Published sources	There are many third parties who collate information on consumerism and then publish this data. This might be online, or in journals, magazines or papers. An example could be a review of the numbers taking part in various classes across the country as a whole.	**Secondary research** This is generic research by a third party which captures useful information but may not be specific to the company.

Trends in sport

Another source of secondary research comes from trends in sport. Sport is an industry heavily influenced by trends: what people perceive as good and what people want to engage in can follow fickle fashions. For example, after the 2012 Olympics and the UK's success in the cycling events, Halfords, the largest bicycle provider in the UK, claimed to have a 15 per cent increase in bike sales.

Many governing bodies publish participation data and this can be a good source of secondary research when you are carrying out your consumer research – can you spot an area where participation is on the verge of booming and position your business to profit from this?

Table 12.7 shows some of the things which can affect the market and the priorities of consumers, and which can provoke different trends.

▶ **Table 12.7:** Trends in sport

Image	Image relates to fashion and how we want to look and act. The media plays a big part in projecting images to which many will end up aspiring. Photos of professional athletes and models in magazines, on television or over the Internet can influence us as consumers. They can affect how we dress, our nutrition and our exercise as we aspire to become like those people in the images.
Health and well-being	The importance of staying healthy is consistently in the news. As we become more educated about the benefits of a healthy lifestyle so we become more susceptible to businesses offering us ways to improve our own health and well-being.
Endorsements	When we see sports celebrities wearing brands and if we look up to those celebrities, we are attracted to those products in a bid to become like their role models.

▶ **Table 12.7:** *Continued*

Finance	The presumed quality of a product is greatly influenced by its cost. Products which are given higher associated costs may in reality not contain an equivalent increase in quality. However, the higher price can make them appear more aspirational and thus desirable. At the other end of the scale, products at a lower price point are more attainable and so easier to access for a wider range of people.
Events	Before, during and after events, publicity surrounding them increases. The sports encompassed in these events will gain more media coverage and so more consumers are likely to be attracted to them.
Success	A successful athlete makes a sport seem more attainable. Success in a sport at a high level brings media exposure to that sport and again consumers are more likely to be attracted to it.

⏸ PAUSE POINT Explain why the sports industry is continually evolving and responding to market trends.

> **Hint** You have two minutes to remember as many factors influencing market trends as you can. Create a list in your notebook.

> **Extend** Order your list according to which factors you believe might have most or least effect on how consumers react to the marketplace.

As a group, discuss which trends are likely to affect you the most. Can you provide any examples of times when you have been attracted to a product or service due to trends in the market?

Local, national and international markets

The world gets smaller every year. As developing countries get high-speed Internet and access to the Web, it has become feasible to run a business that offers a truly international service. The coverage of a business now depends more on the creativity of its owner rather than the limitations of travel and reach. Even products such as nutritional advice or exercise classes can be delivered over the Internet. This means business owners have potential to see their audience continue to grow. Understanding where their market is and how best to target it becomes more important.

If you are selling a physical product such as equipment or sports garments, your reach is almost limitless. However, when considering looking further afield for customers, you need to take into account additional expenses such as delivery and import and export duties.

Realistically, there will always be services within the sports industry which are best delivered face to face and many business owners choose to engage with an audience they can meet and build a relationship with rather than one online.

When considering where your audience is likely to come from there are a few points that should be looked at.

▶ Will your audience come to you or will you need to go to them? Some self-employed people combine the two, such as massage therapists who may hire space in a clinic but also conduct home visits.

▶ If they come to you, how far will they travel from? Are you providing a service that might have a wide reach and people will travel for, such as a dry ski slope or a climbing wall? Is your product more mainstream, such as a gym, with a more limited reach?

▶ If your clients require you to go to them (for example, to deliver one-to-one sessions such as yoga or sports massage), how far are you willing to travel and how far is realistic before expenses outweigh income?

▶ What is your **catchment area**? Are you centred within an area with high numbers of potential clients such as a city or in an area where clients are more thinly spread? Will this affect how far clients are prepared to travel for your product?

> **Key term**
>
> **Catchment area** – the area from which clients are drawn.

Investigating strategies for growth

Market research is important not just when you are looking to start up a business: it is also important when you are looking to expand it. You can have a great idea for expansion, but unless you subject it to the types of market research outlined in Table 12.6, you will be venturing into the unknown and risk the future of your business. No matter how good you think your business idea is, you should always conduct proper market research before launching it.

Generating business ideas

It is very unusual for a business to find a product that is completely new and **innovative**. However, when one does, it can mean instant success and rapid growth. Most businesses take a product that is already available and remodel it in their own style while ideally making innovative improvements.

When looking for a new business idea to start a business or expand an existing one, there are a number of areas to consider which may help your decision making. Undertaking market research into each of these areas will help you to develop and build your own business idea, and build a convincing business case that will help you to attract investment to start up or expand your business.

Gaps and opportunities

There are two sorts of gaps in the market that can be exploited by a new business or self-employed person.

1   You may be able to take a good business idea implemented somewhere else and reproduce it locally where it is not presently accessible.
2   You may be able to identify completely new products or services that are not currently offered by anyone else

When ideas are good, gaps do not tend to remain unfilled for long as business owners will move swiftly to plug the gap.

CrossFit is a brand becoming synonymous with fitness and extreme exercise. It is now a worldwide brand with international competitions, its own merchandise and thousands of affiliated gyms across the globe, all under the tagline 'Forging Elite Fitness'.

It offers high-intensity workouts based on different functional movements derived from gymnastics, weightlifting, running and rowing. Its marketing says: 'The more work you do in less time, or the higher the power output, the more intense the effort. By employing a constantly varied approach to training, functional movements and intensity lead to dramatic gains in fitness.'

CrossFit found a gap in the market and, through a very clever strategy, has ensured growth at a phenomenal pace. Its strategy involves:

* driving a clear aspiration that people should better themselves physically
* affiliated gyms that try to provide environments that are extremely team-focused and encourage participants at both ends of the scale
* providing a competitive element in which individuals within a gym can see how they compare not just with one another, but also with other gyms across the world
* offering graduated levels of participation for individuals across a wide range of abilities
* a very simple image that projects its own values and those which its members buy into.

Check your knowledge

1   What is their logo and what does it make you think of?
2   If possible, take part in a session at the gym or shadow an instructor. What sort of environment do the gym and its staff promote?
3   Can you find any local businesses which are not affiliated to CrossFit but have clearly adopted the CrossFit principles and are using them to generate interest?

Competitors

You can learn a lot from your competitors. Understanding a competitor's strengths can help you identify what you need to do to replicate its success. Equally, understanding its weaknesses can help you identify what you could do differently to attract its clients.

In order for a business to be successful it must stand a chance of competing. Assessing how well a business is managed and financed will help you decide whether you stand any chance of competing with it and, ultimately, whether your own project might work.

Barriers to entry

Making a product more accessible is one of the most common ways of taking an existing product and replicating it more successfully. This might be by halting the need for travel by using online services or bringing the product to the consumer. It could also be by making a task easier to achieve, such as reducing the weight of a piece of equipment, and/or making the product accessible to a wide audience. By overcoming any barriers to entry that customers have, you can grow the market and attract customers to your business who want the product or service but were not previously able to access it.

Pricing strategies

By finding efficiencies in delivering a product you may be able to reduce associated costs and offer the product at a reduced rate. An example of this could be in running a large minimalist gym. Offering a 'no frills' approach on a larger scale provides the opportunity to host higher numbers within an environment that has lower running costs. Offering a lower-cost alternative will attract customers put off by the cost of your competitors' products or services.

 **PAUSE POINT**   Summarise the points made about identifying gaps and opportunities without the help of the book.

> Hint   Generating business ideas needs creative flare and means spotting an opportunity.

> Extend   Can you suggest any strategies to help you identify an opportunity?

Assessment practice 12.2   `B.P4` `B.M3` `B.D2`

You have decided to start a new business within the local sports industry. Conduct detailed research about potential clients, competitors and trends, and attempt to identify a gap in the local market.

Present your research in a written document assessing the results and evaluating the research. Draw valid conclusions about the opportunities that have been identified.

Plan
- How confident do I feel in my own abilities to complete this task?
- Are there any areas relating to business plans I think I may struggle with?

Do
- Do I know what I am doing and what I want to achieve
- Can I identify when I have gone wrong and adjust my thinking/approach to get myself back on course

Review
- Can I explain what the task was and how I approached it?
- Can I explain how I would approach the difficult elements differently next time (i.e. what would I do differently)?

C   Develop a business plan to gain investment and/or contracts

Writing business plans

Once an opportunity or gap in the market has been identified, a business will normally need to either attract investment or win a contract. When attracting investment –

whether it is from a bank, private investors or by any other means – it is likely that a structured and clear business plan is required. Figure 12.1 shows how a strong business plan works.

When writing business plans the key things you need to make clear are:
▶ how you will take advantage of business opportunities
▶ how you will target specific customer groups and identify potential customer demands
▶ the potential cost and profit levels of your business.

You will also need to remember the issues around employment law and registering with HMRC that we looked at in learning aim A on page 76.

Research

There are many ways of displaying the information required within a business plan. Many companies offer online services and free templates to help you structure your thinking. Can you find three examples? Evaluate them choosing one that you feel is most beneficial. Justify your reasons.

 **PAUSE POINT**   Do you understand how the key features of a business plan relate to each other?

Hint   Draw your own flow diagram of the elements found within a business plan.

Extend   What is the most important feature of a business plan?

Describe the nature of the business and associated opportunities

↓

Describe the structure of the business

↓

Project realistic growth, income and expenditure

↓

Explain the strategy for how this growth will be achieved

↓

Describe the investment and support required

↓

Summarise the plan and promote the opportunity

▶ **Figure 12.1:** Structure for a business plan

Nature of business

Describing exactly what the business is and its targets are vital aspects of promoting an idea to investors. Major sectors within the sports industry include:
▶ nutrition
▶ therapy
▶ equipment
▶ clothing and footwear
▶ facility and venue rental
▶ coaching and instruction
▶ fitness development.

These main sectors are supported by more generalised sectors such as marketing, finance, law and human resources businesses.

Whether you are promoting a brand of clothing, a fitness class or rehabilitative therapy, it is likely that within any sector there will be a strong need to sell the product. This is especially relevant from when a business first starts up until the point where recommendations and word of mouth can do much of the promotional work for you. Understanding where a business fits into the sports industry and how other sectors might influence it, service it or be supported by it should be the first task of a business plan.

Remember that one of the things that can attract customers to your business is the additional value you can offer on top of the service. For example, you may run your service on more days in the year than your competitors, or at more flexible times. Or you may be more mobile and be able to visit customers. Any added value you can build in to the service or product you offer will help it to find more customers – and help you to make more sales.

 **PAUSE POINT**   Can you remember the various sectors within the sports industry?

Hint   What sectors are you interested in? Which would you want to work in?

Extend   Are there any additional sectors within the sports industry?

Seasonal patterns

A large proportion of sports businesses experience seasonal patterns, and if this is the case, you should spell it out in the business plan. If a business relies on a specific sport, especially when that sport is conducted outside, there are likely to be seasonal patterns; it may only be realistic to deliver some sports at certain times of the year, such as skiing in the winter or kayaking during the summer. Gyms often have a drop in numbers of users during the summer months when members choose to exercise outdoors and increased numbers over the winter when the weather is poorer and days are shorter.

Businesses that know that they can expect seasonal patterns can react accordingly. Financial projections can be designed to show patterns and there may be opportunity to employ additional staff during busy periods, as well as to reduce other overheads such as facility and resource costs during low seasons.

Business structure

How businesses are structured varies considerably. There are many variable factors that will have an influence on the initial structure and how a business evolves in the future. The structure must be linked to the actual purpose of the business, what it is trying to achieve and what its primary activity is. In any case, the chosen structure should be explained in the business plan. The resources defined in the business structure must be appropriate and directly linked to achieving these goals.

Staffing

The number of staff required by a business will absolutely depend upon what it is trying to achieve. In any business there are a number of key functions which need to be handled, such as:

▸ marketing and personal relations
▸ health and safety
▸ human resources
▸ finance
▸ delivery of services.

It is important that a new business is realistic about how many staff are needed and what it can afford. In an ideal world, a business might employ specialists in all these fields. In reality, small businesses might only have a few members of staff and they must be able to perform a number of functions within the company.

For larger businesses, sometimes it is useful to use a flow diagram to illustrate chains of command and responsibility. Figure 12.2 shows a basic structure for a fitness centre with gym and pool.

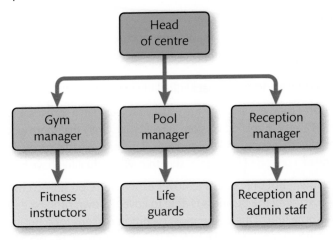

▸ **Figure 12.2:** An organisation chart

▶ People who are in business on their own may need to develop the ability to manage all these functions. It is advisable for any business owner operating on their own to engage specialists from outside the business to assist with key tasks or at least offer advice. This can be organised by contracting specialist companies or consultants.

The business plan should also state which positions will be full time or part time, which will be seasonal and which might be carried out by volunteers.

Resources

Resources can be anything that a business needs to succeed. Resources will have a life expectancy and the business plan should be clear on this fact. Resources can be placed under the following general headings.

▶ **Administration and office** – resources might include laptops, phones, pens and paper, and Internet access.
▶ **Transport** – might include both cars, mini buses and associated costs such as fuel and insurance.
▶ **Licensing and legal requirements** – might include insurance and qualifications.
▶ **Equipment** – might include technical equipment, first aid equipment and teaching or sales resources.
▶ **Uniform** – either to promote a brand or to act as personal protective equipment.

Location and facilities

It is quite possible for a small business to run from an owner's home with no need for any additional facilities. For businesses which need facilities and a physical location, it is important that you are realistic about your requirements both at the present and in future. When choosing a location and facility and justifying your choice in your business plan, these simple questions will help you make informed judgements.

▶ How much space do you need?
▶ What is the nature of the space that you need (for example, outdoors, studio, treatment room?
▶ What is your budget?
▶ How important is location to attracting and retaining clients?

Finance

Projecting both income and expenditure is one of the most difficult tasks of any business owner, but it is an essential part of a business plan. Expenditure on all of the above considerations must be accounted for. From market research, you must judge how well the business is going to perform and how rapidly clients are likely to be engaged.

When considering finance, you must consider:

▶ what initial expenses you will incur
▶ how long it will take before you secure any income
▶ whether initial income will be adequate to cover running expenses and if not how long this will take
▶ how long it will take you to pay back initial investments.

Income (or 'turnover') and expenditure are usually projected in a spreadsheet similar to Figure 12.3. This is a very simplified version. In reality, it is likely that there would be far more examples of both income and expenditure. It is also likely that projections would need to be made of a period of years to ensure that all eventualities have been considered.

The initial investment not only needs to cover expenditure on set-up costs but also cover running costs until the business is able to cover its own running expenses. This could take some time. One of the most common reasons for a business to fail is underestimating how long it will take before it is able to cover its own expenses and **break even**.

INCOME AND EXPENDITURE	Jan	Feb	Mar	Apr	May	Jun	Jul	Aug	Sep	Oct	Nov	Dec	Total
Income													
Merchandise													
One-to-one training													
Group classes													
Monthly memberships													
Total													
Expenses													
Premises													
Professional fees													
Staff													
Equipment													
Maintenance													
Marketing													
Office supplies													
Services and utilities													
Loan for start-up costs													
Insurance													
Total													
Profit or loss													

▶ **Figure 12.3:** An example spreadsheet for calculating income and expenditure

To convince investors that their money will be well spent, it is vital that expenditure of loans is clear and justified.

Contingency

It is very difficult to make a financial projection that is 100 per cent accurate. You may be incredibly lucky and achieve higher profit than expected. It is more likely that you incur unexpected expenses. Ensure that whenever you build a financial projection, you consider the worst case scenario. Make sure there is enough money to cover unexpected expenses and cover running costs for an extended period.

Strategy for attracting clients

Most businesses, unless they are lucky enough to be completely innovative and original, will often try and identify a **unique selling point (USP)**. This USP will add value and appeal or break down barriers that might prevent a client engaging with a product and could be the result of:

▶ reducing cost and providing better value for money for clients
▶ reducing delivery ratios of staff to clients so a better service is offered compared with that of competitors
▶ improving efficiency (i.e. 'getting results quicker')
▶ offering incentives such as additional days for free or merchandise
▶ promoting a lifestyle that is aspirational and appealing to clients
▶ reducing travel needs by using the Internet or bringing the service to the client
▶ offering enhanced quality.

Summary

It is sometimes forgotten that often a primary reason for a business plan is to project a concept or idea. The business plan's summary gives an opportunity to 'sell' the business to secure support or investment. This is the time to really explain why an investor might want to be involved.

Theory into practice

Imagine that you have the opportunity to start a small business as a personal trainer. You have access to £15,000 worth of private investment that must be paid back interest-free over 5 years. You need to ensure that you have all insurance, qualifications and licences in place, purchase resources, access a venue or facilities, cover administrative costs and develop marketing resources.

1 Conduct real-life research into local opportunities to enable you to cost this business.

2 Complete a financial projection for the first year. Be realistic about income and expenditure.

On completion of the projection, make an assessment on whether you feel this business could be sustainable.

Key term

Unique selling point (USP) – something that makes a business or its product different to anything else. It can be projected as a reason for potential clients to buy a particular product or service rather than that of a competitor.

Case study

Outdoor and Fit is a small company that was started in 2013 in Cardiff. Unfortunately, the business failed after two years and had to close its doors. The owner Tris was obviously very disappointed. The business appeared to be busy and he was charging a rate for classes comparable to any other fitness group or centre. On investigation, Tris realised that his expenditure was just too high to allow the company to break even. His expenses could be categorised under the following headings.

- Staff – Tris paid himself a basic wage from the company and employed an administrator 2.5 days a week to respond to emails and take bookings.
- Facilities – the concept behind Outdoor and Fit was to provide circuit training in various outdoor venues including parks, forests and on the beach. Therefore, no venue for delivery was required. The business did lease an office in Cardiff, though.
- Resources – Tris kept office resources to the minimum. For his actual classes, he had a small selection of equipment including resistance bands, exercise mats and kettle bells. These were all well used.

- Insurance and qualifications – Tris was already qualified as a fitness professional before starting the business. However, he did have to ensure his first aid qualification was renewed every three years. Insurance for the business was compulsory and paid monthly.
- Transport – as Tris needed to attend various venues to deliver his classes, he required a car to move around. He bought a Toyota Hilux from new through the company to ensure he looked professional and was able to carry the equipment he required.
- Marketing – the website was built by a friend for a reduced cost. Tris also had flyers which were distributed around sports centres and a budget for local advertising.

Check your knowledge

1 In what ways was Tris successful in saving money and reducing expenditure?
2 Are there ways in which you believe Tris could or should have saved money within the new business?
3 In reality, do you think that this could have been a successful business idea?

Assessment practice 12.3　　　C.P5　C.P6　C.M4　C.M5　C.D3

Think back to the local opportunity that you identified in assessment activity 12.2. You now need to design a business plan that will explain your thoughts clearly and in detail, project finances and promote your ideas to an investor or supporter.

When you have completed the plan, you need to review it, evaluating strengths and areas for improvement. Give recommendations for improvements that you could make in the future.

On completion of your business plan, to get ready for the possibility of presenting it to a bank manager to secure funds, prepare a PowerPoint presentation with accompanying handouts.

Plan
- Am I confident about my ideas and how to illustrate them in a business plan?
- Do I understand all of the considerations when making business projections?

Do
- Do I know how to design my plan and am I confident it will be clear?
- Could I consider both strengths and areas for improvement and make recommendations if I were to re-write my plan?

Review
- Can I explain what the task was and justify my approach?
- Can I explain how I might learn from this task and use what I have learned for future tasks?

Further reading and resources

Barrow, C. (2011), *Starting and Running a Business All-in-One for Dummies*, John Wiley and Sons.

Morton, C. (2013), *A One Person Business: How to Start a Small Business*, Little Brown.

The Prince's Trust (2010), *Make it Happen: The Prince's Trust Guide to Starting Your Own Business*, John Wiley and Sons.

THINK ▶FUTURE

Seb Christy

Self-employed swimming coach

Nothing prepared me for how much work was involved in setting up my business. For the first 18 months, the income wasn't enough to cover my basic living expenses so I had to get a part-time job at a sports centre to supplement it.

Looking back on the experience now, five years later, makes my current situation all the more satisfying. I am now completely self-sufficient. My business has paid back all of the start-up loan that was initially used to fund it. I make a good wage, but more importantly I am able to dictate my own future. I work to my own schedule and book clients to fit around my own lifestyle.

I know that there has been some luck involved in my success. I have friends whose start-up businesses have failed in the first year. However, I know that my hard work and perseverance have been the driving factors behind whether my business worked or not.

Focusing your skills

Identifying an opportunity

A business is only as good as the idea that it is built around. There are many factors which determine whether an idea might be a viable business. The following are tips for identifying and determining whether a business might work.

- Consider the competition. Is the market saturated with similar businesses or is there enough space for yours to find clients?
- Make sure you understand who is in your target market. Conduct plenty of research to get to know them and understand what they want.
- Make your product stand out from the crowd. Find a unique selling point and use this to entice clients to your product.
- Choose a business that you can feel motivated and passionate about. Starting and then running a business is hard work. Unless you are motivated, it is likely you will fail.

Plan your finances

- Ensure that you account for every possible expenditure and always make sure that you have a fall–back built in.
- Look ahead. The further ahead you can build your plan, the better understanding you will have about what you need to do to ensure success.
- Use specialists. Especially in the first year and while you are learning, it might be advisable to use an accountant to help you keep track of finances.
- To secure loans and grants you need to sell the idea. Make sure you believe in any plan you make and ensure it is realistic.

Getting ready for assessment

Keako is in the second year of a Level 3 BTEC in Sport. He aspires to one day own his own business and so was really interested in this unit. Previously he spent some time researching various opportunities within the sports industry to become self-employed and run his own business. For learning aim C, his assignment asked him to:

▶ write a business plan that is realistic and covers all of the key considerations of starting a business.

▶ evaluate its content suggesting improvements for the future.

How I got started

During my course I've had the opportunity to meet a wide range of people in the sports industry. Many of them own their own business and I have taken every opportunity to quiz them on what it is like. A couple of these people offered to give me advice should I ever be looking at setting my own business up. To help me with this task, I contacted them and they were really helpful in making suggestions.

Once I had a sound business concept, I spent time working out how best to structure the information in a business plan. I have realised that as every business is different, so too is every plan.

I wanted my plan to be as accurate as possible and so spent a large amount of time researching costs, resources and facilities. I wanted to be as realistic as possible and so I made savings whereever I could.

How I brought it all together

I made sure my plan was easy to navigate by using a contents page. I also used some images to make my ideas more visual. I remembered that one of the primary reasons for a business plan is to sell an idea. I tried to ensure that my enthusiasm and belief in my ideas were shown in my plan. There are a few things which I did to ensure the plan was thorough and detailed.

▶ I created a flow chart of staffing and then gave a brief job description of each role to ensure that all tasks required within the business were covered.

▶ After completing the financial projections for year 1, I also showed them for years 2 and 3. I realise many businesses don't make money in their first year so it was important to show when I thought mine would.

▶ I tried to be realistic about resources and staff. Sometimes I compromised and reduced spending to make sure costs were as low as possible. At the same time I tried to show how quality could still be kept high.

What I learned from the experience

I always realised that building your own business could be a challenge. I can now see how difficult it actually is. I am still determined to own my own business one day. To make this a reality I can see that I will need to work hard. I am trying to take on board feedback from my tutors and workplace experts that I meet.

There are a number of things that have been highlighted for me to work on and I am going to use the remainder of my course to make improvements. Maths and English are both very important for any business owner. Being able to manage figures, use spreadsheets and communicate thoughts and plans in a written format is crucial. I can't let difficulty slow me down. I need to learn to stay motivated even when faced with a hard task or obstacle. And developing organisational skills is fundamental as hopefully one day I will have to manage my own schedule as well as some employees.

Think about it

▶ Do you know when the submission dates for your assignments are and how you are going to best use your time to complete the tasks?

▶ Have you used every opportunity to research and experience various sectors within the sports industry?

▶ Do you understand all of the features that affect a self-employed person and business owner?

Instructing Gym-based Exercise 13

Getting to know your unit

Assessment
This unit is internally assessed using a series of assignments set by your tutor.

People are more fitness-conscious than ever, leading to a significant growth in gyms around the country. These gyms need instructors to instruct people in the safe use of equipment, work with individuals and plan exercise programmes, and also motivate and support users.

In this unit, you will explore the different types of exercises, including those using cardiovascular and resistance equipment, and how each of these exercises can be performed safely with the correct technique. You will also investigate how to plan and instruct a gym-based exercise session, taking into account clients' needs and how these sessions can be adapted to meet different needs.

Finally, you will explore different methods for collecting feedback on performance, enabling you to identify your strengths and areas for improvement.

How you will be assessed

This unit will be internally assessed through a series of tasks set by your tutor. Throughout this unit, you will find useful assessment activities that will help you work towards your final assessments. Completing each of these will not necessarily mean that you achieve a final grade, but each of them will help you by carrying out relevant research or preparation that can be used towards your final assessments.

To ensure that you achieve all the tasks in your assignments, it is important that you cover all the Pass criteria. Make sure that you check all of them before you submit your work to your tutor.

If you are hoping to achieve a Merit or Distinction, you must consider how you present the information in your assignment and make sure that you extend your responses or answers. For example, to achieve a Merit you must explain your strengths and weaknesses when delivering a gym-based exercise session, providing recommendations on self-improvement. To achieve a Distinction, you must go further by justifying your choices of adapted and alternative exercises, session strengths and recommendations on self-improvement. It is important that you plan your assessments and ensure that you include all the required grading criteria.

The assignment set by your tutor will consist of a number of tasks designed to meet the criteria in the table. This is likely to consist of a written assignment but may also include activities such as:

▶ preparing contrasting clients for a safe gym-based exercise session.
▶ planning and undertaking a safe gym-based session for two contrasting clients, explaining the different methods of training.
▶ evaluating and reviewing your own performance when supervising a gym-based session.

Assessment criteria

This table shows what you must do in order to achieve a **Pass**, **Merit** or **Distinction** grade, and where you can find activities to help you.

Pass	Merit	Distinction
Learning aim **A** Explore the processes of client assessment prior to gym-based exercise participation		
A.P1 Perform client screening for two contrasting clients. **Assessment activity 13.1**	**A.M1** Perform effective screening using methods that are appropriate to the needs of two contrasting clients. **Assessment activity 13.1**	**A.D1** Evaluate the screening from two contrasting clients, justifying suggestions for progression into exercising safely. **Assessment activity 13.1**
A.P2 Interpret the screening results from two contrasting clients.. **Assessment activity 13.1**	**A.M2** Provide recommendations for specific clients on factors affecting their safe exercise participation **Assessment activity 13.1**	
A.P3 Explain factors which can affect safe exercise participation for two contrasting clients. **Assessment activity 13.1**		
Learning aim **B** Examine different types of exercise for a gym-based exercise		
B.P4 Explain different methods of cardiovascular endurance training and resistance training. **Assessment activity 13.2**	**B.M3** Compare and contrast different methods of cardiovascular and resistance training, justifying the use of each for different clients. **Assessment activity 13.2**	**B.D2** Evaluate own performance in the planning and delivery of a gym-based exercise session to specific clients, justifying choices of adapted and alternative exercises, session, strengths and recommendations on self-improvement. **Assessment activity 13.2**
Learning aim **C** Undertake planning and instructing gym-based exercise for individual clients		
C.P5 Prepare a safe and effective plan for a gym-based exercise session.. **Assessment activity 13.3**	**C.M4** Prepare a comprehensive gym-based exercise plan that shows adaptations of each exercise for different clients. **Assessment activity 13.3**	**C.D3** Evaluate the impacts of client assessment and choice of exercise on the planning and instructing of safe and effective gym-based exercise. **Assessment activity 13.3**
C.P6 Deliver a safe and effective gym-based exercise session that includes the performance of safe and effective cardiovascular and resistance gym-based exercises. **Assessment activity 13.3**	**C.M5** Communicate effectively to clients when delivering a gym-based exercise session that offers adapted and alternative exercises for different specific clients. **Assessment activity 13.3**	
C.P7 Review own performance in the delivery of a gym-based exercise session, identifying strengths and areas for improvement. **Assessment activity 13.3**	**C.M6** Review own performance in the delivery of a gym-based exercise session, explaining strengths and providing recommendations on self-improvement. **Assessment activity 13.3**	

Getting Started

Working in a gym can be a demanding but rewarding career, working with a range of clients each with their own personal fitness goals. Write a list of what you think are the key components of designing a gym session and what skills are needed to lead a session. Think of your own current skills and list your strengths as well as areas you would need to improve on to successfully lead a session.

 # Explore the processes of client assessment prior to gym-based exercise participation

Before you allow your client to undertake any exercise, and as part of designing a training programme, you must gain a picture of their exercise history, including any health-related issues or recent illnesses. The client's health and safety before, during and after a training session is of prime importance. Before any exercise sessions commence, you must be certain your client is able to safely complete the session or programme.

Client screening

Before they participate in any exercise session, it is essential that you assess the client's current level of activity as well as their health and any medical conditions or injuries. Each client should complete a screening session. These were covered in depth in Unit 2 but can include:

▶ short, informal interviews
▶ pre-exercise questionnaires such as a Physical Activity Readiness Questionnaire (PAR–Q) and a lifestyle questionnaire
▶ observation.

If you are uncertain about any response given as part of a pre-exercise questionnaire, or interview then you should not allow the client to complete an exercise session until you have resolved the issue to your satisfaction. Remember the health and safety of your client is your primary concern.

You must also obtain the client's informed consent before the exercise session starts – this was also covered in Unit 2.

Contraindications

You must be aware of your client's **contraindications** before they start any exercise programme. Your interview or questionnaires will ensure you are aware of any conditions that are likely to affect your client's ability to train safely. Common examples of contraindications include asthma, pregnancy, heart disease, diabetes and recent operations or injuries.

If you have any concerns regarding the client's health or if there are any contraindications, then you should refer the client to a professional medical expert such as their GP.

> **Link**
>
> Client screening and obtaining informed consent were covered in *Unit 2: Fitness Training and Programming for Health, Sport and Well-being.*

> **Key term**
>
> **Contraindication** – a physical or mental condition or factor that increases the risk involved in an activity.

❚❚ PAUSE POINT   Do you understand the importance of client screening?

> Hint   Write a list of the different methods that can be used to screen a client before exercise and the benefits of each of these.

> Extend   Consider whether there are any disadvantages to each of these methods and why using a combination of methods may be beneficial.

Factors affecting safe exercise participation

All individuals have different needs, abilities, goals, skills, physical attributes, lifestyles, medical histories and exercise preferences. Therefore a training programme should be tailor-made for each individual. Your expectations should be specific to the different individuals.

The pre-exercise questionnaire and interview will allow you to determine the client's current level of activity. This is important and enables you to prescribe exercises that give the client sufficient progression. Never prescribe exercises that are too hard for the client, as this can be dangerous and cause discomfort or injury. Each client must be comfortable with their exercise programme.

Exercise intensity

Exercise intensity is the level of effort required to perform an exercise session – in other words, how hard the exercises are. It can be measured in a number of ways for a variety of exercises. Intensity is sometimes referred to as **overload**. For any improvements to be made, you must work the body beyond what it is normally used to. If overload is not achieved, the best a person can expect is to maintain their current level of fitness.

Percentage of maximum heart rate

Exercise intensity is often measured as a percentage of your maximum heart rate (MHR), with equipment such as a heart-rate monitor valuable in measuring exercise intensity. Commonly, exercises aim for low, medium or high intensity:

▸ **low intensity** – training at up to 70 per cent of MHR – used to improve general fitness
▸ **medium intensity** – training at up to 80 per cent of MHR – used to improve aerobic threshold or endurance
▸ **high intensity** – training at up to 90 per cent of MHR – used to improve strength or anaerobic threshold.

Training zones for cardiovascular health and fitness

Training zones can determine the level of intensity you are working at. This is particularly important for cardiovascular training or exercise. Heart-rate training zones are calculated by taking into consideration your MHR and your resting heart rate (RHR). A simple way to work out your MHR is to subtract your age in years from 220:

MHR = 220 – age.

Your RHR can be measured by taking your pulse at rest, preferably before any form of movement or exercise. Because it is difficult to exercise and measure your heart rate manually, it is useful to use a heart-rate monitor.

Another method of determining heart–rate training zones is the Karvonen formula. The Karvonen formula allows you to determine how fast your heart should be beating when you are in one of the heart-rate training zones (shown in Table 13.1):

desired heart rate (HR) = RHR + [(MHR – RHR) × % intensity]

> **Key term**
>
> **Overload** – working the body systems beyond their normal functional level, which is essential for gaining training benefits.

> **Link**
>
> The aerobic and anaerobic energy systems were covered in *Unit 1: Anatomy and Physiology*.

▶ **Table 13.1:** The four main training zones

Zone	Percentage of MHR	Training
Fitness	60–70%	Develops basic endurance and aerobic capacity – all easy recovery running should be completed at a maximum of 70% MHR.
Aerobic	70–80%	Develops your cardiovascular system – the body's ability to transport oxygen to, and carbon dioxide away from, the working muscles is developed and improved; as fitness improves, it will be possible to run at up to 75% MHR and get the benefits of fat-burning and improved aerobic capacity.
Anaerobic	80–90%	High-intensity – your body cannot use oxygen quickly enough to produce energy so relies on energy that can be used without oxygen, namely glycogen stored in the muscles. This can be used for only a short period – a build-up of lactic acid will rapidly cause fatigue.
Red line	90–100%	Maximum level of exercise – training possible only for short periods, effectively trains fast-twitch muscle fibres and helps develop speed. This zone is reserved for interval running – only for the very fit.

Case study

Otis is an 18-year-old male athlete with a RHR of 70 beats per minute (bpm) and a MHR of 202 bpm. So:

- for 65% intensity: 70 + [(202 − 70) × 0.65] = 156 bpm
- for 75% intensity: 70 + [(202 − 70) × 0.75] = 169 bpm
- for 85% intensity: 70 + [(202 − 70) × 0.85] = 182 bpm.

Check your knowledge

1 How could Otis ensure that he is training at the selected intensity?
2 What intensity should Otis train at to improve his aerobic fitness?
3 Work out your own target heart rate for 65%, 75% and 85% intensities.

Discussion

Heart rate is commonly used to measure how hard somebody will exercise. Discuss why measuring heart rate is important when instructing gym-based exercise and how an understanding of training zones will assist in making an exercise programme.

Research

Research the RPE scale, the categories of exercise intensity and how they map to heart rates. How do you think the RPE scale could be used to plan gym-based exercise programmes?

Key term

Antenatal – during pregnancy (from conception to birth).

Rating of Perceived Exertion (RPE)

The Rating of Perceived Exertion (RPE) is a scale running from 6 to 20 and reflects heart rates ranging from 60 to 200 beats per minute. The participants rate how hard they think they are exerting themselves by giving a number on this scale. For example, if you are exercising and you give a rating of 13 ('somewhat hard'), this gives a rough equivalent heart rate of 130 beats per minute.

Factors affecting safe participation

When planning an exercise programme, you must consider the specific needs of your different clients. Clients can be divided into different categories depending on their age, condition and physical ability. Some of the common groups are described below.

14–16-year-olds

Exercise for children is very important as it provides health benefits such as an improved cardiovascular system and stronger muscles and bones. However, caution should be used when considering the types of training. For example, a 14–16-year-old's bones are still growing so lifting heavy weights should be avoided as the risk of injury is high. However, moderate strength training is beneficial and would be considered low risk.

Antenatal women

The **antenatal** period covers pregnant women from conception to birth. Exercise during pregnancy helps women stay healthy and keep their weight gain within a safe range. Recent studies have identified several benefits of exercise during pregnancy, including:

▶ less backache
▶ increased well-being of the mother-to-be and foetus
▶ improved sleep patterns
▶ improved muscle tone in the upper body and abdominal area.

The better the cardiovascular system, the more stamina a woman will have. Exercise helps circulatory problems such as fatigue and varicose veins. Good circulation supplies the baby with more oxygen and nutrients because mother and baby are linked by the placenta. Exercise reduces the chance of haemorrhoids, cramps and constipation.

Moderate exercise that makes pregnant women feel slightly out of breath is good, especially if the body is already used to exercise. Being fit is excellent preparation for the physical effort required during labour. However, care should be taken during exercise, and exercises involving the abdominal area of the body should be avoided. For example, after 16 weeks of pregnancy, avoid exercises involving the client lying on their front (supine) as this may put too much pressure on the abdominal area. During pregnancy, overhead resistance exercises should also be avoided as this can increase curvature of the lower spine and cause hyper**lordosis.**

Postnatal women

Postnatal refers to the stage after giving birth. Some women have trouble bringing their abdomen back to its original size after having a baby and certain exercises can help. Benefits of postnatal exercise include:

▶ speedier healing and recovery from the birthing process
▶ a faster return to the woman's pre-pregnancy shape
▶ an increase in energy levels to cope with the demands of motherhood
▶ reduced likelihood of stress and depression.

Postnatal exercises help to regain shape, but ligaments and joints will still be soft for at least three months following birth, so vigorous stretching and high-impact activities should be avoided. During pregnancy, the weight of the baby will have altered the mother's centre of gravity. This, combined with the softening effects of the hormone relaxin on her ligaments, may lead to bad posture. Exercise can strengthen abdominal and back muscles, improving posture and reducing chances of backache while carrying the new-born baby.

> **Key terms**
>
> **Lordosis** – a condition in the lower back where there is excessive curvature of the lumbar region of the vertebral column.
>
> **Postnatal** – the period of time after a baby is born.
>
> **Osteoporosis** – a condition that weakens bones due to a loss of stored calcium, which makes bones fragile, brittle and more likely to break.

> **Research**
>
> In a small group, research the different types of exercises that can be safely performed by a pregnant woman. Consider the different stages (or 'trimesters') of the pregnancy and how exercises can be developed to allow exercise to continue.

❚❚ PAUSE POINT   Consider why exercise is important and beneficial to pregnant women.

(Hint)   List the benefits of exercise during pregnancy and explain the main considerations when providing exercise advice.

(Extend)   Now explain why some exercises should be avoided during pregnancy. You should consider the different trimesters.

Older people (50+)

Older adults are defined as those aged 50 or over. Individuals do not grow old in the same way, so this group can have a wide variety of exercise needs. The range of activities is vast, but so too is the range of possible medical conditions, ability levels and client interests.

There are four types of exercise that are key to staying healthy and independent: strength, balance, stretching and endurance exercises. The following should be considered.

▶ Use a longer more gradual warm-up period as older people take longer to warm up as their circulatory system isn't as efficient. A cool-down should also be longer and gradually tapered as part of the recovery period. (You can read more about warm-ups and cool-downs on pages 104–5.)

▶ High-impact exercises such as running and jumping should be avoided, especially where **osteoporosis** has been previously diagnosed. Older people have less dense bones making them more susceptible to impact fractures. Exercise involving balance also has risks of fractures – such as in the hip and pelvis – if the client loses their balance. Support should be on hand to prevent falls.

▶ Exercises should incorporate general everyday movements to aid mobility including:
  • side stepping – to increase leg and hip strength, and balance

- sitting, and getting up and down
- shoulder shrugs – to strengthen back, stretch chest muscles, and improve posture
- toe, heel and leg rises – to improve ankle strength for balance
- eyes-closed balance exercises – to improve posture, balance and range of motion.

Referral to other professionals

If any client, but especially one in a specific group such as those explored above, highlights a contraindication such as a loss of physiological or psychological function during exercise, you should refer them immediately to a medical professional, such as a GP. Any symptoms of a potentially serious disease or health concern highlighted through screening should also be referred to a medical professional.

If your client indicates 'yes' at least once as part of the PAR-Q process or if you have any concerns regarding the welfare of your client starting an exercise programme, you should temporarily defer the session. Remember that it is better that your client is healthy and able to exercise.

▶ Clients over the age of 50 are one group who might need exercises adapted

---

Assessment practice 13.1   A.P1   A.P2   A.P3   A.M1   A.M2   A.D1

You have been approached by a PE teacher who wishes to start an after-school gym class for staff. For this, you have been asked to undertake pre-exercise screening of at least two members of staff: one is described as active and participates in regular exercise, while the other hasn't undertaken any exercise in recent years.

Before the screening takes place, the teachers would like to know what it involves. Prepare an outline for them that explains the screening steps you will take. Based on their profiles, explain possible recommendations that you may make after the screening. You should further explain the factors that can affect safe participation for each of these members of staff and also justify your suggestions to help them progress into exercising safely.

Plan
- I will consider what the differences are in the two selected clients.
- I will design and use pre-exercise paperwork that collects the relevant and necessary information

Do
- I will practise my communication skills and ask my peers to give me advice on how I can improve.
- I will be ready to give feedback to the clients and be able to provide suitable recommendations.

Review
- I can explain what the task was and how I approached the task.
- When I have reflected on my own work and the feedback from others, I will make any necessary changes to my pre-exercise questionnaire.

B   Examine different types of exercise for a gym-based exercise

When designing any training programme, you must consider the factors that will make it safe and effective. These are known as the FITT principles, and you should follow them when devising any fitness or training programme. FITT refers to the following factors.

- ▶ **Frequency** – how often will the client train? The time available will be limited by a person's lifestyle and commitments.
- ▶ **Intensity** – how hard will each exercise be? This should incorporate the 'overload' principle.
- ▶ **Time** – how long will each exercise and session last? Generally speaking, higher-intensity exercises can be performed for a short period, while lower or moderate levels of intensity can be maintained for longer.
- ▶ **Type** – what types of exercises will be included? Your training programme should have the correct exercises to achieve a client's specific goals. You should consider strength, flexibility, muscular endurance and aerobic endurance.

Types of gym-based exercise equipment

When you step into a gym, you will immediately notice the different types of equipment that can be used as part of a training programme. These can be put into three broad categories: cardiovascular machines, free weights and resistance machines.

Cardiovascular machines

Cardiovascular machines are sometimes referred to as cardio machines and are used for improving and maintaining your cardiovascular system. The machines are designed to replicate common exercises to increase heart and respiration rates. They can also be used as part of a warm-up or cool-down.

▶ **Treadmills** have many adjustable features to alter the exercise intensity, including, for example, adjusting the speed or degree of incline. Treadmills are suitable for clients who are used to, or who enjoy, running.

▶ **Static cycles** have adjustable features that affect exercise intensity, such as changes in resistance, making it easier or harder to turn the pedals. Cycling is a low-impact exercise so is a good choice for clients suffering from joint or bone conditions or who may be returning from a skeletal injury.

▶ **Indoor rowing machines** are used to simulate the action of rowing a boat and use the same muscles. This low-impact exercise can help build and tone muscles, strengthen cardiovascular function and increase stamina. The rowing machines are particularly effective for older clients because they place no strain on the back and joints.

▶ Treadmills are a cardiovascular machine common in gyms

Free weights

The most common free weights are dumbbells and barbells. The reason they are called free weights is that there are no pins, cables or pulleys to guide their movement and they rely purely on muscular contractions to move.

▶ **Barbells** are usually 1.2 to 2 m long and have removable weights at each end. The weights attached to the ends of the bar provide resistance while both arms are used to lift the bar. These weights are normally removable so different amounts can be added to the bar. They are fixed in place with a collar.

▶ A **dumbbell** is a short barbell which can be held in one hand. They usually have fixed weights at each end. A range of different weighted dumbbells will be used depending on the goals and needs of the client. Dumbbells enable you to strengthen both sides of your body equally as well as allowing you to do some exercises (like front raises) that can't be done with a barbell.

▶ **Benches** provide a platform to perform weight-based exercises. There are two main types of bench:
  • flat bench – parallel to the ground, ideal for a wide variety of basic free-weight exercises.
  • incline bench – can be adjusted to an angle, allowing different body positions to be used and therefore helping train different muscles.

Resistance machines

Resistance machines combine weights with pulleys and cables, offering a wide range of exercises for many different muscle groups. Because resistance machines use cables and pulleys, they do not require another person to support or 'spot' a client during an exercise. They also enable you to do some exercises you can't do with barbells, such as leg curls, lat pull-downs and leg extensions.

Fixed resistance machines allow individuals to change the load based on their training programme. The variable resistance ranges from 0 to 100 kg on most machines, allowing the programme to include overload and progression. These machines are expensive, making them impractical for use at home. On the positive side, they are safer to use than free weights, and novice trainers can use them to learn different movement patterns as an individual can change the range of movement at a specific joint by adjusting the machine's settings.

Ⅱ PAUSE POINT Do you understand the different uses of cardiovascular equipment, resistance machines and free weights?

Hint Describe the equipment used to train aerobic endurance, muscular strength and muscular endurance.

Extend Explain the advantages and disadvantages of using free weights rather than resistance machines.

Types of exercises

A training programme can include a variety of different exercises depending on the client's goals. These exercises are outlined in the following tables.

Cardiovascular exercises

There are several different cardiovascular exercises as well as different types of equipment that will help improve the cardiovascular system, as shown in Table 13.2.

▶ **Table 13.2:** Cardiovascular exercises

Equipment	Exercise description
Upright cycle	• Can be used as part of aerobic training as well as improving muscular endurance and power. • Places less stress on the joints and is designed to maintain posture while exercising.
Recumbent cycle	• Used to train the aerobic system; the main difference from an upright cycle is the position of the body. • Allows the user to cycle in a reclined position; particularly good if the client suffers from lower back pain. • Also good for those new to cycling as they tend to be more comfortable than upright bikes.
Treadmill	• Can be used as part of a warm-up or cool-down as well as for aerobic and anaerobic training. • To train at high intensities, speed can be increased or the incline made steeper, or both. • Modern treadmills come with a variety of programmes that can be used as part of an interval training programme.
Stepper	• Provides a low-impact aerobic cardiovascular workout targeting the leg and gluteal muscles. • Used to simulate the action of climbing a flight of steps or stairs; it can also target core muscles in your abdomen and lower back.
Rowing machine	• Low-impact machines used as part of a warm-up and cool-down as well as to improve aerobic and muscular endurance. • Can be used to train anaerobically by increasing the speed of the rowing action and the resistance on the pulley chain.
Elliptical trainer	• A low-impact type of cross trainer used to simulate stair climbing without causing excessive pressure to the joints. • Works the upper body by using movable handles and the lower body through moving footplates. • Has adjustable resistance to work at different intensities, and a range of programmes that can be used to vary the exercise session.
Cross trainer	• Another low-impact machine similar to an elliptical trainer. • Used to simulate walking or running without causing excessive stress on joints. • Trains both the upper and lower body and is a common cardiovascular training machine.

Fixed resistance machine exercises

Fixed resistance machines offer a wide range of training options to allow different training methods and goals to be achieved (as shown in Tables 13.3 to 13.5). You can use a number of the training methods that improve muscular strength also to improve muscular endurance simply by doing the training differently. For example, you can alter the weight, the number of repetitions and the number of sets.

Upper body exercises

▶ **Table 13.3:** Fixed resistance machine exercises for the upper body

Type of exercise	Main muscles used	Technique
Seated chest press	Pectorals Deltoid	• Adjust the seat height so the handles are at chest level when you sit down. • Hold the handles ensuring there is a straight line from the hand across to the wrist to avoid injuring the wrist. • Push outwards, straightening the arms (do not lock the elbows) and keeping the back and shoulders in contact with the pad. • Slowly return towards the starting position and repeat.
Bench press	Pectorals Triceps brachii	• Lie on your back on the bench with the feet flat on the floor. • Grasp the handles with the elbows bent and palms facing the feet. The elbows should not be lower than the bottom of the bench. • Push directly upwards to straighten the elbows. • Slowly lower the handles back down, stopping when the elbows are level with your back and repeat.

▶ **Table 13.3:** *Continued*

Type of exercise	Main muscles used	Technique
Pec deck	Pectorals	• Sit on the machine with your back flat on the seat pad and take hold of the handles keeping your elbows at right angles. • Push the handles together slowly as you squeeze your chest in the middle. Breathe out during this part of the motion and hold the contraction for a second. • Return back to the starting position slowly as you inhale until your chest muscles are fully stretched.
Seated row	Trapezius Rhomboids Latissimus dorsi	• Sit on the seat with feet flat on the floor. Knees should be bent and back upright. • Reach forwards to hold the handles; the arms should be straight. • Keep the shoulders back on this exercise and maintain a straight line between the back surface of the hand and the wrist. • Keep the chest against the chest pad and pull back, bending the elbows (which should travel directly backwards).
Shoulder press	Deltoid Pectorals Triceps brachii Trapezius	• Sit on the seat with back and neck supported on the back rest. The handles should be level with your shoulders before you start. • Hold each handle with the palms facing forwards and the elbows bent. • Push the handles straight up above your head, but do not lock the elbows out. • Slowly lower the weight, under control, until your hands are just above your shoulders so that the moving weights do not touch the rest of the stack.
Lateral pulldown (in front of chest)	Latissimus dorsi Rhomboids	• While standing, hold the bar with a wide grip (wider than shoulder width), with the palms facing forwards. • Sit down while holding the bar. • Pull the bar down to chest height. Lean back at your hips slightly as you do so. • Control the bar back to the starting position and repeat. • When you have finished your set, stand up to let the bar move all the way up to its resting position.
Assisted pull-up	Latissimus dorsi Biceps brachii	• Mount the machine so your upper shins are on the pad with the knees bent. • Grasp the overhead bar with a wide grip and pull yourself up until your chin is above the bar. • Slowly lower yourself back down.
Triceps pushdown (high pulley)	Triceps brachii	• Standing upright with the torso straight and a very small inclination forward, bring the upper arms close to your body and perpendicular to the floor. Your forearms should be pointing up towards the pulley as they hold the bar. • Using the triceps, bring the bar down until it touches the front of your thighs and the arms are fully extended perpendicular to the floor. The upper arms should always remain stationary next to your torso and only your forearms should move. • After holding for a second, at the contracted position, bring the bar slowly up to the starting point. Repeat for the recommended number of times.
Triceps press	Triceps brachii Deltoid	• Stand with your legs either side of the seat pad. • Place your palms on the outsides of the handles, facing in, and grip the handle. • Push the handles down so that you can sit on the seat and lean forwards so your stomach is resting on the front pad. • Straighten your arms out while trying to push the handles towards the floor. Keep your elbows close to your body. • Slowly let the handles rise up until your hands are below your armpits and repeat.
Bicep curl (low pulley)	Biceps brachii	• Attach a bar to a low pulley and stand facing the machine about 30 cm away. • Grasp the bar with a neutral (palms-in) grip and stand straight up keeping the natural arch of the back and your torso stationary. Put your elbows in by your side and keep them there. • Using your biceps, pull your arms up until your biceps touch your forearms. • Slowly start to bring the weight back to the original position.
Seated bicep curl	Biceps brachii	• Sit on the seat with your knees bent, feet flat on the floor and chest against the pad. • Place your arms over the angled part of the bench so the backs of your upper arms rest on the pad. • Grasp the handles with palms facing up and bend your elbows to pull the handles up towards your chin. To avoid wrist injuries, do not bend your wrist. • Slowly return the handles back towards the starting position, not allowing the elbows to fully straighten, and then repeat the exercise.

▶ The pec deck is an upper body exercise using fixed resistance machinery

Lower body exercises

▶ **Table 13.4:** Fixed resistance machine exercises for the lower body

Type of exercise	Main muscles used	Technique
Leg press	Quadriceps Gluteus maximus Hamstrings	• Position yourself on the seat with your feet hip width apart on the platform. • In the starting position, there should be approximately 90 degrees (a right angle) at your knee. • Push with your legs to straighten the knees (either the seat will move backwards or the platform will move forwards). Do not lock the knees – leave a slight bend. • Slowly bend your knees back towards the starting position, but do not allow the weights in the stack to touch.
Seated knee extension	Quadriceps	• Sit on the seat so that your back is flat against the back rest and the seat pad supports the whole of your thigh. Position the roller on the front of your lower shin. • Straighten the knees to lift the roller up until your knees are almost straight.
Lying leg curl	Hamstrings	• Position the roller (or pad) so that it is on your lower calf when you lie down. • Lie face down, with the knees straight. • Keep your pelvis down against the bench as you bend your knee. • Once your lower leg is perpendicular (at a right angle) to the floor, stop and return to the starting position.
Seated leg curl	Hamstrings	• Place the back of your lower leg on top of the padded lever (just a few inches under your calves) and secure the lap pad against your thighs, just above the knees. • Hold the side handles on the machine as you point your toes straight and ensure that your legs are fully straight right in front of you. • Pull the machine lever as far as possible to the back of your thighs by flexing at your knees. Keep your torso stationary at all times. Hold the position for a second.
Seated abductor	Gluteus medius Gluteus minimus	• Position yourself in the machine, with your legs together, supported on the outside of your thigh. • Sit with your back against the back rest, ensuring there is a curve in your lumbar spine. • Push outwards to separate your legs, as far as you are comfortable. • Slowly allow your legs to return to the centre.
Seated adductor	Adductor magnus Adductor longus Adductor brevis	• Position yourself in the machine, with your legs apart, supported on the inside. • Sit back against the back rest, ensuring you have an arch in your lower back. • Squeeze your legs in together. • Then slowly allow them to move apart, under full control, only as far as you are comfortable.

Abdominal and back exercises

▶ **Table 13.5:** Fixed resistance machine exercises for the abdomen and back

Type of exercise	Main muscles used	Technique
Abdominal machine	Rectus abdominis	• Position yourself in the machine securely with your feet secured under the support pads. These should rest on your shins. • Lean forward slowly and smoothly using your abdominal muscles. • Slowly return to the start position and repeat.
Lower back machine	Erector spinae	• Sit in the seat with your buttocks at the back of the seat. • Position the roller so that it is against your shoulder blades. • Maintain a curve in the lower back and the shoulders back and chest high throughout the exercise. • Push back from an upright position, to extend the back towards horizontal. Slowly return to an upright position, controlling the movement throughout.

To help understand the variety of different exercises that can be used as part of an exercise programme, it is useful to practise with a friend. Adopt the role of a personal trainer and carry out an induction that demonstrates how to use a variety of machines and exercises.

1 Consider how you will demonstrate and explain each exercise as well as the muscles targeted.

2 Consider what your strengths are when demonstrating.

3 Now discuss with your friend what areas need further development as part of this induction process.

Body weight exercises

Body weight exercises are exercises that only use the body's mass and gravity to provide resistance. The exercises shown in Table 13.6 do not use any additional weights to provide resistance.

▶ **Table 13.6:** Body weight exercises

Type of exercise	Main muscles used	Technique
Chins	Latissimus dorsi Biceps brachii	• Grasp an overhead bar with a wide grip. • Pull yourself up until your chin is above the bar then slowly lower yourself back down.
Press-up	Pectorals Triceps brachii Deltoid	• Kneel on all fours with the hands a little wider than shoulder width. • Straighten your legs out behind you so that your weight is distributed between your hands and toes. • Bend the elbows outwards to lower your chest towards the floor. • Push back up to the starting position.
Lunge	Quadriceps Hamstrings Gluteus maximus Gastrocnemius Soleus	• Step forwards with one foot in a long stride. Make sure your feet are in line and pointing straight forwards. • Keep your back upright as you slowly bend and lower your back knee towards the floor, raising your heel off the floor. • At the same time bend your front knee, making sure it doesn't go past your toes. • Don't let your back knee touch the floor before returning to the starting position.
Squat	Quadriceps Hamstrings Gluteus maximus Gastrocnemius Soleus	• Stand with your feet shoulder width apart and your toes pointing straight forwards. • Keep your back straight as you initiate movement at your hips. • Push your buttocks out behind you and bend your knees. • Do not let your knees move in front of your toes. • Do not squat deeper than 90 degrees (a right angle) at your knee. • Start with shallow squats and increase gradually.
Abdominal curl	Rectus abdominus	• Lie on your back with your knees bent. Place your hands on your thighs. • Lift your head, neck and shoulders off the ground and slide your hands up, towards your knees. • Try to keep the same gap between your chin and chest to avoid straining your neck. • Slowly return to the start position.
Plank	Rectus abdominus Erector spinae	• Lie on your front and place your forearms and palms flat on the floor. • Lift your chest, stomach and legs off the floor and maintain your balance between your forearms and toes. • Keep a straight line from your shoulders, across your back to your feet. • Hold for up to 60 seconds.
Prone back raise	Erector spinae	• Lie on your front with your arms bent and your fingers on your temples. • Slowly lift your chest and stomach off the floor, keeping your hips and legs still. • Hold for 2–3 seconds before slowly lowering your upper body back to the floor. • Movement should only come from your lower back.

Free weight exercises

Dumbbells and barbells allow an individual to have a constant resistance during a **dynamic action**. Free weights increase strength in the short term, but also increase range of movement, specialise in certain movements or muscle groups and can aid training of balance and coordination.

Key term

Dynamic action – any action that involves movement, such as a bicep curl.

Like fixed resistance machines, free weights are used to improve muscular strength and both can be used to produce positive results. However, there is a greater chance of injury while using free weights. For safety reasons when using larger weights, helpers (or 'spotters') are required to oversee (or 'spot') an individual.

Dumbbells

A number of different exercises can be performed using dumbbells, as shown in Table 13.7.

▶ **Table 13.7:** Dumbbell exercises

Type of exercise	Main muscles used	Technique
Front raise	Deltoids	• Position yourself with a wide stance and knees slightly bent. • Hold a dumbbell in each hand with your arms straight by your sides and your palms facing behind you. • Lift your arms out in front, until your hands are at shoulder level. • Return your arms back to the starting position, maintaining control throughout. • Ensure you don't arch your back attempting to lift the weight.
Single arm row	Latissimus dorsi Rhomboids Biceps brachii Trapezius	• Place one knee and the same hand on a bench with your other foot on the floor and dumbbell in your other hand. • Lean forwards so that your spine is straight and approximately parallel to the floor. • Pull the dumbbell upwards, towards your chest. • Do not allow excessive rotation of the back, or shoulder elevation. • Lower the dumbbell back to the starting position under control.
Bent arm pullover	Pectorals Latissimus dorsi	• Lie on your back on a bench with your feet on the floor. • Hold a dumbbell in both hands, with your palms facing each other and your arms straight above your chest. • Lower the dumbbell over and behind your head, with a slight bend in your elbow. • Keep your abdominals braced throughout to avoid arching your back. • Lower to as far as you are comfortable and then reverse the movement.
Shoulder press	Deltoids Triceps	• Position a bench with the back support up and sit on the seat pad, leaning your back against the support. • Hold a dumbbell in each hand at shoulder height. • Push directly upwards until your elbows are almost completely straight. • Slowly return back to the starting position.
Lateral raise	Deltoids Trapezius	• Position yourself with a wide stance and your knees slightly bent. • Hold a dumbbell in each hand with your arms straight by your sides and your palms facing inwards. • Lift your arms out to the sides, maintaining a small bend in your elbow until your hands reach shoulder level. • Return your arms back to the starting position, maintaining control throughout.
Flye	Pectorals Deltoids	• Lie down on a flat bench with a dumbbell on each hand resting on top of your thighs. The palms of your hands will be facing each other. • Lift the dumbbells one at a time so you can hold them in front of you at shoulder width with the palms of your hands facing each other. • Lower your arms out at both sides in a wide arc until you feel a stretch on your chest. Breathe in as you perform this part of the movement. Your arms should remain stationary throughout with the movement only at the shoulder joint. • Return your arms back to the starting position as you squeeze your chest muscles and breathe out.
Prone flye	Pectorals Deltoids	• Lie on your back on a bench with your feet planted on the floor. • Hold a dumbbell in each hand, with the palms facing together, above your chest. • Maintain a small bend in the elbows throughout the exercise. • Take your arms apart, leading with the elbows, until they are just below the level of your shoulders. Maintain control throughout, especially during the lowering phase. • Return to the starting position.
Single arm triceps press	Triceps brachii	• Place one hand and the same knee on a bench and lean over so your back is flat. • Hold a dumbbell in your free hand and hold with your upper arm horizontal next to your upper body, your elbow bent to a right angle and your palm facing in. • Straighten your elbow out behind you, ensuring your upper arm stays still. • Slowly return to the starting position.

▶ **Table 13.7:** *Continued*

Type of exercise	Main muscles used	Technique
Bicep curl	Biceps brachii	• Stand with your feet shoulder width apart, knees slightly bent and back straight. • Hold a dumbbell in each hand with your palms facing forwards and elbows straight. • Bend your elbows to lift the dumbbells from your thighs, up towards your shoulders. • Avoid swinging the weights or arching your back to help lift the weights. • Slowly return the weights back to the starting position.
Lunge	Quadriceps	• Hold a dumbbell in each hand. Step forwards with one foot in a long stride. • Make sure your feet are in line and pointing straight forwards. • Keep your back upright as you slowly bend and lower your back knee towards the floor, raising your heel off the floor. • At the same time bend your front knee, making sure it doesn't go past your toes. • Don't let your back knee touch the floor before returning to the starting position.
Deadlift	Gluteus maximus Erector spinae Hamstrings	• Stand with your feet shoulder width apart, with the bar a couple of inches in front of your shins. • Squat down, keeping your back straight, although lean forwards from your hips. • Grip the bar with your palms facing backwards, at the outside of each knee. • Before you start the lift, ensure your lower back is arched and you are holding your chest up high and looking straight ahead. • Keep your arms straight as you push up using your legs.
Squat	Quadriceps/ hamstrings	• Place your feet shoulder width apart. The weight comes down through your heels. • Drive your hips backwards during the first part of movement. • Don't let your knees come any further forward than your toes. • Face forwards and slightly upwards. • Aim for your knees to be at 90 degrees with the top of your quads parallel to the floor.

▶ The lateral raise is a free weights exercise with dumbbells

Barbell

The range of exercises that can be performed using a barbell include those shown in Table 13.8.

▶ **Table 13.8:** Barbell exercises

Type of exercise	Main muscles used	Technique
Upright row	Trapezius Deltoids Biceps brachii	• Stand upright with your feet shoulder width apart and knees slightly bent. • Hold the bar near the centre, with your hands closer than shoulder width and your palms facing you. Pull the bar up towards your chin. • Slowly return to the starting position.
Bench press	Pectoralis major Deltoids Triceps	• Lie on your back on a bench with your feet planted on the floor. • Grip the bar approximately 2 feet (60 cm) apart (or at a comfortable point, wider than shoulder width) with your arms straight above your chest. • Slowly and under control, lower the bar down to the level of your chest. • Push the bar back up, until your elbows are straight. Keep your lower back in contact with the bench at all times and maintain your natural spine arch throughout.

Type of exercise	Main muscles used	Technique
Supine triceps press	Triceps brachii	• Lie on a bench on your back holding a barbell, with the hands approximately head width apart. • Start with the arms extended at chest level, with the hands pointing to the ceiling. • Keep your upper arms still as you bend your elbows, lowering the bar towards your head. Once the bar reaches a couple of inches (about 5 cm) above your forehead, return to the starting position.
Bicep curl	Biceps brachii	• Stand with your feet shoulder width apart, your knees slightly bent and back straight. • Hold a dumbbell in each hand with your palms facing forwards and elbows straight. • Bend your elbows to lift the dumbbells from your thighs, up towards your shoulders. Avoid swinging the weights or arching your back to help lift the weights. • Slowly return the weights back to the starting position.
Lunge	Quadriceps	• Maintain a neutral spine position, keeping your knees in line with your toes. Your trailing knee just touches the ground. • Drive your elbow forwards to keep the bar stable. Drive your heel in on the way back up.
Deadlift	Gluteus maximus Erector spinae Hamstrings	• Stand with your feet shoulder width apart, with the bar a couple of inches (about 5 cm) in front of your shins. • Squat down, keeping your back straight, but leaning forwards from the hips. • Grip the bar with your palms facing backwards, at the outside of each knee. • Before you start the lift, ensure your lower back is arched and you are holding your chest up high and looking straight ahead. • Keep your arms straight as you push up using your legs. Do not pull using your arms or back.
Squat	Quadriceps	• Hold the barbell across the front of your shoulders, with your elbows bent so that your hands hold the bar with your palms facing upwards. • Keep your torso upright and maintain an arch in your lower back. • Bend your knees and hips, keeping your heels on the floor. Do not allow your knees to move forwards past your toes. • Squat as low as you are comfortable to the point where the thigh is parallel to the floor. Straighten your legs back to the starting position.

Reflect

Consider each main muscle group and identify an exercise that can be used to train them. Try and remember the main techniques used as well as any health and safety points. Work with a friend to practise these techniques and consider how you will explain what you are doing as part of a demonstration.

Ⅱ PAUSE POINT   Do you understand the different muscles of the body, their location and how each can be specifically trained?

Hint   Identify an exercise that can be used to train each of the major muscles groups. Consider the different variations of these exercises.

Extend   When planning a session, you will need to consider the order in which you put each exercise. Using your identified exercise, explain when it should be undertaken as part of a training programme.

Performing exercises safely

There are a number of essential issues that you must remember to incorporate when you are delivering any gym-based exercise session so that your clients perform the exercises safely.

Warm-up

A warm-up is performed before participation in exercise. It generally consists of a gradual increase in intensity of physical activity. Any warm-up should be specific to the following activity, so should prepare the muscles that are to be used and activate the energy systems required for that activity. Stretching active muscles is also recommended after doing a warm-up.

A planned warm-up is important to avoid injury. There are three main functions:

▶ to increase the heart rate – in order to pump more blood around the body to the working muscles, allowing more energy to be produced using oxygen and increasing body/muscle temperature

▶ to raise body temperature – improving the elasticity of the working muscles, making injury less likely

▶ to prepare the major joints of the body for work – with movements that should be specific to the sport or exercise.

In a gym environment, warm-ups often involve the treadmill, a static cycle or a rowing machine.

Cool-down

A cool-down returns the body to its pre-exercise state. There are three main objectives:

▶ to return the heart rate back to normal

▶ to help remove any waste products that may have built up during exercise

▶ to return the muscles to their original state (or length if stretched).

The cool-down keeps the metabolic rate high and capillaries dilated to enable oxygen to flush through the muscle tissue, helping remove lactic acid waste created by exercise. This should stop the blood from staying in the veins, which can cause dizziness if exercise is stopped too quickly. A cool-down can also reduce the effect of **delayed-onset muscle soreness** (or DOMS), which often follows strenuous exercise that the body is not used to.

The final part of the cool-down should include stretching to facilitate and improve flexibility, as the muscles will be very warm at this stage.

> **Key term**
>
> **Delayed-onset muscle soreness** – pain or discomfort often felt 24–72 hours after exercising.

 **PAUSE POINT**   Why are warm-ups and cool-downs such an important part of an exercise programme?

 Hint   Describe the purpose of a warm-up in relation to physiological changes to the body.

Extend   What different exercises can be used as part of a warm-up and why? How could these be adapted for different clients?

Case study

Elizabeth has recently been appointed an assistant gym instructor at a local health club. As part of her duties she is expected to work with a range of different clients and support them in their training programmes. She has been asked by the club's gym manager to prepare an information sheet for the clients on safe gym practice.

Check your knowledge

1 Why is the clients' safety so important?

2 What should Elizabeth include regarding the use of gym equipment?

3 How can Elizabeth ensure that clients are using the correct technique? Why is this important?

Safe alignment of exercise position

The development of 'core stability' is a fairly new phenomenon in the fitness world. It basically seeks to develop an equilibrium or balance throughout the skeletal and muscular systems. Body alignment targets areas of posture and balance to help ensure the body remains functional and efficient. Core stability achieves this by highlighting the core (abdominal and lower back regions) as the framework to generate a solid platform to work from. You should be aware of the benefits of developing this platform, not only in the core, but also throughout the body.

Body alignment also deals with creating a balance between muscle groupings. For example, the quadriceps are capable of producing substantial power output but should not be too powerful for the opposite muscles – the hamstrings – to deal with; otherwise one of the hamstrings is likely to sustain damage.

Alternatives to potentially harmful exercises

Research has shown some exercises are contraindicated and may do more harm than good. As such, these exercises must be avoided and alternatives found. Examples of exercises that must be avoided include:

▶ full neck rolls – previously used as part of a warm-up but can cause compression of the cervical vertebrae which can result in nerve damage
▶ sit-ups with hand behind the neck – can put excessive strain on the neck muscles, especially if a lurching technique is used.

Health and environmental factors

Risk assessments must be performed before a session begins, with all equipment and the environment reviewed and checked. Factors to consider include the following.

▶ **Equipment** – this must be fit for purpose and includes the clothing that is to be worn. Equipment should be checked for quality and condition, and whether it has been maintained correctly.
▶ **Facility** – this includes the space available, whether it was designed for the selected activity, accessibility of emergency exits, noise/acoustics (for example, is there a lot of echo, making instructions difficult to hear?) and accessibility and suitability for people with particular needs, such as wheelchair users.
▶ **Suitability of participants** – if you have planned well, your session will be built around the needs of the people who you are working with. When planning your sessions, consider factors such as:
  • the age and experience of participants
  • the number of participants
  • how well you know the group and how well they know you
  • any specific learning requirements or behavioural issues.

Developing client coordination

Some of your clients will have little experience of exercise or being in a gym environment. As such, you must consider the techniques used to perform an exercise. Any recommended exercises you use should be demonstrated clearly and you should allow clients to develop their movement and exercise techniques gradually so that they develop their coordination and confidence.

In a gym environment, clients could initially do weights work on fixed resistance machines until accustomed to the movements required. Clients could then do the exercises using free weights.

Intensity

For any benefits to be achieved, clients must exercise at a level higher than their normal levels. Most exercises can be adapted to increase or decrease their intensity. For example, in weight-bearing exercises an increase in weight load will increase intensity. This overload will help as part of a strength programme. In this example, by decreasing the weight load but using more repetitions, the training programme will focus on muscular endurance.

The intensity of exercise is particularly important when cardiovascular exercise targets different training zones – refer back to pages 93–4.

Impact

Broadly, exercises can be categorised into two types: high impact and low impact.

▶ **High-impact exercises** put force on the body, especially on bones and joints, for example running. Studies suggest the correct amount of high-impact exercise can increase bone density but too much can place excessive strain on the body and cause injury to bones and joints. Your client should avoid high-impact exercises if they have suffered from previous joint issues, have osteoporosis or are in the latter stages of pregnancy.
▶ **Low-impact exercises** such as walking on a treadmill or using a rowing machine or cross trainer put much less force on the body and are suitable for clients who should avoid the high-impact exercises.

▶ Wall presses are sometimes a useful adaptation for older participants

Alternative exercises for specific clients

Many exercises can be adapted so that they support the requirements of specific clients. For example, a wall press-up will be more suitable for an older adult especially if they have low levels of fitness. For antenatal clients, low-impact exercises such as swimming or walking on a treadmill should be included in a training programme.

 PAUSE POINT   Do you understand how the environment can affect the safe delivery of a gym session?

> Hint   Consider where a session is taking place. Why should the facility and equipment be checked before a session starts?

> Extend   Now consider the specific checks you must undertake before any session starts. What should you do if you are not satisfied that the facility or equipment is suitable?

Assessment practice 13.2   B.P4 B.M3 B.D2

As part of the work for an after-school gym club referred to in assessment activity 13.1, you have now been asked to prepare a leaflet explaining the different methods of cardiovascular endurance and resistance training. Your leaflet should provide information on the different exercises that can be used as well as the different types of equipment to perform these exercises.

Having explained the different training methods and the different exercises, your leaflet should compare and contrast the different training methods, highlighting the benefits of each one. To help you, consider the two members of staff you previously helped and justify the different methods of training for each.

Plan
- How confident do I feel in my understanding of different methods of training? Am I familiar with cardiovascular training and resistance training?
- I will practise using the different types of gym equipment so that I am familiar with the main muscles used.

Do
- I can explain the different methods of cardiovascular training and resistance training.
- I can justify different training methods for different types of client.

Review
- I can explain how I would approach the hard elements differently next time.
- When I have reflected on my own work and the feedback from others, I will make any necessary changes to my leaflet.

C   Undertake planning and instructing gym-based exercise for individual clients

Aims and objectives of the programme

There are several key aims and objectives you must cover when starting to plan your programmes.

▶ **Using information from clients to agree objectives** – one of the biggest problems for anybody trying to improve their fitness is that they often do the wrong type of training or their programme is not structured properly. This leads to a lack of motivation for the individual as well as few training gains. Collecting appropriate information about your client, such as their goals, lifestyle, medical history and physical activity history, means you will produce a more effective programme for them.

▶ **Agreeing goals with clients** – the programme must be flexible but capable of meeting your client's goals and personal needs. Each individual has different ambitions and aspirations – and different potential to develop – and your programme should reflect them. The client's goals should be broken up into short-term (up to one month), medium-term (one to three months) and long-term goals (three months to one year). When designing the programme, set goals that are

Research

Find out more information regarding the importance of health and safety in a gym environment by visiting the Register of Exercise Professionals website (www.exerciseregister.org).

based on SMART (specific, measurable, achievable, realistic, time-bound) targets. The goals should also reflect good practice within the gym instruction industry and your own levels of competence.

▶ **Seeking advice from other professionals** – your client's safety and welfare is your primary concern. If, at any point, you are not comfortable or confident with any information your client has shared and you feel that it would be better for them not to undertake an exercise programme, then you must say so. Remember that it is better to seek professional guidance from a medical expert if any hazards are identified. You should also refer them to a more appropriately qualified instructor if their objectives are beyond your own level of competence.

 **PAUSE POINT**   Why is it important to involve the client closely when putting together a training programme?

Hint   Can you explain what SMART goals are?

Extend   How could SMART principles be used as part of a training programme and why are they important for goal setting?

Gym-based exercise session planning

Identify appropriate exercises

Any fitness programme is based on the 'principles of training' – following these results in the greatest gains through training. The principles of training can be remembered using the acronym SPORTI, which stands for the following.

▶ **S**pecificity – planning your training programme around the needs of the client (such as targeting specific muscle groups) and your client's individual needs. For example, if you are trying to improve your client's cardiovascular fitness then a training programme that involves heavy weights would not be relevant.

▶ **P**rogression – the changes that the client's body makes over the length of the training programme, allowing for your client to achieve steady progress.

▶ **O**verload – exercising just outside your client's normal functional level or 'comfort zone' to stimulate development – it's an essential aspect of gaining training benefits.

▶ **R**eversibility/recovery – any fitness gains that have been made through training will be reversed if the client stops training – they will lose their fitness adaptations.

▶ **T**edium – if you use the same training sessions over a period of time, the client is likely to become bored, so it is best to use a variety of training methods to relieve any tedium.

▶ **I**ndividual differences – this refers to the fact that everybody is different so training plans must consider these individual differences.

In addition to the SPORTI principles, you also need to consider the FITT (frequency, intensity, time and type) principles, one of the most important sets of principles when planning individual sessions and full training programmes (see page 96).

Appropriate sequences of exercises

Structure is very important if the client is to enjoy the exercise and avoid injury. In general terms, a session will follow the order: warm-up, main activity, cool-down (or 'warm-down').

When using resistance training, it is important that corresponding muscles be trained equally. Muscles help stabilise a joint, so if one is stronger than another, this may cause joint instability and injury. It can also cause long-term problems with posture and may affect sporting performance. The main pairs of muscles are:

▶ pectorals and trapezius
▶ bicep and tricep
▶ latissimus dorsi and deltoid
▶ abdominals and erector spinae
▶ quadricep and hamstring.

A simple exercise will involve only one joint (for example, a bicep curl), while a more difficult exercise will involve two or more joints (for example, a chest press). The more difficult exercises will need more focus, so they should be done early in the session before the onset of fatigue. Likewise, you should train the large muscles first. These include:

- trapezius
- latisimus dorsi
- pectorals
- quadricep
- hamstring
- gluteus maximus.

The main reason for exercising these muscles first is that they will require the most effort, so they should be exercised before they start to fatigue. The smaller muscles help the larger muscles work, so should remain relatively fresh when exercising.

Finally, exercise the abdominal muscles last. The abdominal and muscles of the lower back provide support to the main core of the body. These should remain free from fatigue in order to avoid injury to the back and maintain correct posture.

Appropriate timings of each exercise to ensure progression

As we saw with the SPORTI principles, for a training programme to be effective the principles of **progression** and **overload** should be followed. Progression and overload are where the body adapts to training, allowing training to become progressively harder (increasing the levels of overload). Without correct levels of progression and overload, training gains start to level off (plateau).

Be careful when planning progression because poor performances may result from too little progression or a training programme that overloads the system. Excessive overloading may also lead to injury or illness through over-training.

If your client takes a break from training or doesn't train often enough, then their levels of fitness will reverse or **regress**. This means that they will slowly go back to where they were before they started the training programme.

When training, consider the duration of each exercise as well as the total length of the session. Increasing time will increase progression and overload, but it is important to consider recovery between exercises and sessions. Always allow adequate recovery time between sets to allow for repair and renewal of body tissues and to avoid fatigue, which can lead to reduced performance and injury.

Selection of correct equipment

When planning an exercise session, you must check the equipment the client will have available so you can recommend the correct exercises. Make sure you are familiar with all the equipment to be used and how it operates.

It is worth practising using the equipment, especially cardiovascular machines such as treadmills which will have a wide range of different programmes and functions.

Theory into practice

You have been approached by the manager of a local netball team who wishes to plan a pre-season fitness programme that will include cardiovascular, strength and flexibility training. You have access to basic gym equipment including barbells, skipping ropes, dumbbells and a treadmill. What exercises could you use to target the outlined components of fitness? Remember that some exercises can use body weight to make improvements.

Components of a gym-based exercise session

A training programme session will normally follow the order of warm-up, main activity, cool-down (or 'warm-down').

The number of exercises during each stage of a training session depends on the training goals. Generally you need to ensure there are not too many exercises as this could lead to injury. If you use more than one exercise for an area or muscle group, make sure you alternate these exercises with some for other areas or muscles.

Depending on the fitness levels of your client you may have to change the amount of time given to each component of the programme. For example, you may wish to allocate more time to a low-intensity warm-up for a client that has low levels of fitness. As your client progresses, you should review the amount of time allocated to each component to ensure that overload is maintained and that progress is made.

Warm-up

The warm-up can comprise a variety of exercises. These can be categorised as either pulse-raisers or stretches.

Pulse-raisers

A pulse-raiser is a simple cardiovascular exercise that raises a person's heart rate in readiness for further exercise. It should gradually increase in intensity and normally lasts 5–10 minutes leaving the heart rate near to the level expected during the main activity. Common gym-based pulse raisers include treadmill running, static cycling and the rowing machine.

Stretches

Stretches are used as part of a warm-up to improve joint mobility. Stretching induces the body to produce more fluid in synovial joints, in readiness for exercise. The joints will become warmer and allow a full range of motion to be achieved. Stretching should start with small movements and then progress to larger, full ranges of motion. The main joints that should be mobilised by stretches are the shoulders, elbows, spine, hips, knees and ankles. Stretching can be either static or dynamic, as follows.

▶ **Static stretching** stretches muscles while the body is at rest. It uses various techniques that gradually lengthen a muscle to a point of mild discomfort, at which point the position is held for a period of 10–30 seconds. During this holding period – or directly afterwards – participants may feel a mild discomfort or warm sensation in the muscle. Static stretches involve specialised tension receptors in muscles. When done properly, static stretching slightly lessens the sensitivity of these tension receptors, which allows the muscle to relax and to be stretched to a greater length.

▶ **Dynamic stretching** involves moving muscles through their full range of motion in a controlled manner. It keeps the heart rate raised and makes the muscles ready for further exercise. It promotes a form of flexibility that is beneficial in sports using momentum in an effort to propel the muscle into an extended range of motion (not exceeding the static/passive stretching ability).

▶ Stretching is an important part of a gym programme and should not be ignored

Main component

The main component of a session can focus on a range of different areas.

▶ **Cardiovascular endurance** – a physical-related aspect of fitness, also known as stamina or cardiorespiratory endurance. It is the ability of the cardiovascular and respiratory systems to supply muscles with oxygen to maintain exercise. Several events rely almost exclusively on aerobic endurance, such as marathon running, long-distance swimming and cycling. Aerobic endurance forms the basis of fitness for most sports and a reduced aerobic endurance, possibly due to a long-term injury, leads to a decrease in other fitness components such as muscular endurance and poor performance in some sports.

▶ **Muscular strength** – a physical-related aspect of fitness, strength is the ability of a specific muscle or muscle group to exert a force in a single maximal contraction. Strength is required in most sports, in varying degrees. Strength training is typically low repetition with very high loads.

▶ **Muscular endurance** – another physical-related aspect of fitness, muscular endurance is needed where a specific muscle or muscle group makes repeated contractions over a significant period (possibly over a number of minutes). Examples include:
  • a boxer making a repeated jab
  • continual press-ups or sit-ups
  • a 400-metre sprint in athletics.

A number of the training methods used to improve muscular strength can also be used to improve muscular endurance simply by doing the training differently, for example reducing the weight while increasing the number of repetitions and/or number of sets. Common training methods used to improve muscular strength and muscular endurance include:

- resistance machines
- free weights
- medicine ball training
- circuit training
- core stability training.

Cool-down

Stretching as part of a cool-down will allow muscles to return to their normal working length. Developmental stretches involve stretching and holding the working muscle for about 10 seconds until it relaxes. Following this, the muscle should be stretched again but at an increased level, and again held for 10 seconds. This process should be repeated three times.

Using stretching as part of a cool-down will improve flexibility as the muscles will be warm and more pliable. This means that they will be able to extend beyond their normal length and increase the range of motion at the joint.

⏸ **PAUSE POINT**   Cool-downs are often overlooked as part of a training programme as clients feel tired after their workout. Describe why cool-downs are important and list the changes that occur to the body during a cool-down.

Hint   Consider the different types of exercises that can be used as part of a cool-down.

Extend   How can different cool-down exercises be adapted or changed for different types of clients?

Pre-gym-based exercise preparation

Before you start any exercise programme, it is essential that you consider health and safety fully. Before the session starts, check the equipment that is to be used and the facility, as follows.

▶ Check equipment for damage before and after a session, and get any damaged equipment either repaired or replaced before the next session. Never use damaged equipment as this may be dangerous to you and your client. Store all equipment correctly, and in a way that helps you to set up the next session quickly and safely. Keep records of any maintenance work to ensure repairs have taken place or equipment has been replaced.

▶ Inspect the area you intend to use to make sure it is suitable, including checking for hazards, such as slip hazards. If you are training with a group of people, ensure the area is large enough for the group so people have enough space and can exercise freely.

▶ As you exercise, body temperature increases and you will begin to sweat to release excess heat. If the environment you are training in is too hot, then it is harder for the body to remove this heat and the risk of dehydration increases. Therefore, ensure that the environment is a suitable temperature to prevent overheating. Good ventilation will provide 'fresh' air to aid training and prevent overheating.

Preparing clients for gym-based exercise

Before a client can start a gym-based exercise programme, you must prepare them so that they are ready to undertake any prescribed exercise.

▶ **Welcome clients** – remember some of your clients will be unsure or nervous about undertaking a gym session, so you must be friendly and reassuring. Communicate clearly and allow time to determine how people best learn (do they respond best to verbal or visual direction?) and therefore how they will be able to replicate movements that might be new to them and complex.

▶ **Check ability and medical conditions** – collecting appropriate information about your client, such as goals, lifestyle information, medical history and physical activity history, means you will produce a more effective programme for your client. As part of this you can also establish the client's specific exercise goals. This will help with client motivation as well as ensuring your programme presents no danger to the client's health.

▶ **Inform the client of the demands, purpose and value of the session** – consider each planned exercise and explain its physical and technical demands to the client. They should be aware of:
  • what is expected of them and how the exercises should be completed
  • health and safety issues
  • any variations of activities for different participants
  • ability levels or factors that may affect existing/past injuries.

▶ **Confirm or revise plans with the client** – confirm the goals that you originally agreed on and use regular reviews to help them remain motivated and on target.

▶ **Demonstrate any specific movements** – demonstrate and explain each exercise clearly, giving the client an opportunity to practise using the equipment while you supervise. Your demonstration should be non-verbal, allowing participants to observe the movements without a spoken message that might detract from their observation. Allow time for any questions after the demonstration.

▶ **Advise clients of any emergency procedures** – you must be familiar with the facility's emergency procedures and communicate them to the client. Emergencies could include fire evacuation, bomb alerts and injury or first-aid situations. It is good practice to make everybody associated with different activities aware of the procedures to be followed.

Case study

Maureen is a 60-year-old who has not exercised in recent years. She is relatively active and enjoys walking and gardening, and belongs to a ten-pin bowling league where she competes weekly. When she was younger, Maureen was a member of a local netball club and she still enjoys spectating in her spare time. She has also qualified as a netball umpire although she has not officiated a match for at least a year. She doesn't have any specific health-related issues such as illness or injury.

Maureen has been advised by her GP that she should undertake an exercise programme that maintains health and general fitness.

Check your knowledge

1 Using the above information, what exercises would you advise Maureen to undertake?
2 What intensities should she work at and how would you measure and manage this?
3 Write a list of exercises that Maureen could undertake by herself.

Instructing gym-based exercise

Once you have designed your session, with effective warm-up, main components and cool-downs, there are several best-practice techniques you can follow to provide the best service possible to your clients.

Explain and demonstrate each exercise

To demonstrate a session effectively, the abbreviation **IDEA** represents a natural progression suitable for exercise classes, gym inductions, coaching sessions or one-to-one personal training. IDEA stands for introduction, demonstration, explanation and application.

▶ **Introduction** – of the exercise, its purpose, its benefits and basic technique.
▶ **Demonstration** – this should be non-verbal, allowing participants to observe the movements without a spoken message that might detract from their observation.
▶ **Explanation** – of the basics of the exercise – mention perhaps two or three technique-related points but avoid giving too much information.
▶ **Application** – give participants an opportunity to practise the movements and gauge whether there are any potential problems or areas for improvement – it is essential to ensure correct technique, so this is a key phase in the introduction to a session.

Appropriate communication

Communication is essential for developing relationships and interacting. The key to good communication is to provide the amount of information the receiver can use effectively, rather than the amount you would like to give. Your message should be transmitted in a clear voice without any jargon. The use of jargon and slang terms is commonplace, but they can often cause confusion.

Ensure the information you provide provides enough guidance for individuals to take part safely and to establish a good technique. Further information can be delivered over time once the basic principles have been mastered.

Change position to observe clients

When leading an exercise session, you will be able to gauge levels of experience and potential by simply watching. During the session, make sure that you are not static and that you move around the client so that you can observe their technique from different angles.

Monitor the safety and intensity of each exercise

When working with a client, you must monitor the intensity of the session to ensure that it is as effective as possible and so that your client is not at any risk. Common methods of monitoring intensity include the following.

▶ Observation can be used to help monitor the safety and intensity of exercise

▶ **Observation** – how many times have you been training and ended up tired and red-faced? This is just one of the things that you can look for when observing people while training. Observing people is a subjective way of monitoring progress, but can be very useful. When observing people, look for changes in exercise technique, skin colour and, breathing patterns, and excessive sweat levels.

▶ **Talk test** – think about when you're exercising and how much harder it becomes to talk as the exercise continues. The American College of Sports Medicine states that if you are able to hold a conversation at the same time as breathing rhythmically while exercising, you are probably working at an acceptable level for cardiovascular training.

Giving clear instructions and feedback

To ensure your client is training correctly and to ensure their safety, you must provide clear instructions. Avoid technical language as this may be confusing to a client who is new to a gym environment. Any instructions need to be timed correctly so that a client can act on them, or correct their technique to avoid injury or wasted effort. You should also provide clear feedback as this will not only ensure that they are training correctly but also provide motivation and encouragement.

Progression and regression

A fitness programme should be regularly reviewed to ensure that progression is being made according to the client's goals and needs. You should support your client to evaluate their progress to check any prescribed exercises are not too easy or too difficult. Simple questioning after a session will help you and your client review their progress. If your client is finding the programme too difficult, adjustments should be made that allow for controlled regression.

End-of-session feedback

At the end of a session, you should allow sufficient time for your client to recover and reflect on the session.

Once the session has been completed (including the cool-down – see pages 105–6), you have the opportunity to ask clients how they feel it went. This should include how they felt during each exercise, how they felt about the whole programme and whether there are any additional goals they wish to work towards. You should also allow time for your client to ask you any questions about their programme, goals or progress. This will allow you to refine the client's training programme.

This time is important as it gives you valuable feedback for your own personal evaluation.

As your client becomes more confident and competent, they may wish to train without your direct support. Therefore, you should still provide regular feedback on progress including correct technique and specific safety points so that they can continue without direct supervision. Remember any feedback should be clear, and free from jargon or technical language, and always check the client's understanding.

> ### Theory into practice
>
> To help with feedback, it is useful to practise with a friend. Adopt the role of a fitness instructor and prepare a gym-based exercise session. You should conduct a pre-exercise questionnaire and instruct your friend on the exercises you have recommended. During the session you should encourage and motivate your friend.
>
> 1 Following the session, you should reflect on your own performance. What were your strengths and what would you change next time?
>
> 2 Now discuss with your friend the areas of your performance that they thought were good and the areas they suggest you could improve on. Consider how you will improve on these areas.

Leaving the area after a session

Once your training session has been completed, you must ensure that the area and equipment that you have used is stored correctly and ready for the next person or session. Before storing any equipment, check that it is free from damage, clean and assessed for wear and tear, and always report any equipment that is broken.

 **PAUSE POINT**   Communication is an important skill that will underpin your work with clients. Describe the different types of communication.

 Hint   Explain what is meant by 'verbal' and 'non-verbal' communication.

Extend   Now consider how these different types of communication can be used effectively to motivate your client.

Reviewing own performance

To keep developing, it also important you review your own performance. Being open and honest with yourself and considering your strengths and areas for improvement will help you to become better at instructing. You should spend time considering aspects of your personal performance that you think you could improve. These could include your own communication or motivational skills, your knowledge of an exercise, or your knowledge of anatomy and physiology.

Remember you may have to adapt your approach and instructor skills for each individual – what works for one client may not work for another.

Evaluate how exercises meet clients' needs

By reviewing your performance, you can identify whether your selected activities are fit for their purpose. This means making sure the exercises are addressing the short- and long-term goals of the client.

▶ **Track progression** – have clear targets that are measurable, so that any improvements can be tracked. If a specific aspect of the programme is not effective, then changes can be made and the session adapted.

▶ **Adaptation session** – perform regular session reviews. If the client's goals are not being met, then it is important that the session is amended. Such adaptations should take into account the client's needs, and may address whether a client has become demotivated. Adaptations will also allow variety, which can further enhance enjoyment.

▶ **Modify activities** – activities may be modified to take into account factors such as injury, illness, unexpected changes to the length of sessions and client demotivation. Modifications should be discussed fully with clients so that they are aware of what to expect in the future.

Relationship with the clients

Take time to review your relationship with the client. How effective and motivational is it? How well does your instructing style match the client's needs?

A common reason why people leave exercise and training programmes is a drop in motivation. This may be caused by a previous poor experience, lack of enjoyment, or failure to achieve aims and objectives. Therefore, you must motivate your client, especially when the going gets tough. Motivating will involve verbal encouragement as well as considering your own body language.

You must be positive at all times to make sure you are pushing the client into working as hard as is reasonable to achieve their goals safely. Likewise, build a rapport with your clients – being friendly and open with clients will help you to produce effective training programmes. Being honest and respectful will also keep up the clients' motivation. Clients should feel that they can discuss their programmes with you, and feel comfortable in trying to achieve their targets.

Discussion

Building a positive and trusting relationship with a client is an essential part of instructing gym-based exercise. Such a relationship will allow you to give encouragement and motivate the client, especially when they are fatigued or struggling. With a partner, consider how you will build a professional relationship with your clients.

- Consider what is needed to support and encourage clients.
- Consider your strengths and areas for development when communicating with people.
- Consider both verbal and non-verbal language. Why are these important?

Ways to improve personal practice

There are many different ways of reviewing your personal practice. Each method should be understood and used if you are to improve your sessions in the future. Start with getting peer evaluation and handing questionnaires to your clients.

▶ **Peer evaluation** – you can gain information from your peers about your performance. This evaluation can be in the form of interviews or questionnaires. Peer observations are useful because they highlight strengths and weaknesses of performance and give valuable information on how to improve.

▶ **Questionnaires** – these can be given to clients after sessions have been completed. Again, valuable information can be gained about what they enjoyed or disliked. This information can then be applied in future sessions. Here are some examples of questions that can be asked.
- Did the session meet your original objectives?
- Did you enjoy the session, and if not, why not?
- Did you feel safe throughout the session?
- In what ways would you like to see future sessions developed?

You should always ask yourself questions after each session, and you must answer these honestly, even if the answers are likely to identify weaknesses in your performance. Self-evaluation is an important tool as it means future sessions will be safe and effective, and clients will remain motivated and make targeted progression. Self-evaluation will also help you to identify any future training needs to update your skills.

It is important that gym instructors continue with their professional development to ensure that their practice and training methods are up to date and in line with industry requirements. When you are working in a gym you should undertake regular update training, including regular first aid training. Organisations such as the YMCA offer a range of continued professional development (CPD) courses.

Link

CPD is covered in more depth in *Unit 3: Professional Development in the Sports Industry*.

Value of reflective practice

Reflective practice is the process by which you stop and think about your performance and practice, and relate it to how you can improve in the future. Different methods can be used such as:
▶ keeping a diary or journal after each session
▶ discussing the session with colleagues and asking them how you are performing (known as 'peer review')
▶ discussing your methods with your clients and asking for constructive feedback.

The value of reflective practice is that it makes you evaluate your current practice and knowledge, and helps generate new ways of working and ideas. This can help you modify your behaviour, actions and methods, and improve your performance.

Being able to review your own performance is an essential part of working in a gym environment.

Hint   Consider your current skills and explain how these will help your clients in meeting their personal training goals.

Extend   Now consider areas that you need to improve. How will you address each of these and what will the benefits be of improving these areas?

Assessment practice 13.3

C.P5 **C.P6** **C.P7** **C.M4** **C.M5** **C.M6** **C.D3**

Having worked with the two members of staff to identify their specific training goals, you must now prepare a safe and effective gym-based exercise session for each of these 'clients'. You should plan a full induction that demonstrates and explains the different training methods and equipment that can be used. You should clearly communicate the purpose of each exercise to your two contrasting clients.

When you have completed your gym instruction session, write a short report on your own performance. Evaluate your strengths and areas for improvement, and make further recommendations on self-improvement. You should also justify why you have chosen each exercise and any alternative adapted exercises you recommended.

Plan
- How confident am I in undertaking a gym-based induction?
- Can I prepare a checklist of the different muscles and the exercises that can be used to train them?

Do
- Have I demonstrated my communication skills and asked my peers to give me advice on how I can improve?
- Am I ready to justify why I have chosen specific exercises to my clients?

Review
- I can explain what the task was and how I approached the task.
- When I have reflected on my own work and the feedback from others, I will make any necessary changes to the gym-based session.

Further reading and resources

Coulson, M. (2013) *The Fitness Instructor's Handbook: A Complete Guide to Health and Fitness,* London: Bloomsbury.

Crossley, J. (2012) *Personal Training: Theory and Practice,* London: Routledge.

Delavier, F. (2010) *Strength Training Anatomy (Sports Anatomy),* Illinois: Human Kinetics.

Websites

http://www.brianmac.co.uk – Brian Mac Sports coach: a wide range of information related to fitness and training.

http://www.pponline.co.uk – Peak Performance: free advisory newsletter which discusses strength and fitness.

http://www.teachpe.com – Teach PE: a variety of resources to support learners with all aspects of physical education including health and fitness.

THINK ▶FUTURE

Joe Langdon

Gym instructor

I work as an instructor in a local council-run gym. I'm responsible for designing personal fitness programmes for a range of clients who come to use the gym, as well as instructing people on how to use the gym equipment safely.

When meeting clients for the first time, I do a comprehensive client screening. I ask a range of questions depending on the exercise and health history of the client. This information helps me to develop a training programme which takes into account their specific goals. I then demonstrate how to use the various pieces of gym equipment, explaining the different types of exercises and their benefits.

My job also involves the close supervision of clients and providing support throughout an exercise session. On any day, it's quite common for me to be working with clients who range from obese people who need guidance on starting their exercise programmes so that they can lose weight, all the way up to experienced weight trainers who just want somebody there to spot them or watch their technique for them.

I find the job very rewarding. Quite often I get to see people develop their training habits over a long period and it's good to see that I've helped them progress.

Focusing your skills

Working as a gym instructor

Gym instructors work with a wide variety of people, each with different levels of fitness and personal goals. To be successful, you will need to continuously support and instruct clients during exercise. You will need to have a thorough understanding of health and safety, be able to identify the main muscle groups as well as the wide range of exercises that can be used as part of a health and fitness programme. You will also need to be able to give clear and supportive feedback.

- Always have in mind the different reasons why people may wish to undertake a gym-based training programme, and understand the reasons why people may not be able to exercise and what adaptations can be made to suit their needs.

- As part of your ongoing development, regularly practise using different types of gym equipment yourself so that you are familiar with their functions, and practise the techniques that you will be instructing.

- Regularly practise your communication skills and consider how you can motivate people through your own behaviour.

Getting ready for assessment

Nancy is working towards a BTEC National Extended Diploma in Sport and Physical Activity Development. For learning aim C, she was given an assignment with the title 'Plan and instruct a gym-based exercise session for two different clients'. The assessment included:

▶ preparing a safe planned gym-based exercise session
▶ delivering a session that includes cardiovascular and resistance gym-based exercises
▶ reviewing her own performance in the delivery of the session.

Nancy explains how she approached this assignment.

How I got started

First, I collected all my notes on this topic and put them into a folder. I decided to divide my work into three parts: the aims and objectives of a gym-based exercise session, the components of a gym-based exercise session, and the evaluation and review of instructing exercise sessions.

▶ First, I researched the information that I would require from clients before planning a session. This included agreed aims and objectives as well as goals for the programme.

▶ I then researched the main components of a gym-based session including warm-up, cardiovascular and strength training, and cool-down, including the different exercises that can be used for each of them.

▶ Finally, I considered how I was going to instruct each aspect of the programme and what types of communication I could use.

Having identified the different types of exercises that can be included in a programme, I set about practising how to instruct them. I used a range of people to help me practise the instruction and demonstration of them and asked for their feedback on how I had performed.

Once I had completed the practice, I reviewed my own performance and took note of the feedback from the people who had helped me.

How I brought it all together

When I felt confident in how to plan and instruct a gym-based training programme, I identified two suitable clients to induct and instruct. I used a pre-prepared form to identify and record the clients' individual goals.

Following the session, I recorded the exercises that I had recommended as a short summary so that the clients

could continue their training. I paid particular attention to how the summary looked and tried to ensure that it was easy to read and that it looked professional, checking for spelling errors.

What I learned from the experience

I really enjoyed the experience although I realised that being able to remember the different exercises for each of the major muscles is difficult and takes lots of practice. The experience also helped me realise that different people have different training needs and goals, and made me consider how exercises can be adapted to accommodate these. It also made me consider the techniques I can use to instruct, encourage and motivate different clients.

Think about it

▶ Have you practised your gym-based instructing skills? Are you able to select the appropriate exercise for each muscle group as well as cardiovascular fitness?

▶ Consider the components of a warm-up as well as a cool-down and ensure that these are included in your programme.

▶ Have you written your summary report in your own words and have you given clear recommendations? Are you able to justify any recommendations that you have made?

Exercise and Circuit-based Physical Activity

14

Getting to know your unit

Exercise and circuit-based physical activity is a popular method of group exercise that is offered by many fitness providers. To be a successful instructor, you need to know how to establish effective working relationships with different participants. This is needed to develop your reputation as an instructor and to retain participants.

The types of exercise and circuit-based exercise sessions you deliver will differ depending on the participant group, so you need to be able to plan for and adapt sessions to ensure they meet the needs of all participants.

How you will be assessed

This unit will be internally assessed through a series of tasks set by your tutor. Throughout this unit, you will find assessment activity activities that will help you work towards your assessment. Completing these activities will not mean that you have achieved a particular grade, but you will have carried out useful research or preparation that will be relevant when it comes to your final assignment.

In order for you to achieve the tasks in your assignment, it is important to check that you have met all of the Pass grading criteria. You can do this as you work your way through the assignment.

If you are hoping to gain a Merit or Distinction, you should also make sure that you present the information in your assignment in the style that is required by the relevant assessment criterion. For example, Merit criteria require you to analyse and demonstrate whereas Distinction criteria require you to evaluate and justify.

The assignment set by your tutor will consist of a number of tasks designed to meet the criteria in the table. This is likely to consist of a mixture of written and practical assignments and include activities such as:

▶ drawing up session plans for circuit training sessions
▶ preparing a presentation that discusses ways to present a positive image when instructing
▶ demonstrating a range of effective communication skills during a practical assignment.

Assessment criteria

This table shows what you must do to achieve a **Pass**, **Merit** or **Distinction** grade, and where you can find activities to help you.

Pass	Merit	Distinction
Learning aim A Explore how to establish and maintain an effective working relationship with participants		
A.P1 Explain why it is important for an exercise instructor to present a positive self-image when working with participants. **Assessment activity 14.1**	**A.M1** Analyse the methods an exercise instructor can use to present a positive self-image when working with participants. **Assessment activity 14.1**	**A.D1** Evaluate the methods an exercise instructor can use to establish and maintain effective working relationships with participants. **Assessment activity 14.1**
Learning aim B Investigate ways an exercise instructor can support different participants in exercise and physical activity		
B.P2 Discuss effective methods of providing customer service that respond to customer needs. **Assessment activity 14.2**	**B.M2** Analyse the methods required to provide effective customer service to overcome barriers to exercise and physical activity, providing recommendations on how customers can be supported to adhere to an exercise programme. **Assessment activity 14.2**	**B.D2** Justify recommendations on the provision of effective customer service and how to support participants to adhere to an exercise programme. **Assessment activity 14.2**
B.P3 Discuss methods used to overcome barriers to exercise and physical activity. **Assessment activity 14.2**		
Learning aim C Carry out planning of a safe and effective group-based, circuit-based training exercise session		
C.P4 Prepare a safe and effective circuit training plan for exercise sessions with different participants. **Assessment activity 14.3**	**C.M3** Prepare a comprehensive circuit training plan that explains why each exercise is appropriate for each component and the needs of different participants. **Assessment activity 14.3**	**CD.D3** Evaluate own performance in planning, delivering and supporting a range of participants in a group-based exercise circuit session, justifying choices, strengths and recommendations for future practice. **Assessment activity 14.3**
Learning aim D Undertake a group-based circuit training exercise session		
D.P5 Deliver a safe and effective exercise session. **Assessment activity 14.3**	**D.M4** Demonstrate effective communication and motivational skills, taking into account different participants' needs when delivering a group-based exercise session. **Assessment activity 14.3**	**CD.D4** Evaluate the interrelationships between the maintenance of customer relationships, participant support and the effectiveness of group-based circuit training sessions. **Assessment activity 14.3**
D.P6 Review own performance in the delivery of a circuit training exercise session, identifying strengths and areas for improvement. **Assessment activity 14.3**	**D.M5** Analyse own performance in planning and delivering a circuit exercise session, explaining strengths and providing recommendations on self-improvement. **Assessment activity 14.3**	

Getting started

Group exercise is a very popular method of physical activity. To be a successful group exercise instructor you need to have a range of planning and practical skills. Write a list of all the skills you think are required to become an effective group exercise instructor, then, in a small group, discuss the skills you have identified.

A Explore how to establish and maintain an effective working relationship with participants

Presenting a positive and professional image

As a group exercise instructor, you are expected to be a role model for your participants, so presenting a positive and professional image is important. Wherever you are working, it is important that you present a professional image of the organisation and that you work within their policies. This may mean wearing a uniform, promoting other activities that the club offers, and following their health and safety procedures. It is also important that you present a positive image of yourself.

▶ A positive image can help to gain your participants' respect and confidence. Participants need to be confident in your professionalism and feel you are doing everything you can to ensure they are receiving the highest level of service during the group exercise sessions.

▶ Successfully presenting a positive and professional image may lead to participants praising your sessions and encouraging others to attend the session. This will help you to maintain and increase your participant base.

▶ The participants' needs should always be your priority. Participants are paying for a service, so will expect sessions to be planned and prepared in advance. Your plans need to take into account the different needs of the people in the session. You should be encouraging throughout, giving all participants 100 per cent of your attention before, during and after the session.

▶ All sessions should have no tolerance of **discrimination**, either from yourself and others. Anyone practising discrimination should be expelled from the session, and reported to the club's manager.

Discussion

Discuss the potential implications of not presenting a positive image as a group exercise instructor. Do you think the participants are going to be motivated if the instructor is not presenting a friendly attitude? How would you respond if the instructor was not wearing appropriate kit?

Key term

Discrimination – when someone is treated unfairly/differently because of the characteristic(s) they have. The Equality Act (2010) made it illegal to discriminate against anyone for characteristics such as age, sex, race, sexuality and disability.

▶ An exercise class can include people from a wide variety of backgrounds

Look at the photo of an exercise session and discuss what different characteristics each of the participants has. Why is it important to ensure that everyone in your session has the opportunity to take part regardless of the characteristics they have?

Ways of presenting a positive image

Appropriate clothing and footwear

Discussion

Discuss in small groups the type of clothing and footwear that you think is appropriate to wear as a group exercise instructor. Consider the temperature of the environment, the support of the clothing and footwear, and the ability of a group to observe exercise techniques.

An instructor should wear workout and fitness clothing. Close-fitting clothing allows easy movements through a full range of motion and allows participants to correctly follow your technique. Loose-fitting clothing can distort your body position during certain exercises.

Clothing should be breathable to help draw sweat away from the surface of your skin. Cotton is very good at absorbing moisture and can become wet from sweat very quickly. Choosing synthetic materials or a combination of cotton and nylon is usually the best option.
Footwear should be supportive, avoiding fashion trainers as these do not provide stability for the ankle. Many brands now market trainers specifically for gym-based exercise. Training shoes should be light with a breathable mesh and cushioned sole. They should be kept clean and regularly replaced.

Personal hygiene

As a good exercise instructor, you may be delivering several sessions a day. This can often make personal hygiene a challenge, particularly when demonstrating and taking part in the majority of the sessions you lead. Showering regularly throughout the day would be best, but is not always possible. Having spare freshly washed clothes to change into after each session and regularly using deodorant provides another option if time is limited between sessions. Tie any long hair back or pin it back if it won't tie up.

REPs code of practice and continuing professional development requirements

The Register of Exercise Professionals (REPs) is an independent public register that recognises the qualifications of exercise instructors in the UK. Being a member of the REPs register enhances an instructor's professional image and ensures you meet the professional standards in the REPs code of ethical practice. The code defines what good practice is for a professional in the fitness industry by reflecting on the core values of rights, relationships, responsibilities, standards and safety.

To join the REPs register you need to prove you have the appropriate qualifications. To continue as a member, you also need to meet the **continuing professional development (CPD)** requirements. This involves keeping up to date with changes to the industry to ensure they are delivering the most effective techniques to clients.

Research

Visit the REPs website (**www.exerciseregister.org**) for further details about the full code of ethical practice. What are the core values of rights, relationships, responsibilities, standards and safety?

Key terms

Continuing professional development (CPD) – the training and further development of skills and techniques beyond initial training. Usually additional training courses or experience are undertaken.

Empathy – understanding another person's experience from their perspective.

Link

You can read more about CPD in *Unit 3: Professional Development in the Sports Industry*.

Manner

Your own personal manner and attitude can have a positive influence on your image and reputation. Instructors need to be able to relate to all the participants in the session. Key advice includes:

▶ be friendly and welcoming to all participants, making sure you have said 'hello' to all of them
▶ get to know frequent attendees' names and take an interest in their lives, for example by asking them what they have been doing or if they have had a busy day
▶ active listening (making eye contact, nodding and confirming you have listened to what you have been told) is a highly-valued skill
▶ have patience with participants who may need more help with certain exercises – the right encouragement can increase their self-confidence and trust in you as an instructor
▶ try to have **empathy** – show participants you understand that the session or exercise is challenging by adapting or making the exercise less challenging if necessary to support the individual.

PAUSE POINT

As an exercise and circuit-based exercise instructor, what forms of CPD could you undertake?

(Hint) Visit the REPs website. What courses would help you to continue your professional development?

(Extend) Which courses would allow you to accrue enough CPD points to remain a member of REPs in the two years following initial training?

Skills

Group exercise instructors need a variety of skills to make the sessions they lead professional and enjoyable.

▶ **Time management** – this is vital to ensure sessions are well run and do not waste any of your participants' time. Managing your and your clients' time is a key indicator of your professionalism. Make sure there is time for any set-up before the session, including testing any audio system. This will also leave you free to welcome participants as they arrive. Careful planning will be needed for all the individual components of the session including the length of the warm-up, the main session (including the timings on each station and the number of times the station is going to be completed including rest periods) and cool-down – this is covered later in this unit (see pages 143 and 144).

▶ **Methods of motivation** – you need to motivate the participants throughout the session. The participants should find the session challenging so they will benefit from encouragement. Be specific in your encouragement: tell participants what they are doing well (for example, 'good depth in squat') and let them know how long they have left on an exercise station or how many repetitions are left. You should always recognise how well participants have done after a set or round and monitor how well regular attendees are progressing. Giving specific goals at the start of the session to the group or specific participants can also be a good motivator.

▶ **Leadership** – make sure you maintain control of the session and set a good example. You need to be confident and able to raise your voice in a controlled manner to capture the attention of all participants. A good leader will be adaptable and should be able to make quick decisions about whether an exercise is too easy or too hard for the group or a particular participant.

▶ **Organisation** – a good exercise session is a well-planned session: an instructor will have more confidence in delivery and participants should respond positively. Sessions should have structure but the content should be varied as well as having an element of familiarity for participants. Plan for a variety of abilities and fitness levels, and take into account any specific needs or adaptions to ensure **inclusivity**.

▶ **Participant sensitivity relating to physical contact** – you should continually assess the exercise technique of the participants in the session, walking around the space and helping participants if their technique can be improved. If an exercise position is incorrect, it is often easier for an instructor to help by moving them into the correct position. However, you should be aware of a participant's sensitivity to contact and should not automatically touch a participant and move them into a position without asking their permission first.

> **Key term**
>
> **Inclusivity** – making sure that everyone that attends can take part in the planned exercise or that exercises can be adapted to involve everyone.
>
> **Control measures** – actions that are taken to reduce the level of risk associated with a hazard.

Responsibilities and requirements of an exercise instructor

▶ **Customer care** – participants expect you to meet their expectations. A negative experience in a session makes people less likely to return. Keeping participants happy results in a strong client base and positive reputation. Remember they may be nervous about coming to the session and you need to make them feel at ease with you. Always speak to newcomers before, during and after the session. Get to know the participants' names and use their names to encourage them. At the end of the session, make yourself available for questions and let them know you are looking forward to seeing them next week.

▶ **Health and safety** – the health and safety of anyone involved is of the upmost importance. The setting of the session will have policies and procedures in place to ensure welfare. As an employee, you must be made aware of these policies.

▶ **First aid qualifications** – it is the responsibility of an exercise instructor to have an Emergency First Aid qualification and to renew it prior to expiry. If you are employed by a fitness studio or gym, it is likely that you will need to complete a First Aid at Work qualification. First aid qualification requirements will be outlined in a health and safety policy at your place of work.

▶ **Risk assessment** – the area in which the session is taking place must also be checked. An up-to-date risk assessment must be available and the area, and the equipment, must be checked before every session. A risk assessment will identify any hazards and risks, after which **control measures** should be used to reduce the overall rating of hazards (for example, low, medium, high). If you are working for a leisure centre, it is likely the operations manager will have written the risk assessment, so make sure it covers the activities that will be delivered during your session. Any incidents must be logged and recorded.

▸ **Disclosure and Barring Service (DBS)** – a DBS check is provided for people who work with children or vulnerable adults. It is a record of an individual's convictions, cautions, reprimands and warnings or any other relevant information held by the police and/or the DBS that affect an individual's suitability for the job. All employers will require you to complete a DBS check.

▸ **Duty of care** – as a group exercise instructor you have a duty of care for everyone involved in your session. You need to provide reasonable care for the participants in the session, for example by providing regular hydration breaks, access to changing/toilet facilities, and clean equipment and environment, as well as making reasonable adaptations to the session so that everyone can participate.

▸ **Insurance** – REPs members need to provide evidence of an appropriate level of insurance. REPs can provide you with insurance or you can get insurance from another provider. The insurance must provide adequate civil liability insurance which covers your legal liability for death, injury or illness to others and loss of, or damage to, third-party property. The REPs register requires you to hold a minimum annual liability policy with a minimum indemnity of £5,000,000.

> **Link**
>
> Health and safety and risk assessment are covered in more depth in *Unit 4: Sport Leadership*.

> **Link**
>
> You can read more about insurance issues in *Unit 12: Self-employment in the Sports Industry*.

Case study

Jess is a recently qualified group exercise instructor and she would like to set up her own exercise classes. What advice would you give Jess to ensure she meets the responsibilities and requirements of an exercise instructor before she advertises her classes to the public?

Check your knowledge

- What type of insurance should Jess have?
- What type of first aid qualification should she have?
- If Jess is working with vulnerable adults in her session, what type of check should also be completed?

❚❚ PAUSE POINT

Why is it important for a group exercise instructor to have a DBS check, first aid qualifications, insurance and the utmost duty of care for the participants within the session?

> Hint   What implications might there be if an instructor neglected to consider any of these requirements?

> Extend   How might neglecting them have an impact on a group exercise instructor's reputation?

Communication skills for groups

Group exercise instructors are required to communicate with a variety of different groups such as mature people (aged over 60), people with physical disabilities, young people, and ante- and postnatal mothers. Effective communication ensures you can gather information about each participant's needs and expectations.

Verbal communication

Many instructors use head microphones to make it easier for participants to follow instructions. But it is still important to speak clearly and raise the volume of your voice. Repeating instructions can also help participants follow the session. The volume and tone of voice used can depend on the type of exercise session being delivered. A high-intensity circuit training class would require an increase in volume and tone of voice, whereas a yoga class would require a softer quieter tone of voice.

Being enthusiastic can increase the participants' level of motivation. Praise and encouragement is also important. Relating to as many of the participants in the session individually will support their own personal needs and increase their intrinsic motivation.

> **Theory into practice**
>
> Consider how you would alter the volume and tone of your voice if you were delivering a group exercise session to a group of elderly participants compared to a group of young participants.

II   PAUSE POINT   How can you increase motivation? How could you use these methods when you are instructing?

> (Hint)   Consider goal setting, music and tone of voice. How can these all help increase motivation?

> (Extend)   Research other motivational techniques you could use to increase motivation. Would you always use the same techniques?

It is important to not assume anything. Be engaging and ask your participants questions. **Open-ended questions** are usually the best type of questions as they encourage a detailed answer from the participants. Example questions to establish a participant's needs and expectations include the following.

▶ Why have you decided to attend this session?
▶ Do you have any short- or long-term targets?

Example questions to check participants' understanding include the following.

▶ Is there anything in the routine or any exercises you would like me to demonstrate again?
▶ Can you describe to me which part of the body you can feel working?

Example questions to check participant comfort levels include the following.

▶ Where can you feel this exercise working? Can you feel any pain during this exercise?
▶ How hard is this exercise for you?
▶ How do you feel about trying a more challenging exercise?

Non-verbal communication

Demonstrations

Demonstrations are a vital part of group exercise instruction. When the music is loud and you have a large group of participants in front of you, demonstrations allow everyone to follow the session. Repeating demonstrations throughout the session and providing individuals with further demonstrations might also be necessary. You may also need to demonstrate progressions and regressions linked to the main exercise set, or give different participants easier and harder exercise alternatives to help meet their individual needs.

Body language

The body language you use needs to convey enthusiasm. You need to show you enjoy delivering the session and that you want participants to reap the benefits. Often over-exaggerating your body language as an exercise instructor can help increase your participants' engagement with both the session and you as the instructor.

Cueing

As a beginner instructor, **cueing** can be challenging and it is a technique that improves with practice. Cueing

can be split into three different types: verbal, visual and **kinaesthetic** (the photo on this page shows an example of kinaesthetic cueing). Table 14.1 lists different ways to cue as a group exercise instructor. A combination of methods works best because not all participants will learn in the same way. Appropriate consent is needed before conducting kinaesthetic cueing.

> **Key terms**
>
> **Cueing** – the use of visual, verbal and/or kinaesthetic signals to help improve communication between the instructor and participant.
>
> **Kinaesthetic** – learning takes place by carrying out the activity, such as a group exercise instructor helping a participant move through the correct technique.

▶ Kinaesthetic cueing involves supporting a client through a movement

▶ **Table 14.1:** Different methods of cueing

Visual cueing	Verbal cueing	Kinaesthetic cueing
Breaking down an exercise into different parts, e.g. the different joint positions in a squat	Counting down into the next exercise, e.g. '1, 2, 3, change'	Supporting the client through a movement
Pointing in the direction of the upcoming change in direction	Counting down the repetitions or time left on an exercise	Placing your hand on the muscle group that the exercise is working
Pointing to an area of the body that the participants need to focus on, for example, you might point to a participant's elbows during a bicep curl and then show them the correct position	Providing specific feedback to the overall group and individual participants to reinforce technique, for example, 'Try to keep your back straight during this exercise' or 'Avoid dropping your hips during this exercise'	Placing your client in an exercise position or helping them make the exercise more challenging by altering their position

⏸ **PAUSE POINT** Why do you think it is important to combine cueing methods as an exercise instructor?

> **Hint** Think about your own learning style. How do you learn best? Do you learn in the same way as someone else within your class group?

> **Extend** Watch a range of different videos of group exercise. Can you identify when the instructor is using different types of cueing?

Instructing position

For most of the session, you will need to be in a position where all participants can see you and you can see them. This topic is covered in more depth later in this unit (see page 148).

Active listening

Before, during and after the session you should be asking questions – you need to listen to the answers, too. You need to show your participants that you are actively listening to them as this can help you meet their expectations. Demonstrate active listening by:

▶ making eye contact, nodding and smiling
▶ encouraging participants to go on by saying 'hmm' and 'mmm'
▶ providing participants with feedback and clarifying what they have told you to ensure you have interpreted it correctly
▶ remaining neutral and non-judgemental (avoiding judging someone because of their personal characteristics or opinions).

Communicating effectively with clients

As an instructor, you must also have the ability to understand your participants. Participants may willingly provide you with feedback, but it is likely you will need to prompt them for it. This will help you assess how they are progressing and whether you need to make any alterations to the type or intensity of the exercises.

Observing their non-verbal communication will be as important as the feedback they are verbally providing to you. Participants might not be confident enough to tell you how they are feeling, but you should be able to recognise through observing them if they are finding the exercises too easy or too hard.

A range of different participants are likely to attend your sessions and you are also likely to have specific sessions for certain groups of people, for example **vulnerable adults**, mature people (60+) or **ante-** and **postnatal** women. Table 14.2 shows important considerations when communicating with different groups.

Key terms

Antenatal – during pregnancy (from conception to birth).

Postnatal – the period of time after a baby is born. Women will have regular check-ups after birth up until a six-week check-up. At this point a GP will usually let them know if it is safe to gradually re-introduce exercise.

Vulnerable adult – a person who suffers from certain characteristics that prevent them from taking sufficient care or providing themselves with sufficient protection.

▶ **Table 14.2:** Considerations for communicating with different groups

Participant group	Considerations for communication
14–16 year olds, young people and vulnerable adults	• Be clear, lively and enthusiastic. • Engage with the group and get them involved in demonstrations where appropriate. • Introduce an element of competition or a game to increase motivation. • Keep instructions simple until basic technique has been developed. • For vulnerable adults, the nature of their vulnerability will help determine how you communicate with them. For example, if the adult has a development disability, you may need to repeat your demonstrations frequently and guide them through the session.
People with physical disabilities	• A variety of techniques may need to be demonstrated for participants with physical disabilities. The ability of the participants to get into a certain position is the challenge. • Try not to assume that the participants can all do the same exercises. Participants with physical disabilities have varying abilities even if they have the same condition. Ask the participants if they think they will be able to attempt an exercise; if not, adapt it. • Kinaesthetic cueing (if appropriate) will be particularly important.
Mature people (60+)	• Try not to assume that because the participants are mature they cannot attempt certain exercises (unless for individual health reasons). • Repeat demonstrations and slow down the speed of instruction if necessary. • Try to gather as much feedback as possible during the session from individual participants so that you can provide progressions and regressions of exercises as appropriate. • Be respectful – challenge participants but don't expect them to be able to achieve as much as a younger participant.
Ante- and postnatal women	• Adapt exercises to meet the needs of the varying stages of pregnancy. Communicate these adaptations visually and verbally. • Show empathy – show them that you are aware that they may be lacking in energy or be struggling with an exercise that was once easy pre-pregnancy. • Be patient – it may take them longer to complete a set exercise.

Link

Pre-exercise screening processes are covered in more depth in *Unit 2: Fitness Training and Programming for Health, Sport and Well-being.*

Key term

Contraindication – a physical or mental condition or factor that increases the risk involved in an activity.

Gathering personal information

There are several ways to gather information from participants about their needs and expectations. As a minimum, participants must complete a Physical Activity Readiness Questionnaire (PAR-Q) before beginning a series of classes. This gathers personal information and details their exercise and medical history, highlighting any **contraindications**, and gets them to record their needs and expectations.

Ideally, you would ask the participants the questions and guide them through the form, but there is not always enough time to do this. Participants should still fill out a PAR-Q form and you should take the time to look through it and ask the participant any further questions. Even if as an instructor you feel there aren't any further questions, you can still engage with them by asking them why they decided to join the session.

Forming effective working relationships with participants

Building trust with participants is the basis of an effective working relationship. **Confidentiality** is vital to gain your participants' trust. Participants provide you with personal details, details of their medical and exercise history, and their own personal goals. This information is provided so you can support them towards their goals, and they won't want you to share any of this information with other members of the group or other instructors.

Any personal details that you have relating to participants are protected under the Data Protection Act (1998) which means you must not disclose this information to anyone else without the participants' permission and that it must be stored safely and securely.

If you have any concerns regarding your participants, or if they confide in you, you may need to consider whether to refer them to a more appropriately qualified person.

Getting to know participant names, particularly of regular attendees, helps to build a rapport. You should also actively greet new participants and welcome them to the session. New participants might be lacking confidence, so introducing them to a regular member to whom they can direct questions may help them feel at ease.

The participants attending group exercise sessions are likely to vary from week to week. Even regular attendees will miss some sessions due to illness, work or family commitments.

Motivational relationships

As a role model, you need to show participants you are motivated by group exercise. You should be empathetic and understand that they may have had a long day before the session. Set group and individual targets during the session where possible, for example by challenging a participant to increase the difficulty of an exercise in the next round. Participants will look to you to provide them with enthusiasm and motivation. They need to feel they have met targets so that they leave feeling they have achieved something.

❚❚ PAUSE POINT   Where should participants' personal information be stored?

> (Hint)   As a group exercise instructor, how can you make sure personal details are safe and secure?

> (Extend)   If you hold electronic information relating to a participant, how can this be kept safe and secure?

Equality and diversity

Exercise and circuit-based physical activity sessions need to be open to all. However, there may be times when, due to safety or religious reasons, sessions are targeted at specific groups. These could be women-only sessions or classes for mature adults only.

Different organisations may have different policies and procedures relating to **equality** and **diversity**. For example, a council leisure centre may have different policies to a private gym. Ensure you are up to date with the centre's regulations before carrying out any sessions.

You must value diversity when working with participants. All participants want to take part in the session, but they may be there for many different reasons. Being able to support all these different expectations and needs is necessary and shows you are committed to supporting all participants and valuing diversity. Table 14.3 provides examples of different types of prejudice and discrimination, and how you can respond to them.

> **Key terms**
>
> **Equality** – treating people equally, but not necessarily the same.
>
> **Diversity** – recognising and respecting that everyone is different.

▶ **Table 14.3:** Examples of prejudice and discriminatory activity

Prejudice or discrimination	Examples of prejudice/discriminatory comments	Exercise instructor's response
Age (protected characteristic)	'You're too old to take part in this session.' 'You're too young to be out at this time of night.'	'Everybody is welcome in this session as it is adapted to suit everyone's individual needs.'
Antenatal	'Do you think you should be doing this exercise session in your condition?'	'This participant is more than capable of taking part in this session.'
Weight	'You don't need to come to this exercise session – you're skinny enough already.' 'You're too overweight to benefit from this session.'	'Everyone has their own individual goals – you don't need to be a certain size to attend this session.'
Clothing	'You can't wear that in this session.' 'Have you seen that person's trainers?'	'As long as the participant feels comfortable in what they are wearing and it is safe for them to do so, they can take part in this session.'

Assessment practice 14.1 · A.P1 · A.M1 · A.D1

You are an established group exercise instructor. A local college has asked you to deliver a PowerPoint presentation to its sport and fitness learners about the importance, as a group exercise instructor, of presenting a positive self-image, as well as the methods that can be used to maintain effective working relationships with participants. You need to explain to the learners why it is important to present a positive self-image and how it will have an impact on your reputation, increasing your participant base and gaining respect and confidence.

The learners need to know how they can present a positive self-image and the methods they can use to establish and maintain effective working relationships. The presentation should also evaluate the methods that can be used to establish and maintain effective working relationships with the participants. Show how each method may have an impact on establishing and maintaining effective working relationships with participants, to help you consider the strengths and benefits of the methods.

Plan
- What am I learning about and why is it important to present an effective self-image?
- Are there any areas that I might struggle with? What could I do to help avoid this?

Do
- I will spend some time planning the task, researching the different requirements of an exercise instructor.
- I will participate in group-based exercise classes to experience how different instructors approach sessions.

Review
- I can say how I approached the task.
- I can say how my approach helped me meet the task's criteria.

B Investigate ways an exercise instructor can support different participants in exercise and physical activity

Dealing effectively with participants' needs

To support participants effectively, you need to gather background information about them. This information will help you to meet their individual needs. Table 14.4 shows the information you need from participants before they take part in group exercise.

▶ **Table 14.4:** Information required from participants

Personal goals	All participants' goals vary so within a session you need to try to support each participant with their personal goals. You can also gather information about their short-, medium- and long-term goals.
Lifestyle factors	Lifestyle factors are choices a participant makes that affect the quality of the life they lead. Lifestyle factors could include smoking, alcohol consumption, dietary habits, stress levels and amount and quality of sleep.
Barriers to participants	Barriers are usually reasons participants provide for not taking part in exercise. Most commonly reported reasons are lack of time, work and family commitments, and financial reasons. Knowing participants' barriers will help you support the individual needs of a client. You will need to try to provide solutions to help them overcome their barriers.
Medical history	A detailed medical history is required from your clients to determine if it will be safe for them to take part in physical activity or if alterations need to be made in order for them to still participate effectively.
Physical activity preferences	Trying to motivate participants to undertake an exercise that they do not enjoy is going to be challenging. Knowing participants' activity preferences will help you tailor the session to meet their needs, providing them with an alternative exercise if necessary.
Specific learning needs	Knowing if a participant has a specific disability or communication need can help you support them during the session. For example, if a participant within the session has a hearing impairment or is deaf, you will know to stand in a position that makes it easy from them to lip read or view demonstrations clearly.

Case study

A new participant would like to join your exercise group. You have asked them to fill out a PAR-Q health screening form. The information they provide is summarised below.

- **Personal goals** – increase upper body strength and reduce body fat percentage.
- **Lifestyle factors** – high stress and occasionally consumes a moderate amount of alcohol.
- **Barriers to participation** – busy job and two children under the age of 4.
- **Medical history** – tennis elbow. No other previous history.
- **Physical activity preferences** – high-intensity exercise. Does not like too many jumping exercises.

Wants to avoid repetitive elbow flexion and extension to prevent aggravation of tennis elbow.

Check your knowledge

1 What additional information would you like to know before the participant starts training?
2 Would you refer the participant to any other specialists to seek advice prior to training, such as a sports therapist or physiotherapist?
3 What further information would you like to know about their lifestyle factors?

Types of participants

The following participants may need to be supported during group exercise.

▶ **Participants with high and low levels of fitness** – having appropriate progressions and regressions for each exercise will help support both types of participants.
▶ **Experienced and inexperienced participants** – experienced participants will return regularly to the same session and you will be familiar with their specific goals and needs so maintaining their interest and motivation is important. Inexperienced participants may be nervous or low in confidence to start with and need additional guidance, starting with specific exercise techniques.
▶ **Mature participants** – healthy older adults aged 60+ may need exercises to be adapted to suit their needs. As with any group where ability may vary within the session, providing appropriate progressions and regressions may be needed and overall intensity may be slightly lower.
▶ **Children** – children are typically high in energy and may need a regular change in pace and type of exercise to prevent them getting bored.
▶ **Disabled participants** – many exercises can be adapted to suit the needs of a range of disabilities. For example, a participant with cerebral palsy may have difficulty with balance so a seated exercise might be preferred. Try not to assume that just because someone is disabled, they cannot complete an exercise: it is usually best to demonstrate the exercise first and then ask if they think it is possible (possibly with adaptation).
▶ **Ante- and postnatal participants** – pregnant women who regularly take part in the same type of exercise before pregnancy should be able to continue to participate but with some potential adaptations. For example, avoid exercises that involve them lying on their back as the weight of the baby can compress key blood vessels. Postnatal participants are generally advised to wait until after their six-week review with their doctor. However, women who regularly took part in exercise pre-pregnancy may feel they can return sooner. A sensible approach is required to avoid doing too much too soon after giving birth.

Research

Research the different types of exercises to avoid when working with ante- and postnatal women. Why are these exercises inadvisable for this type of participant?

▶ Antenatal women may need to have exercises adapted to enable participation

Responding to participants' requests

Participants may have different requests for the aims of the session or the exercises they do. You must follow the procedures of the organisation hosting the session when dealing with these requests. For example, if a group of participants would like more equipment to be available or suggest the start time of the session is altered, you need to ask them to follow the organisation's procedures to raise this. A participant may wish to make a complaint – if so, you will need to explain the correct procedure, such as making a complaint in writing to the manager.

Sourcing relevant information from different participants

Information can be sourced through the PAR-Q forms that were completed by all new participants and regularly updated by returning participants. Health screening questionnaires may also be used. These tend to source a greater detail of information regarding a participant's lifestyle, medical and activity history as well as their goals. In addition to written detail, you may need to ask additional questions to check it is safe for the participant to participate. For example, if they have recently been unwell or sustained an injury, you would need to ask for additional information on the situation.

Referring participants to other professionals

As a group exercise instructor, it is important to recognise boundaries of your own competence. Participants may come to you for advice on many different topics relating to your job role. However, you may not have the appropriate qualifications or experience to provide the correct advice. It is therefore good practice to refer these participants to an appropriate professional.

▶ **Injury** – during exercise, participants may become injured or over time feel repetitive pain in one area. It is likely they will ask you about this pain and whether you know what it is. It is important to refer participants to their GP, sports therapist or physiotherapist.

▶ **Illness or contraindications to exercise** – if a participant tells you they have an illness or potential contraindication to exercise, it is important that you refer them to their GP as you do not want them to worsen the condition through participating in exercise.

▶ **Screening tests/questionnaires** – before participants take part in exercise they should complete a screening questionnaire. Screening procedures may show participants they have a contraindication that they were not aware of. For example, they may have high **blood pressure** so need to be referred to the GP to get it checked before starting exercise.

Participant objectives

Participants will have a range of individual needs and reasons for participating in exercise and physical activity. These may include:

▶ to improve skills and techniques, for example weight lifting technique
▶ to improve physical fitness, for example aerobic endurance, muscular endurance, strength or flexibility, as well as altering their body composition
▶ to improve skill-related fitness, for example power, balance, coordination, speed and reaction time
▶ to improve sport-specific skills, for example developing physical and skill-related fitness, but with an emphasis on the movement patterns used in the sport – a tennis player, for example, might want to focus on multi-directional speed that matches court movement patterns
▶ to reduce stress levels or the risk of disease
▶ to enjoy social benefits, for example interacting with others, meeting new people and making friends.

Case study

Paul wants to join a circuit-based exercise group to help improve his energy levels and work–life balance. He hopes that the exercise sessions will increase his aerobic and muscular endurance. He has no existing health conditions but he works 50 hours per week as a business manager, so finds this quite stressful and it reduces the time he has available to exercise.

You need to encourage Paul to commit to joining a group.

Check your knowledge

• Would you need any additional information to help encourage Paul?
• Can you highlight key goals for him?

What information do you require from participants before they can take part in your sessions? How could you collect this information?

(Hint)   What personal details and medical history details would you require? Why would you need to know your participants' goals?

(Extend)   If you are concerned about any of the information provided, what should you do?

Providing ongoing customer service

The way in which you provide support to groups and individual participants will differ. Table 14.5 shows these differences. Remember that it is important to recognise any limitations in your experience or qualifications. If you can provide clear information to a participant within the scope of your practice, then do so. However, if you are unsure whether you are able to provide the most up-to-date and accurate information, refer clients to someone who can.

▶ **Table 14.5:** Engaging with groups and individuals

Individuals	**Groups**
Before the session starts, get to know the participants. Take an active interest in them, what they do for a job and whether they have any plans for the weekend.	Address the whole group at the start of the session and at the end. Welcome them all and value their effort for attending.
Can you support their individual targets? Ask them if there is anything that you can do to help them achieve their targets/objectives.	Set group targets at the start of the session, for example: 'In this session I want to reach a combined target of X number of repetitions on this exercise.'
Praise individual efforts during the session. Be specific with your praise.	Set mini competitions within the session, for example: 'If we can all complete another five repetitions, you can have a 1-minute rest.'
Listen to them. If they want to share something with you, it must be important to them so actively listen.	Involve them in the session decisions, for example, would they prefer to have a certain exercise in the circuit or do they have a preferred type of music?
Get feedback from individuals at the end of the session. Ask them if they enjoyed the session, whether there was a particular part of the session they didn't enjoy or found too difficult. You can use this information next time so you know to provide an easier exercise for that participant.	Get the participants to work together on exercise stations or as a team to complete certain exercises. Doing this, particularly when you have a large participant base, can help you engage with all the participants within the smaller groups.

Responding positively to participants and handling complaints

Regardless of a participant's attitude to a session, you must respond positively. You are there to support them and if you respond positively and provide encouragement, you are more likely to motivate them for the session.

Being defensive can be an immediate reaction when someone complains about a session you have planned. Try to avoid taking the comment personally even if it is directed at you. Follow any procedures and tell the participant to make a formal complaint if they wish to. Usually a complaint needs to be referred to the manager as soon as possible. They can then acknowledge and investigate it, probably by contacting the complaining participant to gain further information and offer a solution if possible. Avoid trying to resolve the complaint on your own as this may not be supported by the organisation.

Working with participants to meet their needs

It may take a while to find specific ways of supporting individual needs. However, it is important that you continue to attempt to do this.

Using verbal instruction alongside demonstrations will support most participants during a session. You may need to support participants kinaesthetically, to help them get into different exercise positions. You can also offer one-to-one support before or after a session to any participants who may wish you to increase the challenge of the session or provide them with easier exercises so that they can complete the whole session.

Social media can be used effectively (if the organisation's policy allows it) to support individuals. Posting videos and links to different information or guidance on exercises to complete at home could help support individual needs. Referring participants to personal trainers or other fitness professionals who can support them with their development can also be an option if you are not able to provide additional support.

> **Reflect**
>
> How could you use social media effectively to increase engagement within your sessions and improve your reputation? What should you avoid in using social media as an exercise instructor? How might this damage your reputation?

(❚❚) PAUSE POINT Who should you refer participants to if they have questions regarding pain they are having in their shins during jumping?

Hint Are you qualified to advise them on this situation?

Extend Even though you cannot provide a diagnosis, what would you encourage the participant to do to prevent any worsening of the condition?

Barriers to exercise and physical activity

Barriers are reasons participants provide for not being able to take part in activity. These barriers are often **perceived barriers**, meaning the participant thinks it is a valid reason why they cannot exercise, but support and planning from you as the instructor usually means the barrier can be overcome. Some common barriers are shown in Table 14.6.

▶ **Table 14.6:** Barriers to exercise and physical activity

Barriers	Reasons for the barrier
Time	A commonly cited barrier. However, if participants considered how long they spend watching television or on social media, they may find they choose to prioritise the 'wrong' activities.
Location	Access to nearby facilities can determine whether a participant is going to commit to a session. Often if a session is on the way to somewhere, a participant is more likely to attend, for example if it is on the route home or to work, or close to where they drop their children off at school.
Cost	The benefit of participating in the session has to outweigh the cost; otherwise, a participant is never going to commit to paying for a session they think they will gain no benefit from.
Culture	A participant's culture may have an impact on whether they commit to a session or whether they feel like they want to attend. For example, if a participant is expected to wear certain clothing because of their cultural background, they may not want to attend a session where wearing exercise kit is advised.
Health problems	Certain health problems will determine whether a participant can take part in an exercise session. For example, a participant with high blood pressure or a previous heart condition will not be able to take part in vigorous exercise.
Work patterns	A work pattern – for example changing shifts, night work or long hours – may affect a participant's ability to commit to regular exercise sessions.
Disability	Disability can affect the type of session that a participant can do. However, sessions should be adapted to meet the needs of different disabilities where possible.
Illness	Short-term illness will hopefully only be a barrier for one or two sessions, but it can prevent participants from engaging in sessions.
Level of fitness	'I want to improve my fitness before I go to that exercise class – it looks too hard.' Participants often give this as a reason not to go a session, particularly those who perceive that their own level of fitness is poor.

Strategies to overcome barriers to exercise and physical activity

▶ **Appropriate exercise selection** – if the session mainly includes inexperienced participants with low levels of fitness and the session is too challenging, they are unlikely to return. If the session is adapted to meet their needs, they are more likely to feel like they have achieved something and therefore return.

▸ **Incentives and rewards** – tangible rewards often help motivate participants to commit. For example, if the barrier presented is cost, incentives such as 'Attend 4 sessions and get the 5th for half price' can have an effect. Another incentive is to have a leaderboard for attendance at the sessions, with a prize such as an exercise top for participants when they reach 10 sessions, and then other prizes when they reach 20, 25 and so on. The quality of the prize should improve, the more sessions are attended.

▸ **Differences between everyday lifestyle activity and exercise participation** – everyday lifestyle activity is normally undertaken during the day, for example walking to drop children off at school. Exercise can also require a commitment with an intended purpose. Showing participants the benefits they may be able to gain from increased exercise may help motivate them to overcome barriers such as time and cost.

▸ **Lifestyle changes** – encouraging participants to modify their lifestyles to include more physical activity can also reduce barriers. An example is encouraging them to get off the bus at an earlier stop and walk the remaining distance. Identifying times across the week where they could exercise instead of engaging in a **sedentary activity**, such as reducing TV viewing or social media use, can also have an effect.

> **Key term**
>
> **Sedentary activity** – activity that is low in intensity, for example lying or sitting down.

Ⅱ PAUSE POINT	How could a participant reduce the amount of time they spend watching television or on social media?
Hint	Could they exercise with a friend or partner to help increase their commitment to exercise?
Extend	How could a participant combine television watching with exercise to help increase activity levels?

Methods of supporting participants to adhere to exercise

It is important to recognise your own limitations as an exercise instructor. To support a participant effectively, you may need to refer them to another exercise professional or medical staff to meet their needs. Ultimately, if this is the best way to support them at the time, they may return to you after they have been supported. Avoid providing participants with information and advice if you are not qualified to do so.

Professional relationships

A professional relationship should be formed between you and the participants. It should be based on appropriate advice and support. Ensure the advice you provide to any participant is within the scope of your qualifications and experience. Throughout the sessions, take the time to interact with each of the participants, even if this is just saying hello and goodbye, as well as using their name. This helps reassure the participants that you are there to support them. Prioritise your time during the sessions to support new participants or participants that need further help with an exercise station.

You may be approached before or after a class by a participant who is seeking additional advice or support. You should always be careful to make sure that any advice you give when this happens is appropriate – often it may involve referring a participant to another professional, for example if they have a problem with an injury.

It is not always possible to interact with all participants during the sessions, but social media platforms provide ways to increase communication with your participants. Social media can be an effective tool for contact with participants outside the session, sharing resources and raising the profile of the exercise sessions that you deliver. It can help support exercise adherence, for example by providing participants with reminders about future sessions, praising them after the session and creating a sense of community so participants feel they belong.

Encouraging and using social media to raise the profile of your exercise classes can be an effective tool but it could lead to participants contacting you outside the exercise session. It is important to maintain a professional approach in these situations, so that you do not compromise your reputation. If the social media platform you are using combines professional and public use you need to consider whether certain posts or pictures are appropriate to share with participants. Avoid posting or sharing something that may damage you or your organisation's reputation. Organisations will have a social media policy you need to abide by.

Helping participants take responsibility for their own fitness

The more responsibility a participant takes for their own fitness, the more likely they are to engage with sessions. One of the most effective ways to encourage responsibility is through goal setting. Goals should follow the **SMART** principle.

Goals should be set by the participant with your support. Participants should have short-, medium- and long-term goals. Setting realistic short-term targets can help participants to see progress early, with medium- and long-term targets to help them reach their ultimate goal. This can help motivation as it can be demotivating to see no results. Setting smaller, more achievable targets improves exercise adherence and motivation to achieve their goals.

Case study

Jayne has recently decided to attend your group exercise session because she wants to reduce her body fat levels and increase her aerobic fitness so that she can complete a half marathon. Her long-term goals are to reduce her body fat percentage from 30 per cent to 20 per cent and complete a half marathon in 12 months. She has been running for five years, mainly for enjoyment and stress relief, a couple of times per week, but has never completed a half marathon before. This could be challenging for her as she has family commitments and works four full days per week, but she has dedicated herself to completing the challenge.

- Write Jayne a short-term goal and a medium-term goal.
- Does Jayne present any barriers that may have an impact on her chances of achieving her goals?
- Do you think it is going to be easy for Jayne to achieve her goal? How could you help support her in your exercise sessions?

Reviewing and revising goals

Goals must be reviewed and monitored. Tracking progress allows them to be revised based on the progress made so far. For example, the participant may become unwell or find they are unable to commit to as many sessions as originally planned and therefore the original goals may become unrealistic. One way to review goals is to encourage the participant to keep a diary; for example, for weight loss goals, ask the participant to record their weight weekly.

Methods of overcoming barriers to participation for specific participants

Encourage participants to take ownership of their fitness by considering ways they can overcome any barriers to their participation. Solutions that are identified by the participant are more likely to be successful than ones suggested by you because the participant has suggested them. They should be encouraged to find solutions to any of the barriers identified earlier in this unit (see page 131).

Motivational techniques

You will need to implement a range of motivational techniques, such as those shown in Table 14.7, depending on the type of participant that you are working with.

▶ **Table 14.7:** Motivational techniques

Motivational technique	Who is the strategy targeted at?
Goal setting	Any participant type. However, it is most likely to work with participants who have specific objectives that they would like to achieve, for example participants with sport-specific needs.
Routine	Participants with limited time. Getting participants to include exercise in their routine will help improve their motivation.
Social support	Older participants and participants who are new to group exercise. Linking up participants who have similar goals so they can support each other will help them feed off each other's enthusiasm.
Monitoring progress	Participants that have specific goals should track their progress. This would particularly support participants with a range of different ability levels – it can help to monitor progress and allow them to see how they are progressing individually.
Decision making	Participants who are unsure whether they can commit to the exercise or find the time to participate. Weighing up the pros and cons of an activity might also work with participants with low income, to help them prioritise the importance of exercise.
Competition	Adding an element of competition to sessions will help engage many ages ranges, in particular younger participants.
Variety	Any participants. Keeping the sessions varied and interesting, and adapting sessions to meet specific interests will help motivate participants and prevent them from getting bored.

Ⅱ PAUSE POINT   What methods can you use to improve participants' motivation during the session?

> Hint   Would you use different methods with different participants?

> Extend   If a regular participant has missed two sessions, what could you do to increase their motivation and encourage them to return?

Assessment practice 14.2   B.P2 B.P3 B.M2 B.D2

You have secured a job interview to be a circuit training instructor at a local leisure centre. As part of the interview they have asked you to prepare a presentation on effective customer service and why it is important for supporting participants to adhere to an exercise programme.

The presentation should discuss a range of effective methods of providing customer service and overcoming barriers to exercise. You should then analyse the methods required to do this. Consider whether you think the methods will be effective or will some methods be more suitable depending on the barrier the participant has?

The leisure centre wants to be sure that you understand how to help participants adhere to their exercise programme. Make recommendations on how different customers can be supported and justify these recommendations. Say why the recommendations are important. How are they going to help participants overcome their barriers and improve exercise adherence?

Plan
- Do I understand the different ways I can support participants?
- Can I recognise any areas where I might struggle and identify what I could do to help?

Do
- I will spend time planning the task, for example finding out how instructors use social media effectively.
- I will research the different types of motivational techniques I can use during the exercise sessions, and methods that I can use to help participants re-engage with the sessions.

Review
- I understand how my approach helped me meet the task's criteria.
- I can identify things that I would do differently next time.

C Carry out planning of a safe and effective group-based, circuit-based exercise session

Benefits of circuit-based training

There are several key benefits to circuit-based training. The main benefits are described in Table 14.8.

▶ **Table 14.8:** Key benefits of circuit-based training

Benefit	Description
Combining cardiovascular and resistance training	This enables participants to develop several components of fitness within the same session and prevents tedium. Cardiovascular exercises (shuttle runs, jogging on the spot, jumping jacks, etc.) can be alternated with muscular endurance training stations (triceps dips, lunges and squats, etc.)
Alternating muscle groups to allow rest intervals	Careful planning allows for alternate muscle groups to be targeted, allowing other muscle groups to recover. This maximises workout efficiency and is beneficial for clients who like a whole body workout in a short space of time. For example, circuits focusing on the legs for one exercise (for example, a calf raise) followed by an upper body exercise (for example, triceps extensions) allow for recovery time in the previously active muscle group.
Enabling multiple participants of differing abilities to participate at the same time	A range of exercises at one time allows mass participation. Individual participants can work to their own ability. For example, on an exercise station an experienced participant may achieve 30 lunges whereas an inexperienced participant may only achieve 20 lunges, but each participant can participate to the best of their ability. You can easily adapt exercises to meet the needs of individual participants, progressing them to challenge individuals or adapting them to be more achievable.
Relatively inexpensive to set up	• Low set-up cost in comparison with other group exercises. Basic equipment may be required, for example, mats and resistance bands, but body weight exercises can be challenging enough without any equipment. • The space required depends on your location. An organisation may provide spaces or, if you are self-employed, you may find village halls or sports halls are relatively inexpensive to hire. • A final consideration is music – this may be the costliest set-up. There are legal requirements to consider when playing music for public rather than private use (see page 145–6). Some organisations already have a licence so you will not require one. You may also need to purchase a sound system.
Generic fitness or sport-specific	Usually a circuit-based session in a leisure centre or village hall is designed to meet general needs. An instructor with a sports team or club may adapt the circuit to meet specific needs.

Stations in a circuit

Circuits usually consist of a series of stations and at each station there will be a different type of exercise. The exercises included in the circuit will depend on the objectives of the session and the participants' needs. Table 14.9 includes a variety of exercises that can be used to improve different components of fitness.

▶ **Table 14.9:** Exercises to train different components of fitness

Stations to improve aerobic endurance	Stations to improve muscular strength
• Shuttle runs • Jogging on the spot • Jumping jacks • Spotty dogs • Squat thrusts • Knee lifts • Step-ups • Skipping	• Shoulder presses • Dumbbell flies • Upright rows • Lateral raises • Bicep curls • Triceps extensions • Dumbbell lunges • Barbell squats • Calf raises
Stations to improve muscular endurance	**Stations to improve core strength**
• Triceps dips • Press-ups • Lunges • Squats • Side-bends	• Sit-ups • Crunches • Twisting sit-ups • Planks • Back extensions • Reverse curls

Key terms

Aerobic endurance – the ability of the cardiovascular and respiratory system to meet the demands of extended exercise without tiring.

Muscular strength – the ability of a muscle or group of muscles to overcome some form of resistance.

Muscular endurance – the ability of a muscle or group of muscles to move the body or an object repeatedly without tiring.

Core strength – the ability of all the muscles in the torso to provide stability and balance.

Sport-specific stations

A sport-specific circuit could include a variety of stations from the different components. For example, a running circuit could include leg and core strengthening exercises interspersed with half-mile race-pace runs on a treadmill.

Case study

A basketball player has recently found that she was being easily pushed off the ball. She always tries to maintain a good base of support so that this does not happen, but even doing this she is not intercepting as many passes successfully and is losing the ball easily during a dribble. Her coach has suggested she focuses more on core stability training to try to prevent this from happening.

Check your knowledge

- What type of sport-specific stations could you include in a circuit that will continue to support the demands of her sport but also improve her core strength?
- What exercises are specific to the movement patterns in basketball? How can these help improve her core stability?

Research

Table 14.9 includes a variety of different exercises that can be used to target different components of fitness. Select four different exercises that you don't know from the table above and research to find out what they are. Following this, see if you can create your own list of additional exercises that could be used to improve the different components of fitness.

Circuit cards

Circuit cards are used to help the participants identify the requirements of the exercise station. They should include:

▶ the name of the exercise
▶ a diagram
▶ teaching points
▶ adaptations, including progressions and alternatives.

See Figure 14.1 for an example layout.

Press-up (with wobble board)

Muscles involved:

- pectoralis
- deltoid
- abdominal muscles

- triceps brachii
- serratus anterior
- coracobrachialis

Level 1   **Level 2**   **Level 3**

▶ **Figure 14.1:** An example layout for a circuit card

A range of different circuit training layouts can be used depending on the session aim and the variety you wish to bring to the session. See Table 14.10 for the range of layouts.

► **Table 14.10:** Circuit training layouts

Layout name	Overview	Comments
Square		Exercises can be placed in a square shape. Usually all stations are facing towards the middle.
Lined circuit		Cards are usually placed on the wall at the front with participants lined up behind each other, as shown by the arrows. Participants complete the exercise in their line for the set duration then all move up a station.
Bow tie		Stations are placed in each corner with another station in the middle of the room.
Circular		As many stations as you wish can be placed in a circular layout. The outside circle is also useful as a shuttle run station.
Corners		A corner circuit is where each corner has a target muscle group and three exercises that work that targeted muscle group. It is designed to overload one target area and then move on to another.

PAUSE POINT What type of circuit training layout would you use with a group of 30 experienced participants?

Hint As 30 is a large number, consider this carefully when selecting the layout.

Extend How would you ensure you made the most effective use of the space available?

Planning a group exercise circuit training session

To effectively plan a group exercise session, you need to have clear **aims and objectives**. The aim is the overall goal you want to achieve from the session. An aim tends to be quite broad. For example, the aim of the session could be to improve aerobic and muscular endurance. Objectives, however, state how the session is going to achieve the aim. There are likely to be several objectives for one circuit training session. Examples include the following.

1 Warm up using a range of low- to moderate-intensity cardiovascular exercises including step-ups, walking on the spot and star jumps.

2 Set up the main session in a corners layout: two corners will have cardiovascular exercises and the other two corners will have muscular endurance exercises.

3 Cool down using moderate- to low-intensity cardiovascular exercises with static stretching focusing on a whole-body approach.

(II) PAUSE POINT Without looking back, explain the difference between an aim and an objective.

> Hint One is a broad overview of the session and one provides the specific points the session is going to achieve.

> Extend Write aims and objectives for an upper body strength-based circuit training session.

Other considerations

The practicalities of the session will depend on the number of participants and the space available.

▶ If there are few participants, you may have one person working at each station at a time.
▶ If there are more participants but plenty of space at each station, you may have several people at each station at a time. (If the exercises require specific equipment, you will need to make sure there are sufficient facilities for everyone.)
▶ If there are a lot of participants but limited space at each station, you may have half the group working at stations at any given time, with the rest of the group performing shuttle runs or running laps around the outside of the room.

The time spent at each station can be determined in two main ways:

1 Each participant completes a specific number of repetitions of the given exercise (for example, 20 press-ups) before moving on.
2 Each participant repeats the exercise as many times as they can within a set time (usually between 30 seconds and 3 minutes, depending on the intensity of the exercise) before moving on.

Equipment

You need to know what equipment you will have access to and that there will be enough for your planned activity. Circuit training can be run with minimal equipment, but it is useful to have access to a range of different types of equipment to provide variety within your sessions. Equipment that can be used includes:

▶ dumbbells and barbells – with a range of weight ranges to meet individual needs
▶ mats – needed for floor work, for example planks and twisting sit-ups
▶ resistance bands – useful during muscular endurance circuits to add variety
▶ benches – used to increase the intensity of some cardiovascular exercises such as step-ups but also for triceps dips
▶ stopwatch – to keep track of the overall timing in the session.

Participants

A session plan should be written in a way designed to meet the needs of the participant group and take into consideration individuals with specific needs. For example, if a regular attendee tells you that they have recently found out they are 12 weeks pregnant and they still want to continue with circuit training, in your planning you will need to take this into consideration and provide alternative exercises where needed. Table 14.11 shows considerations for planning for different groups of participants.

▶ **Table 14.11:** Considerations in planning for different participants

Participants	Considerations in planning
Experienced	• Challenging exercises • Range of exercises and circuit layouts • Greater number of stations • Minimal instruction as a group but supporting individuals where necessary
Inexperienced	• Simple circuit layout • Basic exercises with 4–6 stations in the whole circuit • Longer rest times • Lots of group instruction with individual support

Participants	Considerations in planning
Mixed ability and fitness levels	• Lots of progression and regression • Optional stations during rest periods that would challenge higher levels of fitness by reducing rest time • Detailed circuit cards • Pairing up experienced and inexperienced participants (if possible) to support one another
Minimum and maximum numbers	• Space considerations for large groups • More than one exercise per station if minimal space • Body weight stations if minimal equipment for large groups • Pairing up participants when there are minimum numbers to create peer support and competition (if appropriate)
Mature participants	Look at individual ability – remember a mature adult may have been attending circuit training for 20 years and therefore be more advanced than an inexperienced middle-aged adult. However, during initial planning with a new group consider the following: • 4–6 stations • Simple layout • Detailed circuit cards with additional formats available if necessary • Plan progressions/regressions and alternative exercises so everyone can participate
Children	• Variety of exercises • Range of circuit layouts changing half way through to increase engagement • Competition element (include a game) • Visual repetitions board (get children to add their repetitions on a station to a board) • Get children involved in demonstrating and instructing stations
Disabled participants	• Type of disability • Space depending on the disability • Equipment • Rest periods (may need to be longer depending on disability)
Ante- and postnatal participants	• Stage of pregnancy • Range of alternative exercises to meet the needs of individual participants (consider that participants are not likely to be at the same stage of pregnancy so different progressions/adaptions may be required for just one exercise – for example a participant who is 12 weeks pregnant may still feel comfortable lying on their back whereas a participant who is in the later stages of pregnancy should avoid this) • More frequent breaks

Discussion

Discuss in small groups what you may need to consider if you have a range of participants within your session, for example mature, antenatal and experienced participants.

Duration for each station exercise

Typically, a circuit-based exercise session will last 60 minutes with a warm-up lasting 10 minutes, the main session 40 minutes and the cool-down the final 10 minutes. There might be slight variations in these timings depending on the participants – for example, mature and inexperienced participants may need a longer warm-up and cool-down period to reduce the overall intensity of the session.

The duration of each station exercise can be manipulated depending on the participant group, but it is usually 60 seconds per station. For some exercises, particularly beginners, this may be too long. For example, asking a group of inexperienced participants to complete a plank for 60 seconds will be too challenging.

Recovery periods

Recovery between each station is usually minimal. In circuit-based exercise, the stations alternate muscle groups or area being worked, allowing for short recovery periods. Recovery periods are, however, dependent on the group's ability and the session objectives. A strength-based circuit may need to allow for a longer recovery period. For example, if a barbell squat was being followed by a barbell lunge, an extended rest period would be needed. If the weight being lifted is maximal, a 3–5 minute break may be required. Cardiovascular and muscular endurance-based circuit training usually requires minimum rests between the stations, but you should allow for a rest period after a full circuit has been completed.

Structure of a circuit training session

A circuit training session will usually consist of a warm-up and a main session followed by a cool-down.

Warm-up

Every exercise session should start with a warm-up. The function of a warm-up is to prepare the participants physically (the body) and psychologically (the mind). It helps to increase blood flow to the working muscles and reduce the amount of muscle and joint soreness that can be experienced post-exercise. It also increases focus in the session and allows participants to prepare mentally for the higher-intensity periods of the exercise session.

A warm-up should consist of the following components:

▶ A **pulse raiser** – low-intensity exercises that gradually increase in intensity as the warm-up progresses. The pulse raiser should aim to link to the main session. If the main session is focusing on the upper body, the pulse-raising activity should aim to raise the pulse by using the upper body.

▶ **Mobility** – moving a joint through its range of movement. Each joint that is going to be used during the session should have an appropriate mobility exercise, for example circling the arms or torso twists.

▶ **Active and passive stretches** – these are typically static stretches. **Active stretches** are where the participant places themselves into the stretch and has complete control. **Passive stretches** are where a form of resistance is applied to increase the stretch. Static stretching is not often used as part of a warm-up, but if the stretches are interspersed within the pulse raising and mobility exercises, it is acceptable to complete them. Avoid spending 5–10 minutes at the end of the pulse raiser and mobility exercises completing static stretching with the group as they will start to decrease in temperature and return to a resting state.

A warm-up will usually be a minimum of 10 minutes but no longer than 15 minutes. A pulse raiser could last 5 minutes followed by mobility exercises for 5 minutes with stretches, if necessary.

The type of warm-up used may vary depending on the session objective. If the session objective is muscular strength, the warm-up will focus on completing low-intensity versions of the exercises that are going to be completed during the session. This will serve to increase pulse and mobilise the joints through the full range that the subsequent movements are going to use. For example, participants could complete a set of lunges (no weight) that gradually work through the full range of movement.

Main component

The main component of a session will vary greatly depending on the session objectives and the participants within the session. For example, a typical cardiovascular/muscular endurance-based session could include two circuits. The first circuit would focus on cardiovascular exercises and the second on muscular endurance exercises. Each circuit would include 6–8 exercise stations lasting up to 60 seconds (6–8 minutes per circuit with a rest of 3–5 minutes depending on the participant group; fewer stations for inexperienced participants with a longer rest).

Both the cardiovascular circuit and the muscular endurance circuit would be completed twice (four circuits in total, two cardiovascular circuits back to back followed by the rest and then two muscular endurance circuits back to back).

The number of stations, the duration and the rest periods can all be manipulated depending on the neds of the participant group.

When planning a circuit for an experienced group, how many stations and circuits would you include and how long would the duration of each station be?

Hint

An experienced group will be able to complete more stations with a reduced rest time.

Extend

If the group of participants was inexperienced, how would you change the number of stations and the rest time?

Cool-down

The session should always end with a cool-down. The cool-down is intended to help the body return gradually to a pre-exercise state. Physiologically, the cardiovascular system can maintain an increased blood supply to the muscular system, helping to remove the build-up of waste products. The muscles can also act as a muscular pump to help return the blood in veins (venous return) back to the heart and then lungs.

A cool-down should consist of the following.

▶ **Pulse-lower activity** – starting with a relatively moderate- to high-intensity activity then slowly reducing in intensity, for example starting with knee lifts while on the move and jogging, then to on the spot, to walking knee lifts, to just walking on the move. It usually lasts between 5 and 10 minutes.

▶ **Stretches** – **static stretches** are mainly used in cool-down after the pulse-lowering activity. A whole body approach should be taken but if time is limited, have a particular focus on the areas that have been used during the session. A static stretch should be held for approximately 15 seconds in a cool-down, once for each area that has been used, ideally twice if time permits. **Developmental stretches** are also particularly good for improving flexibility. Developmental stretches start with a holding static stretch, but then at the end of the stretch the range of movement is increased a little further to develop the stretch for another 10 to 15 seconds.

▶ A cool-down will usually be a minimum of 10 minutes long, with 5 minutes dedicated to lowering the pulse and 5 minutes focused on stretching.

Adaptations to exercises

There are several ways that exercises can be adapted to suit the needs of different participants.

Reduction or increase in the length of the lever

A reduction in the length of the **lever** will decrease the intensity of the exercise, whereas an increase in the length of the lever typically makes the exercise more challenging. Having a greater surface of the legs in contact with the ball will reduce the length of the lever, reducing the load and making the exercise easier (Figure 14.2(a)), whereas reducing the surface area in contact with the core ball (as in Figure 14.2(b)) increases the load pushing through the fulcrum (the point where movement is occurring) and therefore the challenge is increased.

Key term

Lever – a simple mechanism that allows a force to be applied. In the human skeleton, bones are levers, providing a mechanism to allow heavier forces to be lifted.

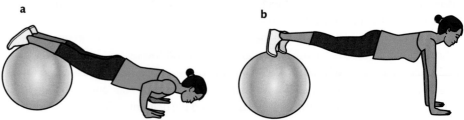

a
b

▶ **Figure 14.2:** (a) Reduced load due to shorter lever arm and (b) increased load due to longer lever arm

Reduce the demand of the exercise

Body positioning for exercises can reduce the demand placed on the body. For example, instead of completing a horizontal press-up, completing a press-up against a wall is significantly easier as the load that is needing to be moved is reduced (see Figures 14.2 to 14.4 for a range of press-up adaptations). Other adaptations to reduce the demand of the exercise include completing squats through a smaller range of movement, for example a half or quarter squat, completing a crunch instead of a full sit-up, and triceps dips with legs bent instead of straight.

▶ **Figure 14.3:** Wall press-up

▶ **Figure 14.4:** Box press-up

Increase the demand of the exercise

To challenge participants within the session, you need to have options to increase the demand of the exercise. See Figures 14.2 to 14.4 for a range of press-up adaptations.

Alternative exercises

Even with adaptations or reducing the length of the lever, some participants may need a completely alternative exercise. This may be due to injury, balance, self-confidence or ability level. The intensity of the exercise may need to be reduced so that they can still participate. For example, instead of jumping jacks they could complete a side lunge or alternate squats with a step tap.

Case study

An experienced participant who has been attending circuit training for several years has recently been told that she is in the early stages of developing osteoporosis (weakening of the bones) and has been advised to reduce the amount of high-impact activity she is doing. She does not want to stop attending circuit training so has approached you to see if you can adapt her exercises and provide alternatives where necessary.

Check your knowledge

- How would you get the participant to document the new diagnosis so you have a formal record of it?
- If you had planned for the session to include box jumps and spotty dogs, what alternative exercises could you provide for the participant?

Use of music

Group exercise sessions often need music to complete the experience and help motivate the participants. However, there are legal requirements associated with playing music in public. If the exercise/fitness centre you work in or where the sessions are delivered already holds a licence to play music, then you as an individual do not need one. However, if you wish to play music in other exercise sessions outside that centre, you will need a licence to do so.

There are two types of licence that the centre or you are likely to need if you are delivering exercise sessions (in the United Kingdom) where music is playing:

▶ a Phonographic Performance Limited (PPL) licence – PPL collects and distributes money on behalf of performers and record companies
▶ a Performing Rights Society (PRS) licence – PRS collects and distributes money on behalf of songwriters, composers and music publishers for the use of their musical compositions and lyrics.

Research

Research how you would obtain a PPL and PRS licence.

Choosing appropriate music

The type of music played during the session depends on several factors. It is important to understand the importance of the speed of the music. Music speed is measured in beats per minute (bpm) and is fixed for most songs, staying the same throughout the whole track. The beats per minute selected can help participants maintain the intensity of an exercise (a faster beat = faster intensity of exercise).

The beat selected is also likely to alter depending on the component of the session. A low–moderate workout could range from 85 to 125 bpm whereas a moderate to high workout may range from 125 to 170 bpm. An 85 bpm song may be played for the warm-up where the participant makes one movement per beat, whereas an 85 bpm song during a main session may require two movements per beat (therefore doubling the intensity). Other factors to consider when selecting music for a session are shown in Table 14.12.

Discussion

Discuss the genre (type of music) and the speed (bpm) of music that you might play to varying participant groups. Do you think it would be appropriate to play the same speed of music to a beginner group as well as an experienced group? How could you alter the genre of music to suit children compared to mature adults?

▶ **Table 14.12:** Choosing suitable music

Session component	Warm-up	Low increasing to moderate speed (85 bpm)
	Main session	Moderate to high speed (125–170 bpm)
	Cool-down	Returning to low intensity (85 bpm)
Component of fitness being trained	Cardiovascular circuit	High intensity = fast-paced music
	Muscular endurance circuit	Lower intensity = lower-paced music
	Core strength circuit	Specific pace based on completing a repetition in time to music, for example, in sit-ups one beat up, one beat down

 PAUSE POINT
What type of music would you choose if you were planning a high-intensity cardiovascular circuit?

Hint
The beats of the music selected should help the participants keep up with the speed of the exercise.

Extend
If the session being planned had a muscular endurance component, how would you alter the music choice?

D Undertake a group-based circuit training exercise session

Introduction to the group-based exercise session

Equipment should be set up before participants arrive, to allow time for it to be checked and to allow time for communication with participants at the start of the session (this is particularly important for a new group or new participants). However, in some cases it may be appropriate for participants to collect their own equipment (for example, collecting weights themselves, or other heavy equipment where you may need help to lift it).

Several health and safety checks should also be completed before the session, including:

▸ a risk assessment for the area and the activity that is going to take place
▸ visual checks of the area and surface
▸ a check of the sound system (including the headset microphone, if used) and any other equipment to be used.

If these checks raise any concerns, these need to be dealt with before the start of the session. If there are any doubts around the safety of the session, it should not go ahead.

The room being used should be appropriately ventilated. Exercise sessions taking place in a specialised fitness organisation are likely to have air conditioning and the temperature can be altered to meet the needs of the participants. Sessions taking place elsewhere may not, and therefore additional breaks and access to hydration points will be required if it becomes particularly warm during the session.

Drinking water should be available, for example from a water fountain, or participants should be encouraged to bring plenty to drink to maintain hydration. A first aid box also needs to be provided, as well as a phone to call emergency services, if necessary.

Greeting a group of participants

After setting up the equipment and carrying out health and safety checks, you are free to greet the group.

▸ **Introduction to the session** – welcome the group to the session and introduce yourself (for new members). Provide them with details on the objectives of the session.
▸ **Health and safety checks** – inform the group of where the toilet facilities and emergency exits are (this can be done individually for new members). New participants must complete health screening forms and you should ensure participants do not have any pre-existing injuries or illness that may have an impact on their ability to participate in the session. Remind participants that they should not be wearing jewellery that could get caught on equipment and that they should be wearing appropriate clothing and footwear.
▸ **Discreet initial screening checks and advice to individual participants** – when asking open-ended questions to the group about injuries and illnesses, some participants may not feel comfortable providing you with information in front of the group. It is important you gather this information discreetly. When new participants fill out health screening forms, ask them further questions if needed. Try to engage with each participant at the start of the session and ask them to let you know then or during the warm-up if they

think you need to be aware of a new injury/illness. This will give you the opportunity to provide advice before the main session.

Delivering the group-based exercise session

Each exercise the participants are completing during the circuit should be demonstrated. These demonstrations must be technically safe and correct, ideally showing progressions, regressions and adaptations.

If for any reason you are not able to show a technically correct demonstration (for example, if you are injured) it may be best to change that exercise or ask another instructor (if available) to support you during the session. Show the demonstration from different positions, usually from the front and side, ensuring you change your position so the whole group can see. In particularly large settings, you may need to be on a raised platform.

Clearly explain the main teaching points for each exercise, for example keeping ankles, hips and shoulders in line during a plank. Try not to overload participants with teaching points for each exercise – these are likely to be on the circuit card and you can move around the group to help individuals, if needed.

During lifting exercises, teach the group correct lifting techniques. Lifting with the legs and keeping the back straight is most important before moving into the position to complete the exercise (see Figure 14.5). Never lift a weight that is too heavy during a demonstration, as you want to demonstrate a good technique. Encourage participants to focus first on their technique before increasing the weight lifted: lifting a weight that is too heavy with poor technique can cause bone and joint problems or injury.

Throughout the session, do not forget to use good verbal and non-verbal communication (refer back to pages 126–7) and motivational techniques to encourage the group (see pages 136–7).

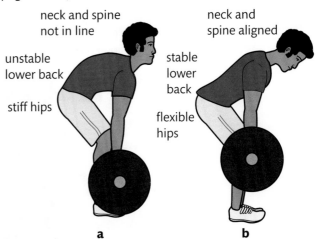

▸ **Figure 14.5:** Lifting technique

Adaptations and alternative exercises

During the initial demonstrations, try to provide adaptations and alternative exercises. However, for time reasons, it might not be possible to provide these on every station – remember you want to try and get participants active as soon as possible and there should be progressions/regressions on each station card.

Provide a demonstration that will meet the needs of most of the group first. After this you can gauge the ability of different group members, providing a more challenging alternative or further regression as you observe. Try to focus support on participants you know will need an adaptation. For example if a participant has injured their shoulder, you may need to change a station for them completely to a lower body exercise to avoid worsening their injury.

Correction of participants' technique

Participants will not always use the correct technique straight away. Inexperienced participants will need additional demonstrations and the teaching points reinforced frequently during the session. Keep eye contact with participants – for example, if they are lifting their heels off the floor during a squat, make eye contact with them and remind them to try and keep the weight through the heel of their foot.

Mirroring can help a participant who is finding a technique difficult. To do this, stand in the same position, in front of them and demonstrate the exercise again, getting the participant to copy what you are doing.

If a participant is still finding it difficult, you may need to help them into a position. Remember this should be within ethical guidelines, so ask participants if they mind you helping them into the position and letting them know where you will need to touch them. For example, this could be the back of the heels or inside the knees to help participants keep their knees over their ankles during a squat. Never move a participant's body position without their consent.

Appropriate teaching positions

For the majority of the session you will need to be in a position where all participants can see you and you can see them. Demonstrating different positions from different angles will also be required. If the group is particularly big, you may need to move around the group to demonstrate the technique. This will allow you to provide specific feedback and assist with an individual participant's technique.

In group-based circuit training, it is best for the instructor to be in the centre of the group (see photo). This does not work well for a lined circuit, but for square and circular circuits it will provide the participants with the best view of you and you will be able to observe and move around the group easily. In a lined circuit, being at the front of the lines and moving up and down the lines will be most appropriate. Ensure that demonstrations are shown from a front and side profile.

▶ Instructing position in the centre of a circular circuit

Ⅱ **PAUSE POINT**   What key points must you remember when you are demonstrating exercises to participants?

Hint   How are you going to ensure all participants can see your demonstration?

Extend   If you have a large group of participants, what additional considerations do you need to take into account?

Concluding and reviewing delivery

The conclusion of a session will be different for you and your participants.

▶ **For participants** – provide them with a summary after the cool-down, congratulating them for completing the session and identifying parts that were particularly challenging. Provide at-home advice, for example drinking water to rehydrate and eating a substantial meal within the next couple of hours. Following this, invite questions, and offer further help with an exercise or advice via additional support after the session.

▶ **For instructor** – once all participants have left, clear away any equipment, checking it is still in good condition. If you need assistance, you can ask participants to help you return any heavy equipment, making sure you all follow correct manual handling procedures. Make sure the area is left in a safe condition for the next user. Remove any rubbish and wipe down any equipment or mats to help maintain hygiene and preserve the equipment.

Methods of review

It is important to review how well the session went, including whether it met the participants' needs and the overall objectives of the session. This will help you to adapt future sessions if necessary. Methods of review include the following.

▶ **Verbal feedback** – encourage verbal feedback from participants at the end of the session, prompting them to approach you with comments or feedback to help you to continue to support their individual needs.

▶ **Questionnaires** – give short questionnaires to participants to fill in. Periodically asking participants to complete session review questionnaires can be useful for the continuing development of the session. Having questionnaires available gives participants a chance to give private written feedback if they do not want to provide the feedback in front of the group.

▶ **Self-evaluation** – it is important for you to reflect on the session and how well you think it went. Keeping a comment book/diary allows you to quickly record notes from the session to help plan the next. For example, you might record that a participant needs extra support or an exercise adaptation, or note that the intensity was too high or rest periods too long for experienced members of the group. Doing this will help support the participants' needs in future sessions and improve your reputation.

Evaluation of the exercise session

As a beginner instructor, a more formal approach to evaluating a session is required. This will help you to progress as a professional instructor. Evaluate what went well and what can be improved upon, looking for strengths and areas for improvement. Consider the following.

▶ Did all participants engage in the session?

▶ Did you have enough equipment?

▶ At any time was the session too easy or too hard for any participants?

▶ Did you ensure health and safety throughout the session?

▶ Were the participants motivated throughout the session?

▶ What modifications might be needed for future sessions? What needs to be changed or are more progressions and regressions needed? Does the layout need to be altered or the type of music changed?

REPs requires that you continue to develop professionally. This can be done by undertaking further training. Attending up-to-date courses ensures you are imparting the correct techniques and information to participants, and helps to build their confidence in your training.

Assessment practice 14.3 · C.P4 · C.M3 · CD.D3 · D.P5 · D.P6 · D.M4 · D.M5 · CD.D4

After an interview at the local leisure centre, you have been short listed to the final two candidates. The interview panel would like you to select, plan and undertake a group-based circuit training exercise session.

1 Plan a safe and effective exercise session for the group. Ensure you can explain to the panel why you have selected certain exercises for the different components of the session.

2 How are the different components of the session going to meet the needs of the group?

3 How are you going to manage time during the session?

After thorough planning, you will be expected to deliver your session.

4 Deliver your session to the group, demonstrating that you can communicate effectively. Use verbal and non-verbal communication, different types of cueing and a range of instructions to support the needs of the group.

Having completed your session, you need to review your own performance.

5 Analyse your own performance in planning, delivering and supporting a range of participants. Justify your choices of activity strengths and recommendations for future practice. Why are they strengths and why have you suggested the recommendations for future practice?

After you have completed the review, the panel would like you to evaluate the interrelationships between maintenance of customer relationships, participant support and the effectiveness of group-based circuit sessions.

6 How does maintaining customer relationships and participant support have an impact on the effectiveness of group-based circuit sessions and how does delivering, effective circuit sessions help to maintain customer relationships and participant support?

7 Consider potential positive and negative impacts of different approaches to planning and delivering and how they might have an impact on instructor–participant relationships.

8 You could give examples of successful and unsuccessful circuit-based outcomes for effective circuit sessions to support your evaluation.

Plan
- Do I understand the characteristics that the group possesses?
- Is there anything else I need to know before I can prepare the session?

Do
- I will attend different group exercise sessions to help me come up with exercise ideas for my session.
- I will produce a selection of different circuit cards to support the participants during the session.

Review
- I can recognise what went well during my session.
- I will evaluate whether the way I approached the task helped me achieve success during the activity.

Further reading and resources

Heyward, V. and Gibson, A. (2014) *Advanced Fitness Assessment and Exercise Prescription*, Illinois: Human Kinetics.

Lawrence, D. and Hope, R. (2015) *The Complete Guide to Circuit Training*, London: A & C Black.

Websites

http://www.exerciseregister.org – Information on the register of exercise professionals.

http://www.ppluk.com – Information on music licensing.

www.publichealth.nice.org.uk – Guidelines on physical activity and different populations.

THINK ▶FUTURE

William Finney

Exercise and circuit training instructor

I have been working as an exercise instructor for two years now. I am a member of REPs and I am currently completing an Exercise to Music qualification so that I can develop the range of classes I deliver. Continued professional development is important as a group exercise instructor. It ensures currency in practice and has given me new ideas I can use in my exercise and circuit training sessions.

At present, I run at least 20 exercise/circuit training sessions per week, mainly in the evenings and at weekends. Sessions at these times attract the greatest number of participants. It has taken me a long time to build up my reputation and now I have a regular client base. Each session takes a considerable amount of planning, not only the type of circuit, layout and the exercises but also the health and safety considerations and music choices including beats per minute. Planning can often take 30 minutes per session and I always arrive 15 minutes before each session, and it can take 15 minutes after each session to clear away equipment. This is an extra hour in addition to the actual delivery of the session. This totals approximately 40 hours per week.

As well as the time delivering the sessions, I maintain a website and often encourage the participants to join Facebook and Twitter groups. These groups provide a sense of belonging to the group, a space to share additional materials and a motivational tool to encourage participants.

Focusing your skills

Recruiting and maintaining a participant base

- Initially how might you recruit participants to sessions, for example advertising, word-of-mouth?

- What can you do to help maintain your participant base, for example organisation, appearance, using adaptations?

- Think about how you could gain feedback from participants to help you review your sessions and maintain your participant base.

Identifying hazards and reducing the level of risk in an exercise session

- Think about what hazards there might be during the session that were not apparent at the start, for example, space, slippery floor from sweat.

- When you are working on your own, setting up or clearing away from a session, how can you ensure your own health and safety, for example mobile phone, heavy weights?

- If an accident did occur during a session you were delivering or a participant became unwell, what would you do?

Getting ready for assessment

Harry is working towards a BTEC National in Sport. He was given an assignment with the title 'Effective relationships' for learning aim A. He had to research the different ways to maintain effective working relationships and consider the importance of these methods in developing a strong reputation as a group exercise instructor. The report had to:

▶ analyse the different methods an exercise instructor can use to present a positive self-image when working with participants

▶ evaluate the methods an exercise instructor can use to establish and maintain effective working relationships with participants.

How I got started

First, I wrote a list of all the methods an exercise instructor can use to present a positive self-image. Following this, I explained all the methods and why they are important in order to present a positive image. I produced a table that listed all the methods and then evaluated the benefits of the methods and the potential implications if the method was not followed on the development of a positive self-image.

To help me understand the importance of self-image, I attended a range of different exercise classes and spoke to the instructors about which methods they felt were the most important for presenting a positive self-image.

How I brought it all together

To start, I wrote a short introduction that outlined the purpose of the work that I was doing. After this, I explained the methods that can be used to present a positive self-image, following this with an analysis of the importance of the method. I then used the table I had produced in the planning stage as a guide to help me evaluate the methods and the potential benefits/ implications the methods might have on the ability to establish and maintain an effective working relationship with participants.

What I learned from the experience

There are many methods that can be employed to maintain effective relationships. Speaking to exercise instructors and attending exercise sessions helped me to evaluate the benefits and implications of not employing the methods effectively. Using tables in the planning stage helped me to evaluate the methods and prepare for the higher grading criteria.

It would have been useful for me to have a more specific structure in my assignment, for example, grouping together methods that can be used together to improve the participants' perceptions.

Think about it

▶ Have you planned your assignment so that you know you will be able to complete it by the submission deadline?

▶ Do you have the recommended resources as well as your class notes to help you to provide evidence and references to support and develop the arguments that you plan to make?

▶ Is your assignment written in your own words? Have you got a reference list that includes all the resources used to help produce the assignment?

Instructing Exercise to Music 15

Getting to know your unit

Exercising to music is a popular way for people to take part in physical activity, helping to raise participants' motivation levels and encouraging them back for repeat classes.

To choreograph an exercise to music (ETM) session, you need to take into account the participants' needs, and adapt sessions and activities to meet those needs. This unit will teach you how to successfully plan and instruct a safe and effective ETM session, including all the different elements required, such as the warm-up, cool-down and the 'aerobic curve'. It will teach you how to review your sessions and identify areas for improvement, as well as how to conduct the essential pre-session checks on participants.

How you will be assessed

This unit will be internally assessed through a series of tasks set by your tutor. Throughout this unit, you will find assessment activities that will help you work towards your assessment. Completing these activities will not mean that you have achieved a particular grade, but you will have carried out useful research or preparation that will be relevant when it comes to your final assignment.

In order to achieve the tasks in your assignment, it is important to check that you have met all of the Pass grading criteria. You can do this as you work your way through the assignment.

If you are hoping to gain a Merit or Distinction, you should also make sure that you present the information in your assignment in the style that is required by the relevant assessment criteria. For example, Merit criteria require you to analyse and assess, and Distinction criteria require you to evaluate.

The assignment set by your tutor will consist of a number of tasks designed to meet the criteria in the table. This is likely to consist of a written assignment but may also include activities such as:

▶ planning and delivering an ETM session

▶ evaluating your own performance in the planning and delivery of an ETM session to meet participant needs

▶ producing a written report justifying your own strengths and making recommendations for self-improvement.

Assessment criteria

This table shows what you must do in order to achieve a **Pass**, **Merit** or **Distinction** grade, and where you can find activities to help you.

Pass	Merit	Distinction

Learning aim **A** Explore the processes of participant assessment prior to exercise participation

Pass	Merit	Distinction
A.P1 Explain the results from client screening, describing their requirements for an ETM (ETM) session. **Assessment activity 15.1**	**A.M1** Analyse the results from the client screening in relation to their requirements for an ETM session. **Assessment activity 15.1**	**AB.D1** Plan an effective ETM session that includes adapted exercises to meet the needs of specific clients. **Assessment activity 15.1**
A.P2 Describe factors which can affect safe exercise participation for contrasting clients. **Assessment activity 15.1**		

Learning aim **B** Plan a group ETM session for participants

Pass	Merit	Distinction
B.P3 Plan a basic ETM session that outlines the exercises used for each component of an exercise session. **Assessment activity 15.1**	**B.M2** Plan a comprehensive ETM session that describes each exercise for each component of an exercise session for a targeted group. **Assessment activity 15.1**	

Learning aim **C** Undertake and review an ETM session

Pass	Merit	Distinction
C.P4 Demonstrate a safe and effective ETM session. **Assessment activity 15.2**	**C.M3** Demonstrate effective communication skills with participants when delivering a safe and effective ETM session. **Assessment activity 15.2**	**C.D2** Demonstrate the ability to respond effectively to the needs of different participants, and modify instruction and exercises to meet the needs of each participant. **Assessment activity 15.2**
C.P5 Demonstrate basic communication skills with participants when delivering a safe and effective ETM session. **Assessment activity 15.2**	**C.M4** Assess strengths of own performance in the delivery of an ETM session, to recommend self-improvement. **Assessment activity 15.2**	**C.D3** Evaluate own performance in the planning and delivery of an ETM session to meet client needs, justifying strengths and recommendations on self-improvement. **Assessment activity 15.2**
C.P6 Explain strengths and areas for improvement of own performance in the delivery of an ETM session. **Assessment activity 15.2**		

Getting started

Group ETM classes have been part of the health and fitness industry for many years and are still very popular. An instructor needs several key skills to plan and deliver a safe and effective ETM session for a range of different participants. Create a mind map of the different ways an instructor can adapt their session to meet the needs of the participants while ensuring it remains safe and effective. When you have completed this unit, revisit your mind map to see if you can add some more ways to adapt a session.

A Explore the processes of participant assessment prior to exercise participation

Link

This unit has particularly strong links with *Unit 2: Fitness Training and Programming for Health, Sport and Well-being,* *Unit 12: Self-employment in the Sports Industry* and *Unit 13: Instructing Gym-based Exercise.*

Link

Participant screening was covered in *Unit 2: Fitness Training and Programming for Health, Sport and Well-being.*

Discussion

What would you do if a participant gave an answer on a PAR-Q or during the screening process that raised concerns? Who can you refer a participant to if this happens?

After referring a participant whose answers during screening raised concerns, what would they need to do before they take part in exercise?

Part of being an ETM instructor is preparing participants for a safe session which meets their individual needs. It is important to screen participants to find out about their specific requirements and whether they have an injury, illness or condition which could affect their safety in the session. You must know how to screen participants and how to interpret the data you collect so that you can adapt your session appropriately.

Screening participants

Before they participate in any exercise session, it is essential that you assess the participants' current level of activity as well as their health and any medical conditions or injuries. Each participant should complete a screening session. These were covered in depth in *Unit 2: Fitness Training and Programming for Health, Sport and Well-being,* but can include:

▶ short, informal interviews
▶ pre-exercise questionnaires such as a PAR-Q and a lifestyle questionnaire
▶ observation.

If you are uncertain about any response given as part of a pre-exercise questionnaire or interview, then you should not allow the participant to complete an exercise session. Remember the health and safety of your participant is your primary concern.

Informed consent and confidentiality

Participants in ETM sessions must give permission before completing a screening method and give their 'informed consent'. Informed consent is the process for obtaining permission from a participant before they undergo the screening process. It can be given verbally (the participant agreeing verbally) or in writing (the participant signing a form).

By giving their informed consent, the participant agrees to give you personal information and for you to collect, store and use this information to design exercises that meet their specific needs. The screening also allows you to get a measure of the participant's fitness level and their suitability for taking part in regular exercise. If a participant has injuries, illnesses and/or medical conditions, then you must know this so that you can make an appropriate decision on the participant's suitability to exercise. By gaining informed consent with the participants agreeing to share this personal information with you, you can ensure their safety.

When collecting personal information, it is important to maintain the participant's confidentiality. Any information given to you by a participant should remain between you and them. They are trusting you to keep their information safe. There are laws, such as the Data Protection Act 1998, protecting people from the selling or using of their personal information. The information you collect cannot be shown to anyone else without the participant's consent and should be kept securely. For example, this could be in a locked filing cabinet if it is stored on paper or in a password-protected file if it is electronically.

Temporary deferral of exercise

The pre-exercise screening may indicate reasons for participants to temporarily defer or delay starting exercise:

▶ one or more concerning responses in the PAR-Q

▶ concerns over health that came to light during the screening processes

▶ **contraindications**, for example pregnancy or treatment for **chronic** health problems.

If this is the case, it is important to defer a participant from starting exercise in order to keep them safe from further injury or illness. Exercise can make existing injuries or illnesses worse and delay recovery. For example, having a muscle strain would be a reason to defer an exercise class – it would be better to first recover from a strain and then continue exercising. Temporary deferral would mean stopping a participant from exercising, but they can resume as soon as they are medically able. Usually, a participant who has been deferred would need to complete another PAR-Q and provide informed consent that they are medically able to take part in exercise.

> **Key terms**
>
> **Contraindication** – a physical or mental condition or factor that increases the risk involved in an activity.
>
> **Chronic** – a health problem that has lasted for more than three months.

❚❚ PAUSE POINT Can you explain the benefits to the participant of completing a screening process before starting regular exercise?

> Hint What is identified by screening participants before starting exercise?
>
> Extend What are the benefits for the instructor of carrying out participant screening?

Factors affecting safe exercise participation

Different participant groups have different considerations for safe participation in ETM sessions. It is important to know some of the main types of participant groups and the common considerations that need to be taken into account, so that sessions can be adapted for their safe participation. Table 15.1 shows the three main participant groups and considerations that should be borne in mind when planning a session, but other individual participants may also need similar adaptations depending on their individual circumstances.

▶ You may have to make adaptations to accommodate pregnant women in your session

▶ **Table 15.1:** The three main participant groups and their considerations

Participant group	Considerations
14–16 year olds	• Should not take part in heavy resistance-based exercises
Antenatal women (pregnant) or postnatal women (those who have recently had a baby)	• Should avoid high-impact and high-intensity exercises • May have issues with stretching • Limit abdominal exercise • Limit the time spent lying on the floor
Older people (50+)	• Should avoid high-impact exercises • May have issues with stretching

Safety tip

If ever you have any doubt about whether to allow a participant to take part in an exercise to music (ETM) session, it is better to refer them to a suitably qualified professional rather than take a risk.

PAUSE POINT — Describe the characteristics of the main participant groups.

Hint — Create a mind map for the key contraindications for each participant group.

Extend — For each contraindication in your mind map, add examples of how a session can be adapted.

Case study

You are working as a fitness instructor's assistant at a local leisure centre. A group of adults aged between 45 and 55 would like to start taking part in the centre's ETM sessions. The group is a mix of men and women. Most of them already take part in some type of exercise at the leisure centre. You have been asked to go through the participant screening questionnaires and to help plan the first ETM session.

Check your knowledge

1 What participant information do you need to collect for each individual?
2 What are the benefits of collecting information during participant screening?
3 Identify any contraindications this group of people may have.
4 How could you adapt an ETM session to meet the needs of this group?

B Plan a group ETM session for participants

Music selection

Music provides the timing for the exercise movements but also makes the class more fun for the participants. The choice of music is a central factor in shaping the type of class you produce, so you must be familiar with the concept of **beats per minute (bpm)** and the appropriate speed for each component of the ETM session.

You can read more about the different components of an ETM session on page 164, but the suggested beats per minute (bpm) for each component are:

▶ 120–135 bpm for the warm-up
▶ 125–150 bpm for the main part of the class
▶ 80–100 bpm for the cool-down and stretching.

The suggested bpm for each component of the ETM session helps the participants to reach an appropriate heart rate for the activity. As a rule, faster music should be used for higher-intensity sections and slower music for lower-intensity sections. For example, during the warm-up it is important for the body to adjust to exercising, so the heart rate needs to increase from its resting rate and the muscles need to begin working harder. Then, as the session enters the main component, the heart rate increases and the bpm also increases to encourage the participants to work harder and at a higher intensity. The bpm should then drop again for the cool-down to help return the heart rate to normal.

If the music is too fast, the participants risk injuring themselves and producing poor-quality movements. If the music is too slow, participants may not work at the right intensity and fail to increase their heart rate sufficiently.

Selecting appropriate music

When thinking about the music selection, as well as thinking about the bpm you also need to consider the group and how they will react to the choice of music. You must consider the lyrics (if there are any) and whether they are suitable for your group. Some types of music, such as pop and dance, work particularly well and allow the body movements to fit well to the tempo. You may find that rap and heavy metal are difficult to **choreograph** movements to and may be less popular choices with some members of your group.

You may want to use pre-mixed ETM compilations while your confidence grows and you become more confident in selecting music. Pre-mixed compilations can save you the time of preparing your own music, but they may not offer the range and type of music that you would want to use for your specific groups.

▶ High-tempo music should be used in the main part of the exercise session

---

 PAUSE POINT   Can you explain why it is important to select the right bpm for each component of your ETM session?

> Hint   What is the role of music in an ETM session?

> Extend   Make a list of songs or music you would use for the different components of an ETM session, explaining why you selected each one.

Legal requirements covering the use of music

You need a licence before you can play music in your sessions. It is illegal to play music in public without buying a licence as without one you have not obtained the permission of the music's **copyright** owners. Paying the licence fee means that the creator of the music gets paid for their music being used and you are given permission to play the music – if copyright fees were not paid then musicians would not be able to make a living from creating their music.

There are two organisations in the UK that issue licences:

▶ **Phonographic Performance Ltd** (often known as PPL) is a non-profit organisation that sells licences for public performance and broadcasting in the UK. It controls the copyright of **recorded music used in public performances**.
▶ **Performing Rights Society (PRS)** is an organisation that sells licences that allow the use of lyrics and composed music to be played in public or copied onto physical products such as CDs or DVDs.

PPL and PRS for Music are separate organisations and you may need a licence from both.

There are also a number of licensed music suppliers, such as FitMixPro, FitPro and Pure Energy, who produce music you can purchase and play in public without having to buy a PPL or PRS licence. These companies have already paid the copyright fee for you to use the music.

Choreography for a group ETM session

To be able to choreograph an ETM session you need to be familiar with the different movements you can use, how to link them together and how to change the intensity of the session. You need to be able to develop **phrases** that can be used in your session which follow the beats of the music. Most music is made up of phrases of 4 to 8 beats and your phrases need to follow this sequence.

Key terms

Choreograph – compose a sequence of steps and moves that flow together.

Copyright – the exclusive and assignable legal right, given to the originator for a fixed number of years, to print, publish, perform, film, or record literary, artistic or musical material..

Phrase – a sequence made up of four or eight beats of music.

Research

Why do you have to buy a licence to play music in public? Where can you get a music licence?

Are there different types of music licence? Are there exceptions to buying a music licence to play in public?

In aerobics, usually 1 beat in the music is equal to 1 step; an 8-beat phrase would be made up of 4 slow steps or 8 fast ones. You can make a 'sentence' or routine by combining 4 phrases or 32 beats together. Work to the phrases of the music, with your session being made up of phrases and each phrase following the beat of the music.

You could choose to 'freestyle' your session, which involves making it up as you go, but you would need to be very quick thinking and have a lot of different moves and phrases to apply quickly and correctly. Instead of doing this, it is best to plan your session in advance. You should think about the following principles when developing choreography for an exercise class to music.

▶ **Types of moves** – what movements will you use to build the phrases in your session? Some steps or moves can easily be built upon, so use them to provide a foundation on which you can build your routine, for example box step (see Figure 15.1), hamstring curl (see Figure 15.2) or grapevine (see Step by step feature below).

▶ **Combining and linking movements** – you can combine/add movements to make a longer phrase. You can link movements together by using marching, toe taps and step touches.

▶ **Changing direction** – this is an important method to make your session more interesting and challenging for the participants.

▶ **Intensity** – can be changed by:
  • changing and adapting the movements to increase or decrease the intensity of the phrase; for example, you could complete a movement twice at double time or complete the movement without using the whole body (for example, a star jump with arms at the side)
  • changing the length of the **lever** used in the movement; for example, a bicep curl when the arms are flexed is lower intensity than a chest fly where the arms are extended
  • changing the speed of the movements which will have an effect on posture and alignment as well as intensity.

▶ **Impact** – by using high- and low-impact exercises you can vary the session to suit all levels of ability in your group and make the movements appropriate for the specific component you are working on. For example, high impact could be lifting knees up as high as possible when performing marching and the low impact for this exercise would be keeping toes on the floor when marching.

You should also think of alternative exercises that you could use to make the class accessible and suitable for all participants. These can be used by specific groups or when participants are feeling fatigued and want to reduce their intensity. Examples would be wall press-ups for the older adult or low-impact exercises for antenatal participants.

> **Key term**
>
> **Lever** – a simple mechanism that allows a force to be applied. In the human skeleton, bones are levers, providing a mechanism to allow greater weights to be lifted.

> **Safety tip**
>
> Make sure you adapt the exercises for the ability of the group and allow time for movement patterns to be learned before moving on to a more complex sequence.

Step by step: Grapevine

1 Stand with feet shoulder width apart.

4 Step to the left with your right foot.

2 Right foot steps over left foot and you move to the left.

5 Put both feet together and hands together.

3 Step to the left with your left foot.

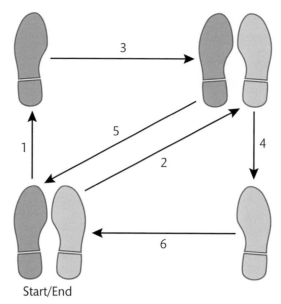

Start/End

▶ **Figure 15.1:** How to perform a boxstep

Cuing

Cuing is used by instructors to let the group know when the next move or phrase will begin. The instructor will use cues to make the group feel confident and part of a team. Cues are often verbal, for example by calling out 'stop', 'now run', 'let's take it up a level' or counting '1, 2, 3, 4'. Verbal cues need to be clear and to the point so that participants can understand them instantly.

Other cues are visual. These include using your hand or head to gesture, and moving forwards or backwards to indicate a change in direction. You can also use toe taps to indicate direction, intensity and timing of phrases.

▶ **Figure 15.2:** A hamstring curl

> **Theory into practice**
>
> When choreographing an ETM session, it is important to consider the types of movement and their intensity and impact so that the session flows and works well with your chosen music.
>
> - Select a song or piece of music you would use for a specific component of an ETM session.
> - Give examples of movement phrases you would use and how you would choreograph them to the music.
> - Identify specific parts of the music and link them to your chosen movement phrases.
>
> **Example**
>
> *One More Time* by Daft Punk (132 bpm) – an example of a 32-beat phrase
>
> | | |
> |---|---|
> | One more time a celebration | 8-beat phrase, e.g. 2 grapevines |
> | You know we're gonna do it right | 4-beat phrase, e.g. a boxstep |
> | Tonight, just feeling | 8-beat phrase, e.g. 4 leg curls and 4 knee raises |
> | Music's got me feeling the need | 4-beat phrase, e.g. a grapevine |
> | We're gonna celebrate | 4-beat phrase, e.g. a boxstep |
> | One more time | 4-beat phrase, e.g. 4 leg curls |

Developing coordination by building up movements gradually

As well as using phrases to gradually build up the intensity and impact of your sessions, you should also use layering techniques and holding patterns to develop coordination by building up movements gradually.

Layering techniques

Layering techniques are used to extend your choreography. Layering allows you to make changes to an existing move or phrase by altering the direction, rhythm, intensity, impact or lever length. You would only change one of these at a time so that the participants can pick up the phrase or movement before you alter it again. For example, a layering technique could extend a phrase by increasing the impact to make movements performed at a running pace instead of a walking pace.

Holding patterns

Holding patterns are short sequences or routines that your group can learn and be familiar with. These can be used when changing the pace of the session or if you have a mental block while delivering the session. The holding pattern should consist of an easy-to-pick-up set of moves or phrases such as a 32-beat, 4-phrase routine, for example 4 touches, 2 grapevines, 4 leg curls, 4 knee raises, 2 grapevines and 4 leg curls.

Theory into practice

When choreographing an ETM session, you need to include layering techniques and holding patterns. These will allow your participants to become familiar with your ETM style and will enable you to build upon your chorography.

- Create a holding pattern which is made up of a 32-beat phrase. This should be made up of basic, easy-to-follow movements.
- Next, add layering to your holding pattern by altering the direction of part of the 32-beat phrase.
- Continue to layer your 32-beat phrase by altering the rhythm, intensity and impact.

Assessment practice 15.1

A.P1 **A.P2** **B.P3** **A.M1** **B.M2** **AB.D1**

As a newly qualified fitness instructor, you are looking to start up an ETM class in your local village hall. You have advertised the classes and have had a good response, with ten people signing up. You need to collect screening information from the participants to adapt your session appropriately. Among the participants are:

- Mary, a 30-year-old pregnant woman with a track record of activity
- Ade, a 65-year-old man who recently retired from a sedentary office role and is looking for a new hobby
- Donna, a 40-year-old woman who has been advised by her GP to do more physical activity because she is overweight.

Once you have interpreted the data from the participant screening, you need to plan the ETM session. Make sure that you have adapted the session to suit your participants' needs.

1. Produce a report that explains the likely requirements for these three participants and describes the factors affecting each one's safety, including the types of exercises they should avoid.

2. Produce a plan for an ETM session that includes a range of different types of exercises adapted to meet the needs of these different participants. The adaptations need to give options that make the exercises easier to follow in terms of coordination, intensity and impact, as well as giving more difficult opportunities to challenge the participants' coordination. They also need to offer higher intensity and high-impact adaptions so that the exercise class can be differentiated to the needs of each participant.

Plan
- What is the task? What am I being asked to do?
- How confident do I feel in my own abilities to complete this task?
- Are there any areas I think I may struggle with?

Do
- I know what it is I'm doing and what I want to achieve.
- I can identify when I've gone wrong and adjust my thinking/approach to get myself back on course.

Review
- I can explain what the report was about and know what to look for in the results from participant screening questionnaires.
- I can explain how to plan a safe ETM session and how to adapt it to meet the needs of the participants.

C Undertake and review an ETM session

Objectives of an ETM session

Before your participants begin their first ETM session, it is important that you know and understand their aims, that is what they want to get from the class. They might want to improve their cardiovascular fitness, lose weight, increase their overall fitness and/or improve their well-being. It is important that you tailor the session to these objectives as well as the level of fitness and ability of the group.

Components of an ETM session

An ETM session is made up of four components. These components ensure that the session progresses and meets the demands of the participants. The four components of an ETM session are shown in Table 15.2.

▶ **Table 15.2:** Components of an ETM session

Component		Aims of the component	Examples of activities/ movements
Warm-up		• Improve mobility • Raise pulse	• Preparatory stretches (dynamic and static stretches) • Basic motor skills moves (e.g. walking, jogging, lunging)
Main component	Cardiovascular endurance	• **Aerobic curve**	• Walking, skipping, jogging, grapevine, knee raises, jumping jacks, lunges, box step, L step
	Muscular strength and endurance	• Exercises to work the core, upper body and lower body	• Sets and repetitions (reps) can be adjusted to focus on muscular strength or endurance – fewer reps with more resistance to target strength or more reps with less resistance to target endurance • Using body weight • Using hand weights, bands and stability balls to add resistance and increase challenge
Cool-down		• Improve flexibility (static and dynamic) • Help prevent blood pooling (when blood has not been returned to the heart and collects in veins)	• Stretches (dynamic, static, maintenance and developmental) • Basic motor skills moves (e.g. skipping, stepping, jogging)

Adapting for different participants

For each component shown in Table 15.2, you need to plan the length of time it will take up in your session. When deciding this, you need to change the length of each component according to the participants' levels of fitness. For example, a group with low levels of fitness will need to spend longer on the warm-up and cool-down, and may need lower-intensity cardiovascular activities during the main component.

You may also need to adapt the types of exercises you use for participants with differing levels of fitness, for example combining stretches for more experienced participants and static stretches for beginners.

Remember to use an appropriate bpm for each component of the class and make sure your music choice is suitable for all participants in the group.

▶ Lunges are often used in the main component of ETM

Case study

William has been working as an ETM instructor in his local leisure centre. He has to include the essential components of an ETM session to make sure that his sessions meet the needs, aims and objectives of the participants. The group of participants are men and women aged over 55. They are all new to regular exercise and have completed PAR-Qs and are fit to take part in the session. The session lasts for 45 minutes.

Check your knowledge

1 What are these participants' common aims for taking part in an ETM session?

2 What can William do to make sure that he meets the participants' aims?

3 Draw up a rough plan, showing how William could apply the components of an ETM session. You should include timings, intensity and examples of activities he could use.

Correcting participants and reinforcing correct techniques

ETM instructors need to instil confidence in their participants. You must be able to correct participants when they perform a movement or activity incorrectly and you must be able to reinforce the correct techniques. You can do this by using the following methods.

▶ **Changing teaching positions** – this will allow the group to see you perform movements in a different position. This will help them to copy your body and help them to perform the movements more accurately.

▶ **Encouraging questions** – reassure participants that it is okay for them to ask for help if they are unclear about something. Encourage an atmosphere of openness, where you, in turn, can ask participants questions about what they are doing and how it could be improved.

▶ **Using effective verbal communication** – you will find that sometimes you need to explain in detail what you are doing and how the participants can do it, such as describing how to carry out a box step. On other occasions, you might just shout a single command, e.g. 'forwards' or 'backwards', to indicate a change in direction. You can also use sounds to indicate a change in intensity or impact, e.g. a whistle or tongue click.

▶ **Using effective visual communication** – this can convey an instruction or information by using a visual aid, such as pointing to a limb or in a certain direction. It is a good way to make the group feel part of a team and to make sure that they are watching you and following your instructions.

▶ **Mirroring** – this is used by most ETM instructors and it is useful for participants to see what to do and then to copy it. It allows you to be part of the session and increases the confidence of the group. Sometimes when delivering a session, you might choose to turn away from the class, showing them your back. This lets them copy the exact movements you are doing. For example, for a grapevine to the left, both you and the group perform a grapevine to the left. This can leave the class feeling removed from you, but can be very useful when demonstrating more complex sequences. In contrast, mirroring is when you face the group and have to remember to reverse or mirror your movements. For example, if you say 'move to the left', you move to your right, and if you do a right-leg toe tap the group will do a left-leg toe tap.

▶ Mirroring involves facing the participants and adjusting your movements so that you all move in the same direction

PAUSE POINT

How can you communicate with a group of beginners in an ETM session?

Hint Create a list of the different ways you can communicate and give examples of how you would do this in an ETM session.

Extend For each method of communicating, explain how you would adapt this for a group who are very experienced and have attended several ETM sessions.

Preparation for an ETM session

Before the participants can take part in their ETM session, there are checks you must carry out. Properly preparing for an ETM session will help reduce risks, help make the group feel welcome, and allow them to enjoy and get the most from the experience. As an ETM instructor you want to make sure everyone feels safe, enjoys the session and comes back again!

Before the session you will need to:

▶ check all equipment that you plan to use is safe and in working order
▶ play a snippet of your music to make sure that you know how the music system works and that all speakers are playing the music clearly
▶ if using free weights, check that they are an appropriate weight and that they can be left somewhere safe but easily accessible when not in use.

It is very important that the area you use for the session is suitable for the class. It should be big enough for the group's needs and safe. If the area is too small there is an increased risk of participants bumping into each other and not carrying out the techniques correctly, increasing the risk of accidents and injuries. If the area is too large, participants may want to spread out too much, especially if they are new to the class and are worried about being too close to people they haven't met before. If the participants are too far away from you, they may not be able to hear you or see what you are doing. This can lead to participants using the wrong techniques, risking injury, feeling left out and not enjoying the session.

You may be asked to lead ETM sessions in a variety of different facilities and rooms. You must make sure that the area can be appropriately ventilated and the temperature changed so that the group remains comfortable. If participants are too hot, they are at risk of **hyperthermia** and if they are too cold they risk injuring themselves if they have not warmed up sufficiently. If the room is too hot or cold, participants may not want to join in.

If the room is not ventilated, participants are at risk from **hypoxia**; this can cause dizziness and fainting because there is insufficient oxygen in their body. There must be an adequate supply of fresh air in the area.

The type of flooring in the facility where you will deliver the session can also affect the exercises you select for your session and whether the area is suitable for a group to use. Table 15.3 shows the different types of flooring and their suitability for an ETM session.

▶ **Table 15.3:** Different types of flooring and suitability for an ETM session

Type of floor surface	Advantages	Disadvantages
Concrete	• Allows good grip between the participants' trainers and the floor • Stops **pronation** during exercise	• Does not absorb impact • Not recommended for medium- or high-impact activities
Concrete with carpet on top	• Allows some grip between the participants' trainers and the floor • Stops pronation during exercise	• Does not absorb impact • Not recommended for medium- or high-impact activities • Can be dangerous because participants think the flooring will be cushioned because of the carpet
Gym mats	• Allow very good grip between the participants' trainers and the floor • Allow impact to be absorbed	• Do not prevent pronation during exercise • Will become slippery when wet • The mats can slip on the floor
Sprung flooring	• Allows good grip between the participants' trainers and the floor • Stops pronation during exercise • Allows impact to be absorbed	• Will become slippery when wet

Research the different types of flooring in a leisure centre near to you. Which types of flooring are available and which activities are carried out on them? Evaluate the floor types' suitability as exercise surfaces.

Theory into practice

Before leading an ETM session, you must make sure that you have carried out a number of checks to prepare for the group and minimise risks.

- Briefly describe the room/area you will be using for the ETM session, e.g. a sports hall, aerobics studio.
- Make a list of the different pieces of equipment you plan to use in your session.
- Describe the checks you would carry out on each piece of equipment before leading the session.
- Identify any factors which you cannot control and who you would work with to make sure they are resolved.

When participants arrive at the beginning of the ETM session, you should carry out the following steps.

- ▶ **Welcome the participants** – you must put them at ease, make them feel confident in you as a leader and make them want to take part in the session.
- ▶ **Advise participants of the facilities' emergency procedures** – you must show the participants where the emergency exits are located in the room/facility and explain the emergency procedures.
- ▶ **Check participants' ability and medical conditions** – any queries from the screening process must be addressed. This is also the time to check if participants have sustained a new injury or are unwell. You should also assess their ability to take part in the session: are they dressed appropriately and fit to take part in the session?
- ▶ **Describe the ETM exercises and session plan** to the group – you should break down what you are going to do in the session. Explain the aims of the session, what participants can expect to do and what they will get out of the session. Say how long it will last, the warm-up, aerobic curve and cool-down.
- ▶ **Confirm or revise your plans** – this is your opportunity to adapt the session plan if needed. There might be more or fewer participants than you expected. There might be more advanced participants or a class full of beginners. When you see who is attending your session you can adapt it to suit their specific needs.
- ▶ **Demonstrate any specific movements** – depending on the ability of the group and their experience (beginners or advanced) you will need to explain and show them how to perform certain techniques. For example, a group of beginners will need to know/see how to carry out a grapevine, while a more experienced group will not.

Instruct a group ETM session

A good exercise instructor will be able to make the group feel confident and valued by instructing each component of the session clearly, providing technically correct and safe demonstrations and checking on the participants to ensure they are following the movements correctly.

Remember that every ETM session you instruct will include a warm-up, a main component (cardiovascular exercise or muscular strength/endurance) and a cool-down with stretching. Refer back to page 164 for more information about these components.

During the session, you will need to remember to do everything outlined in Table 15.4.

Safety tip

Participants must be appropriately dressed for an ETM session. Very loose and baggy clothing may become caught and tangled up on the wearer. Tight fitting clothes may rip, prevent the participant from performing certain movements and cause an injury. You must ensure that you are appropriately dressed and set a good example to the group.

What you should do	Why
Move around the class	Changing your position to observe the participants from different angles allows you to check they are performing the movements and techniques correctly, helping to ensure participants' safety.
Encourage participants to work at their own level of intensity	Participants should not feel pressured to keep up with anyone else as this can increase the risk of an injury or create an unenjoyable experience that might put them off from returning for a future class.
Use clear movements that are easy to follow	Remember to mirror or face away from the class as appropriate.
Be motivational	Give praise and encouragement to help make the session fun and enjoyable.
Give clear explanations of the exercises	Make sure that the participants can see and hear you to help avoid the risk of injury.
Communicate appropriately	Communicate appropriately with both the group as a whole and with individual participants – you want to make sure that everyone feels valued and part of the group.
Provide timely cuing	This will help the participants to follow the sequences and keep in time with the music. See page 162 for more about cuing.
Vary the **pace** and speed of the exercises	The pace and speed should be gradually increased during the warm-up. It can then be varied during the aerobic component of the session and reduced during the cool-down, You should also adapt the pace and speed if necessary. This helps ensure the participants are exercising safely and effectively. If exercises are performed too quickly or participants have to overstretch to complete the movement, they are at risk of injury.
Allocate appropriate timings for each component	A session with a disproportionately long warm-up or cool-down will not leave enough time for participants to reach their aerobic curve and they will not achieve their objectives for the session.

> **Key term**
>
> **Pace** – the length of strides or steps.

Throughout the ETM session, you must check and correct participant's positions where appropriate. As part of this, you must also remember the following.

▶ **Adapt exercises** with appropriate progression and regressions. If a participant is finding the movement or technique too easy, you can demonstrate how to extend and develop the technique. If they are finding it difficult to carry out, you could show them how to make the exercise easier and less demanding.

▶ Use **motivational verbal and non-verbal methods** to show participants how to correct their position. This could be done by you demonstrating the technique, providing an explanation verbally or by moving them into position.

▶ Demonstrate appropriate **leadership styles** for the group. There are times when command-style instruction is appropriate, such as when you are teaching a new technique and when you want the group to do the same movement or sequence. At other times in the session, it may be appropriate for the participants to do their own thing – this could be part of the warm-up or freestyling to a section of the movement sequences.

▶ Pay attention to **how the group are receiving and responding to instructions**. If you present all your exercises in the same way, the group will become bored, they will be able to predict what is happening and will not be interested in what you are doing. You must be able to react to how the group are responding to your instructions and adapt appropriately.

▶ If the group are mainly beginners, they will expect you to tell them what to do and when. A more experienced group may want you to give them some ownership of the session, they might want to lead their own cool-down or to be able to increase the pace or speed of activities when they want.

> **Safety tip**
>
> Check that the participants are following the sequences smoothly and discourage fast/jerky movements as these can cause injury.

PAUSE POINT   How can you provide technically correct and safe demonstrations for all participants in an ETM session?

> **Hint**   Produce a mind map to show the different ways you can provide technically correct and safe demonstrations.

> **Extend**   Explain what you would do to make demonstrations suitable for the different participants in your ETM session?

Ending a group ETM session

At the end of an ETM session, it is important to feed back to the group on how they have performed. This will also allow participants to feed back to you on how they think the session went – they can reflect on the positive parts of the session and ask questions. As an instructor, you want the participants to come back and take part in more sessions. The participants want to feel valued, that they have learned something new and that you can help them meet their exercise goals.

After the participants have left, you must follow the correct procedures for **checking and putting away any equipment** you used in the session. If anything is faulty or broken, you must ensure that you follow this up with the facility staff or make sure that it is replaced. It is your responsibility to make sure the area you used for your session is in an acceptable condition for future use. You must make sure that rubbish is removed, lost property is collected and any equipment moved to make room for the session is returned to its original position.

Reviewing your own performance

To become a better ETM instructor, you must review your own performance. When you first start out, you may make mistakes but as time goes on and you become more experienced, you will learn how to adapt activities with ease and make your sessions more interactive.

After each ETM session you instruct, you should engage in **reflective practice**, thinking about your performance as an instructor and examining how you can use your strengths to build on your weaknesses. You can do this in the following ways.

▶ Evaluate how well the exercises **met the participants' needs**. Did you adapt the session to meet the individual participants' needs? Were participants able to work at a level which was appropriate for their ability?

▶ Consider your **relationship with the participants**. How effective was your leadership style? Did the participants react positively to your commands? Were they motivated? Did they find the session challenging?

▶ Try to find ways to **improve your personal practice**. Consider your strengths and areas for improvement. What went really well during the session and what can you improve? Could your verbal communication be clearer or do you need to practise some of the sequences? Are there any techniques you would consider adding to the session to make it more accessible or more demanding? Were there any music tracks which the participants did not respond well to and are there any types of music you think they would prefer?

> **Link**
>
> Continuing professional development was covered in more depth in *Unit 3: Professional Development in the Sports Industry*.

> **Key term**
>
> **Reflective practice** – reflecting on an action in a process of continuous learning. Reflecting on what you are doing as part of the learning experience.

PAUSE POINT   How could you collect feedback from your ETM session?

> **Hint**   Make a list of the different ways you can collect feedback from an ETM session. Consider who the feedback is from when making your list.

> **Extend**   Explain how you would use feedback to improve your performance as an ETM instructor.

As an ETM instructor, as well as delivering a fun and engaging session, you also need to be able to evaluate your own performance. How well did you plan and deliver your session? How well did it meet the participants' needs and did they enjoy the session and find it met their individual aims?

You must be able to review your own performance to enable you to improve, become a better instructor, meet participants' needs and make sure that they come back to your sessions. If participants do not return, you will not be able to make a living as an ETM instructor!

1 Deliver an ETM session. Make sure that you demonstrate different methods to correct participants' techniques, cover the components of the session and instruct the group by communicating appropriately and using techniques correctly. You should adapt the session to meet all participants' needs and ensure that they remain safe at all times.

2 After delivering your ETM session, produce a written report which identifies your strengths and areas for improvement as an ETM instructor, giving recommendations on how you can meet the needs of the participants.

Plan
- What are the success criteria for this task?
- How will I approach the task?

Do
- What strategies am I employing? Are these right for the task? Are they working? If not, what do I need to do to change this?
- Can I set milestones and evaluate my progress and success at these intervals?

Review
- I can use my written report to identify areas in which I can improve my performance as an ETM instructor to meet the needs of the participants.
- I can deliver an ETM session and demonstrate a range of methods to correct participants' techniques.
- I can make suggestions on how I might make improvements to my communication skills when instructing the group.

Further reading and resources

Books

Champion, N. and Hurst, G. (2000) *The Aerobics Instructor's Handbook: What to Teach, and How to Teach It Effectively!*, London: A & C Black publishers.

Griffin, J. C. (2006) *Participant-centred Exercise Prescription*, Illinois: Human Kinetics.

Norton, K. and Old, T. (1999) *Pre-exercise Health Screening Guide*, Illinois: Human Kinetics.

Woolf-May, K. and Bird, S. (2006) *Exercise Prescription: The Physiological Foundations: A Guide for Health, Sport and Exercise Professionals*, London: Churchill Livingstone.

Journals

Journal of Human Sport and Exercise

Journal of Sports Sciences

Websites

www.bases.org.uk – British Association of Sport and Exercise Sciences: a sports science library

www.topendsports.com – Top End Sports: information about sports, science, fitness and nutrition

THINK ▶FUTURE

Chrissy Sargent

ETM instructor

I have been working in a Fitness Club in a town centre for five years and have recently qualified as an ETM instructor. I really enjoy working with different participants and the challenge of adapting my sessions to meet their individual needs. The ETM classes are very popular and people are always asking me for more! I am hoping in future to run specific ETM classes for the over 50s club, a local ladies rugby team and an antenatal group.

Choreographing the sessions is the best part of the job and I always try to change the music to keep up to date for the participants. They are very motivated by the music and don't notice the increase in intensity because they are enjoying the music so much. It helps the session fly by for some of the participants who don't like exercising as much.

It is important that I match the component of the session to the correct bpm. I don't want people falling over or injuring themselves because the beat is too quick for them.

Focusing your skills

Choreographing your session

To help create a good and effective session, it is important to match the bpm of the music to the component of the session.

- Remember that each component has a different suitable bpm, e.g. the warm-up should be at a lower bpm than the main section.
- Think about the implications of the bpm when choreographing your session.
- Always remember to think about the participants in the group and the type of music and lyrics you may want to avoid and why.

Instructing group ETM

You must be able to give technically correct and safe demonstrations and explanations throughout your ETM session.

- Always make sure that the participants receive technically correct demonstrations.
- Think about each participant's specific needs as well as the needs of the group. What will you need to consider to meet the needs of the individuals and the group?
- Think about how you can adapt exercises with appropriate progression and regressions in response to the participants' needs.
- Different leadership styles can be used with different groups and for different components of your ETM session. You need to be aware of these styles so that you can meet the participants' needs, but also keep the session motivational and fun.

Getting ready for assessment

Danni is working towards a BTEC National in Sport. She was given an assignment for learning aim C with the title: 'How to undertake and review an ETM session.' She had to write a report on her own performance as an ETM instructor and review her ability to respond to the different participants' needs. The report had to:

▶ include information on modifying instruction and exercises to meet the needs of the participants

▶ evaluate her own performance in planning and delivering an ETM session to meet the participants' needs

▶ justify recommendations for self-improvement.

Danni shares her experience below.

How I got started

First, I collected all my notes on this topic and put them into a folder. I decided to divide my work into two sections: undertaking an ETM session and reviewing my performance as an instructor. I felt it would be easier to separate the two parts of the task and to keep the notes for each section together. This also allowed me to check that my notes covered all the topics and that I had enough information to make sure that I achieved all the assessment criteria.

For a previous task, for learning aims A and B, I had to plan an ETM session. For this task, I had to deliver the session and then review my performance as an instructor. I referred back to the notes that I made when I drew up my plan and made sure I had clearly focused my session on meeting the participants' needs and had applied the components of an ETM session.

I also arranged to go to my local leisure centre to take part in an ETM session to see how a professional and experienced instructor leads a session to meet the participants' needs.

How I brought it all together

When I delivered the ETM session, I made sure that I built up the movements slowly, that I followed my aims for the session, that I used the appropriate techniques for correcting participants, and that I instructed the group using appropriate communication skills, both verbal and visual.

For the report, I produced an introduction to myself and the ETM session that I planned and delivered. I then had a section that explained my strengths and areas for improvement and another that evaluated my own performance as an ETM instructor and my ability to meet the participants' needs. Finally, I had a section that covered recommendations for how I could improve my future performance as an ETM instructor.

What I learned from the experience

I used phrases and movements I had observed when I visited the leisure centre in my ETM session, but some of them were quite complex and I wasn't as confident using them as I had thought I might be. Next time, I would only use phrases and movements that I really know and can do the techniques without error.

I also could have spent more time on practising the session so that I knew what was coming next and how the phrases worked with the music. I sometimes struggled to make the phrases and beats fit in time to the music. It's important to think about meeting participants' needs, but I think I focused too much on this when I delivered my session.

Think about it

▶ Have you written a plan with timings so you can complete your assignment by the submission date?

▶ Have you got your notes on the processes of participant assessment prior to exercise participation and how to plan a group ETM session already sorted, so you can refer to them easily?

▶ Is your report written in your own words and have you reflected on your own performance as an ETM instructor and your ability to meet the clients' needs?

Instructing Water-based Exercise 16

Getting to know your unit

Water-based exercise is a popular way for a wide range of people to participate in activity. There are many advantages to exercising in the water and as a result the number of participants taking part in these sessions has gradually increased. Understanding the tools and techniques required to maximise the benefits of water-based exercise is vital for any professional interested in delivering these sessions. The environment in which water-based exercise is delivered can be hazardous and so a solid grasp of how to keep participants safe is a key part of this unit.

How you will be assessed

A number of internally set tasks will be used during this unit to assess your knowledge. It is important that you complete all tasks thoroughly to ensure that you provide enough evidence to enable completion of the unit. When you are asked to demonstrate skills, you must ensure that you are able to show clearly that you possess the required skills and are able to use them appropriately.

It is vital that you ensure that you complete all the Pass level criteria within this unit – even if you intend to try for higher grades, Pass level tasks must be completed as well.

If you are aiming for Merit or Distinction level grades, ensure that you understand the requirements of the criteria and complete them to the level asked for. For example, Merit criteria might require you to analyse and Distinction criteria might require you to evaluate.

Your tutor will set you a variety of tasks within the assignments. They will be designed to cover all subject matter within the unit and enable you to both practise and provide evidence of the skills required within this unit. Tasks might take the form of:

▶ designing an informative poster that describes a swimming pool environment and how this might affect participants

▶ creating a session plan that clearly explains the exercises for each component of the session

▶ delivering a thorough and safe water-based exercise session, demonstrating the appropriate skills associated with this session.

Throughout this chapter, you will find useful assessment activities that will help you work towards your final assessments. Completing each of these won't necessarily mean that you achieve a final grade, but each of them will help you by carrying out relevant research or preparation that can be used towards your final assessments.

Assessment criteria

This table shows what you must do in order to achieve a **Pass**, **Merit** or **Distinction** grade, and where you can find activities to help you.

Pass	Merit	Distinction
Learning aim **A** Understand the principles of exercising in water		
A.P1 Explain the impact of water depth on exercise selection. Assessment activity 16.1	**A.M1** Analyse how the swimming pool environment affects different participants. Assessment activity 16.1	**A.D1** Evaluate the impact of the swimming pool environment on specific clients. Assessment activity 16.1
A.P2 Explain how the swimming pool environment affects participants. Assessment activity 16.1		
Learning aim **B** Develop a water-based exercise session for participants		**BC.D2** Demonstrate the ability to respond effectively to the needs of different participants and modify instruction and exercises to meet the needs of each client in a planned water-based exercise session. Assessment activities 16.2 and 16.3
B.P3 Plan a water-based exercise session that outlines the exercises for each component of an exercise session. Assessment activity 16.2	**B.M2** Plan a comprehensive water-based exercise session that explains each exercise for each component of a water-based exercise session. Assessment activity 16.2	
Learning aim **C** Undertake and review a water-based exercise session for participants		
C.P4 Deliver a safe water-based exercise session. Assessment activity 16.3	**C.M3** Demonstrate effective communication and motivational skills, taking into account different clients' needs when delivering a safe water-based exercise session. Assessment activity 16.3	**C.D3** Evaluate own performance of delivered water-based exercise session against planned session, justifying strengths and recommendations for self-improvement. Assessment activity 16.3
C.P5 Demonstrate basic communication skills with participants when delivering an effective water-based exercise session. Assessment activity 16.3	**C.M4** Analyse own performance in the planning and delivery of a water-based exercise session. Assessment activity 16.3	
C.P6 Review own performance in the delivery of a water-based exercise session. Assessment activity 16.3		

Getting started

Water-based exercise is a fantastic way for many people to take part in physical activity. Write down as many reasons as you can for its popularity.

Obviously, any activity that takes place in or around water needs to be managed effectively to ensure that participants are kept safe. What do you think a leader in charge of a water-based exercise session might need to take into consideration to keep their group out of harm's way?

A Understand the principles of exercising in water

Link

This unit links with *Unit 2: Fitness Training and Programming for Health, Sport and Well-being* and *Unit 14: Exercise and Circuit-based Physical Activity*.

The possibilities for exercising in water are more diverse than many people believe. Swimming remains the most popular participation sport in the UK. But developments in equipment and techniques have led to a variety of other water-based sessions becoming popular too. This has, in turn, helped make exercising in water more appealing and ensured that participation has remained strong.

Table 16.1 shows a range of ways in which individuals and groups can exercise in a swimming pool.

▶ **Table 16.1:** Types of water-based exercise

Type of exercise	Description
Standard swimming	Depending on the size and shape of the pool, the distance of standard swimming can be altered to suit a participant's goals (e.g. they may wish to swim lengths, widths or laps). Distance and timing of the session can be adapted to help train for endurance or short-distance power.
Adapted swimming	Using equipment to make swimming easier, harder or to isolate certain parts of the body allows participants to further develop to meet their goals.
Aqua aerobics	Aqua aerobics is done to music and coordinated by a leader. It can be adapted to meet the needs of the group and will normally involve a range of motions that target a wide range of muscle groups.
Aqua circuits	A combination of either adapted or standard swimming and exercises found within aerobics that creates an adaptable and varied exercise routine.
Water polo	Passing a ball between team members with the objective of getting it in a goal on the pool side. Can be done at all levels of competency. At a low level, it can be participated in with little training but is a fantastic source of exercise.
Paddleboard yoga	Using stand up paddleboards (which are tethered to stop them drifting) to teach yoga is a new activity that is gaining popularity. Taking part in yoga while balancing on a board further enhances the ability to target the core.
Octopush	Underwater hockey in which a puck is passed along the bottom of the pool and into a goal is physically demanding and excellent fitness. There are many local teams that can be joined and participants can take part with little or no training.
Synchronised swimming	Coordinated dance moves in water within various size groups involves core strength and cardiovascular fitness.

▶ Paddleboard yoga is increasing in popularity

Research

Can you locate venues that deliver any of the activities shown in Table 16.1? Which of them would you consider common and which are more difficult to locate? Aside from swimming, which activity do you think is the most popular? Discuss with the rest of the class why this might be, justifying your thoughts.

Case study

Stand-up paddleboard yoga is a new and up-and-coming activity. A large number of pools now offer it within their range of activities.

Lauren had been teaching yoga for eight years and when she heard of paddleboard yoga she was instantly sold on the idea. She claims it allows you to take all the moves from yoga, but brings further challenge to them by adding the additional element of being afloat. Balancing on a board is fantastic conditioning for the core, so when you combine this with yoga it is possible to get some amazing results.

Lauren has invested in eight boards which she uses across five swimming pools within her local area. She pays a set fee for using the pool and having a lifeguard present, but manages the bookings and administration herself. Since starting paddleboard yoga 18 months ago,

she has become busier and busier. She attributes this to it being an activity that is different from the norm and one that people seem to really enjoy.

Check your knowledge

1   Stand-up paddleboarding is usually done outside on open water. What are the advantages of bringing it into a pool environment?

2   Are there any other factors that you could suggest which could account for Lauren's paddleboard yoga sessions being so popular?

3   There is a key safety factor that must be considered when standing on a board in a pool that is not present in most other water-based exercise. What do you think this might be?

Water depth and the effect on participants

Swimming pools are not all the same: they vary in size, shape and, most importantly, depth. Depth is an important consideration to ensure that an appropriate challenge is provided for a group or individual while also keeping them safe.

Shallow water

Shallow water is excellent for those who lack water confidence, are weak swimmers or have limited manoeuvrability. This group can include:

▶   the elderly and the young (children)
▶   pregnant women
▶   injured people
▶   people with conditions that affect their mobility, such as amputees
▶   people who might be considered overweight.

Shallow water allows participants to touch the bottom if they want to, meaning there is a reduced need for them to remain buoyant. This means they can rest as required but also provides confidence that they will not get into trouble, encouraging them to push themselves harder.

For those who are less fit, the reduced gravitational pull provided by being in the water will allow them to make movements they might not be capable of on dry land. Having the bottom of the pool within easy reach means that it can be used to make changes of direction, helping to increase the speed of many movements.

Deep water

As the water becomes deeper, so too does the level of challenge for any movement performed. Deep water can be very dangerous if not treated with respect – even those who are confident and good swimmers can find themselves in difficulty if they become tired. Deep water is most suitable for those who:

▶ are strong swimmers or are water confident
▶ have good levels of fitness and/or good mobility and function.

The challenges provided by exercise within the water are magnified as soon as a participant goes out of their depth. Table 16.2 shows some considerations for when participants are in deep water.

▶ **Table 16.2:** Effects of exercising in deep water

Consideration	Description
Increased buoyancy	Not being able to touch the bottom means that the process of just staying afloat takes both coordination and fitness.
Slower movements and directional changes	Because a participant cannot kick or push off the bottom, all movements must be made without assistance. This again demands additional coordination and fitness.
Reduced levels of choreography	Choreographing movements and keeping time when participants are out of their depth is far harder as the speed at which people can manoeuvre can vary.
Increased resistance	Without the bottom being available, all movements are done against the full force of resistance from the water, meaning that additional energy is required for even basic changes in direction.
Travelling involves higher intensity	Without the bottom of the pool being nearby, travelling any distance involves further expenditure of energy and more coordination.
Reduced impact forces	The bottom of the pool being absent means that no exercises will involve impact with it and so potential impact upon a participant's body is also reduced.

Discussion

In a small group, consider the effect that the depth of the water can have on various categories of participants. What psychological considerations might you have to keep in mind when designing a session for a group?

PAUSE POINT   Think about the appropriateness of delivering a session in either shallow or deep water.

Hint   Consider potential participants and list three reasons you may choose to deliver a session in shallow water and three for deep water.

Extend   What would be the deciding factor if you had a group of mixed abilities?

The swimming pool environment

The swimming pool environment has a drastic effect on the potential performance of participants, as well as significant implications for their health and safety. Understanding these elements is vital for anyone involved in organising water-based exercise.

Water temperature

The recommended temperatures for different types of swimming pool, and the reasons for them, are shown in Table 16.3.

▶ **Table 16.3:** Recommended swimming pool temperatures

Type of pool	Temperature	Reason
Standard swimming pool	26–27°C	In a standard pool, much of the swimming will be of reasonable intensity, so the participants' body temperature will increase due to the activity. This pool is therefore cooler than others.
Leisure pool	29–30°C	The recommended temperature for a leisure pool is higher because much of the pool's use will be less intense and participants will therefore be less active, with their body temperature remaining lower.
Children's pool	31–33°C	In general, children feel the cold and are less well protected against getting cold than adults. Therefore a children's pool is warmer than a standard swimming pool or a leisure pool.

Thermoregulation

The recommended temperatures shown in Table 16.3 rely on several assumptions being made when selecting the appropriate temperature for a pool in relation to its use. In reality, preventing participants from getting cold is a far more complex procedure and subject to small variations in activity levels and the body's compensations as it attempts **thermoregulation**.

> **Key term**
>
> **Thermoregulation** – the body's attempts to maintain an internal temperature of 37°C by various methods, for example by pushing blood to the skin surface to lower body temperature and shivering to generate heat.

Mechanisms of heat loss

There are three ways in which heat can be lost, both by the pool itself and by the human body while in a swimming pool. These are shown in Table 16.4 and Figure 16.1.

▶ **Table 16.4:** Ways heat is lost

Method	Description
Conduction	Heat is transferred through a substance or from one substance to another. In a swimming pool, heat can be lost as it passes from the body into the surrounding water and from the water into the pool walls.
Convection	This happens in two ways: • **Heat is lost into the air above a pool** – as this air has heat transferred to it from the pool water and the exposed human body, it rises away from the surface only to be replaced by cooler air which in turn is heated by the water and body – and the cycle continues with heat continuously being lost from the body to the pool and then to the air. • **Water passing over the body draws off heat** – the body's movement through water causes water to flow past it – if this water is cooler, then heat will be transferred from the body to the water. Even a gentle current, such as water being pumped into the pool, will generate enough flow for convection to take place.
Evaporation	If the body becomes too hot, it begins to sweat. Sweat draws heat away from the body and as it is released, it evaporates away into the surrounding air.

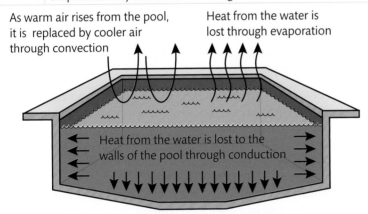

▶ **Figure 16.1:** Heat loss from a pool happens through a combination of conduction, convection and evaporation

Water is a good conductor and more efficient at heat transfer than air, so loss of body temperature can happen more quickly in water than when the body is surrounded by air.

People with higher levels of fatty tissue will find their body is better insulated from the water, so their heat will be lost more slowly. The body is warmest within its core and when threatened with cold it draws all available heat into itself and behind whatever barrier of fat that it might possess. This fat is a poor conductor and does not easily attract nor release heat. This prevents the water from drawing off the body's precious warmth. In simple terms, this means someone who is very lean and contains less body fat is likely to become cold much faster than someone who has large reserves of fat.

⏸ PAUSE POINT   Consider the three different ways that heat can be lost.

Hint   Different clients that might use a pool. Who would benefit from a warmer pool and who from a cooler pool?

Extend   Are there any specific activities that might require the pool to be heated differently?

Impact on session planning

As no two people will lose heat into a swimming pool at the same rate, it is important when conducting water-based exercise to be aware of who the participants are and how they might be affected by water temperature. For people who might become cold faster, it is important that the following considerations are made:

▶ a level of exercise is maintained that will ensure that their bodies generate enough heat to keep them warm

▶ rest periods are kept short so that body temperature is maintained

▶ total immersion time might need to be reduced to limit exposure to the water and its resulting heat loss.

Humidity and air temperature

The relative temperature of the air in a pool environment and its **humidity** are also important in maintaining a suitable water temperature. Cool air and cool surfaces draw heat to them. If the air surrounding a pool is cooler than the water temperature, then it will attract heat from the water, resulting in a loss of average temperature. The cooler the air and the larger the difference between it and the water temperature, the faster this process will take place.

▶ Although most heat is lost from the body to water, it is also important to consider the air temperature as a factor relating to participants' body temperature. Exposed parts of the body will lose heat into cool air above the surface. This will also happen to the warm water on the surface of the pool. As this heat is lost, the average pool temperature might lower, meaning that conduction of heat from a participant's body into the water is sped up.

It is recommended that the air in a pool environment is kept 1°C higher than the water temperature. Keeping it just higher than the water will mean that heat loss from the water to air is kept to a minimum and the pool temperature is maintained, reducing any need for additional heating.

There are two additional effects on participants of this optimum air temperature.

▶ They will feel less difference between pool and air temperature and so the process of getting in and out should be less of a shock.

▶ Participants with asthmatic tendencies will find that their symptoms are reduced because of the warmer air temperature.

Ⅱ PAUSE POINT Do you understand how the temperature of the water and the air around the pool can ensure a safe environment suitable for exercise?

Hint What are the reasons why it is recommended you keep pools at different temperatures?

Extend What type of person is most likely to be affected by the cold?

Size and shape of pool

Pools can vary a lot in both size and shape, although in competitive swimming a 'long course' pool is a regulation 50 metres long and a 'short course' pool is 25 metres long. When organising and managing a water-based exercise session, the size and shape of the pool will have considerable bearing on how the activity is conducted.

▶ Ensure that the pool is large enough to accommodate the group and any other potential water users.

▶ Avoid potential blind spots in the pool where you are prevented from seeing the whole group.

▶ Ensure that a location is found for you to conduct the session from where you are easily visible.

▶ Check whether there is potential to rope off or divide the pool to help manage the group and segregate it from other water users.

Pool side

The pool-side environment is where a large percentage of 'water-based' injuries actually happen, and you must do all you can to reduce the chances of these happening during any session you run. There are two considerations and factors that you should continually check for.

▶ Sharp edges from broken tiles can be very hazardous – this is especially true on the very edge of the pool where bodies might slide in or swimmers might grab the side for support or to rest. You should make a visual check before each session.

▶ Slippery surfaces around the pool should be prevented – wet flooring can become very slippery. Ensure that the side is either treated with a non-slip substance or covered with a non-slip mat to avoid accidents. Good coverage should be checked before each session.

Depth and level

As with size and shape, there is also a great deal of variation in pools' depth and water level. Most pools will have a variety of depths, gradually sloping from shallow to deep to ensure a challenge for all levels of participants.

However, there are exceptions and you must be very familiar with the depths in your pool to ensure safety and to use the pool to the best benefit of your participants. Other examples of pool depth profiles might be:

▶ shallow and without any **gradient**

▶ shallow with a gentle gradient that leads into a rapid change of depth and much deeper water

▶ movable floor resulting in an adjustable depth.

The actual water level compared to the edge of the pool is another factor that can have a significant effect on the safety of participants.

▶ A pool that has a water level close to the height of the walls will mean that increased water is lost over the edges and the sides are likely to be more slippery.

▶ A pool that has a level significantly below the edge will mean getting out of the pool becomes harder for participants – a ladder might be required and as such exit points will be limited.

> **Safety tip**
>
> Make sure you know the depth of the pool and understand how it might affect your group: a shallow pool may be dangerous to jump or dive into, but a deep pool could be dangerous for swimmers who lack confidence.

> **Key term**
>
> **Gradient** – the incline of a slope.

 **PAUSE POINT**   Close the book. Can you list the pros and cons for both a shallow pool and a deep pool?

> Hint   Consider who might use both.
> Extend   What gradient profile do most pools have?

Electrical equipment

The combination of water and electricity is inherently dangerous. Any electrical equipment used within a pool environment must be selected and managed carefully. The most likely piece of electrical equipment to be used at the pool-side is a music-playing device, to help you to deliver aerobic sessions. Some pools have music-playing equipment integrated into the design of the pool surroundings, but others do not. If so, the equipment should be kept completely away from the pool side and any risk of getting wet, or selected to be low voltage and waterproof. You should also be extremely careful when packing up after your session to avoid touching the equipment with wet hands.

> **Research**
>
> A stereo is a vital piece of equipment for many water-based exercise leaders. Can you identify any brands and designs that would be suitable to use? What makes the device suitable for this purpose?

Storage

At the pool side, there is already potential for slips without any additional obstructions being introduced. Any equipment that might be used in delivery of a water-based activity should be stored so that it is clear of walkways and people who might stumble on it. It should preferably be kept in a lockable cupboard, away from the pool side, and stored so that it can dry before the next session.

First aid

On the pool side, a first aid kit with relevant supplies should be both clearly marked and easily accessible. This first aid kit should be regularly checked and kept full of the required supplies. There should also be a way to call for assistance if needed. This could be a walky-talky for direct communication, an alarm or a phone for calling medical support, such as paramedics.

Qualified personnel

Delivering exercise in a water-based environment has the added complication of keeping individuals safe from drowning. Professionals delivering a session are likely to need training both to deliver exercise sessions and to provide lifeguarding assistance if needed. Alternatively, there could be an exercise specialist present as well as a separate lifeguard.

Assessment practice 16.1   A.P1   A.P2   A.M1   A.D1

You work for a local sports complex that includes a large indoor swimming pool. The pool is very busy with a wide range of exercise classes on offer. Your line manager has asked you to design a training package for all new water-based exercise instructors.

Create a leaflet that will help them consider the pool environment. Ensure the leaflet explains the impact of both water depth and other pool environmental factors that affect participants and water-based exercise. It should go on to evaluate the impact of different swimming pool environments on:

- an 81-year-old man who is typical body weight for somebody of his age
- a pregnant 30-year-old woman
- a toddler.

Plan
- Do I understand the task?
- Do I have any gaps in my knowledge that mean I might need to do further research?

Do
- I know what I need to do and how I am going to go about it in a clear and detailed manner.
- I can adjust my leaflet while producing it if I feel something is not working to ensure my final piece is of a high standard.

Review
- I can explain what this assignment was and what I have learned from it.
- If I were to do this task again, I can explain what I might do differently to make improvements.

B   Develop a water-based exercise session for participants

Designing a water-based exercise session is something that takes practice and thought. Not only does a session need to meet the requirements of the participants but it is also done in an environment that is potentially highly hazardous.

Pre-session checks for ensuring that safety is maintained should be conducted and managed by the team responsible for overall management of the pool, but this should not stop you from doing your own checks too. The pool management team is likely to have an operating procedure that covers:

- the process for raising an alarm and procedures for evacuation
- first aid locations
- child protection policies
- ratios of pool-side staff to pool users.

There will also be a risk assessment that clearly defines hazards and the actions that might be put in place to minimise risk or eradicate it completely.

Theory into practice

Swimming pools can be very hazardous environments unless proper guidelines are met and suitable rules are adhered to. A risk assessment for a swimming pool is shown in Figure 16.2.

- Complete the risk assessment in Figure 16.2, suggesting precautions to be taken to reduce the risks.
- Can you identify any further risks that should be incorporated into a risk assessment?
- What do you feel is likely to be the largest cause of accidents in a pool environment?

RISK ASSESSMENT SHEET

Hazard	Immediate risk	Precautions to be taken	Ultimate risk
Slippery pool side	Medium risk	Maintain non-slip matting. Ensure participants are briefed not to run and to watch their footing.	Low risk
Shallow water	High risk	Brief all participants not to jump or dive into shallow end. Ensure warning signs are clearly visible.	Low risk
Collisions with other pool users	Low risk	Use swim lanes to regulate the flow of swimmers.	Low risk
Entanglement in ropes for buoyed areas	Low risk		
Participants getting cold	Medium risk		
Water becoming dirty and hazardous to health	Medium risk		
Difficulties due to historic medical conditions	Medium risk		

▶ **Figure 16.2:** A risk assessment for a swimming pool

Equipment

The range of equipment available to use when delivering water-based exercise is diverse and continually expanding. Equipment can be roughly split into two categories:

▶ equipment to increase buoyancy
▶ equipment to increase intensity.

Examples of these two types of equipment are shown in Table 16.5.

▶ **Table 16.5:** Equipment used in water-based exercise

To increase buoyancy	
Buoyancy or float belts	Fit round a participant's waist and back, helping them float in a variety of positions.
Woggle (noodle)	A long buoyant cylinder usually made of foam. They are versatile and can be bent to provide a variety of buoyancy options.
Kickboards	A compressed foam board that can be held in the hands or gripped between the legs for a variety of outcomes.
Jog belts	Fit round a participant's waist and encourage them to adopt a position in the water where their head and shoulders are upright and clear.
Stand-up paddleboard	A large surfboard that might be inflatable or solid that can be used to paddle around or – more likely in a swimming pool environment – be used to practise yoga.
To increase intensity	
Aqua dumbbells	Dumbbells designed to get wet without deteriorating or damaging the pool sides or bottom.
Weight cuffs	Weights that can be attached to wrists or ankles to increase resistance and reduce buoyancy.
Webbed gloves	Gloves that can be used to increase the surface area of a person's hand and therefore generate more power per stroke.
Sinking objects	Any object that readily sinks and can be used to chase or pick up from the pool bottom.

▶ Woggles or noodles can be used to increase buoyancy

PAUSE POINT Without looking at this book, quickly write down six items of equipment that might be used to help deliver water-based exercise.

Hint   Think about items that are both held and worn.

Extend   If you had to choose just one item as being most useful and versatile, what would you pick and why?

Water-based exercise routines

Any water-based exercise routine should be planned in advance but may need to be adjusted to meet the needs of individuals and the group as you go along. A routine or training session should be appropriately challenging without taking a participant to the point of exhaustion. Remember, the session is based in water so over-exerting participants may be hazardous.

As you get more experienced at delivering water-based sessions, you will learn more movements to teach, develop better group control and be able to tailor sessions to accurately meet a group's or an individual's needs. But no matter how experienced you become, you should still use the following questions in your planning of the session:

▶ What is the desired outcome from this session?
▶ How can I ensure that my session is delivered to the best of my ability and meets the desired outcome?
▶ How will I keep my team and the participants safe?

Planning and choreographing

When planning a session, the whole group must be considered to ensure the session meets their exercise needs without over-exerting them. The following need to be considered for all participants.

▶ **Ability** – experienced participants need less guidance and direct instruction. It may be that a group has a variety of abilities. If so, you might consider splitting the participants into smaller groups or finding another way in which participants can be grouped to ensure that everyone is challenged.

▸ **Fitness** – fitter participants can be pushed harder. A wider range of motions can be used. Your choice about where to position yourself within the pool to deliver appropriate challenge could be affected.

▸ **Age** – age will have both physical and psychological effects on participants. Younger participants will have less strength and speed; they may have less focus and may not be able to maintain attention for as long as more mature participants. Older participants are more likely to have an injury history and less stamina.

▸ **Gender** – as males and females get older, their different physical strengths become more noticeable. While younger groups can easily be taught in mixed-gender classes, it might be appropriate for older groups to split the genders into separate groups. As an instructor, you will have to judge on a group-by-group basis whether it is best to teach the group together or separately, although your teaching environment may also have guidelines based on age.

▸ **Cultural issues** – cultures are diverse and different customs must be respected. Without compromising safety, adjustments can be made to accommodate cultural differences such as dress and beliefs. For example, Muslim women may choose to wear full-cover swimwear.

▸ **Medical issues** – some medical conditions such as asthma and diabetes are relatively common, others less so. Medical forms should be used before a session so you know any relevant medical details. This will then allow you to make adaptations to protect participants from harm, such as ensuring they have their inhaler to hand or avoid placing strain on damaged limbs.

▸ **Disabilities** – for many people with a disability, integration into mainstream activity is possible and welcomed. For example, someone with a visual impairment could take part in aqua aerobics by listening to the instructions, rather than by following visual cues. But it may be that dedicated sessions are more appropriate. For example, for an activity for paraplegics you might need a higher ratio of staff to participant to ensure safety.

▸ **Size of group** – the number of participants may mean that additional staff and resources are required. Larger groups are challenging, and maintaining supervision and a safe environment can be difficult for even the best of water-based exercise leaders.

(❚❚) **PAUSE POINT**	Shut the book. Can you remember different considerations that should be made when thinking about the group?
Hint	There are eight main ones relating to individuals in a group. How many can you remember?
Extend	Are there any that you feel may be more important than others to ensure the group stays safe.

Environmental considerations should also be borne in mind. This will include assessing the size, shape and depth of the pool. It could be that the pool has additional equipment that might be available for use, such as woggles or float belts, which might enhance the session.

When planning or choreographing a session, the basic guidelines shown in Table 16.6 should be used.

▸ **Table 16.6:** Guidelines when planning a water-based exercise session

Tip	Reason
Keep things simple	Do not over-complicate a session; instead focus on keeping it flowing and consistent.
Include a warm-up	As in any exercise, allow time for participants to warm up and their bodies to prepare for more vigorous exercise – see pages 187–8 for more information about the components to include in a water-based exercise.
Vary the intensity	Allow for rests by slowing down the routine or session in an appropriate way for the group.

Tip	Reason
Choose movements that can be replicated on dry land	This will allow you to demonstrate where necessary from the pool side and be able to explain them more easily.
Choose the right music	If using music, ensure that the routine is in time to the music and consider the rhythm – see page 187 for more about using music in water-based exercise.

Discussion

Individually, choose three basic exercises that you might consider to be the most widely used and useful when teaching water-based exercise. Compare your thoughts with the rest of your group. What makes a valuable movement when instructing water-based exercise?

Development of the routine

As participants and groups become more experienced in water-based exercise, they are likely to want greater challenge so that they continue to progress. The following examples are some ways in which you can develop a class to provide additional challenge.

1 Add exercises that further challenge coordination, such as balancing on one foot while performing another action.
2 Lengthen sequences of movements, shortening rest times and making the routine more complex.
3 Increase the intensity and/or the number of repetitions of any given exercise.
4 Increase the range of movement found within an exercise, adding further resistance and a greater need for flexibility.
5 Increase directional changes, increasing the complexity of the routine and potentially further challenging coordination and increasing resistance.

Adapting and differentiating

Almost all water-based exercises can be adapted to either increase or decrease resistance and intensity. For many people, their attraction to water-based exercise stems from its ability to provide a range of resistance training without creating high levels of impact on their body. Intensity and resistance can be increased by:

▶ lengthening levers, for example performing an exercise with arms outstretched rather than held in tight by the body
▶ making movements faster
▶ transitioning movements from being performed above the water, with no resistance, to on the surface with a little resistance, to under the water with more resistance
▶ moving from shallow water to deep water
▶ increasing the distance travelled in a movement
▶ removing buoyancy assistance
▶ introducing weights.

Table 16.7 shows basic movements that can be incorporated into a water-based exercise routine and ways that the difficulty might be adapted.

▶ **Table 16.7:** Exercises for use in a water-based exercise routine

Exercise	Method	Adding further challenge
Shallow water squat	Drop the body to a seated position, keeping the back upright.	Keep one foot raised and out in front, turning the exercise into a pistol squat.
Tip toes	Stand as tall as possible with arms above the head, reaching for the sky.	Hold for extended periods to test balance or perform on one leg.
Body twist	Rotate at the core, looking over one shoulder and then the other.	Hold arms out in front to increase resistance.
Stationary swimming	Hold the edge of the pool and then use the legs to kick.	Increase intensity of the kicking.
Stationary jump	Squat and then jump as high as possible, extending the body as you do so.	On each jump perform a star shape with your body. Move into deeper water.
Arm circles	Hold arms out horizontally to the side and move hands in circles, either forwards or backwards.	Make circles larger and faster for increased resistance.
Treading water	Possibly using a float belt for buoyancy, hold the position by using hands and feet to keep afloat in one spot.	Remove the float belt. Ask advanced participants, to hold their hands above their heads.

▶ Stationary swimming is a simple exercise to use in water-based sessions

Choosing appropriate music

For many routines, music can be used to enhance delivery, helping participants' coordinating, timing and motivation. Exercises are timed by the number of beats per minute (bpm) within the music. When selecting music, the bpm should be considered to ensure it is correct for:

▶ the ability and range of participants in the group (considering their age)
▶ the range of exercises most appropriate for achieving the desired outcomes from the session (whether they will be performed quickly or slowly)
▶ the depth within the pool where the exercise will be performed, and consequently the speed at which movements might be performed
▶ the component part of the class – a range of music might be required to increase intensity from warm-up through to the core routine and then slow back down into a cool-down.

Ⅱ PAUSE POINT   Before you design a session, you must understand who you are delivering it to. Create a spider diagram to show six considerations you should be aware of when looking at a group.

> Hint   Think about both personal characteristics and how the participants might respond when in the water.

> Extend   Explain how each consideration may affect your session planning.

Components

A water-based exercise routine can be split into component parts, each with a required outcome. From a delivery perspective, it might not be obvious to the class when they transition from one part to another: a good session will flow and movements and exercises will feed into one another.

▶ **Warm-up** – as in any exercise, this should raise the pulse, stretch out the body through a variety of dynamic and static movements, and allow time to practise any complex movements required in the class.
▶ **Main component** – the core part of the session could either focus on cardiovascular or muscular performance, develop a skill or technique, or incorporate a variety of elements. It should provide a challenge for the group without over-exerting them. Allowing for differentiation within the exercises will mean that provision can be made for individuals, with routines adapted so everyone feels happy with the session.
▶ **Cool-down** – after intense exercise the body should be brought back down to rest slowly. Intensity should be reduced and stretches performed on muscles to prevent them tightening up; the latter could lead to restricted movement.

Adapting length

The actual length of the component parts of any exercise routine will vary depending on the individual or group. Those who are less fit might need longer to warm up and cool down and, for them, higher-intensity exercise may be less appropriate, leading to a shortened main component. Those who are very fit may have a short warm-up and cool-down but very intense main components.

Assessment practice 16.2 — B.P3 B.M2 BC.D2

You are starting a new job at a local leisure centre, contributing to their award-winning water-based exercise programme. You are going to be delivering your first session to a small group of expectant mums. You have met them before: they are a friendly bunch who all know one another, are all reasonably fit but obviously have some manoeuvrability problems.

Plan a comprehensive water-based exercise session that lasts 45 minutes and includes all the components. Explain each exercise within the components individually, including why you have chosen it. Explain any choices that you would make in the use of equipment and where in the pool you would choose to deliver each exercise from.

Plan
- Am I familiar with the challenges faced when providing water-based exercise to pregnant women?
- Can I structure my plan and present the information required?

Do
- I have taken the opportunity to gather experience by shadowing other leaders and have plenty of ideas for how to complete this task.
- I can suggest the use of specific equipment that might enhance my session.

Review
- I can justify why I approached the task as I did.
- I can suggest ways I might improve my plan if I were to rewrite it.

C Undertake and review a water-based exercise session for participants

As with leading any session in sport and exercise, practice makes perfect. Even the most experienced water-based exercise leaders should not be complacent and should be continually reviewing their performance and improving their delivery. A strong water-based exercise leader will have a variety of skills and qualities to provide a session that is challenging, fun and motivational. These skills and qualities are likely to include:

▶ excellent verbal and physical communication skills
▶ patience, professionalism and approachability
▶ personal motivation
▶ strong background knowledge
▶ good organisation and safety awareness.

Pre-session preparation

Before any session, make sure that you are properly prepared. This will give you the confidence to deliver your session knowing that everything is in hand. You can then project this confidence onto your group, building their confidence in you. Before any session, carry out the following checks.

▶ Inspect equipment to make sure that it is both appropriate for the session and well maintained. Prepare sufficient equipment for the number of participants in the group.
▶ Check that the delivery area is free from obstructions and other water users and appropriate for the session.
▶ Check that the environment is at the correct temperature and the water is appropriately cleaned.

PAUSE POINT Do you understand how to deliver an exercise session and keep clients safe in a potentially hazardous environment?

> Hint List eight skills and qualities that a water-based leader should possess.

> Extend Which of these skills and qualities are your top three and why?

Participant preparation

Preparing participants for the water-based exercise session begins well before they actually start. Many water-based exercise sessions are run as part of an extended series, and you will often build a strong relationship with the participants and aim to build trust through an in-depth knowledge of the individual.

The main steps for preparing participants for the session are shown in Figure 16.3.

> **Welcome**
> Greet the participants, set them at ease and ensure they are introduced to other members of the group.

> **Safety**
> Point out any hazards and introduce emergency procedures such as evacuation in the event of a fire.

> **Checks**
> Ensure that you have checked individuals' abilities and highlighted medical conditions where appropriate.

> **Session brief**
> Explain the session plan and the desired outcomes. Give the participants the opportunity for feedback.

> **Adapt plans**
> If potential problems are highlighted in the feedback, ensure that you can adapt the session to meet everyone's requirements.

> **Demonstrate**
> Ensure everyone is familiar with the movements required within the session, using demonstrations as required. It may be useful to get participants to practise some moves on the pool side.

▸ **Figure 16.3:** Steps to prepare participants for a water-based session

Delivering an effective demonstration

To give an effective demonstration, you should remember the following.

▸ A demonstration is visual, so keep your commentary to a minimum to allow participants to focus on what you are showing them.

▸ Many exercises can be demonstrated from the pool side but you may need to enter the water for more complex movements.

▸ Avoid distractions by positioning the demonstration appropriately – consider what is going on in the background and move the group around so they are able to focus on the task in hand rather than something in the distance.

▸ Where possible, demonstrate slowly and smoothly. If the subject matter is something that can be broken down into bite-sized chunks, then clearly identify each chunk so the group understands its significance.

▶ You can use another person to do the demonstrations, providing commentary yourself.

Case study

Aqua aerobics

Sean is new to teaching aqua aerobics but has lots of ideas and is very keen on developing his skills. He works for a small hotel that has its own swimming pool and delivers his aqua aerobics sessions at 8.30 a.m. Thursday to Sunday. His classes are mainly attended by women but the age range can be varied.

In general, the class is good fun. Some clients for his lessons are local people who pay the hotel a membership fee to use the facilities, but most are hotel residents and as such only attend one or two sessions before leaving.

Sean tries to inject lots of energy into every session that he runs. He wants to ensure that everyone he teaches leaves having enjoyed the experience, and he takes real pride in his classes.

Every morning, Sean arrives early to ensure his session

is well planned for and that any equipment is ready for use. He can access his clients' details from the hotel's central booking system.

Despite his best efforts, Sean finds it a real challenge to plan for his sessions.

Check your knowledge

1 What challenges do you think Sean might face when planning for a water-based exercise session in the hotel pool?

2 Sean's pre-session brief is often longer than he would like. Why do you think this could be?

3 What strategies could Sean use to ensure that his sessions challenge all his clients?

4 Is there anything that the hotel could do to make the process of planning his sessions easier for Sean?

 **PAUSE POINT** Do you understand what information must be delivered before a class, so a group or individual can participate safely and effectively?

 Hint Draw your own flow diagram of the elements you should cover before a session starts.

Extend Which element might you consider removing to help you maintain structure in your first few sessions?

Instructing the session

Any session you deliver should include the components discussed on pages 187–8.

To deliver an effective exercise class, you should fully understand the elements within the session, the challenges they might present for individuals and how movements might be broken down to allow individuals to master them. The best way to achieve this is through practice and experimentation. A leader who is both confident and competent in delivering water-based exercise will have spent a large amount of time in the water themselves, evaluating movements and potential routines.

Theory into practice

The following is a very basic routine that can be tried by you and your fellow learners in chest-deep water.

- Walk on the spot for 1 minute, and then gently bounce for a further 30 seconds with your arms raised above your head.

- Keeping your feet planted firmly, rotate your body from the waist, first left, then right, looking over your shoulder each time. For the first 30 seconds, do so with your arms by your side and then for the next 30 seconds, hold them out at right angles.

- Stand on tip toes with your hands out to your side, making circles just under water. Increase the intensity every 10 seconds for a total of 30 seconds.

- Squat until your chin is at water level. Jump as high as you can, clapping the air above your head. Repeat this 10 times.
- Run on the spot for 40 seconds, then 10 seconds faster and then 10 seconds slower, before repeating.
- Repeat the squat exercise, but this time do it so your head goes under the water each time.
- Gently perform five hops on your left foot, and then five on your right.
- Follow this immediately with running on the spot for 20 seconds, kicking your feet towards your backside as hard as you can.
- Gently bounce on both feet for 30 seconds.
- Walk on the spot for a final 1 minute.

How did you find this routine? Did it offer enough challenge to you and your fellow learners? Were there any movements that were easier or more difficult than others? How could you adapt the movements to differentiate for various participants? Discuss your thoughts with the rest of the group.

Techniques and coaching points

When coaching a technique, you should be aiming to deliver a movement to participants in a way that is:

▶ clear and concise
▶ will enable participants to keep their bodies safe
▶ will allow participants to succeed and progress to more complex versions.

Case study

Teaching an underwater forward roll

Nancy has a class that she teaches regularly every Wednesday evening. They are all becoming water confident, and are able and keen to push themselves. However, none of them has much experience in swimming pools. She has been asked to teach them to do an underwater forward roll from standing.

Although Nancy has done a forward role many times, she has never taught it. To enable her to better understand the elements required to be successful, she chooses a quiet time in the pool to practise it herself, taking notes as she goes along.

These are the key points that she comes up with.

- From standing, lie out on your stomach with your face underwater and arms out stretched.
- Tuck your knees in to your stomach and chin into your chest.
- At the same time, draw your hands strongly down past your sides trying to force your head towards your feet.
- Remain curled as you go head over heels and you feel yourself coming back to the surface.
- Extend your legs and stand up to catch your breath.

Check your knowledge

1 What safety concerns might you have if teaching this move?

2 Can you suggest any equipment that might be useful to make the move more comfortable for people to learn?

3 Are there any manoeuvres that are complex and which you might need to practise yourself to break down into coachable points?

Principles of group behaviour management

There are a number of key principles that you should follow to provide a session that meets the aims of the group and is conducted in a safe and timely manner.

▸ Move round the pool-side environment to ensure you are visible to the whole group and you can demonstrate clearly and effectively.

▸ Use a variety of communication techniques, depending on what you are trying to achieve and the nature of the session. Communication techniques include:
  • verbal, making sure you project your voice over any background noise
  • using a whistle to indicate you want to gain attention or to indicate a change in movement
  • using written signs clearly stating the next movement
  • visually demonstrating the movements.

▸ Constantly motivate the group with positive encouragement and open and energetic body language.

▸ Provide timely cuing – giving the group a warning of what might be expected next. Use a countdown where possible rather than introducing a new movement or change of direction suddenly.

▸ Vary the pace of the session to meet the needs of the group and maximise the effectiveness of the exercise. Use changes in pace to allow rest periods to ensure no participant is exhausted or unsafe. Remember that the pace should also reflect the depth of the water that participants are exercising in.

▸ Constantly monitor the intensity of the session and how individuals are coping with it. Test their responses to ensure that they are not being over-exerted.

▸ Adapt exercises with appropriate progression and regressions that you can introduce in response to participants' performance, using equipment where required.

Monitoring intensity

A simple way of monitoring exercise intensity is the **talk test**. It can be easily used in a pool environment to ensure participants are working at a safe threshold. Roughly speaking, all the following observations are true but they will vary between individuals to a certain extent.

▸ If a person can talk and maintain a light conversation, they are within a low-intensity threshold.

▸ If a person needs to take a breath every few words, they are in a medium-intensity threshold.

▸ If a person struggles to speak at all, they are in a high-threshold – this is too high for safe water-based exercise.

You can also enourage the group to use **Rating of Perceived Exertion (RPE)** techniques to check their own intensity and be responsible for their own safety. Using a scale of 1 to 20, they can assess how hard they are working, considering how tired they are, how difficult it is to breathe and how difficult the exercise is. For most people, working within the range of 12–15 is most effective and also maintains safety in a water-based environment.

Research

Research the RPE scale. How do you think the RPE scale could be used to maintain effective and safe water-based exercise programmes?

Discussion

Discuss the talk test and RPE techniques for assessing a participant's level of intensity. What do you feel are the strong points and potential weaknesses for each technique? Which technique do you think is most valuable? Justify your thinking.

Methods of correcting participants

Whether the session is focused on teaching a new skill or purely delivering exercise, at some point it is likely that you will have to correct a participant's technique. This may be to ensure that the session is more effective or so that they remain safe. The following are basic methods for correcting participants.

▸ **Projecting positivity** – ensure any criticism or corrections are softened by making them positive. You may like to use the 'praise burger' technique to do this: for every point you pull out as needing improvement, highlight something that the individual is doing well.

▸ **Moving position** – adjust where you are positioned in relation to the group. Ensure everyone can see you during coaching points, especially when demonstrating. When talking to a specific individual, try to get as close to them as possible.

▸ **Asking questions** – much of what is happening in the water may not be visible from the pool side. Have an open conversation with the participant as to how they feel they are performing. You may only have indications from the shoulders up that their technique needs adjusting and you may need to fill in the rest of the picture using directed questioning.

▸ **Verbal communication** – water-based environments can be noisy and sometimes verbal communication is hard. You might like to use a whistle and hand signals to draw attention to yourself. Project your voice and ensure that you are facing the class.

▸ **Non-verbal communication** – using hand signals, a whistle, whiteboards or an air horn are all useful forms of non-verbal communication. They do rely on a solid brief at the start of the session to ensure everyone understands what a signal or sound means but an entire session could potentially be run with no speaking at all.

▶ **Visual communication** – this includes many of the features of non-verbal communication as well as demonstrations (see pages 189–90).

▶ **Mirroring** – this is particularly useful for showing a group what you want from them, especially when it comes to keeping time. From the pool side, you can demonstrate the movements in real time and ask the group to copy you exactly maintaining your pace and rhythm.

Ⅱ PAUSE POINT Can you name the different elements involved in leading water-based exercise?

Hint What are the fundamental principles involved in delivering a good water-based exercise session?

Extend What two techniques might you implement to ensure exercise is implemented at a suitable intensity?

Ending a water-based exercise session

Ensuring that a session is finished professionally and neatly is essential when leading a water-based exercise class. Make sure any equipment used is checked, repaired if needed and then stored away correctly for future sessions. Check the environment around the pool, looking for sharp edges and ensuring any non-slip matting remains in place. Any trip hazards or rubbish should be cleared away to ensure the safety of other pool users.

Debrief

After the session, you should lead a debrief with the group to discuss how it went. This should achieve three main points.

1 Highlight successes from the class and congratulate positive performances. You want people to leave the session feeling as though they have achieved success. Make this easy for them by explaining clearly what they did well.

2 Point out areas for improvement and where participants should focus to improve. This should be a two-way process with them having the opportunity to take ownership of their own paths and suggest things that might be useful to help them succeed in the future. Allow them to give feedback on the session and ask questions, and where possible suggest ways you might be able to incorporate their ideas into future sessions.

3 Point them towards a progression route. This should be an opportunity to sell further sessions positively and capture momentum built during the session. Explain clearly long-term goals and how attending further sessions will help them achieve this.

Use the debrief to help make notes on what was achieved in the session, any areas for improvement or things you were not happy with, and what might be included in the following session. Where possible, incorporate suggestions from participants to show them that you take their feedback seriously.

Ⅱ PAUSE POINT Every session should be finished professionally and with structure. In no more than 30 words, explain why an effective debrief is important.

Hint How do you display professionalism? Think about jobs or work placements where you may have had to act professionally.

Extend What strategies might you use to ensure that a participant comes back for further sessions?

Reviewing your own performance

The process of reviewing your own performance as a leader of water-based exercise is vitally important. All leaders should avoid complacency and always aim to improve and learn. When reviewing your session, it might be useful to use the following questions to give structure to your thoughts.

▶ Was my preparation for the session thorough and organised? Did I make appropriate checks and prepare my equipment? Did I check my group information documents so I understood who was attending and their individual needs?

▶ Was my brief clear and did I project energy from the start, inspiring my participants to succeed?

▶ Did I position my group and myself effectively in the water-based area and at the pool side? Did they have space to move and were they able to see me at all times?

▶ Were the exercises I chose appropriate to my group and did they push them sufficiently? Was there enough variation in the session and did the session feel smooth and well structured?

▶ What was my relationship with my group like? Did I communicate effectively? Did I maintain positivity and motivate them at all times? Have I built trust? Was I able to make adjustments as we went along?

▶ Did I keep the group safe and were there any issues highlighted during the session?

▶ Did I use the debrief effectively to ensure that my group left feeling happy that they had achieved and keen to return for further sessions?

Improving personal performance

> **Link**
>
> Ways of improving your personal performance were covered in more depth in *Unit 3: Professional Development in the Sports Industry*.

After any session, you should be able to identify areas for improvement, no matter how experienced you might be. The next task is to ensure that you can identify strategies for improving your personal performance in the future. Table 16.8 shows three examples of areas in which new water-based exercise leaders might need to improve, with suggestions on how to develop skills for the future.

▶ **Table 16.8:** Areas to focus on for improving personal performance

Organisation and preparation	• There is nothing worse than starting a session in a panic because you do not feel adequately prepared. Start to consider your session days before it is due to happen. Allow time to make a plan, but then consider its effectiveness and adjust it as necessary. • If in any doubt, check your equipment the day before. If you know that something is not available or out of action, it is better to know sooner so you can adapt your plans. • On the day, turn up early enough to get ready and then have time to relax and calm any nerves before the group arrives.
Choice of exercises	• Practise any exercises before you ask a participant to do them. Ensure you understand the challenges of the movement. • Develop strategies to break a movement down into smaller chunks if you find it difficult. • Shadow other water-based exercise leaders and, if possible, take part in their class. Take their strong points and make them your own by mixing them with personal ideas.
Inspiring participants	• Your participants must believe you are highly motivated and want to be there. In reality, there will be some days when you are more motivated than others, but you must always project positivity. • Practise projecting positive body language in your day-to-day life. When you are doing a task you particularly dislike, focus on personal motivation and maintaining an energetic posture and expression. • Observe other leaders and discuss with them how they maintain motivation.

▶ Checking equipment beforehand is a way to help improve performance

The SWOT technique is a useful way to structure your review, focusing on four areas to target your improvements.

▶ **Strengths** – a session's positive elements should be recognised so that you can use them again in the future.

▶ **Weaknesses** – no matter how minor, areas for improvement should be highlighted so that you can eliminate weaknesses from future sessions.

▶ **Opportunities** – change is an important part of the leadership process. Learning new techniques, developing or improving resources, or gaining access to new venues are all opportunities that a good leader will look out for and try and integrate into their delivery.

▶ **Threats** – elements that might prevent success are varied. They might be time constraints, access to appropriate resources or potential injury. Identify threats early so you can put preventative measures in place to eliminate or lessen their impact.

Assessment practice 16.3

`C.P4` `C.P5` `C.P6` `C.M3` `C.M4` `BC.D2` `C.D3`

In consultation with your tutor, identify a group and deliver a water-based exercise session to it. Plan and deliver a session during which you will demonstrate effective communication and motivational skills, taking into consideration the needs of individuals in the group. Ensure the session is managed in a safe and structured way.

Afterwards, evaluate your performance in delivering the session, justifying strengths and areas for self-improvement that you have highlighted.

Plan

- I have ensured that I have gained valuable experience by shadowing other leaders.
- I am confident in my own abilities and believe I have chosen a sensible group to practise on.

Do

- I know what I am trying to achieve in my session.
- I have a strong plan but am prepared to adapt it if I need to.

Review

- I can recognise the value of this exercise.
- If asked to deliver another session, I could make valuable improvements to my performance.

Further reading and resources

Katz, J. (2003) *Your Water Workout*, New York: Broadway Books.

Pappas Baun, M. (2008) *Fantastic Water Workouts*, 2nd edition, Illinois. Human Kinetics.

Tamminen, T. (2007) *The Ultimate Guide to Pool Maintenance*, 3rd edition, New York: McGraw-Hill Education.

THINK ▶FUTURE

Grant Richards

Swimming coach and water-based aerobics instructor

I have been teaching water-based exercise for many years. It was my love of the water that drew me to this discipline of exercise instruction. I actually teach open water swimming as well as pool-based exercise. Both come with their challenges.

My teaching is done through my own company Aqua Fit Pro. I have spent a long time building the reputation of my company and now I have good demand from pools for me to come and deliver sessions for them. I deliver a wide range of activities and sessions. I like to ensure that this is always the case as it means that I do not get bored and can find challenge in developing new sessions.

My experience has allowed me to build a wide range of skills including communication, patience and motivation. But the skill that I rate as most vital is adaptability: you never know what might happen in a lesson and you must be ready to make changes as needed.

Focusing your skills

Maintaining safety

Water-based exercise sessions must be conducted in a controlled and safe manner. The challenges for a new water-based leader are diverse and making mistakes can result in serious consequences.

- Ensure that the pool is kept at an appropriate temperature so the group are kept safe and able to perform.
- Consider your group and how a session may need to be adapted to keep them safe while meeting their group and individual needs.
- Always consider the features of a swimming pool and how it might be best used to keep the group safe and ensure they have a positive experience.
- Practise techniques for monitoring the intensity of a session and how participants are reacting to it so that you get into the habit of doing this.

Delivering a session

A well-delivered session is one that has been planned for and prepared for. Delivering a good session relies upon a wide range of leadership skills.

- Don't be afraid to use a checklist to ensure you prepare everything that you need.
- Practise delivering your session brief and check it contains all the information that you need to convey to participants.
- Always look for opportunities to develop your coaching, both through 'hands-on' practice and by carrying out observations of other coaches.

Getting ready for assessment

José is working towards a BTEC National in Sport. He was given an assignment for learning aim B with the title 'Planning a water-based exercise session'. He had to design a session plan that met the needs of his client group, ensuring they had a quality experience in a safe environment. He had to:

▸ provide information on who the client group were and how he developed the session to meet their specific needs

▸ discuss the precautions that should be taken to keep the group safe.

José shares his experience below.

How I got started

I have had plenty of experience in planning exercise sessions during my BTEC course. I also volunteer for a children's hockey club at weekends so this helped. Although I like the water, I hadn't ever led a session in this environment. My first task was to gain some experience. I managed to shadow a swimming coach at my local pool. I also signed up for three weeks' worth of aqua aerobics.

This was invaluable to my development. I had opportunities to ask the leaders questions and discuss challenges that they faced. They also gave me some fantastic pointers on designing a session and considerations for structuring it appropriately for my client group.

How I brought it all together

To produce a session plan that I was comfortable with, I took a plan pro forma provided by my tutor but adapted it so I was confident using it and it highlighted all the particular areas I wanted to focus on.

I then started to fill in my plan. I decided to keep things simple so that I could deliver the session with confidence. I ensured that I had an in-depth knowledge of my group and understood the individual participants and their goals in joining my session. I also considered the pool environment where the session would be taking place and how I could use it to my group's best advantage and maintain sight of them and good communication.

I had a few doubts about some of the exercises I was thinking about including, so I made time to go and try them in the pool. I tried to break them down and understand the challenges that they might present to my class so that I could deliver it to them successfully.

What I learned from the experience

This whole experience has really pushed me. Because this is an environment that I am not used to, I was nervous, but I feel that challenging myself has really helped my overall leadership and coaching ability.

It was useful having shadowed sessions before making my plan. This meant that I could incorporate the strengths of others' sessions into my own. I will definitely follow this approach again.

I allowed myself plenty of time to create my plan. I'm glad I did this as I needed to make a number of adjustments in order to get it exactly how I wanted it. Having the background information on my group and understanding the environment and resources available to me helped me generate a plan that I felt happy with.

Think about it

▸ Have you allowed adequate time to complete your plan and make amendments as required?
▸ Have you got access to all the information that you require to generate a thorough plan?
▸ Have you provided all the information asked for to achieve the best grade possible?

Sports Injury Management 17

Getting to know your unit

For personnel involved in any aspect of sport, experiencing or witnessing an injury is common. Depending on your role within sport, an appreciation and understanding of sports injuries and their symptoms is essential to ensure appropriate treatment is administered. Injury prevention is vital and the risk of injury can be reduced by understanding the mechanism of injury, the role of biomechanics and effective preventative measures. For those participants who are suffering an injury, effective treatment may result in a quicker return to their chosen activity or on to rehabilitation.

How you will be assessed

This unit will be internally assessed through a series of tasks set by your tutor. Throughout this unit, you will find assessment activities that will help you work towards your assessment. Completing these activities will not mean that you have achieved a particular grade, but you will have carried out useful research or preparation that will be relevant when it comes to your final assignment.

For you to achieve the tasks in your assignment, it is important to check that you have met all the Pass grading criteria. You can do this as you work your way through the assignment.

If you are hoping to gain a Merit or Distinction, you should also make sure that you present the information in your assignment in the style that is required by the relevant assessment criteria. For example, Merit criteria require you to assess and apply, and Distinction criteria require you to analyse and justify.

The assignment set by your tutor will consist of a number of tasks designed to meet the criteria in the table. This is likely to consist of written assignments but may also include activities such as:

▶ presenting the various risk factors of sports injury and preventative measures

▶ creating a rehabilitation programme

▶ observations of applying sports injury treatments

▶ responses to oral questioning.

Assessment criteria

This table shows what you must do to achieve a **Pass**, **Merit** or **Distinction** grade, and where you can find activities to help you.

Pass	Merit	Distinction

Learning aim A Understand common sports injuries and their associated physiological and psychological responses

Pass	Merit	Distinction
A.P1 Discuss common acute, overuse sports injuries and symptoms, and red flag symptoms. **Assessment activity 17.1**	**A.M1** Assess common acute, overuse sports injuries and symptoms, with specific examples of injury mechanism and aetiology. **Assessment activity 17.1**	**A.D1** Analyse common sports injuries and symptoms, and the physiological and psychological responses to these with specific examples of injury mechanism and aetiology **Assessment activity 17.1**
A.P2 Explain how the body responds physiologically and the mind psychologically to sports injuries. **Assessment activity 17.1**	**A.M2** Assess the physiological and psychological response to sports injuries, with regard to the stages of injury, using specific examples. **Assessment activity 17.1**	

Learning aim B Explore common treatment and rehabilitation methods

Pass	Merit	Distinction
B.P3 Apply appropriate protocols when performing a range of common treatment methods to four contrasting scenarios. **Assessment activity 17.2**	**B.M3** Apply appropriate protocols in a confident and effective manner when performing a range of common treatment methods to four contrasting scenarios. **Assessment activity 17.2**	**B.D2** Justify the rehabilitation programme design, including future recommendations and considerations. **Assessment activity 17.2**
B.P4 Review the performance of officials, using assessment methods in selected sports, identifying strengths and areas for improvement. **Assessment activity 17.2**	**B.M4** Design a detailed safe and appropriate rehabilitation programme for a specific sports injury, including adaptations and alternatives. **Assessment activity 17.2**	

Learning aim C Investigate risk factors which may contribute to sports injuries and their associated prevention strategies

Pass	Merit	Distinction
C.P5 Explain how extrinsic and intrinsic risk factors contribute to sports injuries and how they can be prevented, using specific examples. **Assessment activity 17.3**	**C.M5** Assess preventative measures for intrinsic and extrinsic risk factors selected, using specific examples. **Assessment activity 17.3**	**C.D3** Analyse intrinsic and extrinsic risk factors which may contribute to sports injuries, using the sequence of prevention model. **Assessment activity 17.3**
		C.D4 Evaluate the importance of sports injury management, justifying its role in helping sports performers prevent or overcome common sports injuries. **Assessment activity 17.3**

Getting started

Taking part in sport and exercise is really good for your health. However, by taking part you also increase your risk of sports injury. When we sustain a sports injury, it affects us physically and psychologically. Think about an example of a high-profile injury. Who was injured? What do you think were the physical signs they were injured? How do you think the injury would affect them psychologically?

A Understand common sports injuries and their associated physiological and psychological responses

Link

This unit has particularly strong links with *Unit 1: Anatomy and Physiology* and *Unit 6: Sports Psychology*.

Research

What does the term 'injury incidence' mean? Why is this a better term than 'injury rate'? In pairs or small groups, research these two terms and report back to the rest of the group.

To effectively manage injuries, it is important for sports injury practitioners to know what a sports injury is and the different types of injury that their athletes might sustain.

What is a sports injury?

A sports injury is often defined as any physical complaint that occurred during a scheduled training session or performance. Usually the injury will require some form of medical attention and require the athlete to have a period of time when they cannot take part in training and competition. It is often the time loss from being unable to train or compete that determines the severity of the injury.

Types of sports injury

There are two main types of sports injury. These are determined by the mechanism of injury, or the way it is caused, and how quickly the symptoms show themselves.

▶ **Acute injuries** tend to occur because of sudden high force to the tissue, for example contact with another player or a direct blow, and the symptoms occur quickly. Most of the dramatic injuries we see on television are acute injuries.

▶ **Overuse injuries** tend to occur because of repeated force to the tissues, for example repeated movements with little recovery, and the symptoms occur gradually. These are in comparison far less dramatic than acute injuries but can have the same severity.

Acute injuries

These are the injuries that most of us have seen when an athlete requires medical attention in sport. Sports that involve frequent contact, collisions, and high-intensity changes of direction have high rates of acute injuries, for example rugby, football and basketball. Acute injuries can affect bone, joints, muscle, bursae (in the knee), and connective tissue. In fact, some acute injuries can involve more than one tissue type. For example, high-grade ankle sprains involving lateral ligaments can also cause avulsion (or tearing) fractures to the fibula.

Usual signs and symptoms of acute injuries include:
▶ swelling
▶ pain
▶ bleeding (internal or external)
▶ loss of function
▶ redness
▶ heat
▶ increased joint laxity (or looseness).

Table 17.1 highlights the major types of acute injury by tissue type.

▶ **Table 17.1:** Common acute injuries

Tissue type	Acute injury types	Brief description
Bone	Fractures including: • Transverse fracture • Oblique fracture • Spiral fracture • Comminuted fracture	A crack or full break in bone/s. The shape of the break describes the type of fracture.
Cartilage	Osteochondral tear	An injury or small fracture of cartilage surface of bone
	Meniscal tear	Injury to the fibrous cartilage between joint surfaces
Joint	Dislocation	Complete separation of joint surfaces
	Subluxation	Partial separation of joint surfaces
Ligament	Sprain (grades 1–3)	Tearing of ligament fibres
Muscle	Strain (grades 1–3)	Tearing of muscle fibres
	Haematoma (intra- and intermuscular)	Localised bleeding within muscles (intra) or between muscles (inter) – see Figure 17.1
	Cramps	Painful involuntary muscle contractions
	Acute compartment syndrome	Increased pressure due to swelling within a body compartment, e.g. the compartment of the lower leg
	Delayed onset muscle soreness	Microtrauma to muscles as a result of overloading the muscle
Tendon	Tear (partial to complete)	Injury where tendon fibres are damaged
Bursa	Traumatic bursitis	Inflammation of a bursa caused by a collision or fall
Skin	Abrasions, lacerations and puncture wounds	Open wounds caused by scraping, cutting or piercing the skin
	Contusions	A direct blow causing muscle damage and bleeding below the skin surface

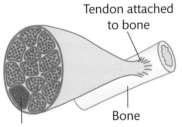

Intramuscular haematoma: bleeding is confined to one bundle of muscle fibres

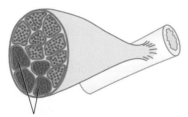

Intermuscular haematoma: bleeding has spread to several bundles of muscle fibres

▶ **Figure 17.1:** Intramuscular and intermuscular haematoma

Types of fracture

A fracture is a partial or complete break in a bone and is a common hard tissue injury. The way the injury takes place (its mechanism) causes the bone to break differently. Most fractures are due to direct impact such as a fall or a direct blow. The site of the injury and how it occurs results in different types of fracture.

Fractures may be open or closed and complete or non-complete. **Open fractures** protrude through the skin, while **closed fractures** do not. **Complete fractures** involve the bone being snapped into at least two pieces and can have large displacement, while with **incomplete fractures** the bone is not totally snapped and has little or no displacement.

There are four common fracture types based on the shape of the break. These are:

▶ **transverse fracture** – a break that is perpendicular (at right angles) to the length of the bone
▶ **oblique fracture** – similar to the transverse fracture, but the break occurs diagonally across the bone and can result in sharp ends where the break is
▶ **spiral fracture** – the break is in a spiralling pattern along the bone
▶ **comminuted fracture** – a break with multiple fragments of bone.

Grades of strain and sprain

The severity of strains and sprain are commonly referred to in grades of the injury. Grade 1 is the least severe and has the least number of symptoms and loss of function. Grade 3 is the most severe and has profound symptoms and loss of function. Important symptoms include pain, swelling, and laxity (looseness) of joints. Loss of function often refers to muscle strength and the range of motion at the joints.

Overuse injuries

Overuse injuries tend to occur from repetitive frequent forces through the tissues with little recovery time. They typically occur:

▶ in sports that have monotonous training regimes such as swimming and distance running
▶ in sports that have repetitive similar movement patterns such as cricket or tennis
▶ in sports where there is a rapid increase in training/competition load such as in football and handball.

Youth athletes may be particularly susceptible to overuse injuries at periods of growth. Just as with acute injuries, overuse injuries can affect a number of tissue types.

Table 17.2 highlights common overuse injuries and describes each one briefly. While acute injuries have clear signs and symptoms, overuse injuries tend to have symptoms that are less obvious. This means they can be a challenge to manage.

▶ **Table 17.2:** Common overuse injuries

Tissue type	Overuse injury types	Brief description
Bone	Stress fracture	A micro fracture in bone Inflammation of bone–muscle attachment site
	Osteitis	Inflammation of bone–muscle attachment site
	Apophysitis	Inflammation of growth plate
Cartilage	Chondropathy	Degeneration of cartilage
Joint	Synovitis	Inflammation of synovial membrane
	Osteoarthritis	Painful and stiff joints usually caused by injury or general wear and tear – it is a degenerative condition (i.e. it gets worse over time)
Ligament	Inflammation	Pain and swelling caused by repetitive loading
Muscle	Chronic compartment syndrome	Long-term increased pressure in a body compartment due to repetitive exercise
	Muscle focal thickening	Chronic change to muscle causing reduced range of motion
Tendon	Tendinopathy including: • Tendinitis • Tendinosis • Paratenonitis • Tenosynovitis	Painful conditions of the tendon
Bursa	Bursitis	Swelling of a bursa
Skin	Blister	A pocket of fluid caused by repetitive friction
	Callus	Chronic change to skin from repetitive friction making it hard and thickened

Osgood-Schlatter disease

Osgood-Schlatter disease is an example of an apophysitis injury that is common in youth athletes. An apophysitis injury affects where a tendon attaches to a bony growth plate. In Osgood-Schlatter disease it is where the patellar tendon attaches to the tibial tuberosity.

Overuse of the quadriceps causes repeated strain on the tendon attachment causing irritation, pain, redness, swelling and, in some cases, a bony bump to develop below the knee. This bony bump is permanent but becomes painless as the tibia bone matures.

Red flag symptoms

Sometimes an athlete may mention they are getting symptoms that make you think something more serious might be wrong with them, and that they need referring to a specialist immediately. These are known as red flag symptoms and suggest a severe underlying condition. Examples of conditions and symptoms include:

▸ a spinal injury – indicated by saddle anaesthesia (numbness in the groin region) or saddle paraesthesia (sensation changes in the groin area, for example pins and needles), bowel/bladder dysfunction, muscle weakness, gait abnormalities (for example drop foot), severe bilateral radiating pain

▸ **deep vein thrombosis (DVT)** – indicated by severe pain and tenderness (usually in the calf), red warm and shiny skin, swelling, pain on movement

▸ **vertebrobasilar insufficiency (VBI)** – indicated by dizziness, fainting, struggling to talk, struggling to swallow, double vision, numbness, nausea, unable to coordinate eyeballs.

All the above conditions can be life threatening or life changing so you urgently need to refer on in a safe and effective manner.

Physiological response to injury

As soon as an injury takes place, the body responds in a number of ways. There are three phases of responses as shown in Figure 17.2. The length of time at each stage depends on a number of factors and may be different for different athletes. These stages start as soon as the injury happens and usually continue well after the athlete has returned to sport.

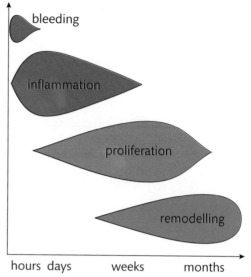

▶ **Figure 17.2:** Stages of tissue repair. Does each stage occur separately or are they overlapping?

Phase 1: The inflammatory stage

The **inflammatory response** stage is an essential part of tissue repair (see Figure 17.3). This stage happens quickly following injury (0–3 days), peaks after 24–72 hours, and can last for a few weeks. It is the protective stage involving vascular and cellular changes where chemicals are released that cause pain, swelling, **vasoconstriction** and then **vasodilation** of blood vessels, and cell debris that has to be removed. The rest of the healing process will not occur normally if there isn't an inflammatory stage.

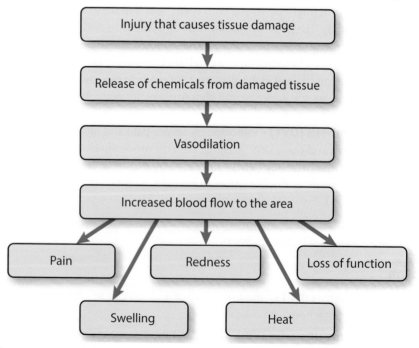

▶ **Figure 17.3:** Signs and symptoms of inflammation. Why does the body react to injury in this way?

Signs and symptoms

The inflammatory stage has five major signs. Knowing these signs and regularly checking them on an injured athlete helps us understand how severe the injury is and how the healing process is progressing. The five signs are:

▶ **pain** – due to increased pressure and chemical irritation of sensory pain receptors (**nociceptors**)
▶ **swelling** – due to bleeding and chemicals causing the area to swell
▶ **redness** – caused by increased blood flow to the area by vasodilation
▶ **heat** – caused by increased chemical activity in the injured area and an increased flow of blood
▶ **loss of function** – due to the swelling and pain caused by the injury.

Loss of function can be partial, such as limping, include some loss of strength or be complete, such as being unable to weight bear or move the body part at all.

Phase 2: Tissue formation

The **proliferation** (tissue formation) stage is important for generating repair material and has two main events. Firstly, around the injury site there is a development of new capillaries to promote healing. This is called **angiogenesis**. Secondly, cells (**fibroblasts**) start to lay down a supportive network to stabilise the injury site. This is called **fibroblastic repair**.

At this stage, the supportive network develops into scar tissue and is much weaker than normal uninjured tissue and its fibres are laid down in a random order. The scar tissue at this stage is made up from a fibre called type III **collagen**.

The tissue formation stage can last from 24 hours to 6 months (peaking in 2–3 weeks).

Key terms
Nociceptors – pain-sensing receptors.
Collagen – a protein-based building material used in the repair of tissues.

⏸ PAUSE POINT The stages of tissue healing are like rebuilding a broken bridge.

Hint Create a step-by-step process to rebuilding a broken bridge.

Extend Explain your process to a classmate to see if your sequence is correct or if you have missed any steps out.

Phase 3: The remodelling phase

In the maturation (remodelling) stage, the scar tissue is refined. This means that fibres are constantly reabsorbed and repaired making the scar tissue stronger and less randomly arranged. The randomly arranged type III collagen is replaced with more functional type I collagen. Over time the scar tissue resembles non-injured tissue as closely as possible.

The remodelling stage lasts from 7 days up to 12 months.

⏸ PAUSE POINT How does injured tissue heal?

Hint Put this book to one side. Using only drawings or images (no words), describe the stages of tissue healing.

Extend Explain your drawing to another person and see if they understand the process.

Factors affecting the healing process

There are a range of factors that can positively or negatively influence the duration of the healing process. These include:

▶ **nutrition** – food (for example protein) and fluid intake – a well-balanced diet will speed up recovery
▶ **type** of treatments used – such as electrotherapy, exercise therapy, manual therapy
▶ **age** – young versus old - a younger athlete will recover quicker from an equivalent injury than an older athlete, all other things being equal
▶ **tissue type involved** – tissues with a good blood supply will heal more quickly than tissues with a poor blood supply

Research
Research how bone heals and draw a flow diagram of this. What are the similarities and differences with soft tissue healing?

▶ **sleep** – both the quality and quantity of sleep affect recovery

▶ **psychology** – the athlete's psychological state will also affect recovery – the following section of the unit looks at this in more detail.

Psychological response to injury

Link

This content links to *Unit 6: Sport Psychology*.

As well as physiological responses of the body to injury, there are also psychological responses. Psychological responses influence physical responses and vice versa. Psychological responses change a lot through an athlete's rehabilitation and vary between individuals based on personal and situational factors.

▶ Personal factors include pain tolerance, mental toughness, resilience, gender, age and injury history.

▶ Situational factors include level of competition, relationship with the coach, social support network and team environment.

Psychological responses to injury can be categorised as being **emotional** (relating to feelings), **cognitive** (relating to thoughts) and **behavioural** (relating to how we act) – examples are given in Table 17.3. These responses can be beneficial or detrimental to successful rehabilitation. For example, a high level of self-confidence is an important psychological factor in returning to sport after injury. Alternatively, anxiety or fear over re-injury is detrimental when returning to sport.

Theory into practice

Monitoring athletes' psychological responses throughout sports injury rehabilitation is really important. This is because they can affect rehabilitation progress but may also have a wider impact on athletes' health. Responses to sports injury can be placed on a continuum from mild to severe.

Discuss the following with a classmate.

• How could you monitor an athlete's psychological responses to injury?

• Give examples of responses you think are normal or mild.

• Give examples of responses you think are more severe and may need referring.

▶ **Table 17.3:** Psychological responses to sports injury

Emotional responses (feelings)	Cognitive responses (thoughts)	Behavioural responses (actions)
• Anxiety/fear • Anger • Frustration • Helplessness • Depression	• Self-esteem • Self-confidence • Altered identity • Loss of control • Over-motivation	• Adherence to rehabilitation • Avoidance coping • Malingering • Removal from team setting • Altered diet and alcohol intake

Psychology and injury risk

Key term

Stressor – an activity, event or other stimulus that causes stress.

An athlete's psychological make-up can make them more or less prone to getting a sports injury. Williams and Andersen (1998) created the Stress and Injury Model to explore this (see Figure 17.4). An athlete's personality, history of **stressors** and coping resources all affect how likely they are to get injured.

▶ Personality factors include trait anxiety, risk taking, hardiness, optimism and perfectionism.

▶ History of stressors consists of sport-related and non-sport related hassles, and previous injury history.

▶ Coping resources related to the athletes 'tools' to deal with high levels of stress include sleep, stress management skills and their social support network.

When an athlete appraises a sporting situation as stressful, these psychological factors combine to influence the athlete's stress response. The stress response leads to changes that are both physiological (such as increased muscle tone and spasm) and psychological/attentional (such as loss of concentration, poor decision making and narrowed attention focus). It is thought that these changes affect whether the athlete gets injured or not. Sports psychology can be used to reduce the effect of the stress response and help reduce the chance of potentially harmful changes happening.

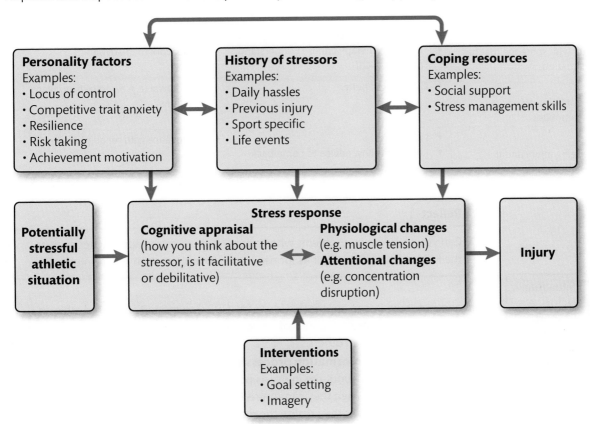

▶ **Figure 17.4:** The stress and injury model. Which psychological factors might give you an increased risk of injury?

Psychology and injury rehabilitation

There are two main approaches to understanding the psychology of injury rehabilitation: stage-based and cognitive appraisal approaches.

Stage-based approaches

Of the stage-based approaches, the most popular is the Kübler-Ross (1969) Grief Response Model. This was originally created to describe a patient's experience of terminal illness but has been applied to sports injury. The model suggests the athlete progresses through five stages of reaction to injury in a predictable pattern. These stages are shown in Table 17.4.

The time spent at each stage varies according to the athlete's psychological factors and the support that they have access to. An athlete that progresses through the stages more quickly will recover psychologically from the injury experience in a shorter period of time.

> **Discussion**
>
> Discuss examples of injury-prone athletes with a group of your classmates. What psychological factors might have increased their risk of injury?

Table 17.4: How grief response affects rehabilitation

Grief response stage	Associated thoughts	Associated behaviours
Denial Not acknowledging injury and carrying on regardless	• I'm not injured. • I can carry on. • It won't stop me.	• Continue to participate despite loss of function and pain
Anger High levels of frustration about getting injured and being reliant on others	• It's the opposition's fault. • It's the coach's fault.	• 'Storming off' • Potentially aggressive behaviour towards others
Bargaining Trying to negotiate with someone that has control over the situation	• If I do more, I'll recover faster. • The sports therapist doesn't understand, I'm fine, coach!	• Not following advice (e.g. doing more rehab work than advisable)
Depression Low mood from not being able to participate with teammates	• I'll never get better.	• Withdrawal (e.g. removal from team situations)
Acceptance Finally, acknowledging injury and the importance of rehabilitation.	• I am injured. • I need to follow advice to come back from this.	• Compliance with rehab plan

> **Reflect**
>
> Can you think of any problems when applying stage-based approaches such as the Kübler-Ross (1969) Grief Response Model to athletes with sports injuries?

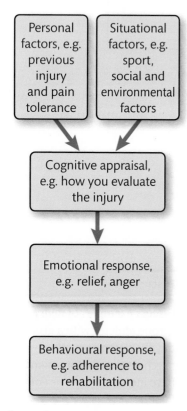

Figure 17.5: Cognitive appraisal process. What are your own personal and situational factors affecting cognitive appraisal?

In another stage-based approach, Udry et al. (1997) suggested all injured athletes progress through three categories of response. Some athletes will progress through these more quickly than others.

1 **Injury-relevant information processing stage** – where the athlete wants as much information about the injury as possible. For example, what's involved in the recovery and when they can return to playing. It is the stage with the greatest negative emotions as they realise the disruption the injury will cause.

2 **Emotional upheaval and reactive behaviour stage** – where the athlete has intense emotions such as being agitated, irritable and physically tired. An athlete might feel isolated from the team while being very anxious.

3 **Positive outlook and coping stage** – where the athlete starts to accept that they are injured and adapt to the injury. They feel like they can cope with the injury demands and develop a positive outlook as they sense progress is being made.

Cognitive appraisal approaches

Cognitive appraisal approaches are more supported with research than stage-based models. These approaches include the Cognitive Appraisal Model (Brewer, 1994) and the Integrated Model of the Response to Sport Injury (Wiese-Bjornstal, 1998).

In the Cognitive Appraisal Model (see Figure 17.5), the athlete's thought processes about their injury are affected by personal and situational factors, for example age, injury history, gender, team environment, stage in career and social support network. This is in addition to the standard responses outlined earlier in Table 17.4. These factors make the athlete appraise their injury in a certain way, which determines their emotional and behavioural responses. For example, an athlete might appraise their rehabilitation progress as not being quick enough, and become frustrated and anxious. This may cause non-adherence and prevent them following the exercises the practitioner has given.

The Integrated Model of Response to Sport Injury is the most widely accepted model and combines pre-injury and post-injury factors. In this model, cognitive appraisal, behavioural responses and emotional responses influence each other in a cyclical manner. It is this cycle of responses that ultimately determines rehabilitation outcomes. Rehabilitation outcomes can be physical or psychosocial. The cycle is dynamic and should be seen as a three-dimensional spiral. If the responses are favourable, the spiral will lead to positive rehabilitation outcomes. In comparison, if responses are unfavourable, the spiral leads to negative rehabilitation outcomes.

There are intermediate recovery outcomes and sports injury recovery outcomes. Intermediate outcomes include improvement in strength, adherence, less pain, greater range of motion and perceptions of recovery. Sports injury recovery outcomes include functional performance, quality of life, treatment satisfaction and readiness to return to sport.

> **Reflect**
>
> Going through injury rehabilitation is often seen only as a negative experience. What might be some of the positives of going through this experience?

Assessment practice 17.1 A.P1 A.P2 A.M1 A.M2 A.D1

You are working as a freelance sports therapist for your local sports club. You have been asked to write a blog on the sports club's social media site about common sports injuries. The blog should be short and to the point, containing images of each injury. In the blog, they would like you to:

- identify the five most common acute injuries and the five most common overuse injuries in the sport
- analyse for each of the injuries what its usual signs and symptoms are, and the likely mechanisms of the injury
- discuss what red flag symptoms are
- analyse physiological and psychological responses to injury.

The blog can be based on a sport of your choice.

Plan
- What is the task? What am I being asked to do?
- What does a blog look like?
- How confident do I feel in my own abilities to complete this task? Are there any areas I think I may struggle with?

Do
- Do I know where I can find out more about specific sports injuries and mechanisms of injury?
- For physiological responses to injury, can I use the stages of tissue healing (bleeding, inflammation, proliferation, and remodelling)?
- Can I apply the models of psychological response to injury (e.g. Grief Response Model, categories of response and different reactions to injury)?

Review
- I can explain what the task was and how I approached the task.
- I can explain how I would approach the hard elements differently next time (i.e. what I would do differently).

B Explore common treatment and rehabilitation methods

Rehabilitation is the process of restoring sport function following an injury. It starts as soon as the injury occurs and finishes after the athlete has successfully returned to sport. Understanding the basics of early trauma management (first aid) and selecting effective methods to improve the athlete's function (a rehabilitation plan) is important for a successful rehabilitation.

Common treatment methods and the need for medical referral

To make sure that injuries can be dealt with effectively, each sports team should have a medical emergency action plan (EAP). This action plan is a detailed breakdown of what should happen if an athlete suffers an injury during sport. It should include minor injuries (e.g. muscle strains) and more severe injuries/conditions (e.g. spinal injury or cardiac arrest).

The first aid care of an injured athlete is usually a real team effort involving many people (e.g. coaches, sports injury practitioners, club doctors, parents) so everyone needs to understand the EAP to provide the best care possible. The EAP should answer the following basic questions.

▶ Who are the qualified practitioners at the venue?
▶ How can injured athletes be safely removed from the field of play?
▶ What medical equipment is available and where is it kept (e.g. defibrillator, stretcher)?
▶ Who calls for the ambulance if an athlete needs transferring into hospital care?
▶ Where is the nearest hospital with an accident and emergency department and head trauma unit?
▶ Where is the ambulance access?

Principles of first aid

First aid is the immediate treatment given to an injured person. The severity of sporting injuries can vary, from minor cuts and bruises to life-threatening problems. Some knowledge of first aid can potentially save an athlete's life, and can also help with minor problems to speed the recovery process and limit potential complications. In the application of first aid, you should follow the 4Ps approach. In order of importance you should:

▶ P – **protect** yourself, the athlete and others
▶ P – **preserve** life
▶ P – **prevent** deterioration
▶ P – **promote** recovery.

With potentially serious accidents, a specific primary survey should be carried out.

Primary survey

This is a dynamic process to address the life-threatening injuries before moving to minor, less life-threatening issues. It is of paramount importance that it is carried out first and repeated to monitor the athlete.

▶ **Danger** – check the area for potential danger to yourself. Another casualty will worsen the problem. Also, remove any potentially hazardous objects from around the casualty.
▶ **Response** – check if there is any response from the injured person. If not, call for help immediately. Do not leave the injured person.
▶ **Airway** – gently tip the head backwards to open the airway and check if there are any foreign objects in the person's mouth, blocking the airway.
▶ **Breathing** – check to see if the person is breathing 'normally' (for up to 10 seconds). If not, send someone for an ambulance (dial 999 or 112) and to get the automated external defibrillator (AED).
▶ **Circulation** – can you confirm the presence of a pulse (for up to 10 seconds) and the strength/rate of this (in beats per minute)?
▶ **Disability** – have they got a head or spinal injury? Determine consciousness status. Is there any seizure activity, for example involuntary jerking movements of arms and legs?
▶ **Environment/exposure/extrication** – do they need moving? Keep them warm, wait for the emergency services. Reassess all the time.

Theory into practice

For a sports team you are involved with, create your own medical EAP.

Safety tip

Completing this unit does not qualify you as a first aider. If you do witness a serious accident, the most qualified and experienced individual should be the one who carries out the first aid procedures. Do not crowd the injured person, but assist in any way that the first aider asks.

Secondary survey

A secondary survey should be carried out if an unconscious person is breathing normally and if life-threatening conditions have been identified and dealt with. This is done to check all areas of the body for damage. The process should be carried out quickly and in a systematic way.

▶ **Bleeding** – check the area, and check the patient head to toe for blood.
▶ **Head and neck** – check for bruising and/or deformity. Gently feel the back of the neck for damage.
▶ **Shoulders and chest** – compare the shoulders; feel for fractures in the collarbones and ribs.
▶ **Abdomen and pelvis** – feel around the abdomen for abnormalities and to see if the person feels any pain.
▶ **Legs and arms** – check legs, then arms, for fractures and any other clues.
▶ **Pockets** – check the person's pockets to make sure there are no items that could injure them when you roll them into the recovery position. Be very cautious of sharp objects (for example, needles). If possible, have a witness if you remove anything from their pockets.
▶ **Recovery** – make sure you do not cause further damage to the person when placing them in the recovery position. If a neck injury is suspected, as long as their airway is maintained, do not move them and instead stabilise the head either side with your hands.

▶ **Figure 17.6:** The recovery position in which the athlete is turned onto their side with the airway opened and supported

> **Safety tip**
>
> • Be aware of jewellery or sports equipment (e.g. GPS monitors) to make sure it is not worsening the problem – remove it in such cases. Also look for medic alerts (such as diabetes bracelets/necklaces).
>
> • Make a mental and/or written note of anything you have observed during the primary and secondary surveys. This information should be passed on to the emergency services to help with treating the patient.

The recovery position (see Figure 17.6) is a way of positioning an unconscious casualty, minimising the risk of their airway becoming compromised. Two potential dangers that are to be avoided are:
▶ the tongue relaxing and blocking the airway
▶ the patient vomiting and the vomit blocking the airway.

Cardiopulmonary resuscitation (CPR)

CPR should be performed when a person is not breathing and shows no signs of circulation. This process keeps the vital organs alive until help arrives. An oxygen supply to the brain is essential to sustain life, via inhaled air and the movement of blood in the body. If a person is not breathing and their heart is not beating, this will need to be done for them.

CPR involves breathing for the casualty and performing chest compressions at a ratio of 30 compressions to 2 breaths for adults and children (see Figure 17.7). Early access to an Automated External Defibrillator (AED) is vital to the success of this process with CPR being carried out to buy time until the AED can be used.

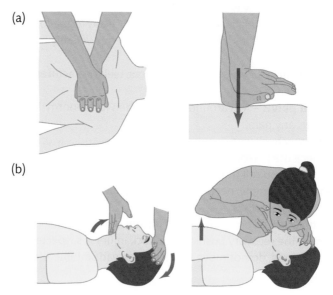

▶ **Figure 17.7:** The CPR process. What is the ratio of compressions (a) to breaths (b)?

Shock

Shock is caused by a drop in blood pressure or blood volume. Shock can be a secondary reaction to many serious injuries (for example, with major blood loss). There are three classifications:

- ▶ **cardiogenic shock** – the most common type, caused by the heart not pumping effectively
- ▶ **hypovolemic shock** – caused by a loss in bodily fluids resulting in low blood volume (can be common for traumatic injuries such as major sports injuries)
- ▶ **anaphylactic shock** – caused by a severe allergic reaction.

The signs and symptoms of shock include:

- ▶ increased pulse rate (can become weaker as the condition worsens)
- ▶ pale and clammy skin, sweating as shock worsens (lips can become blue)
- ▶ fast, shallow breathing
- ▶ nausea or vomiting
- ▶ dizziness and/or feelings of weakness
- ▶ with severe shock, deep breathing can develop, with confusion, anxiety and possibly aggression
- ▶ casualties can become unconscious.

To treat shock:

- ▶ the cause of shock must be addressed (for example, a fracture must be immobilised)
- ▶ lay the person down and, if possible, raise the legs (keeping the flow of blood to the vital organs)
- ▶ keep the person warm and loosen any tight clothing.

Blood-loss treatment

Loss of blood is common in many sports. Causes of blood loss can vary from minor scratches to serious lacerations and puncture wounds. With all cases of blood loss, you should prevent infection in both the casualty and the person treating the wound. Wear disposable gloves when dealing with blood. The main priorities are to stop the bleeding, prevent the person from going into shock and reduce the risk of infection.

Safety tip

With all cases of shock, the emergency services should be contacted immediately. The casualty should be monitored continuously (for breathing, pulse and response).

To treat bleeding, apply direct pressure to the site of bleeding using an appropriate bandage or gauze. Do not remove any large, impaled objects from a person. If an object is imbedded in a person, you can apply pressure at either side of the object. Use an absorbent, sterile dressing large enough to cover the wound completely and apply it firmly without restricting the blood flow to the rest of the body.

Further considerations

▸ Special attention needs to be paid in certain situations following an injury.

▸ For an unconscious casualty, you must be aware of the possibility of both head injuries and concealed injuries. These can be identified through the primary and secondary surveys already discussed.

▸ If fractures are a possibility, it is essential to minimise the movement of the injured area.

▸ Where the risk of infection is high, this risk must be minimised, often through appropriate covering of the injury. For example, an open wound (such as a friction burn from artificial turf) should be washed and sterilised to prevent infection.

With any of these injuries, it is important to summon qualified assistance and the emergency services.

Whether an accident takes place in the workplace or during a sporting competition, it is essential to complete an accident report form if treatment is required. This process is a legal requirement for insurance purposes.

> **Safety tip**
>
> If you are in any doubt about a condition or injury, it is better to be cautious and refer it to a specialist.

⏸ PAUSE POINT A player collapses unconscious without any contact in a match for which you are providing medical support. As you approach the athlete, what would you think is wrong? How would you feel?

    (Hint) How would you act in this situation?

    (Extend) Create a bullet-pointed list of exactly how you would deal with this situation.

Pitch-side assessment of sports injuries

If an incident occurs during a sporting event, you have ruled out the injury being life threatening and the athlete is fully conscious, then you can assess them to find out what is wrong with them, how it happened, how it affects their function and whether they could continue or not. This is usually done using a 'look, feel, move' approach or the SALTAPS process.

▸ **S** – get the athlete to **stop**. Did you see how the injury was caused and mechanism of injury?

▸ **A** – **ask** questions about the injury, where it hurts, how severe the pain is, how they thought it happened.

▸ **L** – **look** for specific signs such as redness, swelling or foreign objects.

▸ **T** – **touch**/palpate the area for heat and tenderness.

▸ **A** – ask the athlete to perform **active movements** of the body part to check pain and range of motion.

▸ **P** – gently move the body part with **passive movements** and check how it feels, how severe the pain is, and the range of motion.

▸ **S** – test the **strength** of the body part by providing light resistance. Can the athlete stand on it? Can they walk, run, jump, and sprint? Can they return to action safely?

> **Safety tip**
>
> It is important to stop the SALTAPS process as soon as it indicates that an injury might be serious.

In the treatment of all sports-related injuries, the most appropriate individuals to give treatment are the most experienced. The aim of the SALTAPS process is to make an accurate assessment of the type, severity and location of an injury. This can be difficult for some sports injuries – even experienced practitioners can find an initial on-site diagnosis difficult.

Treatment of sports injuries

After most common sports injuries are suffered, the immediate treatment should follow the acronym of PRICED. This means that even at this early stage of injury, the healing process can be enhanced. The guidelines are there to manage the inflammatory response, **not** to remove it completely.

▸ **P**rotect – the person and injured part of the body to minimise the risk of further injury.
▸ **R**est – allows healing and prevents any further damage.
▸ **I**ce – stops the injured area from swelling and reduces the pain.
▸ **C**ompression – acts as support and prevents swelling.
▸ **E**levation – reduces blood flow to the area, reducing swelling with the aid of gravity.
▸ **D**iagnosis – needs to be done by a qualified sports injury professional or through a scan.

> **Theory into practice**
>
> Recently, the PRICED acronym has been adapted to POLICE to reflect the importance of exercise in rehabilitation.
>
> - What does the POLICE acronym stand for?
> - How does it differ from the PRICED acronym?
> - Create a tweet (with a maximum of 140 characters) about why 'optimal loading' is important in sports injury rehabilitation.

Other immediate care treatments

There are a range of other treatments that can help manage the symptoms in the early stages of injury. These treatments can be categorised into cryotherapy (cold treatments), thermotherapy (heat treatments), stability treatments, and electrotherapy (electric-based treatments). Examples of these include the following.

▸ **Cryotherapy** – use of bagged ice, ice packs, ice sprays, frozen peas, ice bandage, cryo-compression equipment.
▸ **Thermotherapy** – heat packs, radiant heat lamps, heat creams/gels, heat pads, paraffin wax, spa baths.
▸ **Stability treatments** – athletic tape, kinesio tape, bracing, joint supports, slings, crutches, splints.
▸ **Electrotherapy** – ultrasound, shockwaves, transcutaneous electrical nerve stimulation (TENS).

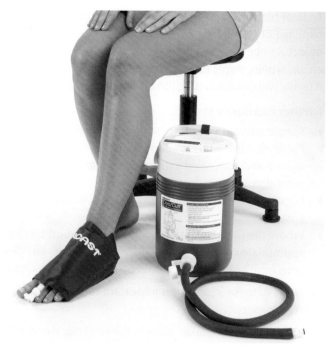

▸ Example of a cryo-compression device. What are the advantages and disadvantages of this treatment?

Some practitioners may combine several of these treatments as opposed to using them on their own, for example with hot and cold treatments including contrast bathing. This is alternating heat with cold treatments to quickly take the blood vessels from vasodilation to vasoconstriction in order to remove swelling and cell debris, lessen pain and improve range of motion. It is often known as the Lewis hunting response.

It is important to understand this response when applying cryotherapy to athletes. Applying ice causes narrowing of the blood vessels in the injured area (vasoconstriction). After a number of minutes (approximately 10–15 minutes) blood vessels start to re-open (vasodilation) to prevent tissues dying from a lack of oxygen. This can mean applying ice to an injured area for too long can increase bleeding and swelling, albeit less than if ice was not applied.

> **Safety tip**
>
> You must be qualified to use treatments and know for which conditions a treatment is not appropriate for the athlete. Some treatments, if used at the wrong time, may slow down tissue healing. For example, using thermotherapy in the very early stages of healing may increase or re-start bleeding.

Medical referral

Depending on the nature of the injury, it may be necessary to refer an individual to a specialist. Such individuals could include:

▸ General Practitioner or club doctor

- St John Ambulance or other person qualified in first aid
- local accident and emergency departments via a lift or paramedics (e.g. to access radiology department)
- local minor injuries clinic
- sports therapist or physiotherapist
- soft tissue therapist or sports massage therapist
- specialist consultant and/or surgeon
- podiatrist, osteopath or chiropractor.

You can also phone 111 to gain medical advice on non-life threatening issues.

Principles of rehabilitation

The overall aim of rehabilitation is to restore physical and psychological functioning to the level seen prior to injury, or even better. Any treatment or rehabilitation plan should be based on accurate diagnosis by a qualified practitioner.

For each treatment that you may use, there are particular reasons to use it (indications) or not to use it or adapt its use (**contraindications**). The overall programme should be well rationalised with a clear specific aim based on which stage the athlete is at, their progress and how the injury occurred. For example, if the injury was caused by overstretching tight hamstrings, the programme should seek to lengthen the hamstring group on both sides to prevent re-injury.

Research

It is important that the transfer of care to the emergency services is effective. This usually follows the ATMIST acronym. What does each letter stand for?

Key term

Contraindication – a physical or mental condition or factor that increases the risk involved in an activity.

Discussion

Discuss with a group of your classmates how the body responds to a period of time without training. Create a mind map about the impact this has on rehabilitation.

▶ **Table 17.5:** Aims of each stage of rehabilitation with examples of treatments

Stage of rehabilitation	Aims of each stage	Suggested treatment
Acute stage	Manage the inflammatory process and reduce the pain	Ice, compression, elevation, cryo-compression and TENS
Sub-acute stage	Try to encourage full range of motion, and also optimal loading and weight bearing	Massage, stretching, crutch walking (double to single), ice, heat and exercising non-injured limbs
Early rehabilitation stage	Start to fully weight bear, start to restore strength and activate muscles, proprioception and neuromuscular control	Passive mobilising, strength exercise (isometric at first), muscle activation treatments, e.g. electronic muscle stimulation, closed chain exercises, cardiovascular exercises, walking/jogging in straight lines and balance exercises
Late rehabilitation stage	Develop muscle power, endurance and multidirectional movement	Introduce isotonic or isokinetic exercise and add greater load and more intense cardiovascular exercises
Functional rehabilitation stage	Introduce sports-specific function, mirroring the demands of competition, e.g. intensity and frequency of sports-specific movements	High-intensity, multidirectional and unpredictable movements, e.g. diagonal cutting, landing and sprinting and combining many movements in drills

Rehabilitation is hard work for an athlete so it is important to use key principles to guide yourself and them. Any good rehabilitation plan is well explained, contains goals, provides a precise prescription, and makes the most of the available resources. An effective rehabilitation programme should also use the acronym ATCISIT.

- **Aggravation** – avoid aggravation of the injury and monitor signs of aggravation.
- **Timing** – start as soon as possible as too much rest can slow down healing.
- **Compliance** – encourage the athlete to do the plan as you have prescribed.
- **Individualisation** – based on the athlete's own demands and individual needs.

- **Specific sequencing** – the plan should follow a sequence of events in line with the stage of healing.
- **Intensity** – this should challenge the athlete and not aggravate the injury.
- **Total patient** – trying to recognise the athlete holistically, not just physically, and optimise trainability.

For rehabilitation to be successful, tissues need to be appropriately loaded (exercised) for them to adapt positively to this loading. You should base loading on the tissues that were injured and monitor it regularly. The Specific Adaption to Imposed Demands (SAID) principle means you need to think about:

- What type of loading am I doing?
- How heavy should I load it?
- How long should I load it for?
- How frequently should I load it?

If the loading is too little, the athlete may not progress as quickly as expected. Alternatively, if the athlete is overloaded, they may break down and suffer setbacks in their rehabilitation. The loading from the rehabilitation plan should be relatively pain-free during and after the session.

Progression of rehabilitation exercises

An effective rehabilitation plan should use physical and psychological criteria to progress between stages, and should not be purely based on time. A sports injury practitioner can progress rehabilitation load by adapting the following key training variables.

- **Type of activity** – exercises that do not directly stress the injured area versus those that do.
- **Duration of the activity** – time spent performing the exercise.
- **Frequency of the activity and rest** – how many times per day or week will they do this, and what will they do on rest days?
- **Intensity of the activity** – how hard to exercise is based on perceived exertion, resistance, time to completion.
- **Complexity of the activity** – performing simple, unidirectional exercises versus high-speed, multidirectional and multi-joint exercise.

The athlete can then follow a pathway to eventually returning to sporting action, as shown in Figure 17.8.

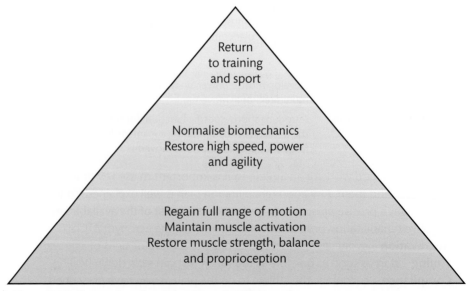

▶ **Figure 17.8:** Progression of exercises in a rehabilitation plan

Case study

Footballer David Silva sprains his ankle playing for Spain

David Silva suffered a lateral ankle sprain playing for Spain versus Luxembourg in October 2015. This is a common injury that is often suffered by footballers. Lateral ankle sprains have also affected athletes from other sports such as Sachin Tendulkar, Rafael Nadal, and LeBron James. Poor rehabilitation of this injury can lead to long-term losses in function and re-injury. The injury affects the three lateral ligaments of the ankle and in more severe cases causes an avulsion fracture.

1 What is the likely mechanism of injury for David Silva's ankle sprain?

2 Name the lateral ligaments that could be strained.

3 Create a flow diagram of how you progress an athlete from walking with two crutches to finally being able to sprint in different directions, jump and land.

Psychological factors associated with rehabilitation

Following a rehabilitation plan properly is an essential factor in determining whether an athlete will be successful or unsuccessful in their recovery. It is an important intermediate rehabilitation outcome. For example, an athlete who does not follow the exercises set by a practitioner following an ankle sprain may end up with a reduced range of motion in the long term.

Getting athletes to **adhere** to rehabilitation advice is challenging, so identifying the psychological factors affecting rehabilitation and using techniques aimed at improving adherence is important.

> **Key term**
>
> **Adherence** – continuing to perform a behaviour, such as completing a rehabilitation plan.

Psychosocial factors affecting rehabilitation adherence

Rehabilitation takes place in a social environment. Whether an athlete adheres to a rehabilitation plan is affected by a range of psychosocial factors, shown in Table 17.6. These factors can be classified as either personal or situational.

▸ **Table 17.6:** Personal and situational factors related to injury adherence

Personal factors	Situational factors
• Pain tolerance • Mental toughness • Self-motivation • Independence • Goal orientation	• Belief in the sports injury practitioner process and treatments • Comfortable environment • Convenient appointments and facilities • Quality of social support

Psychological techniques used to enhance adherence

Identifying and modifying the factors that affect rehabilitation adherence is vital to the rehabilitation plan's success. Some of the techniques that can lead to greater rehabilitation adherence are goal setting, social support, education, imagery and self-talk – see Table 17.7.

Technique to improve adherence	Description of technique	Purpose in rehabilitation
Goal setting	Creating, implementing, and evaluating short-, medium-, and long-term goals (performance, process, outcome-related) through rehabilitation. Goals should be: • S – shared • M – measurable • A – attainable • R – realistic • T – time-orientated • S – self-determined.	• Increases motivation to adhere to the rehabilitation plan • Manages expectations • Helps break down longer rehabilitation periods • Promotes faster recovery • Enables the athlete to view injury as a positive developmental experience
Social support	The support network available to an injured athlete in order to meet their demands. Providers of social support include family, friends, team mates, sports injury practitioners, coaches and social media.	• Reduces injury-related stress • Increases confidence • Enables sharing of experiences • Reduces feelings of isolation
Patient education	Getting the athlete to understand what the injury is, the purpose of each treatment, and the process in which injury will get better, e.g. use of leaflets, Internet and plenary tasks.	• Manages expectations • Improves adherence • Gives a greater sense of control
Imagery	Getting the athlete to use polysensoral (involving all senses) mental images to enhance their injury experience. Different types in rehabilitation are: • healing imagery • pain imagery • performance imagery • motivation imagery • relaxation imagery.	• Aids the healing process • Reduces negative emotions • Improves motivation • Helps regain skills • Manages pain • Increases confidence
Positive self-talk	Using positive statements throughout rehabilitation at challenging times, when the injury is painful, or when they are frustrated with the progress of rehabilitation.	• Changes negative thoughts • Reduces injury stress • Improves adherence • Helps retain focus
Motivational interviewing	A counselling-based technique is where the athlete is supported in exploring the pros and cons of taking part in rehabilitation rather than being prescribed an intervention.	• Improves adherence • Gives a greater sense of control • Helps generate rehabilitation goals

Types of coping resources

Coping resources are the athlete's own ways of dealing with the stressors placed upon them. As different stressors occur from the time of an injury to returning to action, an athlete must have a range of coping resources. Not being able to deal with the stressors of rehabilitation by having insufficient coping resources will result in negative outcomes.

The three main types of coping resources used by an athlete are:

▶ **avoidance coping** – where the athlete doesn't acknowledge there is a problem and carries on, or removes themselves from stressful situations and does something else instead

▶ **emotion-focused coping** – where the athlete uses strategies to help regulate the emotional upheaval of injury, for example using social support, imagery or stress management skills

▶ **problem-focused coping** – where the athlete uses strategies to address injury problem, for example. gathering information or seeking out practitioners who can help.

Reflect

Often avoidance coping is thought to be negative. Can you think of an example when avoidance coping might be beneficial for an athlete?

Stress management skills such as imagery, progressive muscle relaxation and positive self-talk are emotion-focused coping strategies that athletes should develop to allow them to deal with the stressors of rehabilitation. These may lead to a more successful rehabilitation and prevent future injury. Some of the benefits of stress management skills include:

▶ reduced anxiety
▶ increased confidence
▶ pain management
▶ increased adherence.

⏸ **PAUSE POINT**   Getting injured is a stressful experience for all athletes no matter what gender, ability level or sport.

> **Hint**   Describe what you think the stressors might be in the early stages of rehabilitation.

> **Extend**   Describe what you think the stressors might be when the athlete nears returning to action. Are these the same?

Psychological factors associated with the return to sport

Returning to action after an injury is a stressful time for athletes. When an athlete returns to sport, they have to deal with many physical, social and performance stressors (also referred to as concerns or anxieties).

▶ Physical stressors – these include the risk of re-injury, being unfit compared with others and not having match fitness.
▶ Social stressors – these include feeling isolated, increased pressure from the coach, players and the crowd.
▶ Performance stressors – these include not being at the same level as prior to injury, falling behind the rest and losing their place in the team if they are underperforming.

Case study

Paul O'Connell (Ireland captain)

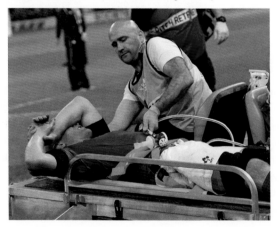

During the group stages of the Rugby World Cup 2015 versus France, Ireland captain Paul O'Connell suffered a severe hamstring injury ruling him out of the tournament and for an anticipated 8 months. To make matters worse, this would turn out to be his last game for Ireland, as they lost the next match against Argentina in a quarter final they were expected to win. It was O'Connell's fourth World Cup and he had never been beyond the quarter finals of the tournament. As a result of the injury, O'Connell had a delayed start to playing for his new club.

An old teammate was quoted as saying: "What a captain he has been. He is the first second row I have played with who has been the complete player [...] I have never met anybody like him. He demands the highest of standards from everyone within an organisation to make sure the team succeeds."

1 Based on Paul's personal and situational factors, what do you think his psychological responses to being injured might have been?

2 What techniques could you use to help a player with these responses?

3 What psychological issue might O'Connell have faced when he first played for his new club?

Monitoring rehabilitation programmes

How the athlete is responding to the rehabilitation programme must be monitored regularly using subjective and objective feedback/measures. Key factors to be monitored include:

▶ perceived exertion and how the athlete is feeling
▶ any pain and discomfort during and after exercise
▶ biomechanical or technical faults and range of motion
▶ swelling, heat and redness
▶ their progress in performing exercises and functional activities
▶ number of sets, repetitions and contacts until fatigue, technique worsens or pain is caused
▶ any concerns or, for example expectations placed upon them or compliance.

Any adverse reactions should prompt the plan to be re-evaluated and modified.

All rehabilitation documents and information should be recorded as they form a legally binding document. The plan should include the precise prescription of what you planned to do and also any changes that were made during the rehabilitation based on how the athlete responds to your intended exercises. Things to consider when documenting a rehabilitation programme include:

▶ background information about the athlete (for example, medical issues, injury history and specific requirements of rehabilitation)
▶ the activities undertaken
▶ the levels and development of the athlete
▶ problems or issues arising from the session
▶ complications (for example, allergies or illness) that affect progress during the session
▶ important legal documents and forms such as parental consent for younger sports players
▶ dates for review/functional testing (aims, objectives, etc.)
▶ accurate and up-to-date information that may change during the treatment
▶ specific objectives including appropriate and measurable timescales and review dates.

 **PAUSE POINT** Can you explain how and why rehabilitation plans must be progressive?

 Hint Create a rehabilitation plan for rotator cuff strain in the sub-acute stage of rehabilitation. Try and be as specific as possible.

 Extend How would you know the athlete was ready to progress? What type of factors would you progress?

Methods of rehabilitation

When an athlete sustains an injury, it has an immediate effect on their fitness levels. Specifically, the athlete's range of motion, flexibility, muscle condition, neural control over their muscles and ability to perform skills with good technique are all deconditioned. Therefore, knowing a range of effective methods that can address reduced fitness levels is important when working with injured athletes. An effective practitioner will make the exercises engaging, and have a flexible approach with progression and regression exercises. Progression exercises will further challenge the athlete, and regression exercises will be less challenging if you find your exercises are overly difficult for them.

Methods to improve joint range of motion

Joint **range of motion** refers to the amount of movement permitted at the joint. This is very specific to each joint and the athlete's make-up. It is limited by joint-based and soft tissue structures. The early restoration of range of motion is extremely important in rehabilitation. The following methods help to restore range of motion.

▶ **Continual passive motion (CPM)** – this is using a specially designed machine to put the joint through continual and controlled movement. It is mostly used on athletes that have suffered severe knee injuries requiring surgery.

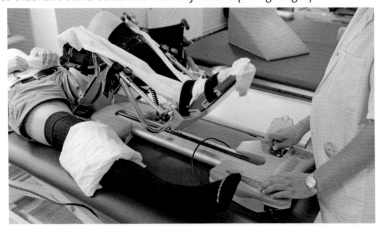

▶ CPM machines can be used to put a joint through continual and controlled movement

▶ **Passive mobilisation techniques** – these are joint-specific techniques where the practitioner will perform different grades (1–4) of joint mobilisation repeatedly to improve pain-free range of motion and joint nutrition.

▶ **Passive exercises** – passive exercises allow for a joint to be moved through the available range of motion without any effort required by the athlete. These exercises can be performed by the practitioner or by the athlete using their non-affected limb to support the movement.

▶ **Active exercises** – these involve the athlete moving the joint through its available range of motion by themselves. For example, repeatedly flexing and extending the knee joint within the constraints of pain and swelling.

▶ **Active assisted exercises** – this is where the athlete performs the range of movement exercise themselves involving the injured joint and then uses the non-injured limb to support the movement, allowing the athlete to move further. For example, if the right knee is injured, the athlete might use the left leg to support active flexion and extension.

Improving musculotendinous flexibility

Musculotendinous flexibility refers to the ability of the soft tissue to lengthen, which influences joint range of motion. Muscles and tendons work together so stretching has an effect on both. The beneficial effects of stretching do not last very long. Therefore, to improve flexibility, stretching should be carried out repeatedly and regularly, for example every day.

There are three main types of stretching techniques and all should be done with a feeling of tightness but not pain. The athlete should breathe normally with all stretching techniques rather than holding their breath. Flexibility is gained by altering biomechanical and neurological properties of the tissues.

▶ **Active stretching** – this involves the athlete stretching their muscles to their active bind point (the point of resistance or tightness) and holding the stretch statically for a period of time (minimum of 30 seconds). The stretch is then taken off the bind point. The process is repeated a minimum of three times. The bind point should be further along each time.

▶ **Passive stretching** – this involves a practitioner stretching the athlete's muscles for them. Often the amount of flexibility gains with passive stretching can be greater than active stretching. The practitioner finds the passive bind point of the muscle, holds it for 45–60 seconds, releases, and then repeats up to five times.

▶ **Proprioceptive neuromuscular facilitation (PNF) stretching** – there are a number of types of PNF stretching techniques. These techniques try to improve flexibility by reducing the neural input to the muscle and therefore flexibility can be gained. The most commonly used PNF technique is contract–relax, which is described as follows.

- The practitioner finds the target muscle's passive bind point and holds for 15 seconds.
- In this position, the athlete performs an isometric contraction of the target muscle (where the muscle contracts without changing in length) between 25–75% of their maximum. The contraction is held for 10 seconds.
- The target muscle is taken off the bind point for 3 seconds.
- The target muscle is then put back on a stretch to a new further bind point.
- The process can be repeated up to four times.

Ideas for effective stretching

▶ Include stretching after a gentle warm-up or a soft tissue massage.
▶ Combine with thermotherapy-based treatments.
▶ Always ensure correct technique.
▶ Cryotherapy prior to stretching might reduce pain and spasm.
▶ Stretching must be pain-free, not discomfort-free.
▶ To progress stretching, think about the type of stretching and its duration, frequency and intensity.

Link

Fitness testing is covered in *Unit 4: Field- and Laboratory-based Fitness Testing.*

 PAUSE POINT   Without looking at this book, list the different stretching-based techniques used in rehabilitation.

   Hint   Why do stretching-based exercises need to be carried out on a regular basis?

   Extend   What are the strengths and weaknesses of each of the stretching techniques?

Methods to improve muscle conditioning

There are three main components to muscle conditioning:

▶ **muscle strength** – ability to exert force on an object
▶ **muscle power** – rate at which a muscle can exert force
▶ **muscle endurance** – ability to contract repeatedly without excess fatigue.

It is important to restore all of these to near pre-injury levels before the athlete returns to full training and returns to action. When performing muscle conditioning work, the technique must be good to avoid **secondary injury** or causing re-injury.

The key to effective muscle conditioning is with the loading, both resistance and repetitions. Having pre-injury base line scores is a good way to check the progress of the rehabilitation programme. In the absence of these scores, using an injured versus non-injured comparison from testing can be useful.

Muscle strength

Muscle strength is gained by the athlete performing high-weight/low-repetition exercises. The type of muscular contraction the athlete has to perform progresses throughout rehabilitation.

▶ In the early stages of rehabilitation, the athlete should perform **isometric** contractions to maintain muscle strength as this does not involve moving the joint through a full range.
▶ As rehabilitation progresses, **isokinetic** contractions which are slow and controlled can be used.
▶ Finally, **isotonic** contractions, involving a **concentric** and **eccentric** phase and that mirror the demands of sport much more, should be used.

Using whole body strengthening exercises is often safer and more functional than overly isolating vulnerable tissues too soon in rehabilitation. It is important that the athlete is both concentrically and eccentrically strong on returning to training and sport.

Key terms

Secondary injury – an injury to another part of the body as a result of the initial injury, for example through compensating.

Isometric – when the muscle contracts without a change in length.

Isokinetic – when the muscle contracts with constant speed and resistance.

Isotonic – when the muscle contracts with a lifting and lowering phase.

Concentric – when the muscle contracts and shortens.

Eccentric – when the muscle contracts and lengthens.

Muscle power

Muscle power is gained by increasing the speed of contraction or using exercises with rapid transition between eccentric and concentric contractions. For example, with repeated squat jumps the landing phase is the eccentric contraction and the upwards jump phase is the concentric contraction.

These exercises should clearly be avoided in the early stages of rehabilitation because of high loading of the tissues. Power-based exercises could include:

▶ fast isotonic or isokinetic movements
▶ increased speed of functional exercises. for example calf raises, squats
▶ **plyometric** exercises, for example hopping, bounding, counter movement jumps.

Muscle endurance

Muscle endurance is developed by performing low- to moderate-weight/high-repetition exercises (for example body weight squats, lunge walking) or sustained high-intensity, low-intensity exercise (e.g. cycling with high-resistance intervals, performing exercise in a swimming pool using buoyancy aids). Incorporating many rehabilitation exercises into a circuit training session for the athlete is another good way to improve muscle endurance.

With sustained muscle endurance exercises, remember to monitor how fatigue affects technique and pain.

Ⅱ PAUSE POINT   How can we plan safe and effective muscle conditioning exercises for hamstring injuries?

Hint   Give five examples of specific muscle conditioning exercises for an athlete with a strained hamstring.

Extend   Explain why muscle conditioning exercise must be carried out with the correct technique.

Methods to improve neuromuscular control

Neuromuscular control refers to the ability of nerves to sense and then affect the muscles in order to stabilise joints and maintain balance. It also plays an important role in further injury prevention. This can be developed by the athlete taking part in balance, coordination, and **proprioception**-based exercises. These exercises enhance joint stability through interplay between sensory **mechanoreceptors** (detecting joint and body position) and the central nervous system (CNS).

Exercises such as single leg stands, tandem stance, and jumping and landing exercises can all improve neuromuscular control. You can progress the different surfaces you use through rehabilitation (for example trampoline to sprung flooring to harder surfaces), and use equipment such as wobble boards, BOSU balls, and Swiss balls to challenge the body's ability to maintain stability.

Methods to improve skill acquisition and functionality

Once the athlete has regained their muscle conditioning, range of motion and neuromuscular control, you can incorporate sport-specific skills and functional exercise into their rehabilitation plan. These can then be progressed until the athlete returns to full training and sport. The exercises should involve combining all other types of exercise, but in a realistic environment based on specific sport demands, mimicking the movements and skills that form the basis of their sport. The sooner sports equipment (for example rackets and balls) is introduced, the quicker sports skills and confidence in executing these skills will be restored.

For example, progression of functional exercise for a footballer who has suffered a severe lower limb injury may follow the pattern of:

▶ walking with a gradual increase in intensity and distance (without and with the ball)
▶ jogging with a gradual increase in intensity and distance (without and with the ball)
▶ running with a gradual increase in intensity and distance, for example 20–30–40 m (without and with the ball)

> **Key terms**
>
> **Plyometric** – an explosive contraction with rapid transition between eccentric and concentric phases.
>
> **Proprioception** – the ability to sense where the body is in space.
>
> **Mechanoreceptors** – movement sensing nerves.

- linear sprinting with a gradual increase in intensity and distance (without and with the ball)
- curvilinear sprinting e.g. figures of eight
- agility and change of direction drills, for example narrow (45 degrees) and wide cutting (90 degrees).

As the athlete nears returning to training and sport, the rehabilitation plan needs to mirror the demands of that sport. Factors to consider include intensity, movement patterns, surface, work/rest ratios, duration and distance covered.

PAUSE POINT	How can we make rehabilitation sport-specific to help athletes prepare to return to sport after injury?
Hint	Create three sport-specific drills (for a sport of your choice) that an athlete might complete in the late stages of their rehabilitation.
Extend	Justify your drills in terms of intensity, distance, movement patterns, surface and work/rest ratio.

Return to sport criteria

An athlete should return to training and sport when they are both physically and psychologically ready to do so. Put criteria in place to help practitioners make this decision. These criteria could include:

- full pain-free range of motion and flexibility
- no persistent swelling
- muscle conditioning comparable to the non-affected body part
- fitness levels the same as baseline pre-injury measures or better
- the athlete being psychologically ready (low anxiety, good confidence)
- the coach satisfied with training form
- sport skills having been regained.

Assessment practice 17.2

B.P3 B.P4 B.M3 B.M4 B.D2

Two important aims of sports injury management are to provide immediate sports trauma care and then to provide safe and appropriate rehabilitation plans. You are working as head sports therapist for a rugby union team. You want to conduct a professional development event aimed at upskilling your medical team on the treatment and rehabilitation of sports injury.

Part one

Sports trauma care needs to be pre-planned and follow a logical process. Produce flow diagrams showing how you manage the scenarios below:

- a dislocated shoulder
- an unconscious athlete
- a bleeding athlete with potential shock
- sprained lateral ligaments (grade 2) of the ankle.

The flow diagrams should be clear and identify the process you would follow and who you would refer on to. Explain them to a class-mate and get feedback. Could they follow the flow diagrams?

Now role play each scenario with some classmates – did you manage the four injuries safely and confidently?

Part two

For an athlete who has a grade 2 sprain of their lateral ankle ligaments, design a progressive rehabilitation plan for each of the five stages of rehabilitation to ensure that they return to training and sport physically and psychologically ready. Be as specific as possible, and provide progression and regression alternatives for the exercises you choose. You should be able to justify your rehabilitation plans and try to support the plans with evidence.

Create some criteria that you could use to determine their ability to return to training and sport, and give some future recommendations for the athlete by explaining how re-injury to the ankle could be prevented.

Plan
- What is the task? What am I being asked to do?
- How confident do I feel in my own abilities to complete this task? Are there any areas I think I may struggle with?

Do
- I know what it is I'm doing and what I want to achieve.
- I can identify where I've gone wrong and adjust my thinking/approach to get myself back on course.

Review
- I can explain what the task was and how I approached it.
- I can explain what I would do differently next time.

C **Investigate risk factors which may contribute to sports injuries and their associated prevention strategies**

To repeat an old phrase, it is better to prevent injuries than to cure them (or rehabilitate). Before you can effectively prevent injuries occurring, you must understand the factors that might cause an injury to occur. Once you have understood these factors and how they interlink, robust preventative measures can be put in place to reduce injury risk.

Aetiology of sports injury

The word 'aetiology' broadly means the science of causation – it is the study of factors that cause a sports injury to occur. Sports injury can be caused by a variety of factors which fall into two categories – **intrinsic** and **extrinsic**. These factors all combine during sport to cause an injury. Identifying the risk factors could dramatically reduce the chances of an athlete suffering the different types of injury.

Intrinsic risk factors

These risk factors originate within the athlete's body and predispose them to either an increased or decreased chance of getting injured during sport or exercise. Intrinsic risk factors include the following.

▶ **Muscular factors** – this includes having muscle imbalances leading to difference between dominant and non-dominant limbs, and also between agonist (causing an action) and antagonist (blocking an action). A common example is a poor quadriceps to hamstring strength/power ratio. A weaker muscle is more prone to fatigue and injury. The body may have to compensate due to muscular weakness. Muscle weakness and leg length discrepancies also fall into this category.

▶ **Lack of flexibility** – competitive sport often requires athletes to execute movement patterns right at the end of their range of motion, for example stretching to catch a ball in cricket or lunging to make a tackle in football. Generalised muscle tightness that is focal areas of muscle thickening due to repetitive loading or restricted range of motion, can increase the risk of injury. It can affect muscles, tendons and joints. For example, over-tight hamstrings may tear during rapid deceleration or over-tight quadriceps may irritate the patellar tendon causing tendinopathy symptoms.

▶ **Individual variables** – these are unique characteristics of the athlete contributing to injury. Injury patterns are different based on an athlete's age, growth and development, and gender. For example, younger athletes are more at risk of apophysitis injury and older athletes of strains. The period of **peak height velocity** (PHV) in youth athletes is a time where injury risk is high. Females are more at risk of anterior cruciate ligament (ACL) sprains. One of the biggest risk factors is previous injury history, for example a history of lateral ankle sprain, ACL sprain, or hamstring strains. These would increase your risk of further injury. Body size and composition are also risk factors with under-weight (low body fat percentage) or over-weight having an increased risk. Unfit athletes will fatigue quickly and have an increasing risk of injury compared with an appropriately conditioned athlete.

▶ **Postural defects** – abnormal curvature of the spine is a potential risk that can become degenerative and restrict sporting potential. Examples of such malalignment of the vertebrae include **scoliosis**, **flat back**, excessive **kyphosis** and excessive **lordosis**. These problems can occur both independently and together (to a certain degree). Overuse and insufficient recovery following exercise and excessive strain on a body part can also exacerbate injuries and worsen existing postural defects. As we get older, our intervertebral discs become thinner which can also increase the risk of injury.

Key terms

Intrinsic factors – the factors within the body that increase the risk of injury.

Extrinsic factors – factors outside of the body that increase the risk of injury.

Peak height velocity (PHV) – the period when growth rate is at its fastest or the growth spurt.

Scoliosis – an abnormal lateral shift or curve in the spine.

Flat back – insufficient curvature in the spine to distribute forces.

Kyphosis – a condition in the back where there is an outward curve of the spine.

Lordosis – a condition in the lower back where there is excessive inward curvature of the lumbar region of the vertebral column.

Research

Why might females be more at risk of ACL injury than males? Create a Twitter status (140 characters) of your results. What have your classmates written?

▸ **Malalignment** – asymmetry or malalignment within the athlete can lead to excessive forces going through the body as the athlete compensates. Examples include changing running technique due to one leg being longer than the other (leg length discrepancy) or knees collapsing inwards on landing (genu valgum) due to a broad pelvis (wide quadriceps or Q angle). Common malalignment examples include: pes planus, pes cavus, rearfoot varus, tibial vara, genu varum, genu varus, patella alta, tibial torsion and femoral neck anteversion.

▸ **Psychological factors** – an athlete's psychological make-up can make them at risk of injury. This includes their personality, stressors (sporting and non-sporting), and coping resources. Having high life stress, little social support, high trait anxiety, and overusing avoidance coping resources are linked with increased injury risk.

Extrinsic risk factors

These risk factors originate outside the athlete's body and mean they have either an increased or decreased chance of getting injured. Together with intrinsic factors they determine how susceptible to injury the athlete is. Extrinsic factors include the following.

▸ **Training errors** – excessive training load (volume, intensity) often with little or no recovery is a common factor in athletes suffering injury, causing fatigue. Any sudden increase or changes to training load (volume, intensity, type) are also important risk factors. Training frequently involves repetitive movements, sometimes with resistance or weights, so doing these movements with poor technique can increase the risk of injury. Competing too often (for example twice per week or more) can also increase the risk of getting injured.

▸ **Coaching and social factors** – the types and number of injuries their team suffers tend to follow a coach from club to club. This means your coach is an injury risk factor. The coaching style, style of play, communication, expectations, adherence to rules and professional body guidelines may all influence whether athletes get injured. The attitude and culture of the team and the sport may also be an injury risk, for example, playing to hurt the opposition.

▸ **Incorrect technique** – an athlete that moves well is less at risk of injury and vice versa. Sports skills are made up of fundamental movement patterns, and if these are poor becasue the athelete is fatigued or has to do them with intensity, the risk of injury increases. For example, the defending position in football is the same as a semi-squat. If a player can't perform a semi-squat correctly, they are at risk every time they get into the defending position. Poor manual handling and lifting techniques can increase risk of injury in sports where this occurs, such as in a line-out in rugby union.

▸ **Clothing and footwear** – not wearing the correct clothing or having the correct equipment for your sport will create major extrinsic risk factors. Examples include the wrong footwear for the activity or playing surface, damaged, or too much or too little, protective equipment, or the wrong protective equipment for the sport.

▸ **Safety hazards** – it is important for coaches, support staff and players to be aware of hazards and risks associated with the activities being undertaken. Various health and safety considerations must be applied to all activities both before and during participation. For example, risk assessment, medical emergency action plans and health screening (sometimes including electrocardiogram screening) should all be implemented.

▸ **Environmental factors** – closely linked to safety hazards are environmental factors. The weather conditions can affect the likelihood of an injury. For example, rain may make the playing surface slippery, which will increase the chance of injury. The playing surface itself also has an impact (whether it is hard or soft).

▸ **Misuse of equipment** – the misuse and abuse of equipment causes risks to sports players, as it is specifically designed to do a particular job. Tampering with or modifying equipment will make it less useful and often dangerous.

▶ **Inadequate nutrition and hydration** – having too little energy from an inappropriate pre-match meal increases time to fatigue and the risk of injury. A regular energy deficit for an athlete may increase the risk of injury and other health issues. Taking part in sport when dehydrated is also linked to early fatigue and can cause heat-related illness. Poor nutrition after training and competing will delay recovery and over time become injury risk factors as tissue fails to repair.

Theory into practice

To reduce the impact of sports injuries, it is important that the practitioner helps prevent them from occurring. Many practitioners may have a role to play in injury preventions. Using the information on extrinsic risk factors, create a list of 'do's and don't's' for rugby union players to follow with the aim of reducing injuries.

Ⅱ PAUSE POINT   Can you explain the process of how sports injuries occur?

> Hint   What do you think your own unique predisposing/intrinsic risk factors are?

> Extend   What are the extrinsic risk factors in your sport?

Preventative measures

One of the most important roles of a sports injury practitioner is to prevent injuries and thus the physical, mental, social and financial harm that goes with them. **Primary prevention** is preventing injuries in a certain sport/team. **Secondary prevention** is working with an injured athlete and working out how to reduce further injury or re-injury. Any approach to preventing injuries should be well informed, logical and use a framework.

Principles of injury prevention

There are two major sports injury prevention frameworks – created by Van Mechelen et al. (1992) and by Van Tiggelen et al. (2008). The four-step model of injury prevention (see Figure 17.9) suggests a cycle of stages going from establishing the injury problem to ultimately evaluating if the preventative measure has affected the number and type of injuries.

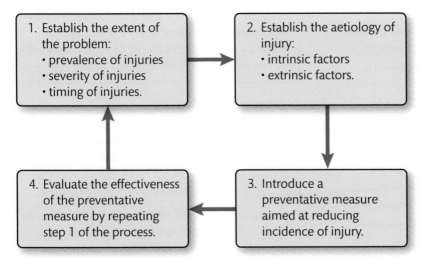

1. Establish the extent of the problem:
   • prevalence of injuries
   • severity of injuries
   • timing of injuries.

2. Establish the aetiology of injury:
   • intrinsic factors
   • extrinsic factors.

3. Introduce a preventative measure aimed at reducing incidence of injury.

4. Evaluate the effectiveness of the preventative measure by repeating step 1 of the process.

▶ **Figure 17.9:** The four-step model of injury prevention

More recently, Van Tiggelen et al. (2008) suggest an additional process which sports injury practitioners need to take into account. Before implementing preventative measures, this involves thinking about:

- **efficacy** – does research say it will work?
- **efficiency** – what are the time and resourcing demands?
- **compliance** – are athletes likely to adhere to it?

> **Theory into practice**
>
> For a sport of your choice, explain how you would go through the four steps of injury prevention. Why is the Van Tiggelen et al. (2008) approach to prevention beneficial for sports injury practitioners?

Responsibility for preventative measures

Many preventative measures vary based on the demands of the sport, the level of competition, resources available and contact time with athletes. But many individuals are responsible for injury prevention including the coach, players, sports injury practitioners, referees, sports scientists and conditioning coaches – it should be a real team effort. Some general preventative measures are covered in this section.

The role of the coach

The coach has a huge role to play in preventing injuries. A coach should have up-to-date qualifications and knowledge of the sport and their athletes. This includes monitoring of loading (physical and cognitive), and each athlete's strengths and weaknesses. They should be able to adapt their coaching style, communication style and expectations to the athlete's ability, age, fitness, gender and motivation. For example, they should not coach children as if they are mini adults, and should stress the dangers of early specialisation in sport.

The coach also has a role in reinforcing health and safety, making sure athletes wear protective equipment, surveying the playing surface and ensuring equipment is safe to use.

Equipment and environment

A thorough risk assessment of the training and competition environment must be carried out. It is also important to go through this procedure for the equipment that is used (for example, protective equipment). In many sports, protective equipment has changed dramatically as technological advances in the materials available and biomechanical analysis techniques (research and analysis of movement) have allowed improvements in quality. Advances have been made in both protecting of specific body parts and limiting the negative impact of the protection on playing performance (such as excess weight and decreased range of movement).

Sports players need to ensure that any sport-specific or specialist protective equipment is used correctly. If it is used incorrectly, it can be a hazard, putting yourself and other athletes at risk. When using different types of protective equipment, you should:

- ensure that the equipment is thoroughly checked prior to use

- use the equipment only for the sport for which it is designed
- use only the correct size
- not make modifications to the equipment
- be aware that protective equipment does not make you invincible
- use the equipment for both practice and competition.

Environmental conditions should also be considered to help reduce injury risk. For example, a training session held on grass might reduce the risk compared with the same training session on a hard surface. If weather conditions change, perhaps with rain making a surface slippery, then the session could be moved indoors.

Performer preparation

Properly preparing the athlete to take part in training and competition will also reduce their risk of injury. An effective warm-up should prepare the athlete to work at game pace. A good warm-up should follow the RAMP acronym.

- **R** – **raise** the blood flow, breathing rate and heart rate.
- **A** – **activate** key muscle groups using dynamic stretches.
- **M** – **mobilise** the major joints.
- **P** – **potentiate** muscles to improve effectiveness through jumping and landing, sprinting, cutting movements.

An athlete who has been sitting down or standing still for a period of time (for example a substitute) should be encouraged to re-warm. All athletes should also take part in a cool-down after training or competition.

Measures to improve mobility should be taken on most days. These measures only work if they are done on a regular basis. They could include stretching, foam rolling or having a regular sports massage.

> **Theory into practice**
>
> For your sport, create a warm-up routine that could reduce the risk of injury. Carry this out and gain feedback from coaches and athletes. Did they enjoy it? Would they do it again? What would you change?

Appropriate training

Athletes should be appropriately trained to meet the demands of the sport and have sufficient recovery after training and competition. This means carefully following periodised training without rapid increases in the frequency, duration, intensity or type of training.

Training methods should be as specific to the demands of the sport as possible. Preventative exercises usually try to develop core stability for postural control, proprioception and balance, muscle strength, such as eccentric hamstring strength, and good landing control.

Correction of biomechanical abnormalities

Each player should be screened to identify any potential

abnormalities that could lead to injury. For example, screening athletes for adequate range of motion at major joints (too little or too much), limb length discrepancy (such as leg length), posture and gait analysis, and assessing the quality of fundamental movement patterns will highlight any issues that might need to be addressed. This may then lead to the athlete needing one-to-one strength and conditioning support, engaging in a programme of suitable core stability training or stretching, or being referred to a **podiatrist** to correct these faults.

> **Key term**
>
> **Podiatrist** – a practitioner who takes care of people's feet and treats foot diseases.

Other measures

▶ Taping and bracing certain 'at risk' joints or muscles (for example using athletic tape or kinesiology taping) may prevent injuries through correcting biomechanical issues by providing stability to joints or addressing muscle weakness and tightness.

▶ Ensuring an athlete's diet contains plenty of energy facilitates adequate recovery, and making sure they are fully hydrated will help prevent injury and illness.

▶ Psychological skills training (PST) such as imagery, progressive muscle relaxation, and self-talk will also reduce the physical and mental impact of stressors and reduce injury risk.

Sleep (both its quality and quantity) is an important part of recovery and following good sleeping practices that improve sleep patterns may reduce injuries (for example no mobile phones in the bedroom, avoiding big meals before bed).

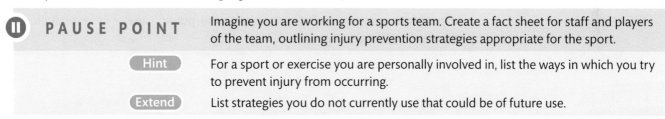

Ⅱ PAUSE POINT
Imagine you are working for a sports team. Create a fact sheet for staff and players of the team, outlining injury prevention strategies appropriate for the sport.

Hint
For a sport or exercise you are personally involved in, list the ways in which you try to prevent injury from occurring.

Extend
List strategies you do not currently use that could be of future use.

Assessment practice 17.3
`C.P5` `C.M5` `C.D3` `C.D4`

The manager of the team you are working with has read that the most successful teams suffer fewer injuries compared with others. He has asked you to produce an information sheet that evaluates the role of sports injury management within the team and outlines your plan for injury prevention for the upcoming season. You have decided to use the four-step model of injury prevention by Van Mechelen et al. (1992) to help structure your decisions. On the information sheet, you need to explain each step using examples.

Introduction – what is the role of sports injury management, and what impact might effective sports injury management have on the team?

Step 1 – assess the extent of the problem and how you would go about doing this.

Step 2 – assess the common intrinsic and extrinsic risk factors in the sport, and how these interact.

Step 3 – suggest three specific preventative measures you would introduce and how these would work.

Step 4 – state how you would evaluate the preventative measures.

The sport on which this activity is based is your choice.

Plan
- What information do I need to put on my information sheet?
- Which sport am I basing this on?
- How confident do I feel in my own abilities to complete this task?

Do
- I know how effective sports injury management can have an impact on a team.
- I know the four steps of the model and can apply these to my sport.
- I know where to get evidence from to support my information.
- I am aware of the possible consequences for athletes who do not have access to sports injury prevention methods.

Review
- I can explain how I would improve the content on the information sheet next time.
- I can identify the assessment criteria I have achieved on my work.
- I know what I did well and what I need to improve upon.

Further reading and resources

Brukner & Khan's Clinical Sports Medicine: Injuries: Vol. 1 (2017), Australia: McGraw-Hill Education.

Forsdyke, D., Gledhill, A., Mackay, N. and Randerson, K. (2011) *Foundations in Sports Therapy*, London: Heinemann.

Joyce D. and Lewindon D. (2015) *Sports Injury Prevention and Rehabilitation: Integrating Medicine and Science for Performance Solutions*, London: Routledge.

Websites

http://www.physioroom.com – sports injury website with educational content and specialist terms explained.

http://bjsm.bmj.com/site/podcasts – an international peer-reviewed journal of sport and exercise medicine.

http://www.electrotherapy.org – information on various aspects of electrotherapy and tissue-healing written by experts

https://www.resus.org.uk/information-for-the-public – advice on resuscitation guidelines for the general public.

THINK ▶FUTURE

Shane Rafferty

Academy
movement coach

I've been working as a movement coach for the past two years since graduating with a degree in Physical Education and Sports Coaching. The role involves working with young footballers and coaching fundamental movement patterns to make each player more athletic, hopefully reducing the risk of injury in the future. My role involves working alongside both the technical team and the medical and science team.

I first became interested in the prevention of sports injuries because I have had a few injuries myself and my BTEC Diploma had some injury-related units which I loved. My degree was great as I learned about the theory of coaching good movement patterns with youth athletes as an essential part of their long-term development.

I am really passionate about my role because when I played sport no one taught me how to move effectively, which I think is why I suffered so many injuries. I am part of the science and medical team which monitors each player's movement abilities and reports back to them regularly.

Focusing your skills

Interpersonal skills

When working with youth athletes, effective interpersonal skills are very important.

- What might happen if you don't have effective interpersonal skills?

- What specific interpersonal skills do you think are important?

- Which of these skills do you need to develop?

- Try and observe a practising sports injury practitioner or strength and conditioning coach, and reflect on the interpersonal skills they use. Create a list of these skills.

- A good way to develop sound interpersonal skills further is to ask athletes which skills they would want a movement coach to have.

- Do the same with a technical coach of a team about the skills they would want from a movement coach. How do they compare?

Effective movement patterns

It is important that athletes can perform basic movement patterns. This will help them with their sport performance and to remain injury-free.

- What do you think basic movement patterns are?

- Which professionals might be involved in helping coach effective movement patterns?

- At what point during a player's development might movement patterns become poor? How can effective movement patterns improve sport performance? How can effective movement patterns reduce the risk of injury?

Getting ready for assessment

Mo is working towards a BTEC National in Sport. He was given an assignment for learning aim C with the title 'Prevention is better than cure'. He had to design a poster on how to prevent sports injury in a specific sport which had to outline the four-step sequence of injury prevention.

▶ Stage 1 – research the common injuries in your chosen sport.

▶ Stage 2 – what is the aetiology and mechanism of these injuries?

▶ Stage 3 – suggest three preventative measures and how these might work.

▶ Stage 4 – how could the impact of these preventative measures be measured?

Mo shares his experience below.

How I got started

First, I collected all my notes on this topic and put them into a folder. I decided on my sport pretty early on and began to research the information I needed on injury rate, injury types, and injury causes using the Internet and textbooks. I made sure I used a few sources to find this information to make sure the information on the poster was reliable. My tutor said this was a very wise thing to do.

I chose a sport that I am interested in because I knew this would make me more motivated and committed to do a good job. I created a plan of action so I could spend the week before the deadline just checking things over, and so I wasn't rushing to get it finished.

How I brought it all together

I thought about how I was going to present the poster and what an effective poster looks like. I even asked my mum and dad what they thought. I decided to use a variety of colours and pictures to make people want to read the poster. I planned what I wanted the poster to look like on an A4 sheet of paper before starting. I created an eye-catching title for the poster, then:

▶ created an introduction section that evaluated the role of sports injury management in my sport

▶ used an image of the four-step sequence image as a template to put my information into – this meant my tutor could easily see how I had applied the theory

▶ got feedback from my mum and dad about how the information was presented and how the poster looked

▶ made sure I put the references from the Internet, books, and the journals I used on the back of the poster.

What I learned from the experience

The key things I learned from this experience were that researching on the Internet is really good but always to cross-check the reliability of information as different sites said different things. I found this quite confusing to start with, so I asked my tutor what he thought. He said sometimes books and journals are more reliable. It took me a long time but I found and included some information from a journal article about how effective the FIFA 11+ warm-up is. My tutor highlighted this in my feedback.

Chatting to my classmates about my progress and sharing ideas was really good as they reassured me my work was good quality.

Despite me trying to make my poster look effective, it has too much small writing on it meaning people might not want to look at it. In the future, I will think about the amount and size of my information.

Think about it

▶ Have you written a plan with timings so you can complete your assignment by the submission date?

▶ Do you have notes on injury risk factors, and the theories of how injuries can be prevented?

▶ Is your information written in your own words and referenced clearly where you have used quotations or information from a book, journal or website?

Work Experience in Active Leisure 18

Getting to know your unit

This is your chance to discover what it is like to work in the sports and leisure industry. The aim of the unit is to equip you with the skills to complete a work experience placement.

Sport and leisure is a growth industry with diverse opportunities. There are many career opportunities related to sport including management positions, coaching and fitness, sports development, sports science jobs, teaching, sports attendants and lifeguards. Work experience gives you the chance to progress your career. It looks great on your CV – it is an opportunity for somebody to give you a glowing reference and it will help you make career decisions.

How you will be assessed

This unit will be internally assessed through a series of tasks set by your tutor. Throughout this unit, you will find assessment activities that will help you work towards your assessment. Completing these activities will not mean that you have achieved a particular grade, but you will have carried out useful research or preparation that will be relevant when it comes to your final assignment.

For you to achieve the tasks in your assignment, it is important to check that you have met all of the Pass grading criteria. You can do this as you work your way through the assignment.

If you are hoping to gain a Merit or Distinction, you should also make sure that you present the information in your assignment in the style that is required by the relevant assessment criteria. For example, Merit criteria often require you to analyse whereas Distinction criteria require you to evaluate.

The assignment set by your tutor will consist of a number of tasks designed to meet the criteria in the table. This is likely to consist of a mixture of written and practical assignments and include activities such as:

▶ researching where you might have the opportunity to get a placement and designing a personal action plan related to your placement

▶ completing online or paper applications for your placement, composing letters and CVs and being interviewed by a panel for your placement

▶ keeping a record, such as a diary or a logbook, that details what you have done on your placement and how you feel at the time

▶ completing a self-appraisal that analyses your performance during the placement, identifying both the skills that you have learned and used and those that you now realise you need in order to attain employment in this or a similar position.

Assessment criteria

This table shows what you must do in order to achieve a **Pass**, **Merit** or **Distinction** grade, and where you can find activities to help you

Pass	Merit	Distinction

Learning aim A Undertake in-depth preparation for an active leisure work experience placement

Pass	Merit	Distinction
A.P1 Create a fit-for-purpose work experience action plan. **Assessment activity 18.1**	**A.M1** Explain how a chosen active leisure work experience placement is relevant to own career development as identified in work experience action plan. **Assessment activity 18.1**	**A.D1** Justify the appropriateness of the selected active leisure work experience placement against career aspirations and development identified in work experience action plan. **Assessment activity 18.1**
A.P2 Summarise own suitability for the chosen active leisure work experience placement. **Assessment activity 18.1**		

Learning aim B Undertake a job application process for an active leisure work experience placement

Pass	Merit	Distinction
B.P3 Assess own performance in the job application and workplace placement selection interview process. **Assessment activity 18.2**	**B.M2** Analyse own performance in the job application and interview process. **Assessment activity 18.2**	**B.D2** Evaluate own performance in the job application and interview process, justifying strengths, areas for improvement and the next steps necessary to make the identified improvements required. **Assessment activity 18.2**

Learning aim C Carry out work experience tasks to meet set objectives from work experience action plan

Pass	Merit	Distinction
C.P4 Demonstrate work-related skills to meet set objectives for work experience tasks. **Assessment activity 18.3**	**C.M3** Demonstrate work-related skills with confidence and proficiency to meet objectives in different situations. **Assessment activity 18.3**	**CD.D3** Evaluate the impact of preparing for, participating in, and reviewing an active leisure work placement on own future plans for personal and professional development, justifying further opportunities that this and similar organisations could provide to develop own skills and knowledge. **Assessment activity 18.3**

Learning aim D Investigate the impact of an active leisure work experience placement on career development

Pass	Merit	Distinction
D.P5 Discuss chosen active leisure work experience organisation providing evidence of research into history, structure, culture and opportunities offered by the business. **Assessment activity 18.3**	**D.M4** Compare roles and opportunities offered by chosen active leisure work experience organisation to other similar organisations. **Assessment activity 18.3**	
D.P6 Review own work experience performance, identifying strengths, areas for improvement and impact on own career development. **Assessment activity 18.3**	**D.M5** Analyse own work experience performance in applying work-related skills and impact on own career development, providing recommendations for future development. **Assessment activity 18.3**	

Getting Started

Work experience is a great way to practise working in a career that you may want to pursue. The sports and leisure industry is very diverse and includes therapists, managers, coaches, teachers, engineers and lifeguards to mention just a few. The organisation that represents the industry and ensures that standards are established for sport in education is called SkillsActive. Take a look at what it does and who it represents. This will help you to understand better the extent and range of what you could take on as a placement.

A Undertake in-depth preparation for an active leisure work experience placement

Work experience action plan

Link

This unit has strong links with *Unit 3: Professional Development in the Sports Industry*.

Before you research where and when you might carry out a work experience placement, you need to prepare a formal work experience action plan to help you move in the right direction. This is particularly important if you are not exactly sure what direction you might want your career to move in. It is not essential you secure a placement in the job of your dreams, but it would be useful if your placement helps you to reach that end goal.

There are many different templates for a work experience action plan, but as a minimum they should include:
- your personal details
- what kind of placement you would like
- which job roles you would like to work alongside or with
- your overall aims for the placement (which could be as simple as practising basic skills or observing other professionals)
- your current strengths and weaknesses from the employers' perspective.

Your plan will also set out the aims and goals for your work placements and the sort of experience and skills you will want to develop during the work experience, as well as help to identify any particular skills or knowledge you need to have before beginning.

Before putting together a plan, you will need to look at your own interests and skills, and put together a series of goals for your career. Ask yourself the following questions.
- What do you want to do? What are your current career aspirations?
- What are your sporting interests and what are your specific skills, both personal and sports-based?

This self-evaluation is a crucial part of any work experience action plan, as you will need to continually review your own skill set and goals throughout your career.

Content of a work experience action plan

Your work experience action plan should cover the following.
- **Short-term goals** might be achieved in the immediate future, and could include completing your BTEC course, achieving some coaching qualifications or training in software applications relevant to the industry. You should have some idea of your career aspirations.
- **Medium-term goals** are more concerned with the next 6–12 months and are likely to see you either employed or at university on your way to achieving your longer-term aims.

▶ **Long-term goals** look ahead to 2–5 years' time, perhaps at the end of a university course, a training programme or following an apprenticeship or internship.

▶ **Work-related aims** are specific to the role you are interested in, such as learning massage techniques for a sports therapist or coaching techniques for an archery instructor. You should have some vision of your future career direction and how work experience will help to achieve this.

▶ **Personal skills** are related to your own current knowledge and skills. They might relate to specific qualifications or be connected to areas like organisation, communication or teamwork. Sport-specific skills are also personal skills. There will be several areas you may be looking to improve in, or new personal skills you need to develop, and your plan should include opportunities and goals for developing these.

▶ **Self-assessment summary statements** might look at your current career motivators plus both your existing work-related skills and competencies and those that you still need to develop.

▶ **Development activities and experiences** illustrate your commitment and lead you towards actions required for your eventual career goals. These actions should include:

- **success criteria** – these will detail how you know that your target has been completed and could include completing an apprenticeship, completing stages of a training programme or the first year of a higher education course
- **target completion dates** – an idea of the order in which you will complete your targets.

You will need to have a clear idea of what resources you might need to achieve any goals, aims and outcomes.

Remember your goals need to be SMARTER (see Table 18.1). Some versions of this SMARTER abbreviation replace 'evaluated' with 'exciting' or 'recorded' with 'reviewed'.

▶ **Table 18.1:** SMARTER targets including review

Element		Meaning	Example
S	Specific	Your targets should relate to something in particular that you want to achieve.	I want a work experience placement in a leisure centre.
M	Measurable	You should be able to measure them.	I want to find ten contacts for work experience placements.
A	Achievable	You must be able to attain them.	I am going to set myself a task and a date that are real so that they will be met.
R	Realistic	You must set your sights on something you can achieve; otherwise you will be put off.	I must be realistic – will I be able to find myself a placement with a PE teacher in a school?
T	Timed	You must set deadlines that can be met.	I want a placement by 3 January.
E	Evaluated	Afterwards you should complete a review of your target, considering all aspects of them.	I will complete a logbook or diary throughout my placement.
R	Recorded	Afterwards you should complete any necessary documentation.	Along with my diary, I will add information and reports from my colleagues and my supervisor.

Aims and objectives

Aims are 'large' in size and relate to your career and life aims. They are usually challenging such as 'I want to be a PE teacher and I am going to find work experience to find out what it is like'. Objectives are 'medium' in size and are related to how you will achieve your aims. They are medium-term and achievable, such as 'I am going to contact three schools by the end of the week and send my CV with a covering letter' or 'I want to be able to run a whole session by myself'. You will usually have more objectives than aims.

Your goals or targets should be related to **outcomes**. They should satisfy answers to the following questions.

1 What are the aims of my placement? What do I want to get from my placement: skills, knowledge, experience or a mix of each?

2 How does all of it relate to what I want to do as a career in the long term?

Outcomes should be reviewed to make sure there is progress throughout your placement and, critically, at the end. To ensure that you are constantly evaluating, you should ask yourself the following questions.

▶ What progress have I made since last week?
▶ What evidence have I got that proves this?
▶ What else could I do to improve, especially if things are not progressing?
▶ How could I overcome any obstacles?

Prior knowledge and experience

It is important to detail any experiences you already have that might be relevant for your career. For example, if you have volunteered as a sports coach with a group of children, this can relate to the role of lifeguard in a busy swimming pool: it demonstrates your experience with young people, managing behaviour issues and communicating with children and parents.

This is also the best place in the action plan to highlight any leadership experience, perhaps with the scouts or guides, or from helping new players in a tennis club. Sometimes even travelling abroad can be relevant as experiencing other cultures and customs can help you appreciate the needs of a diverse population.

Qualifications are important in any industry, and in the sports industry academic qualifications such as GCSEs – particularly in Maths, English and PE – will help you to progress through further and higher education. In addition, you should also consider other specialist qualifications such as canoeing instructor, tennis coach or what are generally termed National Governing Body (NGB) qualifications for particular sports.

Generic work-related skills

While most occupations and placements have very specific duties, there are some work-related skills required by all jobs in the sports and active leisure industry – and beyond! Your placement is not only about being an effective lifeguard, assistant teacher, technician or fitness assistant; it is also about developing the skills that are required in almost all jobs. These include:

▶ communication skills and ability to work with others
▶ problem solving and organisational skills
▶ ability to work to deadlines
▶ management and leadership skills
▶ negotiation skills
▶ motivational skills
▶ good decision making
▶ research skills.

Technical work-related skills

Technical work-related skills are skills that are specific to the job role you are taking on in the placement. The kind of technical skills you need for your placement will depend on the placement itself and the activities that you do. Here are some examples of typical placement job roles with some of the activities you could be expected to carry out.

▶ Sports coach – planning, setting up and delivering coaching or activity sessions.
▶ Recreation assistant – dismantling and checking equipment and resources, assisting with accident and emergency procedures, and dealing effectively and courteously with colleagues, customers and clients.
▶ Assistant fitness trainer – planning and reviewing a personal training programme and using leadership skills in the session.

Theory into practice

With your intended placement in mind, look at each of the generic work-related skills and describe how each applies to that role. For each skill, try to imagine an example specific to your placement or the job you would like to pursue.

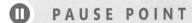

PAUSE POINT What are the important steps in the route to your chosen sport-related career?

> Hint   Make a list of generic skills that would be useful in any sports profession and then rank them in order of importance.

> Extend   From the list of generic skills that you have just devised, appraise your current performance, giving yourself a score out of ten for each. Use this as a set of comparative strengths and areas for improvement.

Case study

Chloe is a BTEC sport student who is preparing to go on a work placement and has been given an action plan to complete. She is not sure whether what she has completed is sufficient.

Check your knowledge

Look at Chloe's action plan (Figure 18.1) and respond to the following.

1 Complete the actions required section for Chloe.

2 Suggest ways in which her plan could be improved.

3 Consider how you would use the plan for yourself and how you would go about completing each section.

▶ **Figure 18.1:** Chloe's action plan so far

ACTION PLAN		
Current career motivators • To be a personal trainer • Working full time in fitness • Eventually to own my fitness business • Providing one-to-one guidance to clients to help them achieve their fitness goals	**Current skills and competencies** • Experience of assisting instructors in a variety of exercise classes • Full first-aid qualification • Qualified tennis coach	**Personal skills** • Excellent communicator • Self-disciplined and motivated • Organisational and leadership experience • Awareness of equality/diversity • Ability to successfully train, motivate and encourage individuals from a range of backgrounds • Excellent knowledge of gym specialist training equipment
Short-term career-related goals (in the next few weeks and months) • Complete BTEC course • Participate in as many fitness sessions as possible • Gain a work placement in a fitness centre where I can shadow a fitness professional(s)	**Medium-term career-related goals (in the next 2 years)** • Consider a university degree in a fitness- or business-related field • Maintain industry links by working part time (at least) in recognised fitness employment • Complete as many health and fitness short courses as possible including Personal Trainer qualification, Exercise to Music, and Exercise for Special Populations	**Long-term career-related goals (beyond 2 years)** • To have started and be working towards completing university degree • To have a comprehensive set of qualifications as part of my CV • To have a business plan for my own fitness business fuelled by my experience and qualifications • To have a small staff and support the local community
Resources required to meet goals Training that allows me to: • devise fitness programmes for weight loss, muscular gain and rehabilitation etc. • conduct fitness and exercise classes and use demonstrating equipment • measure and assess blood pressure, heart recovery rate, body fat ratio • design and advise on dietary programmes.	**Actions required**	

Selection of an appropriate placement

When thinking about suitable work experience placements, it is vital to select a placement that meets your own needs and interests. You should be looking for opportunities and employers that are related to or in the fields or areas of the sports industry in which you would like to develop a career.

There are several different sectors in the sports and leisure industry that you may be interested in working in.

▸ The **health and fitness sector** is made up mainly of centres where clients can use a gym, swim, eat a healthy meal, have a massage and take a fitness class. These centres vary in size, with a range of jobs. See Table 18.2 for example job roles in this sector.

▸ The **sport and recreation sector** includes coaching jobs in a range of specialist sports such as football and ice skating. This sector also includes general leisure centre work, physical education teaching and sports development officers. See Table 18.3 for example job roles in this sector.

▸ **Outdoor education** is a growth area in the sports industry. There are many centres around the country where you can take part in activities such as sailing, surfing and rock climbing. See Table 18.4 for example job roles in this sector.

▸ **Sport and exercise science** is a specialist area of sports provision which works on areas such as the psychology of athletes and analysis of how the body works, suggesting small changes to technique to refine performance. Nutritional advice and injury treatment is also part of this sector. See Table 18.5 for example job roles in this sector.

Research

Identify the careers or jobs you might want to do in the sports industry. Where can you find these jobs locally? Make a list of the name, address, telephone number, email address and contact person at each potential placement in which you are interested.

▸ **Table 18.2:** Health and fitness sector job examples

Job	Outline of role
Sports masseur	Pre-performance massage, post-performance massage and injury rehabilitation.
Personal trainer	Works one to one with a client encouraging and motivating them through their personal workout and exercise plan.
Sports therapist	Works with individuals helping to rehabilitate them from injury.

▸ **Table 18.3:** Sport and recreation sector job examples

Job	Outline of role
Sports attendant/ recreation assistant	Puts out equipment and tidies it away. They keep the centre clean, deal with customers and have a good awareness of health and safety. They may work on the pool side.
Fitness instructor	Most centres have a fitness instructor based at their gym to advise clients about their training programmes and progression.
Sports centre management	Runs the centre on a day-to-day basis. They will open and close the building, deal with any problems, organise the staffing and be responsible for cashing up and developing the centre.
Sports development officer	Responsible for the development of sport in a local area and improving participation. They may specialise in a particular sport and provide opportunities to participate in that sport.
PE teacher	Will have been to university and completed a degree and have QTS (Qualified Teacher Status), and may have completed a PGCE (Post Graduate Certificate in Education). They will have a range of knowledge of sports they will be expected to teach.
Sports coach	Usually specialises in one sport such as football or rugby and could coach a range of different age groups and levels.

▶ **Table 18.3:** – Continued ...

Job	Outline of role
Coaching and fitness instructor	Works with a team or individual to improve the team's performance with drills and fitness tests specifically designed for that sport.
Professional sports performer	Will have a talent for a particular sport such as cycling and will train, usually full time, in that sport to achieve the highest standard possible.
Sports promoter	Could represent a particular performer or team and arrange the team sponsorship deal. They may represent an event to raise its profile, such as the rugby world cup.

▶ **Table 18.4:** Outdoor education job examples

Job	Outline of role
Specialist sports instructor	Specialises in a sport such as canoeing. They could teach children, people with disabilities or adults on a range of courses.
Ground facility worker	Has a specialist knowledge of the physical nature of the playing surfaces. All sports grounds need to be maintained.

▶ **Table 18.5:** Sport and exercise science job examples

Job	Outline of role
Exercise physiologist	May provide scientific support to sportsmen and women in a club or team setting. They might work with cardiac rehabilitation patients and chronic diseases, providing expert advice.
Biomechanist	Uses the scientific principles of mechanics to study the effects of forces on sports performance. They will use this information to improve, refine and develop techniques for sports.
Sports psychologist	Helps with the mental/cognitive components of the performance of sports performers.
Sports dietician	Devises nutritional programmes to help the sports performer to reach their potential by adapting their diet.
Sports scientist	Helps to maximise the performance of an individual, working on small areas of technique or fitness and devising programmes to improve performance.
Sports medicine	A qualified doctor who has decided to specialise in sport. They will diagnose, make recommendations, prescribe and refer.

❚❚ PAUSE POINT   Do you understand what the four main sectors of the sport and active leisure employment sector are?

Hint   Can you name two different job types for each sector?

Extend   Can you provide local examples of specific positions in local sport or leisure organisations for each sector?

SWOT analysis for work experience

Using a **SWOT** analysis can help ensure you have fully considered all aspects of the placement and provide a starting point for reviewing the placement later.

SWOT analysis is carried out to identify internal strengths and weaknesses, as well as external opportunities and threats. The aim is to provide a framework for targets to improve the situation. In this example, it helps identify any improvements required before taking on a work placement.

Key term

SWOT – Strengths, Weaknesses, Opportunities Threats.

Case study

Sohail is hoping to begin a work placement with a sports therapist. His tutor has confirmed there is a placement available but that the therapist would like to speak to him first. Sohail needs to be prepared to discuss why he should have the placement and demonstrate some analysis of his own strengths and weaknesses. He has completed a SWOT analysis (see Figure 18.2) to prepare for the discussion.

Check your knowledge

1 How will this SWOT analysis help Sohail prepare for his placement?

2 Explain why identifying your weaknesses could be seen as a strength when looking at work placement opportunities in sport.

3 Look at the last threat in this case study and see if you can address the issue and come up with a suggestion related to taking every opportunity.

▶ **Figure 18.2:** Sohail's SWOT analysis

SWOT ANALYSIS	
Strengths	**Weaknesses**
• I have a flexible approach to work • A positive attitude to problem solving • A working interest in anatomy and physiology • High level of personal fitness • Experience of working with athletes and competing	• No qualifications in Sports Therapy • No hands-on treatment experience • No previous work experience
Opportunities	**Threats**
• Planned work-based placement as part of my BTEC National in Sport course • Personal involvement with local rugby club shadowing their physiotherapist • Could take out a student membership of The Society of Sports Therapists • Link with the local authority sports development team	• Difficulty remembering detailed anatomical information • The cost of my university course and the debt that I will have afterwards • The number of available work opportunities for therapists compared to the number that qualify every year

Contacting a work experience placement

After you have completed your work experience search, telephone, write to or email the places you have identified. Be very careful how you speak to staff: begin the conversation by saying 'good morning/afternoon', introduce yourself and ask to speak to the person who deals with work experience. If they are not there, ask for the name of the appropriate person and when it will be convenient to call again.

Remember, they may have many enquiries about work experience so remember to call back and if possible leave a message (although do not assume your call will be returned). After a suitable interval, call again, asking for them by name, introducing yourself, what course you are doing, where you are doing it, what your work experience requirement is and when you would like to do it. Have a pen ready to take down any information you may need. Always be polite, enthusiastic and interested in the organisation.

PAUSE POINT   Do you understand why goals are used to help plan your work experience?

    Hint   When writing aims and objectives, why is it important for them to be SMARTER? Try and provide an example.

    Extend   Identify the appropriate specific technical skills of a placement by researching the demands of the position.

Assessment practice 18.1

To demonstrate your ability to plan effectively, design and complete a template for a work experience placement action plan. You will need a sport-specific placement on which you can focus the detail of your action plan. Your plan should demonstrate your current career aspirations, your skills and experience to date, and, where possible, justify the appropriateness of this work experience placement for your chosen employment pathway.

Your plan should show a clear vision of how and where you plan to spend the next few years in terms of career development and when you expect to complete each stage, including the resources that you might need.

Plan
- Have I used a variety of sources to build up my work experience plan?
- Have I built up the work experience plan with details of my own interests and reviewed in which direction I am interested in progressing my career?

Do
- I will complete the work experience action plan in as much detail as possible, with a clear focus and structure.
- I will justify why I have included each step on my action plan in terms of my future career interests.

Review
- I will review the action plan once completed, and continue to review it as my knowledge grows around the sector.

B   Undertake a job application process for an active leisure work experience placement

Completion of the application and interview process

After you have identified your work experience placement, you will probably need to complete an application process to secure the placement. The application process for jobs in the sport and active leisure industry is much the same as with any job. You will need to make sure you have carefully researched the job you would like to apply for, that you understand what the job would entail and that you know how you can convince an employer you are the best person for the role.

Application methods

Application forms

Application forms are the most common way of applying for a job. They are considered good practice because all candidates complete the same form, helping to make sure that they are all judged on the same criteria and fairly on their merits. You may be asked to complete an application form before your work placement.

Online application forms are an increasingly common way to apply for jobs. Employers use these as they can be easily stored, passed on to colleagues or scored against a list of criteria. Online applications are also less expensive and time-consuming, and are increasingly replacing paper-based application forms. **Paper-based application forms** ask for much the same information as online applications, but are completely in writing and kept offline.

When completing an application form, there are several key steps you should follow.
- Read all questions carefully and make sure you answer them fully.
- Write a draft of your answers and check it yourself for spelling and grammar. If possible, ask someone else to check it as well. Computer spell checks will pick up spelling errors, but not incorrect word usage. After you have completed your draft, you can copy your answers onto the form.

- If you are using similar answers for several application forms, make sure you remember to change the name of the company and any details specific to the company (such as the job role).
- Be clear and to the point in your answers – avoid waffling.
- Use any job description or person specification provided by the employer as a guide for what you should include in your answers. (For more about job descriptions and person specifications, see below.)
- Include key verbs linked to the job like 'organised', 'supervised' and 'liaised'. Some employers will scan forms for these words and discard those that don't include them.

CVs

- A curriculum vitae or CV is a summary of yourself, your achievements and your qualifications for a job role – both academic and personal qualifications and experience. A CV should be typed on a single side of A4, although as you gain more experience this will extend to two pages. There are no strict rules about layout, but your CV must be neat, logical and easy for the employer to read and understand.
- Your CV should contain all your personal and contact details, as well as presenting any employment history you have, details of your education and your key achievements (these can be personal, but make sure they are relevant to the job). You will also need to include one or two referees who the employer can contact to check what you have said in your CV is true and accurate.

Adapt your CV for the job you are interested in – different jobs will need you to emphasise different experiences and skills. Leave out any irrelevant information. As with an application form, you can do this by checking against the job description and person specification.

Letter of application

- A letter of application contains much of the same information as a CV but in letter form. Some employers ask for this to see if a candidate is committed enough to the work placement to take the time to write a letter.
- When you send your CV or application form, you will also need to send a short letter with it, sometimes called a **covering letter**, in which you can say something about the role and why you are suitable for it. This is your opportunity to 'sell' your suitability for the role.

Personal statements

- Most application forms give you a generous space to write a personal statement. A personal statement will describe your strengths, skills, attributes, achievements and any other relevant information for the job that you have not covered in another part of the form. This is an extremely important part of the application as candidates are free to write whatever they want; this is where a candidate can make themselves 'stand out from the crowd'.

Job descriptions and person specifications

When applying for jobs or work experience placements, it is important to consider how well your own skill set and personal qualities match those required for the job. You should have already identified your own skills and personal qualities as part of your action planning. To discover the skills and personal qualities needed by the job, you will need to look at the role's **job description** and **person specification**. You may find a job description in the advert for the job or you may be sent it when you apply for the role. The employer may also send you the person specification.

The **job description** describes the duties and responsibilities of a particular job. A job description is likely to include:

Key terms

Covering letter – a short letter sent with a CV or application form.

Job description – an explanation of the duties of a particular job (sometimes called a 'job specification').

Person specification – description of the ideal person for the job in a job description.

- the job title and a brief summary of the job
- who you would report to, for example an assistant manager
- who and what you would be responsible for.

A **person specification** is based on the personal skills, knowledge, qualities, attributes and qualifications needed to do the job as it is described in the job description. It will include:

- personal attributes and qualities
- vocational and academic qualifications
- expected competences and experiences.

Each of these will be identified as being either 'essential' or 'desirable'. This will help you to decide if you have the skill set required for that job role.

The main reason job descriptions and person specifications are used is to give an interviewer a clear and objective basis on which to assess each candidate.

Discussion

In a group, choose a particular active leisure job role. Prepare a job description and a person specification for that role. What are the key areas you need to focus on? Why are these areas important?

Ⅱ PAUSE POINT

Interviewers can use a range of different types of interviews depending on the type of job, time and resources available. It is as well to consider each type so that you are best prepared.

Hint

What are the different ways in which an employer might invite people to apply for a job?

Extend

Prepare a short presentation slide that considers the advantage of online applications over paper-based ones, then another slide that sets out the advantages of paper-based applications.

Interviews

The final stage of many application processes is an interview. In this stage, you will be asked a series of questions based on the details contained in the job description and person specification. The questions will aim to determine whether you have the qualities the employer is looking for. There are several different types of interview that you might experience, shown in Table 18.6.

▶ There are several different types of interview that you might experience

▶ Table 18.6: Types of job interview

Interview type	Description
Group interview	Several candidates at a time meet with one or more interviewers. More companies are starting to use this as a way of quickly removing unsuitable candidates from the process.
Individual interview	The candidate meets with one (or more) interviewer(s) alone. Usually there are several representatives from the different parts of the company that the candidate will be working with. Many people find this type of interview intimidating, so good preparation is essential.
	Some jobs require just an interview – in some cases this might be a phone or online interview, for example via Skype, rather than face to face.
Interview with presentation	Many employers will ask candidates to put together a short presentation to give at the interview which can then be used as the basis for further discussion. This is a good opportunity for you to demonstrate some key work skills, such as communication, organisation and presentation skills, and for you to demonstrate your ideas, dedication and thoroughness. This sort of interview can show what you could bring to the company on a day-to-day basis.
Interview with micro-coach	This interview will also have a short session where you are required to coach to a peer group. It is a good opportunity to demonstrate your skills, knowledge and understanding to the interviewers. The key thing to remember is that the focus is on the learning taking place with those you are coaching, not on the coach. It is always best to rehearse these sessions in advance.
Interview with task performance	This interview will also require you to perform a job-specific task, or series of tasks, related to the job. These might be problem-solving exercises, short presentations to prepare or a short written report.

Interview preparation

There are several key things you can do in advance to prepare for an interview.

▶ You should carry out research into the organisation to find out everything you can about it. This is one of the most important steps and is often overlooked. You might have an idea of what the organisation does (for example, providing after school coaching for primary schools) but you should also know why it does this work (for example, to close the achievement gap) and the organisation's values (such as direct communication and including parents in decision making). An interviewer will expect you to know about the company and the job you are applying for. It will not reflect well on your dedication and interest in the job if you do not have these facts.

▶ Are you a good match for the job? Do you honestly think that you would be the right person for the role? Use the job description and person specification and compare these to your own skills and competencies – is there a good overlap between these? If so, the job will probably be right for you.

▶ Once you have assessed your match for the job, you will need to adjust your CV, personal statement and any other documents to focus on the key skills and experiences asked for by the employer – this will help to show quickly your suitability.

▶ Prepare answers to common questions. You will probably be able to make an educated guess about some of the questions you might be asked for a particular job role, for example if you were applying for a role as a lifeguard. Having prepared answers will help you feel confident for the interview and make sure your answers sound well thought out and professional.

▶ Prepare questions to ask the interviewer – this is another step a lot of people forget to do. All interviewers will give you the opportunity to ask questions – having prepared, relevant questions to ask shows you are interested in, and have thought about, the role in advance.

Interview participation

We can all improve at interviews – the more you practise, the better you will become. Mock interviews can be very good practice to help you relax. They are also a good opportunity to go through the job description and person specification, and try and work out questions that might be asked.

When practising, go through the whole interview process so you can get used to it. When talking to your mock interviewer, practise 'active listening' – this is when you look at the person talking to you, follow what they are saying and show your interest.

Verbal communication

Your verbal communication skills need to be good – you must be clear and not use slang or jargon. You need to be confident and use appropriate language for the industry. If you are not sure about the question you have been asked, ask for clarification from the interviewer.

The interview will have a prepared format, and the format and questions should remain similar for all candidates as the panel will compare the answers.

Tips for clear verbal communication at an interview

Remember the following tips.

- Speak slowly and breathe naturally, and pause if you feel you are speaking too quickly.
- Vary the tone in your voice which will help engage the panel.
- Do not read from your notes – this rarely helps your vocal delivery. Think about what you want to say and then say it clearly.
- Know when to stop talking – it can be very easy to fill an uncomfortable silence with too many words.

Non-verbal communication

Non-verbal communication is very important. Sit forward and sit up straight – do not cross your arms and make sure you smile. Look as though you are interested. Your body language, facial expressions and posture will indicate your interest to the interviewer.

Appropriate presentation

For an interview, you must dress in a suitable manner – do not wear jeans or smart/casual clothes, but dress professionally and smartly. Clothing choice is important as it gives an impression of your professionalism and how seriously you are taking the interview. A tracksuit or low-cut top would be inappropriate.

Theory into practice

Ella is outgoing and enthusiastic. She went for a work experience interview to work with a personal trainer. It is what she wants to do for a career but she was so nervous in the interview that she answered the questions much too briefly and did not represent herself well.

- What could Ella do to overcome her nerves in an interview?
- How can she 'sell' herself more?

 PAUSE POINT   There are several different stages to applying for a job. Can you describe them?

> **Hint**   What are the different types of interview? Try to describe a unique feature of each.

> **Extend**   Have a go at producing a set of questions that you are likely to be asked in an interview, and prepare your responses.

Assessment practice 18.2   `B.P3` `B.M2` `B.D2`

You are to apply for a work-based placement with a sport or leisure focus. The application will be in three stages.

1 Your potential employer will want you to produce a copy of your CV and will expect you to include an introductory covering letter. Find a real-life job advert and produce a personal CV and covering letter that are tailored to this job role. Print out the CV and covering letter as evidence.

2 Ahead of an interview, prepare a set of answers to anticipated questions and a set of questions you want to ask the interviewers. With other learners playing the role of interviewer(s), conduct and record a mock interview, demonstrating your ability to respond under pressure.

3 Afterwards, complete a report that evaluates your own performance in the job application and interview process, identifying strengths and areas for improvement.

 Plan

- Have I reviewed the job description and used it to plan my application form?
- Have I practised my interview technique and prepared what I want to say?

Do

- I will adapt my CV and covering letter to reflect the nature of the job.
- I will use my preparation to communicate clearly in the interview, and prepare a set of questions to ask.

Review

- I will review my performance in the job application process and use it to improve in the future.

C Carry out work experience tasks to meet set objectives from work experience action plan

Work experience tasks

There are a number of tasks that you might be expected to perform during a work placement. A lot of this will depend on the type of placement and the host organisation's policy on work placements. The tasks may be sport-specific or general work-related tasks.

Sport-specific tasks

There is a wide range of sport-specific tasks that will vary depending on the sector you are working in. The case study shows an example of the tasks that can be found during a placement as a recreation assistant in a sports centre.

Case study

The King's Sports Centre

This sports centre is a busy, well-equipped sports centre on the edge of a large town. Work placements have been in place for a number of years, with learners on work placement fulfilling the role of a recreation assistant, so the activities required are quite clearly defined. They include the following.

- **Coaching** – depending on their ability and experience, some learners have the chance to, for example, assist the tennis coach in after school tennis clubs.
- **Leading** – most learners can lead a toddler gym-based activity session that lets 3–4-year-olds become more confident in their surroundings. Leading allows for greater safety and mostly involves close contact with parents, carers and the children themselves.
- **Instructing** – some learners can work alongside experienced gym instructors, for example, to help new members familiarise themselves with gym equipment.
- **Setting out and clearing away equipment for sports events** – this is a very important role that

ensures the smooth running of the sports centre and protects the equipment from damage.
- **Cleaning and maintenance** – this is not always popular but is an essential part of sport and leisure to ensure health and safety. For example, cleaning and maintaining fitness equipment is a legal requirement.

Check your knowledge

1 In busy sports centres, leisure professionals often carry mobile communication with them. Why might it be important to have this kind of communication? See how many different examples you can provide of uses for these walkie-talkie radios.

2 It is 6.59 p.m. during an evening shift. From 7 p.m., a badminton club has booked the sports hall but the footballers who are booked into it from 6–7 p.m. do not want to leave until exactly 7 p.m. How do you make sure that this is never an issue and what could you do about this problem?

General work-related tasks

While many of the tasks you take on will be specific to a particular role or to the sector of the industry you are working in, there are also some less obvious work skills that you will need to demonstrate in all placements.

- ▶ **Working as part of a team** – you need to become as much a part of the team as possible, and develop the ability to understand the needs of others and how you could best help in a range of scenarios.
- ▶ **Problem solving** – this requires initiative. You might have to think quickly and be able to prioritise, balancing the needs of your colleagues, clients and customers – or even yourself.
- ▶ **Communication** – there are many different types of communication, including interpersonal (verbal and non-verbal) and written communication. At all times, you need to be clear and honest, and make sure your message and tone is appropriate for the audience.
- ▶ **Following instructions** – work placement coordinators need to know they can trust you to follow instructions, often so that health and safety can be maintained.

▶ **Completing tasks following guidelines and within timescales** – to do this, you will need to demonstrate that you can prioritise and manage your time effectively. This may be one of the most important skills in determining your suitability for future employment.

▶ **Using ICT** – technology in the sports industry is widespread and integral, from advanced programming in fitness machines to chemical dosing in swimming pools. An understanding and interest in technology is a must. As well as sport-specific technology, all offices expect you to understand, apply and use spreadsheet applications. You should also be able to produce basic marketing material and word process.

▶ **Following health and safety practices** – the main concern for any business is that both customers and staff are kept safe and healthy. An induction process will explain the health and safety procedures in the workplace. Many placements will want you to undergo basic health and safety training that relates to emergency evacuations, first aid, identifying hazards and risks, and reporting accidents.

▶ **Asking for help** – if you are unsure of what you are doing or are concerned about something, find a way to ask. Most workplaces will respect you more for asking than for pressing ahead regardless and getting it wrong.

Promoting person-centred approaches

A person-centred approach focuses on an individual's personal needs, desires and goals so that they become central to the normal operating process of the work placement. Being person-centred in the workplace is likely to produce a much happier place for the staff and for the paying customers.

Adopting a person-centred approach at your placement is not just about giving people whatever they want or providing information. It is about considering people's desires, values, family situations, social circumstances and lifestyles – seeing the person as an individual, and working together to develop appropriate solutions.

It is particularly important in roles where you have sustained contact with customers such as:
▶ treating injured athletes
▶ coaching people on a one-to-one basis
▶ working in challenging settings – for example, ensuring everyone is safe when a swimming pool is close to its maximum bather load (the number that has been determined as a safe maximum of swimmers) can place considerably more pressure on a team of lifeguards.

Importance of supervision

On your work placement, you will be likely to be allocated to a supervisor or mentor. This person will support you through the work experience and will be your first point of contact for explaining what is required of you and to answer any questions. This supervisor, or mentor, can be the key factor in the success or otherwise of your placement.

▶ Your supervisor will play a key role during your placement

Your work placement supervisor will:

▶ ensure that you are able to handle the responsibilities you are given
▶ give you a chance to try things out
▶ ask the right questions and get you to think for yourself
▶ listen to your ideas
▶ teach you to have a positive attitude towards your work.

Ⅱ PAUSE POINT

What are the most important tasks for sports placements? Which of the generic skills apply to most work placements?

Hint

Devise a list of five skills you think everyone should have before they go on a work placement.

Extend

Choose a placement opportunity and list as many non-sport specific skills as you think are necessary for someone to have an outstanding experience.

▶ Work shadowing can be useful for observing specific procedures, such as those used by a sports massage therapist

Work shadowing and observation

Work shadowing is when you simply observe a sports professional doing their job to get a better understanding and insight into that role. It involves being with the professional through their normal working day, observing what they are doing and asking questions as they do the work. In turn, the professional will make sure they are explaining clearly what they are doing, and involve you as much as possible during the day to help you learn.

Work shadowing is suitable when the job role requires a great deal of practice and training, and when there are specific procedures involved. Many work experience roles are more appropriate for this kind of approach due to the nature of the work, for example:

▶ personal trainers (due to the personal relationship with the client)
▶ sports nutritionist (for the same reason)
▶ jump jockey (for health and safety reasons)
▶ football referee (for the level of skill required and the unique nature of the performance).

Many professionals approached for placements can be reluctant to consider placements at all, but suggesting a balance of shadowing and hands-on tasks can help to secure an opportunity for a placement.

Shadowing and observation can lead to getting some practical experience if you are enthusiastic, reliable, helpful and use your initiative. For example, if you are shadowing in a school with a PE teacher, ask if you can help take warm-ups. Plan them, show your plans beforehand, discuss them and then refine them. Build on this and by the end of your placement you might be involved in running a session.

Case study

Maisy's work experience

Maisy managed to find a placement working as a football coaching assistant. The placement included working with elite athletes. Because of the very specialised nature of the coaching and the interventions the coach must carry out, it was not appropriate for Maisy to do anything other than shadow the coach on this occasion. It is very important that the relationship between coach and performer is not interrupted in any way.

Check your knowledge

1 Maisy was not disappointed about not being able to coach in this scenario, even though she is a qualified

coach. Why do you think that she was not concerned?

2 Observing an expert can be as beneficial as completing tasks in isolation or under supervision. See if you can identify specific tasks within placements for the following roles where it is either advisable or essential that shadowing is the most appropriate action:
   • sports massage therapist
   • trampoline coach
   • PE teacher.

Reflecting on your work placement

Reflective practice involves looking at all your experiences in depth to learn more for next time. It will develop your personal and professional growth and also your ability to link theory and practice.

For your placement, you will be required to set targets and reflect on your progress towards achieving your targets. You will also have to reflect on your experiences during your placement. Reflective practice is essential to help you learn from your experience and to develop. This process should be continuous both on a personal and professional level, and not just during this unit.

When on your work experience placement, you should keep a reflective journal to record what you have learned and experienced, and how this affects your personal development. You should also reflect on the procedures used by the work placement organisation so that you can gain an understanding of why things are done this way.

When reflecting on your work placement, it is important any reflection is structured and organised. Gibbs (1988) suggested a model that is appropriate for work placements since it is one of the few reflective models that takes into account how you feel – see Figure 18.3 for an overview. There are six key steps to this process.

Step-by-step: the Gibbs reflective cycle

6 Steps

1 Description – describe exactly what happened during your placement, keeping a log on a regular basis. Depending on the nature of your placement, you may have a timetable to follow, e.g. you may be delivering coaching sessions on the hour every hour in the morning – if so you may choose to describe each session individually.

2 Feelings – for each of your descriptions, document what you were thinking and feeling at the time. Comment on how confident you felt. Did you feel you could not answer a question because of a lack of knowledge or that you could not communicate effectively with an athlete or parent?

3 Evaluation – for each experience, list good and bad points. For example, it may be good you are gaining experience coaching children under 9 years, but when you witnessed an injury you may have been unsure exactly what to do and had to look to others for guidance.

4 Analysis – analyse what sense you made out of the situation. What does it mean? You could analyse that your knowledge of dealing with injuries is poor and, due to your lack of experience, you were unable to control the situation.

5 Conclusion – conclude and document what else you could have done, or should have done, during that experience. Do you need to complete a first aid course, or revise a course you have already done?

6 Action plan – if the situation arose again, what would you do differently and how will you adapt? For example, if you had witnessed an open fracture, actions could include gaining more supervised pitch-side experience and attending a refresher first aid course.

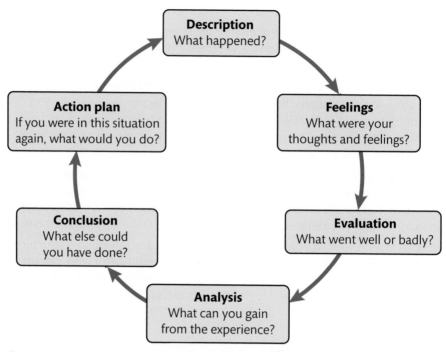

▶ **Figure 18.3:** The Gibbs reflective cycle

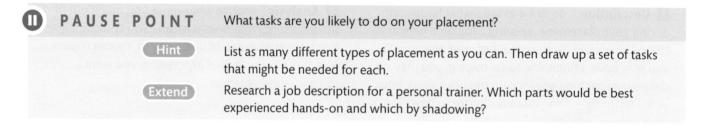

❚❚ PAUSE POINT   What tasks are you likely to do on your placement?

Hint   List as many different types of placement as you can. Then draw up a set of tasks that might be needed for each.

Extend   Research a job description for a personal trainer. Which parts would be best experienced hands-on and which by shadowing?

D   Investigate the impact of an active leisure work experience placement on career development

You need to review your performance both during and after your work experience. When you are doing this, you need to critically analyse what you have done, what you can learn from any situation and how this will be useful in terms of building up your skills and knowledge of the industry.

There are many ways you can reflect on your placement, but it is useful to base your review on your original aims and outcomes from your action plan, including any opportunities to apply both generic knowledge and skills – such as communication and problem solving – as well as specific technical skills – such as coaching, mentoring or setting out equipment.

> **Reflect**
>
> Think about some of the activities you carried out on your work placements. What did you enjoy and not enjoy? Why? What new skills did you learn? How has this affected your career plans?

It is also important to consider your achievements linked to the SMARTER framework (see page 239), paying particular attention to the last two components concerned with evaluation and recording.

Case study

Leisure centre duty manager

Jordan completed ten days' work experience at his local leisure centre. He was offered a job as a part-time lifeguard and sports attendant. He finished his BTEC National in Sport and now works full-time as a duty manager.

Jordan works hard and takes every opportunity. Depending on his shift, he arrives at the centre at 6 a.m. to open up at 6.30 a.m. or closes it late at night, which also involves 'cashing up' the day's takings – the centre shuts at 11 p.m. and he aims to leave at 11.30 p.m. The shifts he does are either early or late, and he has one weekend in three off. He has completed his Pool Plant course, a management development course and four different governing body awards.

The skills he uses most are customer service skills, organisation and management techniques. He loves being in contact with the public and being responsible for the smooth running of the centre and planning and running

events, like wedding receptions. He also enjoys managing and organising the staff, and thrives on the challenge of working to a deadline and getting the set-up perfect.

He is now 19 and wants to apply for the job as centre manager. He has had some training but wants to progress to be a centre manager.

Check your knowledge

1 What does Jordan need to do to prove he is suitable for the manager position?

2 Before going for an interview for a similar position, what must Jordan consider and include as a result of this placement?

3 How can he make himself stand out from other candidates who might want to become a centre manager?

4 How can he persuade the interview panel that, at 19, he is ready for the manager's position?

Reviewing your work experience

You can base your review around the following considerations.

▶ **Activities** – what activities did you do during work experience? Were they what you expected? Did you do what you hoped to do? Were you given more responsibility than expected? Did you feel you were an unpaid member of staff? Did you feel challenged but not abandoned?

▶ **Achievements** – what did you achieve? Were you pleased? Has it changed your mind about what you want to achieve?

▶ **Aims and objectives** – did you achieve the goals you set yourself before your work experience? Did you achieve them fully or partially?

▶ **Strengths and areas for improvement** – what do you now consider to be your strengths and what are your areas for improvement? Refer back to the work skills (see pages 250–51).

▶ **Evidence and techniques** – how did you use evidence, such as photographs or video footage, to support your review conclusions?

▶ **Interviews and use of witness testimony** – interview staff about your placement and performance. A witness testimony is a brief outline statement of what you did, written by your supervisor, and signed by them and you. Interview the staff – how did they reach that position? What qualifications have they got? What is their biggest achievement to date? This will help you to identify how to develop in the future.

Future career development

After the placement, you should complete a personal development plan that reflects the aims and objectives you set at the start of the placement. The development plan should support your overall career ambitions as well as helping you achieve the aims and objectives you set yourself before the placement.

Consider what you could do next to support your development and attain your overall goal. To do this, consider what else you could have done to achieve the aims and objectives you set yourself before the placement. You might try to spend more time at the placement or seek part-time employment.

▶ **Experiences** – you should consider what other experiences you could get to meet your career ambitions or aims and objectives.

▶ **Training** – work experience may make you aware of specific training courses which could support your development. These could be included in your personal development plan.

▶ **Qualifications** – there may also be specific qualifications which can help you achieve your future goals. In your development plan, highlight these and provide yourself with targets of how and when to attain them.

Reflecting on your work placement

Reflective practice involves looking at all your experiences in depth to learn more for next time. It will develop your personal and professional growth and develop your ability to link theory and practice.

For your placement, you will be required to set targets and reflect on your progress towards achieving your targets. You will also have to reflect on your experiences during your placement. Reflective practice is essential to help you learn from your experience and to develop. This process should be continuous both on a personal and professional level, and not just during this unit.

When on your work experience placement, you should keep a reflective journal to record what you have learned and experienced and how this affects your personal development. You should also reflect on the procedures used by the work placement organisation so that you can gain an understanding of why things are done this way.

When reflecting on your work placement, it is important that any reflection is structured and organised. Gibbs (1988) suggested a model appropriate for work placements since it is one of the few reflective models that takes into account how you feel – see Figure 18.3 for an overview. There are six key steps to this process.

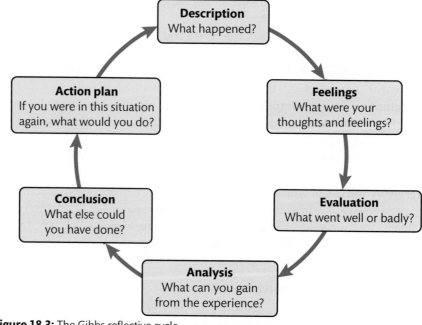

▶ **Figure 18.3:** The Gibbs reflective cycle

After reflection and should the situation arise again, you will have developed personally and professionally to deal with the situation and the new event will become the focus of the continuing reflective cycle. Remember, development is a continuous process.

Ⅱ PAUSE POINT   What tasks are you likely to do on your placement?

> Hint   List as many different types of placement as you can, then draw up a set of tasks that might be needed for each.

> Extend   Research a job description for a Personal Trainer. Which parts would be best experienced hands-on and which by shadowing?

Research into leisure organisations

After completing your placement, you are in an ideal position to understand not just the organisation where you did your placement but also other employers in your local area that have a similar purpose and offer similar job roles, services and/or products. This will help you appreciate the wider industry and the opportunities that exist for you locally as you develop your career.

> **Research**
>
> Using the example in Figure 18.4, design a similar template and look at two active leisure organisations in your area, making sure that you understand what makes them function, and how you might be positioned for future employment.

EVALUATION			
Name and type of organisation	Organisation history	Structure	Mission and aims
Cobdown Golf Club Private golf facility with public authority support	Opened 1967 when a landowner bequeathed land in their will to the council for sport or recreation	Private company runs the facility on behalf of the local authority, with executive board, trustees and management structure including duty managers, golf instructors and ground staff	To provide high-quality facilities at affordable prices for all of the local community
Culture	Workplace roles and responsibilities	Standards of behaviour and presentation	Opportunities for professional development, skills and knowledge
Friendly yet professional and fully inclusive including a balance of private societies with local school use	Duty manager attends to all matters including finances, staff management, booking systems, grounds maintenance and improving the business	Staff uniform for all staff that reflects club standards and to act professionally at all times	• Management training including financial management • Qualifications in golf course management with the Institute of Greenkeepers • Golf coaching qualifications with professional organisations • ScUK qualifications in generic coaching subjects such as Child Protection and Equity in Coaching

▶ **Figure 18.4:** Appraising a local employer

Step-by-step: the Gibbs reflective cycle

1 Description – describe exactly what happened during your placement, keeping a log on a regular basis. Depending on the nature of your placement, you may have a timetable to follow, e.g. you may be delivering coaching sessions on the hour every hour in the morning – if so you may choose to describe each session individually.

▼

2 Feelings – for each of your descriptions, document what you were thinking and feeling at the time. Comment on how confident you felt. Did you feel you couldn't answer a question because of a lack of knowledge or did you feel you could not communicate effectively with an athlete or parent?

▼

3 Evaluation – for each experience, list good and bad points. For example, it may be good you are gaining experience coaching children under 9 years but when you witnessed an injury you may have been unsure exactly what to do and had to look to others for guidance.

4 Analysis – analyse what sense you made out of the situation. What does it mean? You could analyse that your knowledge of dealing with injuries is poor and due to your lack of experience you were unable to control the situation.

▼

5 Conclusion – conclude and document what else you could have done, or should have done, during that experience. Do you need to complete a first-aid course, or revise a course you have already done?

▼

6 Action plan – if the situation arose again, what would you do differently and how will you adapt? For example, if you had witnessed an open fracture, actions could include gaining more supervised pitch side experience and attending a refresher first aid course.

How career aspirations have been influenced

Having thoroughly reviewed your experiences, you may have new thoughts about your career aspirations, taking into account your own self-reflection, the research you have done into the organisation and others in the area, plus comments from the employer and colleagues.

Your reflection is, of course, personal but should be honest, as it probably represents your best opportunity to reflect on what career might suit you. You could structure your reflection with questions, looking at three key areas.

Career choice

Your work placement can be the confirmation you needed that the career path you have chosen is the right one – or the wrong one – for you. Either way, the placement is useful in that purpose. Try questions like the following.

▶ What were your main activities and responsibilities during your work experience placement?

▶ Why did you select this placement and did it meet your expectations?

▶ What did you learn about the organisation you were working for?

▶ What was the greatest challenge you encountered during your work experience? How did you overcome it and how might you approach a similar situation differently in the future?

▶ Describe a situation from your work experience when you used your initiative. What did you do and why, and what was the outcome?

Confirming or changing your career aspirations

▶ Do you think it is the type of organisation you would like to work for in the future and why?

▶ What aspect of your work experience did you find most satisfying and why?

▶ What aspect of your work experience did you find least satisfying and why?

▶ What is the most significant thing you have learned through your work experience and how do you think it will help you in the future?

Plans for your next steps to pursue a career

Your reflection following your work placement will allow you to update your original action plan so that you can embark on the next steps towards your chosen career – whatever it may be.

 PAUSE POINT　　How would you review your work placement?

> **Hint**　　This chapter describes six points of focus for a review for a placement. What are they?
>
> **Extend**　　Provide examples from your own experience from your placement, providing specific detail for each review point.

Assessment practice 18.3　　　C.P4　C.M3　D.P5　D.P6　D.M4　D.M5　CD.D3

Part 1

Design a logbook that contains key elements to complete which will be useful for your actual placement, such as:

- what you have picked up by observing, doing, listening and discussing
- examples of what you have done well and not so well
- thoughts and feelings from the placement
- suggested improvements to what you are doing or have done and to the placement
- where you have demonstrated teamwork
- examples of resilience when things are not easy
- evidence of planning for the future for interviews or by questioning professionals.

The next part of your logbook is concerned with two major elements: firstly, your reflections while on your placement and secondly, specific details related to your placement including information about the organisation history, what its main aims are, how its staff are structured and the implied standards that it has for itself that reflect the industry standards. You should also say who the company is responsible to for the upkeep of those standards; for example, lifeguards and those who employ them must comply with legislation and recommendations from the Royal Lifesaving Society.

Part 2

Having completed your placement, it is important to begin post-placement reflection. You will have the opportunity to reflect on what you did, what you did and did not enjoy and, most importantly, what it has helped you decide about your future career. Start by looking back at your work experience action plan and particularly the aims and outcome you have established.

Produce a template form to add to your presentation that allows you to adequately reflect on all your experiences. In particular, note any changes of attitude or future aspirations relating to your career. Justify the kind of opportunities presented as a result that will develop your own career related knowledge and skills. You must compare similar organisations and establish what opportunities there might be in these or similar organisations.

Plan

- What is the task?
- How much time do I have to complete the task?

Do

- I can seek others' opinions.
- I can make connections between what I'm doing and the task, and identify the important information.

Review

- I can explain which elements I found hardest.
- I can explain what skills I employed and which new ones I have developed.

Further reading and resources

Masters, J. (2011) *Working in Sport*, 3rd edition, Oxford: How To Books.

Wells, M. et al. (2010) *A Career in Sports: Advice from Sports Business Leaders*, M. Wells Enterprises.

Swee Hong, C. and Harrison, D. (2011) *Tools for Continuing Professional Development*, London: Quay Books.

Websites

http://www.careers-in-sport.co.uk – advice for young people embarking on a career in sport

https://nationalcareersservice.direct.gov.uk – information, advice and guidance to help you make decisions on learning, training and work

http://www.uksport.gov.uk/jobs-in-sport – the UK's high-performance sports agency investing in Olympic and Paralympic sport

THINK ▶FUTURE

Jo Shilling

BTEC learner
and keen golfer

I've been into golf since I was four years old – I loved watching it on television and thankfully my parents supported me to take it up when I was still young. When I started my BTEC National in Sport, I decided to base as much of my studies on golf as I could.

I've always wanted to work as a golf professional and for this unit my coach helped me get a work placement at a local golf course. I've been splitting my time between the pro shop, coaching on the range and even some time with the grounds staff improving and repairing the course – it's all helped me gain a wider picture of what happens at a golf course, the customer's overall experience and how a golf professional can fit into that.

It was strange to see things from the other side. Usually I am a customer but on my placement I saw things from a different perspective. Each of the customers has a set of expectations that range from caddy service, disability access or just making sure that play is not too slow and that everyone follows the rules with respect for each of the other users.

While I could have guessed that I would be serving in the shop, helping with the coaches and helping in the restaurant, I didn't appreciate the work that goes into making sure that everyone is happy and ready to play, from 5.30 a.m. to the late-arriving twilight golfers. The operation of a successful golf club requires a great deal of effort and planning but I still enjoyed it all.

Focusing your skills

Working with others

Your placement will help develop work-related skills such as working with others to form a strong team.

- Make an effort to build working relationships with all around you – take an interest in their work and how it fits into the business, and offer to help them if you have time available.

- If you find that you are not getting the experience that you were promised, request a meeting with your supervisor to discuss this and suggest some ways in which you could make a better contribution.

- Ask your employer for a reference before you leave, while your contribution is fresh in their mind. This could be included as part of your logbook.

Self-reflection is important not just during your placement but throughout your career

- Watch for opportunities that might arise on your placement, and listen to people who are talking about opportunities.

- Make a note of all the skills that you learn during your placement but particularly those which can be transferred to other employers.

- Make sure that you ask as many co-workers as possible about how to go about finding a good job.

Getting ready for assessment

David is working towards a BTEC National in Sport Development, Coaching and Fitness and is a keen basketball player who has managed to secure a work placement at a national league basketball club based locally, spread over a few weeks for a few hours at a time.

David knows that he needs to prepare an action plan, apply and be interviewed by the club, undertake the placement hours and then complete a review.

David shares his experience below.

How I got started

First, I collected all my notes on this topic and put them into a folder. I decided to divide the work into four parts: the action plan, the application and interview, the placement at the basketball club and finally the review of the placement

Really it was about just following the process. First, I put together the action plan with all my skills and qualities listed, including my passion for basketball, then I researched the basketball club and contacted them to arrange an interview, helped by the fact that my friend Robbie plays in the junior team, The Silver Foxes. I then completed an application and sent it to the club secretary.

How I brought it all together

The work was then presented as required as a report, and action plan and eventually a presentation, and all of this was ready before I had even started.

After a successful but nervy interview, I began the placement and throughout used a logbook that my tutor had provided that kept a record of everything that I had done.

What I learned from the experience

I am happy to say that the club are allowing me to carry on as a volunteer on game days where I perform a range of functions, including greeting the away team and supporting the match officials, and I am now training in how to take statistics from the game that are fed to the league so that the latest information on the games is available on the Internet.

I have realised that full-time careers in what I have done in my placement are not very common but I have had a good look at coaching, player development and event management, and at the moment I am split between wanting to become involved in sports event management and being a performance analyst.

My review has allowed me to reflect on both what I have done at the club and how it might shape my future career choice.

Think about it

▶ Plan your work carefully. Think about all the different tasks you need to complete, then add completion dates for them so you can be sure you will finish everything by the deadline.

▶ Ensure that you use your logbook on a daily basis as it is very easy to leave till later – and also very easy to forget what you have done on a particular day.

▶ Make sure that you check for spelling and grammar in all areas and have some others review your work before you submit it.

Development and Provision of Sport and Physical Activity

19

Getting to know your unit

Nelson Mandela once said: 'Sport has the power to change the world. It has the power to inspire. It has the power to unite people in a way that little else does. Sport can awaken hope where there was previously only despair.'

Sport and physical activity have a number of physical, psychological, social and financial benefits, among others. This unit is about how developing and enhancing the provision of sport and physical activity plays a central role in helping to improve the health of the modern world.

How you will be assessed

You will be assessed by a written task set and marked by Pearson. Your assessment will take place under supervised conditions. A set period of time ahead of this you will be given a scenario around which to base your written answer. You should spend time researching this independently and making notes. You cannot receive any feedback during this preparation period. Your teacher will tell you the amount of time you have, and the length and format of notes you can take.

When you are preparing for your case study, you should consider the following questions.

▶ What are the key principles and wider concepts of sports development?
▶ What is the role of media and commercialisation within the development and provision of sport and physical activity?
▶ What are the key considerations you need to take into account when writing a sports development proposal, such as for an event, an initiative or for facility development?

You are expected to complete a set task during the supervised assessment period. The set task will assess your ability to produce a sports development proposal.

As the guidelines for assessment can change, you should refer to the official assessment guidance on the Pearson Qualifications website for the latest definitive guidance.

The assessment outcomes for this unit are:

▶ **AO1** Demonstrate knowledge and understanding of sports development and its measurement, the role and functions of sports development organisations, and the relationship between commercialisation and the media in wider sports development

Command word:

- **Demonstrate** – To show knowledge and understanding.

▶ **AO2** Apply knowledge and understanding of sports development and its measurement, sports development organisations, and the relationships between commercialisation and the media to familiar and unfamiliar contexts

▶ **AO3** Analyse and evaluate the impact of sports development proposals in the wider sports development context

Command words:

Analyse – Learners present the outcome of methodical and detailed examination either:

- breaking down a theme, topic or situation in order to interpret and study the interrelationships between the parts and/or

- of information or data to interpret and study key trends and interrelationships.

Analysis can be through activity, practice, written or verbal presentation.

Evaluate – Learners' work draws on varied information, themes or concepts to consider aspects such as:

- strengths or weaknesses

- advantages or disadvantages

- alternative actions

- relevance or significance.

Learners' enquiries should lead to a supported judgement, showing the relationship to its context. This will often be in a conclusion. Evidence will often be written but could be through presentation or activity.

▸ **AO4** Be able to develop a sports development proposal with appropriate justification

Command word:

Justify – Learners give reasons or evidence to:

- support an opinion; or

- prove something right or reasonable.

There are several key terms you will need to understand as part of your assessment, and these are shown in Table 19.1.

▸ **Table 19.1:** Key terms in this unit

Key term	Definition
Commercialisation	The way something is managed or exploited in order to make a profit
Infrastructure	The basic physical and organisational structures and facilities (e.g. buildings, roads, and power supplies) needed for the operation of a society or enterprise
Interrelationship	The way in which each of two or more things is related to the other
Key Performance Indicators (KPIs)	A performance measure used to evaluate the success of a situation, organisation or particular activity
Proposal	A detailed description of aims, KPIs, proposed activities and resources aimed at developing sport
Sports development	Work with individuals, groups and organisations to increase participation in sport and physical activity of all kinds
Sports development stakeholders	Anyone who has an interest in the value that the organisation creates. Stakeholders may be owners, customers, sponsors, employees, volunteers and government agencies
Wider sports context	The wider community and other organisations in the same sport, i.e. participants, volunteers, owners, customers, sponsors, employees, volunteers and government agencies

Getting started

Sport is used the world over to contribute to social change and development. It has contributed to enhancing gender and age equality, reducing the spread of HIV and Aids, crime reduction and community regeneration. Produce a mind map of the different ways participation in sport and physical activity could contribute to these social considerations.

A Principles of sports development

Link

This unit has strong links with *Unit 10: Sports Event Organisation, Unit 11: Research Project in Sport* and *Unit 24: Provision of Sport for People with Physical and Learning Disabilities*.

Research

Research your school or college's sports activities. Do they have recreational sport on offer as well as competitive sport? What do they say are the key benefits of this?

'Sport development' has the following three key principles behind it which are explored in this section.

1 To increase **participation** levels
2 To increase levels of **inclusivity**
3 To help people **progress** their level of sport along a 'sport development continuum'.

Participation

There are different ways to take part in sport, and sport development aims to increase participation levels in all of them. As well as participating in sports as an athlete or performer, people can coach the sport, be an official or an administrator or volunteer to help at an event or with a sports club. Participation is at three levels: recreational, competitive and professional.

Recreational

Recreational sport is a sporting activity that people engage in during their free time, that they enjoy and that has some form of social benefit. It is often played without a competitive element, but may still be played within the established rules of the sport. A key feature of recreational activity is that the activity itself is less important than the reasons for participating, such as for enjoyment or for the social aspect.

Competitive

Competitive sport is played within the set rules of the sport. An example is a local rugby team that competes in a local league or runners who compete for a local athletics club. Competitive sport has the ultimate aim of winning, but there can be other, far greater benefits from competitive sport. Taking the attention away from winning or losing can be beneficial for young athletes, as it can shift their attention to factors such as effort and learning and development, which are better for their longer-term development.

Professional

Professional sports are those in which athletes receive payment – in the form of wages or a salary – for their participation. In many cases, it is likely to only be elite athletes who participate in sport in this way, but there are other paid job roles in professional sport as well, such as working in administration, as a sports official or as a coach.

Inclusivity

Inclusivity refers to the development and provision of sport and physical activity that encourages all sections of society to participate. Although the aim is to encourage everyone to participate, there are also **target groups** within society that have lower levels of physical activity or sport participation. They are often defined in relation to gender, age, **socio-economic** status, ethnicity or disability. Sport England's Active Lives Survey monitors the activity levels of different sections of society to help direct funding towards different target groups and increase their levels of activity.

Gender and age

Sport England has reported a significant gender gap in sports participation and physical activity between males and females. In England, they estimated that two million fewer females aged 14–40 play sport regularly, despite 75 per cent of women saying they would like to be more active. They highlighted that this disparity does not occur in other European countries. As a result, Sport England produced the 'This Girl Can' initiative to try to enhance levels of female participation.

The 'This Girl Can' initiative was based on research findings that fear of judgement – on appearance, ability or how they chose to spend time on themselves – puts women of all ages off exercising. Therefore, Sport England produced their very successful 'This Girl Can' video, which has since been viewed over 9 million times. By February 2017, almost 250,000 females were more active on a weekly basis.

▶ An example of a This Girl Can poster designed to encourage women and girls to become more active

Older males are also a target group for increasing participation. As men get older, their participation in sport and physical activity decreases. This may be due to illnesses, injury, frailty or a lack of confidence in an ageing body. As a result, a number of organisations, such as the Older Men's Network, have worked in partnership with local authorities to set up 'walking sport' initiatives for older men. These include walking football and walking rugby events with the intention of encouraging older men to participate in 30 minutes of activity at least once per week.

Socio-economic factors

An individual's socio-economic status is defined by the **National Statistics Socio-economic Classification** (NS-SEC). People with a socio-economic status classified as 5–8 (the lowest half of the NS-SEC, those with lower household incomes) tend to be less active than those classified 1–4. In 2015, Sport England reported that only 25.9 per cent of people in the 5–8 NS-SEC classification were active. This is compared to 39.1 per cent of people in the higher classifications.

Key term

Socio-economic – relating to a person's social and economic background. Social factors include their cultural background and where they live, while economic factors include the amount of income that they have.

Discussion

Go to **www.thisgirlcan.co.uk**. You can also search the hashtag #thisgirlcan on social media. What are the key aspects to this initiative that try to encourage females to become more active? How do you think they might be effective?

Key term

National Statistics Socio-economic Classification – a scale used to classify the socio-economic status of people in the UK.

Ethnicity

Across the UK population as a whole, only 11 per cent of people who participate in sport and physical activity are from non-white backgrounds.

For males, participation in sport (defined as four sessions of 30 minutes of moderate intensity sport per week) varies little. According to the Active Lives Survey, most ethnic backgrounds hover around the 40–43 per cent figure for participation, with males of mixed race being the only ethnic group that exceeds 50 per cent participation.

For females, however, the picture is different, which is why females in different ethnic groups are often considered target groups to increase participation. For example, females of an Asian ethnic background report participation levels as low as 21 per cent. Within ethnicity, faith and religion are also considerations for target groups. For example, participation rates of Muslim females are as low as 18 per cent.

Disability

Participation in sport and physical activity for disabled individuals is less than half that of the general population. According to Sport England, people aged 16 or over with long-term life-limiting illnesses or injuries, or a disability, have activity levels of 17.2 per cent. Those with a sensory impairment (such as loss of sight or hearing) have activity levels of only 13.4 per cent.

Youth disability sport has become a target group for elite sport development, and recent years have seen an increase in funding and governmental interest in disability sport in the UK. The Paralympic World Class Performance Programme funding increased from approximately £10 million in 2000 to almost £73 million to support athletes in their preparation for the 2016 Paralympics in Rio de Janeiro.

There are also instances where people may fall into more than one target group and therefore face multiple challenges. For example, Muslim women from low socio-economic backgrounds and with a disability face a 'triple-challenge' of engaging with sport and physical activity.

The sport development continuum

The sport development continuum is a model that shows the different levels of sport development. The four levels of the sport development continuum are shown in Table 19.2 and Figures 19.1 and 19.2.

▶ **Table 19.2:** The levels of the sport development continuum

Level	Description
Foundation	• Aimed at primary school children or complete beginners • Provides basic skills education (e.g. throwing, catching) and an introduction to basic rules • Emphasis is on fun to encourage continued participation
Participation	• Aimed at a variety of individuals • Focuses more on community sport participation, trying to engage people with more regular activity
Performance	• Emphasis is on improving skill level through practice or competition, to enhance overall performance • People at this stage may be selected for trials and take up places in academy sports environments, and will be likely to perform in county-level sport
Excellence	• Aimed at national and international-level competition • Focuses on developing talented athletes into elite athletes with realistic chances of winning at major international tournaments, such as winning medals at the Olympic Games

Progression along the continuum

Talent identification has the important function of helping athletes progress through the sport development continuum. The role of talent identification is, as early as possible, to identify athletes with the potential to progress to an elite level. The criteria that talent scouts use to select athletes varies: some organisations invite athletes from a high-level sporting background and with certain physical characteristics (for example over a certain height) to attend talent camps, while other talent scouts rely on intuition and their own experience of previously identifying talented athletes.

▶ **Figure 19.1:** A simple sports development continuum. Arrows show the possible paths between levels

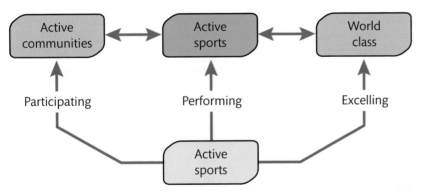

▶ **Figure 19.2:** Sport England's sport development model reflecting its interpretation of the continuum

Participation barriers, solutions and impacts

This section looks at common barriers to participation, some suggested solutions to reduce or remove these barriers, and some of the potential impacts of these on society. A barrier to participation is anything that might stop an individual from participating fully in a sport or physical activity.

Remember, any barrier associated with these groups is a 'socially constructed' barrier – none of them should ever actually stop people from taking part in sport or physical activity. Because of this, there is some debate about whether some commonly identified barriers should actually be considered barriers. For example, your gender should not stop you from participating. However, how a person may feel about participating in different settings may stop them. As a result, it is the perception of the individual in certain environments that becomes the barrier, rather than the actual gender of the individual. You should ensure that any perceived barriers connected with these groups are overcome smoothly and effectively to help encourage participation.

Barriers to participation

Some of the common factors where barriers to sport and physical activity can be seen are shown in Table 19.3.

▶ **Table 19.3:** Barriers to participation

Participation factor	Description of barrier
Gender	Gender-related considerations may affect the overall development of female sport. For example, in many cultures, sports traditionally played by males take priority over those played by females, having greater funding, prize money and media attention. This then has an impact on the perception of females within sport. This can become a barrier as it can convey a message that only certain sports are 'for girls'. Initiatives (such as This Girl Can) have aimed to redress this gender imbalance.
Age	Anybody of any age can be active to some degree – however, there are certain age-related potential barriers that need to be addressed in order to facilitate physical activity and sport participation. From childhood to adolescence, a lack of involvement of friends is an age-related barrier. For younger children, lack of parental consent can also be a barrier. Understanding research findings is important for development and provision of sport and physical activity for adults. For example, in a recent series of studies, between 53% and 100% of adults aged between 20 and 80 years old reported at least one barrier to activity associated with their age (e.g. health concerns, fear of injury and lack of confidence).
Socio-economic status	According to the 2014 Health and Fitness Omnibus Survey, cost is still said by many people to be a significant barrier to participation, which partly explains why those in lower NS-SEC classifications are less active. While this may be applicable to activities such as organised sport where athletes pay fees to play or commercial gyms with expensive memberships, other forms of activity do not require any financial outlay. In addition to cost, those in lower NS-SEC classifications may also work more hours than those in higher classifications and have less free time available for sport or physical activity.
Ethnicity	Certain ethnic backgrounds have very low participation rates in sport and physical activity. However, some ethnic groups show above-average representation in some sports. For example, there is a significant under-representation of Asian males in professional English football leagues, in comparison to their representation within cricket in England.
Disability	Recent research by the English Federation of Disability Sports (EFDS) highlighted disabled people classified barriers to participation as either: • physical (e.g. facilities, equipment, and health and safety considerations) • logistical (e.g. geographical location, expense and suitability of activities) • psychological (the strongest barrier) – this included perceptions of self (e.g. self-confidence and having had negative experiences in the past) and the attitudes of others (e.g. lack of awareness of opportunities and an unwillingness to make changes to facilitate participation). Disability itself is not a barrier to participation, but the EFDS findings suggest social influences and perceptions of the disability can become significant barriers for disabled participants.

PAUSE POINT   What are the barriers to participation?

 Hint   Produce a table that summarises each of the barriers.

Extend   Discuss how the perceptions of these different barriers can affect participation levels.

Solutions to barriers

For every perceived barrier to participation in sport and physical activity, some potential solutions have been suggested.

▶ **Concessionary rates** can be introduced for different groups to make sport and physical activity less costly and therefore more accessible. It is thought that making entry rates cheaper for people in particular target groups, such as those earning lower incomes, those in receipt of certain state benefits or those over 16 and still in full-time education, may encourage them to participate more.

▶ **Promotions** can be used, often at particular times of the year. For example, it is common for gyms and leisure centres to offer promotions on memberships immediately after Christmas and in the lead-up to summer holidays as these are times when people will be thinking about becoming more active. These promotions encourage people to become more active.

▶ Evidence suggests **facilities** which are more welcoming, have social spaces and are well maintained and regularly updated are more likely to encourage people to participate. Facilities in close proximity to where target groups live are more likely to encourage participation. Always consider the quality, design and proximity of facilities to the target users when planning a sport or physical activity development initiative in order to reduce a potential barrier.

▶ **Accessibility** of facilities for all social groups is an important way of increasing participation. The Equality Act (2010) requires sports clubs and other providers to make 'reasonable adjustments' so that everyone has access to the facilities. In 2015, the English Federation of Disability Sports released an updated guide, *Access for All: Opening Doors*, to support sports clubs in improving physical access for disabled people. This was with the main aim of removing the biggest barrier to people with disabilities: accessibility of facilities.

▶ Adapting **equipment**, such as using smaller equipment and soft play equipment for young children, can increase participation as well as maximising their safety. Equipment can also be adapted to meet the needs of different disabilities, for example in blind football the ball contains ball bearings so that the players can locate the ball when it is rolling by the sound it makes.

▶ The development of clothing and changes to rules regarding sports uniforms has also reduced potential barriers to participation. For example, Islamic cultural dress codes include requiring women to cover their head, hair, arms, legs and sometimes feet, making their participation in sports such as swimming and gymnastics challenging. However, recent innovations such as the burkini (which covers an athlete's entire body) are likely to help to reduce these barriers further.

▶ **Transport** dependency can be a barrier, particularly with certain types of individuals. For example, a recent study of lower limb amputee competitive and non-competitive athletes found that unreliable transport arrangements and greater travelling time were barriers to their participation. Equally, in a study of barriers to participation by children, being dependent on parental transport was also seen as a barrier. Investment in transport infrastructure (such as cycle lanes and rail networks) often forms part of bids for major sports events, so increased transport links to sports facilities will remain after the event.

▶ **Staffing** in some areas may be a barrier to the development and provision of sport and physical activity. For example, if there is a shortage of coaches or volunteers, it might not be possible to run as many sessions. Equally, a shortage of duty staff may make it difficult to cater for people with different accessibility requirements.

▶ **Training staff** to understand the needs of individuals helps reduce barriers. EFDS research with a cross-section of disabled athletes highlighted the fact that they felt a lack of staff awareness regarding impairment-specific needs was a barrier to effective participation. Research with children showed that when they were treated like 'mini-adults', they were more likely to drop out of sport. Therefore, it is important that sports organisations such as the English Football Association now provide specific coaching education to meet the needs of different populations, with courses like the FA Youth Award and providing mentors such as regional disability coach mentors.

▶ **Education** on the benefits of a physically active life has become more common and more widely publicised. Publicity activities usually include educational messages regarding the health and well-being factors of being physically active, with the intention of encouraging people to become more active. By empowering people through education, it is believed that barriers to participation can be reduced.

Research

Search online for the EFDS *Access for All: Opening Doors* guide. What are the key tips provided and how would they be helpful when planning a sport or physical activity development initiative?

The 2010 Youth Olympics

In the 2010 Youth Olympics, FIFA (the world's football governing body) had originally banned the Iranian female football team from participation over a disagreement relating to headwear. For religious reasons, the Iranian team wanted to wear headscarves to cover the players' heads. However, FIFA banned this (and subsequently the team) from participating, giving as the reasons player safety and not wanting religious symbols on the football pitch.

Following this, FIFA and the Iranian Football Federation reached an agreement where players could wear amended headwear which would respect the religious and cultural beliefs of the players as well as being within FIFA's rules on player safety. By making this change to playing equipment, FIFA had a positive impact on the Iranian female football players' sport participation.

Check your knowledge

- Why do you think it is important for people to consider religious and cultural beliefs when planning sports and physical activity initiatives?

PAUSE POINT   What are the solutions to barriers to participation?

> Hint   Produce a table that summarises each of the barriers.

> Extend   Provide specific examples of how you think these solutions can reduce barriers.

Impact of sports development

The impact of sports development is measured against specific outcomes. While the specific outcomes will vary for different initiatives, they usually have links with community cohesion, health and well-being, regeneration, crime reduction and education. An example of a model of sports development planning and its impacts can be seen in Figure 19.3.

Community cohesion

The notion of community cohesion became prominent in the early to mid-2000s in response to disturbances in multi-cultural areas, such as Bradford, Burnley and Oldham. The government defined community cohesion as having four key points.

▶ There is a common vision and sense of belonging for all communities.

▶ Diverse backgrounds and personal circumstances are appreciated and valued positively.

▶ There will be similar life opportunities, regardless of social backgrounds.

▶ Strong, positive relationships are developed between people of different backgrounds in the workplace, schools and different neighbourhood settings.

> **Key term**
>
> **Power dynamics** – the ways people use power to exert influence in relationships and how this process changes in different circumstances.

Sport has the benefit of being seen as a common or safe ground where people, particularly young people, can engage without being dominated by traditional or pre-existing social barriers. Sport provides an opportunity for people to engage with each other under pre-existing rules that are known, understood and accepted. This helps reduce the possibility of different **power dynamics** affecting cohesion, and provides an opportunity for different people within the community to come together with a shared purpose and work towards common achievements. As such, sport can play a central role in enhancing community cohesion.

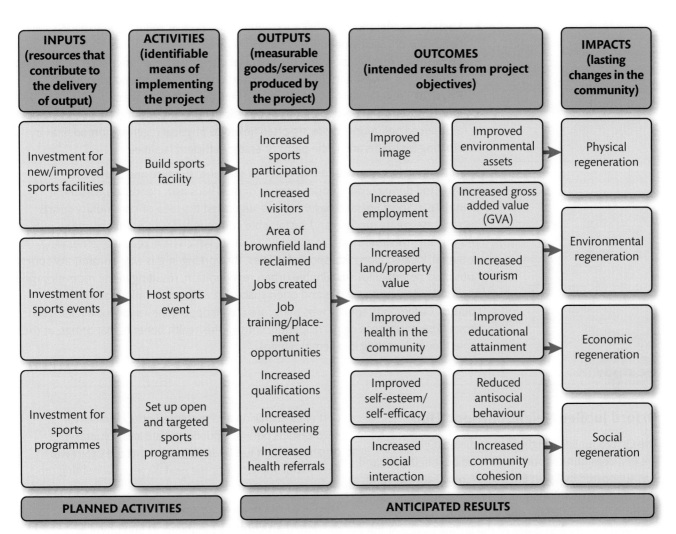

▶ **Figure 19.3:** A model of the planned activities and associated outputs and impacts of a sports development initiative, based on the Orford Jubilee Neighbourhood Hub

Health and well-being

Improving the health and well-being of the nation is a key rationale behind initiatives such as Sport England's document *The Framework for Sport in England: Making England an Active and Successful Sporting Nation: a Vision for 2020.*

Participation in sport and physical activity has a number of benefits: physical (for example increased cardiovascular health, reduced risk of obesity and/or diabetes), psychological (for example reduced risk of mental health conditions), social (for example social integration) and technical (for example increased sporting ability). Success in major sporting events can also inspire people to become more active and take up sport, so Sport England's vision of sporting success and improving health and well-being by increasing participation is made up of two distinct aspects that can influence each other strongly.

Regeneration

Urban **regeneration** has become a central feature of government policy, with large sporting events (for example Glasgow Commonwealth Games in 2014), development of sports infrastructures (for example building new sports facilities) and the development of sports initiatives (for example targeting increased participation in different social groups) contributing greatly to this notion of regeneration. The success of regeneration projects is often judged with reference to regeneration in the following areas.

Discussion

While there are many benefits of sport for community cohesion, there are also suggestions that sport may be divisive. How do you think that sport may also divide local communities and how can you reduce the chances of this happening?

Key term

Regeneration – the long-term and sustainable social, economic, physical and environmental transformation of an area that has previously experienced degeneration.

- **Social** – regeneration that has social outcomes, such as reducing antisocial behaviour or making people feel safer in an area.
- **Economic** – regeneration that has financial outcomes for an area, such as increased employment, investment in the area or additional education and training.
- **Physical** – regeneration of buildings and facilities within an area.
- **Environmental** – changes that have beneficial outcomes for the environment, such as reduced pollution – these are often linked to physical regeneration, such as by creating footpaths and cycle paths or energy-efficient facilities.

Sport England has recognised that much of the infrastructure and provision constructed during leisure boom periods of the 1980s now needs re-investment to update it. Sport England has therefore suggested the idea of 'community sports hubs'. These create modern and sustainable community facilities that combine public and private investment with community services, which have revenue-generating potential, located alongside sports facilities. By working in this way, community sports hubs have potential for sustainable urban regeneration, resulting in the redevelopment of various sites, such as parks and open spaces, in different locations across the country. Community sports hubs therefore create opportunities for social change in urban areas by increasing participation, with all the health benefits that brings, at the same time as boosting local employment.

Case study

Orford Jubilee Neighbourhood Hub

The Orford Jubilee Neighbourhood Hub (OJNH) was the first community sports hub to be built in the UK and was supported by Sport England's Iconic Facilities fund, in partnership with other local, regional and national partners. It was officially opened by the Queen in 2012 and was seen as a sign of the lasting legacy of the London 2012 Olympics.

OJNH is a multi-sport facility that was designed with a four-court sports hall, squash courts, 100-station fitness suite, a 25-metre eight-lane swimming pool and a learner pool with moveable floor. Outside there are a number of grass pitches, including a full-size artificial grass pitch and five-a-side pitches, three floodlit bowling greens, a bowls pavilion, BMX/skatepark facilities and outdoor exercise stations. As can be seen from the range of facilities, it was designed to meet the participation needs of a diverse range of community members.

As well as being a multi-sport facility, the OJNH also houses non-sport facilities and services, such as libraries and health, education, and child and adult services facilities.

Part of the reason a successful bid was made for funding for the OJNH is that Orford – at the time – was one of the most deprived areas of the country. The OJNH was built on a former landfill rubbish tip at a total cost of £27.3 million and presented opportunities for partnerships between public, private and voluntary organisations. It has been estimated that the OJNH will have social impacts over the next 20 years, benefiting the wider community.

The OJNH has been reported a success. It achieved:

- more than double its initial sport and physical activity participation targets
- 53 per cent of its memberships being concessionary for specific target groups (14 per cent higher than the average for the other local facilities)
- physical and environmental outcomes including the successful regeneration of a large park with improved transport links
- a threefold increase in park users post-development
- increased employability within the community hub
- decreased antisocial behaviour.

Check your knowledge

1 Why do you think that Orford was selected as a location for this community hub?
2 Why do you think that the OJNH has been successful since opening?
3 What do you think are the key benefits of community hubs?
4 Are there any community hubs near you and how do they compare to OJNH?

Crime

There is a growing appreciation that involvement in sport reduces crime, particularly in young people. To understand how sport does this, you need to think about the combination of the type or level of risk of crime (see Table 19.4) and the ways that sport can help reduce the risk (see Table 19.5).

▶ **Table 19.4:** Level of risk of crime

Level of risk of crime	Explanation
Primary	People may be subject to different conditions (e.g. personal or social circumstances) that may increase their risk of offending. Sport development programmes focus on community cohesion and enhancement, to reduce perceived levels of social disadvantage.
Secondary	Sport development initiatives try to target 'at risk' groups of young people to reduce their likelihood of committing crime.
Tertiary	Work with people who have already been identified as offenders aims to reduce the risk of re-offending. Sports development initiatives are likely to take referrals from organisations such as a Youth Offending Team.

▶ **Table 19.5:** Ways sport can reduce risk of crime

Mechanism of reduction	Explanation
Diversion	Sport is used to move people away from a time or place where they are more likely to commit offences. It can also include diverting people away from boredom (which can lead to adolescents engaging with crime). For example, a number of sports initiatives are run in school holidays as this is a time when some young people are likely to get bored or have time available, leading to an increased risk of crime.
Deterrence	People are less likely to commit crime if they feel they will get caught. Supervised sports programmes reduce the likelihood of crime as the people running the programme are more likely to get to hear about incidents that have taken place.
Development	Increasingly, initiatives focus on **pro-social development** of young people. This type of programme is most commonly used with identified offenders as it develops pro-social skills, such as self-esteem, teamwork, leadership, increased sense of control and increased moral values. Sports development initiatives underpinned by this mechanism tend to be long term as developing these skills can take time.

Education

Providing opportunities for sport and physical activity participation can enhance educational potential and achievement for young people. Young people who take part in physical activity and sport are more likely to be able to select, organise and initiate goal-directed behaviours (for example decide what they need to work on and work harder towards it) and research shows that young people who are more active often achieve higher grades in education.

A report commissioned by Sport England also showed that the educational benefits of sport and physical activity participation included lower levels of absenteeism and drop-out from education as well as greater progression into higher education.

Key term

Pro-social development – developing positive, helpful behaviours that benefit different aspects of society.

Research

Research 'midnight football leagues'. How can initiatives like these be used to reduce crime and antisocial behaviour? Make reference to the level of risk and mechanism of reduction.

Discussion

What do you think would be the pros and cons of reducing formal class contact time in schools and replacing this with sport or physical activity sessions?

Sports development stakeholders

If you plan on working within sport and physical activity development, it is important to know the different people and organisations ('stakeholders'), their function, and the different personnel involved. Understanding these stakeholders is important so that you know how sport and physical activity is run on a national and international level, but also because you might find it useful to start thinking about a potential job and career.

Stakeholders

Local authorities

Local authorities (LAs) play an important role in the development and provision of sport and physical activity as they take into consideration all types of target group. LAs ensure facilities and opportunities are inclusive and often work with other service providers and agencies (for example health authorities, voluntary sports clubs, police, welfare agencies, charities and neighbourhood groups) to maximise opportunities for the widest range of people within the community.

LAs also have a role in monitoring the success of sport and physical activity development projects, by examining areas like health outcomes, crime rates and antisocial behaviour. You can read more about methods of measuring the success of sports development starting on page 281.

Sport England

Sport England is the government agency responsible for the development and provision of sport and physical activity in England, from grass roots to excellence. At grass roots, Sport England plays a key role in developing the community sport system through developing local clubs and facilities, coaches and volunteers. Currently, 53 per cent of all volunteer work in England takes place in sport.

Sport England work with other stakeholders (such as national governing bodies and education providers) to create a sporting culture in England to help sports be sustainable, grow and be promoted from participation to excellence. During 2014/15, Sport England invested £324.9 million, with £200.3 million being invested in sport participation.

Similar organisations doing a similar job exist in Scotland, Wales and Northern Ireland.

UK Sport

UK Sport was founded by the Royal Charter in 1997 and supports athletes and sports to compete for, and win, medals at the Olympic and Paralympic Games. It does not have any direct involvement in community or school sport, but success by Olympic and Paralympic athletes does often see a spike in participation. Therefore, although UK Sport does not have a direct involvement in community or school sport, its work does have an indirect impact.

UK Sport has supported Great Britain in developing its reputation in Olympic and Paralympic sports. In the 1996 Olympics, Great Britain were 36th overall in the medal table; by the London 2012 Olympics Great Britain finished third. Figure 19.4 shows the relationship between UK Sport funding and medal tallies.

Most of UK Sport's funding (over 70 per cent) goes into the World Class Programme. UK Sport states that this programme operates on two specific levels.

▶ **Podium** – this is focused on supporting athletes who are seen as having realistic medal winning capabilities at the next Olympic/Paralympic Games. These athletes are seen as being a maximum of four years away from achieving a 'podium place'.
▶ **Podium potential** – this is focused on supporting athletes whose performances suggest that they have realistic medal winning capabilities at subsequent Olympic and Paralympic Games. These athletes are viewed as being a maximum of eight years away from a podium place.

Discussion

Why do organisations such as UK Sport place so much emphasis on talent identification in sport?

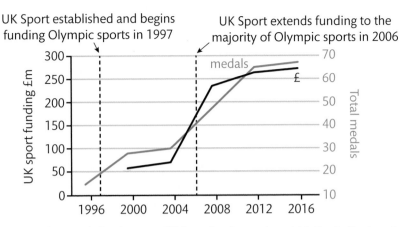

▶ **Figure 19.4:** The correlation between UK Sport funding and medal tallies in Paralympic and Olympic sports since 1996

Politicians

Politicians have realised over time the potential for growth in infrastructure, economic/ wealth development, health benefits and social development that are all associated with increased sports participation. The Secretary of State for Culture, Media and Sport is a senior politician, appointed by the Prime Minister, who takes charge of a large department (the Department for Culture, Media and Sport, or DCMS) which oversees sport development among other issues. The Under Secretary of State for Sport, Tourism and Heritage also spends time on sport-specific issues.

In late 2015, politicians published the government's latest sport strategy, called *Sporting Future: A New Strategy for an Active Nation*.

Facility management

Facility managers must demonstrate that their facilities are being used in the intended manner, as well as showing how they are working to increase their facility's use within its capacity. They play a role in the development and provision of sport and physical activity by producing different ways of encouraging inclusive and progressive participation.

National governing bodies (NGBs)

NGBs are responsible for running different sports within a country. They have vision statements, mission statements and plans for the overall development of the sport, and sometimes for different variants of the sport. For example, the English Football Association released its Game Changer strategy, which is a development plan aimed specifically at women's and girls' football in England.

World governing bodies

World governing bodies are responsible for the governance of specific sports at a continental and world level, in much the same way as a national governing body is at a national level. For example, where the English Football Association is responsible for football in England, UEFA is responsible for football across Europe and FIFA is responsible for football on a worldwide scale. Again, world governing bodies will have their own plans for developing their sport.

Voluntary/public/private sector

Over 50 per cent of all volunteering in the UK takes place in sport. It is a valuable way of developing life skills and experience in working environments, which can then increase your chances of becoming productive in later life (for example gaining a job, contributing to society further, supervising younger volunteers). This can have an impact on the role you may play in the private and public sectors.

Research

What is the NGB for your favourite sport? What are its vision and mission statements? Does it have any specific development plans for the sport?

The **public sector** and **private sector** are both stakeholders in the development and provision of sport and physical activity as they provide significant funding for sport and physical activity. The public sector wants to ensure that public funds are not wasted, while the private sector is often concerned with an economic return on their investment.

All of those involved in volunteering and in the public and private sectors have their own perspectives on maximising the social impact of sport.

Education providers

Education providers such as schools and colleges are stakeholders on a variety of levels. By providing different sport and physical activities, education providers can gain extra funding. In addition, over the past 20 years, sport and physical activity courses – like your BTEC course – have become seen as being equal in importance to other subjects.

In addition, increased sport and physical activity development is linked with positive youth development and prosocial behaviour, which can have an impact on the wider social learning environment. More recently, studies have shown that people who are more physically active can experience greater academic achievement.

Healthcare providers

Healthcare providers are stakeholders as increased participation has significant positive impacts on people's health and well-being. Increased physical activity is linked with decreased obesity, decreased risk of type 2 diabetes, decreased cardiovascular disease and decreased risk of mental health conditions, as well as being an effective treatment and management method for each of the above conditions. However, sports injuries do account for a significant number of accident and emergency visits, particularly at weekends.

▶ Parkrun events are run by volunteers but their start-up costs are often subsidised by local authorities or healthcare providers

 **PAUSE POINT**

Stakeholders exist at local, national and global level. For one of the categories of stakeholder above, try to think of a local, national and global example.

 Hint

What is a stakeholder?

Extend

Consider why they are stakeholders: what is their interest in the development and provision of sport and physical activity?

Stakeholder functions

Funding

One of the most important functions of stakeholders is to find funding: without this, there would be no way of developing sport and physical activity provision. Sport

England plays a key role in funding sport and physical activity provision. Figure 19.5 shows the breakdown of Sport England funding in 2014/15.

Stakeholders either use this funding themselves or pass it on to other organisations for spending on specific projects.

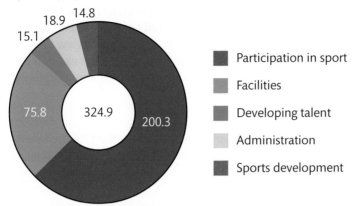

▶ **Figure 19.5:** Breakdown of Sport England funding in 2014/15 (£m)

Resourcing

One of the reasons funding is so important is that it helps provide necessary resources for sport and physical activity initiatives and events to take place. The resources required by these projects will usually come under three headings.

▶ **Human resources** – the people that the stakeholder needs to engage, employ and therefore pay, ranging from administrators to coaches. Even organisations that rely on a large number of volunteers will often have a 'core team' in a head office providing the overall direction for the stakeholder.

▶ **Physical resources** – not just spending on the equipment needed to deliver sports development projects, such as sporting equipment for coaching sessions, but also resources needed in the stakeholder's headquarters such as photocopiers and other office equipment and supplies.

▶ **Financial resources** – money needed to help the stakeholder meet its financial obligations, such as paying for staff and equipment.

Promoting

Stakeholders have a key role in promoting sport and physical activity to different groups of people. For example, UK Sport has used different promotional strategies such as 'Tall and Talented' as part of their talent identification programmes for specific sports. Sport England has played a significant role in promoting sport and physical activity participation through mass media promotions, such as 'This Girl Can'.

Coaching

Stakeholders play a key role in coach development. National Governing Bodies provide coach education courses. Different stakeholders can also offer subsidised coaching qualifications, making them more accessible to coaches from different backgrounds. Some stakeholders have also introduced coach development programmes aimed at particular target groups, such as women-only coaching courses, to increase the representation of these groups.

Strategic planning

With increasing pressures on public funding and the tendency for private organisations to fund only the most popular sports, the need for strategic planning has become even more prominent. This involves stakeholders clearly planning ways in which sport and physical activity can be developed within target groups or communities to make the

Theory into practice

What is the UK Coaching Framework and how does it have an impact on the development and provision of sport and physical activity?

best use of funds available. This strategic planning will include prioritising decisions to maximise the beneficial impact of funding on development and provision.

Research

Stakeholders pay significant attention to research into levels of participation in sport and other relevant areas. Stakeholders such as Sport England and National Governing Bodies have research budgets that are distributed among research organisations (such as universities or private research organisations) with a view to enhancing the development and provision of sport and physical activity. For example, Sport England's Active Lives Survey is a large-scale research programme that is used to identify priority areas for growth in participation.

Consultation groups

Consultation groups consist of people who are approached for their views on different sports development initiatives, events, clubs or facilities. Consultation groups can vary in size. One example of a large-scale consultation regarding sport and physical activity was conducted by the Department for Culture, Media and Sport who, before producing the government's new strategy, released a national-level consultation paper. Within this paper, they asked for public views on specific areas relating to factors such as participation, funding, sustainability and commercialisation.

See Figure 19.6 for the different roles of a consultation group.

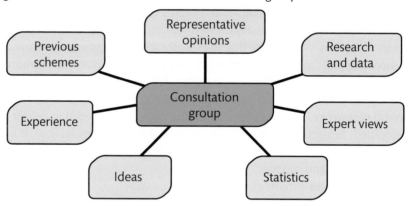

▶ **Figure 19.6:** The roles of a consultation group

Key stakeholder personnel

There are numerous key stakeholder personnel who play a role in the development and provision of sport and physical activity. Without these personnel, there would not be any provision of sport or physical activity – they include the following.

▶ **Sport-specific development officers** – who work to increase participation in and provision of specific sports.
▶ **Community development officers** – who work to enhance overall participation and provision within specific local communities.
▶ **Community leaders** – who take responsibility for the well-being and improvement of their communities.
▶ **Local authority councillors** – local elected politicians who are influential in approving funding for sports initiatives, events and facilities. In the case of facilities, they will also play a role in local strategic planning.
▶ **Club officials** – people such as club secretaries and welfare officers who work with other stakeholder personnel, such as administrators and development officers, to support and develop different levels of sport.
▶ **Administrators** – who fulfil administrative responsibilities within organisations and competitions, such as league fixture secretaries who organise league fixture schedules.
▶ **Participants** – the people who take part in sport.

Discussion

Which factors do you think will play a role in decisions being prioritised?

Theory into practice

Using a search engine, find the DCMS document entitled 'A New Strategy for Sport: Consultation Paper'. What were the key areas for consultation? Why do you think these areas were prioritised?

Link

Measuring sports development has links with *Unit 9: Research Methods in Sport*.

Measuring sports development

Purpose of measuring sports development

The success or failure of sports development is measured for a number of reasons. Doing so allows us to see:

▶ whether our plan for the development and provision of sport and physical activity is meeting its intended aims

▶ areas for improvement within the sport and physical activity development initiative/project

▶ whether the initiative meets the standards required, or whether it is producing outcomes of a comparable standard to other similar projects

▶ the impact of the plan that has been put in place.

We will often consider different **success measures** to help us determine whether a project has or has not been successful. Success measures will aim to be either increased or decreased. Success measures to be increased could include effects on participation, inclusion and progression, regeneration, education, community cohesion, and health and well-being. Success measures to be decreased could include crime rates, antisocial behaviour and recreational drug use.

Methods of measuring sports development

Benchmarks

Benchmarks are standards set to allow organisations to compare themselves against similar organisations or against standards set nationally compairing performance and service delivery. Benchmarking is designed to provide sports development providers with the opportunity to identify strengths and areas for improvement, in support of continual improvement.

For instance, at elite level an organisation might take its sport's performance at a specific Olympic Games as a benchmark. For example, if they have won an average of four gold medals in recent Olympics, they might use this as a benchmark figure: if they win more than four gold medals at the next Olympics, their sports development would be judged successful.

Quality schemes

Quality schemes can be used to determine how successful you have been within the definitions of that scheme. They are usually assessed through **key performance indicators (KPIs)** against which your performance can be judged. There are a number of quality schemes used in the sport development industry.

Quest

Quest is an industry standard developed by Sport England and it measures specific elements of sports development work including research, management, customer service and partnership working. It can be used to assess the management of sports development schemes.

Quest covers sports development units in local authorities, governing bodies and voluntary organisations. Sports development organisations can either use a self-assessment and improvement programme, or they can submit themselves to an independent external assessment in their pursuit of an award. The administration of

Key term

Key performance indicators (KPIs) – a performance measure used to evaluate the success of a situation, organisation or particular activity.

the scheme is overseen by an independent consultancy to ensure it is fair.

The assessment is based on criteria such as:

▶ objectives and the actions targeted at achieving these
▶ timekeeping, workmanship and coaching
▶ quality of equipment
▶ problem-solving techniques
▶ organisational culture – elements of pride, professionalism and standards.

Investors in People

The Investors in People (IIP) award follows many of the same principles as Quest. It focuses on organisations achieving specific standards for training and development of their staff, in turn helping to achieve the objectives of the sports development programme. During the process of achieving the standards, the organisation should improve its performance. Organisations that have achieved IIP standard often find it easier to attract and retain high-quality staff, which can improve their productivity and therefore the quality of their sports development work.

The IIP standard provides a national framework for improving performance and competitiveness. It involves a planned approach to setting and communicating objectives, and developing people to meet these objectives. The scheme provides:

▶ the opportunity to review current policies and practices against a recognised benchmark
▶ a framework for planning future strategy and action
▶ a structured way to improve the effectiveness of training and development activities.

It is based on:

▶ a commitment to invest in people, such as by providing training
▶ effective planning to set down how skills, individuals and teams are to be developed to achieve these goals
▶ effective action being taken to develop and use the necessary skills
▶ evaluating the outcomes of training and development for individuals' progress towards goals, such as checking that what was planned has been achieved.

Clubmark

By mid-2016, over 12,000 community clubs had achieved Clubmark status. The scheme demonstrates to partners, parents and young people that Clubmark-accredited clubs are:

▶ active – getting the best out of young people
▶ accessible – giving everyone a sporting chance
▶ accredited – have attained the Sport England mark of high quality.

Clubmark aims to provide more and better opportunities for children and young people to participate in sport in their local community. This shows that a sports development scheme at a club is safe, effective and child-friendly. It gives a nationally adopted set of standards for NGBs. Sports clubs must set and meet standards that will lead to better-quality provision for children and young people.

The scheme applies across a wide range of sports. It is promoted nationally to enable parents, carers and young people to quickly recognise a club that is committed to providing a quality experience.

Clubmark sets out standards for:

▶ duty of care and child protection
▶ coaching and competition
▶ sports equity and ethics
▶ club management.

Charter Standard scheme

In the case of the FA Charter Standard, its goal is to raise standards in grassroots football and support the development of clubs and leagues, recognising and rewarding them for their commitment and achievements. The FA's Charter Standard section of its website provides detailed guidance on Charter Standard applications and criteria.

> **Discussion**
>
> Choose one of the quality schemes named above and look at the requirements in more detail. How do you think that you would prepare for one of its assessments?

Primary data

Primary data is original data that you collect about a particular project. For example, you might monitor the number of people accessing and engaging with sport and physical activity within a specific location before and after an initiative, to assess the effectiveness of the initiative.

Secondary research

Secondary research uses previously published data found in books, journals, government publications, websites and other forms of media. For example, you might compare levels of sport and physical activity participation in your area to the normative (standard) levels from national data.

 PAUSE POINT   It is important that you can measure the impact of developing sport and physical activity provision. What are the different ways of doing this?

Hint   Produce a table that identifies the different ways of measuring sport development.

Extend   For each method, produce one strength and one limitation of that method of measurement.

 B   Wider sports development

Whenever a sporting development takes place – ranging from developing a facility or club to hosting or having hosted a major international sports event – this will have a wider impact on society. These impacts can be felt at local, national or global level, depending on the nature of the project.

The key areas that they can have an impact on are **infrastructure**, environmental, political, ethical, cultural, and economic. We have already looked at the political, ethical, cultural and economic effects of sports development in this unit, but we now need to look at infrastructure and environmental impacts.

Infrastructure

Major sporting events such as the winter and summer Olympic Games or the FIFA World Cup require host cities to include **legacy** elements as part of their bids to host the events. Infrastructure benefits are an important element of the event's legacy. For example, some of the infrastructure legacy from the London 2012 Olympics was the production of almost 3000 homes (almost 1400 affordable housing) from the athletes' village; as well as 10 railway lines, 30 new bridges and a £10 million investment to improve London's pedestrian and cycle routes.

> **Key terms**
>
> **Infrastructure** – physical and organisational structures and facilities required to run an event, such as buildings, roads, power supply, communication networks.
>
> **Legacy** – the lasting impact of the sports event at local, regional and national levels.

Similarly, the 2016 Olympic Games in Rio de Janeiro saw the development of a new Light Rail Transport system, while the 2022 FIFA World Cup in Qatar includes almost 200 infrastructure projects (ranging from health and education to roads and sewerage, to social security considerations).

▶ Improved transport links were an important part of the Rio de Janeiro 2016 Olympics

Environmental

One of the roles of the United Nations Environment Programme (UNEP) is to consider the environmental impact of sport. Whether developing a facility or hosting a major international tournament such as the Olympic Games or the FIFA World Cup, they suggest that there are positive and negative environmental impacts. The Sydney Olympic Games in 2000 were the first 'green games' (Olympic Games that consider the environmental impact and sustainability) and since then, all Games have considered their environmental impact as part of their reporting on the Games. According to UNEP, the following are all environmental considerations:

▶ loss of fragile ecosystems or scarce land for sport development
▶ noise and light pollution from sport
▶ consumption of non-renewable resources (fuel, metals, etc.)
▶ consumption of natural resources (water, wood, paper, etc.)
▶ emission of greenhouse gases by consuming electricity and fuel
▶ ozone layer depletion (from refrigerants)
▶ soil and water pollution from pesticide use
▶ soil erosion during construction and from spectators
▶ waste generation from construction of facilities and from spectators.

There are also some straightforward environmental benefits of introducing initiatives aimed at enhancing physical activity. If you successfully introduce an initiative that increases the number of people walking or cycling to work, you are likely to reduce the amount of environmental damage caused by pollution from cars. For example, Amsterdam has one of the most successful cycling initiatives in the world where cyclists collectively travel 2.3 million kilometres per day. This has a big impact on the environment as every four kilometres travelled by bike instead of by car results in one kilogram less of CO_2 released into the environment.

 **PAUSE POINT** Major sports events have wide implications for society at local, regional and national levels. Why is legacy development important when planning events?

> **Hint** Write down the different ways that major sports events of your choice have left, or plan to leave, a lasting legacy.

> **Extend** For each, justify why this an important aspect of the legacy for a major sports event.

C Media and commercialisation in sport

The media has a significant role to play in the development and provision of sport and physical activity. Different media outlets have a number of uses, including coverage and reporting of sport, advertising and promoting events, helping with recruitment, and providing funding.

Different types of media can have both positive and negative impacts on sport, at both economic and social levels. For example, the media has been criticised for focusing on female athletes' appearance or attractiveness as opposed to their ability and talent. This has been seen as demeaning the role of women in sport by not recognising or promoting the role they have.

Types of media, their impact and uses

There are many different types of media that have an impact on the development and provision of sport.

Television and satellite

Television and satellite deals have played a significant role in the development of sport, particularly in English football. Owing to the recent record Premier League television deal worth over £5.1 billion, the English Premier League is the richest league in the world. It is estimated that by 2018, almost all 20 of the English Premier League football teams will be in the richest 30 football teams in Europe. Putting this into context, in 1997, the television deal with the English Premier League was £670 million. This has meant that football in England has grown significantly due to its ability to attract the biggest names and best players from across the world. However, there are also suggestions that this has hindered the progress of the English men's national senior team due to a lack of English players playing at the highest level in England.

As well as in men's football in England, television and satellite have played a significant role in promoting women's football on a global scale. For example, the FIFA Women's World Cup final in 2015 was the most watched football match in United States television history and by 2014, 99 of FIFA's 209 member nations had television coverage of the national football league.

Television and satellite is important for generating global interest in sport which, in turn, increases coverage, reporting and funding of different sports. television and satellite organisations also use sport as a way of generating income for their company through selling advertising time.

In addition, television and satellite can be used for promoting different sports and events. Mega events such as the Olympics and FIFA World Cup are given significant promotional time in the lead-up to events, to generate interest and increase viewing figures. The same principle applies to smaller local and regional sporting events; however, they are almost exclusively restricted to local television stations and programmes.

Social networks

Since the advent of popular social media, social networks have become increasingly important for the work of sport development practitioners. In 2017, Facebook claimed to have approximately 1.94 billion people logging on every month. Social networks such as Facebook, Twitter, Instagram, Vine, LinkedIn and Google+ all provide an opportunity for marketing and promoting new events, initiatives, clubs and facilities.

> **Discussion**
>
> What are the economic and social implications of not representing women as athletes or recognising their athletic ability in the media?

As a sports development practitioner, you must be aware of common trends in social networks – particularly the emergence of new social networking tools – as these can be used to reach different elements of communities. Using tools such as designated 'hashtags' is a way of promoting the work of development organisations as well as generating interest in new sport development plans. For example, in 2016, FIFA (the world's governing body for football) used the hashtag #askFIFAMayi to host a question and answer forum about the role of FIFA in women's football development.

Social networks can also be used to gain feedback from your consumers and stakeholders, deal with any queries and complaints, and circulate information to staff within an organisation. One of the key benefits of using social networks is that they are free, so are a cost-effective method of enhancing the development and provision of sport and physical activity.

As social networks have progressed, organisations now use them for recruiting staff. It is common for organisations to advertise jobs, internships and voluntary positions across their various social networks in order to ensure the widest reach. In addition, people are more commonly using social networks such as LinkedIn as an online CV that can be easily distributed to potential employers, or that can be used to attract potential employers.

Discussion

Given the wide-ranging uses of social networks, why do you need to be careful about who can see your social network profiles and what you use them for?

Press and newspapers

The press and newspapers have considerable influence over the popularity both of a sport and individual athletes. As a result, they have an influence over the development and provision of sport and physical activity. Coverage of the success (or lack of it) of an athlete or team can influence an individual's motivation to become involved with a particular sport, so newspapers and the press have a social responsibility to report sport fairly. However, press and newspaper coverage tends to report the sports and athletes that will sell their publication to the reader, which creates a bias towards certain sports and types of athletes as well as the use of sensationalist headlines to attract the reader.

Apart from mega sporting events such as the Olympics and Paralympics, there is a significant bias towards the reporting of male sports with much less attention paid to female or disabled athletes. By devoting significant coverage to more popular sports, this supports their popularity while potentially making it difficult for other sports to develop.

▶ Newspapers devote a lot of coverage to sport – but the coverage is not always positive

Specialist press

In addition to general press and newspapers, there are also sport-specific magazines such as *Runner's World*. These sport-specific publications are a good place to advertise and promote upcoming sports events or initiatives as they are likely to have a more captive and interested audience, given that they generally require subscriptions or a specific purchase. These types of publications can also offer coverage of different events and initiatives within a specific sport, which helps to increase interest and can have an effect on participation.

Local press

Local press outlets are useful for promoting initiatives, events, clubs and facilities in your area. Organising press releases, giving sports coverage, providing adverts for local sport and leisure facilities, and promoting upcoming events are all important roles of the local press that can enhance interest in different approaches to the development and provision of sport and physical activity.

The local press can be particularly useful as it can help to highlight key outcomes of initiatives and events by releasing stories about them, such as developments in community cohesion or 'feel-good' stories about achievements within events, initiatives or clubs. This can have dual benefits as coverage at a local level can then generate coverage at regional or national level, aiding the growth of an initiative, event, club or facility. By increasing this interest, you are likely to have more opportunities to gain funding through different revenue streams (for example sponsorship or crowd funding) which may then support your sport development event, initiative, club or facility development further.

Online media

Online media at local, national and international levels play significant roles in the development and provision of sport and physical activity. From a local blog to a large international corporation's website, online media can influence people's perceptions of sport and physical activity, as well as perceptions of their ability to participate.

Having some form of online media to promote your event, initiative, club or facility is an important element of increasing participation. However, simply having online media does not guarantee success. Different methods can be used to increase traffic through online media and to expose your sport development topic to a wider audience. One of the most common ways of doing this is to include video within your online media.

Using video within online media increases traffic and, in the case of selling products or services or trying to generate increased funding, can also increase **conversion rates**. By increasing traffic through your online media, you are also increasing your opportunities to sell advertising space on your online media, which provides a further source of income and can make your initiative, event, club or facility more sustainable.

Videos can enhance your online media traffic mainly because with videos:
- you can simplify complex topics into clear messages
- it is easier for your audience (for example your consumers or stakeholders) to connect with you
- you are able to demonstrate your event, initiative, club or facility in action
- people tend to prefer watching videos as opposed to reading text
- people are more likely to share or comment on videos than text-based content, which further increases your potential audience.

Theory into practice

Look at a selection of local and national newspapers' sport sections. What types of headlines and stories are included? How do you think they will positively and negatively affect the development and provision of sport and physical activity?

Key term

Conversion rates – the ratio of people who purchase goods or services after visiting a website or shop.

Theory into practice

Why do you think that combining online media with social networking can be a really useful way of enhancing the development and provision of sport and physical activity?

Hint   Produce a mind map of each of the different types of media.

Extend   Discuss how each type of media can enhance the development and provision of sport and physical activity.

▶ Commercialisation of sport is visible with competitors such as Roger Federer wearing Nike clothing

Key terms

Commercialisation – the general process by which a product or service is evaluated for its potential to have economic impact or financial value.

Sustainable – something that can be maintained at a required level over an extended period of time.

Commercialisation in sport

Commercialisation is the process where a product is evaluated for its potential economic or financial value within a target market. Many people argue that certain sports are now primarily commercial businesses with enormous financial potential. However, as a sports club or organisation becomes more commercial, it increasingly depends on sporting success to maintain a brand value and enhance its commercial interests. For example, Manchester United are seen as one of the world's leading sport brands and commercial sports organisations. They recently signed the largest commercial shirt agreement in history with Adidas for a reported £750 million over ten years. However, as a result of their declining success within football, Sky Sports recently reported that Manchester United's value as a football club had decreased by approximately £650 million.

Professional sports – particularly professional team sports – are now viewed as a 'micro-economy' made up of a set of independent and interdependent markets. One independent market is where teams buy players and coaches that will not only enhance their sporting prowess, but also their brand value. Supporters of sports teams will buy tickets to go to see games, refreshments at games, team kits, and subscriptions to team magazines, websites and television channels. Because of fan identity with their teams, they will often buy into this market regardless of their team's success, or whether they buy new players or coaches (making this an independent market).

However, when success increases or famous 'brand names' are signed, consumer engagement with aspects of this market – such as merchandise sales – will increase (making it an interdependent market). For example, when David Beckham signed for Real Madrid from Manchester United, Real Madrid experienced a significant increase in their commercial activity.

Typically, sports organisations that have more successful commercial activities – from small-scale fundraising in local amateur sport to international-scale global sponsorship partnerships – tend to be more **sustainable** organisations and can often experience more success.

Sustainable commercialisation

Sustainable commercialisation is important for the long-term health of an initiative, event, club or facility. Sustainable commercialisation does not seek to make as much money as possible, but seeks to generate some income – such as through charging participation fees or through sponsorship – in order to help fund the project's survival.

Sports development organisations also have to show awareness of commercial requirements regarding managing their finances, including funding sources, budgeting, income and expenditure, and the distribution of these funds across maintenance, staffing, resources and investments.

Sources of funding

The Department for Culture, Media and Sport (DCMS) increasingly encourages sport development organisations to explore various sources of funding for their projects.

Sport England in its funding guidance document also suggests that being aware of local funding streams and how to access them is an important aspect of developing sport and physical activity. There are a number of available sources of funding, such as Sport England itself, the Football Foundation, the National Lottery and local authorities.

In addition, private investment from companies (for example sponsorship and other partnership agreements) plays a role in the development of sport and physical activity.

Finally, social investment is a modern way of gaining funding from **social investors**, with the UK now being the most developed social investment market in the world. The DCMS estimated in 2015 that there was over £1 billion of private capital currently working towards social impact through social investments. This has been aided by the UK government's Social Investment Tax Relief scheme where those investing private capital in social schemes can gain tax relief on the amount they invest.

In 2014, Forbes SportsMoney discussed how crowdfunding was becoming more established for funding athletes and clubs. One example of this type of funding in the UK is 'Street League' which raised over £600,000 from a social investment scheme and used sport as a way of supporting unemployed young people and those from disadvantaged backgrounds.

Using funds

To show how you will use funding effectively, you need to demonstrate how you will budget your projects to avoid overspend but use all of the money. You should provide details of your income and expenditure, including where the funds will be distributed (for example investment in maintaining existing or investing in new facilities, staffing requirements, and other resources such as sports equipment and technological support). Figure 19.7 shows an example of how you might provide budgetary details of expenditure when requesting funding.

> **Research**
>
> Research Sports Coach UK's 'ten tips for successful funding'. How can Sports Coach UK support you in finding and planning your funding for the development and provision of sport and physical activity? How similar is it to other organisations, such as Sport England or the Football Foundation?

> **Key term**
>
> **Social investor** – somebody who invests finances in social projects with a view to seeing both social and financial benefits.

SOCIAL CLUB BUDGET					
Planned initiative	**How will this be achieved?**	**Outcome measures including target date**	**Person (s) responsible**	**Individual costs**	**Cumulative costs**
12-week initiative to develop a new goalball club	Two-hour facility booking, per week	Facility booked by January 2017 for a 12-week booking	Lead sport development officer supported by disability sport coordinator	£50 per hour, two hours per week, 12 weeks	£1,200
	Goalball coach employed	Coach employed for a 12-week block by November 2016		£30 per hour, per week, 16 weeks (4 weeks' preparation prior to 12 weeks' delivery of the programme)	£480
	Volunteer assistant secured	Volunteer assistant secured for 12-week block by December 2016	Head coach supported by disability sport coordinator	£25 per week expenses, 12 weeks	£300
	Clarify goalball equipment requirements from *www.goalballuk. com/the-sport/ equipment* and purchase as required	Equipment purchased, delivered and checked for health and safety considerations by December 2016	Head coach supported by disability sport coordinator	Negotiated package, included maintenance, consumables and replacements	£3,000
Total estimated expenditure					£4,980

▶ **Figure 19.7:** Example outline costs

Ethics of commercialisation

The ethics of commercialisation is a key concern for the development and provision of sport and physical activity. There are high-profile examples of when the commercial activities of sports organisations have been viewed as unethical. For example, in 2014, the BBC reported the English FA was widely criticised for fans having to pay up to £90 for the new England football shirt for the 2014 World Cup.

Appropriate sponsorship and funding

One of the key topics within the ethics of commercialisation is appropriate sponsorship and funding. Some people within sports development have concerns over large companies such as Coca-Cola and McDonald's sponsoring major sporting events watched by children. This is because their products are seen as unhealthy food options due to large amounts of sugar (Coca-Cola) and saturated fat and salt (McDonald's), which are significant contributors to childhood obesity.

A key agenda for the government is balancing the benefits of private financial and commercial investment in sport and physical activity, with the potential pitfalls of promoting different types of organisations, such as gambling, alcohol and high fat, salt and sugar (HFSS) foods.

Fairtrade resourcing

The Fairtrade Foundation and Fairtrade International are organisations that promote fair trade on an international level. They work to promote the rights of farmers and workers, and to organise better deals for the products they produce. The Fairtrade Foundation structures its work around four key areas:

- Providing independent certification of the trade chain for products, and licensing the use of the FAIRTRADE Mark on products as a consumer guarantee
- Helping to grow demand for fairtrade products and empowering producers to sell to traders and retailers
- Working with partners to support producer organisations and their networks
- Raising public awareness of the need for fair trade and the significant role of the FAIRTRADE Mark in making trade fair.

When planning a sport development event, initiative, club or facility, by considering how fairtrade products can be included within your plan, you can contribute to supporting ethical trading. For example, could your kit or equipment be sourced from fairtrade suppliers, or your refreshments?

Impact of media and commercialisation on sports development

The media and commercialisation have an impact on the wider sport development context. They can affect participation, inclusion and progression. For example, media coverage of successful British tennis players during Wimbledon tends to increase participation in tennis during the tournament. Further, the London Paralympic Games saw a significant increase in national attention to various forms of different sports, contributing to a more inclusive approach to development and provision of sport and physical activity.

Media coverage of disputed decisions in football has often drawn on the commercial aspects of the game (for example, the amount of money gained or lost through promotion or relegation, or qualifying for the UEFA Champions League) to justify the need for goal-line technology.

Research

Research a local sports team of your choice, either professional or amateur. Who are their sponsors and why do you think these sponsors would want to be associated with that sports club?

Theory into practice

Investigate Bala Sport. What is their relationship with fair trade and how has this had an impact on the economy?

Case study

The FIFA World Cup decisions

Think about the role of the media in the build-up to the 2018 and 2022 FIFA World Cups in Russia and Qatar respectively. A significant amount of media coverage has been targeted at the alleged corruption surrounding the decisions to award the World Cups to these countries, as well as some of the alleged poor working conditions in Qatar particularly.

For example, media coverage in 2015 reported that the then FIFA President Sepp Blatter claimed a decision had been made to award the 2018 World Cup to Russia without voting having taken place. Media coverage surrounding the 2022 World Cup in Qatar has raised concerns about modern-day slavery and poor working conditions, as well as making disputed claims about injury and loss of life during Qatar's preparations for the World Cup.

Collectively, the media coverage in the build-up to the events has distracted much of the public attention away from football.

Check your knowledge

1 How do you think the media coverage may affect the popularity and funding of these World Cups?

2 How do you think the timing of the media coverage may have had an impact on the monitoring of rules and regulations (such as health and safety) in preparation for these events?

3 How do you think the media coverage has raised our awareness of the different facilities to be used at these World Cups?

4 Many of the media outlets recounting the World Cup stories of Russia and Qatar were from countries who failed in bids to win World Cups. Some have since printed corrections or retractions about their stories. What does this suggest to you about the role of popular media within the wider sports development context?

On a local level, media and commercialisation can be used to support the development of clubs, initiatives and facilities. Local news outlets and social media can be used to draw public attention to these new facilities or initiatives, whereas commercial activities can be used to ensure that they are sustainable. There is also a link between media and commercialisation, whereby the media can be used to promote commercial activities.

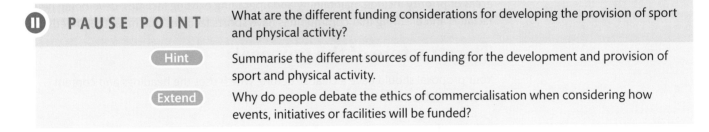

PAUSE POINT What are the different funding considerations for developing the provision of sport and physical activity?

Hint Summarise the different sources of funding for the development and provision of sport and physical activity.

Extend Why do people debate the ethics of commercialisation when considering how events, initiatives or facilities will be funded?

 ## D Proposal writing

This section links with *Unit 9: Research Methods in Sport*.

Before you start writing your sport development proposal, you should conduct research to identify a need for a particular initiative. You will need to consider how sport development initiatives have an impact on local, regional or national environments and start to create a **rationale** for the event, initiative or facility you are planning. Each decision you make when writing the proposal should have a clear rationale.

Key term

Rationale – a reason for a decision.

Preparatory research for proposal writing

Before you start writing your proposal, you should conduct research. During your preparatory stage, you should consider the different sources of research that reflect current trends (for example Sport England Active Lives Survey, published papers and reports that investigate participation levels). When viewing this information, consider how you interpret the data presented. For example, national-level trends demonstrate an overall picture, but a specific locality may fall above or below these national trends, meaning that there may be a different need in different areas of the country.

Your research should focus on other events, initiatives or facilities that are available within your area, any that are already planned or under development, and what the potential benefits of your planned sports development activity would be. You should also think about some of the guidance documents that are available to support you in writing sports development proposals, such as the funding guidance documents from Sports Coach UK and Sport England.

Creation of relevant aims

Your proposal should have relevant aims, based on your research. As organisations such as Sport England provide the majority of the funding for participation, your aims should be based around increasing participation in sport or physical activity. Other areas of priority include maintaining and upgrading existing facilities, developing new facilities and ensuring that communities have sports facilities that meet their needs.

The structure of the proposal

Your proposal should have a clear structure, which uses the headings and content shown in Table 19.6.

PAUSE POINT   What are the required resources you need to plan a project or proposal?

Hint   Produce a table of the human, physical and financial resources required for your plan.

Extend   Justify the inclusion of each of these resources, using evidence where appropriate and possible.

▶ **Table 19.6:** Structure of a proposal

Section of the proposal	Purpose
Aim(s)	These should be: • based on your research • linked to increasing participation • inclusive and encouraging participation from diverse target groups • linked to the development of an event, initiative, facility or club.
Performance indicators	These are the criteria you will use to determine the success of your plan. They might include: • total participation rates • participation rates from different target groups • a reduction in antisocial behaviour and crime rates • the successful development of a new facility or club. There should be a clear link between these, the aims and your research. Performance criteria would benefit from some justification, for example linking increased participation rates with health benefits.
Proposed activities	Again, based on research, these should have been identified as fulfilling a particular need and be supported by evidence showing they will be beneficial to achieving the programme aims. Types of activities could include participation events, spectator events, promotional events, social events, charity events, or events focused on health and well-being. Many events 'tick a number of different boxes'. For example, a charity cycle ride for a large group of people would cover participation, social, charity, focus on health and well-being, and promoting cycling as a method of physical activity.
Timeframe	You should ensure you have an appropriate timeframe to achieve the aims of the planned activity. For example, if your aim is to increase long-term swimming participation in 50+ females, you are not likely to achieve this within two months. What you might do in that timeframe is review initial participation levels.
Realistic costs	The proposed costs in your plan should be realistic. If your cost projections are too low, funding providers are unlikely to believe you will be able to achieve them and less likely to fund your work. If you over-estimate costs, they may not believe they are getting value for money. Again, this would affect your chance of funding. Conduct detailed research into costs, exploring different options, and negotiating costs and rates to provide a balance between realistic costs and value for money. Factors affecting cost include logistics and the need for any technical competence (e.g. appropriate levels of coaching and appropriate ICT support).
Resources	The resources required fall under three headings. For each, budgeting should be realistic. • Human resources – the people required to deliver the project. This may include: coaches, administrators, officials and staff to look after security, medical support, reception and promotion. • Financial resources – the investment needed to deliver the plan. • Physical resources – the facilities and equipment needed to deliver the plan.

Relationship between proposals and the wider sport development context

Throughout this unit, we have discussed factors in the wider sports development context that will influence your planned activity. In a plan aimed at the development and provision of sport and physical activity, you should also show its wider impacts. Table 19.7 shows some questions to consider when thinking about both how your plan influences the wider sport development context and how the wider sport development context can influence your plan.

▶ **Table 19.7:** Interrelationship questions

How does your plan influence the sport development context?	How does the wider sport development context influence your plan?
• How does your plan fit with the aims of sport development organisations? • How will your plan contribute to the development of participation, inclusivity or the progression of the sport? • How will your plan influence infrastructure, environmental considerations, political considerations, ethical and cultural considerations, or the economy? • What impact will your plan have on media and commercialisation?	• How will the aims of sport development organisations influence your plan? • How will the development of participation, inclusivity or the progression of the sport influence your plan? • How will infrastructure, environmental considerations, political considerations, ethical and cultural considerations, or the economy influence your plan? • What impact will media and commercialisation have on your plan?

Further reading and resources

Government publications

Department for Culture, Media and Sport, Tracey Crouch MP (2015) *Sporting Future: A New Strategy for an Active Nation*. Available from: **https://www.gov.uk/government/publications/sporting-future-a-new-strategy-for-an-active-nation**

Books

Byers, T., Slack, T. and Parent, M. M. (2012) *Key Concepts in Sport Management*, London: Sage.

Nichols, G. (2007) *Sport and Crime Reduction: The Role of Sports in Tackling Youth Crime*, London: Routledge.

Robson, S., Simpson, K. and Tucker, L. (2013) *Strategic Sport Development*, London: Routledge.

Journal

The International Journal of Sport and Society

Websites

www.lotterygoodcauses.org.uk/funding – information about how National Lottery money is distributed and which organisations make the decisions

www.theguardian.com/teacher-network/series/pe-and-school-sport – articles from *The Guardian* on PE and school sport

www.sportanddev.org/en – a resource and communication tool dedicated to sport and development

www.sportengland.org – the website for Sport England, which works to get more people doing sport and activity and increase participation across all groups in society

www.uksport.gov.uk – the website for UK Sport, the nation's high-performance sport agency

Assessment practice

Your local community hub wants to run a sports initiative to help reduce antisocial behaviour in local teenagers. Young people in the area complain that there is nothing to do in their locality and statistics highlight the fact that the sport and physical activity participation levels in boys and girls are below the national average. There have been reports of drinking late at night as well as graffiti and high noise levels. The community hub wants to try to use sport as a way to reduce this, but is keen for the sport to be available at a time that the antisocial behaviour usually occurs. They have asked you to plan an initiative with this in mind.

Plan
- What am I being asked to do?
- What resources do I need to complete this task and can I access them at times when I will be doing my work?

Do
- I can make connections between what I am reading/researching, the task, and the context in which I need to apply the information.
- Am I confident that I know what I am doing and what I should be aiming to achieve?

Review
- I can explain how I approached completing this task and why I approached it in this way.
- I can explain how my applied knowledge of sport development has changed or developed through completing this task.

THINK ▶▶FUTURE

Helen Robinson

Sport development officer

I've been working as a sport development officer for three years. During this time, I have encountered so many different opportunities for developing sport and physical activity, with many different parts of my local community.

After I completed my BTEC Level 3 in Sport, I went to university and completed a degree in sport development and coaching because my main interests are increasing the range of sporting opportunities and helping support coaches to meet the needs of different people who might access these opportunities.

Having an understanding of the needs of your local community as well as the wider regional, national and international scope of sport development is important for being an effective sport development officer. You need to be able to identify sources of funding – sometimes your job depends on it! You also need to know how this funding can best be used to meet the needs of different target groups and the wider community.

Because of this, having the ability to develop and maintain effective working relationships with different people is key. By having these relationships, you are more likely to be able to meet the aims of different plans, as well as being able to negotiate better deals on things like products and services. In doing so, you are more likely to provide a value for money plan that meets the needs of your stakeholders, meaning you are more likely to get funding.

Focusing on your skills

Designing effective plans

It is important to be able to design effective plans for the development of sport and physical activity. Here are some tips to help you do this.

- Make sure that you know the needs of the area that you are responsible for.
- Keep up to date with sources of funding that are available.
- Network locally, regionally and nationally – having contacts is good for forming wider partnerships and for developing ideas.

- Make sure you are able to provide a clear rationale for the aims of any plan to develop the provision of sport and physical activity, supporting your suggestions with appropriate evidence.
- Review the progress of your planned programmes as you go along and evaluate their effectiveness. This is important for showing how you are meeting the original aims and that you are measuring the impact of your work.

Getting ready for assessment

This section has been written to help you do your best when you take your assessment task. Read through it carefully and ask your tutor if there is anything you are still not sure about.

In your externally set assessment, you will have some extended answer questions. The extended answer questions will be phrased to allow you to highlight key pieces of information and start to think about how you can plan your answer. Completing the preparatory work before the externally set assessment is vital in getting to know the topic area, in the context of the set question.

When approaching the question, remember the following.

- Make sure that you read the question carefully.
- Identify the key words in the question.
- Focus on the words that tell you what you need to write about.
- Read the case information and highlight key parts that will help you answer the question.

An important part of the extended answer questions is that you are assessed against qualitative improvements in your answer. This means the number of marks you get will not necessarily be based on the number of points that you make, but the **quality** of the points that you make.

- Avoid simply repeating information included in the scenario. Make sure you use the information in the context of the set question, to demonstrate how your plan has been produced and why it will be beneficial.
- Provide an answer that relates to all the key parts of the question.
- If there is more than one perspective on a topic, ensure that you produce a balanced answer.
- Draw links between the scenario and the wider sport development context.

Example

You are a sports development officer for a local athletics club. The athletics club has a range of members from children to senior, elite, international competitors. However, you are concerned about the falling number of members renewing their annual subscriptions as this pattern may lead to a significant reduction in the athletics provision in the town and potentially the closure of the club.

Members are required to pay annual subscriptions, purchase their own athletics kit and pay event fees. Recently, the club has been losing competitions because it was not able to field enough athletes. The athletics club is located centrally within the town and is within reach of the local school and colleges. The athletics track has several service routes, including road and bus routes, but the cycle track and footpath leading to the track

---

Continued...

both get heavy use so require restoration due to wear and tear. There are also several sites with graffiti, and many of the grass areas and trees that line them have become overgrown.

You are required to produce a proposal for an event that aims to develop the sport in the scenario. Your event should be structured as follows:

- aims
- performance indicators
- proposed activities
- resources
- interrelationships between your proposal and the wider sports development context.

Aims: The aims of this event are to increase membership and participation at the local athletics club. Sport England provides most of its funding for increasing participation; therefore we are more likely to gain funding if we target our event at increasing participation. By increasing membership it will mean that the club is more sustainable and the athletics club can continue; by increasing participation there will be a number of different social, psychological and health-related benefits for the athletes.

> What are these different benefits and how might they result from increased participation in athletics?

Performance indicators: The performance indicators for the success of the event will be an increase in membership and then, increased participation. We would see this as a success if we got 100 new memberships and then those people attended the athletics club and were active every week.

> Is there any information in the scenario that suggests this is needed?

> This lacks a rationale. How have you decided on this number? Are you targeting any specific groups or just 100 people from any social group?

Proposed activities: We will organise an event that can be run for the local schools and colleges, which can attract more children to the club. We will also run this at a time when parents or carers can attend with their children as it would be good to increase adult participation as well. There is also some research that shows family interventions in physical activity can increase participation levels. The first event will be that we will host an inter-school sports day focused on athletics events and then the same type of event for colleges. The events will be open to anybody of any ability level or background. This way, we are being inclusive.

> When using phrases like this, it is good practice to provide the specific reference.

> It would be good to say how family interventions can increase physical activity levels.

Resources: We will need a combination of human, physical and financial resources to run these events. The human resources will be officials and administrators to run the events and update the scoring as the event progresses. We will also need first aid qualified staff at the event to make sure that everybody is safe.

The physical resources will be the kit required to run all the events and the venue to host the events. We would be able to buy the appropriate amounts of kit once we have the number of confirmed attendees, and the cost of the kit would be dependent upon this. The venue would not cost anything as we already have a venue close to the schools.

> Would there be any costs associated with running the venue for the days of the events?

We would also put on free transport for the schools so we would need enough coaches to collect them and take them back. This is because research says that people are more likely to participate in sport and physical activity if the transport to get there is better.

The financial resources would be the money required to pay for the kit, staff and transport.

Interrelationship between proposals and wider sports development context:
These events could have wider impact on the local area. The scenario says that the cycle track and footpath have graffiti on them, which might be because young people in the area either don't have enough to do in their spare time or they don't know about the different activities available, so they have started vandalising things. By putting these events on, we might be able to get them more interested in taking part in sport and physical activity, and reduce the chances that they will continue with vandalism and antisocial behaviour. This mechanism of crime reduction is known as diversion because it moves young people away from times or places where they might otherwise become involved with crime or antisocial behaviour.

The scenario also talks about the footpath and the cycle path being in need of restoration. As part of our proposal, we would work with the local council to restore the footpath and the cycle path, which might make it safer and easier to travel to the athletics venue. We would also work to get the graffiti removed from there so that people feel safer when they go down the paths. This might then increase the likelihood that they'll use them to access the athletics club more regularly. This means that we would be benefiting the infrastructure and the environment within the local area, which would have the benefit of community regeneration.

Having this event on in the run-up to the Olympic Games might help because people become more interested in a sport when there is a major sporting event happening. This means that we might be able to get people to take out more club memberships and take part more in their sports. By running this event now, we can contribute to the progression of the sport by increasing the grassroots participation. This can have an added benefit because if we have more people taking part in sport, then we have a potentially bigger talent pool to select talented athletes from which then might make the sport better at higher levels.

This section contains valid points but lacks supporting evidence from research.

The links back to the information in the scenario, making it easier to see the purpose of statements that you make.

Investigating Business in Sport and the Active Leisure Industry

22

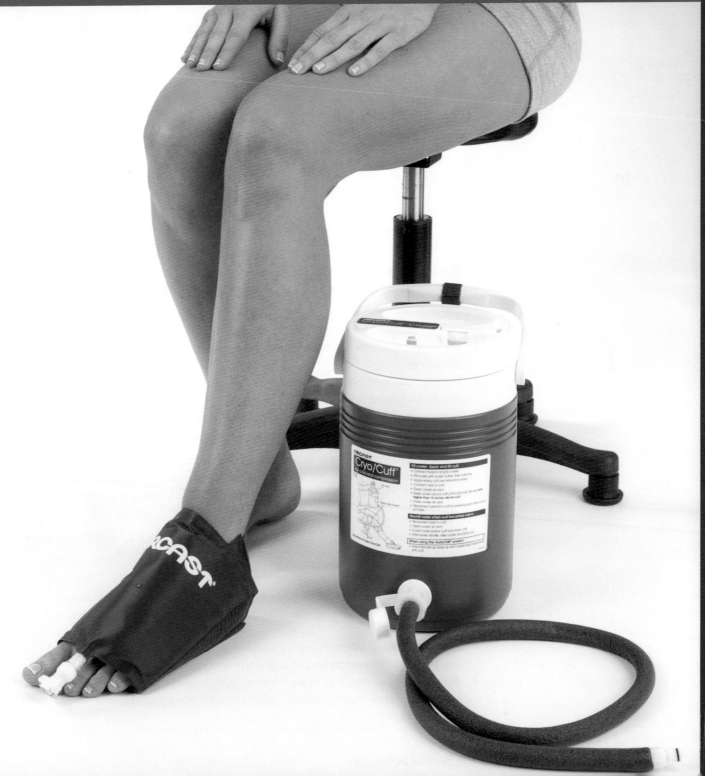

Getting to know your unit

In this unit, you will explore how sports businesses are always planning for growth and expansion. You will look at the skills needed to work in businesses that operate in areas such as professional sport, private, public and voluntary sports clubs, community and active leisure programmes, the sporting goods industry, and all aspects of the media. You will also investigate trends, changes and developments that influence the potential success of any sports-related business.

This unit is an externally assessed unit as it covers many of the processes that are carried out in the industry. You will need to draw on learning from across your qualification to complete your assessment.

How you will be assessed

This unit will be assessed externally using an examination set by Pearson. The examination will contain two parts.

▶ **PART A** is supplied a set period of time before your examination so that you can carry out independent research about a scenario based on a fictional sports business.

▶ **PART B** is a written examination carried out under controlled conditions in which you can use your research notes to complete a task that builds on Part A.

As the guidelines for assessment can change, you should refer to the official assessment guidance on the Pearson Qualifications website for the latest definitive guidance.

You will be assessed for your understanding of:

▶ business operations and how to respond to trends and internal and external influences

▶ business information and data, and their potential impact and influence on a sport and active leisure business

▶ synthesising business ideas and evidence from several sources to support arguments.

Throughout this unit, you will find activities that will help you work towards your assessment. Completing these business-based activities will not mean you have achieved a particular grade, but you will have carried out useful research and preparation that will help you later when you do your external assessment.

Unit 22 has four assessment outcomes (AOs) which will be included in the external examination. Certain command words are associated with each assessment outcome. Table 22.1 explains what these command words are asking you to do.

The assessment outcomes for this unit are:

▶ **AO1** Demonstrate knowledge and understanding of sport and active leisure business operations and how to respond to trends and internal and external influences

▶ **AO2** Analyse and interpret business information and data, and their potential impact and influence on a sport and active leisure business

▶ **AO3** Evaluate evidence to make informed judgements on how a sport and active leisure business should be developed, diversified or adapted

▶ **AO4** Be able to make justified recommendations for a sport and active leisure business, synthesising ideas and evidence from several sources to support arguments.

The command words or key terms shown in Table 22.1 may be used in the assessment.

▶ **Table 22.1:** Command words / key terms used in this unit

Command word	Definition
Analyse	• To examine in detail in order to discover the meaning or essential features of a theme, topic or situation. • To break something down into its components or examining factors, methodically and in detail. • To identify separate factors, say how they are related and explain how each one contributes to the topic.
Business models	Two business models need to be understood: • SWOT (strengths, weaknesses, opportunities, threats) • PESTLE (political, economic, social, technological, legal, environmental).
Interpretation	To draw the meaning, purpose or qualities of something from a given stimulus.
Justification	To give reasons or evidence in order to: • support an opinion and/or a decision • prove something right or reasonable.
Research	To carry out careful and organised study or gather information about a specific topic.
Review	A process for learning (knowledge or skills).

Getting started

Sport is big business. We are all familiar with the products and services of global retailers of sports equipment and clothing, media organisations, Premier League football clubs, stadia and arenas, and the many chains of private gyms that have emerged from an increased public awareness of health and fitness. But many sports businesses are small, employing just a few people – often a single manager has to have all the business skills that in a larger business would be spread across several departments. Consider these smaller types of business and how many you have come into contact with. Does your local football team need to run like a business and if so, how does that differ from a Premier League football club? Why are business skills important for anybody who wants to work in the sports industry?

A Features of sports and active leisure businesses (business operations)

Features and organisation of sport and active leisure businesses

People on the commercial side of sport organise their companies to accommodate:
- the products or services they will offer
- the way they wish to operate (the company structure)
- the requirements to comply with the law.

> **Reflect**
>
> Think of a sports club you are (or have been) involved in. Consider the organisation that goes on behind the scenes to allow you to play a sport or receive coaching. What organisation do you think is involved, from advertising, hiring coaches or pitches, arranging for kit and equipment and so on? Now consider the amount of business knowledge required to operate this sports club. Get together in small groups and discuss your thoughts, focusing on the differences between various clubs you are all involved in.

Types of sports and active leisure businesses

Any sports and active leisure business will belong to one of three types: private, public or voluntary.

Privately owned businesses

Privately owned businesses are not owned by local or national governments, but are owned by an individual person or by a group of people, potentially up to thousands of them. There are a number of different ways that a privately owned business can be set up.
- **Sole trader** – This is when a person, such as a personal fitness coach (offering a service) or a small sports shop run by an individual (selling products), trades as an individual. They will be the decision maker and run the business as they wish, enjoying the profits but also having **unlimited liability** for any debts. People wishing to set themselves up as sole traders can get advice from HM Revenue & Customs and a bank to ensure they are properly informed and have a sensible **business plan**.

> **Key terms**
>
> **Unlimited liability** – where a person (usually a sole trader) has no limit to the amount of debt that they are responsible for. If someone working as a sole trader makes a regular loss and gets into debt, they are personally responsible for repaying all of that debt.
>
> **Business plan** – a document that outlines the objectives and goals for a business, explains how they will be achieved, and forecasts business performance.

▶ **Partnership** – This business arrangement is used when two or more people wish to come together to form a business. They all have to share responsibilities which are written into a contract called a deed of partnership. Advice for setting up this type of business can be obtained from Companies House, where registrations are logged to make them legal. The partners share the profits but are responsible for any debts, again on an unlimited liability basis.

▶ **Private limited companies** – These are generally smaller businesses organised with shareholders who invest money to buy a share of the company. With a private limited company, the shares cannot be bought openly on the stock market but only by coming to a deal with an existing shareholder. Often the shareholders will appoint a board of directors to make the business decisions, while a managing director will deal with the everyday running of the company. If the company does not succeed, shareholders will lose their investment but have **limited liability** for any company debts. Their status is indicated by the company name ending with 'Ltd'. One sporting example of this type of company was the London Organising Committee of the Olympic Games and Paralympic Games Ltd (better known as 'LOCOG').

▶ **Public limited companies** – Known as PLCs, these companies tend to be larger businesses with shares offered for sale to the general public and investors on the stock market. Shareholders can vote on general policies, but the organisation is run by a board of directors who are experienced business practitioners. Shareholders are paid a dividend from profits if they are made, but if the organisation makes a loss they are not likely to get a payment. Shareholders are not liable for debts; however, directors may be subject to limited liability under certain financial circumstances. One example of a plc in the sports industry is shown in the case study on this page.

> **Key term**
>
> **Limited liability** – where if a company gets into debt an individual shareholder is only responsible for the amount of debt that matches their investment. For example, if a shareholder bought £10,000 of shares when a company was formed, they would only have to cover £10,000 of that company's debts.

Case study

Sports Direct

Sports Direct International plc is a well-known sporting goods retailer that sells sports equipment and clothing through its network of stores and via the website sportsdirect.com.

It owns a number of sport and leisure brands including Dunlop, Everlast, Kangol, Karrimor, Lonsdale and Slazenger.

▶ Sports Direct founder Mike Ashley

Sports Direct was 'floated' as a plc on the London Stock Exchange in 2007 making nearly £1 billion for majority stakeholder and founder Mike Ashley.

Check your knowledge

1 How do you think the founder acquired the capital to build up the business prior to Sports Direct becoming a plc?

2 Can you find out what the share price was worth in 2007 and what it is worth now?

3 Thinking about where you buy your sports equipment and clothing, would you say Sports Direct plc has a monopoly, squeezing out other retailers? Explain why you think this.

▶ **Co-operatives** – A co-operative is where a business is owned and run by its members. In the sport and leisure industry, a number of professional football clubs are co-operatives, from AFC Wimbledon and Portsmouth FC to FC Barcelona. An example of a non-sporting retail co-operative is The John Lewis Partnership. A key point of a co-operative is that employees have a say in how the business operates and its future, all of which is done without institutional shareholder input.

Carry out some Internet research to find out which type of sport and active leisure business is most common as a new business or start-up.

Hint   Can you list the five categories of business operations and explain which one would suit a new business or start-up and why?

Extend   Can you trace a well-known company's progress from its humble beginnings to its current status? Can you determine under what category that company started out and under what category it is currently operating?

Public bodies

These organisations (sometimes called quangos) have been set up and are funded by the government. Examples include the Youth Sport Trust, Sport England, UK Sport and the English Institute of Sport. They are intended to function 'at arms' length' from the government, running their respective areas semi-autonomously, but with funding guaranteed, usually drawn from lottery sources. They are not-for-profit organisations and work in a business-like manner to fulfil their role.

Public bodies also include local authorities that deliver public provision in-house or sometimes contract these services to other companies. Some local authorities operate their sports and active leisure facilities as co-operatives (see above).

Voluntary sector

Charitable trusts are created for the public good to promote areas such as public health, education and relief from poverty. Charitable trusts operate on a not-for-profit basis and, as a consequence, are exempt from most taxes.

Scope and size of businesses

It is important not to get confused between the 'scope' and the 'size' of a business that operates in sport and active leisure.

The 'scope' of a business refers to the extent of the business's activities and how far it extends around the world. The scope of the business will influence which type of business structure (see previous section) is best suited to that business.

▶ **Local** – A local sports business may be a personal training business that aims to help clients lose weight, based in a specific town or its surroundings. A business like this is likely to be a sole trader, a partnership or a private limited company.

▶ **National** – A national sports business or organisation is one that operates throughout a particular country. An example is Sport England which is tasked with promoting physical activity throughout England. At national level and above, a business is unlikely to be a sole trader or partnership.

▶ **International** – An international business trades across international borders. For example, most Premier League football clubs sell merchandise to fans in different countries.

▶ **Multi-national** – A multi-national business has assets and activities in at least one other country other than its home country. For example, Nike has manufacturing and retail outlets around the globe.

The 'size' of a business generally refers to its total number of employees. The categories that are commonly used for grouping businesses are shown in Table 22.2.

Key term

Public bodies – organisations funded by the government that deliver on a not-for-profit basis.

▶ **Table 22.2:** Size of sport and active leisure businesses

Category of business	Number of employees	Example
Micro	Up to 9	A local independent gym run by an owner-manager may employ 4 to 5 additional instructors.
Small	10 to 49	A local leisure centre that employs a management team, a range of lifeguards, office staff, caterers and recreation assistants.
Medium	50 to 249	A Football League club that employs the players, manager, coaching staff, medical staff, ground staff, stewards, catering staff and administration staff.
Large	250+	A large sports retail company such as Sports Direct which employs thousands of people in the manufacturing process, warehousing and retail staff in its shops.

Aims and objectives of sport and active leisure businesses

All businesses in this industry will want to increase participation (which either helps them raise more income or meet participation targets), raise awareness (to help attract people to their services) and meet current trends (to stay relevant by keeping their product or service up to date and popular). But the businesses are likely to have other aims and objectives, too, and these will vary from sector to sector and be used to help judge whether or not the business is successful.

As you will have discovered in other units in your BTEC in Sport, the best objectives are **SMART** – and that applies as much when designing a business plan or strategy as it does to setting sports targets. See Table 22.3 for a reminder of what SMART targets are like.

> **Discussion**
>
> Which classification of size of business do you think accounts for most sports businesses in the UK? Try to justify your answer by giving as many examples as you can for each classification.

▶ **Table 22.3:** SMART targets in a business context

Abbreviation	Meaning	Example
Specific	They say exactly what you mean.	To increase the profit margin for the business
Measurable	You can prove that you have reached them.	To increase profit by 20%
Achievable	They are actions you can in fact achieve.	To increase the business profit margin by employing increased service provision with a strong customer service focus
Realistic	You will be able to achieve them but they will still challenge you.	The increase in profit must be manageable – 100% in 2 months is not achievable
Time-constrained	They have deadlines.	To reach the target by the next financial year

Private sector

The fundamental aim of any private sector business is to make money for its owners or shareholders. But the circumstances that the business finds itself in will affect the aims and objectives that it chooses in order to try and achieve this.

▶ **Making profits** – successful companies will end their year with a **gross profit** figure, which is income from sales minus any costs incurred in creating the goods or services they have sold. A better figure to use is **net profit** as that is the amount which is left over after deducting all costs of supplying the goods or services **and** additional costs such as rent, taxes and rates. You can roughly judge the profitability of a company by measuring the difference between its costs of producing something and how much profit it has produced. Private sector companies require high net profit as this will not only define the success of their company, but it determines how much:

- can be taken as earnings by the owner

- will go to shareholders
- will be reinvested in the business.

In a climate of recession, a company may have a much lower profit margin; if no profit is made, the company may have to restructure to stay in business.

▶ **Break-even** – the point at which the total revenue or income of a company matches the total outgoings, so the business is neither making a profit or loss. For some businesses, especially new ones, this is an important target.

▶ **Survival** – just surviving can be an important target when a business continues to trade through difficult economic times, for example a recession. Occasionally, a bank may set up an overdraft or loan facility to extend a business's survival through tough economic times so long as the business has a robust business plan and capacity for longer-term growth.

▶ **Growth** – most businesses will ultimately want to grow in size, whether that is measured by recruiting more people or increasing profits. Business growth comes through increased revenue allowing expansion. Private sector companies that show a year-on-year growth can be considered successful. However, if growth is not resourced properly, for example by recruiting more employees, staff can become overstretched. Many sports businesses have experienced growth during the past decade as demand for their products has increased due to influences such as the 2012 Olympics. However, it is less apparent during a recession when for many businesses survival or restructuring is more often the aim.

▶ **Market leadership** – a company may aim to become the one with the largest market share or highest profit margin in a given sport or active leisure market.

▶ **Diversification** – this is a strategy whereby a company aims to enter a new market. For example, a sports clothing company might decide to diversify into sports footwear.

▶ **Service provision** – a company might aim to have additional specialised staff available to deliver a particular service to its customers. For example, a private health club might employ a physiotherapist to offer treatment to its members.

▶ **Strong customer service / satisfaction** – almost all private businesses will emphasise strong customer service and satisfaction. This is achieved by having good policies and procedures for staff to follow and a customer charter. Successful private sector businesses often have a quality system aimed at customer satisfaction which is applied throughout the business, viewing customer service as a team effort that must come from everyone in the business. There are many business advantages which come from good customer service (see Figure 22.1).

▶ **Figure 22.1:** Advantages of good customer service

Public sector

Public sector businesses are run by national or local governments, their agencies and other associated organisations using public money (money raised through taxes). The fundamental aim of any public sector business is to be successful in providing a service. However, unlike a private sector business, this is not achieved by making a profit, but by adopting strategies such as cost control, value for money and quality service provision and standards.

▶ **Cost control** – because they are spending public money, many public sector businesses aim to keep down the costs of delivering services that meet customer needs. While a private company may opt for a high-cost supplier because they can charge more to cover that cost, a public sector business may choose to go with an alternative, cheaper supplier.

▶ **Value for money** – given that public sector businesses deliver services using public money (taxes), it is important that those services do not waste money but are still fit for purpose. They also have to make sure that the services or facilities offer value for money for participants, in order to help encourage participation.

▶ **Service quality** – it is important that the quality of public sector business service is of a high standard. This demonstrates that public money is being used effectively by meeting customer needs, while also providing value for money. The business may also be judged against surveys asking customers what they think of the quality of the services offered.

▶ **Meeting government standards** – the use of taxpayers' money requires businesses to meet the required government standards for both provision and customer service. For example, the Disclosure and Barring Service (DBS) is a government organisation that helps other organisations make safer recruitment decisions.

Government guidelines require that sports coaches working with children in regulated sports and leisure activities have undergone a DBS Enhanced Criminal Records check. This process should take between 6 and 8 weeks and is designed to prevent individuals with a criminal history from working with children.

⏸ PAUSE POINT

How do the aims of private sector businesses differ from public sector organisations?

Hint   Can you list the common aims and objectives of each sector?

Extend   Where can you find examples and information about successful businesses/organisations from each sector and what dictates their respective measures of success?

Voluntary sector

The voluntary sector aims to support local communities by running projects, providing volunteers and establishing links to consult or advise on regional or national sport and active leisure issues. This is often achieved on a minimal budget (funded by private or public sector) with no aim to make a profit.

But a common aim in the voluntary sector is to support communities and encourage participation. For example, volunteer skills and expertise are often used to support local projects or sport and active leisure initiatives, such as grassroots junior football that relies on qualified coaches to run teams for free that can then exist financially on subs and small amounts of sponsorship.

Another example is parkrun, a not-for-profit organisation that puts on free-to-attend weekly 5k runs in many countries around the world. Although there is a small central team of employees that provides basic services such as the organisation's website, each event relies on volunteers who have to raise money locally to get their event off the ground. This money often comes from local health authorities that have targets to encourage activity in order to tackle health issues such as obesity. Parkrun can support its community by contributing to these objectives.

Research

The sport sector comes under the government's Department for Culture, Media & Sport (DCMS). Research what percentage of the DCMS budget is allocated to 'sport' and how this spending is broken down. You should be prepared to present your findings as a small group to the rest of your class.

▶ parkrun UK is a volunteer-run organisation that puts on weekly free 5k runs around the UK

Investigating Business in Sport and the Active Leisure Industry

Provision of sports facilities, programmes and services

Public sector funded facilities, programmes and services are paid for by local and national government out of taxes and through additional funding such as the National Lottery. Large **multi-use facilities** such as leisure centres, outdoor pitches and swimming pools are designed for the wider public use.

Private sector facilities, programmes and services are set up and funded by private companies. These include health or fitness clubs and golf or tennis clubs. They are often **members-only clubs** and likely to be more expensive to use compared with public-sector facilities.

The purpose of provision of services

National and local government promote participation by employing sports development teams who arrange events that offer coaching and competition, and develop links with existing facilities. This is often done to encourage more people to live an active lifestyle and to promote healthy living. The private sector will often use more business-orientated approaches by offering discounted rates or additional incentives to encourage people to pay to use their facilities. The ultimate reason that the private sector encourages participation is to increase their profits.

Programmes to promote participation

Health and fitness programmes

These programmes increase a person's fitness levels, help them to lose weight or simply encourage greater social interaction, but all will have potential health benefits.

▶ **Individual training** – occurs both in public and private sectors, mostly at private clubs or leisure centres. Personal training or one-to-one coaching is more expensive due to the fact that one person is taking up the time of one coach/instructor. In the public sector, personal training to improve strength and fitness is available and fitness programmes are often written for new members or those new to training. In the private sector, individual training is much more commonplace. Personal training at private health clubs is a core business and tailored to the needs of the client. Tennis and golf clubs offer one-to-one coaching which often includes video analysis to correct faults. In all cases, this comes at a cost and those with a higher disposable income are the only people likely to be able to afford this level of individual attention.

▶ **Group exercise activities** – occur both in public and private sectors, mostly at private clubs or leisure centres. Group exercise activities can be classes (for example spin or yoga) operating out of leisure centres or private health clubs, or children's sports clubs in which a variety of exercise activities or sports are undertaken. Another example is a local authority country park that offers a speed walk group activity for the over 50s.

▶ **Water-based activities** – occur in both public and private sectors but rely on a swimming pool. Water-based activities can include swimming lessons, aquatic exercise classes or more specialised activities such as scuba diving or canoeing. For example, a local scuba diving club that runs diving excursions overseas may hire a local swimming pool to introduce and train people to use scuba gear.

Educational/schools programmes

Physical Education (PE) and sport is a key issue in schools. Targets have been set for schools to create more time for PE, and for secondary schools in particular; the aim is for a range of activities for a minimum of two hours per week. Therefore, schools are increasingly looking towards working with the public and private sectors to provide an increased and flexible sport and active leisure provision. Secondary

Multi-use facilities – leisure centres incorporating additional facilities, such as outdoor pitches and swimming pools.

Members-only clubs – private or fee-paying clubs that offer leisure or sports facilities for the exclusive use of members.

▶ Water-based activities are often popular with different groups of participants

schools increasingly look to local leisure centres to plug gaps in the PE curriculum. For example, classes may be held at leisure centres to teach sports such as badminton, volleyball or basketball, all of which require a specific space and equipment. This might relieve pressure on an already busy school sports hall timetable or provide classes which would otherwise not be possible.

Sports programmes

Schools are increasingly 'buying in' expertise in the form of specialised sports coaching. For example, private coaching companies may run after-school football clubs, or local authority sports development staff may coach children at local leisure centres in sports such as basketball, volleyball or trampolining.

Gym programmes

Public and private sector gyms will often draw up a basic training programme for new members after induction. These programmes will often be updated or amended by a gym instructor as the client increases their fitness levels. This is also a good way of ensuring the client continues with their membership. Public and private sector gyms and leisure centres often have themed gym challenges for their members. These might include weight loss programmes, running a specified distance over a period of time or simply a number of gym visits in a month.

Swimming pool programmes

Swimming pools are expensive to operate and maintain. However, both public and private sectors recognise their potential to engage the public and generate revenue. Large leisure centres often have 25-metre swimming pools and schedule swim sessions according to people's work patterns. For example, many pools operate a lunchtime swim session for people at work. Private sector health clubs will promote a swimming pool as an additional membership benefit.

Programmes to match demand

Popular sports such as football are often oversubscribed. For example, both public and private sectors offer holiday or after-school clubs that allow children to experience football coaching. There is little difference in terms of the provision, though private football coaching businesses often hire other private facilities which generally include 3G artificial pitches. Football courses are often run by local football clubs as a method of generating revenue but also to meet a wider demand. When demand is great and football clubs cannot meet it, courses are sometimes put on by small businesses.

Programmes to serve specific groups

▶ Programmes may be run for people in specific groups, such as people with Down's syndrome

Both public and private sectors will often accommodate specific groups. Children or adults with learning or behaviour difficulties are often granted specific times to engage in sports activities that will not give the participants cause for concern and will allow them to exercise without worry.

Services

Many sports businesses are set up specifically to provide a service, such as instruction or sports injury treatment. But other businesses can increase their attraction to possible customers by arranging for these services to be offered within their facilities, too, either by using their own staff or by 'contracting in' one of the businesses set up to specialise in this area.

Instruction

No matter what the sport or activity, there is usually potential for a business to deliver instruction in it. For example:

▶ a running coach might give advice on gait analysis to improve running form

▶ an indoor climbing business might employ people to teach customers how to climb safely

▶ an outdoor activities centre might coach people on how to recover a capsized canoe before letting them out on the open water

▶ a business might deliver football coaching through a private academy

▶ a fitness instructor might work with gym users to instruct them on the safe use of the equipment.

The instruction could be provided on a one-to-one basis by a sole trader, offered as an extra service by private businesses, or offered through public and voluntary organisations, such as the national governing body of the relevant sport.

Anybody considering offering instruction as part of their business activities should check out the coaching requirements of the relevant governing body: many will require coaches to have appropriate qualifications. Even if they do not, it can be worthwhile taking relevant qualifications to make sure you offer high-quality instruction that helps build a good reputation among customers.

Therapeutic services

Physiotherapy and sports injury treatment is offered through the **National Health Service** via your **General Practitioner (GP)**; this is free when you get it, but there will be a waiting period of days or even weeks for an appointment. So, many public and private sport and active leisure businesses will offer therapeutic services, though a private club may offer these services as part of a membership package, whereas a public leisure centre will charge for them. Quite often, the therapeutic practitioners will work for both public and private businesses on a freelance basis.

Customer service

Customer service is important for all businesses regardless of whether they are public or private, a big or small company, or a sole trader. Good customer service can range from the welcome desk at a facility providing an efficient and friendly welcome, to any issues being followed up on promptly and resolved to the customer's satisfaction. Earning and maintaining a reputation for good customer service is important for any sport and active leisure business.

Additional facilities

One way that a business can distinguish itself from its competitors is to offer additional facilities.

▶ **Refreshments** – these provide an additional attraction to the overall provision of a leisure centre or private sports club and provide an excellent potential source of additional revenue if marketed correctly. The refreshments provided might range from a vending machine to a full café.

▶ **Car parking** – this can be a vital area of provision. Many people travel to leisure facilities by car, so without parking provision, any sports facility whether private or public will lose custom and revenue.

▶ **Changing areas** – these are important as users need a place to wash and change. These areas should be clean and presentable at all times. Family changing areas should be made available as appropriate.

▶ **Lockers** – these are important so clients can store their belongings safely and securely. In the majority of leisure centres or private health clubs, lockers are integrated within the changing areas.

▶ **Crèche** – an increasingly important area of provision as it allows parents to exercise or use the facilities offered even if they have young children. A crèche must be staffed by appropriately trained employees.

Key terms

National Health Service (NHS)– National Health Service: the collective term for health services in England, Wales and Scotland.

General Practitioner (GP) – a doctor who treats a range of illnesses and provides preventative care for patients at a designated surgery.

Discussion

Do you think that paying an increased amount to access facilities in the private sector is a guarantee of a better overall service and of achieving fitness goals outcomes?

Customer groups

Businesses often think of customers as fitting into different distinct customer groups to help promote participation and understand some of the perceived barriers to undertaking sport and physical activity. Some businesses will try to appeal to a broad range of groups, while others will target just a small group or **niche market**.

Breaking down the target customers into groups can also help with marketing, by allowing companies to tailor their marketing activities to match the target group. For example, a marketing campaign aimed at people aged 16–20 will probably be very different from one aimed at people aged over 65.

There are two ways that sport and active leisure businesses break down their customer base: by demographic and by purpose. **Demographic** refers to a specific part of the population that has shared characteristics or needs, for example, the same age, gender, ethnic origin or disability. Common ways of grouping people by demographic are shown in Table 22.4. **Purpose** refers to the reason why that group is looking to take part in sport or active leisure. Common ways of grouping customers by purpose are shown in Table 22.5.

Key term

Niche market – a small, specialised market for a particular product or service.

Link

You can read more about marketing later in this unit.

▶ **Table 22.4:** Common customer groups – by demographic

Demographic	Explanation
Age classification	Allows people of a specific age group to exercise together on the basis that they are of a similar ability. For example, leisure centres of fitness clubs might offer a yoga class for the over 50s.
Gender	Allows people of the same gender to exercise together, often for a sense of comfort and lack of intimidation. For example, swimming pools often offer a women-only swim session.
Ethnic minority grouping	Research by Sport England suggests that a lower proportion of people from ethnic minorities are often keen to partake in sport or active leisure, but access to facilities is limited. Sports businesses will often target ethnic minority groups to tackle potential inequality and provide access to sports such as basketball, without stereotyping.
Disability	Sports businesses are encouraged to become more welcoming and accessible to people with disabilities. For example, organisations award accreditation to leisure facilities that get more people with disabilities physically active.
Socio-economic group	For example, displaced people (individuals seeking asylum and recent refugees) who may find access to sport facilities difficult. A key business and marketing driver is an individual's income (i.e. a private business is likely to target a higher-income individual who is more able to afford the fees).

▶ **Table 22.5**: Common customer groups – by purpose

Purpose	Explanation
In specific activity or sport	Individuals or groups who are aiming to improve or gain new skills in a particular sport or activity.
Recreational	Individuals or groups who want to participate in recreational sporting activities.
Weight loss	Those who want help with weight reduction using exercise and dietary advice.
Personal image	Those who want to regularly undertake exercise to improve their personal image.
Health maintenance	Those who want regular exercise to help improve health and maintain the body's functions.
Training for performance	Regular sports performers or elite athletes who want to undertake more prescribed training to aid performance.
Charitable	Those who are undertaking activities which engage and inspire, children in particular, to undertake sports or active leisure activities and those who have signed up to do a charitable event such as a marathon.

Programming to meet the needs of customers

Once the business's target customer group or groups are known, the business can put together a programme that meets their needs. There are three key areas that the business has to consider: provision, staffing and legal requirements.

▶ **Provision** – it is vital that the appropriate facilities to undertake a sport or active leisure activity are available and fit for purpose. For example, there is little point in hiring UEFA qualified coaches during the school holidays if the playing fields are not suitable to coach or play on. The provision also has to be made available at the relevant time. For instance, it would be pointless for a company that wants to deliver football coaching sessions to young children aged 11–16 to schedule its sessions for during the school day (unless they were working with a school or group of schools). It would be much more sensible for them to run their sessions in the early evening, at weekends or during school holidays.

▶ **Staffing** – businesses need to ensure they employ an adequate number of properly qualified personnel to coach or instruct their client base. For instance, some age groups will require more supervision and so the business will need more staff to be working when those groups are being catered for. It is also important that these employees project a professional image that further inspires the client base.

▶ **Legal requirements** – all employees must have undergone the appropriate Disclosure and Barring Service (DBS) checks, especially if working with children. All health and safety protocols must be observed with risk assessments carried out (and the nature of the risk assessment may vary depending on the nature of the customer group being catered for). Employees must be paid at least the relevant minimum wage. Depending on the customer group and the activity, there may also be governing body requirements regarding the minimum level of qualifications that members of staff must have in order to deliver an activity or coaching session.

Research

Investigate a local sports or activity club that is available for school children during the summer holidays in your area. Examine its advertisement claims and compare this with the club's provision, staffing and legal requirements to undertake its activities. You should be prepared to present your findings as a small group to the rest of your class.

Link

Many of the legal requirements faced by sport and active leisure businesses are covered in *Unit 20: Leisure Management*. See also the section on laws, legislation and safeguarding later in this unit.

Stakeholders and their influence

Whatever the nature of the sport and active leisure business, it is likely to have a number of **stakeholders**. These stakeholders will all have an effect on the business's business plans, aims and objectives.

Types of stakeholders

There are two types of stakeholders: internal (those within the business) and external (those outside the business). The following sections give examples of both types.

Internal stakeholders

▶ **Managers** – working at management level means making decisions, keeping staff motivated, ensuring standards are met, dealing with complaints, and interpreting and applying new instructions. You have to be a good leader, organised and knowledgeable to be effective. A manager is often the link between employees and senior stakeholders, such as owners or a **chief executive**.

▶ **Employees** – are staff employed by the business or organisation on a full-time, part-time or temporary contract? All should have a personal investment in the business or organisation for which they are working. It is ideal to aspire to work for a company or organisation that you both enjoy and are proud to represent.

▶ **Owners/shareholders** – owners or shareholders wish to see a business or organisation succeed as they have both a financial and a personal investment, and wish to see that success transform into profit. Sometimes, owners or shareholders will wish to see a business or company succeed because its aims and objectives reflect their own aims, such as encouraging people to take up a particular sport or activity.

External stakeholders

▶ **Suppliers** – will have regular contact with the business, supplying the sports business or company with items it needs, for example, from football equipment for a junior football team to toiletries for a fitness club.

▶ **Competitors** – the business's competitors can actually help increase awareness of the service or facility that your own company offers. Think of them as 'friendly competition': it is in their own interest for the service that both your businesses provide to be well known by the public, as that way you can all prosper. For example, a business offering taekwondo instruction in one town may help make more people in the wider area aware of the sport and seek out instruction in their own town.

▶ **Creditors** – a creditor is a person or company owed money by your business or company. It is in creditors' interests that your company succeeds; if the business goes bust, they are unlikely to be paid the full amount they are owed.

▶ **Customers** – customers will wish to return to a business that sells them a product or service they want at a reasonable price. If a customer likes the product or service that you offer, they have an interest in seeing your company survive.

▶ **Government agencies and departments** – these have a general interest in seeing the health of the nation improve. They also set frameworks and policies that might affect businesses in some areas, such as by introducing new legislation that affects businesses or by changing taxation rates.

▶ **Communities** – wish to see successful businesses and companies employ local people to help create a vibrant local community.

▶ **Interest groups** – wish to see successful businesses and companies addressing their particular interests and those of the people they represent. For example, this might include a group of people who are 'friends' of a local country park and actively engage in promoting the interests and activities of the park.

▶ **Trade associations** – organisations such as the Federation of Sports and Play Associations (FSPA) want to see their area flourish and thrive, so they are always keen to encourage success in their particular sport or business type at a local and national level.

▶ **Fundraisers** – will raise money for local interest groups (for example, a local gymnastics club) so they can continue to use the facilities offered by local sports and active leisure businesses.

Relevant laws, legislation and safeguarding issues

Any business operating in the sport and active leisure industry must make sure that it meets the requirements of any relevant laws, legislation and safeguarding issues.

These laws are not always sport-specific but may be general legislation applying to any business, such as equality and diversity legislation. Numerous laws, such as the Sex Discrimination Act (1975), Race Relations Act (1976), Disability Discrimination Act (UK 1995 and 2002) and Equality Act (2010), have been passed by successive governments in order to make it illegal for companies to discriminate against employees on the grounds of race, gender, disability, religion or sexual orientation.

The main piece of health and safety legislation is the Health and Safety at Work Act (1974), which ensures that all companies have health and safety policies and provide training for their staff. It is enforced by the Health and Safety Executive (HSE) which has powers to fine or close down companies or imprison individuals if standards are judged to be unsafe (see **www.hse.gov.uk**).

The proper treatment of employees is enforced through the Working Time Regulations Act (1998) and the Employment Act (2002), which govern working hours and practices.

Legislation that has an impact on some or all sport and active leisure businesses is summarised in Table 22.6.

▶ **Table 22.6:** Business legislation

Name of legislation	Examples of what it covers	Impact on sport and active leisure businesses
Personal Protective Equipment (Clothing) (EU 1992)	Crash hats, gloves, protective goggles	Investment in safety gear
Manual Handling Operations (EU 1992)	Lifting gear	Training staff in the safest techniques
Working Time Regulations (EU 1998)	The hours staff can work and their breaks	Adjusting shift patterns and breaks to suit legislation
The Employment Act (2002)	Guidelines on how employees should be treated	Permitting employees to request flexible hours, leave requests, etc.
Control of Substances Hazardous to Health (UK 2002)	Chemicals and cleaning fluid	Creating safe storage systems/locations
Occupiers' Liability (Duty of Care) (UK 1984)	Requires premises to be safe for customers	Ensuring buildings and rooms for hire comply
Data Protection Act (UK 1988)	Requires information held on clients to be confidential	Secure IT systems
Disability Discrimination (UK 1995 & 2002)	Adaptation of premises and working practices	Investment in disabled-friendly fittings and access routes – an equality policy
Sex Discrimination Act (1975)	Protects individuals from discrimination on grounds of gender	Creating an equitable working environment for employees
Race Relations Act (1976)	Protects individuals from discrimination on grounds of race	Creating an equitable working environment for employees
The Safety at Sports Grounds Act (UK 1975) Fire Safety and Safety of Places of Sport Act (UK 1987)	Safety inspections and certification required	Investment, time to train staff and equipment
Consumer Protection Acts	Goods must be fit for purpose	A returns and complaints procedure

Write down examples of real-life businesses that undertake one of the activities below and research what you think is the appropriate piece of legislation that covers the activity.

- Gaming or gambling
- Running adventurous activities
- Staging sports events with large crowds
- Selling goods

▸ Health and safety is the responsibility of all the business's employees

 PAUSE POINT How might the legal and financial influences on sports businesses help and protect you as a worker or employee?

Hint Can you list examples of the legislation that are designed to protect you and explain briefly how they do so?

Extend Where can you find information about the various levels of minimum wage and what is it for an under-18 employee?

B Business models in sport and active leisure

Business models

Business models are strategic plans for the operation of sport and active leisure businesses that identify customer bases, products to sell, sources of revenue and good financial management. A business model is the basic template for the business to compete and survive in a particular marketplace. In other words, it reflects the vision and ability of a business to reward its investors or backers.

When business owners put together their business model, they often use two common analysis tools to help them work out where they are now and where they want to go. These are known as **SWOT** and **PESTLE**.

SWOT

SWOT analysis is used to evaluate the strengths, weaknesses, opportunities and threats that face a business. The analysis should help its owners and/or managers understand the demands placed on the business, the environment in which it competes with other businesses and the strengths and weaknesses compared to the competition.

- ▸ **Strengths** – what does the business offer that is out of the ordinary?
- ▸ **Weaknesses** – what does the business require in order to be successful?
- ▸ **Opportunities** – is there an existing or potential new market available?
- ▸ **Threats** (including competitor threats) – is local competition or pricing likely to have a significant impact on the business plan?

Table 22.7 shows an example SWOT analysis for a recently qualified personal trainer who wants to set up a business that accommodates the health and fitness needs of business professionals working in the financial district of a city. This business requires initial investment and will target a wealthy audience by offering **bespoke** fitness and health assessments followed by training packages that fit around their working day.

▶ **Table 22.7:** Example SWOT analysis for a personal training business

Strengths	Weaknesses
Expertise: excellent level of training knowledge, including performance physiology and weight loss approaches *Customer need*: increasing number of busy professionals with disposable income who are willing to pay for specific training expertise	*High start-up costs*: hi-tech measuring equipment (e.g. digital body fat analysis) is expensive but required for specific training expertise *Lack of funding*: requires investment to fund the first two years of operation
Opportunities	**Threats**
Untapped market: only approximately 1% of professional people over 30 have a personal trainer *Fast growth*: the demand for personal training expertise is on the increase	*Competition*: personal trainers of similar ability competing for a small market pool *Pricing*: increased competition likely to push prices down over time

PESTLE

PESTLE analysis looks at factors that influence a business environment. Each letter denotes a particular factor that has an impact on the business's activities and success:

▶ **Political** – takes into account the political situation in the host country. For example, is the host country sympathetic or actively promoting sport and active leisure?

▶ **Economic** – takes into account the components of an economy and their likely impact on a business. For example, **inflation**, **interest rates**, and even **foreign exchange rates** if the business trades overseas. Is the economy in a downturn, which may affect how much people want to spend on sport and active leisure? Or is the economy booming?

▶ **Social** – each nation or region has a particular culture, demographic or approach to business. This culture can affect how business services are offered or how they are transacted. Social may also take into account trends in sport and active leisure, and how these trends increase or decrease in popularity.

▶ **Technological** – technology is continually changing so businesses need to be aware of how to use and integrate these changes to their benefit. Technological factors could be business-related, such as new computer systems that allow the business to operate more efficiently, or they might relate to sport and active leisure, such as the introduction of new equipment.

▶ **Legal** – businesses operate within a legal framework. This framework often changes so businesses must be aware of any new or existing legal requirements.

▶ **Environmental** – Geographical location, weather and climate are different components that will affect different locations, and will influence the types of trade businesses will conduct. The sports and active leisure industry often works around the environment. For example, a business in the UK might offer professional athletes or customers winter training in Spain where the weather is generally warmer and more conducive to fitness and conditioning gains.

Key terms

Bespoke – written or adapted for a specific participant or purpose.

Inflation – the rate at which the cost of goods and services rises.

Interest rates – the amount of a loan that is charged to a borrower.

Foreign exchange rates – the rate at which one currency is exchanged for another, such as British Pound (£) to US Dollars ($).

Link

Social and technological trends are explored in learning aim F, of this unit.

PESTLE for Nike Inc.

Table 22.8 shows what a PESTLE analysis for a large sports business such as Nike Inc. might look like.

▶ **Table 22.8:** A possible PESTLE analysis for Nike Inc.

Political	Nike has benefited from stable components of the US economy including low interest rates and a steady dollar international exchange rate.
Economic	Nike has weathered challenging trading conditions by outsourcing manufacturing to countries where advantage is taken of lower wages while retaining the strategic and design components in the US.
Social	Nike has benefited from a growing awareness of individual health and fitness. Nike was criticised for outsourcing manufacturing to emerging economies and paying low wages. Nike has since addressed these issues and attempted to make its manufacturing practices more transparent as it cannot afford to be the subject of a global consumer boycott.
Technological	Development of a social media platform, increasingly sophisticated design and manufacturing techniques and an increase in online or mobile payments have all increased Nike's productivity.
Legal	Nike's growth as a worldwide brand has relied upon **globalisation** and the capacity to adapt to the legal requirements of its trading and manufacturing areas.
Environmental	Nike has a positive approach to green issues and **ISO 14000**-compliance is a key component of its global brand.

Check your knowledge

1 Compare Nike with other global sports clothing manufacturers and make a list from one to five in terms of worldwide sales.

2 What are your influences for choosing a brand of sports clothing? Do you wear Nike, Adidas or some other brand and what do you think it says about you as a sportsperson?

Key terms

Globalisation – when businesses and organisations develop international operations and influence.

ISO 14000 – a series of standards that provide a framework for businesses and organisations to improve their environmental management and green credentials.

Discussion

How far do you think a need for a healthy and active lifestyle can form the basis of a business opportunity? Do you think it is right that businesses seek profit on the back of people wishing to become healthier or do businesses have a legitimate role in promoting this important issue? Discuss this complex issue as a group.

Assessment practice 22.1

You are about to apply for jobs at two different sports companies: one private and one public. Choose the two companies. To help your application and give yourself a better understanding of the two companies, investigate both companies and prepare a presentation looking at business models, organisation, aims and objectives, provision of facilities, stakeholders and the legislation that governs them.

Plan
- What is the task? What should my presentation address?
- How confident do I feel in my own abilities to complete this task? Are there any areas I think I may struggle with and what can I do to improve on these areas?

Do
- I know how to examine the business operations of both public and private organisations. In particular, I can identify the various differences in terms of business models, organisation, aims and objectives, provision of facilities, stakeholders, and the legislation that governs them.
- I can identify where my presentation may have gone wrong and adjust my thinking/approach to get myself back on course.

Review
- I can explain what the task was and how I approached the investigation and construction of my presentation.
- I can explain how I would approach the more difficult elements differently next time (i.e. what I would do differently).

C Human resources

Job roles and person specifications

Staff are often described as the key element in any business, and that is especially true in sport and active leisure where they must be qualified enough to be able to instruct customers as necessary while also giving good customer service.

The number and extent of job roles will vary depending on the precise nature and size of the individual sport and active leisure business. In medium-sized and large companies, members of staff will usually be organised into teams and departments with a 'chain of command'.

Common job roles and responsibilities

Common job roles in sports and active leisure companies are shown in the list below, alongside their typical responsibilities.

▸ **Executive/owner/manager** – decides on the sports business's **strategy** and overall direction, taking responsibility for the overall success or failure of the business.
▸ **Supervisor** – implements the organisation's strategy by adopting good tactics in day-to-day activities, leading a team of other members of staff.
▸ **Qualified sports leader, instructor, coach** – carries out the daily coaching or training schedules under the guidance of the supervisor.
▸ **Support staff** – provide additional support to the instructors and coaches. Four typical support-staff roles are:
  - Administrators – often involved in the implementation of the planning, organisation and budgeting of a business, as directed by the overall company strategy, or processing sales and bookings
  - Security staff – ensure information held is always secure as this is vital to the reputation and productivity of a business. To achieve this, IT systems and premises should always be secured and access limited to those who need it to execute their duties

> **Key term**
>
> **Strategy** – how a business plan is implemented.

- Cleaning staff – important from a health and safety and presentational viewpoint. Business premises or equipment should always be maintained to a hygienic or safe standard
- IT staff – most businesses operate on various IT platforms. IT staff will ensure that email, accounts and databases are maintained and accessible throughout the working day.
▶ **Trainees** – often employees who are being trained to perform a particular role or function within a business.
▶ **Volunteers** – volunteers offer their time freely and often perform a particular role or function without payment. They are more often found in voluntary organisations than in public or private businesses.

▶ Reception staff are often also involved in handling sales and bookings in leisure centres

Person specifications and job descriptions

Any job in sport and active leisure will be accompanied by a person specification (minimum requirements for the job) and a job description. The job description gives a clear definition of titles, roles and responsibilities, lines of communication and who is in authority. The type of structure adopted by a sports business will depend on a number of factors, such as the nature of the operation, the type(s) of products and services it offers, its locations and its number of employees.

All job descriptions will list the following criteria.
▶ Post title – what the role is (for example, customer services manager)
▶ Salary – how much the role pays (for example, £24,000 p.a.)
▶ Job purpose – an overview of the main accountabilities (for example, a finance director will be responsible for all financial aspects of a company)
▶ Principal responsibilities – detailed breakdown of the role's decision making and accountability (for example, a development manager will be responsible for the career development and training of all employees of a company)
▶ Knowledge, skills, training and experience – the level of education and experience required to perform the role (for example, a project manager is likely to be required to be educated to degree level and possess previous experience in managing sport and active leisure projects).
▶ An example of a job description for a leisure operations manager, including most of the criteria mentioned above, is provided below:

Job Description	
Post title:	Leisure Operations Manager
Salary:	£35,000 to £45,000
Responsible to:	Senior management
Responsible for:	Leisure Facilities Operational Teams
Hours of work:	37 hours per week
Job purpose:	The Leisure Operations Manager role is about providing leadership to the Leisure Facility Teams along with a business focus. The Leisure Operations Manager will have responsibility for the financial and operational performance of the leisure facilities, ensuring that excellent customer service is delivered at all times and that the facilities meet all specified quality and performance standards.
Principal responsibilities:	• To lead, manage, motivate all staff and carry out recruitment, induction, training, appraisal, development and performance management of staff • To be the lead contact for all facilities (operational) • To produce weekly staffing rotas • To liaise with the Finance Director to develop the membership activity and attendance, and organise advertising in the local area, and attract new customers through special offers • To carry out market research • To deal with complaints and general queries • To deal with general feedback from members of the public • To undertake the role of Premises Manager for the leisure facilities. • To implement procedures and systems to ensure the highest standards of: – cleanliness throughout the buildings – environmental conditions (water treatment, building temperature) – plant and equipment – repair and maintenance • To keep records of stock and re-ordering • To write reports on the progress of the leisure facilities • To ensure risk assessments and all health and safety procedures are kept up to date, and to ensure staff are fully briefed on health and safety legislation and industry guidelines. • To ensure inventories of equipment and stock are maintained • To ensure safeguarding procedures are in place and adhered to, particularly in relation to the Disclosure and Barring Service (DBS)
Supervision/ management of people	The post holder will supervise and directly manage the Leisure Operational Teams through allocating and monitoring work, mentoring, development and training.
Knowledge, skills, training and experience	Education to degree level, or equivalent relevant experience (operational management of leisure facilities, project delivery, evidence of effecting cultural change, events organisation and marketing and service improvement, etc.)

Types of employment

There are several ways that sport and active leisure businesses can hire staff, and the best type will depend on the nature of the business.

Full-time staff

Full-time employment involves working a minimum number of hours as contracted by an employer. Companies generally require 35 to 40 hours per week to be defined as full time. For example, a general manager at a leisure centre will likely be a full-time employee. Full-time contracts often include benefits such as paid sick leave, annual leave and health benefits.

Part-time staff

Part-time employment involves a person working fewer hours per week than a full-time role. Companies generally consider fewer than 30 hours per week to be part-time work. An added advantage of part-time work is the flexibility it offers the employee. A fitness instructor at a private gym may work rotational shifts amounting to, for example, 24 total hours over a 4-day period.

Seasonal roles

Seasonal roles are temporary, short term and unlikely to have the benefits of full-time work despite working long hours over a short duration. For example, ski resorts often hire workers during the winter to help with the increased participation.

Consultants

Consultants are experienced practitioners who offer specialised advice to businesses to help improve their performance or productivity. Consultants are likely to offer specialised sport or active leisure knowledge, or more business-specific advice such as IT, finance or HR expertise.

Volunteers

Volunteers carry out unpaid work for organisations such as charities or sports clubs, but can also work for public sector bodies. Volunteers usually sign an agreement instead of an employment contract, though they should undertake a level of training appropriate to their role, for example a Level 1 or Level 2 FA Coaching qualification to coach grassroots football teams.

Franchisees

Instead of expanding by hiring employees directly, a sport and active leisure business may choose to expand by allowing other business people to set up as a franchise of their brand. This is when an individual or outside business buys a contract or licence to access an established company's knowledge and trademarks, and use these to provide a sport or active leisure service under the company's name or banner. Setting up as a franchise can be a low-risk way of starting a business as the franchisee is guided by the franchisor to follow a proven trading method with a proven product or service, for example, golf breaks, or health and fitness products. The franchisee can also benefit from the fact that the brand name is already established. An example in the sport and active leisure industry is the clothing retailer, InterSport.

Benefits and risks of different types of employment

There are a number of ways a business may decide to employ staff, though the key consideration is what best suits the business and its circumstances. If a business runs on traditional hours, for example 9 a.m. to 5 p.m., then full-time employees are probably the best option. However, full-time employees are expensive as you will not simply pay a salary, but also pay sick leave, annual leave, **pension** payments and health benefits.

A retail business may be open for much longer hours, for example 7 days per week and 8 a.m. to 9 p.m. In this situation, a team of part-time workers may have to be employed to cover late shifts.

Other businesses, for example tourism, may have busy times when seasonal workers need to be hired over a short period.

Consultants are often hired to address an area of business weakness or to develop a particular service to increase the business's **capacity**. Consultants are expensive and fees of £500 per day are not uncommon. Therefore, it is imperative a business hires the right consultant at the right time to address the right issue; otherwise, a lot of money may be wasted.

> ### Key terms
>
> **Pension** – a tax-efficient method of saving during working life to provide an income once retired.
>
> **Capacity** – the output or performance that a business can provide in a given timeframe.

> ### Research
>
> See if you can identify real-life examples for each of the types of employment listed above. Identify the business or organisation each type works for and see if there is any trend or link between the types of employment and the type of sports or active leisure business. You should be prepared to present your findings as a small group to the rest of your class.

Human resource management

Human resource management is the formal system of managing people within a business or organisation. Many larger businesses will have a whole department dedicated to human resource management; smaller businesses will often give this responsibility to a single manager.

Roles and responsibilities of human resources

Human resource (HR) management is a large and important component of any business that employs staff. Its main roles and responsibilities are as follows.

Timetabling staff

If a business has a number of staff performing different roles and functions, it is essential that each employee knows where they are working and what roles they are performing at any one time. For example, a football coaching company may employ several coaches during the week. Each coach needs to know what school or club they are to be at and at what time. HR management involves timetabling staff to make sure that the staffing requirements of the business are covered.

Salaries

The payment of salaries is an important HR role. Salaries, including National Insurance, tax deductions and pension contributions, must all be calculated prior to being sent to employees' bank accounts. These details will be filled out on a payslip that the employee receives for their records. A lot of the processes are usually computerised and automated, but the HR management has ultimate responsibility for ensuring that everything happens correctly.

Conditions of employment

Conditions of employment are often written up as a contract and include important HR items such as the employee's job description, pay details, disciplinary processes, working hours and any holiday entitlement.

Physical resource management

The range of physical resources needed by a sport and active leisure company can be huge, from everyday disposable items such as pens and paper to the equipment needed in order to provide its service to the customer. Physical resource management involves planning to make sure that the business is never without the resources that it needs at any one moment, and ensuring that the resources it does use are properly maintained.

Resource planning

Resource planning involves identifying the resources that the business needs in order to operate effectively and ultimately succeed. Proper resource planning needs to consider all of the following.

▸ **Supplies and materials** – these generally account for consumable items that are required to enable the smooth-running of the business. For example, a water-cooler at a health club will be regularly restocked with fresh water for clients by a fitness instructor.

▸ **Contracting** – this involves the short-term hiring of people, often with particular skills, to help your business with a project, for example. Money and the HR management function both need to be available to undertake contracting.

▸ **Changes in staffing needs** – each time a position within your business becomes available or a new position is created, you should plan to fill the vacancy. A manager or owner should consult with HR (if the company has or contracts one) and begin a carefully planned recruitment process.

▸ **Events and foreseen risk control** – it is important to understand that there are numerous potential risks involved with setting up or running a business. Risks are unknown events that have yet to occur and could cause problems for your business. The benefits of risk control mean you can plan to tackle and deal with these events as and when they occur.

Resource maintenance

Resource maintenance involves creating a business plan that looks after the physical business and personnel resources required to deliver a service to customers.

▸ **Emergency cover** – a prudent business will consider in advance emergency cover if a resource does become unavailable, such as hiring a generator or similar power unit to cover for electricity loss, or other actions taken to cover the loss of physical resources or equipment due to flooding or accidental damage.

▸ **Health and safety** – as maintenance means keeping the workplace safe, including any equipment, furniture and facilities operating correctly and making sure their condition does not decline, it is imperative to do so safely so as not to place the customers or staff in unnecessary danger.

▸ **Assets** – business **assets** can range from cash, to buildings, to intellectual property, but all count towards the overall value of the business. Assets such as equipment or buildings should be maintained regularly (and replaced if need be) so long as they are used by employees and customers.

▸ **Leasing options** – leasing options allow a business to hire or rent resources such as equipment or a vehicle, rather than purchasing outright. Leasing allows a business to spend a smaller amount of its **cash flow** on the equipment it needs. The disadvantage is the equipment leased does not belong to the company and is not considered an asset towards the company's value.

▸ **Maintenance and refurbishment** – it is important to maintain all equipment, furniture and buildings of

---

PAUSE POINT   Do you understand the likely risks to a business if human resource (HR) management is ignored or not considered?

Hint   Close this book and try to recall the main responsibilities of HR.

Extend   Find out from the various web sources the likely risk of penalties or legal action if a business ignores its HR responsibilities.

a business from the point of view of presentation and health and safety management. Employees are entitled to work in a safe and comfortable environment and fee-paying customers will not want to continue using a service that does not invest in the maintenance and refurbishment of its resources.

- ▶ **Budgetary restraints** – budgetary restraints set limits on how much your business can spend on particular areas. For example, if it can only spend a certain amount on resource maintenance (see above), spending beyond this level may put the business in financial difficulties.

> **Key terms**
>
> **Assets** – property or equipment owned by a business or organisation with a specific value.
>
> **Cash flow** – the amount of money flowing in to and out of a business or organisation.
>
> **Productivity** – the economic measure of a business's potential output.
>
> **Wastage** – service or stock that are not used to their potential resulting in a monetary loss to the business.

Importance of resource management

Resource management involves the development of business resources. These can include finance, human resource, IT or staff development of capacity and skills.

Maximising skills, productivity and capacity

It is important to keep staff trained so that they can carry out their role to the best of their ability. When staff are well trained, knowledgeable and motivated, their **productivity**

is likely to increase. It is also important to provide staff with physical resources to help them maximise their skills. For example, fitness instructors at gyms should use the most up-to-date fitness testing equipment the budget can afford, which will maximise their capacity and contribute to enhancing the overall customer experience. Similarly, cleaners should have access to deep cleaning equipment for use in changing areas and the gym equipment for the same reason and as part of a more efficient overall business model.

Reducing risk, costs and wastage

A fundamental aim in business is to make a profit. By reducing risks, costs and wastage, a business can increase its profits. Risks are unknown events yet to happen and they are often expensive to deal with when they do so.

Having a proper maintenance programme and ensuring that physical resources work properly is a method of risk control: it decreases the chances of a physical resource breaking or not being usable, and also lessens the likely financial impact when this does occur.

Costs and **wastage** are closely linked. It makes sense to consider carefully what a business requires to operate at an optimal level and without overspending. For example, for a business that uses approximately 200 bottles of hand wash in its changing room each month, there is no business case in purchasing 400 bottles per month from the supplier as this will lead to overspend and financial wastage.

Assessment practice 22.2

You have been asked to give a talk to a group of new staff who have just joined a sports business, as part of their induction process. Your boss has asked you to cover the impacts of human resources on the business and why it is such an important area. You are given 20 minutes to design a poster that you can refer to during your talk.

Plan

- How am I going to successfully plan my time and keep track of my progress?
- Do I need clarification about anything?

Do

- I know how to explain the various components of a business's human resource management. In particular, I can identify the various job roles and specifications, types of employment and the importance of physical resource management in a sports or active leisure business.
- I can identify when my talk is going wrong and adjust my thinking/approach to get myself back on course by referring to my notes.

Review

- I can say whether I met the task's criteria and whether I succeeded.
- I can explain how I would approach the more difficult elements differently next time (i.e. what I would do differently).

D Marketing

Marketing is a vitally important activity for any sport and active leisure business. You might have the best product or the best service in the area, but unless your potential customers know about you, your business will fail. Marketing is the process that sport and active leisure businesses use to tell their cusotmers about their products and show how they can meet their needs and expectations.

Link

When marketing, companies often aim to target a specific customer group or groups. Refer back to the section on customer groups earlier in this unit.

Marketing 7 Ps

When planning their marketing, many people find it helpful to think of the marketing '7 Ps' shown in Figure 22.2 and explained in the text that follows.

▶ **Figure 22.2:** The marketing 7 Ps

Product

Product life cycles, unique selling points (USPs) and product range – the most successful businesses find out what their customers want: there is no point developing or trying to sell customers something they do not want.

Price

Pricing strategies – a product is only worth what a customer is willing to pay for it. Pricing should be competitive but remember not to price yourself out of the market or sell something at a loss – do either of those and you will go out of business quickly.

Key terms

Product life cycle – the stages a product goes through from the initial idea, through usage, to it being withdrawn from the marketplace.

Unique selling point (USP) – something that makes a business or its product different to anything else. It can be projected as a reason for potential clients to buy a particular product or service rather than that of a competitor.

Logistics – the coordination, movement and storage of products or services.

Promotion

The 'promotional mix' – a marketing term describing various promotion methods such as the use of advertising, digital promotion, social media, target market, brand image (celebrity endorsements), above-the-line (mass media methods, for example, TV advertising) and below-the-line (specific, memorable methods focused on groups of customers, for example, direct marketing at individuals) promotion – how your business communicates with your customers. It includes advertisements, social media and promotions, in other words, everything the customer needs to know in order to be able to choose your product over someone else's.

Place

Supply chains, the processes involved in the production and distribution of a product, **logistics** and customer needs – the place where you supply or deliver your product must be convenient for the customer. Moreover, your product must be available at the right time.

People

Staff training, consistent and reliable customer service, relationship between people and brand image – your staff are your biggest asset as they, more than any other factor, determine a good level of customer service and satisfaction. Remember that many customers will not distinguish between your product or service and the staff that deliver that product or service.

Process

Managing customer interactions consistently, as shown in the model of service consumption (see Table 22.9, opposite) – customers will not simply invest in a product or service; in many cases, they will invest in an experience or lifestyle choice. For example, a gym or health club membership is not simply about the exercises the client will undertake to keep fit – it can also be a social investment to meet people, a leisure investment if they have something to eat or drink at the health club, or simply a part of their weekly routine.

▶ **Table 22.9:** The model of service consumption

Stage	Description
1	Pre-purchase (expectations of a product or service)
2	Purchase-use (consumption of the product or service)
3	Post-purchase (evaluation of the customer experience of the product or service)

Physical environment

Reflecting brand image in the physical environment, appropriateness to offering – it is always important that customers can see what they are buying. Health club membership or weekly football coaching for children is a financial commitment and customers will be keen to like what they see, and to believe they are getting value for money. It is important that staff are clean and smart, and the surroundings are welcoming and well maintained. Both these factors (and others besides) create a good impression that leaves the customer feeling confident that they are making the right decision buying into your product or service.

Discussion

Sports retailers are particularly good at using their shop windows to promote offers. Why do you think they run these types of deals?

Meeting the needs of the customer

The marketing process for a sports product or service starts with the identification of customers and their needs. This requires research which, in turn, will contribute to a plan for the promotion of the business. This could relate to anything from the sale of a health drink to an expensive personal training service. In all cases, the method of research has to be reliable, the marketing activities appropriate, and any promotional plan flexible and fit for purpose.

Being knowledgeable about services, equipment, activities and facilities

Sports businesses have good reasons for planning their marketing – they need to build up knowledge of customers, competitors, their market, demand, trends, opportunities and pricing. If you understand these concepts and are knowledgeable about the services the business can offer or the equipment it uses, you can make informed judgments and plan marketing strategies to tell your customers all about it.

▶ **Customer knowledge** – you need to understand the characteristics of customers and which particular demographic they fall into, analysing preferences and sporting habits of demographics. Thereafter, you can tell customers about the products and services best suited to them.

▶ **Competitors** – knowing what your competitors are doing in the short term, and what their strengths and weaknesses are, is important to sports businesses. For larger sports organisations, this is important for pricing decisions; for smaller businesses, quality of service may be the key. Research may show that there are gaps in the market which may present opportunities.

▶ **Market** – you need to be aware of what is going on in the market for your particular goods or services, but also in the general business environment. Market analysis is often carried out using the PESTLE analysis.

▶ **Demands and trends** – demand is the quantity of goods or services that a customer will buy at a given price. Trends can often offer business opportunities or give an early warning that something is no longer popular or is becoming more and more popular.

▶ **Opportunities** – a PESTLE analysis will indicate opportunities as well as new trends.

▶ **Pricing** – Three broad approaches are often considered:
 • Low price to try to gain a foothold in the market or to try to increase market share – this can produce a price war with rivals.
 • Prices set at the market rate – usually for frequent purchases.
 • A high-price strategy – usually for upmarket or high-end goods or services.

Link

Trends are covered in learning aim F.

Key term

AIDA – Awareness, Interest, Desire and Action: a model used to describe the steps involved when a customer engages with a new business or organisation.

Highlighting benefits for the customer of promotions (special offers, customer loyalty schemes)

Sales promotions are usually short-term activities aimed at raising awareness or to compete with other similar products and services. They follow the model acronym **AIDA** by raising awareness, interest, desire and action to buy. The activities typically involve seasonal promotions such as sales and special offers, gifts and incentives to loyal customers, competitions or offering the product at a very attractive introductory price. Popular seasonal approaches are the

'New Year' deals to new members that offer, for example, one month free membership or no administration fee. These types of deals often come with additional benefits for customers such as a free personal training session, or customers can select their own bespoke membership package to meet their personal fitness goals. It is often worth prospective customers shopping around for the best deal, or existing customers taking advantage of any loyalty or bonus scheme. These benefits culminate in the customer being satisfied and the business gaining new or continued revenue.

With any of these circumstances, a business needs to adopt a managed and controlled approach, targeting the message and activities, so that later you can identify which was the most successful in meeting customer needs. Similarly, customers also need to adopt a managed and controlled approach when selecting their chosen promotion or loyalty scheme to ensure that it meets their needs and satisfies their personal goals.

Ⅱ   PAUSE POINT   Why do you think marketing is important to the success of a business or organisation?

> Hint   Can you recall the reasons for a sensible and productive marketing strategy?

> Extend   Can you find an example of a sport or active leisure business (large or small) whose marketing strategy prompted you to purchase a product or service?

Taking the initiative in communicating with customers

The success or failure of a marketing plan lies in how well it communicates with existing or potential customers, but any business should always look to take the initiative to communicate with customers in all areas of their operations. This does not just help the business promote itself, it also helps it get to know its customers and be able to respond to their wishes and desires. The various ways of communicating with customers are shown in Table 22.10.

▶ **Table 22.10:** Ways of communicating with customers

Type of communication	Explanation
Verbal Employing direct speech – stress and tone is important	Verbal communication might include face-to-face chats with existing and potential customers or a simple telephone call asking them a number of questions as part of a questionnaire to determine the level of customer service received. Verbal communication might also include an interview at a local radio station that might provide a much needed advertising opportunity.
Non-verbal Employing written or image communication	Non-verbal communication might include a press release to a newspaper, website or magazine. This represents free publicity and is a simple story about what a business is doing. It might also include a feature article in a written publication. This is designed to target a specific market (i.e. publication readers) and will be likely to contain a unique selling point (USP) to further enhance publicity. Other methods of non-verbal communication include posters and information leaflets displayed in the business's premises.
Listening Simply hearing what customers want and say	Often the best and certainly an appreciated method of communication is listening to what customers say. For example, take time out to meet and chat to customers at a private health club and ask them if there are any improvements they would like to see introduced.
Responding to complaints	Every business should have a complaints policy that outlines how customers who have concerns are responded to. This policy should detail the response time and level of employee who will deal with the complaint. Complaints should always be responded to by letter (as well as verbally if appropriate) with an apology if it is required and the likely recompense or actions to follow should the complaint be upheld.
Recognising if customers have special requirements	In theory, all customers have special requirements. Simply ensure that your business or company finds out about and acts upon any specific special requirements a customer may have.

You have been asked by a local sports centre to review their marketing activities. Pick a local sports centre. Carry out some research into their marketing activities, analyse the outcomes, and then make proposals based on the research for promotion of an aspect of their business (e.g. 25 m swimming pool usage or after-school football clubs).

Plan

- What is the task? What is my role and how will I address the marketing activities that will produce the research necessary for a report?
- How confident do I feel in my own abilities to carry out these activities and analyse the outcomes relating to what is being asked? Are there any areas I think I may struggle with?

Do

- I know how to examine the various components of marketing and meeting the needs of customers.
- I can identify when my talk may have gone wrong and adjust my thinking/approach to get myself back on course by referring to my notes or this textbook.

Review

- I can explain what the task was and how I approached the construction of my report and reached my recommendations.
- I can explain how I would approach the more difficult elements differently next time (i.e. the analysis – what I would do differently). For example, I might look at a different type of questionnaire for use with customers.

Finance in the sport and active leisure industry

Financing a business in sport and active leisure

Financing a business requires the ability to review financial statements and assess budgeted figures to determine if the business is developing, improving or making a profit. If careful analysis of the figures is not carried out, the business may suffer a decline or cease trading. The key things to know and understand are outlined here.

Content and purpose of cash flow

Cash flow is important for a sports business – it is what accountants call 'liquidity'. It allows the organisation to buy in goods and services, to support its own activities, pay its debts and save for contingencies or future developments. A sports business must plan its cash flow to ensure it has enough money to carry out its plans and meet needs such as wages, loan repayments and utility bills.

Fixed and variable costs of a business

Fixed costs are those a business pays regardless of how much of its service the business sells. For example, overheads such as rent for premises are fixed costs that must be paid.

Variable costs are those often related to sales. As sales go up, then so do the variable costs. For example, the more customers a health club gets through the doors, the more water is drunk from the water cooler, the quicker the water will need replacing at additional cost.

Capital costs and operational costs

'Capital' can have a dual meaning, but in the context of a sports business it would be cash or raw materials invested in order to generate income (working capital). This allows the business to know how much it will be operating with at least initially, but it can vary with the inflow and outflow of cash.

> **Key term**
>
> **Cash flow** – the total amount of money flowing into and out of a business – a business needs regular money coming in, in order to pay for regular items such as monthly bills.

Operational costs are the expenses relating to the day-to-day running of a business. They can include all staffing, utilities, rental, IT, security and maintenance expenses.

Equipment costs, including upgrading equipment

Budgets should be set aside or factored in for equipment costs and potential upgrading. Equipment is a variable cost and, at times, it may break down beyond a period of scheduled maintenance. Such an occurrence must be addressed immediately as a lack of equipment may have an impact on overall customer service.

▶ Businesses must plan to cover their equipment costs

Financial records

Businesses – even sole traders – are subject to audits, where their financial records are checked, so it is important to keep accurate financial records. This enables accountants or human resource departments to calculate the businesses, salaries, taxation, expenses and costs accurately.

Businesses are legally required to keep financial records for:
▶ all sales and income
▶ all business expenses
▶ VAT records – VAT or 'value added tax' is a tax on certain goods and services that is collected at every stage of production and distribution. The current VAT rate is 20%
▶ PAYE records (if the business has employees) – PAYE stands for 'pay as you earn' – it is a tax that employees pay to the government but it is deducted by the company from the staff members' monthly pay.

Ultimate Personal Training

Profit and loss account. For the year ending 31 March 2017

	Expenditure (£)	Income (£)
Sales		38,500
Less cost of sale		
Purchase of equipment	(2,250)	
Hire of gym facilities	(12,500)	
Accreditation fees	(1,500)	
Gross profit		22,250
Less expenses		
Loan repayment	(2,400)	
Office expenses	(1,250)	
Tax	(2,650)	
Advertising	(1,500)	
Insurance	(600)	
Travel (inc. fuel costs)	(1,975)	
Net profit		11,875

▶ **Figure 22.3:** Example financial records for a personal training business

Sales

Business sales might be broken down into different units such as fees, merchandising and hires, and you might keep an accurate stock control of any product or service being sold to give a more accurate picture of the business's financial health. These records will also guide the payment of any taxes and help sales forecasts. They enable you to calculate monthly sales projections, perhaps based on previous years or predicted trends.

Payment of tax

It is important to keep accurate financial records so that the business is sure it is paying tax correctly. Keeping these records will also ensure that when the payments of tax become due, the business has enough cash at hand to be able to pay the bill.

As well as VAT and PAYE mentioned earlier in this section, businesses can also be liable for **corporation tax** (paid on limited companies' income and profits) and **National Insurance** (a deduction from employees' earnings to fund government welfare schemes).

Purchasing and ordering records

All purchases and orders should be recorded to enable the payment or claiming back of VAT, depending on how much money the business or organisation makes. For this reason, it is essential to keep an accurate stock control of any product being sold.

Wages for employees

All businesses need to calculate salary and wage payments for each month, which should include National Insurance deductions, PAYE deductions and often pension contributions too, for the year. Wage rates may also fluctuate if staff are asked to work a lot of overtime. The more of this that can be predicted, the better.

Trends in the sport and active leisure industry

It is essential that sport and active leisure businesses keep an eye on activities that are increasing in popularity among the general population, and which they may be able to cater for within their business. They should also watch those activities that are generating less attention or engaged in less. These trends can be affected by several different factors.

Trends

New technologies

Technologies are continually changing, as are their application in the sport and active leisure industry. Technological innovations may relate to the improvement of existing technology, such as upgrading of gym equipment to make it more durable, or may involve completely new developments. For example, 'Zwift' is a company that created a digital indoor cycling training tool using 3D graphics and a social element that allows customers to ride together online around various courses on a static cycle at home or at work.

Many recent technological developments incorporate the widespread use of mobile phone technology. It is also possible to download apps that can monitor your heart rate, fitness and exercise levels while maintaining and developing a live fitness or exercise programme. It's now possible to develop apps that allow gym customers to sign up to classes online and the gym equipment used is often compatible with customers' own HRM straps.

The advent of portable digital cameras has added a new dimension to sports participation and fitness training. Rather than traditional camcorders which record video footage, new portable cameras can provide a live image from the viewpoint of the participant, a bird's-eye view of an individual's performance. This new stream of technology can also be adapted using software to further analyse performance.

Influence of the media, including social media

Social media has allowed the increased dissemination of information to a much wider audience beyond that of watching or observing sports or active leisure. Video footage can be quickly uploaded or discussions and/or advice held live at any time.

Mainstream media – for example, satellite television, radio and print media – will regularly bring news or issues to the notice of participants. The mainstream media also use social media extensively to further engage viewers, listeners and readers.

Social and mainstream media can have a direct role in affecting participation rates. The coverage of the 2012 London Olympics witnessed a rise in sports participation that sports businesses were able to exploit.

Changes in national participation rates for different activities

Fitness-based activities, team games and recreational activities have all benefited from the advent of new technologies, in particular mobile phone and social media platforms. For example, the boom in road cycling has led to cycling retailers and peripheral industries (such as clothing manufacturers and gadget companies) benefiting from increased participation rates. Other businesses (for example, gyms offering spin classes) will try to tap into this boom with promotions such as 'Avoid cycling in the winter cold by coming to our spin classes'.

> **Discussion**
>
> Do you think social media is changing the way we do business? Discuss as a whole class and exchange your views.

Changes in participation and spectator numbers

Mobile phone apps and social media have enabled the instantaneous dissemination of footage, comment and results of sporting activities, achievements and events. For example, the results and comments on football matches, professional or otherwise, can now be uploaded to social media by mobile phone and discussed between fans. On a more individual level, performance figures for gym activity can be uploaded to ranking tables or charts for comment.

Developing products/services to take advantage of trends

Sport and active leisure is subject to change and development like every other industry. Business will always take advantage of these trends so long as money is there to be made. Sports nutrition is currently a huge growth sector, particularly protein supplements. Professional coaches of athletes through to casual users of a local gym have all embraced the use of protein supplements to aid recovery and enhance muscle-building capabilities. As a consequence, there has been an increase in the number of businesses manufacturing and distributing protein supplements. It is a competitive industry with many businesses promising training gains for those who use their products.

▶ Many established products have been re-versioned to capitalise on the current trend for protein products – here, Cheerios and the Protein Cheerios variant, made by General Mills in the USA

Benefits

Improvements and diversification of products, services and customer experience

The development of new products will ultimately lead to the diversification of the services offered. Customers will have a wider choice of products on offer as businesses compete to sell their products. The wider choice may also lead to a reduction in price as rivals aim to place their products at an increasingly competitive price and provide an added customer experience as an incentive.

Business growth – development of new target markets, offering USPs and improved reputation

As trends change, it is important for businesses that they understand the potential of these trends and develop new target markets. A business should assess whether a target market fits with a new strategic direction and target this market via a USP accordingly. For example, football is becoming increasingly popular in China. Consequently, businesses from clothing manufacturers to qualified football coaches are looking to exploit the new market in China and grow business there.

Risks

Diversifying and developing new products comes with a financial risk and with no guarantee of success.

Failing to meet customer needs

When developing a new product or service, there is always the possibility that customer needs will not be met. For example, there have always been changes in health and fitness trends; some prove popular (for example spin classes) and some less so (for example, sauna suits). The key is market research and proof that the product or service can actually have a benefit to the customer and meet their needs.

▶ Sauna suits have not proven popular

Failing to anticipate competitor activities

To stay one step ahead of competitors, it is often prudent to anticipate their next target or USP, and develop your own to counter this development. The risk here is that you are letting a part of your business strategy be led by what you think your competition is going to do, rather than developing your own ideas.

Failing to achieve a return on investment

Often the development of new target markets, offering USPs, improved reputation and so on. will require a financial investment in marketing, research and trialling a product. All these functions come with a cost and there is no guarantee that your new development will achieve a financial return. Therefore, there is always a financial risk to factor into the business plan if you are looking to expand, diversify or offer something new.

Hint   Can you recall the potential risks when developing new markets or USPs?

Extend   Can you find an example of a business (large or small) which underwent an unsuccessful period of development or promotion associated with a new development or USP?

Assessment practice 22.4

You have inherited some money, which you have decided to invest by buying shares in a sports business. You need to carry out some research to assess which one will give you the best prospects of success and some future dividends.

In the form of a report you need to:

1 explain what makes a financially successful business

2 explain how a business successfully adapts its practices to accommodate new trends in the sport and active leisure industry to enhance growth.

Plan

- What is the task? How will I address the issue of what makes a business financially successful? What aspects of finance should I consider?
- How confident do I feel in my own abilities to carry out an assessment of the successful utilisation of trends such as new technology? Are there any areas I think I may struggle with?

Do

- I know how to examine the various components of financial management and identify trends, and what helps these factors succeed.
- I can identify when my report may have gone wrong, or when I am not happy with the description of financial or trend success. I can get myself back on course by referring to my notes or this textbook.

Review

- I can explain what the task was and how I approached the construction of my report and the recommendations I had reached, providing examples as appropriate.
- I can explain how I would approach the more difficult elements differently next time (i.e. in the analysis of a company's finances – what I would do differently). For example, I can examine existing reports on a company's performance.

Further reading and resources

Arthur, D., Beech, J. and Chadwick, S. (2017) *International Cases in the Business of Sport*, 2nd edition, Abingdon: Routledge.

Smith, A. and Westerbeek, H. (2003) *Sport Business in the Global Marketplace*, Hampshire: Palgrave Macmillian.

www.bbc.co.uk/news/business – Daily business news stories and information from the BBC.

Websites

www.bbc.co.uk/news/business – daily business news stories and information from the BBC.

THINK ▶FUTURE

David Ingram

Personal trainer
(as a sole trader)

I studied for Level 3 BTEC National Sport at a further education college from 2006 to 2008. Soon into the course, I knew that when I finished I wanted to be a personal trainer. I took my Level 2 gym instructor award and my Level 2 FA football coaching award while at college and started up my own after-school football fitness group for school children. The content of the BTEC course helped me with the knowledge of how to set up this small business and what I needed to do beforehand, such as DBS checks, public liability insurance and equipment.

When I completed the BTEC course, I had saved up enough money to enrol on a Level 3 Personal Trainer course. This took me around 12 months to complete and it was hard work, but I'm now a fully qualified advanced personal trainer with a list of clients that I train out of the same health club.

The role is varied and many of my clients I see either early in the morning or later in the evening as most work regular hours during the day. The free hours during the day are invaluable to me as they allow me to plan my weekly schedule, send out invoices, manage my cash flow and ensure all my administration is up to date. I also catch up on the latest research and articles on fitness and business, for the benefit of my clients and to stay one step ahead of my competitors.

Personal training is my dream job, but it is only part of it: the other part is running a business and that's tough. But I make a good living and I'm now considering expanding the business and hiring additional personal trainers to cope with the business's growth, when I might switch from being a sole trader and set up a limited company.

Focusing your skills

Understanding business information and data

It is important to be able to analyse and interpret business information and to know how to research and adapt your business according to the needs of your customer base.

- The ability to review and analyse financial data will help you determine whether or not the business is in a healthy position.
- Ensure all financial records are accurate and up to date. These include all sales figures, tax returns, purchase orders and any additional wage costs.
- Emphasise your competency when handling cash payments or direct debits from customers: make sure they are given receipts and any payment is quickly entered into your accounts.

Marketing knowledge

You need a good understanding of the market and how to identify potential customers and their needs.

- Carrying out either a SWOT or PESTLE analysis of your business will help indicate new potential business opportunities.
- When promoting your business, it is important to use a plan with clear objectives followed by coordinated advertising and publicity.
- Understand how good public relations works, enhancing your relationships with customers, suppliers, the media, potential investors and the general public.

Getting ready for assessment

This section has been written to help you do your best when you take the assessment test. Read through it carefully and ask your tutor if there is anything you are still not sure about.

About the test

The assessment test is in two parts. Part A will contain a case study based on a fictional fitness club that requires a review of its business model and a detailed set of recommendations for how to improve it. This will be released to you a set period of time before Part B which includes supplementary stimulus information building on the scenario information in Part A.

As the guidelines for assessment can change, you should refer to the official assessment guidance on the Pearson Qualifications website for the latest definitive guidance.

Preparing for the test

To improve your chances on the test you will need to make sure you have revised all the key assessment outcomes that are likely to appear. The assessment outcomes were introduced to you at the start of this unit.

To help plan your revision, it is very useful to know what type of learner you are. Which of the following sounds the most closely matched to you?

Type of learner	Visual learner	Auditory learner	Kinaesthetic learner
What it means	• Need to see something or picture it to learn it	• Need to hear something to learn it	• Learn better when physical activity is involved – learn by doing
How it can help you prepare for the test	• Colour code information on your notes • Make short flash cards (so you can picture those notes) • Use diagrams, mind maps and flow charts • Use sticky notes to leave visible reminders for yourself	• Read information aloud, then repeat it in your own words • Use word games or mnemonics to help • Use different ways of saying things – different stresses or voices for different things • Record short revision notes to listen to on your phone or computer	• Revise your notes while walking – use different locations for different subjects • Try and connect actions with particular parts of a sequence you need to learn • Record your notes and listen to them while doing chores, exercising, etc. – associate the tasks with the learning

Do not start revision too late! Cramming information is very stressful and does not work.

Sample answers

You will be given some background information on which the questions are based. Look at the sample questions which follow and our tips on how to answer these well.

- Read the question carefully.
- Highlight or underline key words.
- Note the number of marks available.
- Make additional notes that you can include in your answer.
- Make sure you make the same number of statements as there are marks available. For example, a 2-mark question needs two statements.

Worked example

Look carefully at how the question is set out to see how many points need to be included in your answer.

Ultimate Fitness Club opened in 2008 and has quickly built a reputation as a friendly, clean and professional facility in the local town.

The facilities include:
- fully equipped gym containing cardiovascular machines, free weights and resistance machines
- 25 metre swimming pool
- several studios for classes.

Other products or services include:
- sauna and steam room
- coffee bar
- shop selling fitness equipment and clothing
- personal training
- nutritional therapy.

The club is open from 8 a.m. to 8 p.m. Monday to Saturday – membership details are as follows:

Membership	Price	Joining fee	Notes
Individual	£40 per month off-peak	£50	Couple = £70 per month
Individual	£50 per month peak	£50	Couple = £90 per month
Children under 5 go free			
Non-members can pay £10 a day to use the club's facilities			

Ultimate Fitness Club operates as a private limited company (Ltd). The club recruits its own staff, ranging from full time to seasonal. The club is owned by the Managing Director and Finance Director. They employ a full-time club manager who is responsible for HR, staff training and the general day-to-day operations of the club.

Ultimate Fitness Club maintains a database of all customers (past, present and casual) and sends them details of new promotions and services. The club website is regularly updated to reflect any new promotions and services, together with the times of classes. Ultimate Fitness Club advertises in the local press and online.

In light of the above, Ultimate Fitness Club is viewed as a premier club and it claims its unique selling point (USP) is 'the leisure experience' – customers use the gym, have a swim then enjoy a coffee and relax. There is a nutritional therapist available for consultation at limited times, and this is popular with many customers.

The club is located in a town with a population of just over 50,000 people. In the town, there are four secondary schools (one of which is a specialised sports college), an amateur cricket club and a semi-professional football club. There is a local authority leisure centre nearby that has a swimming pool and a small gym. The town has a large business park where staff work in several office buildings and small manufacturing outlets.

Table of demographics of the town

Age	Year 2005	Year 2010	Year 2015
0–5	3162	3328	3382
6–10	3004	3204	3414
11–15	2900	3089	3196
16–20	3152	3459	3643
21–30	4914	5045	5362
31–40	5220	5508	5942
41–50	6061	6504	7286
51–60	5864	6925	7737
61–70	5560	6308	7231
70+	5663	5809	6418
Total population	**45,470**	**49,279**	**53,611**

Review the current status of Ultimate Fitness Club using your research on the sports and leisure industry and the given data (45 minutes)

You should consider:
- the purpose of the existing sports and leisure business, Ultimate Fitness Club
- what the data says about the existing business. [16]

Answer: *Sports and leisure businesses are either private or public companies. Private companies tend to be run to make a profit (i.e. make money) and public companies are publicly funded (i.e. from taxpayers' money) to provide a service to a community. When you look at the provision of the sport and leisure industry, private and public sector companies will often have the same goal but achieve it in different ways.*

Both types of business aim to get people fit and healthy by engaging in exercise and reducing potential or longer-term health risks such as obesity or heart disease. Private companies will try to do this by making a profit when providing a good service. Public companies will try to do this by providing a service that is value for money and profit is less of an issue. A further difference is found in the people who use the private and public companies. The private sector is aimed at those people who can afford it (e.g. pay monthly fees to use sport and leisure facilities in a private environment), whereas the public sector tries to cover as many people as possible by making its services affordable.

Ultimate Fitness Club is a private limited company with two shareholders who will take much of the profit after paying wages and overheads. It is classed as a small business because it employs between 10 and 49 people. Its goal is to make a profit, have a strong customer focus and be a market leader in its local area by providing a unique selling point (USP) which is 'the leisure experience'. The costs of a peak membership (£600 per year) may not be available to everyone, so the membership numbers are always going to be limited. However, the business is making money so it is doing okay and needs to hold onto its membership.

This answer demonstrates a clear review with sound references to the sport and leisure industry, demonstrating a clear understanding of the purpose for the business in question. It shows some understanding of the data provided though **it does not cover** some of the more detailed use of the data provided and further research (i.e. products available, town demographics and wider discussion around the facilities) and compare these to what might be available in the public sector.

11 marks awarded

Analyse the internal and external influences that are currently affecting Ultimate Fitness Club (45 minutes).

You should:
- use an appropriate business tool
- refer to the possible impact of the nearby public sector leisure centre.

[16]

Answer: *To analyse the internal and external influences effectively, I will use a SWOT analysis. A SWOT analysis analyses the Strengths, Weaknesses, Opportunities and Threats to a business.*

- *Strengths – excellent facilities (fully equipped and modern gym; 25 m swimming pool; coffee bar and affordable membership).*
- *Weaknesses – dependent on members renewing their membership; needs to encourage new membership to promote profit and growth; limited market as town has population of 55,000 and customers unlikely to come from much further afield.*
- *Opportunities – data suggests membership can be offered to a variety of demographic groups (large 60+ population); membership incentives and partnerships with employers at local business park.*
- *Threats – nearby public sector leisure centre may be able to offer more affordable membership packages and may advertise this, which may be viewed as negative publicity for Ultimate Fitness Club; possible job losses or company closure/relocation at business park.*
- *In view of the SWOT analysis, it is recommended that Ultimate Fitness Club embark upon a concerted publicity effort (local newspaper advertisement; local radio and billboards) to get in first and promote the benefits of membership to stay ahead of the competition.*

This answer demonstrates a detailed analysis of internal and external factors, including competitor activity that influences the business. It takes into account how a SWOT analysis works and this further highlights a detailed knowledge of the business model used. Perhaps a more detailed discussion of pricing and profit forecasts might have earned more marks.

13 marks awarded

Recommend how Ultimate Fitness Club can develop and market itself (60 minutes).

You should consider:

- meeting the needs of the customers
- meeting the current trends of the industry
- meeting the needs of the business. [20]

Answer: Firstly, ask customers to complete a short questionnaire to ask how the club might improve its service. The club will also leave a suggestion box at reception for people to suggest ideas. The results of the questionnaire suggest two items: customers would like to see newer CV and resistance machines in the gym and the option to eat a quick healthy snack at the coffee bar.

The gym has decided to hire the latest CV and resistance machines, both of which are fitted with the latest technology which allows their workout to be recorded on an app on their mobile phones. After much research, the management of the gym have also employed a new member of staff to serve healthy meals from a carefully formulated diet plan to serve to customers. Both initiatives look at the developing trends and new markets for app-tracking exercise and healthy eating. As such, the gym has embarked upon an advertising campaign that promotes Ultimate Fitness Club as a reactive and customer-focused business, However, the business has planned this growth carefully and ensured the cash position of the business can meet these new initiatives; one is a fixed cost, one is a variable cost. The risk is the expenditure and the publicity is forecast to increase membership which will cover the expenditure.

This answer demonstrates recommendations that are relevant. They demonstrate clear consideration for meeting customer needs, meeting current trends and the meeting of the business needs in order to expand. Perhaps a more detailed discussion of other aspects of the gym, a more detailed analysis of industry trends and justification for the initiatives chosen would ensure new membership and financial stability and would therefore have earned more marks. 10 marks awarded

Skill Acquisition in Sport 23

Getting to know your unit

In this unit you will explore how the characteristics associated with skill and ability contribute to performance. You will investigate the information processes that enable learning to take place and how coaches use feedback to aid these processes. You will also examine theories of teaching and learning, and the phases a performer undergoes when learning a new skill. Finally, you will need to demonstrate a plan showing how all these components fit together and develop learning strategies for successful skills performance.

This unit is an internally assessed unit and, as it covers many of the processes that are carried out in the sports industry, you will need to draw on learning from across your qualification to complete your assessment.

How you will be assessed

This unit will be assessed by a series of internally assessed tasks set by your tutor. These tasks might take the form of written documents, presentations or short projects.

The assignments set by your tutor may take the following forms.

▶ Produce a report on the effectiveness of information processing models in showing how sports performers produce skilled performance.
▶ Create a presentation evaluating the effectiveness of selected behaviourist and cognitive theories of learning when teaching skills to sports performers.
▶ Carry out an evaluation of the effectiveness of your use of teaching and learning strategies to develop selected sports skills.

The exercises within this unit are designed to help you practise and gain the skills that will help you complete your assignments. The theories you will learn will give you the background information to enable you to complete the unit but not necessarily guarantee you a particular grade.

Assessment criteria

This table shows what you must do in order to achieve a **Pass**, **Merit** or **Distinction** grade, and where you can find activities to help you.

Pass	Merit	Distinction
Learning aim **A** Investigate the nature of skilled performance		
A.P1 Discuss the qualities of skilled performers. Assessment practice 23.1	**A.M1** Assess how abilities contribute to the production of sports skills. Assessment practice 23.1	**AB.D1** Evaluate the effectiveness of information processing models in showing how sports performers produce skilled performance. Assessment practice 23.1
A.P2 Explain the characteristics of skills and abilities. Assessment practice 23.1		
Learning aim **B** Examine ways that sport performers process information for skilled performance		
B.P3 Explain how a sports performer processes information in a given situation. Assessment practice 23.2	**B.M2** Assess the stages of information processing models. Assessment practice 23.2	
B.P4 Discuss the value of different types of feedback to learning. Assessment practice 23.2		
Learning aim **C** Explore theories of teaching and learning in sport		
C.P5 Describe two contrasting theories of teaching and learning. Assessment practice 23.3	**C.M3** Analyse how selected theories of skill learning can be used when teaching skills to sports performers. Assessment practice 23.3	**C.D2** Evaluate the effectiveness of selected behaviourist and cognitive theories of learning when teaching skills to sports performers. Assessment practice 23.3
C.P6 Explain the three phases a sports performer experiences when learning a new skill. Assessment practice 23.3		
Learning aim **D** Carry out teaching and learning strategies for sports skills		
D.P7 Produce a plan showing how a skill can be taught to meet the needs of different sports performers. Assessment practice 23.4	**D.M4** Demonstrate the effective use of teaching and learning strategies appropriate to specific situations when developing sports skills. Assessment practice 23.4	**D.D3** Evaluate the effectiveness of your use of teaching and learning strategies to develop selected sports skills. Assessment practice 23.4
D.P8 Demonstrate the use of different types of teaching and learning strategies to develop sports skills. Assessment practice 23.4		

Getting started

Success in a chosen sport is dependent on how well an athlete learns specific skills. Athletes need to process information they are being told, execute skills they are learning and refine these with practice. How do your tutors or coaches teach you sport skills and how might their methods either differ or be similar to professional coaches, in, say, professional football?

A   Investigate the nature of skilled performance

Learning and performance

There are some key differences between how we learn to do something, and then how we perform that skill later. Key among these differences is understanding the connection between the theoretical knowledge that underpins teaching and learning and the practical application of that theory in a sports or active leisure setting.

▶ Measuring learning – when a coach measures an athlete's learning, they do so by a combination of observation and practice. For example, a coach might teach an athlete a new skill and ask them to perform it. This will provide the coach with an indication of how the athlete has changed their capability to execute this new skill. The extent and process by which this skill will have been learned can be demonstrated by various learning curves (see below).

▶ Measuring performance – performance differs from learning insomuch as it refers to the execution of the skill after learning. Performance is often measured using learning curves which show performance changes against the time spent practising. Performance is often difficult to measure accurately because of the impact external factors can have on it, for example the environment, the health of the performer or their motivation.

▶ Performance plateau – a period during training or learning of a skill when there is no apparent improvement in performance. This is a common occurrence during which training or performance improvements level off.

> ### Theory into practice
>
> Think of a coaching session you have gone through recently. How did your coach or tutor plan and carry out the session: did they explain things clearly; set learning outcomes; demonstrate the skills or correct any faults in technique; set practice?
>
> Consider the amount of preparation time that would have gone into delivering the session. Get together in small groups and discuss your thoughts, focusing on the different coaching styles experienced and the amount of preparation you think went into each session.

Learning curves

Learning curves are a simple way of graphically demonstrating the different rates of learning by an athlete. They can be used to demonstrate how quickly athletes acquire different skills, and if there are any variations in how they learn over the time they are being taught the skill. Each graph is constructed by a y-axis indicating the amount of learning, and an x-axis indicating the time taken.

▶ A linear learning curve, as shown in Figure 23.1, demonstrates a proportional increase in learning over time, meaning as the time increases, the expertise at a skill, or the number of skills learned, increases at the same rate.

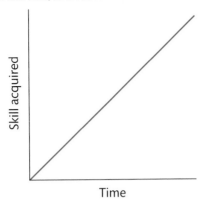

▶ **Figure 23.1:** Linear learning curve

▶ A negatively accelerated learning curve, as shown in Figure 23.2, demonstrates rapid early learning, but slows during the late time component. This means that a person learns a great deal quickly, but as time increases, their rate of learning slows – this might be because the skill(s) learned become more complex as time goes on meaning more time is needed to master them.

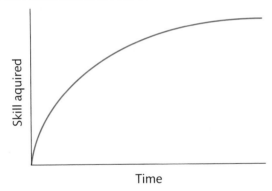

▶ **Figure 23.2:** Negatively accelerated learning curve

▶ A positively accelerated learning curve, as shown in Figure 23.3, demonstrates a small early learning gain followed by a rapid rate during the late time component. This is the reverse of the negatively accelerated curve and would mean a person takes a long time learning the basics of a skill but once they master it, they are very quickly able to build on it.

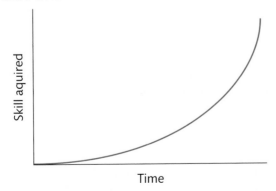

▶ **Figure 23.3:** Positively accelerated learning curve

▶ The S-shaped learning curve, as shown in Figure 23.4, is a combination of positive and negative performance curves. In the example shown, the learning started slowly, then had a period of rapid acceleration, before plateauing again.

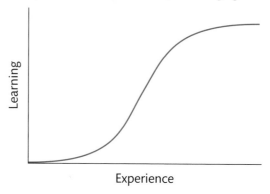

▶ **Figure 23.4:** S-shaped learning curve

ⅠⅠ PAUSE POINT   Consider your process of learning when working on a set of skills for a sport with which you were previously unfamiliar. Which of these charts most closely matched your experience?

Hint   Think how easy you found it to understand the new skills you were learning.

Extend   What do you think you could do to transform your learning pattern from one type of learning curve to another?

Characteristics and classification of skills

Sports are composed of a variety of skills that can be classified and broken down. A skill is defined by Knapp (1963) in her book *Skill in Sport – The Attainment of Proficiency*, as 'The learned ability to bring about predetermined results with maximum certainty, often with the minimum outlay of time or energy or both.'

A skill is the ability to produce a combination of movements using a variety of muscles and joints to produce a coordinated action. Skills are acquired through learning and perfected through practice and observation. Athletes develop skills through support and feedback from coaches or other athletes. Mastering a skill means being able to continually produce it successfully with little effort.

Skills vary; however, some can be transferred from sport to sport. For example, an athlete who masters the skill of throwing in athletics can transfer this skill to other sports such as cricket, softball or baseball.

Qualities of a skilled performance

A skilled performance requires a number of key qualities to act (often together) to reach a desired outcome. These qualities include the following.

▶ Fluency – this enables the execution of the skills to look smooth and natural, not disjointed or uncomfortable. For example, Ronnie O'Sullivan's cue action in snooker appears very relaxed because it is so fluent.

▶ Control – movement control requires a combination of the correct blend of speed, accuracy and distance. For example, a fielder in cricket throwing the ball directly to the wicket keeper from the boundary to execute a runout illustrates control.

▶ Economy of efficiency of movement – the execution of a skill needs to be successful, often in the least amount of time (efficient) and done with the minimum of errors (economic). An example would be several members of a rugby team combining to pass the ball from one side of the pitch to the other without errors.

▶ Consistency of outcome – this is important when executing high levels of performance repeatedly. For example, Novak Djokovic may hit several shots around the court but always within the tramlines so he has more chance of winning the point.

▶ Energy expenditure meeting the demands of the task – minimising energy expenditure by reducing unwanted movements during skill execution – so energy is not wasted on unnecessary movements. For example, a gymnast might hold a handstand for several seconds.

Types of skill in sport

There are three main types of skill in sport.

▶ Cognitive skills – these require thought processes and are sometimes referred to as intellectual skills. For example, a rugby captain, in the context of the game, might decide whether to take a penalty as a scrummage for a possible seven points (from a try and conversion) or a kick for three points.

▶ Perceptual skills – these require the interpretation of external stimuli by the brain. For example, a boxer may interpret his opponent backing off as weakness or getting tired, and decide to attack. The opponent, on the other hand, may simply be employing cognitive skills and back off to enable counter-punching.

▶ Motor skills – these require movement or muscle control. For example, sprinting the 100 m inside a narrow lane requires excellent motor skills.

Effect of the environment on skill classification

Skills can be classified according to the environment in which they are performed. They may be open or closed.

Open skills

Open skills are those the athlete is constantly adapting, according to what is happening around them. Examples of open skills include:

▶ Team sport – a footballer dribbling a ball, unaware of the location of all members of the opposing team. Defenders will challenge the player to try to get possession of the ball. The decisions the player dribbling the ball makes depend on the actions of the opponents.

▶ Individual sport – a return shot in badminton: the receiver is unaware where the shuttlecock will be played by the returnee, so will have to react to their opponent's moves to select an appropriate return. The choice of return shot will be affected by the position of the opponent on the court.

Key terms

Open skills – skills continually adapted according to the situation.

Closed skills – skills carried out in a pattern regardless of the environment in which they are performed.

Fine skills – skills requiring delicate and accurate muscle control in specific parts of the body.

▶ Badminton players use open skills

Closed skills

Closed skills are pre-learned patterns of movements which the athlete can follow with very little reference to the surrounding environment. Examples of closed skills include:

▶ Team sport – a rugby player taking a conversion during a match. The movement pattern remains the same every time the player performs the skill.

▶ Individual sport – when an archer takes aim, pulls back the bowstring and releases the arrow towards the target.

We also classify skills by the pace with which the athlete controls the timing of an action. Skills are said to be self-paced, externally paced, or somewhere between the two.

▶ Archers use closed skills

Precision of movement and skill classification

Skills can also be classified by the muscles involved in completing the skill. In this style of definition, skills are defined as fine and gross.

▶ **Fine skills** involve small movements of specific parts of the body. For example, taking a close-range shot at goal in netball will only require the goal shooter and goal attack to move their fingers and wrist to produce the required skill. An individual shooting a rifle on a shooting range will only move their trigger finger.

▶ **Gross skills** involve large muscle groups and movement from the whole body. An example of this form of skill in a team sport is the bowling action in cricket, while an individual example is the javelin throw. In both cases, many muscle groups are involved, as well as movements that run through the whole body.

Distinctiveness of beginning and ending of movement

Skills can also be classified by how easy it is to identify their beginning and end.

▶ **Continuous skills** are those which have no obvious beginning or end; they can be continued for as long as the performer wishes, with the end of the skill becoming the beginning of the next, for example, running.

▶ A **discrete skill** has a clear beginning and end. The skill can be repeated, but the athlete will start the full action again in a controlled and timely manner. An example of a discrete skill in a team sport is a rugby conversion, while an individual example is a golf putt.

▶ A **serial skill** is a series of discrete skills put together to produce an organised movement. The order of the movement is often important, but the requirements of each part of the skill will require specific development. An example from a team sport is when a footballer dribbles with the ball, steps over it to beat a defender and then shoots at goal at the end of the movement. An example from an individual sport is a gymnastic tumble.

Theory into practice

In groups, identify whether a golf shot is:
- an open or closed skill
- a fine or gross skill
- a self-paced or externally paced skill
- a continuous, discrete or serial skill.

List the skills in your own sport and identify which categories they fall into.

Timing and pacing of skills

Skills can also be classified by looking at the time needed to complete them, and the pace at which they can be executed.

▶ Self-paced – where the performer determines the pace, time and execution of the skill. For example, taking a throw-in during football, the player has complete control over the timing when they release the ball and the level of force and direction they apply to its execution.

▶ Externally paced – where external factors set or influence the pace, time and execution of the skill. For example, the pace by which you return a serve in tennis, will be affected by the serve of your opponent (its speed, direction etc.).

 **PAUSE POINT** Carry out research into the type of skills involved in your chosen or favourite sport.

Hint Do any of the types of skills suit your chosen or favourite sport more than the other two?

Extend Can you choose a different sport and list its key skills? Try to describe these types of skill and link them with qualities of skilled performance. For example, a key skill in football is passing; although it requires cognitive and perceptual skills, it is largely a motor skill requiring control and consistency of outcome.

Characteristics and classification of abilities

- A sportsperson will have a wide range of different types of abilities. Abilities should not be confused with skills. Skills are considered complex and coordinated. A performer is not born with skills such as being able to hit a tennis backhand or take a free-kick in football; skills need to be learned and practised in order to be executed.
- Abilities, however, are generally considered to be innate, that is, a performer is born with different abilities inherited from his or her parents that help the performer to learn and execute skills.
- Abilities and skills are closely linked, and in order to perform many skills, you will need to have developed certain key abilities.

Differences between abilities and skills

There are several core areas that help to define the differences between skills and abilities, as well as fuelling debate within the sport and activity industry.

- Natural level of skill – performers can perform a skill immediately and consistently without previously attempting it. This is thought to be due to a natural ability where the performer possesses the genetics (or movement patterns) to execute the skill without having to practise or follow a process to learn it.
- **Nature** versus **nurture** – whether nature or nurture is the major determining factor in skills acquisition. All skills can be learned, and this is considered nurture, for example, an athlete can learn the long–jump technique. However, all athletes possess a certain amount of 'natural level of skill', which helps them learn to carry out sporting skills, or helps them reach a certain level of physical fitness or achievement.
- There is an ongoing debate about the extent to which our development of skills and abilities is determined by our genetic make-up (nature) or from the environment and influences that a person encounters around them while they are growing up and throughout their life (nurture). For example, could a child whose parents are athletes become athletic because of the genes they have inherited from the parents, or would the fact that they would be more exposed to athletic performance day-to-day make them more likely to become interested in sport?
- Stable verses unstable – how a performer thinks and behaves when executing a skill. The 'stable' component is the performer's ability to execute the skill. The 'unstable' component is the performer's attitude when executing the skill. In order for a skill to be executed correctly, both stable and unstable components have to work together effectively. In other words, the performer must have the ability to execute the skill and the confidence (or correct attitude) to do so.
- A combination of abilities is required to perform skills. For example, a combination of coordination, reaction time, balance and fine motor skills is required to catch a ball. Each of these abilities will need to be developed (or be present already in the athlete) before the skill itself can be learned correctly.
- Many abilities are learned during our growth and development throughout childhood and onwards, and the more opportunities there are to practise these while growing up, the more proficient a person will be later in life.

Key term

Nature – innate qualities inherited from parents.
Nurture – the influence of life experiences and the environment on development.

Research

What do you think is more important for the achievement of skill mastery – nature or nurture? Is high-quality coaching more important than natural ability, or do performers require innate abilities before skill mastery can take place? You should be prepared to present your findings as a small group to the rest of your class.

Psychomotor abilities

Psychomotor abilities are associated with performing movements associated with fine motor skills. The possession of a high aptitude of these abilities will make executing a number of skills much easier.

▸ Reaction time – the ability to react quickly between receiving a stimulus to make a movement, and the start of the movement being made by the body. For example, a sprinter in the 100 m must be able to react quickly to the starter gun in order to begin running.

▸ Coordination – the ability to use different joints and muscles in a specific order or sequence to perform a task. For example, a basketball player when approaching the net to shoot will need to coordinate both the movement of their steps, the bouncing of the ball, the timing of their jump and the release of the ball.

▸ Balance – the ability to maintain stability or equilibrium when performing. For example, a rugby player running with the ball will need a good sense of balance in order to weave between opponents and avoid tackles.

> **Key terms**
>
> **Psychomotor abilities** – abilities that combine mental activity and muscular movement.
>
> **Gross motor abilities** – abilities that require the coordination of many muscle groups at the same time.
>
> **Perceptual abilities** – abilities in which a performer is highly dependent on recognising a changing environment and adapting motor skills accordingly.

Gross motor abilities

Gross motor abilities are associated with larger body movements such as running. They are usually acquired while a child is growing up and involve controlling and using the body.

▸ Strength – the ability of a group of muscles to exert a force to create a movement.

▸ Speed – the ability to move over a distance in the quickest time. Sprinting in sports is an obvious example of speed at work.

▸ Flexibility – the ability of muscles and joints to achieve maximum range of movement. In many sports, flexible movement is vital to allow the body to move smoothly and complete skills.

> **Link**
>
> You can discover more about psychomotor and gross motor abilities in *Unit 2: Fitness Training and Programming for Health, Sport and Well-being*.

Perceptual abilities

Perceptual abilities involve interpreting and making use of information the body receives from its senses. This could involve using things in your environment that you can see, hear, feel or even smell. For example, on a windy day, deciding what direction to hit a golf ball off the tee to land nearest to the flag will depend on how you evaluate the environmental information around you. Two examples follow.

▸ Interpreting information – a golfer will review the wind speed and direction alongside the distance. The greater the wind speed, the more likely that it will cause the ball to move in the air. Therefore, the golfer will need to include this when they aim so that the movement of the ball in the direction of the wind will allow it to end up near the target.

▸ Decision making – a golfer makes an adjustment to factor in the wind speed and plays their shot. This will be based on their judgement of the conditions and combined with their experience of previous situations.

▸ How would you use the information from your immediate surroundings to make a decision about the direction to hit a golf ball?

PAUSE POINT   How do abilities affect the development of skills?

>   Hint   When you carry out a skill specific to your sport, what is your body doing?

>   Extend   How could you help to develop certain abilities you may need for sports?

In pairs or small groups, write down a sporting example for each type of skill. Then explain the difference between a skill and an ability. Lastly, list the skills and abilities for a sport of your choice.

Assessment practice 23.1

A.P1 A.P2 A.M1 AB.D1

Create a pamphlet or handout that selects a skill in a sport (for example, the serve in tennis). This pamphlet or handout should identify and assess the abilities that will influence the development of the technique(s) required to execute the skill correctly. Furthermore, how will this skill contribute to the performer's ability to compete in the sport? Your handout should explain how the performer's abilities underpin the specific sporting skills they will need to develop.

Plan

- What is the task? What is my pamphlet or handout being asked to address?
- How confident do I feel in my own abilities to complete this task?

Do

- I know how to examine the qualities of a skilled performance within a chosen sport.
- I can identify the abilities that contribute to the successful execution of the skill.

Review

- I can explain what the task was and how I approached my investigation and construction of my pamphlet or handout.
- I can explain how I would approach the more difficult elements differently next time.

B Examine ways that sport performers process information for skilled performance

In any sport, performers learn and execute a range of skills. However, being skilful is not always sufficient in itself. What is as important is selecting the correct skill for the correct occasion or moment. This key decision making is achieved through **information processing models**.

Information processing models

When performers execute a skill, decisions must be made. These decisions are often made based on the environment and circumstances the performer happens to be in, so will have many factors that are outside the performer's immediate control.

For example, a performer must decide whether or not to smash a high bounce in table tennis, in which direction to hit the ball and what position to take up after the smash. These decisions and the processes involved are demonstrated in the examples below.

Simple model

The simple model, as shown in Figure 23.5, describes how a performer takes in information (input stage), decides on a course of action (central stage) and executes the skill (output stage). A footballing example would work as follows.

▶ Input stage – the performer sees a football moving in his or her direction.
▶ Central stage – the performer decides to hold the ball up and look to pass rather than shoot.

▸ Output stage – the performer takes a touch with his or her right foot and passes to another player.

In this process the performer uses the information he or she has received to make a decision about an action to take and then completes that action.

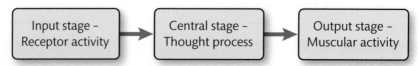

| Input stage – Receptor activity | → | Central stage – Thought process | → | Output stage – Muscular activity |

▸ **Figure 23.5:** Simple information process model

Expanded information process model

In this model, the central stage can be further expanded into three sub-stages (**stimulus** identification, response selection, response programming). So, the same footballing example would work as follows.

▸ Input – the performer sees a football moving in his or her direction.
▸ Stimulus identification – the performer detects and decides a stimulus has occurred, that is, the performer sees a football moving in his or her direction.
▸ Response selection – the performer acts on information received from stimulus identification and a decision is made about which movement the performer will take, for example, the performer decides to hold the ball up.
▸ Response programming – the decision is received by the body and the performer organises themselves to carry out the movement. For example, he or she might decide to take a touch with his or her right foot and pass to another player.
▸ Output – the decision is executed. For example, the performer takes a touch and passes the ball on.

Using information process models

Information processing systems are an essential part of any performance as they help to explain the difference between decisions made by performers.

The simple model, as its name suggests, helps to explain simpler decision-making processes required for straightforward movements or responses, such as a footballer seeing the ball in the air and deciding to head it.

The expanded model allows the performer to consider and evaluate a range of responses which the simple model does not consider according to the variables presented by the environment. For the footballer heading the ball, these would be the weather, the player's positioning, the speed of the ball, etc. For example, a footballer sees the ball in the air and decides to head it, notices there are no teammates within heading distance, so he decides to head the ball out for a throw-in as the safest course of action.

The introduction of the computer and its associated language provided information processing systems with the necessary terminology to help us understand how the human mind handles information from the environment. Terminology that we often associate with computing, such as 'input' and 'output', is easy for people to comprehend. However, the use of such language has been criticised as many believe that the human mind is far more complex than any computer system. Information processing systems are useful to a point, but they cannot fully explain how complex issues such as human instinct, emotions or feelings have an impact on our decision making.

Perception

Perception is the ability to become aware of something or the surroundings via the senses. The perception stage of any information processing system is important when executing skills. Differences occur between beginners and experts as the latter can differentiate between the various inputs much more quickly and efficiently.

Stimulus features that affect perception

The stimuli you receive as a sports performer will affect you in different ways, depending on the circumstances in which you receive them. Different factors will affect how you respond.

▶ Familiarity of stimulus – when a performer is familiar with a stimulus, perception levels are likely to be heightened, as they will be expecting the stimulus to occur and their body will already be ready to respond, for example, a sprinter being aware of the starting pistol in the 100 m.

▶ Speed – the speed of a stimulus can affect a performer's perception. If a performer has a long time to decide on an action, they can consider a greater range of responses. However, a short period of time requires quick responses. For example, snooker players take time to consider options for the best shot available, whereas a table tennis player has a fraction of a second to consider a shot in response to their opponent's play.

▶ Loudness and colour brightness – the stronger a visual display or louder the sound, the more likely a performer is to respond quickly, as they are more likely to draw focus and attention from the performer. This is why tennis balls are luminous yellow or the starting pistol is a loud 'bang'.

Individual factors impacting on perception

Perception can also be affected by a number of personal factors that are unique to an individual or the situation an individual is in.

▶ Attention level – this involves the withdrawal from certain possible stimuli to deal effectively with others, in other words, focusing on certain stimuli at the expense of others. Information processing models contend that a selective filter in the brain can restrict the levels of information that can be dealt with effectively at any one time.

▶ Arousal level – the state of general preparedness for activity. When perception levels are heightened, this is likely to impact on **arousal**.

▶ Attention capacity – this can be learned for specific sports that include certain stimuli on which a performer should concentrate. It can also be the ability to shift the individual's perception and focus from one stimulus to another when appropriate.

> **Key term**
>
> **Arousal** – state of preparedness of the body for action.

Case study

Practical sport

Olympic diver, Tom Daley, competes in a sport that requires high levels of perception to execute a dive to perfection. Tom is required to undertake the following to perceive and adapt to the competitive situation.

• Attention level: as Tom stands on the springboard,

he will ignore all but a few key external stimuli and concentrate on his body position and mental state in preparation for his dive.

• Arousal level: Tom will focus on the dive, relax himself via mental rehearsal of the practice routine he has executed hundreds if not thousands of times previously, then almost instantaneously raise his arousal levels in preparation for the beginning of the dive.

• Attention capacity: Tom needs to be aware of the movements of the springboard (however small) and focus on key sight points to aid the dive execution.

Can you think of any circumstances that might have an impact on Tom's attention and arousal levels, or his attention capacity, while preparing to dive?

How do you think Tom might deal with these circumstances?

Discussion

Experienced performers have often been shown to respond more quickly and accurately than inexperienced performers. In small groups, discuss the merits of this argument and the likely impact of this on team and individual sports. Be prepared to make your case to the rest of the class.

Decision making and reaction time

A performer's ability to react demonstrates how effectively he or she can make decisions and carry out sport-specific actions. There are several factors that affect reaction time and the ability to make decisions.

▶ Number of stimulus-response alternatives (Hick's law) – the more choices that are available to a performer, the more reaction time increases, as they choose which choice to take. A performer's ability to react demonstrates how effectively he or she can make a decision quickly and deal with these choices.

▶ Stimulus-response compatibility – if the stimulus is expected by the performer, the reaction time is quicker than if it is not expected. For example, when Lewis Hamilton approaches a left-hand turn (stimulus) on lap 48, he adjusts the steering wheel of his car to the left, because he knows the track and is expecting the car to need to turn left. If Lewis had never driven the track before, his reaction time at the same left-hand turn would be marginally slower as the turn (stimulus) would be less familiar.

▶ Practice and anticipation – practice can decrease reaction time as a performer becomes more skilled at anticipating stimuli. For example, sprinters regularly practise starts to improve their reaction time to the starting pistol.

▶ Psychological refractory period (PRP) – this is the time taken to react between one stimulus and the next. For example, imagine a badminton player anticipates a low drive return from their opponent, but the shuttlecock clips the top of the net on the way and slowly falls to the other side. The player must react quickly to the sudden change. The time between the player's initial anticipation of the drive and their realisation that the shuttlecock is now falling from the net is the PRP.

Theory into practice

Following a practical sport session, identify a set of circumstances when you were performing a skill in a specific sport or situation. For example, blocking in volleyball.

Thinking about the sensory inputs you were exposed to throughout the skill, list the factors affecting:

1 perception

2 decision making and reaction time.

When considering the above points, are there any factors that would require you to do more work or additional practice to improve performance?

Types of feedback

Feedback is often associated with guidance and for performers to learn and develop their skills, feedback and guidance are a necessary component of sports coaching. A major skill for any sports coach is to be able to feed back to their sports performers in a way that helps to both inform the performer of ways they can improve, and also motivates them to do so.

Some of the key types of feedback you will use include the following.

▶ Knowledge of results (KR) – feedback about the success of a performer's action(s) related to the goal of a particular skill. For example, if a footballer scores a penalty, feedback may reflect this.

▶ Knowledge of performance (KP) – feedback about the correct execution of a skill. For example, a coach may provide a springboard diver with feedback about his or her somersault rotation.

▶ Continuous feedback – feedback given throughout the course of a performance, usually from a coach.

▶ Terminal feedback – feedback given at the end of a performance.

▶ Extrinsic feedback – feedback from outside the performer, for example, a coach or tutor.

▶ Intrinsic feedback – feedback from within the performer, often referred to as an internal response or feeling. You could ask the performer to give their own honest feedback on their performance.

▶ Positive feedback – feedback about a performance that concentrates on what was done correctly so the performer knows to repeat the same process. For example, a coach will tell a cricket bowler his technique was correct if he or she bowls at off-stump.

▶ Negative feedback – feedback about a performance that concentrates on what was done incorrectly so the performer knows not to repeat the same process. This method can be demotivating for the performer and should be used sparingly.

Link

Feedback is also covered in *Unit 4: Sports Leadership* and *Unit 8: Sports Coaching*.

Theory into practice

During your next practical sports sessions or training sessions for your chosen sport (perhaps at weekends), write down the types of feedback you received from your tutor/coach over the next few weeks. Is there a particular type of feedback your coach uses more than others? Which type do you think you respond best to? Are the answers to these points the same, and if not, what might you recommend as a possible course of action or intervention?

In pairs or in small groups, compare your findings and try to assess your own ability to process information and what type of feedback is most popular.

 PAUSE POINT   Watch a piece of sport footage on TV and try to identify the type of feedback a featured coach is giving to the performer(s).

 Hint   Can you list the different types of feedback available to coaches and tutors?

 Extend   Are some types of feedback more suited to different types of sport? Choose a sport and list the feedback you think would be most suitable to the participant(s).

Assessment practice 23.2   B.P3   B.P4   B.M2   AB.D1

You have been asked to give a talk to a group of new coaching staff who have just joined a football coaching business. The company's owner has asked you to give a presentation on how children process coaching information and how this helps improve the children as performers.

Design a poster that you can refer to during your presentation. Your presentation should include information about how information processing models work at each stage, their strengths and weaknesses, and a judgement of how useful they are when practising skills.

Plan
- How am I going to successfully plan my time and keep track of my progress?
- Do I need clarification around anything?

Do
- I know how to explain the various components of information processing models. In particular, I can identify the various models, how to improve decision making and reactions to coaching feedback.
- I can identify when my talk is going wrong and adjust my thinking/approach to get myself back on course by referring to my notes.

Review
- I can say whether I met the task's criteria and whether I succeeded.
- I can explain how I would approach the more difficult elements differently next time (i.e. what I would do differently).

C   Explore theories of teaching and learning in sport

There are several different types of theories that can be used to help teaching and learning of sports skills. Each theory has its own advantages and disadvantages and you should carefully consider these, as well as the situation and the performer(s) you are working with, before selecting which one to use.

Behaviourist theories

Behaviourism is a branch of psychology that studies the principles of learning, through scientific experimentation, to understand and manipulate human behaviour. The main principle of behaviourism is that only observable behaviour can be scientifically studied.

Classical conditioning

> **Key terms**
>
> **Unconditioned response** – an original or innate response.
>
> **Conditioned response** – a response that is established by training or learning.

Conditioning is a method of learning in which a neutral stimulus becomes a conditional stimulus that creates a response after being presented with an unconditional stimulus. For example, the psychologist Pavlov conducted an experiment where a bell was rung (unconditional stimulus) whenever a dog was about to be fed. At first, the dog would salivate at the sight or smell of the food (**unconditioned response**). Eventually the dog would salivate at the sound of the bell (**conditioned response**), even when the sight or smell of food (unconditional stimulus) was absent. This was because the dog had learned to associate the sound of the bell with food – it had been 'conditioned' to expect food when the bell rang, so reacted when it heard it.

In sports, many performers (in football, rugby, hockey, and so on) could be said to automatically react to the sound of a whistle blown by a referee.

Classical conditioning demonstrates the importance of learning from the environment and supports the nurture over nature argument. It suggests that our environment and experiences lead us to expect certain things and to react in certain ways to certain stimuli. For example, 100 m sprinters react to the sound of a starting pistol. However, this approach can underestimate the complexity of human behaviour and information processing. For example, 100 m sprinters will not react in the same way to all sudden, loud noises.

Operant conditioning

Operant conditioning is a form of learning in which rewards and punishments are used to modify behaviour. This process can have both positive and negative outcomes. Skinner (1938) researched operant conditioning using experiments on rats, introducing a learning method in which certain behaviours were reinforced or punished. Skinner's experiment involved placing a rat in a box. Within this box were a lever and two lights (red and green). If the green light was illuminated, the rat would be able to press the lever and receive food as a reward. If the red light was illuminated, the rat would press the lever and receive an electric shock. The results were as follows.

▶ Relationship of action and consequences – over a period of time, the rat learned that the green light was associated with food (positive) and the red light was associated with an electric shock (negative).

▶ Role of feedback in learning – this process enabled the rat to understand the relationship between visual stimulus and consequence (positive or negative).

▶ Reinforcing desirable actions – the rat was conditioned to wait for the green light and receive food rather than act on the red light and receive an electric shock.

Thorndike's laws argued that the fundamental point to all learning was strengthening the relationship between stimulus and response.

▶ Law of exercise – suggests that a performer cannot learn a new skill simply by watching others but must practise the skill.

▶ Law of effect – suggests rewarding a behaviour of the execution of a skill increases the chance that the behaviour or skill will be repeated.

▶ Law of readiness – suggests that learning is dependent on the performer's readiness to act and this strengthens the relationship between stimulus and response.

Cognitive theories

Cognitive theories describe the mental processes that explain the thought processes that show performers learn about themselves and the environment in which they compete/train, and how they interpret this information.

Closed loop theory

The closed loop theory (see Figure 23.6) is a cognitive theory of skill learning that emphasises the role played by feedback. This theory explains slow skill movement in which decisions are made in the brain where a set of executive or cognitive processes are carried out, though not all the information is sent out in the same package of actions. This information is sent to the muscles or effectors (body glands or organs) to initiate movement.

Feedback (as a comparator that compares two or more situations or predicaments) is available to the performer from the environment and their own analysis of their actions, and is vital to correcting or amending movement patterns. For example, a footballer may make adjustments when dribbling a ball past an opponent, depending on the actions and position of their opponent.

Open loop control

This theory (see Figure 23.6) explains the control of rapid, discrete movements of which the performer is not consciously aware (that is, the performer does not pay any attention, he or she just carries out the movement – for example, reaction reflexes). Neither do they require any feedback from the environment or themselves to have an impact on their performance. These movements involve decisions that are made in the brain; all the information is sent to the muscles in one message and they act accordingly. This is usually seen most clearly in swift and fluid movements. For example, with a tennis serve, there is little time to read and change the movement once the serve is under way.

OPEN FEEDBACK SYSTEM   **CLOSED LOOP FEEDBACK SYSTEM**

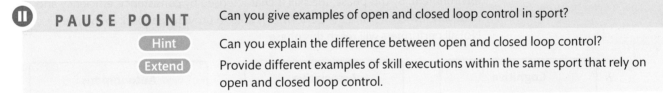

▶ **Figure 23.6:** Open and closed loop feedback systems

⏸ **P A U S E P O I N T**   Can you give examples of open and closed loop control in sport?

> Hint   Can you explain the difference between open and closed loop control?

> Extend   Provide different examples of skill executions within the same sport that rely on open and closed loop control.

Schema theory

Schema theory outlines a set of rules, which have been acquired from practice or experience, which determine your motor responses in a given situation. It is believed that there is a schema for each class of movement and the success of any skill execution is dependent on the efficiency of the schema. Schmidt (1975) suggested that the learning of skills came about by understanding the following areas of information.

▶ Recall schema – occur before a movement skill is initiated and include the following which the performer must know to build a schema.
  • Knowledge of initial conditions – the situation and initial position, for example, the starting position when about to throw a javelin (i.e. javelin held above the head and ready to run forwards);
  • Response specifications – the pattern of movements required to perform a skill, for example, the various stages when throwing a javelin.
▶ Recognition schema – occur during and after the execution of a skill. To correct a future response, the performer needs to know:
  • the sensory consequences – what was the result of the skill execution? For example, did the javelin achieve a distance over 50 m?
  • the response outcomes – how did the performer feel after the throw?

Schema theory is useful because it goes some way toward explaining how performers are able to execute relatively new skills or tasks with some success. However, the theory is limited as it implies motor movements are generalised and do not accommodate individual differences when executing the same skill.

> **Key term**
>
> **Schema** – rules that have been acquired from practice or experience that determine motor responses in a given situation.

Phases of skill learning

In its simplest form, learning a new skill is the progression of a performer from a position where he or she cannot execute a skill to a time when he or she can. Learning a new skill involves practice, and correct practice will lead to improvement. To get to this stage requires the performer to pass through different stages of learning (see Figure 23.7).

Cognitive/plan formation phase

This is the initial phase of learning and vital to the performer if he or she wants to move on to the next stage where the skill can be executed consistently well. This phase involves the focus on what to do and how to do it. The performer tries to understand the requirements of the skill and the most effective method is demonstration. With practice, the performer's practice will be characterised by **gross errors**, which will be complemented and corrected by feedback and further instruction until the skill is learned.

Associative/fixation phase

The performer's focus is on practising the newly acquired skill. The execution of the skill will be characterised by fewer errors and an awareness of how to correct errors. The performer starts to rely on their own internal feedback, as they become more and more aware of what is involved in good execution of the skill. This phase can be lengthy depending on the complexity of the skill.

Autonomous/automatic phase

When the performer reaches this stage, the skill becomes automatic and performed without thought. Instead attention focuses on how to apply the skill in a given environment. By this phase, the skill is characterised by consistency, efficiency and relatively few errors, and the performer is able to provide feedback to themselves. Not all performers will reach this phase.

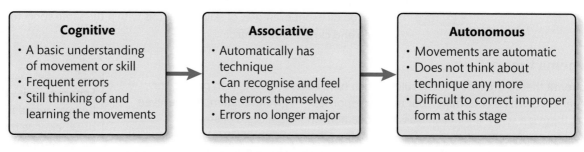

Cognitive	**Associative**	**Autonomous**
• A basic understanding of movement or skill • Frequent errors • Still thinking of and learning the movements	• Automatically has technique • Can recognise and feel the errors themselves • Errors no longer major	• Movements are automatic • Does not think about technique any more • Difficult to correct improper form at this stage

▶ **Figure 23.7:** Cognitive, associative and autonomous phases of learning

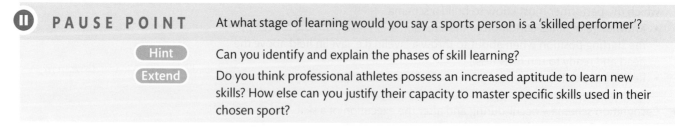

PAUSE POINT At what stage of learning would you say a sports person is a 'skilled performer'?

Hint Can you identify and explain the phases of skill learning?

Extend Do you think professional athletes possess an increased aptitude to learn new skills? How else can you justify their capacity to master specific skills used in their chosen sport?

Transfer of learning

Skills that have been learned and developed in one situation can be used in others. This is why you often find that some individuals excel at many sports. For example, Sir Ian Botham is perhaps England's most famous cricketing all-rounder, having also played professional football for Scunthorpe United FC. It has been argued that this is perhaps due to a natural ability, but it can also be explained by the transfer of learning.

Types of transfer

There are several factors that affect the transfer of skills from one sport to another.

▶ Positive – when two skills are similar, becoming proficient at one skill makes the learning of the second easier. For example, a football goalkeeper may utilise their skill and knowledge of goal kicking to take penalty kicks in rugby.

▶ Negative – the learning of one skill makes the learning of a second skill more difficult. For example, a badminton player may find the use of the wrist shots not beneficial for tennis shots, which require fuller arm movements.

▶ Zero – there are no transferable components between a previously learned skill and a new skill to be learned. For example, somersaults in trampolining and batting in cricket.

How transfer occurs

Transfer of skills can occur in several ways as follows.

▶ Inter-task – the learning and performance of a new skill influences the learning and performance of another new skill in a similar environment or sport. For example, a tuck somersault in trampolining may influence the learning of a piked somersault.

▶ Intra-task – the learning and performance of a skill in one environment or set of conditions has an impact on the learning and performance of the same skill in a different environment or set of conditions. For example, a footballer may practise a direct free kick from a variety of distances from goal.

▶ Near transfer – the learning and performance of skills between two similar environments or scenarios, for example, catching in netball and basketball.

▶ Far transfer – the learning and performance of skills between two unrelated environments or scenarios. For example, a performer who understands wind conditions in sailing may be able to adjust a penalty kick in rugby during windy conditions.

▶ Bilateral transfer – the learning of one skill can be transferred from one limb to another. For example, most football academies now encourage all footballers to use both feet.

Transfer and generalisation

Sometimes learning can be transferred, or picked up, from one person to another.

▶ Stimulus generalisation – learning that is likely to have a similar response after the response has been conditioned. For example, a child that has learned or been conditioned to view violence as bad is more likely to transfer this learning and not enjoy watching boxing on television.

▶ Response generalisation – learning that is likely to spread the effect of a stimulus. For example, in a class of children, if it is cold and one child puts on a coat, the remainder of the class are likely to follow suit.

Theory into practice

Select a skill for a sport and create a profile for this skill, listing the abilities and techniques you would expect to see as a perfect model. Next, make a further list of the phases of learning for your skill. Alongside these, list the level of technique and ability you would expect to see demonstrated at each learning phase.

Compare your results with a working partner and see if you have reached common ground on what is required for each phase.

Case study

Practical sport

Consider as many of the practical sport sessions or coaching sessions as you have had for various sports over the past few months. Make a list of skills you have learned for at least three of the sports (for example, chest pass in basketball, front crawl technique in swimming and throw-in in football). Limit the skill list to approximately 10 skills per sport.

1 Thinking about the skills you have listed, how many of these do you think can be transferred from one sport to another?

2 Identify the types of transfer employed for these skills.

3 Do the sports you have chosen have much else in common?

Your tutor has asked that you produce two sets of resources that will help other learners to understand teaching and learning theories, and how these theories are applied in sport.

For the first set, you are asked to create a series of flash or revision cards for use by other leaners that describe two contrasting theories of teaching and learning. These cards should detail key aspects of behaviourist and cognitive theories.

For the second set, you are asked to create a series of posters for display in a classroom that visually explain the three phases of skill-learning and how these theories aid the teaching and learning of new sports skills.

Plan

- What is the task? What information must the flash cards and posters contain?
- Given these resources will be used by other learners, how much planning should I put into the illustration and presentation of these materials?

Do

- I know how to describe the key factors of behaviourist and cognitive learning theories, and how best to present these on flash or revision cards.
- I can identify the phases of skill learning, then analyse, evaluate and illustrate how these work (using a step-by-step process) when learning new sports.

Review

- I can explain each component of the task, how I approached construction of my resources and any analysis or evaluation of the skill-learning processes.
- I can evaluate how to undertake the learning of different sports skills using the same poster format if required. For example, I could analyse, evaluate and illustrate learning to execute a tennis serve instead of a volleyball serve.

D   Carry out teaching and learning strategies for sports skills

Link

More information on delivering coaching and learning, and presenting new skills for coaching, can be found in *Unit 4: Sports Leadership* and *Unit 8: Sports Coaching*. These units also provide more information on styles of learning and types of practice.

Teaching and learning skills can be affected by a number of different situations and strategies. All of these will affect which teaching and learning theories you plan to apply when teaching sports skills to performers.

Presentation skills

▶ Part of teaching and learning is knowing the most effective way of presenting your teaching to the people you are coaching. You will need to know how a task can be analysed and then match this analysis with the most appropriate method to facilitate it being learned.

▶ How would you present your teaching to performers?

Analysis of task

Tasks are analysed in the following key ways:

▶ Complex or simple – an easy way of analysing skills is to define them as either complex or simple. Skills that can be easily divided into their component parts are known as simple skills. Those that are difficult to divide are known as complex skills. Complex skills are likely to need more in-depth and detailed coaching.

▶ Number of parts – skills can also be broken down by the number of 'parts' they contain when they are delivered. As a rule of thumb, the more component parts a skill contains, the more complex it is likely to be.

▶ Performer's skill level – it is important for a tutor or coach to understand the performer's own skill level, both in terms of what they are capable of achieving and what they have already achieved. This will affect what they ask the performer to do, and the methods that they use to ask them to deliver.

Methods of presenting skills to facilitate learning

Once you have determined the complexity of a skill, its number of parts and the performer's skill level, you will need to select the best method of presenting new skills to learners. There are several approaches.

▶ Part method – this identifies the subroutines of any skill. The performer learns, practises and perfects each component before moving on to the next, and eventually is able to complete the whole skill.

▶ Whole method – the complete skill is demonstrated, and the performer learns it as one complete movement.

▶ Progressive part method – this involves an initial experience of the skill that then permits a mental picture to be created for the performer of what the skill involves.

▶ Whole-part-whole method – this is similar to the part method but it involves an initial introduction or demonstration of the whole skill before it is broken down into its components.

Types of practice

A major factor influencing the development of a skill is practice. Different types of skill require different types of practice. There are two main types of practice.

▶ Fixed practice – this involves the repetition of the skill, allowing the movement to become second nature through muscle memory. This type of practice is appropriate for a skill that is always performed in the same way and is unlikely to be influenced by the environment. It tends to benefit closed skills such as putting in golf.

▶ Variable practice – this involves a variety of situations and environments. This type of practice is beneficial for developing open skills where initial movement patterns are adapted according to the circumstances. For example, dribbling in football should be executed in different scenarios (such as varying pace, distance and gameplay scenarios).

Regardless of whether the practice is fixed or variable, a coach should also take into account the performer's level of experience and motivation when performing the skill: too difficult and the performer may get disheartened and lose interest; too easy and the coach may not challenge the performer enough.

The two main types of practice that can be used to help develop skills are:

▶ massed – a continuous session with no breaks and, as such, best used for experienced performers

▶ distributed – a session divided into its component parts and designed to give performers a rest or provide natural breaks according to the type of skill being undertaken.

Styles of teaching

Each tutor is likely to have a different style when delivering learning. The personality of the tutor is a major factor that will affect the style of learning delivery. Fiedler (1967)

identified two categories of leader which can be applied to teaching and the style of learning.

▶ Task-orientated – leaders/tutors who have activity-/skill-related knowledge who can lead a group of people (learners) during a task.

▶ Person-orientated – leaders with strong inter-personal skills who are able to get the best out of each individual rather than concentrating on a task.

In addition, it is also important to consider the personality of learners, their skill levels, the size of the learner group and the time and resources available to the coach/tutor to enable the development of performance skills. Once these aspects have been considered, a method of teaching can be adopted that takes all these relevant points into account.

Mosston and Ashworth's (1986) spectrum of teaching styles

Mosston and Ashworth argued that teaching styles were more concerned with a framework of relationships that existed between tutor and learner rather than any teaching techniques or approaches.

This framework of relationships has a spectrum made up of a number of styles along a continuum that is based around the importance of decision making, as illustrated in Figure 23.8.

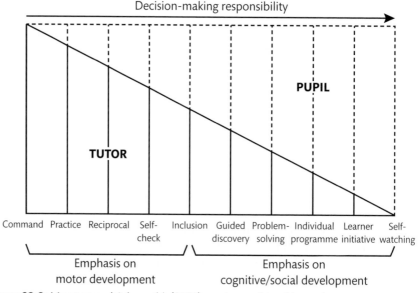

▶ **Figure 23.8:** Mosston and Ashworth's (1986) spectrum of teaching styles

Each stage of the spectrum shows a slightly different teaching style. These are arranged in order with the most tutor-led at the left end and the most learner-led at the right end. So the scale runs from the tutor instructing every step, to the learner teaching themselves. Some of the key stages you will encounter are the following.

▶ Command – the tutor has responsibility for all decision making and the learner follows instructions, for example, a coach or tutor giving instructions and demonstrating a sports skill.

▶ Reciprocal – after the instruction and demonstration, the learner would replicate the skill as demonstrated to them by the tutor. This allows a certain level of self-teaching.

▶ Guided discovery – a learner gains knowledge about a topic or subject without tutor guidance. This method allows the learner to develop their own understanding of the topic or subject.

▶ Problem solving – this requires a certain amount of instruction from the coach or tutor before the learners are required to conduct their own research to solve problems. Under these circumstances, the learners develop more cognitive skills, as well as greater independence.

Discussion

It is often said in sport that practice makes perfect. Use your knowledge of cognitive theories, phases of skill learning and transfer of learning to support or reject this argument. Get together in small groups and discuss the merits of both arguments and be prepared to make your cases to the rest of the class.

Theory into practice

Identify and discuss leaders in sport, from your coach or tutor to high-profile professional coaches. Are they person-orientated or task orientated?

Refine your list to three leaders and discuss the qualities of each; what makes them a good leader in your view and what characteristics or personality traits do you think they exhibit to be an important leader?

Discuss your views in groups and write your findings on the whiteboard for comparison with other groups.

Styles of learning

Everyone finds it easier to learn information if it is presented in certain ways. You will have your own ways of learning things, and will find there are certain ways of working that help you to remember things. Learners can usually be characterised as either visual (seeing and observing things), auditory (listening to things) or kinaesthetic (learning by doing).

Visual learners

Visual learners enjoy visual stimulation so they want to read, see or observe things. They prefer pictures, diagrams and colour-orientated images while viewing a tutor's body language to reinforce their learning. Visual learners tend not to enjoy lectures that involved the tutor talking at length, and often daydream if visual prompts are absent.

Visual learners require a clear view of their tutor and need a quiet place away from noise disturbance to concentrate fully. Visual learners often benefit from using images and mind maps in their written work. When memorising material, it often helps if visual learners write the same material over and over to commit to memory.

Auditory learners

Auditory learners interpret the underlying meanings of speech through listening to the voice, tone and pitch of tutors or speakers. They prefer their instructions to be given orally and rarely write things down or take notes, so they prefer lectures to reading.

Auditory learners enjoy participating in class discussions/debates and making presentations. Auditory learners retain information by discussing ideas with friends of colleagues or reciting information over and over to better memorise material.

Kinaesthetic learners

Kinaesthetic learners need to handle materials and objects while studying. They are generally good at sports or practical activities, often adventurous in their outlook/ nature and find it difficult to sit for long periods. Kinaesthetic learners often count using their fingers and doodle while listening.

Kinaesthetic learners require frequent study breaks to prevent boredom. It is important to try to make their study more physically orientated by allowing them to study while moving. Kinaesthetic learners like their classrooms to have posters or work displayed on the walls or with music played in the background. When reading, they should first skim read their work, then go back to read in more detail.

Methods of guidance

When learning guidance is provided by the tutor or coach, there are various ways and methods in which learning may be undertaken. Often the best method will depend on what best suits the learner.

Learners are individuals so there is no perfect model to teach any one performer. It is important that a coach takes into account the personality, motivation and skill level of the learner, which learning style (auditory, visual or kinaesthetic) is preferred, the type of skill being taught (for example, cognitive, perceptual or motor), the environmental factors in which the skills are being taught and refined and, finally, the stage of learning the learner is at (for example, cognitive, associate, autonomous), which is closely linked to the learner's progress.

Types of guidance

▸ Visual guidance involves the transfer of information by video, visual aids (for example, posters or photographs) and webcam footage. Visual guidance is useful when introducing new information and material that allows the learners to create a mental picture of what is to be achieved.

▸ Verbal guidance is beneficial so long as it is clear and concise. Beginners can have problems with verbal guidance and it is often more useful when a performer is more experienced and more receptive to a one-to-one chat with a coach or tutor explaining (in depth) what needs to be done to address any problems.

▸ Manual guidance involves a more hands-on approach during which the coach or tutor may physically manipulate the performer into the correct position to aid **muscle memory**.

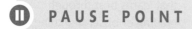

Key term

Muscle memory – when muscles become familiar with particular movements over time.

Ⅱ PAUSE POINT

What factors might you need to keep in mind when giving an athlete guidance on performance?

Hint Do you think it is possible to impart too much information at once?

Extend How might you break down your guidance into categories or components?

Assessment practice 23.4

D.P7   D.P8   D.M4   D.D3

Your tutor has asked you to produce a two-part assignment that will be shown/distributed to next year's new sports learners as preparation for how they will learn new sports skills next year.

Part 1 is a presentation that explores the teaching and learning theories in sport.

Part 2 is a collection of video clips that give examples of the teaching and learning strategies being carried out at college. Both parts should be completed on a PowerPoint presentation.

Plan
- What is the task? What is my role and how will I address the two parts to produce the research necessary for a presentation?
- How confident do I feel in my own abilities to carry out these activities and analyse the outcomes relating to what is being asked? Are there any areas I think I may struggle with?

Do
- I know how to examine the various components of teaching and learning theories, and video examples of teaching and learning strategies being carried out at college.
- I can identify where my talk may have gone wrong and adjust my thinking/approach to get myself back on course by referring to my notes or this textbook.

Review
- I can explain what the task was and how I approached the construction of my presentation and the recommendations I reached.
- I can explain how I would approach the more difficult elements differently next time (i.e. the analysis — what I would do differently). For example, I could look at alternative filming methods to review teaching and learning strategies being carried out at college; perhaps interviewing learners to get their views.

THINK ▶FUTURE

Sarah O'Leary

Trainee
secondary
school PE tutor

I studied Level 3 BTEC National Sport at a further education college from 2010 to 2013. I soon knew that, when I finished, I wanted to be a PE tutor. I took my Level 2 gym instructors award and my Level 2 Basketball coaching award at college and really enjoyed going into schools and delivering coaching sessions as work experience. The BTEC course helped me with the knowledge of how coaching works, the different ways children learn and, most importantly, how to get the best out of PE sessions, make them enjoyable and witness improvement in children's sporting achievements.

When I completed the BTEC course, I got a job as a teaching assistant in my local secondary school. I worked mostly with the PE department and enjoyed every moment. After one year, I felt I had gained sufficient knowledge and saved enough money to go to university. I studied PE and had a fantastic three years. I am currently working towards my postgraduate Certificate of Education (PGCE) and working at a secondary academy preparing Year 11 learners for their GCSE practical performance examinations.

My role is varied and many of the learners look to me for additional help with their PE portfolios and extra revision. This, together with lesson preparation and marking (all of which my teaching mentor checks), means hours of hard work, but it's worth it and great to see learners achieve.

PE teaching is my dream job. In the short term, I want to continue as a class tutor, but in the longer term I would consider becoming a Head of Department and developing PE teaching and coaching further for the benefit of the learners.

Focusing your skills

Understanding the nature of skilled performance

It is important to be able to analyse and interpret the characteristics of skilled performance and the contribution of skills and abilities to its production. You need to:

- review and analyse the learning process and performance when coaching/teaching performers new skills or developing existing ones
- recognise how skills are classified and what a skilled performance looks like, which requires in-depth understanding of the qualities of skilled performance, the component parts of a skill and analysis of them
- understand the characteristics and classification of

abilities, how these differ from skills, how they are viewed in terms of nature versus nurture and how they are categorised and linked to components of fitness.

Theories of teaching and learning in sport

You need a good understanding of how the theories of teaching and learning can be applied to sport, which involves:

- understanding how behaviourist and cognitive theories explain how people learn new skills
- understanding how learning new skills goes through different phases of learning, and the features of each phase
- understanding how learning can be taken from one skill and transferred towards learning a new task or skill.

Getting ready for assessment

Reece is working towards completing the second year of his BTEC National Extended Diploma in Sport. He has been given an assignment to create a presentation examining the methods for skill acquisition in sport. The presentation may be in a format of his choice (PowerPoint, posters, slideshow, etc.), but must address the following key points.

▶ The nature and process of information for skilled performance

▶ Theories of teaching and learning in sport

▶ Teaching and learning strategies for sports skills

Reece shares his experience below.

How I got started

First I wrote down a list of everything I learned during my lectures at college. I started by structuring my presentation under four key headings.

▶ What is skilled performance?

▶ How performers process information for skilled performance

▶ Theories of teaching and learning

▶ Learning strategies

I decided upon a PowerPoint presentation as that allowed me to include photos. The first part was quite easy – I looked through my notes and compiled a framework of what constitutes skilled performance. The remaining headings were a little more difficult because, apart from the few bits and pieces of theory we'd done at college, I wasn't too sure what else I could include. I asked my tutor if I could photograph and film a few lectures/lesson to get images of learning taking place. This helped visualise the different methods of learning taking place. However, the most important thing by far was being able to film practical sessions of fellow learners being coached, so their skills and skill level could be referred to in my presentation. My tutor also suggested I include diagrams in my presentation as this would create a visual representation of the complex theories under discussion.

How I brought it all together

Although my course taught me a great deal about skill acquisition and learning styles, I'm so glad I sought permission to pick up a camera to film lectures and learning taking place and sports coaching. What I saw

there put everything into perspective. A combination of the two approaches allowed me to:

▶ investigate the nature of skilled performance

▶ examine ways that sport performers process information for skilled performance

▶ explore theories of teaching and learning in sport

▶ carry out teaching and learning strategies for sports skills.

What I learned from the experience

I'm glad I gave myself plenty of time to plan my presentation. Had I left everything to the last minute, I wouldn't have had the opportunity to film lectures, learning taking place and sports coaching. Studying this unit made me realise the complexity and amount of skill involved in sport and, equally as complex, how skills are learned. I also learned how useful a camera and camcorder can be to record footage that can prove beneficial as evidence for assessments.

Think about it

▶ Make sure you give yourself enough time to plan and write your assignments

▶ Do not be afraid to use IT equipment at your school or college for ideas and inspiration, but always consult your tutor beforehand about what you intend to do.

▶ Remember you are a sports learner. Examine sports coaching and teaching at school or college, and consider not only accomplished athletes but those performers who are just starting out or learning new skills.

Rules, Regulations and Officiating in Sport 25

Getting to know your unit

Being an official is seen by many as a thankless task, but most officials are content in the knowledge that they are making a difference and providing an essential service. Many report not only enjoying the role but also enjoying knowing that they have been part of the development of players and learning how to improve themselves under pressure.

This unit allows you to fully explore the roles and responsibilities of officials in a range of sports from tennis umpire to rugby referee, from gymnastics judge to track official.

You will also develop and maintain your own ability to apply sport-specific rules in their intended spirit, as well as taking a historical look at the development of officials.

The unit should provide you with the opportunity to maintain and develop your ability as an official, including a final evaluation of your own performance as an official.

How you will be assessed

This unit will be assessed by a series of internally assessed tasks set by your tutor. Throughout the unit, you will find assessment activities that will help you work towards your assessment. Completing these activities will not mean that you have achieved a particular grade, but you will have carried out useful research or preparation that will be relevant when it comes to your final assignment.

To achieve the tasks in your assignment, it is important to check that you have met all of the Pass grading criteria. You can do this as you work your way through the assignment.

If you are hoping to gain a Merit or Distinction, you should also make sure that you present the information in your assignment in the style that is required by the relevant assessment criteria. For example, Merit criteria require you to analyse whereas the Distinction criteria require you to evaluate.

The assignment set by your tutor will consist of a number of tasks designed to meet the criteria in the table. It is likely to consist of a mixture of written and practical assignments, and include activities such as:

▶ a written report discussing how officials' roles and responsibilities have evolved

▶ a written report or video analysis of officials' performance that identifies how the rules, laws and regulations were applied

▶ a practical demonstration where you apply the correct rules and regulations in a controlled environment

▶ a written report analysing your own performance when officiating in a selected sport.

Assessment criteria

This table shows what you must do to achieve a **Pass**, **Merit** or **Distinction** grade, and where you can find activities to help you.

Pass	Merit	Distinction
Learning aim **A** Understand the development of the roles and responsibilities of the officials involved in sports		
A.P1 Explain how and why the current role and responsibilities of the official have evolved over time. Assessment activity 25.1	**A.M1** Analyse how and why the current role and responsibilities of the official have evolved over time. Assessment activity 25.1	**A.D1** Evaluate the influences contributing to the evolution of and impacts on the current roles and responsibilities of the official. Assessment activity 25.1
Learning aim **B** Explore the performance of officials in a selected sport		
B.P2 Explore the performance of officials in a selected sport. Assessment activity 25.2	**B.M2** Analyse the strengths and weaknesses of officials' performance in selected sports. Assessment activity 25.2	**B.D2** Evaluate the performance of officials officiating in selected sports for recommended good practice. Assessment activity 25.2
B.P3 Review the performance of officials, using assessment methods in selected sports, identifying strengths and areas for improvement. Assessment activity 25.2		
Learning aim **C** Undertake the role of a match official in a competitive sport		
C.P4 Perform two officiate roles in a selected sport, applying rules, laws and regulations in a competitive practice correctly. Assessment activity 25.3	**C.M3** Perform two officiate roles in a selected sport, applying the rules, laws and regulations appropriately and accurately in a competitive situation. Assessment activity 25.3	**C.D3** Evaluate own performance, strengths and areas for improvement, using feedback from others and two different assessment methods to recommend improvements for personal development. Assessment activity 25.3
C.P5 Review own performance in officiating in a selected sport, using two assessment methods, identifying skills gained. Assessment activity 25.3	**C.M4** Assess own performance, identify strengths and areas for improvement, using feedback from others and two different assessment methods. Assessment activity 25.3	

Getting started

Officials, referees, judges, starters, linespeople, assessors and umpires are all an essential part of sport. All are responsible for managing the performers of their sport and ensuring their health and safety. Many are unpaid volunteers. Consider the Sunday League rugby referee, the gymnastics judge or the starter at an athletics event. What duties will they have in common and what will be different?

 A # Understand the development of the roles and responsibilities of the officials involved in sports

Link

This unit has links with *Unit 3: Professional Development in the Sports Industry, Unit 4: Sports Leadership, Unit 6: Sports Psychology* and *Unit 12: Self-employment in the Sports Industry*.

Discussion

Consider derivative sports and as a group discuss the implication for the other versions of each sport. How might the officiating be different? Could you devise your own derivative sport from an existing one? What modifications to the rules could you make?

History of rules and regulations

Many of the sports that exist today have a long history and often started as recreational activities long before becoming international favourites. Football is, by some way, the most popular global team sport, played and watched just about everywhere in the world. It might surprise you to know the earliest form of the game in medieval England had virtually no rules and was played by teams of entire towns!

Many sports – including rugby, football, tennis, squash and netball – have their roots (as we would recognise them) in 19th-century British schools. Players from these schools devised first their own school rules, and eventually a single set of rules to which everyone must comply (so schools could compete against each other). This gradual process is usually referred to as 'codification'. From here, as sports moved into the wider world, national governing bodies (NGBs) were formed to standardise a single set of rules.

This process itself has had an influence on the rules of most sports: for example, half time is often thought to be a necessity for a rest, but, in fact, was originally employed as a way of dividing the rules for schools – the first half played by one school's rules, the second by those of the other, usually administered by teachers from the two schools and eventually by neutral officials.

More recently, NGBs for newer sports have developed rules for other reasons. A number of these sports can be called 'derivative sports', usually modern versions of existing established sports introduced to attract new attention to sports with falling numbers or because they are perceived as more exciting. Examples include five-a-side football, beach volleyball, T20 cricket, 7s rugby and 3-on-3 basketball.

▶ The role of a rugby referee has changed a lot since the late 1800s

NGB rules/laws and regulations in different sports

One of the key considerations and main roles of an official is their knowledge and working application of the rules, regulations and laws. Sports differ depending on a variety of factors, but generally rules are established and communicated as part of a process similar to the basketball example shown in Figure 25.1, starting at a global level and filtering down to local level.

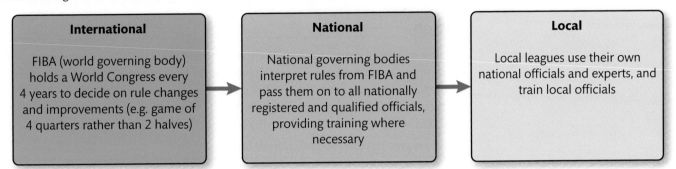

International	**National**	**Local**
FIBA (world governing body) holds a World Congress every 4 years to decide on rule changes and improvements (e.g. game of 4 quarters rather than 2 halves)	National governing bodies interpret rules from FIBA and pass them on to all nationally registered and qualified officials, providing training where necessary	Local leagues use their own national officials and experts, and train local officials

▶ **Figure 25.1:** The process of basketball rules management, from global to local league level

Current-day rules/laws for different sports

As seen in Figure 25.1, sport rules are usually determined first internationally and then nationally. Examples of the organisations involved in different sports are shown in Table 25.1.

Sometimes, rules are interpreted differently according to the level of the competition. For example, rules in place related to clothes and equipment for cricket are very particular at international level where the image of the sport is in the limelight. These rules are relaxed in local competition, where players and teams are less restricted about what they wear.

▶ **Table 25.1:** Bodies involved in setting rules/laws for different sports

Sport	International governing body	National governing body	Local organisation (example names, not real organisations)
Badminton	Badminton World Federation	Badminton England	West Yorkshire Badminton Association
Football	FIFA (Fédération Internationale de Football Association)	Football Association (FA)	Devon County Football League
Judo	IJF (International Judo Federation)	British Judo Association	South East Region Judo
Rugby Union	IRB (International Rugby Board)	Rugby Football Union	Manchester Rugby Union League
Rugby League	RLIF (Rugby League International Federation)	Rugby Football League	London Rugby Football League
Tennis	ITF (International Tennis Federation)	Lawn Tennis Association	Kent Tennis Association
Cricket	ICC (International Cricket Council)	England and Wales Cricket Board	Sussex Village League
Netball	INF (International Netball Federation)	England Netball	Cumbria County Netball
Basketball	FIBA (International Basketball Federation)	Basketball England	Kent Basketball Association
Volleyball	FIVB (International Volleyball Federation)	Volleyball England	Wessex Volleyball Association

There are also versions of many of these sports for people with physical or mental impairments, such as wheelchair basketball, blind football and wheelchair tennis. For example, boccia was originally played by people with cerebral palsy but has been adapted to include a wide range of motor skill disabilities. Players throw leather balls as close as possible to a white target ball known as the jack (similar to bowls). The player who lands closest to the jack is awarded a point. Balls can be thrown or kicked, or a ramp can be used. Boccia can be played by individuals, pairs or in groups of three.

> **Research**
>
> In a pair or a small group, research the sports shown in Table 25.1 and prepare a short report about the key rules and regulations in each of those sports. Focus on the following questions: How do the sports work in competition? What rules are there around factors like play and scoring? How is misconduct in the sport punished? How large should the playing area be?
>
> Hockey is given as the *Worked example* below.

Worked example

Hockey is a team game with 11 players on each side and up to 5 substitutes. The aim of the game is to hit the ball into the opponent's goal, between the goalposts and under the crossbar, with the team scoring the most goals being the winner. They can only be scored from inside the shooting circle – a semi-circular area in front of the opponent's goal. Goals scored from outside this area are disallowed. If both teams score the same amount, the match is a draw. A game starts with a push-back from the centre spot.

Each game is split into two halves of 35 minutes each. Each half begins with a pass from the centre of the halfway line. After a goal, the match is restarted in the same way. There is a 5-minute half-time interval, or longer if previously agreed.

Every team must have a goalkeeper with the other ten players being outfield players.

Hockey is played with a hard ball and there is a strong emphasis on safety. Players must not play the ball dangerously or in a way which leads to dangerous play. A ball is considered dangerous when it causes legitimate evasive action by players. Officials and players must ensure the spirit of the game's laws is followed.

PAUSE POINT   What are the most important rules for a sport?

Hint   Can you identify the top ten rules for your sport? Produce a list in order of importance. Think what someone might need to know if they had never played before.

Extend   For one of the rules, draw a storyboard that illustrates the rule clearly and demonstrates the reason for the rule.

Current-day regulations

What kinds of rules are common to most sports? Rules need to be very specific about what is and is not allowed, and how to decide whether a rule has been broken or not. But some principles are common to most sports.

- **Playing area or dimensions** – the size of the playing surface can vary within a range determined by the governing body, which explains why some football or rugby pitches are smaller compared to others and why table tennis tables differ in size. But some sports are stricter: for example, all tennis courts should be exactly the same size.

- **Playing surface** – in some sports, like tennis, surfaces can vary from grass, concrete and clay to cement, all within the rules, while others, such as judo, must always take place on the same kind of surface.

- **Number of players** – sports can vary from individual to team sports, with teams being different sizes. The number of players may also include substitutes who replace players either on a permanent basis (such as in football) or on a regular switching basis (such as in ice hockey or basketball).

- **Time** – sports can be played in real time (such as golf or badminton) but also in artificially controlled time where a clock shows when game time has been stopped and restarted (such as for basketball). Recently, Rugby Union effectively suspended or stopped game time, particularly towards the end of a game, for certain instances such as injuries or for remote officials' decisions (video reviews).

- **Facilities and equipment** – these can vary from sport to sport and can either be very specific (such as protective equipment for ice hockey players) or quite generalised (for example a cricket or tennis player can choose what kind and size of bat or racket they prefer).

- **Scoring system** – sports scoring systems can vary, such as goals (for example football), points (for example netball or rugby) or number of shots taken (for example golf).

- **Officials** – numbers of officials can vary from sport to sport. The regulations will say who is responsible for which decisions and also cover remote officials who use video playback, if relevant.

- **Health and safety** – this is a vital role for each official but is not their responsibility alone since players, coaches and fans must also take responsibility for their own safety and that of those around them.

- **Player discipline and sanctions** – all sports have different sanction systems for fouls or aggressive play, for example card systems for hockey and football, technical fouls in basketball or sin bins in rugby.

Effects of the media

The media, Internet, printed media, radio, etc. have a huge impact on how society views everything, including sport. This is also true for how society views sports officials at all levels. Not only has it become normal in a number of sports for players to challenge officials but the portrayal of the officials' role in the outcomes of contests has never been more apparent.

Perhaps the most obvious way in which the media influences officials is when the rules are adapted to allow for media interruption, such as in the case of TV timeouts in sports like basketball where the game is stopped to allow commercial breaks to satisfy broadcast sponsors. In these situations, the officials are expected to learn new signals and even communicate with the broadcasting team as well as their co-officials.

There are several ways in which the media can affect officials.

- The presence of the media can add to stress and anxiety, and have a direct influence on perceived stress.

- Journalists, pundits and commentators often exaggerate the impact of officiating 'mistakes', some of which are not mistakes but legitimate (though disputable) interpretations of the rules of the game. However, it should be pointed out that some sports have very supportive media professionals who make an effort to support the actions of the officials, such as in cricket commentary.

- Media technology can analyse repeatedly (and at length) the faults made by officials, but it rarely gives the same coverage to any quality decisions that have been made.

However, the technology that the media use, in particular television, has often been adopted to try and improve officiating decisions, as the next section explores.

Effects of technology

There are several ways in which technology has influenced the role of the official, with the rules and regulations of sport updated to include modern developments which aim to make the officials' decision making more accurate.

- **Timing technology** – in sprinting, the use of a hand-held stopwatch has been replaced by an electronic timing system that can accurately measure to within 0.0001 seconds and cameras sophisticated enough to determine the order of up to 3000 events in a single second can surely only help the official. Timing technology also includes chips that transmit data to sensors so that large numbers of runners can be tracked over long distances with pinpoint accuracy. For example, the annual London Marathon employs delicate sensors stored in plastic matting at the start and finish lines to accurately track runner times for its 30,000 runners.

- **Heat sensors** – these are used in cricket to detect barely distinguishable touches of the bat. Heat sensors are also used in endurance cycling events to attempt to catch cheating by the use of small motors hidden in the bike frame that unfairly add an additional power source.

- **Microphones** – these are now often linked to public address systems so that officials can communicate with the crowd. This happens in many American sports but also through Reflink radios used by rugby officials during elite rugby matches.

- **Video reviews** – by far the largest modern application of sport technology in officiating is the video review. In its simplest form, it is used to validate a decision in a sport that could be crucial and has been adopted by tennis, fencing, rugby, basketball and cricket. The video review process does not always have to be 'official' to have an impact – see Table 25.2

▶ **Table 25.2:** Examples from different sports that have used video review to help make decisions

Sport	Application of video review (VR)
Gymnastics	The first time that a video review had an impact on an Olympic medal decision, Japanese gymnast Kohei Uchimura fell from a pommel horse in the 2012 Olympic final. VR demonstrated that the initial deduction of points was too harsh and the routine was regraded with an additional 0.7 points added, which meant that Japan won silver instead of no medal.
Golf	At the BMW championship in 2013, Tiger Woods had shots added to his card since video revealed that when moving a twig next to his ball, he had caused the ball to move slightly.

Case study

Hawkeye

Developed in Britain by mathematician Paul Hawkins in 2001, the Hawkeye system uses a series of cameras that surround the playing surface and track the movement of the ball. Since 2006, tennis has used Hawkeye to decide whether a ball was in or out with a simple playback decision. To prevent players contesting every shot, tennis adopted a challenge system where each player could challenge up to three times per set, only losing a challenge if they were incorrect.

Hawkeye has also added extra unintended elements to the game. Firstly, the challenge itself often leads to crowd participation, adding enjoyment to the spectacle. Secondly, and less obviously, the rules are stretched when a player looks to break the rhythm and concentration of an opponent by challenging where the outcome is obvious.

Many see systems like Hawkeye as detrimental and disrespectful to the officials, one of the main reasons that goal-line technology was so long in being adopted in top flight football in England. Others say that, if managed properly, Hawkeye and others can only help the officials to make correct, quality decisions.

Check your knowledge

Discuss the impact of this system in a small group and answer the following questions.

1 What impact could a replay screen in a large sporting arena have on the officials, and how might they best prepare for this effect?

2 Are there any applications in other sports where this kind of technology is not presently used but where it could be used to help officiating? Try to identify either aspects of a sport that already uses video reviews but which could use them to help with other decisions, or a sport that does not use video reviews at all but which could adopt them.

 **PAUSE POINT** | Is video replay essential in sport?

Hint | Describe how video replay has been adopted by four different sports.

Extend | For one of the sports, analyse the value of the video review system, considering its effect on players, coaches and spectators. Describe the advantages and disadvantages, and try to make suggestions for improvement.

Officials and their historical development

As the perceived importance of the outcome of sports events increases, there is an impact on the attention paid to the training, management and analysis of officials. Football referees have only been full-time professionals since the 1990s in England. Before that, part-time officials combined their role with other full-time jobs. In many other sports, referees do not make a living from the role and are therefore technically amateurs.

But all officials perform a vital function and go to great efforts to train, qualify and have access to support and assessment. As we have seen in the previous section, the media and technology have had an impact on the role of officials, with some of the changes for netball, football and rugby shown in Table 25.3. Changing roles over time also mean that officials have needed different skills at different times in the sport's history, with the introduction of new technology, for example, meaning that officials have to be trained in its use.

▶ **Table 25.3:** Development of officials in sport

Role	Outline	Origins	Current role
Netball umpire	Two umpires, one who manages each half, records goals and first centre pass order	Developed as a school sport so early umpires almost always teachers	Very little change in roles from early days of sport
Football referee	Originally amateurs, only recently have the elite become professional	Originally settled disputes between gentlemen players	Since 1891 have had support first from linespeople and now third, fourth, fifth and sixth officials, all with unique responsibilities
Rugby referee	1 x referee, historically a public schoolmaster from the home school	Eventually a neutrally-appointed official	Now supported by a team that includes a touch judge and a third match official (TMO)

There are many different types of official in different sports. As well as referees, officials include umpires in cricket and tennis, line judges in tennis, referee's assistants in sports like football, time keepers, scorers, linespeople, fourth officials, video referees and judges – many of these being roles that have been introduced as the rules and regulations of a sport have changed over time.

Roles of officials

Since all sports are different, at least in a small way, it is clear that the roles and responsibilities of officials depend not only on the way that the sport is played but also on the expectations placed on its officials. We can distinguish between two main roles required of an official: on the one hand, they can be **arbiters**, mainly responsible for officiating in disputes; on the other hand, they can be **disciplinarians**, applying the rules. The reality for most officials is that they must be both at different times and for different scenarios – sometimes in the same contest.

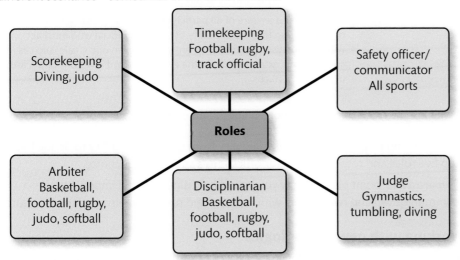

▶ **Figure 25.2:** The role of officials in selected sports

Research

Using the examples provided in Table 25.3, research the development of officials in a sport of your choice. You must consider the roles and responsibilities of officials in the early days of the sport compared with today. You will need to try to outline the reasons for the changes, e.g. societal, influenced by the media, as part of a process of the updating of rules or due to technology. The roles of many officials will be very different for some, such as basketball referees, but hardly changed for others, such as athletics track officials.

Key terms

Arbiter – a person who settles dispute between two parties – in this case players or teams on the field of play.

Disciplinarian – the person responsible for ensuring fair play and issuing disciplinary sanctions, such as red cards and technical fouls.

Impact of and relations with the media

As a result of the pressure that can be exerted by the media, it has become critical for officials – particularly at the highest level – to consider their communication with the media. All professional officiating organisations and NGBs have guidelines on dealing with the media that include, for example, not being interviewed or answering questions with any organisation other than their own regulating authority, who will prepare a statement on behalf of the organisation if necessary.

There is rarely a reason for active officials to communicate with the media, but there is a growing trend to have expert pundits in the shape of retired ex-officials who offer their unofficial but expert opinion to satisfy the demand of the media to answer questions related to officiating and decisions taken by officials.

Responsibilities of the officials

There are seven main responsibilities expected to be displayed by any official, regardless of their specific sport. These are shown in Table 25.4.

▶ **Table 25.4:** Responsibilities of officials

Responibility	Description
Communication	Communicating with players, co-officials, managers, coaches and sometimes crowds is a key role. This can include non-verbal signals and speech, and may sometimes include having a microphone and an earpiece to communicate with other officials.
Appearance	Officials must look like professionals and behave in a professional way.
Application of the rules	It is not enough to know the rules; officials must know how to apply them fairly and in the right context, for example, deciding which rules must be applied in certain situations and how these decisions are communicated.
Fair play	Having an instinct for what is right and a highly developed sense of justice and fairness is crucial for all officials.
Relationships	Establishing and maintaining relationships is a characteristic of all good officials, who continually communicate and lay clear boundaries while respecting the players, the competition and their role within it.
Scoring	Some officials, such as those in netball and football, are required to keep details of the score of the contest and the scorers, though this role is often carried out by additional officials.
Health and safety	The safety and welfare of all participants, including coaches and co-officials, is also the responsibility of the main official who must act within recognised guidelines to ensure that everyone is safe, such as in conditions of extreme heat, in the event of crowd invasions or in cases of slippery surfaces.

▶ NBA referees like Karen Holtkamp use radio as well as their whistle to communicate

---

PAUSE POINT   What are the main roles and responsibilities of an official in your sport?

   Hint   The roles and responsibilities of officials vary from sport to sport. Try to define the top five roles and responsibilities for officials in a sport of your choice.

   Extend   Prepare a five-point plan for how you would help a new official improve their communication and relationship with coaches and players within your chosen sport.

Working with new technologies

As new technologies are introduced into sport, officials have to learn how to use them and interpret what they show. This can lead to either an increase or a decrease in the responsibilities of the officials. There is no doubt that in almost all cases modern-day officials are under more pressure than their predecessors: the advent of televised sport and even mobile video technology has meant that our officials have never been under such scrutiny. Coupled with a change in attitude towards officials in some sports – where competitors think nothing of verbally abusing or surrounding an official during or after a contest – this only adds to perceived pressure on match officials.

Examples of a decrease in responsibility generally arise when either a rule is changed – for example, the removal of a goal-line decision in football — or when extra officials or technology are added, such as in the case of video replay systems.

Video replay systems

Video replay systems (VRS) are now used across many sports, with many trialling their use in a variety of scenarios. Their role is increasingly important. For example, Rugby Union uses a television match official (TMO) primarily in try/no try situations, while basketball (NBA only) uses video reviews of out-of-bounds and ball–hand–clock ('buzzer beater') scenarios. In game 2 of the 2016 Western Conference NBA basketball play-off game, Steven Adams of Oklahoma City Thunder tipped a last second shot to apparently win the game away from home in front of a packed crowd. The officials reviewed the decision with the help of VRS and overturned their original call; the result of the game went in favour of the Dallas Mavericks which had a direct impact on one of the most important series in professional basketball.

Discussion

As sports continue to evolve, so too must officiating, and as decision making over important elements of a competition comes under increasing scrutiny, the search for solutions continues. Take a look at the following ideas.

- Video assistant referees in football – IFAB (International Football Association Board), a body made up of Great Britain's football governing bodies and FIFA, will be trialling the use of video assistants in the 2017/18 season, proposed to help referees make decisions about whether to send a player off, to review penalties and offside decisions and to alert them to foul play.
- Virtual reality (VR) in cricket and other sports – as the use of VR becomes commonplace, so too do its applications. Essentially VR allows a user to have 360-degree vision of stitched-together videos, gathered in this case at the sports arena. This allows fans, and potentially officials, to experience the action (albeit with some time lag, known as latency). It also potentially allows officials to look at critical decisions from a variety of angles in order to improve decision making. Research has been carried out in basketball, cricket, American football and baseball, and its applications are at the experimental stage.

In a pair, discuss the advantages and disadvantages of one or both ideas. Try to imagine the experience for supporters, coaches, players and, most importantly here, officials. Can you suggest any other ideas?

Wireless communication technology

Football, American football and rugby are among those sports that now regularly have officials communicate wirelessly during the game, or at least at an interval communicate and share information in order to make better-quality systems. Some believe that this approach interrupts the natural rhythm of the sport. Sports, such as baseball, prefer to stick with umpire decisions, though run-out decisions are supported by video review.

For example, football uses goal-line decision-making software including wireless communication to judge whether the ball has crossed the goal-line so that the match officials are informed of the outcome in fractions of seconds.

Current issues in officiating in sport

Abuse of officials

For some time, there has been a decline in respect for match officials at all levels of sport, particularly in football. Many point to the way Premier League footballers are perceived to abuse and question referees as the root cause. The scale of the issue at grassroots level is widespread and increasing, in spite of recent campaigns such as Respect (2008).

One study identified that 60 per cent of officials have experienced serious verbal abuse, while others have been physically attacked. It reported 3731 cases of misconduct by adults in children's football in England, though many feel that the actual number of incidents is higher. The Football Association is attempting to deal with this issue in a number of ways, including by punishing those responsible and persisting with its line of no tolerance. Nevertheless, such incidents are still on the increase. It is not uncommon for officials to be abused not only by children on the field of play, but also parents and coaching staff.

Case study

Ultimate frisbee – a team sport with no officials

Ultimate frisbee has grown rapidly in recent years, perhaps because of the simplicity of the game. Two teams attack opposite end zones. Players score when they catch the frisbee in their opponent's end zone. Players must learn to pass, defend and attack – the only equipment you really need is one frisbee.

What is unique about the sport is that it is the only team sport that has no officials. The sport is very proud of this and says that it embodies the true spirit of sport: of fair play. The idea that players are responsible for fair play is a simple one and is based on mutual respect, and keeps the focus on the pleasure of play. Players make their own calls and it is not unknown for players of one team to congratulate those of the other team for good play.

Ironically, it is this unique feature that keeps the sport out of the Olympics and Paralympics, in spite of the ideals of those organisations promoting fair play.

Check your knowledge

1   What is the unique feature of ultimate frisbee from an officiating point of view?

2   What impact do you expect this unique phenomenon has on the players of the sport?

3   The international governing body of ultimate frisbee is considering introducing officials, which divides the sport. Many say the change is necessary and will improve the sport; others that the concepts of no officials and honesty are at the heart of the game and should not change. What are your thoughts?

Recruitment and retention of officials

When asked why they continue to officiate, the three main responses across all sports are the same:

1   for excitement
2   out of enthusiasm for the sport
3   from a desire to contribute to player learning.

Officiating can be very rewarding: it can help you stay in touch with changes and developments of the sport, allow you to have access to elite athletes and competition, and keep you fit and part of a productive and progressive community.

Being an official also allows you to test yourself in many ways: officials are expected to remain emotionally detached and objective, and to make fair and consistently accurate decisions under pressure. The best officials see the sum of these expectations as a challenge.

Yet there is an acute recruitment crisis for new officials in many British sports, particularly football, cricket, rugby and basketball. Why might this be the case?

- The verbal and sometimes physical abuse of officials is increasing.
- Those involved in sport would rather play or coach.
- There is not enough value placed on the positive aspects of officiating.
- Good sportsmanship is declining.

So what is the solution? This does not seem to be an easy issue to solve, but the following strategies have been gaining popularity in the USA (which suffers from similar recruitment issues).

- Market the job to encourage people to take it up.
- Set officiating standards and evaluate and continually support new officials.
- Set up mentoring programmes.
- Create incentives and a structure where new officials can see opportunities for promotion.
- Hold fans, parents, players and coaches responsible for their behaviour.

Other issues

Political

International sport is a complex network of differing levels of competition, separated by age group and ability, not to mention geographical distance and political disputes. This has an impact on international officials since on top of all of their existing roles and responsibilities, they must also consider and respect the values and cultural differences of other competing nations.

In recent times, countries have tried to suggest that sports officials are corrupt and that decisions made against their nation's performers are biased towards a Western-focused way of thinking. There have been a number of high-profile media stories concerning international officials including the following.

- Brazilian footballer Hulk accused Russian referee Alexei Matyunin of racial abuse in a Champions League fixture in 2015 during Zenit St Petersburg's 1-0 defeat to Mordovia Saransk. Russian Football Union ethics committee head Vladimir Lukin ruled 'a serious personal conflict took place' but said there was no 'direct proof' of racist behaviour by Matyunin, who denied the accusation, and there were no other witnesses.
- In an international badminton match, Chinese badminton head coach Li Yongbo accused Danish referee Torsten Berg of causing an injury to player Wang Xin, after the player slipped and fell on a sweat

patch that she had previously asked to be removed. The Danish official had assumed that the player was intentionally delaying the match.

- At the London Olympic Games in 2012, the Great Britain men's hockey team progressed at the expense of a Spanish team to reach the semi-finals. Immediately afterwards, the Spanish coach Dani Martin accused the New Zealand and Australian umpires of bias, pointing out that they had twice changed their minds over two penalty corners in the closing part of the contest with no reason. The Spanish Olympic team demanded an explanation from the officials immediately after the game but the result remained the same.

Social

In addition to political pressure, officials may also feel subject to the following social pressures.

- **Litigation and legislation** – as the number of legal cases being brought against officials is on the increase, so too are the lengths to which organising bodies will go to support their own officials. Such bodies now offer third-party liability and other legal protection as well as increased training, CPD materials and events to improve knowledge, particularly for children's competitions. Nevertheless, the risk of being taken to court if an incident occurs can be at the back of officials' minds when they are officiating.
- **Professionalisation** – in the UK, the idea that officials are employed full time only exists in football. In all other sports, officials are expected to balance their work and home commitments with those of officiating in their sport of choice. At the very least, this represents a disproportionate approach to investment in improving sport. If sports, including football, want to improve as more money comes into them, should there not be a proportionate increase in investment in officials?

Research

In pairs, research the challenges faced by officials in your sport. This could be an interview with an experienced official, even a phone conversation with a few well-considered questions, as well as traditional sources of research and articles from sports officials' organisations.

You could create a poster that depicts visually the challenges faced, which might include consistent abuse, lack of time to prepare, other commitments, feeling disrespected or any other issue that you are able to identify. As an extension activity, you might try to offer solutions to the issues identified.

PAUSE POINT What are the main issues related to the abuse of officials?

> Hint
>
> Try to identify the main problems concerned with the abuse of officials. What is the impact and on whom?

> Extend
>
> Devise an official recruitment strategy for your sport. Keep the focus local and describe how you are going to attract new officials and support them in a sustainable way.

Assessment practice 25.1   A.P1   A.M1   A.D1

You have been asked by your local authority to present a display at a local sports careers fair. You have to create a poster detailing the current roles and responsibilities in a sport of your choice. Your poster should include details of the evolution of the role of the official in your sport. From the first ever officials and how the games were managed right up to the current day, detail aspects of the role such as game management, appearance, communication, and respect for the official. You might want to research details of early officials and present imaginary officials from the start of competitive officiated games to the modern day.

To get the best grade possible, make sure that you provide a careful analysis of the roles and responsibilities, drawing comparisons for each successive change in focus for the officials. Try and populate your report with images of officials through the ages to help ratify your discussion. Produce a full evaluation of each of the influences, whether they are rule changes or those imposed by society. It is also important to consider the impact that these changes have had on the current roles and responsibilities of officials, such as the change to the game of basketball when the three-point line, 3 second rule and 4 quarters were introduced.

Plan
- What am I learning? Why is this important?
- How will I approach the task?

Do
- I understand my thought processes and why I have decided to approach the task in a particular way. I can explain this reasoning when asked.
- I can question my own learning approach.

Review
- I can draw links between this learning and prior learning.
- I realise where I still have learning/ knowledge gaps and I know who can (and how to) resolve them.

B Explore the performance of officials in a selected sport

Applying rules/laws and regulations to different situations

One of the main responsibilities of any official is to enforce the rules in given situations. This obviously depends on the sport as the skills and rules are different for different sports. Table 25.5 gives some examples from different sports.

▶ **Table 25.5:** Examples of law infringements in different sports

Sport	Situation	Type of issue	Action required of official/outcome
Basketball	Player commits a foul on an opponent in the act of shooting	• Unfair contact	• Charge foul against player who committed that foul. • Inform scorer of that foul. • Award free throws to opposition.
	Attacking player in zone for more than 3 seconds	• Players in illegal positions	• Call violation and offer the ball out of bounds to the opposition.
	Player jumps from out of bounds, catches ball and lands	• Ball out of play	• Call violation and offer the ball out of bounds to the opposition.

▶ **Table 25.5:** *Continued*

Sport	Situation	Type of issue	Action required of official/outcome
Rugby Union	Player not binding correctly at the ruck	• Injuries to players • Poor discipline	• Award penalty kick to the opposition.
Netball	Player in attacking semi-circle who is not entitled to be	• Players in illegal positions	• Give opponent free pass.
Football	Player offside	• Players in illegal positions	• Award free kick to opposition.
	Diving	• Simulation (feigning an injury)	• Book player (yellow card).
	Ball hit by defender against attacking player and over goal line	• Ball out of play	• Award goal kick.
Ice hockey	Head injury	• Injuries to players	• Stop play until injury correctly dealt with by medical staff. • Allow game to resume depending on who was responsible.
Rugby League	Serious foul play	• Illegal challenges • Poor discipline	• Depending on the severity, make a sin bin or sending off decision.

Effective decision making

Judgement and decision making are at the heart of all sports officiating; these are perhaps the most important attributes of any official. Whether it is a travel call in basketball, offside in football or a foot fault in tennis, the process of decision making should be straightforward.

If it were that easy we would all be excellent officials and great decision makers. It is worth considering that the decision-making process is affected by a number of factors.

▶ **Memory** – many officials talk about having a mental library of images that constitute all the key decisions that they make on a regular basis, e.g. fouls, out of bounds.

▶ **Visual perception** – how and at what angle did you see the incident that requires a decision?

▶ **Embodiment perspective** – this is the idea that officials should know what it feels like to be an athlete in that sport to be able to make an accurate decision.

▶ **Pre-judgement** – for example, trampolinists in their finals appear in reverse order which creates the idea that the judge should only see improved performance throughout the competition, which may not be the case.

▶ **Prior knowledge of performers** – this can easily influence potential decisions based on the judgements made even before the start of games.

▶ **Unwanted distractors** – crowd noise, player interference after the event, the official's own feelings and emotions – even the colour of the team's shirt.

Effective communication

Another key role of an official is in communication which could be as simple as holding a scorecard or flag or as detailed as a verbal exchange or signal.

Verbal communication

This includes spoken language, **paralanguage** and delivery. Language is simply the vocabulary that we use as officials to say what we want to say; put simply, the words and their order.

Paralanguage includes such aspects as:

▶ volume – the loudness

▶ articulation – how clear the message is

▶ pitch – the quality of the sound

▶ emphasis – the amount of expression behind what we are saying

▶ rate – the speed at which we communicate the message.

> **Key term**
>
> **Paralanguage** – non-verbal communication that emphasises body language and vocal tone.

This is known as the VAPER model and it helps us to identify the emotion and stress in our communication. An official who reports a clear message, at the right pace and with the right emphasis is more likely to have their decision valued than one who communicates their message in a high pitched, quick and over-emotional way.

Non-verbal communication

Non-verbal communication is quite simply anything that is not words. Many consider non-verbal communication to be more important than its verbal equivalent. It includes the following.

- **Body language and posture** – such as effective use of in-game signals as well as a confident approach (that is, not looking at the floor when talking to participants or slouching in a chair).
- **Eye contact** – making strong eye contact while talking to a participant reinforces the strength of the message.
- **Facial expressions** – very personal but can be used to demonstrate authority and compassion, and even reinforce other forms of communication.
- **Appearance** – such as a professionally turned-out official being subconsciously more efficient based on appearance alone.
- **Proximity** – how close to the action you are – the closer you are, the more believable your calls. It is hard to respect a decision as right or wrong if it is made from a distance.
- **Haptics** – the science of applying touch, such as reinforcing a message via a hand on a participant's shoulder.
- **Orientation** – the way the referee is facing, linked to mechanics and proximity but an indicator of reading the game as an official.
- **Use of whistle and signalling** – the strength of a blow on a whistle can communicate a lot of meaning. Consider the official who makes sharp and clear use of both whistle and signals compared to one who is casual with signals and empties their lungs into the whistle for a minor offence.

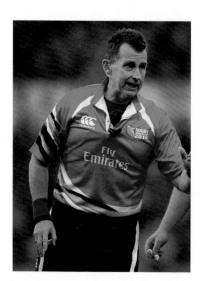

▶ Rugby referee Nigel Owens uses a wide variety of verbal and non-verbal communication techniques

 PAUSE POINT   What are the main ways in which officials communicate?

Hint   Can you name all aspects of non-verbal communication that apply to officiating?

Extend   Produce a short leaflet, or short video, to guide new officials on effective communication.

Behaviour management

It is perhaps inevitable that, at some point, most sports officials will need to deal with conflict, either aimed at themselves or among the performers and coaches.

In these circumstances, some regulatory authorities and governing bodies have quite different views on how best to deal with the conflict situations. But it is important to be aware of the fact that, particularly for sports that offer you the choice in how to manage these situations, there are a number of strategies or styles that you can employ for any given situation to manage the conflict.

Conflict management styles

The researcher Ralph Kilmann has identified a number of different ways of responding to an imaginary player who says, 'Come on, ref: he's offside, that is ridiculous!' The type of the response illustrates a different conflict management style, as shown in Table 25.6.

▶ **Table 25.6:** Conflict management styles in action

Style	Example
Forcing	'Sorry, I don't need your help: I'm penalising your team 10 metres.'

▶ **Table 25.6:** *Continued*

Style	Example
Collaborating	'Skipper, I can't continue with a running commentary from your team all afternoon.' 'Tell your players they must leave it with me, please, okay?'
Compromising	'You play it, I'll referee it, thanks.' This involves give and take – it lets them get away with it in this instance, but reinforces who is in charge.
Avoiding	Saying nothing but making a mental note for future reference.
Accommodating	'Thank you, you've had your say – let's get on with it.'

Clearly good officials will know when to apply these approaches in the right context. You could say that this is part of the official's tool kit and officials need to know which tool to use for which situation.

Game control

It is worth thinking about the skills and qualities required to be successful in managing a game and keeping the players under control. The skills that officials need to have are outlined in Table 25.7.

▶ **Table 25.7:** Skills and qualities needed for game control

Skills and qualities	Justification	How would they be developed?
Motivation, confidence and concentration	One of the key characteristics recognised in elite officials in all sports is their apparent dedication, commitment and ability to focus on only the most important aspects of the role.	Motivation needs to be nurtured by constantly revaluating and striving to be the best you can be. It is vital to have the support of peers in this process. Confidence is generally a by-product of experience which implies that you must officiate and reflect with peers more often. There are a number of so-called 'cue utilisation interventions' that can help you focus on only relevant cues in pressure situations. Techniques like these are covered in *Unit 6: Sport Psychology*.
Good working knowledge of the sport's rules	This seems obvious, but in many sports, slight changes to rules and, more likely, changing interpretations of those same rules, will alter from time to time, for example before a tournament.	Briefings for officials are often held pre-season, pre-tournament and at other times, and will contain points of focus for the season ahead. NGBs also offer refresher courses for those officials who need updating on the latest changes.
Excellent communication skills	An official who has little focus on this aspect will only progress to a certain level, even if they have technical ability. At some point in one's sport, as an official one must relate to the feelings and 'feel' of a contest and be able to react appropriately.	Officials are unlikely to be offered courses or even guidance on this critical skill – the best ideas come from talking to players and coaches in a non-threatening context to discuss how they understand the role of communication.
Anxiety control strategies	All officials are in stressful situations and, as a result, may experience pre-game, in-game and post-game anxiety which can have serious implications to key roles such as decision making.	Sports psychologists (see *Unit 6: Sport Psychology*) have a number of interventions or techniques to help with anxiety that include mental rehearsal, biofeedback, breathing techniques or simple centring. Techniques such as these are explored in *Unit 6: Sport Psychology*.
Ability to read and 'feel' the game and well-developed anticipatory skills	'They haven't come here to see you …' Fitting in with the flow of the game is an important part of the craft. Some say that only those officials that have played can truly appreciate the finer points and have this kind of 'feel'.	Watching how a game is set up, understanding and appreciating tactics and applying fair play come from officiating more and reviewing post-game, asking yourself questions such as 'What could I have done differently?'

▶ **Table 25.7:** *Continued*

Skills and qualities	Justification	How would they be developed?
Mental toughness	At all levels, the perception of success and failure felt by officials is critical to the view of their performance. An official needs the ability to remain calm under pressure and to follow logical mental processes to maintain control if they are to be effective for the entire game.	Several NGBs offer guidance on mental toughness and detail positive behaviours pre-, mid- and post-competition.
Physical fitness	This is not essential for all sports officials but increasingly measured and assessed for those expected to keep up with play, e.g. in rugby, football and basketball.	This is quite simply observing the principles of maintaining personal fitness that match the pace of the contest that you are officiating. This might include some aerobic endurance training, running, swimming or cycling such that performance measures can be assessed easily. For example, VO2 max (maximal oxygen uptake) is measured in football, rugby and basketball officials pre-season.
Emotional control	The official who has seemingly lost control, shouting and becoming red-faced or even abusive, will quickly lose the respect of the competitors and may not be able to continue or be allocated high-pressure contests.	There are many techniques (e.g. simulation training) to artificially create high-stress situations either in a contrived training session or more likely as part of a mental rehearsal. Officials must prepare their most appropriate response and deliver it, in the same way that an athlete rehearses physical skills.

Research

Take a close look at Table 25.7. Choosing a specific role, e.g. tennis chair umpire or rugby touch judge, research key elements of their performance as listed above. Construct research that can be simplified into a guidance leaflet for officials that provides advice on developing each of the following aspects specific to that official:
- fitness (if appropriate)
- emotional control
- mental toughness
- communication
- keeping up to date with the rules.

 **PAUSE POINT**   How do you control a contest?

 Hint   Can you name all five of the main approaches to handling conflict as an official?

Extend   For one of the approaches, produce a three-sentence summary describing it to someone who knows nothing about the theory. Explain what it is and how it applies to sport.

Analysing officials in different sports

Match officials are evaluated in a similar way to players and coaches in terms of their performance. As part of this unit you will be analysing your own performance and will be assisted in your evaluation by other observers to help you improve. Even fully qualified officials are regularly reviewed as national governing bodies seek to make sure that standards are maintained. Generally speaking, it is those officials who are new to the role and those at the higher end who are most frequently assessed in their performance.

The evaluation of performance depends largely on the sport and on the official's level in that sport. Table 25.8 gives some examples of what can be assessed for different officials in different sports.

▸ **Table 25.8:** Elements of officials' performance that can be assessed

Sport/official	What can be assessed
Basketball referee	<ul><li>Mechanics (position)</li><li>Court coverage (fitness)</li><li>Communication</li><li>Game management</li><li>Rule interpretation</li></ul>
Football referee	<ul><li>Game control</li><li>Appearance</li><li>Attitude to players and coaches</li><li>Field mechanics (position)</li><li>Fitness</li><li>Communication</li></ul>
Cricket umpire	<ul><li>Appearance</li><li>Organisation</li><li>Interaction with players</li><li>Knowledge of rules</li><li>Interaction with co-officials</li><li>Clarity of decisions</li></ul>
Netball umpire	<ul><li>Communication</li><li>Positioning</li><li>Vision</li><li>Control</li><li>Fitness</li><li>Decision making</li></ul>
Tennis line judge	<ul><li>Accuracy</li><li>Consistecy</li><li>Voice</li><li>Appearance</li><li>Reliability</li><li>Cooperation</li><li>Professionalism</li></ul>
Rugby touch judge	<ul><li>Communication</li><li>Vision</li><li>Movement and fitness</li><li>Cooperation</li><li>Professionalism and appearance</li></ul>
Football fourth official	<ul><li>Pre-match administration</li><li>Dealing with substitutions</li><li>Control of replacement balls</li><li>Completion of post-match reports</li></ul>
Rugby Union TMO (video referee)	<ul><li>Knowledge of rules and interpretations</li><li>Communication</li><li>Technical ability</li><li>Ability under pressure</li><li>Cooperation</li><li>Professionalism</li></ul>
Gymnastics judge	<ul><li>Knowledge of key performance competencies, e.g. full body involvement, movement skills</li><li>Accuracy</li><li>Consistency</li></ul>
Boxing timekeeper	<ul><li>Knowledge of rules</li><li>Ability to keep time under pressure</li><li>Accuracy</li><li>Professionalism</li></ul>

Methods of analysis

There are many ways in which an official can have their skills analysed in order to improve them. The purpose of this is to recognise both strengths and weaknesses, and to further develop their officiating skills.

▶ **Observation** – at the highest level, officials are assessed by experienced officials appointed by the league or governing body. They usually produce a report and often provide post-event feedback.

▶ **Video analysis** – another way of analysing performance is simply by having your performance filmed. This will provide you with an objective record of what happened with the advantage of being able to analyse your performance in slow motion or real time.

▶ **Notational analysis** – this studies movement patterns in team sports and is primarily concerned with strategy and tactics. However, it can be a useful method for officials to analyse their movement during a match as well as the number of decisions made. Patterns of play can then be identified, and strengths and weaknesses highlighted. This information can then be used as a strategy in subsequent matches to improve performance.

▶ **Performance profiling analysis** – this can be used to document, assess and predict the ability of the official to meet the demands of performance, covering various aspects of technical skill, tactical awareness, physical capacity and psychological factors. Performance profiling is a way of giving an official information of what actually happened in their sport rather than what they think happened. This provides an insight into the official's state of mind. For example, there may be occasions when the official has underperformed due to nerves or lack of concentration. Therefore the purpose of performance profiling is to:

- help the official with their psychological needs
- improve the official's motivation and performance.

Performance profiling will assess the official before and after the match, and should address the following important psychological factors: confidence, concentration, commitment, control and ability to refocus effort. Understanding each of these will allow you to prepare a strategy that can address any issue highlighted as part of the profiling.

Reflect

While each role in sports officiating is different, there are some common areas of emphasis. Look at each of the officiating roles below and then the attributes/skills. Rank the attributes/skills in order of importance for each role, from 1 to 8 where 1 is the most important and 8 the least. Be prepared to debate your rankings with your peers.

	Football assistant referee (score 1–8)	Table tennis umpire (score 1–8)	Ice hockey referee (score 1–8)
Physical fitness			
Communication			
Mental toughness			
Experience			
Being in position			
Decision making			
Appearance			
Humour			

Identifying strengths and areas for improvement

The purpose of any performance analysis is to identify any strengths and weaknesses. Having done this and identified areas for improvement, the official can choose strategies to develop these areas. This may involve enrolling on recognised courses or taking refresher sessions. Regular evaluation is needed to ensure that skills are up to date and suitable for a variety of match situations address.

One of the key ways of identifying strengths and areas for improvement is to use a SWOT analysis based on the assessment of their performance.

SWOT analysis is used to evaluate the strengths, weaknesses, opportunities and threats involved in the performance of an official. The observer should understand the technical demands of the officiating that they are analysing. Normally, experienced officials carry out this process, although as officials develop, it is also beneficial for them to carry out SWOT analyses so that they can compare and contrast their findings with those of their peers and agree on targets for future performance.

▶ **Strengths** – the observer/assessor should identify the official's strengths in a SWOT grid like the one in *Unit 18: Work Experience in Active Leisure*, Figure 18.2 (page 244). This information could come from objective data or subjective observations. The coach should compare the performance against an ideal model for each performance demand. It is important the observer/assessor has clear criteria against which to assess the performer(s) when carrying out the performance and SWOT analysis. It is most likely that a system like this will be employed by your observer after a contest, leaving you with action points.

▶ **Weaknesses** – with the support of the data, the assessor/observer should identify any weaknesses such as technical inefficiencies in the performance of specific competencies or the incorrect application of officiating techniques in a game or a simulated practice.

▶ **Opportunities** – the assessor/observer should note any opportunities that the official has to develop their performance, such as access to training sessions or specific videos to support technical development. It may also include information about any additional training such as objective data on previous performances or subjective assessments of their effectiveness, possibly in the form of extra match reports.

▶ **Threats** – the assessor/observer should identify any short- or long-term threats to the performance of the official.

Strengths and weaknesses could be observed in communication, fitness, rapport with players, emotional control or any of the other identified aspects previously mentioned in the section 'Game control', describing the skills and attributes of top officials. Naturally, there will be a different focus for each sport.

Opportunities are sport-specific but could include face-to-face officiating, training, membership of officials' associations, officials' social media groups, Internet video sites with instructional videos, officiating camps and clinics.

Threats could include poor mental strength, inability to control emotions, verbal abuse from participants, perceived pressure and injury.

Identifying ways for future development

The way in which officials develop and improve in sport in the UK largely depends on the size of the sport and the organisation that is responsible for that sport. A sport with a relatively small following might only be able to offer general guidance and the occasional referee or judge course based on local interest.

In contrast, football, rugby and, to a lesser extent, cricket are able to offer training courses, clinics and camps, professional advice and guidance, mentoring systems and even video analysis. It is no coincidence that these are the three sports that pay more for officials than any other in the UK, purely because of numbers.

Other forms of future development, with examples, are as follows:

▶ **Practice** – simply making yourself available for more fixtures (if you can) will raise your profile and get you noticed on a local circuit, and though practice does not necessarily make you perfect, it certainly helps you reflect and improve, in the same way that a player needs match practice.

▶ **Training** – in Rugby Union, referees and other officials are expected to retrain and update on a regular basis, train and be tested for fitness. They are given video clips from a referee's perspective in order to make a decision or start a discussion with their peers as to the best outcome for each decision, a lot like the hazard perception videos you might watch when learning to drive.

▶ **Qualifications** – sometimes, especially where there are no camps, limited fixtures and a shortage of material, officials can learn by taking additional courses at the next level of progression. They can also provide an extra motivation or reward for those identified as having talent in officiating.

▶ **Self-analysis** – post-game analysis is encouraged in most sports and regardless of experience, all officials can aim to be honest in their evaluation of themselves and even identify ways in which they can improve.

▶ **Mentoring** – particularly in team sports, and usually at the start of an official's career, the official can be supported by a more experienced co-official. In fact, some sports do not qualify officials until an experienced colleague signs them off as competent.

▶ **Buddy systems** – similar to mentoring but less formal, a buddy system will provide a point of contact for a new or returning official. While their feedback will be less formal, they will offer moral support, particularly after tough games.

PAUSE POINT

Can you list four methods of analysing an official's performance?

Describe four ways in which an official's performances may be evaluated and analysed during a contest. Provide examples for a sport of your choice

Design an action plan template for evaluating an official's performance which contains examples of the kinds of actions that could result from a poor performance by a new official.

Assessment practice 25.2

B.P2   B.P3   B.M2   B.D2

1 Select two sports. Consider how these sports are officiated and their key rules or laws. Then identify a set of parameters against which you could measure the performance of an official, e.g. mechanics or communication.

2 Complete the review of two selected officials in your sports and add either video clips or still images to emphasise their performance in a selected contest, scoring the criteria you identified in Task 1. Make suggestions related to the improvement of the officials based on your assessment of their performance.

Plan
- What are the success criteria for this task?
- What aspects of the task do I think will take the most/least time? How will I balance these?

Do
- I can seek others' opinions.
- I am recording my own observations and thoughts.

Review
- I can explain how I approached the task.
- I can describe my thought processes.

C   Undertake the role of a match official in a competitive sport

Once you have completed your research, you will be ready to practise officiating. Remember, even the greatest of officials started where you are now, so you need a checklist, like the one shown in Figure 25.3, before you go out and try it for real.

Reviewing your own performance

To continue to develop as an official, it is vital to always be reviewing and evaluating your own performance, and using this to identify areas where you can develop performance (refer back to page 387), getting feedback from others is a crucial way of collecting information for your review.

▶ Participants and players are often a useful source of feedback but you must remember player reports can be biased and less than objective, particularly from those who have not been successful. It might be best to wait rather than collect feedback immediately after a game.

▶ Supervisors are perhaps the most reliable sources of critique and guidance. As they are usually experienced themselves, they should leave you with some targets to achieve from discussions after your performance.

▶ Observers can also be objective experts with much to offer, and will probably leave you with a checklist or suggestions for future improvements.

Strengths and areas for improvement

It is important when analysing performance that you do not solely concentrate on weaknesses. Through observation and discussion, your strengths should also be highlighted. To further aid this, it is useful for you to observe an experienced or elite official so that you can identify their strengths and skills.

There are two types of assessment:

▶ **formative assessment** – takes place informally and should support the development of an official

▶ **summative assessment** – takes place formally to assess the performance of an official – this form of assessment is often used to assess the ongoing training needs of an official.

Development plan

After you have planned, officiated and obtained feedback from a competition, you need to reflect on your performance and produce a development plan for improvement. This will include targets which you have set for yourself and which address the areas identified for improvement. This will increase your ability to officiate effectively.

Personal reflection

This can take several forms: a diary, logbook or even an audio or video diary. Reflective logs and increasingly online records are a good way to record your feelings. It is often surprising to look back on these performances after a length of time and identify what you thought was important at that time; you will make a better analysis by looking back.

Effects on participants' performance

It is also important to consider the effect that you have had on the performance of the participants (but just as important for them to reflect on their own actions).

Conversations about critical decisions can be useful but are always best away from the heat of the moment.

Rules
· Know the rules – check the rule book.
· Apply the rules fairly.

Game management
· Keep control of the players and coaches.
· Control spectators if necessary.

Scoring
· Keep a record of the score or make sure those who are responsible for keeping score know what they are doing.

Health and safety
· Make sure the court, pitch or playing area is safe.
· Reduce the risk of injuries and monitor equipment.

Communication
· Demonstrate effective relationships with others, including coaches, performers, spectators and other officials.

Conflict
· Resolve conflict in a way that is best for the scenario and that suits your style.

▶ **Figure 25.3:** Key officiating requirements

 PAUSE POINT   Identify four ways that an official might access continuing professional development for their sport.

Hint   Where do you go to improve?

Extend   Devise a flow chart presentation for a sport of your choice, detailing an imaginary official's pathway to officiating excellence that includes training expectations and mentoring, and establishes a clear three-year plan.

Assessment practice 25.3

C.P4   C.P5   C.M3   C.M4   C.D3

For this part of your assessment, you will keep a logbook of evidence of officiating on your own in a tournament at your school or college. You will need to officiate in two different sports. Design and complete a logbook that includes:

- an explanation of why you have chosen these sports, a brief summary of the key rules of both sports and details of the matches you will officiate
- details of how you prepared and what you consider to be your strengths and areas of improvement before the tournament
- details of the location, a video of your performance and an observation checklist that can be completed
- a reflection on and analysis of your performance, which could include notation, SWOT analysis, etc.
- where possible, reflective comments from your peers and the competitors.

Design an action plan detailing what aspects of your performance you intend to improve and why those particular components are so important.

Plan
- How confident do I feel in my own abilities to complete this task?
- What aspects of the task do I think will take the most/least time? How will I balance these?

Do
- I am recording any problems I am experiencing and looking for ways/solutions to clarify queries.
- Am I using all of the support available to me?

Review
- I can use this experience in future tasks/learning experiences to improve my planning/approach and to monitor my own progress.
- I realise where I still have learning/knowledge gaps and I know how to (and who can) resolve them.

Further reading and resources

Ager, D. (2015) *Soccer Referees Manual*, 4th edition, London: Bloomsbury Sport.

Trevillion, P. and Holder, J. (2009) *You Are The Umpire: An Illustrated Guide to the Laws of Cricket*, London: Guardian Books.

American Sport Education Program (2011) *Successful Sports Officiating*, 2nd edition, Champaign, Illinois: Human Kinetics.

Websites

www.sportsofficialsuk.com – recognised as the organisation responsible for representing and supporting officials across all sports in the UK

www.naso.org – US version of the above with some interesting research links and articles

www.sportsofficialsworldwide.com/supporting-organisations – organisation that seeks to develop officials across the world

https://playonref.co.uk/what-we-do – great resource aimed at schools that encourages new referees taking the first step to becoming an official

THINK ▶▶FUTURE

Tim Dickson

Learner and
basketball referee

I have been a basketball referee for a few years now, doing it alongside my studies at university, and have been very passionate about every aspect. I have studied the psychology of officiating and as well as refereeing myself I have watched hundreds of games and always study the way in which my colleagues behave as officials. I am particularly interested in how officials work under pressure.

In my view, it is the duty of an official to prepare mentally in the same way that you would emphasise physical preparation. Physically, basketball is a tough sport to officiate but I would argue that it is every bit as tough mentally. The pressure that we all put ourselves under is really a choice, and we are responsible for keeping calm, controlling our emotions, keeping confident and alert, and staying positive.

There are many ways in which you can train these factors and improve each of them. I always tell new referees to reflect not just on the practical elements of their officiating but also on psychological factors. The tips I give them for mental game preparation are:

- prepare for all possible scenarios
- try some mental rehearsal before the game and make it a regular habit
- remember that you are where you are because you deserve to be
- look forward to the buzz
- anticipate that you will enjoy the game, you will be in control and you can handle all situations.

Focusing on your skills

What's involved?

- Take a look at how you can become involved in the sport of your choice, perhaps volunteering at a local club in some low-level competition or practice.
- In all officiating roles, communication is the key. Some referees practise signals in the mirror, while others imagine pressure situations to mentally rehearse how they would deal with them.
- Try and be friendly and approachable as players respond better to people than decisions.

What makes a good official?

- Being decisive and assertive but never aggressive. Do not perceive challenges to your decisions as personal attacks.
- Never try to balance justice – just make the right decisions and let the justice take care of itself.
- If you make a mistake, admit it: people will respect you for that.

Getting ready for assessment

Ian is working towards a BTEC National in Sport Development, Coaching and Fitness, and is a keen rugby player who has been identified as having some talent. While helping his local club, Ian noticed that he really enjoyed refereeing in some small-sided young player tournaments and decided to take a rugby officials course alongside studying this unit. He explains how he prepared for this unit.

How I got started

First, I collected all my notes on this topic and put them into a folder. I decided to divide the work into three parts: the history of rugby officiating, the measurement of rugby officiating performance, and finally, the reviews of my officiating performances.

Really it was about just following the process. Once the rugby club knew what I was doing, I was able to volunteer as a referee in order to get plenty of experience and practice. First, I put together the action plan listing all of my officiating skills and qualities, including my passion for rugby, and then I organised with the club to get some refereeing experience at one-day tournaments. I then submitted my action plan to my tutor.

How I brought it all together

The first task was to build a set of notes that I would use for my poster related to the history and development of rugby officiating. I was lucky enough to take some time out on a school trip to Twickenham to ask our tour guide about the history of officials. He gave me some ideas which really added to my research. I was easily able to put an interesting and detailed poster together.

For the second part, a multimedia presentation on the performance of an official, I was able to ask a local senior team referee at our club if I could analyse his performance, and he was only too happy to help and very interested in the results.

Lastly, I constructed a detailed logbook with a variety of different bits of information, all of it with a view to providing me with an evaluation of my performances. The coaches at one tournament all provided me with some good feedback which really helped my work.

What I learned from the experience

I'm happy to say that the club are allowing me to carry on as a volunteer on game days where I perform a range of functions but mostly as an official which I am able to do without it interfering with my playing time.

I've realised that full-time careers in officiating are not very common but the experience has led me to look at coaching, player development and event management, all of which I could do alongside officiating. At the moment I am split between wanting to become involved in sports event management and being a performance analyst.

My review has allowed me to reflect on both what I've done at the club and how it might shape my future career choice.

Think about it

▶ Plan your work carefully. Think about all the different tasks you need to complete, then add completion dates for them so you can be sure you will finish everything by the deadline.

▶ Ensure that you use your logbook on a daily basis as it is very easy to leave it for later and also very easy to forget what you have done on a particular day.

▶ Make sure that you check for spelling and grammar in all areas, have others review your work before you submit it, and ask them for any tips.

Glossary

A

Accuracy – how close your measurement is to the 'gold standard'.

Adherence – continuing to perform a behaviour, such as completing a rehabilitation plan.

Aerobic curve – increasing the intensity level during aerobic exercise to hit your target heart rate.

Aerobic endurance – the ability of the cardiovascular and respiratory system to meet the demands of extended exercise without tiring.

Agenda – items that need to be discussed during a meeting.

AIDA – Awareness, Interest, Desire and Action: a model used to describe the steps involved when a customer engages with a new business or organisation.

Antenatal – during pregnancy (from conception to birth).

Arbiter – a person who settles dispute between two parties – in this case players or teams on the field of play.

Arousal – state of preparedness of the body for action.

Assets – property or equipment owned by a business or organisation with a specific value.

Auditory learner – a person that learns best through listening and talking.

B

Bespoke – written or adapted for a specific participant or purpose.

Blood pressure – the pressure placed on the walls of the blood vessels when the heart is contracting and relaxing. High blood pressure could increase the risk of someone having a heart attack.

Break even – where a company's income is equal to expenditure.

Business plan – a document that outlines the objectives and goals for a business, explains how they will be achieved, and forecasts business performance.

C

Capacity – the output or performance that a business can provide in a given timeframe.

Capital resources – resources that may lose value over time but will hold some value, such as a rowing machine or squat rack.

Cash flow – the amount of money flowing in to and out of a business or organisation.

Catchment area – the area from which clients are drawn.

Causality – the relationship between a cause and its effect.

Chairperson – the person tasked with keeping a meeting focused and ensuring that all agenda items are met.

Chief executive – the highest-ranking executive in a company who is appointed to lead the company on a day-to-day basis.

Choreograph – compose a sequence of steps and moves that flow together.

Chronic – a health problem that has lasted for more than three months.

Closed questions – questions that are worded to provoke a single-word response, such as 'yes' or 'no'.

Closed skills – skills carried out in a pattern regardless of the environment in which they are performed.

Collagen – a protein-based building material used in the repair of tissues.

Commercialisation – the general process by which a product or service is evaluated for its potential to have economic impact or financial value.

Competence – having knowledge, skills and experience within a given area and recognising your associated limitations.

Concentric – when the muscle contracts and shortens.

Conditioned response – a response that is established by training or learning.

Consumables – resources that have a limited life expectancy, such as pens and paper or cleaning products.

Continuing professional development (CPD) – the training and further development of skills and techniques beyond initial training. Usually additional training courses or experience is undertaken.

Continuous skills – skills that have no recognizable beginning or end.

Contraindication – a physical or mental condition or factor that increases the risk involved in an activity.

Control group – a group of participants who undergo the control condition in an experiment or study, for example receiving no treatment or 'sham treatment' when they think they are being treated.

Control measures – actions that are taken to reduce the level of risk associated with a hazard.

Conversion rates – the ratio of people who purchase goods or services after visiting a website or shop.

Copyright – the exclusive and assignable legal right, given to the originator for a fixed number of years, to print, publish, perform, film, or record literary, artistic or musical material.

Core strength – the ability of all the muscles in the torso to provide stability and balance.

Corporation tax – the tax levied on companies' income and profits.

Covering letter – a short letter sent with a CV or application form.

Cueing – the use of visual, verbal and/or kinaesthetic signals to help improve communication between the instructor and participant.

D

Deep vein thrombosis (DVT) – the formation of a blood clot in a deep vein that can then become detached.

Delayed-onset muscle soreness – pain or discomfort often felt 24–72 hours after exercising.

Dependent variable – a variable whose variation depends on that of another.

Disciplinarian – the person responsible for ensuring fair play and issuing disciplinary sanctions, such as red cards and technical fouls.

Disclosure and Barring Service (DBS) checks – checks carried out by a government agency to make sure that someone has no history that might pose a risk to youngsters or vulnerable adults.

Discrete skills – skills containing a single activity with a beginning and an end.

Discrimination – when someone is treated unfairly/ differently because of the characteristic(s) they have. The Equality Act (2010) made it illegal to discriminate against anyone for characteristics such as age, sex, race, sexuality and disability.

Diversity – recognising and respecting that everyone is different.

Dynamic action – any action that involves movement, such as a bicep curl.

E

Eccentric – when the muscle contracts and lengthens.

Empathy – understanding another person's experience from their perspective.

Equality – treating people equally, but not necessarily the same.

Ethics committee – a panel that looks at research proposals and decides whether they are safe and ethical.

Evidence-based practice (EBP) – making sure that evidence uncovered in research is included in your everyday work practices for the benefit of your clients.

Extraneous variable – a variable outside the scope of a study that could adversely affect the results, reducing the validity and reliability of findings.

Extrinsic factors – factors outside of the body that increase the risk of injury.

F

Feasible – when a plan, idea or method is possible and likely to work.

Fine skills – skills requiring delicate and accurate muscle control in specific parts of the body.

Flat back – insufficient curvature in the spine to distribute forces.

Foreign exchange rates – the rate at which one currency is exchanged for another, such as British Pound (£) to US Dollars ($).

G

General Practitioner (GP) – a doctor who treats a range of illnesses and provides preventative care for patients at a designated surgery.

Globalisation – when businesses and organisations develop international operations and influence.

Gradient – the incline of a slope.

Gross errors – large inaccuracies in the performer's execution.

Gross motor abilities – abilities that require the coordination of many muscle groups at the same time.

Gross skills – skills that involve the action of muscle groups and the movement of the whole body.

H

Humidity – the amount of water vapour found in the air.

Hyperthermia – a medical condition where body temperature is increased above the normal range.

Hypothesis – the predicted, testable relationship between two or more variables, for example imagery training will improve basketball free throw performance.

Hypoxia – a medical condition where the body has too little oxygen and the blood concentration of oxygen becomes too low.

I

Inclusivity – making sure that everyone that attends can take part in the planned exercise or that exercises can be adapted to involve everyone.

Independent variable – a variable whose variation does not depend on that of another.

Inflammatory response – the cellular and vascular changes the body makes when faced with harmful stimuli.

Inflation – the rate at which the cost of goods and services rises.

Information processing models – a framework used to describe how people make decisions based on their reactions to things around them.

Infrastructure – physical and organisational structures and facilities required to run an event, such as buildings, roads, power supply, communication networks.

Innovative – introducing new ideas and using creative thinking.

Interest rates – the amount of a loan that is charged to a borrower.

Interval size – the range of values that each group will cover.

Intrinsic factors – the factors within the body that increase the risk of injury.

ISO 14000 – a series of standards that provide a framework for businesses and organisations to improve their environmental management and green credentials.

Isokinetic – when the muscle contracts with constant speed and resistance.

Isometric – when the muscle contracts without a change in length.

Isotonic – when the muscle contracts with a lifting and lowering phase.

J

Job description – an explanation of the duties of a particular job (sometimes called a 'job specification').

K

Key performance indicators (KPIs) – a performance measure used to evaluate the success of a situation, organisation or particular activity.

Kinaesthetic – learning takes place by carrying out the activity, such as a group exercise instructor helping a participant move through the correct technique. **Kinaesthetic learner** – a person that learns best through handling materials and objects.

Kyphosis – a condition in the back where there is an outward curve of the spine.

L

Legacy – the lasting impact of a sports event at local, regional and national levels.

Legally binding – an obligation, by law, for parties to deliver their side of an agreement and give all parties protection.

Lever – a simple mechanism that allows a force to be applied. In the human skeleton, bones are levers, providing a mechanism to allow greater weights to be lifted.

Leverage – when you are able to offer something to enable you to encourage a supplier to give a better price. This could be by buying in bulk or by offering useful brand exposure.

Limited liability – where if a company gets into debt an individual shareholder is only responsible for the amount of debt that matches their investment. For example, if a shareholder bought £10,000 of shares when a company was formed, they would only have to cover £10,000 of that company's debts.

Logistics – the coordination, movement and storage of products or services.

Lordosis – a condition in the lower back where there is excessive inward curvature of the lumbar region of the vertebral column.

M

Mechanoreceptors – movement sensing nerves.

Members-only clubs – private or fee-paying clubs that offer leisure or sports facilities for the exclusive use of members.

Minutes – records of a meeting.

Multi-use facilities – leisure centres incorporating additional facilities, such as outdoor pitches and swimming pools.

Muscle memory – when muscles become familiar with particular movements over time.

Muscular endurance – the ability of a muscle or group of muscles to move the body or an object repeatedly without tiring.

Muscular strength – the ability of a muscle or group of muscles to overcome some form of resistance.

N

National Health Service (NHS) – the collective term for health services in England, Wales and Scotland.

National Insurance – a contribution from a person's income towards nationally distributed benefits, which might include a state pension, maternity allowance and bereavement benefits.

National Statistics Socioeconomic Classification – a scale used to classify the socio-economic status of people in the UK.

Nature – innate qualities inherited from parents.

Niche – an event or product that has a small, specialised audience or consumer base.

Niche market – a small, specialised market for a particular product or service.

Nociceptors – pain-sensing receptors.

Nuance – a very slight, hardly noticeable difference in manner or meaning.

Nurture – the influence of life experiences and the environment on development.

O

Open skills – skills continually adapted according to the situation.

Osteoporosis – a condition that weakens bones due to a loss of stored calcium, which makes bones fragile, brittle and more likely to break.

Overload – working the body systems beyond their normal functional level, which is essential for gaining training benefits.

P

Pace – the length of strides or steps.

Paralanguage – non-verbal communication that emphasises body language and vocal tone.

Peak height velocity (PHV) – the period when growth rate is at its fastest or the growth spurt.

Pension – a tax-efficient method of saving during working life to provide an income once retired.

Perception – a mental process during which the brain gives meaning to the information it is receiving via the senses.

Perceptual abilities – abilities in which a performer is highly dependent on recognising a changing environment and adapting motor skills accordingly.

Person specification – description of the ideal person for the job in a job description.

Phrase – a sequence made up of four or eight beats of music.

Plyometric – an explosive contraction with rapid transition between eccentric and concentric phases.

Podiatrist – a practitioner who takes care of people's feet and treats foot diseases.

Power dynamics – the ways people use power to exert influence in relationships and how this process changes in different circumstances.

Postnatal – the period of time after a baby is born.

Precision – how fine or small a difference a measuring device can detect.

Price point – the retail price of a product or service, chosen to compete with prices of other similar products. The price point can alter depending on current demand and competition.

Private sector – companies that make a profit for the company's owners. Sometimes they run a service, such as a leisure centre, on behalf of the public sector.

Probe questions – questions used to explore a topic further when it appears as part of an interview. Examples of probe questions include elaboration, clarification and prompts to continue.

Productivity – the economic measure of a business's potential output.

Product life cycle – the stages a product goes through from the initial idea, through usage, to it being withdrawn from the marketplace.

Pronation – walking or running with most of the weight on the insides of the feet.

Proprioception – the ability to sense where the body is in space.

Pro-social development – developing positive, helpful behaviours that benefit different aspects of society.

Psychomotor abilities – abilities that combine mental activity and muscular movement.

Public bodies – organisations funded by the government that deliver on a not-for-profit basis.

Public sector – organisations that usually work on a not-for-profit basis and reinvest any money they make back into developing their sport or facilities. These organisations are often funded by taxpayers' money, such as local councils and government agencies.

R

Rationale – a reason for a decision.

Referral – when you recognise that you are not competent to work with a particular client or conduct research in a particular area based on your skill set, contacting another professional who is competent so that they can conduct that work.

Reflective practice – reflecting on an action in a process of continuous learning. Reflecting on what you are doing as part of the learning experience.

Regeneration – the long-term and sustainable social, economic, physical and environmental transformation of an area that has previously experienced degeneration.

Reliability – the consistency or repeatability of a measure.

Rule for inclusion – a statement used to define which data is included in a category.

S

Schema – rules that have been acquired from practice or experience that determine motor responses in a given situation.

Scoliosis – an abnormal lateral shift or curve in the spine.

Secondary injury – an injury to another part of the body as a result of the initial injury, for example through compensating.

Sedentary activity – activity that is low in intensity, for example lying or sitting down.

Serial skills – skills containing numerous components that, when combined, produce a single movement.

SMART – Smart, Measurable, Achievable, Realistic and Time-bound.

Social investor – somebody who invests finances in social projects with a view to seeing both social and financial benefits.

Socio-economic – relating to a person's social and economic background. Social factors include their cultural background and where they live, while economic factors include the amount of income that they have.

Stakeholder – someone who has an interest in a business.

Stimulus – an event that alters the behaviour or action of a performer.

Strategy – how a business plan is implemented.

Stressor – an activity, event or other stimulus that causes stress.

Subjective – based on or influenced by personal feelings, beliefs or opinions.

Sustainable – something that can be maintained at a required level over an extended period of time.

SWOT – Strengths, Weaknesses, Opportunities, Threats.

T

Table of critical values – a table that compares statistical testing results to find out if they are significant at a given level.

Thermoregulation – the body's attempts to maintain an internal temperature of 37°C by various methods, for example by pushing blood to the skin surface to lower body temperature and shivering to generate heat.

Treatment group – a group of participants who undergo the treatment condition in an investigation.

U

Unconditioned response – an original or innate response.

Unique selling point (USP) – something that makes a business or its product different to any thing else. It can be projected as a reason for potential clients to buy a particular product or service rather than that of a competitor.

Unlimited liability – where a person (usually a sole trader) has no limit to the amount of debt that they are responsible for. If someone working as a sole trader makes a regular loss and gets into debt, they are personally responsible for repaying all of that debt.

V

Validity (in data analysis) – the soundness of the interpretation of results.

Validity (in data collection) – whether you are measuring what you intended to measure.

Vasoconstriction – a reduction in the diameter of blood vessels.

Vasodilation – an increase in the diameter of blood vessels.

Vertebrobasilar Insufficiency (VBI) – reduced blood supply to the hindbrain.

Visual learner – a person that learns best through reading or observing things.

Vulnerable adult – a person who suffers from certain characteristics that prevent them from taking sufficient care or providing themselves with sufficient protection.

W

Wastage – service or stock that are not used to their potential resulting in a monetary loss to the business.

Index